Lecture Notes in Computer

Edited by G. Goos, J. Hartmanis and J

Advisory Board: W. Brauer   D. Gries   J. Stoer

Springer

Berlin
Heidelberg
New York
Barcelona
Budapest
Hong Kong
London
Milan
Paris
Tokyo

Selim G. Akl Frank Dehne
Jörg-Rüdiger Sack Nicola Santoro (Eds.)

Algorithms and Data Structures

4th International Workshop, WADS '95
Kingston, Canada, August 16-18, 1995
Proceedings

 Springer

Series Editors

Gerhard Goos, Karlsruhe University, Germany

Juris Hartmanis, Cornell University, NY, USA

Jan van Leeuwen, Utrecht University, The Netherlands

Volume Editors

Selim G. Akl
Department of Computing and Information Science, Queen's University
Kingston, Canada K7L 3N6

Frank Dehne
Jörg-Rüdiger Sack
Nicola Santoro
School of Computer Science, Carleton University
1125 Colonel By Drive, Ottawa, Canada K1S 5B6

Cataloging-in-Publication data applied for

Die Deutsche Bibliothek - CIP-Einheitsaufnahme

Algorithms and data structures : 4th international workshop ;
proceedings / WADS '95, Kingston, Canada, August 16 - 18,
1995. Selim G. Akl ... (ed.). - Berlin ; Heidelberg ; New York ;
Barcelona ; Budapest ; Hong Kong ; London ; Milan ; Paris ;
Tokyo : Springer, 1995
  (Lecture notes in computer science ; Vol. 955)
  ISBN 3-540-60220-8
NE: Akl, Selim G. [Hrsg.]; WADS <4, 1995, Kingston, Ontario>; GT

CR Subject Classification (1991): F.1-2, E.1, G.2, I.3.5, H.3.3

ISBN 3-540-60220-8 Springer-Verlag Berlin Heidelberg New York

© Springer-Verlag Berlin Heidelberg 1995
Printed in Germany

Typesetting: Camera-ready by author
SPIN 10486509   06/3142 – 5 4 3 2 1 0   Printed on acid-free paper

Preface

The papers in this volume were presented at the 1995 Workshop on Algorithms and Data Structures (WADS '95). The workshop took place from August 16 to August 18, 1995, at Queen's University in Kingston, Ontario and was sponsored by the Natural Sciences and Engineering Research Council of Canada, Carleton University, ITRC, and Queen's University.

In response to the program committee's call for papers, 121 papers where submitted. From these submissions, the program committee selected 40 for presentation at the workshop. In addition to these papers, the workshop included 5 invited presentations.

August 1995

S. Akl
F. Dehne
J.-R. Sack
N. Santoro

Program Committee

Co-chairs: S. Akl, F. Dehne, J.-R. Sack, and N. Santoro.

A. Apostolico, R. Baeza-Yates, C. Bajaj, B. Bhattacharya, J.-D. Boissonnat, P. Eades, F. Fich, D. Gries, S. Hambrusch, D. Kirkpatrick, R. Klein, S. R. Kosaraju, D. Krizanc, M. Li, A. Lingas, R. Lins, E. Lodi, M. Loui, E. Mayr, J. Peters, G. Plaxton, A. L. Rosenberg, P. Shor, J. Stolfi, S. Song, R. Tamassia, R. Tan, S. Whitesides, P. Widmayer, S. Zaks, N. Ziviani.

Conference Chair

H. Meijer

Table of Contents

Lower Bounds to Processor-Time Tradeoffs under Bounded-Speed Message Propagation

Gianfranco Bilardi*　　　　　Franco P. Preparata**

Abstract. Lower bounds are developed for the processor-time tradeoffs of machines such us linear arrays and two-dimensional meshes, which are compatible with the physical limitation on speed propagation of messages. It is shown that, under this limitation, parallelism and locality combined may yield speedups superlinear in the number of processors. The results are obtained by means of on a novel technique, called the "closed-dichotomy-size technique", designed to obtain lower bounds to the computation time for networks of processors, each of which is equipped with a local hierarchical memory.

1 Introduction

As digital technology continues to improve, there is an emerging consensus that physical limitations to signal propagation speed and device size are becoming increasingly significant. It is therefore justified to analyze a hypothetical environment where – provocatively – the limits of physics have been attained. Such analysis [BP92] forces a breakdown of several standard models based on instantaneou signal propagation. We denote such hypothetical environment the "limiting technology".

Typically, the classical processor-time tradeoff embodied by Brent's Principle [B74] (whereby a computation running for T steps on n processors can be emulated in at most $\lceil n/p \rceil T$ steps on $p < n$ processors of the same type), no longer holds. Informally, when communication delays are proportional to physical distances, the deployment of p processors has the potential to lead to speed-ups both through p-fold parallelism and through reduction of processor-to-memory distance (exploitation of data locality).

In [BP95a], we have developed simulations of machines with n processors by machines with $p < n$ processors, in the framework of the limiting technology. The slowdown of such simulations takes the form $O((n/p)\Lambda(n, p, m))$, where parameter m denotes the number of memory cells in unit volume and plays an important role. It is natural to interpret the factor n/p as due to the loss of parallelism (*Brent's slowdown*) and the factor $\Lambda(n, p, m)$ as due to the loss of locality (*locality slowdown*).

* Dipartimento di Elettronica e Informatica, Università di Padova, Padova, Italy. Supported in part by the ESPRIT III Basic Research Programme of the EC under contract No. 9072 (Project GEPPCOM), by the Italian Ministry of University and Research, and by Brown University. email: bilardi@artemide.dei.unipd.it

** Department of Computer Science, Brown University, 115 Waterman, Providence, RI 02912-1910. Supported in part by NSF Grant CCR94-00232 and ONR Contract N 00014-91-J-4052, ARPA order 2225. email: franco@cs.brown.edu

In this paper we present lower bounds to the slowdown of any simulation, which match the upper bounds of [BP95a], thereby showing that the locality slowdown is an inherent feature of the limiting technology and providing a quantitative characterization for it.

More specifically, let $M_d(n, p, m)$, $d = 1, 2$, denote a d-dimensional mesh of p nodes, each of which is a CPU equipped with a hierarchical memory module of mn/p locations (see Section 2 for a formal definition). Clearly M_1 and M_2 have the topology of the conventional linear array and two-dimensional mesh, respectively. We will establish:

Theorem 1. *For $d = 1, 2$, in the worst case, the slowdown of any simulation of $M_d(n, n, m)$ by $M_d(n, p, m)$ satisfies*

$$T_p/T_n = \Omega((n/p)\lambda(n, p, m)),$$

where ** $\lambda(n, p, m) = \min((n/p)^{1/d}, m \, \ell og(n/m^d)/p^{1/d} + m \, \ell og(n/pm^{2d}))$.

We note that the term λ, corresponding to the locality slowdown, increases with m up to a certain value, and then only depends on n and p. To observe this phenomenon more clearly, let us consider the special case arising when $p = 1$, for $d = 2$. We have $T_1/T_n = \Omega(n \min(n^{1/2}, m \, \ell og(n/m^2)))$. When $m = 1$ (as is the case for cellular-automaton and many systolic computations), the worst-case locality slowdown is $\Omega(\log n)$. When $m \geq n^{1/2}$, the locality slowdown is $\Omega(n^{1/2})$.

As mentioned above, the lower bounds embodied by Theorem 1 match the upper bounds of [BP95a] for most values of the parameters n, p, and m.

The present paper also contributes a new method, of independent interest, called the *closed-dichotomy size technique*, to obtain time lower bounds for machines with hierarchical memory. Whereas alternative techniques were already known ([HK81],[S95]) for uniprocessors, our method also applies to multiprocessor networks where each node is equipped with a hierarchical memory, by capturing the tradeoff between inter-node and intra-node access costs.

In the remainder of this paper we develop the models (Section 2) and the techniques (Section 3) needed to derive the results for linear arrays and meshes (Section 4) . We conclude (Section 5) by comparing upper and lower bounds. Due to space constraints, proofs will be either omitted or sketched, and the reader is referred to [BP95b] for details.

2 Model

We shall consider parallel machines built as interconnections of (processing-element, memory-module) pairs. Such a pair is modeled as a Hierarchical Random Access Machine, or H-RAM [CR73],[AACS87], [S95].

Definition 2. An $f(x)$-H-RAM is a random access machine where an access to address x takes time $f(x)$.

** Hereafter, we let $\ell og(x)$ denote $\log_2(x+2)$. Note that $\ell og(x) \geq 1$ for any nonnegative x.

According to this definition, a (processing-element, memory-module) pair is an $f(x)$-H-RAM. In $d \leq 3$ dimensions, denoting by m the number memory cells in a unit cube, the access function takes the form $f(x) = (x/m)^{1/d}$.

Definition 3. For $d \geq 1$, we denote by $M_d(n, p, m)$, a d-dimensional near-neighbor interconnection of p $(x/m)^{1/d}$-H-RAMs where each H-RAM has memory size mn/p and the geometric distance between near neighbors is $(n/p)^{1/d}$.

Next, we consider a fully-connected set of H-RAMs.

Definition 4. A *clique of H-RAMs*, denoted $(f(x), \ell)$-CH$_p$, is a completely interconnected network of p nodes, each an $f(x)$-H-RAM (with unlimited memory); an access by a given node to a memory location in another node takes ℓ steps.

By assimilating each (processor,memory module) pair to a node of an $((x/m)^{1/d}, (n/p)^{1/d})$-CH$_p$, access time within such a pair is correctly modeled, whereas the access time outside the pair is conservatively underestimated. Hence, we have:

Proposition 5. An $((x/m)^{1/d}, (n/p)^{1/d})$-CH$_p$ is strictly more powerful than an $M_d(n, p, m)$. Therefore, a time lower bound for the former also holds for the latter.

The main goal of this paper is to establish lower bounds to the slowdown of a simulation of an $M_d(n, n, m)$ (the guest) by an $M_d(n, p, m)$ (the host). The general approach consists in considering a computation whose execution time we can be bounded from above for the guest and from below for the host. The ratio of these two bounds provides an existential lower bound to the slowdown of any simulation.

The computations we shall consider for the above purpose will be modeled by appropriate directed acyclic graphs (dags) $G = (V, A)$, where:

- A vertex v with no incoming arc represents an input operation;
- A vertex v with k incoming arcs is labeled with a k-argument operator;
- The values associated with the vertices in a designated subset are regarded as outputs .

3 The closed-dichotomy technique

The time performance of $M_d(n, p, m)$ whose memory system is distributed and hierarchical depends not only on the number of memory accesses, but also upon their "distance" from the executing processor. Therefore, the following quantity pertaining to H-RAM computations plays a key role.

Definition 6. Consider the execution of a computation on an H-RAM with memory cells numbered $\{0, 1, \ldots\}$. For $S \geq 0$, we call *access complexity*, denoted $Q(S)$, the number of accesses made to addresses $\{S, S + 1, \ldots\}$.

In this section, we focus on lower bounds to access complexity which will be translated into lower bounds to running time. The basic idea behind our technique is simple: if the execution of a given dag requires each of β values to be written before any of them is read, then at least $\beta - S$ of these values must be written to and read from an address no lower than S, thus contributing to $Q(S)$. Furthermore, this argument can be separately applied to each member of a family of disjoint subsets of dag vertices, thus capturing the need for multiple use of the storage. The quantity β itself can be related to the graph-theoretic notion of closed-dichotomy size, defined below.

Definition 7. Given a dag $G = (V, A)$, a subset of its vertices, $W \subseteq V$, is called *closed* if whenever $v \in W$ the predecessors of v are also in W.

Definition 8. Given dag $G = (V, A)$ and $W \subseteq V$, let $B_{out}(W)$ denote the set of vertices in W that have a successor in $V - W$. The *closed-dichotomy size* of G is the function β of the integer variable $w \in \{0, ..., |V|\}$ defined as

$$\beta(w) = \min\{|B_{out}(W)| : W \subseteq V, W \text{ closed}, |W| = w\}. \tag{1}$$

The closed-dichotomy size provides a lower bound to the access complexity of a dag computation.

Lemma 9. *Given dag $G = (V, A)$, let $\beta(w)$ denote the closed-dichotomy size of G. For any w, with $0 \leq w \leq |V|$, the access complexity $Q(S)$ of G satisfies*

$$Q(S) \geq 2(\beta(w) - S). \tag{2}$$

The preceding lemma is easily generalizable to the case where rather than to set V we choose to refer to a collection $\{U_1, U_2, \ldots, U_k\}$ of disjoint subsets of V, each of which is the vertex set of a dag defined as follows:

Definition 10. Given dag $G = (V, A)$ and $U \subseteq V$, we denote by $G(U)$ the subgraph (U, A_U) of G induced by U, where $A_U = \{(u, v) \in A : u, v \in U\}$.

We then immediately have:

Theorem 11. *Given dag $G = (V, A)$, let $U_1, U_2, \ldots, U_q$ be disjoint subsets of V and let β_i denote the closed-dichotomy size of $G(U_i)$, for $i = 1, \ldots, q$. The access complexity of G satisfies*

$$Q(S) \geq \sum_{i=1}^{q} 2(\beta_i(w_i) - S), \tag{3}$$

for any $w_1, ..., w_q$, with $0 \leq w_i \leq |U_i|$.

The analysis developed above is clearly inadequate for the multiprocessor case, since it does not capture the communication requirements of the computation. To cover such aspect, we now develop an extension of the closed-dichotomy technique, where both local and remote accesses are taken into consideration.

Definition 12. For a given computation on an CH_p, for $j = 0, 1, ..., p - 1$, we denote by $Q_j(S)$ the *internal* access complexity of node j (the number of accesses to local addresses $\geq S$) and by R_j the *external* access complexity of node j (the number of accesses to other nodes).

Our results will expose a trade-off between internal (local) accesses and external (remote) accesses. To capture this trade-off quantitatively, we need to extend the notion of closed-dichotomy size to apply to situations where the computation dag can be partitioned among different processors, and an upper bound is placed on the amount of inter-processor communication. The next definition formalizes the observation that a value is communicated whenever the vertices u and v of an arc of the computation dag are executed by different processors.

Definition 13. Given a dag $G = (V, A)$ and a partition $\{V_0, V_1, ..., V_{p-1}\}$ of V into (possibly empty) subsets, $u \in V_h$ is a *communication vertex* if and only if there is an arc (u, v) such that $v \notin V_h$. The *communication number* r of a partition is the number of its communication vertices. A subset $U \subseteq V_j$ of a block of the partition is referred to as a *monochromatic* subset of V.

A monochromatic set is executed by a single processor. Intuitively, we expect a tradeoff between internal and external access complexities, in the sense that, as communication decreases, there will typically be monochromatic subsets with significant internal access complexity. A measure of this property of a dag is provided by the following extension of the notion of dichotomy size.

Definition 14. Given dag $G = (V, A)$, and integers $0 \leq w \leq |V|$ and $r \geq 0$, the *distributed closed-dichotomy size* (DCDS) $\beta(w|r)$ of G is the maximum integer b such that, for every partition $\{V_0, V_1, ..., V_{p-1}\}$ of V with communication number no greater than r, and for every closed subset W of V with size $|W| = w$, there is a $j \in \{0, 1, ..., p - 1\}$ such that at least b vertices in $W \cap V_j$ have a successor in $(V - W) \cap V_j$.

The following theorem expresses the internal/external access tradeoff alluded to above.

Theorem 15. *Given a dag $G = (V, A)$, let $\{U_1, U_2, ..., U_q\}$ be disjoint subsets of V such that the induced subgraphs $G(U_1), ..., G(U_q)$ all have the same DCDS function $\tilde{\beta}(\cdot|\cdot)$. Then, for any execution of G on CH_p with $R = \sum_{j=0}^{p-1} R_j$ we have*

$$\sum_{j=0}^{p-1} Q_j(S) \geq q(\tilde{\beta}(w|2R/q) - S) - R, \tag{4}$$

for any value of w.

Sketch of proof We underestimate the contribution of each individual set U_i (which may be shared by several nodes of CH_p). There are at least $q/2$ values of i for which at most $2R/q$ external accesses involve transmission of values of vertices in U_i. Clearly, any such U_i contains at most $2R/q$ communication vertices. Next we argue as for Lemma 9. For any node j executing (a portion of) U_i, a value is either stored locally or at some other node. Since at most $2R/q$ accesses are available, at most R/q values can be stored remotely. Therefore, at least $\tilde{\beta}(w|2R/q) - R/q - S$ cells with addresses $\geq S$ are being used, i.e., the contribution of subset U_i is $2(\tilde{\beta}(w|2R/q) - R/q - S)$. Since there are at least $q/2$ such disjoint subsets, relation (4) is established. □

Note the different roles of subsets $\{V_0, V_1, ..., V_{p-1}\}$ and $\{U_1, U_2, ..., U_k\}$ introduced above. $\{V_0, V_1, ..., V_{p-1}\}$ is an *arbitrary* partition of V and V_j is the subset assigned to processor j (node j of clique CH_p) for execution, whereas $\{U_1, U_2, ..., U_k\}$ are *selected* disjoint subsets of V (usually, a partition of V), selected on the basis that they generate well quantifiable demands on the simulation effort.

We use now the notion of access complexity to obtain lower bounds to dag execution time on H-RAMs and cliques of H-RAMs, which in this context are adequate models of uniprocessor and multiprocessor machines, respectively.

We begin by relating $Q(S)$ to the computation time of an $f(x)$-H-RAM.

Proposition 16. Let $f(x) = ax^\alpha$, with $0 < \alpha \leq 1$. Let $S_h = \sigma 2^h$, for $h = 0, 1, ..., g-1$. Then, for a computation with access complexity $Q(S)$ the computation time T of an $f(x)$-H-RAM satisfies

$$T_{\text{H-RAM}} \geq (1 - 2^{-\alpha}) \sum_{h=0}^{g-1} Q(S_h) f(S_h). \tag{5}$$

Proof Let $\sigma 2^h \leq x < \sigma 2^{h+1}$. An access to address x takes time $f(x)$. It is easily shown that

$$f(x) \geq f(\sigma 2^h) = a\sigma^\alpha 2^{\alpha h} > a\sigma^\alpha (1 - 2^{-\alpha}) \sum_{i=0}^{h} 2^{\alpha i} = (1 - 2^{-\alpha}) \sum_{i=0}^{h} f(S_i) \tag{6}$$

i.e., the quantity $(1-2^{-\alpha}) \sum_{i=0}^{h} f(S_i)$, which is the contribution of the considered access to x to the right-hand side of (5), is a lower bound to the time to access x. □

Proposition 16 suggests an effective bookkeeping of the access cost. Indeed, an access to address x in the $f(x)$-H-RAM is interpreted as follows. A collection of imaginary nested barriers is defined on the memory real-estate, separating memory regions of geometrically increasing sizes. Traversal of barrier S_j incurs a charge $(1 - 2^{-\alpha})f(S_j)$. The access time is no less than the sum of the charges across the traversed barriers.

Proposition 16 can be generalized to the clique of H-RAMs.

Proposition 17. *With the notation of Proposition 16, the computation time on an $(f(x), \ell)$-CH$_p$, satisfies*

$$T_{\text{CH}} \geq (1 - 2^{-\alpha}) \sum_{h=0}^{g-1} Q(S_h) f(S_h/p)/p. \tag{7}$$

We now turn our attention to the communication aspects. We let $\tau_j = \sum_{S \geq 0} f(S)(Q_j(S) - Q_j(S+1))$ and $\rho_j = \ell R_j$ denote the time spent by node j in local and non-local accesses, respectively. Finally, we let

$$\tau = (1/p) \sum_{j=0}^{p-1} \tau_j, \text{ and } \rho = (1/p) \sum_{j=0}^{p-1} \rho_j.$$

Clearly, the overall *running time* T_p of the computation satisfies the inequality

$$T_p \geq \tau + \rho. \tag{8}$$

The following theorem gives quantitative substance to the sought τ-ρ trade-off. The setting to which the theorem is to be applied is a uniform tessellation of the computation dag (a $(d+1)$-dimensional cube partitioned into identical $(d+1)$-dimensional cubes). For notational convenience the access function $f(x)$ of the CH$_p$ node is compactly expressed as ax^α.

Theorem 18. *Consider an $(f(x), \ell)$-CH$_p$ where $f(x) = ax^\alpha$ ($0 < \alpha \leq 1$), and let $S_h = \sigma 2^h$, for $h = 0, 1, ..., g-1$ (as in Proposition 16). Given dag $G = (V, A)$, for $h = 0, 1, ..., g-1$ and for some constant η, let sets $U_1^h, U_2^h, ..., U_{q_h}^h$, all of size $\eta 2^{h(\alpha+1)}$, form a partition of V (thus, $q_h = |V|/(\eta 2^{h(\alpha+1)})$), and be such that $G(U_1^h), ..., G(U_{q_h}^h)$ all have DCDS $\tilde{\beta}_h(w_h|2R/q_h) \geq 2S_h$, for suitable values of w_h and R. Then, the time T_p to execute G on an (ax^α, ℓ)-CH$_p$ satisfies the inequality*

$$T_p \geq (1/p)\min_{R \geq 0}\max(\lambda|V| - \mu R, \ell R), \tag{9}$$

where $\lambda = (1 - 2^{-\alpha})a\eta^{-1}\sigma^{(\alpha+1)}g$ and $\mu = a(\sigma/2)^\alpha 2^{\alpha g}$.

An important aspect of the preceding result is that it is totally independent of the arbitrary assignment of processors to dag vertices (as specified by the partition $\{V_0, V_1, ..., V_{p-1}\}$) and that it hinges exclusively on partitions $\{U_1^h, U_2^h, ..., U_{q_h}^h\}$, for $h = 0, 1, ..., g-1$, which can be conveniently selected.

4 Computation dags for the analysis of simulations

As mentioned in Section 2, we specify below the computations for which we establish upper bounds for their execution on the guest (in this section) and lower bounds for their execution on the host (in the two subsequent sections). Conservatively, these computations are modeled as dags, so that, for a given input size, the pattern of memory references is *static*, that is, independent of the input values. Since in many applications memory references are *dynamic*, with addresses determined only at "run-time", our results will show that the difficulty of the simulation is not due to the unpredictability of the accesses.

We begin by observing that an arbitrary T-step computation of a network $H = (N, E)$, where each node has one word of state information, can be conveniently modeled by a dag as follows:

Definition 19. Given an undirected graph $H = (N, E)$ and an integer $T \geq 1$, we let $G_T(H) = (V, A)$ denote a directed acyclic graph where:

$$V = \{(v, t) : v \in N, 0 \leq t \leq T\},$$

$$A = \{(u, t - 1), (v, t)) : u = v \text{ or } (u, v) \in E, 1 \leq t \leq T\}.$$

A simulation of H can be viewed as the execution of graph $G_T(H)$. In our arguments, however, we shall make use of the following more general type of dag, modeling a specific computation of a network $H = (N, E)$ with m cells of memory at each node.

Definition 20. Given an undirected graph $H = (N, E)$ and integers $m, T \geq 1$, we let $G_T^m(H) = (V, A \cup A_m)$ denote the directed acyclic graph where V and A are as in Definition (19), and

$$A_m = \{((v, t), (v, t + m)) : (v, t) \in V, \ t + m \leq T\}.$$

It is straightforward to verify the following statement.

Proposition 21. Dag $G_T^m(H)$ can be executed by $H = (N, E)$ in T steps, with processor at node $v \in N$ evaluating vertex $(v, t) \in V$ at step t and storing the result in its private memory at location $t \bmod m$, for $1 \leq t \leq T$. Input value $(v, 0)$ is assumed to be stored at location 0 of node v at $t = 0$.

Of particular interest to us are the dags $G_T^m(M_d(n, n, m))$, for $d = 1, 2$, for which the above proposition provides the upper bound T to their execution time on the guest $M_d(n, n, m)$. It is the objective of the two next sections to establish lower bounds to their execution time on the host $M_d(n, p, m)$.

For notational convenience, we let:

$$L_T^m(n) \stackrel{\triangle}{=} G_T^m(M_1(n, n, m)), \qquad (10)$$

It is also convenient to let $L_{k-1}^m \stackrel{\triangle}{=} L_{k-1}^m(k)$. If the superscript m is omitted, it will be assumed that $m = 1$.

5 Lower bounds for simulations

Below, we shall consider in some detail linear arrays and apply the closed-dichotomy technique to dags representing computations of $M_1(n, n, m)$ to obtain lower bounds to the number of "remote" accesses required by any execution of such dags. When the cost of the accesses is chosen to reflect the memory structure of the host linear array, we obtain the desired simulation lower bounds.

Lemma 22. *Let $X \subseteq V$, be a closed subset of vertices in dag $L_{k-1} = (V, A)$. Then*

(a) *For suitable values of $\tau_0, ..., \tau_{k-1}$, $X = \{(h, t) : 0 \leq h < k, 0 \leq t < \tau_h\}$.*
(b) *For $h = 1, 2, ..., k - 1$, $|\tau_h - \tau_{h-1}| \leq 1$.*

Next we state an easily established relationship between the boundary of a closed $X \subseteq V$ and its size (number of vertices).

Lemma 23. *Let $X \subseteq V$, with $|X| = \lfloor |V|/4 \rfloor = \lfloor k^2/4 \rfloor$, be a closed subset of vertices in dag $L_{k-1} = (V, A)$. Then $\tau_h < (3/4)k$, for any $0 \leq h < k$.*

Intuitively, as we decrease the size of closed set X, the upper boundary $\{\tau_h\}$ of X is correspondingly bounded.

We shall show below that dags of type L_{k-1} possess desirable properties for our objectives. Therefore they will be used as *standard* dags in forming partitions like $\{U_1, U_2, \ldots, U_k\}$, which are instrumental to establish lower bound to the execution time. We shall separately consider the single-processor and the multiprocessor case.

A. Single-processor simulation. Based on the preceding lemmas we begin by showing a result on the closed-dichotomy size of suitable subsets of L^m_{k-1} (recall that L^m_{k-1} is the dag of a $(k - 1)$-step computation of an $M_1(k, k, m)$).

Lemma 24. *For $m \leq k/4$, the value of the closed-dichotomy size of L^m_{k-1} at $\lfloor k^2/4 \rfloor$ satisfies the inequality*

$$\beta(\lfloor k^2/4 \rfloor) \geq mk/4. \tag{11}$$

Sketch of proof A set $X \subseteq V$ is closed in L^m_{k-1} if and only if it is closed in L_{k-1}. The subset $B_{out}(X)$ of the vertices in X with a successor in $V - X$ satisfies

$$|B_{out}(X)| \geq \sum_{h=0}^{k-1} \min(\tau_h, m). \tag{12}$$

Since $\tau_h < (3/4)k \leq k - m$, each vertex (h, t) in X, if $t \geq \tau_h - m$, is the origin of an arc terminating in $V - X$. It is easy to show that $|B_{out}(X)| \geq mk/4$, . $\square$

Essentially, Lemmas 1 and 2 together establish that, as long as $4m \leq k \leq n$, any closed subset of L^m_{k-1} of size $k^2/4$ has a closed-dichotomy size at least $mk/4$.

Next we combine this result and Theorem 11, to obtain a lower bound to the access complexity of $L_T^m(n)$. Specifically for any value of S in a suitable range (in all cases address S cannot exceed nm), a value of $k \leq n$ can be chosen as a function of the threshold S in order to maximize the lower bound to $Q(S)$.

Lemma 25. *Let $n \leq T$. The access complexity of $L_T^m(n)$ satisfies $Q(S) \geq Tnm^2/(32S)$, for any S in the range $m^2/2 \leq S \leq nm/8$ (which constrains $m \leq n/4$).*

Sketch of proof We partition the vertices of $L_T^m(n)$ into $q = Tn/k^2$ "squares' of sidelength k. By Lemma 24, the closed dichotomy size of any such square at $w = \lfloor k^2/4 \rfloor$ satisfies $\beta(w) \geq mk/4$, so that $Q(S) \geq q2(\beta(w) - S)$. We select k to maximize the lower bound to $Q(S)$, i.e., $k = 8S/m$. This choice yields $Q(S) \geq (Tn/k^2)2((mk)/4 - S) = Tnm^2/(32S)$. $\qquad\square$

The preceding lower bound to $Q(S)$ is now translated into a lower bound to computation time of a suitable H-RAM.

Theorem 26. *Let $m \leq n/4$ and $n \leq T_n$. The time T_1 to execute dag $L_T^m(n)$ on an (x/m)-H-RAM (or, equivalently, an $M_1(n, 1, m)$) satisfies*

$$T_1 = \Omega(Tnm\log(n/m)).$$

Proof We apply Proposition 16 with $f(x) = x/m$, ($\alpha = 1$, $a = 1/m$), and select $S_h = (m^2/2)2^h$ for $h = 0, 1, ..., \log(n/4m)$. $\qquad\square$

Arguments analogous to those of Lemmas 23, 24, and Proposition 16 can be applied to the case $m \geq n$ to obtain the following result.

Theorem 27. *For $m > (3/2)n$, the slowdown of any simulation of $M_1(n, n, m)$ by $M_1(n, 1, m)$ satisfies*

$$T_1/T_n = \Omega(n^2).$$

B. Multiprocessor simulations. We begin by considering the lower bound which obtains by using in Proposition 17 the lower bound to $Q(S)$ given by Lemma 25.

Proposition 28. *In the worst case, the slowdown of any simulation of $M_1(n, n, m)$ by $M_1(n, p, m)$ satisfies*

$$T_p/T_n = \Omega(nm\log(n/m))/p^2).$$

Next, by appropriately modifying the argument of Lemma 24, we obtain a lower bound to the distributed closed-dichotomy size of dag L_{k-1}^m for particular values of closed subset size and communication number.

Lemma 29. *For $m \leq k/4$, the value of the distributed closed-dichotomy size of $L_{k-1}^m = (V, A \cup A_m)$ at $\lfloor k^2/4 \rfloor$ with communication number $k/8$ satisfies the inequality*

$$\beta(\lfloor k^2/4 \rfloor | k/8) \geq mk/8. \tag{13}$$

We can now use sets of type L_{k-1}^m, for appropriate values of k, to form the partitions $U_1^h, U_2^h, ..., U_{q_h}^h$, which appear in the statement of Theorem 18, in order to prove the following theorem (the main result of this section).

Theorem 30. *Let $m \leq n/4$. In the worst case, the slowdown of any simulation of $M_1(n, n, m)$ by $M_1(n, p, m)$ satisfies the inequality*

$$T_p/T_n = \Omega((n/p)m \log(n/pm^2)). \tag{14}$$

Sketch of proof For any value of the communication number R, we try to maximize the local access complexity. Therefore we establish a geometric progression of thresholds S_h, $h = 0. \dots, g-1$, and for each h construct a tessellation of $L_T^m(n)$ into q_h "squares " of sidelength k_h. We select the maximum g compatible with the condition $\tilde{\beta}_h(\lfloor k_h^2/4 \rfloor | k_h/8) \geq mk_h/8$ and select $S_h = mk_h/8$. With these choices, all assumptions of Theorem 18 hold. Minimizing with respect to g yields the result. $\qquad\square$

Combining Proposition 28 with Theorem 30 and with a simple generalization of Theorem 27 to a p-processor host, we summarize the results of this subsection.

Theorem 31. *In the worst case, the slowdown of any simulation of $M_1(n, n, m)$ by $M_1(n, p, m)$ satisfies*

$$T_p/T_n = \Omega((n/p)\min(m\ell og(n/m^2 p) + m\ell og(n/m)/p)).$$

The structure of the arguments developed above for linear arrays can be applied to mesh networks, although the combinatorial lemmas require independent and somewhat more involved proofs. The results are reflected by the selection $d = 2$ in Theorem 1 in the Introduction.

6 Conclusions

Within the context of the limiting technology, a scenario where the time to transmit a signal is proportional to the traveled distance, we have shown that both the deployment of parallelism and the exploitation of locality jointly afford speed-ups that are superlinear in the number of used processors, for one- and two-dimensional arrays. Specifically, we have shown that, when simulating a computation of an n-processor array by a p-processor array, in addition to the standard slowdown attributable to loss of parallelism (Brent slowdown), there exists a slowdown due to loss of locality. The necessity of this additional slowdown has been shown for a maximally connected network of processors, which represents a very conservative approximation of linear arrays nad meshes.

It is therefore surprising that, for most values of the parameters, the lower bounds to slowdown match the corresponding upper bounds. Indeed, as mentioned in the Introduction, in a companion paper [BP95a] we have described simulation strategies of an $M_d(n, n, m)$ by an $M_d(n, p, m)$, for which the locality slowdown $\Lambda(n, m, p)$ has the following behavior in four significant ranges of the parameter m:

- (1) for $m \leq (n/p)^{1/2d}$, $\Lambda(n, m, p) = (m/p^{1/d}) \log m + m \log(2n^{1/d}/p^{1/d}m^2)$,
- (2) for $(n/p)^{1/2d} \leq m \leq (np)^{1/2d}$, $\Lambda(n, m, p) = (m/p) \log(n/p)^{1/2d} + 2(n/p)^{1/2d}$,
- (3) for $(np)^{1/2d} \leq m \leq n^{1/d}$, $\Lambda(n, m, p) = (m/p^{1/d}) \log(2n^{1/d}/m) + n^{1/d}/m$,
- (4) for $n^{1/d} \leq m$, $\Lambda(n, m, p) = (n/p)^{1/d}$.

Note (Theorem 1) that the lower bounds match the upper bounds in Ranges 1,3, and 4. Only for Range 2 proving a matching lower bound remains an open problem. The conclusion we reach is that the demonstrated locality slowdown is an inherent feature deriving from fundamental physical laws.

References

[AACS87] A. Aggarwal, B. Alpern, A.K. Chandra and M. Snir. A Model for Hierarchical Memory. In *Proc. of the 19th ACM Symposium on Theory of Computing*, (1987), 305–314.

[ACS90] A. Aggarwal, A.K. Chandra and M. Snir. Communication Complexity of PRAMs. *Theoretical Computer Science*, 71:3–28, 1990.

[BP86] G. Bilardi and F.P. Preparata. Area-Time Lower-Bound Techniques with Application to Sorting. *Algorithmica*, 1:65–91, 1986.

[BP92] G. Bilardi and F.P. Preparata. Horizons of Parallel Computing. In *Proc. of INRIA 25th Anniversary Symposium*, invited paper, 1992, LNCS Springer-Verlag. To appear in Journal on Parallel and Distributed Computing.

[BP95a] G. Bilardi and F.P. Preparata. Processor-Time Tradeoffs under Bounded-Speed Message Propagation: Part I, Upper Bounds. TR, CS Dept., Brown University, May 1995.

[BP95b] G. Bilardi and F.P. Preparata. Processor-Time Tradeoffs under Bounded-Speed Message Propagation: Part II, Lower Bounds. TR, CS Dept., Brown University, May 1995.

[B74] R.P. Brent. The Parallel Evaluation of General Arithmetic Expressions. *Journal of the ACM*, (21)2:201–206, 1974.

[CR73] S.A. Cook and R.A. Reckhow. Time Bounded Random Access Machines. *Journal of Comput. System Science*, 7:354–375, 1973.

[HK81] J.W. Hong and H.T. Kung. I/O Complexity: The Red–Blue Pebble Game. In *Proc. of the 13th ACM Symposium on Theory of Computing*, (1981), 326–333.

[S95] J.E. Savage. Space-Time Tradeoffs in Memory Hierarchies. TR, Dept. of Comp.Sci., Brown University, 1995.

[S86] L. Snyder. Type Architectures, Shared Memory, and the Corollary of Modest Potential. *Annual Review of Computer Science*, 1:289–317, 1986.

The Two-Line Center Problem from a Polar View: a New Algorithm and Data Structure

Jerzy W. Jaromczyk[1] and Miroslaw Kowaluk[2]

[1] Department of Computer Science, University of Kentucky, Lexington, KY 40506
[2] Institute of Informatics, Warsaw University, Warsaw, Poland

Abstract. We present a new algorithm for the two-line center problem (also called unweighted orthogonal L_∞-fit problem): "Given a set S of n points in the real plane, find two closed strips whose union contains all of the points and such that the width of the wider strip is minimized." An almost quadratic $O(n^2 \log^2 n)$ solution is given. The previously best known algorithm for this problem has time complexity $O(n^2 \log^5 n)$ and uses a parametric search methodology. Our solution applies a new geometric structure, *anchored lower and upper chains*, and is based on examining several constraint versions of the problem. The anchored lower and upper chain structure is of interest by itself and provides a fast response to queries that involve planar configurations of points. The algorithm does not assume the general position of the input data points.

1 Introduction

We present a new algorithm for the minmax orthogonal L_∞-fit problem in the two-dimensional space with respect to two lines. Cast in the geometric language, the problem is:

"Given a set S of n points in R^2, find two strips bounded by parallel lines whose union contains S and such that the width of the strips is as small as possible."

This problem is known in the literature as the *two-line center problem*.

We will show the following results:

1. A deterministic algorithms that solves the two-line center problem in $O(n^2 \log^2 n)$ and $O(n^2)$ space. That is the best up-to-date solution to the two-line center problem.

2. A new data structure, *anchored upper and lower chains*, to support efficiently the following queries:

- for a given point $p \in S$ and a (directed) query line h and l passing through p, find the tangents to the convex hull of $S^-(l)$ (the subset of those point in S that are in the left open half-plane of l) that are parallel to h.

- for a given point $p \in S$, a (directed) query line l passing through p, and a point $q \in S$, find the tangents to the convex hull of $S^-(l)$ that passes through q;

14

- for two given lines l and h passing through given points in S, find the common tangents to the convex hulls of $S^-(l)$ and $S^-(h)$.

The structure can be built in $O(n)$ time and $O(n)$ space per point when the polar order sorting for all the points is done in the preprocessing. The query time is $O(\log n)$. The total cost, for all the points in S, is $O(n^2)$ time and $O(n^2)$ space.

In addition to the above listed main results, the structure allows us to solve in $O(n^2 \log n)$ time the decision version of the two-line center problem: "given $r > 0$ determine if there are two stripes of width r whose union contains S". It automatically leads to an improvement by the factor of $\log^2 n$ in the parametric search algorithm by Agarwal and Sharir [AS] and results in $O(n^2 \log^3 n)$ time and $O(n^2)$ space complexity solution. (Note that our main result is even better than this improved parametric solution.)

2 Background

The problem is an unweighted two-dimensional instance of the minmax orthogonal L_∞-fit, that is: for a set of points S find

$$\min_{l_1,l_2} \max_i \min\{dist(p_i, l_1), dist(p_i, l_2)\}$$

where minimization is over all pairs of lines l_1, l_2.

Minimization with respect to just one line creates the one-line center problem known in the computational geometry literature as the *point set width problem*. This problem has several optimal $O(n \log n)$ solutions; see [PS]. When the convex hull of S is available then the width can be found in $O(n)$ time. On the other hand, if k is a part of the input and minimization is with respect to k lines the problem is $NP-hard$ in the strong sense; see [MT82, MT 83]. This follows from the strong $NP-completness$ of the point line cover problem: for any n and k, decide whether n given points can be covered with k straight lines. More discussion on the important problem of hyperplane approximation and its application can be found in the survey by Korneenko and Martini [KM93]. A weighted version of the problem is discussed, for example, in [HIIR89].

The $O(n^3)$ bound for the two-line center problem has been broken by Agarwal and Sharir [AS91] . They provided an almost quadratic solution $O(n^2 \log^5 n)$ that is based on the parametric search technique and a data structure that supports queries about the width of sets. Our solution does not use parametric search. Instead, it utilizes a new data structure that is applied to solve a few constrained versions of the problem; the best of the solutions for the constrained versions provides the global optimum.

3 Anchored lower and upper chains

The algorithm will rely on a data structure that maintains information about the convex hulls for those subsets of S that belong to halfplanes determined by lines passing through points of S. The structure is defined for each point p in S; this point will be called the *anchor* of the structure. Let l be an oriented line passing through p. Let $S^- = S^-(l)$ and $S^+ = S^+(l)$ be the points of S that lie in the left and right, respectively, open halfplanes determined by l. We are interested in the convex hulls $CH(S^+)$ and $CH(S^-)$. For each l, the set of edges of $CH(S^-)$ can be divided into two sets: edges that are invisible from p (we will call them *anchored (at p) upper chain*), and edges that are visible (*anchored (at p) lower chain*). In degenerate cases of the convex hull being a segment, the edges belong to both chains. For simplicity of presentation we will discuss only points in general position; without any technical difficulties the solution applies for any configuration of the input points.

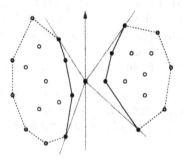

Anchored chains.

We are interested in the structural changes in the anchored upper and lower chains when line l is rotated clockwise about point p. We can think about this process as a special case of an off-line dynamic sequence of delete/insert operations. Points are added or deleted in the process of rotating l. Our goal is to have a structure that makes both anchored upper and lower chains readily available for every position of l; there are no more than n such positions in the discrete sense. From that point of view there is a resemblance with the existing structures for maintaining planar configurations, see for example Overmars and van Leeuwen, Overmars [OvL81], Herschberger, Suri [HS91]. Typical for those structures is that the upper and lower convex chains are determined with respect to a (arbitrarily) selected coordinate system; in other words, edge visibility is defined with respect to the point in infinity. Our anchored chains, which are defined with respect to a given point of S, have distinctive features that make them suitable for the two-line center problem.

There are two questions that we need to address:
- how to construct and represent the sequence of lower and upper chains?
- what is the space and time complexity of the representation?

As the result of rotating l, the subset of S to the left of l changes (clearly, the subset to the right of l changes as well). Let S_t^- denote this set at the moment t, where t corresponds to the number of deletion/insertions at the given stage of the rotation. In particular, S_0^- is S^- and S_{n-1}^- denotes the set to the left of the line after rotating by π. Note that to obtain all the convex hulls to the left of l the rotation must be performed about 2π; it is more convenient than working simultaneously on the left and right sides of l. In this process new edges are created as the result of deleting or inserting points. For classification purposes we will color vertices in the anchored upper an lower chains of $CH(S_t^-)$:*black* when the point is inserted (it becomes a vertex of the convex hull), *white* either if it is a vertex of $CH(S_0^-)$ (for the initial position of l), or if it is in the interior of $CH(S_{t-1}^-)$ and becomes a vertex of $CH(S_t^-)$ after some point is removed at time t. Other points are uncolored at time t. The colors may change during the rotation. The black points can get uncolored (if they get into the interior of the convex hull) and they can get colored white later, after some point is deleted. This process creates new edges in the anchored chains. We call an edge *white* if both their ends are *white* at the time the edge is created, *black* if the both ends are *black*, and *grey* otherwise. For $CH(S_t^-)$ the upper and lower chains may consist of white, grey, and black edges. Note that black and white edges are not interleaved within the chain. The union of all the lower chains for p is denoted by $LC(p)$, for the the upper chains by $UC(p)$.

Now we can answer the combinatorial question posed earlier:

Lemma 1. *For every point p the cardinality of the set (not multiset) of the edges in the entire sequence of the lower chains is bounded by $7n - 10$. That means, the cardinality of $LC(p) = \bigcup_{t=0}^{2n-3} LC(S_t^-)$ is bounded by $7n - 10$. The same bound holds true for $UC(p)$.*

PROOF: We will count the number of edges after rotation by π and will perform this counting with respect to line l at its initial position. Denote the number of points to the left of l by L and their number to the right by R. Clearly $L + R = n - 1$. The number of edges crossing l is not bigger than $n - 1$; they are created only if a point is added or removed. The number of *grey* edges is not bigger than the number of the chains minus 1; each chain contains at most one *grey* edge; the first chain contains only white vertices and edges. To count the number of the remaining edges, that is, the edges with both their endpoints either in S_0^+ or in S_0^-, observe that they do not intersect each other except perhaps at their endpoints. Assume otherwise and consider a pair of crossing edges in the right halfplane and their four endpoints. They are inserted during the rotation and can never be deleted as the rotation stops after sweeping π radians. Then the line containing the edge connected to this point which is inserted last separates the remaining two points. This is not possible for an edge on the convex hull - a contradiction. For the left halfplane the argument is similar. In fact, these edges do not only form a planar graph, which is sufficient for the linearity of the structure, but the *white* edges as well as the *black* edges form a forest. Hence, the estimate is $(n - 1) + (n - 1) + (L - 1) + 2(R - 1)$ (no black nodes in the left halfplane). By symmetry, the total number of edges in the anchored lower chains for the remaining part of the rotation from π to 2π is bounded by $(n - 1) + (n - 1) + (R - 1) + 2(L - 1)$ which together with the above proves the $7n - 10$ upper bound.

□

Remark: Note that edges crossing l can mutually intersect and they can also intersect other edges of the collection; it is irrelevant to our counting, however.

3.1 Constructing the anchored lower chains

The structure will be built incrementally with insert/delete determined by the angular order. We start with finding for each $p_i \in S$ the ordering of $S \setminus \{p_i\}$ with respect to the polar angle around p_i. It can be accomplished in $O(n^2)$ time and space; see [LC85]. This preprocessing will be useful for constructing anchored chains for all of the points in S. In the next step, we build an auxiliary structure for S_0^+ by running the standard Graham's scan algorithm [G72] using the polar order of points with respect to p (in the counterclockwise direction), and separately for S_0^- (in the clockwise direction). The resulting structure consists of a tree of the candidate edges that are created during the Graham scan. For the anchored lower chains we need to consider only those candidate edges that are visible from the anchor point p. The size of this auxiliary structure is $O(n)$. The time to build the auxiliary structures is $O(n)$, after preprocessing. Note that after the rotation is completed, the auxiliary structures can be discarded. The auxiliary structures will be useful to modify the current chain when, after deleting a point and its corresponding edge, some points from the interior of the convex hull become visible. Note that the auxiliary structures contain all edges with both endpoints in the left and right halfplanes, respectively, which can potentially become visible for some position of the rotating line. Now the anchored lower chain structure is constructed as follows. The $LC(S_0^-)$ is found directly as a side effect of running the Graham's scan.

Assume inductively that chain $LC(S_t^-)$ is available and consider the structural changes it undergoes at time $t + 1$:

- a point q is inserted. It becomes the beginning of $LC(S_{t+1}^-)$ (and is colored *black*). The end of the edge beginning at q is found by scanning $LC(S_t^-)$. The scanning starts at this point v of $LC(S_t^-)$ which is next to q in the angular order with respect to p. The rest of the chain remains unchanged. The cost is proportional to the total number of scanned edges; note that the discarded edges will not be considered again.

- a point q is deleted. There are two possibilities. The (only) edge attached to q in $LC(S_t^-)$ has its other end v in S_0^-. Then the newly visible portion of the convex hull can be restored from the auxiliary structure for S_0^- starting at v. The cost is proportional to the number of edges scanned in the auxiliary structure. Although vertices in this structure can be examined several times, each edge is scanned at most once.

The second possibility is when v is in S_0^+. Then, after removing this edge and adding edges that become visible (using the above approach) we will need, in addition, to find the edge that bridges both sides. Here the auxiliary structures for both sides are helpful; note that it useful that the Graham's scan has been performed in different directions for S_0^- and S_0^+. The ends of the bridging edge can be found in $O(\log n)$ time using a standard search in the auxiliary structures, if these structures are augmented with additional pointers. However, it can be done in the amortized $O(1)$ per point, using the standard technique of finding the lower bridge for two convex chains, similar to the merging algorithm for a divide-and-conquer construction of the convex hull of a set of points; see [E87].

The complexity of the whole process is $O(n)$. Insertions and deletions scan edges in the anchored chains and in the auxiliary structures in constant cost per edge. Those edges never reappear in the chain. Hence by Lemma 1 the amortized cost of those operations is $O(n)$. An example illustrating the anchored chain construction is given in the Appendix.

The process is repeated for the rotation of l from π to 2π to construct the complete set of the anchored lower chains to the left of l. The similar construction is carried out for all the points in S serving as the anchors. The upper chains are constructed similarly.

3.2 Constructing an efficient representation for the anchored chains

The standard methods allow us to represent the union of all the upper and lower chains obtained in the process of rotating l, with pointers that provide fast traversal, in $O(n \log n)$ space per anchor point. We will use instead a structure that resembles an interwoven collection of skip lists and requires $O(n)$ space per point. For each chain, the sequences of black and white edges are represented separately. The chains have well defined beginnings and ends. We maintain an array of all the possible slopes for lines passing through $p \in S$ and every other point in S. (It corresponds to times in our rotation process.) The pointers from the corresponding slopes point to the beginning and ends of the chains. Each edge in the union of the anchored lower chains is represented only once in the structure. In fact, if the chains for white and black nodes are stored separately, there is no need for explicit representation of the grey edges. The pointers between nodes of the structure allow us to traverse the chains quickly. It requires some care to organize the pointers while maintaining the linear size of the structure. In our approach we utilize the fact that the white and the black edges form a forest of rooted trees. In each tree, in the order of the decrementing lengths of paths, the vertices along each path are labeled with integer numbers. These labels are distinct along each path and are the smallest natural numbers that satisfy the following invariant: for every two vertices v with label $2^k x$ (x being an odd number), and w with label $2^p y$ (y being an odd number), that are equally distant from their lower common ancestor in the tree, if v is on the path not longer than the path containing w, then 2^k divides 2^p. The labels are auxiliary and they determine the number of pointers launching at node v labeled with $2^k x$ to be $k + 1$. Similarly to skip lists, pointers point to vertices at the distances being powers of two. The total number of pointers is linear. An example of the structure (rotation by π) is given in the Appendix. Similar representation is used for the anchored upper chains.

To find, for example, the tangent line to $S^-(l)$ (p being the anchor) given direction s, we can proceed as follows. First, compare s with the slopes of the *grey* edges of $S^-(l)$ to decide whether the tangency point is among the black or white vertices. Then, in the appropriate chain we perform a walk along the pointers in a binary search fashion to locate the vertex of tangency. Due to the structure of the pointers this process requires a logarithmic time.

Theorem 2. *The collection of all anchored upper and lower chains for set S of n points can be constructed in $O(n^2)$ time and $O(n^2)$ space. The structure supports the basic queries (see Introduction) in $O(\log n)$ time.*

4 Algorithm for the two-line center problem

Let h_1, h_2 denote the boundary lines of the first stripe, and let $S(h_1, h_2)$ stand for the subset of S that is in this strip. Similarly, h_1^* and h_2^* are the boundary lines of the second stripe and points contained in this stripe, as well as the stripe itself, is denoted by $S(h_1^*, h_2^*)$. The boundary of each stripe is determined (supported) by at least three points - two on one line and a third on the other one. Otherwise, by a small rotation, the stripe could decrease its width. (Again, the case when one stripe reduces to a line is not difficult to handle.) When the stripes intersect each other their boundaries are divided into pieces; those unbounded pieces will be called *the boundary halflines*. The points determine the stripe in the sense that after removing any of them, the stripe can be narrowed without leaving any point of S outside; we will call these points *determiners*. Mutual positioning of the determiners categorizes the input sets into several cases. The top-level classification depends on whether one of the boundary lines of the optimal stripes contains an edge of the convex hull of S. If not, then the triples form configurations that can be grouped into three groups. This classification is based on how the determiners are placed on the boundary halflines. Groups 1 and 2 include cases where there is a halfline that contains two of the determiners or the stripes are parallel. In group 3 each of the (eight) boundary halflines contain at most one of the determiners. In our approach we find the optimal pair of stripes for each type of the configurations; look at them as the solutions to constrained versions of the problem. The best among those constrained solutions provides our global minimum. Let us emphasize that the above classification not only allows us to use individual algorithmic techniques for each configuration, but also provides additional information that guides the search. Namely, the search is guided both by balancing the widths of stripes and by checking that the next candidate for the stripes is determined by points forming currently analized configuration.

The key idea behind our algorithm is to select a few points as a candidate subset of determiners and then to propagate implications of this choice to find the remaining determiners. This selection depends on the constrained version being considered. For example, when the search is within configurations where one of the edges of $CH(S)$ supports a stripe then endpoints of the $CH(S)$ edges are selected as two candidate determiners. For other configurations we select a point and the endpoints of one of edges in the upper or lower chains associated with this point. The crucial observation here, in virtue of Lemma 1, is that the number of candidates to consider is $O(n^2)$ (the number of points times the number of edges in the anchored chains). Finally, we also consider all pairs of points. Three quite different algorithmic methods, which we will call *dissecting and touching*, *dissecting line* and *rotating stripe*, are used to tackle the constrained versions. Below we will briefly review these techniques.

The case when the endpoints of some edge e in $CH(S)$ support h_1 is probably the simplest. To find the optimal stripes meeting this constraint, we perform the following operation for each candidate e. Select h_1 as the line containing e. Sort the distances between h_1 and the remaining points in S. Place h_2 with respect to the distances at a point p in binary search fashion to find $S(h_1, h_2)$. The complementary set S^* lies outside $S(h_1, h_2)$. Its convex hull is readily available from the anchored upper and lower chain structure determined by p and h_2 and its width can be computed in $O(n)$ time. The binary search will provide the optimal pair of stripes for h_1 determined by e. Note that the widths of the stripes change monotonically during this search. The cost is $O(n \log n)$ for sorting and $\log n$ steps of the binary search iterations with $O(n)$ per iteration. Running this process for all the possible edges of $CH(S)$ costs $O(n^2 \log n)$.

Now, two different cases arise depending on whether some of the eight halflines in the arrangement of the boundaries of the stripes contains two of the determining points or does not. In the former case our approach is to select h_1 based on those points and to continue with finding the remaining lines (*dissecting and touching* and *dissecting line* techniques are used here). Only pairs of points that are the endpoints of the edges in the anchored chains must be considered. If none of the boundary halflines contain a pair of determiners then we select two points in S and draw through them parallel lines - candidate boundaries for $S(h_1, h_2)$. The *rotating stripe* technique is used here to find the optimal stripes. We will present each technique describing how it works for representative configurations. For the reference, figures illustrating the discussed cases are included next to the corresponding descriptions. Some notations will be useful here. Let p be a point and l be a line. $H(l, p)$ denotes the set of those points of S that are in the open halfspace determined by l and containing p. The remaining points of S, except for those on l, are denoted by $C(l, p)$. That is, $C(l, p)$ is the set of those points in S that are in the open halfplane determined by l and not containing p.

Dissecting and touching : We will begin with a case when there is exactly one boundary halfline that contains a pair of determiners t_1, t_2. These points are the endpoints of an edge in the upper chain for some point p which is a determiner for the second stripe. Therefore we can limit our analysis to considering p and edges in its upper chains and we do not need to analyze edges in the lower chains. Boundary line h_1 is determined by t_1, t_2. Boundary line h_1^* is one of the tangents to $C(h_1, p)$ passing through p. It leads to two subcases. For the first subcase consider this of the two tangents whose intersection with h_1 is closer to t_1. Boundary h_2 is found as the tangent to $H(h_1^*, t_1)$ and parallel to h_1. If $p \in S(h_1, h_2)$ then we stop the analysis as it leads to a configuration different from one being considered; p must be outside of the stripes in this configuration.

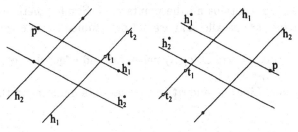

Boundary h_2^* is selected as the farther to h_1^* tangent to $H(h_2,p)$ or to $C(h_1,p)$ and parallel to h_1^*. For the second subcase consider that of the two tangents whose intersection with h_1 is farther to t_1. Boundary h_2^* is selected as the tangent to $H(h_1,p)$ and parallel to h_1^*. Now, if either of t_1, t_2 is in $S(h_1^*, h_2^*)$ then we stop the search for this case as it leads to a configuration different from one being considered; both t_1, t_2 must be outside of the stripes in this configuration. Boundary h_2 is selected as the parallel to h_1 and tangent to $H(h_2^*, t_1)$. It determines both the stripes. This case is concluded with a test that verifies if all the points in S are in the union of stripes; it can be done in cost $O(\log n)$ with the use of the anchored chains by checking if the points that are not in one stripe are between the boundaries of the other one. If S is not in that union then the chosen set of points p and t_1, t_2 is not a valid choice of determiners for this configuration and does not correspond to any solution.

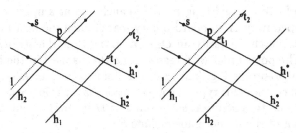

The second case arises when there are two pairs of points lying on the boundary halflines. Then one of these pairs t_1, t_2 belongs to some upper or lower chain for each of the points p, s in the other pair, with p being closer to the line passing through t_1, t_2. For this p we will analyze all pairs of points t_1, t_2 (edges) that are in its upper or lower chain. Boundary h_1 is selected as the line containing t_1, t_2. Let l be a parallel to h_1 passing through p. Using the polar order with respect to p we find points s_1 and s_2 on the convex hull of $C(l, t_1) \cup \{x \in S : x \in l\}$ that are vertices of this convex hull connected with p. These points are candidate points that together with p will determine h_1^*. We will analyze both cases rejecting, as previously, lines h_1^* that separate t_1 from t_2 as not being in the current configuration. Boundary h_2 is selected as the parallel to h_1 tangent to $\{H(h_1^*, t_1) \cap H(h_1, p)\} \cup \{t_1, t_2\}$, if t_1, t_2 is in the upper chain of p, or as the parallel to h_1 tangent to $\{H(h_1^*, t_1) \cap C(h_1, p)\} \cup \{t_1, t_2\}$, if t_1, t_2 is in the lower chain of p. Boundary h_2^* is selected as the parallel to h_1^* and tangent to $H(h_1, p)$ or $H(h_2, p)$, depending on whether t_1, t_2 is in the lower or in the upper chain, respectively. This determines both the stripes. Again, we need to verify if the union of the stripes contains all the points in S. Similar method is used when the optimal stripes are parallel and are not determined by an edge of the convex hull of S.

The entire process costs $O(\log n)$ per point and edge; the total cost for this configuration is $O(n^2 \log n)$.

Dissecting line: Lines h_1 and h_1^* in this case are found as in the above technique.

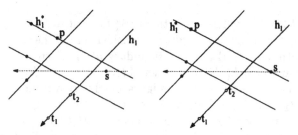

The major difference with respect to the case of *dissecting and touching* is that h_1 and h_1^* form here "outer" boundaries of the stripes and the "inner" ones must be found. The key observation is that the widths of stripes are monotonic with respect to a line l passing through s which is on the opposite side of h_1 than p; such a point always exists, otherwise $t_1 t_2$ is an edge of $CH(S)$ which is the case considered earlier. That is, candidates for h_2 and h_2^* are found as the parallel to h_1 or h_1^*, and tangent to the anchored at s upper chain of $S^-(l)$ and $S^+(l)$, respectively. A standard binary search finds the best balance for the widths; in this search we verify, in $O(\log n)$ time, that the stripes contain the whole set S. The polar order with respect to s that is used in the binary search is known from preprocessing. The cost per point p and an edge is $O(\log^2 n)$, and the overall cost for this type of configurations is $O(n^2 \log^2 n)$. Note that not every search leads to a solution since some of them may result in a situation where the union of stripes does not include S.

Rotating stripes: for each pair of points $p, q \in S$ draw a line through p and q. Think of that line as a pair h_1, h_2 of lines that split when rotated around p and q, respectively.

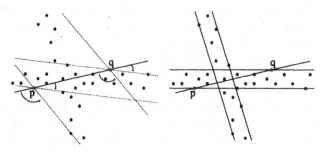

Rotating stripes and the optimal solution.

They form a strip whose width changes during the rotation. Lines h_1^*, h_2^* border the points that are not in $S(h_1, h_2)$. These points are on the both sides of

$S(h_1, h_2)$ (otherwise, we have another configuration) and one of h_1^*, h_2^* must be tangent on both sides to the convex hulls of these points, as well. These lines can be found in $O(\log n)$ time from the anchored chain structure. Note that, in order to be in the configuration, the stripes must intersect between p and q. The angle of rotation is therefore limited in both directions and such a rotation preserves the set inclusion monotonicity of $S(h_1, h_2)$ and $S(h_1^*, h_2^*)$ respectively, during the rotation. The angles are determined in such a way that the complementary stripe $S(h_1^*, h_2^*)$ does not contain either of p, or q. Lines h_1, h_2 are rotated in a binary search fashion to find the best balance of the widths. The combined cost of the binary search and finding the second stripe is $O(\log^2 n)$ per pair of points, and results in the total of $O(n^2 \log^2 n)$ for this group of configurations. This leads to the following theorem:

Theorem 3. *A pair of two stripes whose union contains a given set S of n points, such that the width of the wider strip is minimized, can be found in $O(n^2 \log^2 n)$ time and $O(n^2)$ space. Moreover, all optimal pairs can be found within the same bounds.*

5   Conclusions

We have presented a solution to the two-line center problem for the Euclidean real plane. The problem is of interest in the context of the approximation for sets of points. Our method can find all the optimal solutions and is based on applying three different algorithmic techniques to a few constrained versions of the problem. The overall $O(n^2 \log^2 n)$ time and $O(n^2)$ space complexity is the best known up-to-date and improves the previous result by $\log^3 n$ factor. Our solution depends on a new structure of the anchored upper and lower chains. This structure supports basic convex hull queries that involve convex hulls of subsets dissected from the given set S by straight lines. Organization of the structure is determined by the polar (angular) order of points with respect to each other. Its construction, both on the geometric and abstract levels, uses several interesting ideas combined with earlier techniques. The structure can be applied to the decision version of the two-line center problem, thus providing $O(n^2 \log n)$ decision time and reducing the time complexity of the earlier parametric search solution [AS91] by $\log^2 n$ factor and its space requirements by $\log n$. Furthermore, similar methods can be used to solve in the same time a more general decision problem whether two stripes of prescribed (different) widths can cover a given set of points. Additional applications of the anchored chains can be found in the geometric optimization related to the coordinate-independent two-center problem in the L_∞-metric and covering a set of points with two rectangles; see [JK95]. The question about the optimality of the presented algorithm is open.

Acknowledgement
    The authors would like to thank the Center for Computational Sciences of the University of Kentucky for supporting this research.

References

[AS91] P. K. Agarwal and M. Sharir. Planar Geometric Location Problems and Maintaining the Width of a Planar Set, *Proc. of the Second ACM-SIAM Symp. on Discr. Alg.*, (1991), pp. 449-458,

[E87] H. Edelsbrunner. Algorithms in Combinatorial Geometry. Springer Verlag (1987).

[G72] R. L. Graham. An efficient algorithm for determining the convex hull of a finite planar set, *Inform. Process. Lett.*, 1 (1972), pp. 132-133,

[HIIR89] M. E. Houle, H. Imai, K. Imai, J.-M. Robert. Weighted orthogonal linear L_∞-approximation and applications, *Lect. Notes Computer Sci.*, 382 (1989), pp. 183-191,

[HS91] J. Hershberger and S. Suri. Offline Maintenance of Planar Configurations, *Proc. of the Second ACM-SIAM Symp. on Discr. Alg.*, (1991), pp. 32-41,

[JK95] J. W. Jaromczyk and M. Kowaluk. Coordinate-system independent covering of point sets in R^2 with pairs of rectangles or optimal squares, *Manuscript*, (1995).

[KM93] N. M. Korneenko and H. Martini. Hyperplane Approximation and Related Topics, *New Trends in Discrete and Computational Geometry (Janos Pach Ed.)*, (1993), pp. 135-161,

[LC85] D. T. Lee and Y. T. Ching. The power of geometric duality revised, *Inform. Process. Lett.*, 21 (1985), pp. 117-122,

[MT82] N. Megiddo and A. Tamir. On the complexity of location linear facilities in the plane, *Oper. Res. Lett.*, 1 (1982), pp. 194-197,

[MT83] N. Megiddo and A. Tamir. Finding least-distances lines, *SIAM J. Algebr. Discrete Math.*, 4 (1983), pp. 207-211,

[OvL81] M. Overmars and J. van Leeuwen. Maintenance of configurations in the plane, *Journal of Computer and System Sciences*, 23 (1981), pp. 166-204,

[PS] F. Preparata, M. I. Shamos. Computational Geometry: An Introduction. Springer Verlag (1985).

6 Appendix

This Appendix contains figures that further illustrate concepts and structures described in this paper.

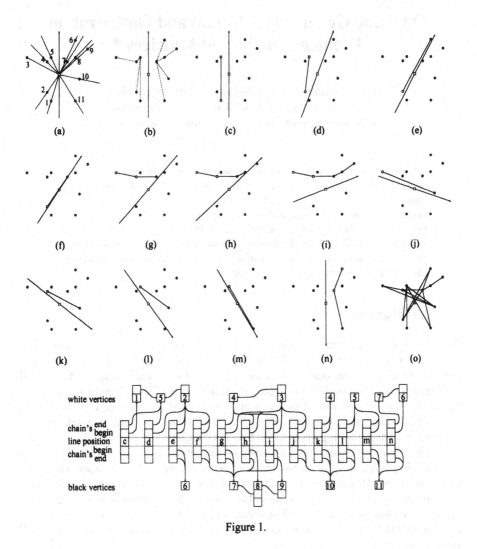

Figure 1.

Figure 1: Computing the anchored lower chains for a given anchor (marked with a square). Figure 1a shows the points and the polar order, Figure 1b shows the auxiliary structure obtained from Graham's scan, Figures 1c-n show the consecutive lower chains in rotation by π, Figure 1o shows the union of the edges in the anchored lower chains constructed in steps c-n. Note that edges with two their endpoints in the halfplane determined by the rotating line at its original position do not intersect. Then the corresponding representation of the anchored lower chain is given. Letters correspond to the slopes, numbers correspond to the points.

On Some Geometric Selection and Optimization Problems via Sorted Matrices *

Alex Glozman   Klara Kedem   Gregory Shpitalnik

Department of Mathematics and Computer Science
Ben-Gurion University of the Negev, Beer-Sheva 84105, Israel

Abstract. In this paper we apply the selection and optimization technique of Fredrickson and Johnson to a number of geometric selection and optimization problems, some of which have previously been solved by parametric search, and provide efficient and simple algorithms. Our technique improves the solutions obtained by parametric search by a $\log n$ factor. For example, we apply the technique to the two-line-center problem, where we want to find two strips that cover a given set S of n points in the plane, so as to minimize the width of the largest of the two strips.

1 Introduction

Consider a set S of arbitrary elements. *Selection* in the set S determines, for a given rank k, an element that is k^{th} in some total ordering of S. The complexity of selection in S has been shown to be proportional to the cardinality of the set [2]. Fredrickson and Johnson [9] considered selection in a set of sorted matrices. An $m \times n$ matrix M is a *sorted matrix* if each row and each column of M is in a nondecreasing order. Fredrickson and Johnson have demonstrated that selection in a set of sorted matrices, that together represent the set S, can be done in time sublinear in the size of S. They have also observed that given certain constraints on the set S, one can construct implicitly a set of sorted matrices representing S. For instance, the sorted matrix corresponding to the sums of the pairs $X + Y$ of two input sets X and Y, can be represented implicitly by means of the sorted input vectors X and Y [7]. In [8], [9], [6] a number of selection and optimization problems on trees were considered. For example in [8] they presented an $O(n \log n)$ time algorithm for selecting the kth longest path in a tree with n nodes.

More generally, their algorithm for selecting the kth smallest item in an $m \times n$ sorted matrix M runs in time $O(m \log(2n/m))$ [9]. When M is sorted by columns only, their algorithm runs in time $O(n \log m)$.

The optimization technique via sorted matrices follows the general idea of the parametric search [15], although this technique has a number of advantages over the parametric search technique: it does not require parallelization of the decision algorithm and, usually, it produces more efficient algorithms than the ones obtained by the parametric search technique. Assume we have a decision problem $\mathcal{P}(d)$ that receives as an input a real parameter d and we need to find the minimal value d^* of the parameter d such that $\mathcal{P}(d)$ satisfies certain properties, depending monotonically

---

* The work of the second author was supported by AFOSR Grant AFOSR-91-0328, while working at the Department of Computer Science at Cornell University, Ithaca 14853, NY

on d. Assume, furthermore, that the set S of all values that d can get are presented in a sorted matrix M and there is a decision algorithm A for $\mathcal{P}(d)$, which in time T decides whether the given d is equal to, smaller than, or larger than the desired value d^*. Frederickson and Johnson show [6, 8] that the overall runtime consumed by the optimization algorithm is $O(T \log m + m \log(2n/m))$. If the matrix M is sorted by the columns only then the overall runtime of the optimization algorithm is $O(T \log m + n \log m)$.

There have been some attempts to apply these techniques to geometric selection and optimization problems (e.g., [4], [13], [5]). In this paper we show some more such applications. In general our approach is the following: We examine geometric properties of the optimal solution for the particular problem. This leads to the determination of constraints on the set S of potential solutions for the problem. The constraints allow us to partition the set S into subsets, with a total or partial ordering defined on their elements, and to represent the subsets implicitly, as a set of sorted matrices. Next we apply the technique of Fredrickson and Johnson, using as subroutines the linear time selection algorithm of [2] and the decision algorithm for the particular optimization problem. Below we present a list of the problems which we solve in this paper:

The Two-Line Center Problem. Given a set S of n points in the plane, find two strips Δ_1 and Δ_2 that together cover the set S such that the width of the larger strip is as small as possible (see Figure 1.a).

Agarwal and Sharir [1] presented an $O(n^2 \log^5 n)$ time algorithm for this problem, based on the parametric search technique [15]. Recently this result has been improved by Katz and Sharir [14], [12] to $O(n^2 \log^4 n)$ using an expander-based approach. In Section 2 we present an $O(n^2 \log^4 n)$ algorithm which is significantly simpler than the Katz-Sharir algorithm. Our algorithm is based on new observations regarding the geometry of the problem which allow us to perform an efficient search in the set of strips that are candidates for the optimal solution.

The kth Triangle area problem. Given a set S of n points in the plane, determine which three points define the triangle with the kth largest area. This problem was stated and solved by Chazelle [4]. He presented an $O(n^2 \log^2 n)$ time algorithm based on the Cole's scheme [3] for searching among similar lists, combined with the Fredrickson and Johnson selection algorithm. Chazelle has conjectured that this bound can be improved to $O(n^2 \log n)$. In Section 3 we show that the geometric observations and structures which we use in our solution for the two-line center problem lead to the improved $O(n^2 \log n)$ time algorithm for the kth triangle area problem.

The Min-Max Two Rectangle Problem. Given a set S of n points in the plane, find two axis-parallel rectangles r_1 and r_2 that together cover the set S and minimize the following expression: $\max(\mu(r_1), \mu(r_2))$, where μ is a two-argument monotone, nondecreasing in each argument function of the height and width of a rectangle (e.g., area, perimeter or diagonal length).

Hershberger and Suri [11] consider a *rectangular measure* $\mu(r)$ which is a two-argument, nondecreasing in each argument function of the height and width of a rectangle r. They solve the following clustering problem: Given a planar set of points S, a rectangular measure μ acting on S and a pair of values μ_1 and μ_2, does there exist a bipartition $S = S_1 \cup S_2$ satisfying $\mu(S_i) \leq \mu_i$ for $i = 1, 2$? They have presented an algorithm which solves this problem in $O(n \log n)$ time.

We use a modification of their algorithm as a decision algorithm for the min-max two rectangle problem. Then we show that the set of potential solutions for the min-max two rectangle problem can be represented implicitly as a constant number of sorted matrices. Eventually, applying the optimization technique of Fredrickson and Johnson we obtain an $O(n \log n)$ algorithm for the min-max two rectangle problem (see Section 4).

The kth L_∞-interdistance problem. Given a set S of n points in the plane, determine which pair of points of S defines the kth distance in the L_∞ metric. Salowe [16] has solved this problem based on parametric search in $O(n \log^2 n)$ time. In Section 5 we present a simpler $O(n \log^2 n)$ algorithm based on our technique.

2 The Two-Line Center Problem

2.1 Geometric observations.

To proceed further we need some notations and definitions. Let us denote the subset of points covered by a strip Δ by S_Δ. We denote the width of a set S by $\omega(S)$ and the width of a strip Δ by $\omega(\Delta)$. We call a pair of strips Δ_1 and Δ_2 a *two-line configuration* and denote it by $\mathcal{C}(\Delta_1, \Delta_2)$. The width $w_{\mathcal{C}}$ of a configuration $\mathcal{C}(\Delta_1, \Delta_2)$ is defined by $max(\omega(\Delta_1), \omega(\Delta_2))$. We assume wlog that $\omega(\Delta_1) \geq \omega(\Delta_2)$. We denote an optimal two-line configuration by $\mathcal{C}^*(\Delta_1, \Delta_2)$ and the corresponding optimal width by w^*. Let us also denote the convex hull of a set of points S, by $CH(S)$. An edge-vertex pair (e, p) of $CH(S)$ is called an *antipodal pair* if there is a supporting line to $CH(S)$ through p which is parallel to e. We state without proof

Lemma 1. *The width of of the optimal two-line configuration $\mathcal{C}^*(\Delta_1, \Delta_2)$ is defined by an edge-vertex antipodal pair of $CH(S_{\Delta_1})$.*

Lemma 1 implies that there is a triple of points $p_1, p_2, p_3 \in S$ that together defines the width of the optimal two-line configuration. More precisely, the line (p_1, p_2) defines the slope of strip Δ_1 in the optimal configuration and the point p_3 defines its width w (see Figure 1.b).

We call the set of all values of the parameter w, induced by the triples $p_1, p_2, p_3 \in S$, the *set of potential solutions* of the two-line center problem, and denote it by $\mathcal{W}$. We will perform a binary search over the set $\mathcal{W}$ using the decision algorithm of [1] as an oracle. In order to do it efficiently we will present the set $\mathcal{W}$ in a certain implicit form.

We denote by $\mathcal{L}$ the list of lines, passing through pairs of points in S and sorted by their slopes. Clearly, there are $N = n(n-1)/2$ such lines. We associate with each line $l_i \in \mathcal{L}$ $(i = 1, \ldots, N)$ another line $\bar{l}_i \perp l_i$. Also we denote the list of points of S ordered from left to right according to their orthogonal projection on $\bar{l}_i$ by L_i. The following observation is straightforward

Observation 2 *Given two consecutive lines $l_i, l_{i+1} \in \mathcal{L}$ and the list L_i, then the list L_{i+1} can be obtained from L_i by a single swap of points $p', p'' \in S$, where p' and p'' is the pair of points which defines the line l_{i+1}.*

Observation 3 *Given the list L_i and the pair of points $p', p'' \in S$ which defines the line l_i, the point $p \in S$ having the kth distance from line l_i and lying on the right (left) side of line l_i can be found in constant time. (Here $i = 1, \ldots, N$ and $k = 1, \ldots, n$).*

Proof. We consider the point $p \in S$ to the right of l_i, the case where the point p lies to the left of l_i is symmetric. Clearly, the index of the point $p \in S$ with the kth distance from l_i in the list L_i equals to the index of the point p' in L_i plus k (see Figure 1.d). If the resulting index exits the list L_i we assume the corresponding distance to be equal to $+\infty$.

2.2 The Representation of $\mathcal{W}$.

We build a list $\mathcal{R}$ of N records. The first record $r_1 \in \mathcal{R}$ consists of a pointer ptr_1 to the list L_1, which has to be prepeared beforehand. Each record $r_i \in \mathcal{R}$ $(i = 2, \ldots, N)$ consists of a pointer ptr_i to the list L_{i-1} and indices i', i'' of the two elements in L_{i-1}, which have to be swapped in order to produce the list L_i. Clearly, with this structure available, we can produce all the lists L_i $(i = 1, \ldots, N)$ successively by proceeding from one record r_i of $\mathcal{R}$ to the next one, each time performing a single swap of two elements of L_i. The next Lemma follows immediately from Lemma 1 and the description of $\mathcal{R}$

Lemma 4. *The structure $\mathcal{R}$ implicitly contains all the values of the set $\mathcal{W}$.*

In the following preprocessing algorithm we build the structure $\mathcal{R}$. We use a dynamic auxiliary array, *Index*, which maintains, at the i-th step, the ordered list of points along $\bar{l}_i$.

The Preprocessing Algorithm:

1. Choose a line passing through a pair of points of S and denote it by l_1. Sort the set of points S along the line $\bar{l}_1$ and store the result in lists L_1 and *Index*. Set the pointer of record r_1 to the list L_1.
2. Produce the list $\mathcal{L}$ by sorting all the lines l_i by their slopes. Each line in $\mathcal{L}$ is defined by a pair of indices of two points from the set S.
3. For each record r_i $(i = 1, \ldots, N)$ do:
   (a) Assume that the line l_i is defined by a pair of points with indices $1 \leq j_1, j_2 \leq n$. Perform $i' = Index[j_1]$ and $i'' = Index[j_2]$.
   (b) Swap the elements with indices i', i'' in the list L_{i-1}.
   (c) Set the pointer ptr_i to point to the list L_{i-1} (now L_{i-1} is assumed to be L_i).
   (d) Perform $Index[j_1] = i''$ and $Index[j_2] = i'$.

Lemma 5. *The preprocessing algorithm above builds correctly the structure $\mathcal{R}$ in $O(N \log N)$ time, $\mathcal{R}$ requires $O(N)$ space.*

Proof. The correctness of the algorithm can be proved by induction on Step 3, applying Observation 2 $N-1$ times. Step 1 of the algorithm requires $O(n \log n)$ time. Step 2 consumes $O(N \log N)$ time. Steps 3(a) – 3(d) require a constant amount of time each. Clearly each record r_i ($i = 1, \ldots, N$) is of constant size. This completes the proof.

Corollary 6. *The structure $\mathcal{R}$ can be traversed record by record in $O(N)$ time, allowing access to the list L_i at each step i, $i = 1, \ldots, N$.*

2.3 The Algorithm.

In this section we present our algorithm which solves the two-line center problem. It uses the following result of Frederickson and Johnson [7], [6]: Given a matrix M of size $m \times n$ with each column sorted in ascending order, and provided a constant time access to each element of M, one can solve the optimization problem over the values of the matrix M in time $O(T_D \log m + n \log m)$, where T_D is the runtime of the decision algorithm.

The structure $\mathcal{R}$ is an implicit representation of a sorted matrix M of size $n \times N$, which provides a constant time access to elements of single column $c \in M$ at a time. It follows from Corollary 6 and Observation 3. This representation is sufficient for the application of the optimization algorithm of Frederickson and Johnson. We sketch our algorithm:

1. Perform the preprocessing algorithm described in the previous subsection.
2. Perform the following steps until there is one element in each column of the matrix M:
   (a) Produce the columns c_i of the matrix M one column after the other starting from the first column of M. Partition each column c_i into four subarrays of equal size and select the minimum and maximum elements from each subarray as in [8], [6].
   (b) Form two lists: one of the minimum values and one of the maximum values respectively, of the subarrays of M, as in [8], [6].
   (c) Select the median from each list.
   (d) Run the decision algorithm of [1] on each of the two selected values.
   (e) Produce the columns of the matrix M successively again. This time, reject at least half of the subarrays according to the answers of the decision algorithm of the previous step as in [8], [6]. Mark the remaining subarrays in each column c_i by means of auxiliary pointers to the list L_i.
3. Find the optimal value w^* by performing a binary search over the $O(N)$ remaining values (one from each column $c \in M$), using the decision algorithm of [1].

2.4 Analysis of the Algorithm.

Step 1 requires $O(N \log N)$ time as was shown in Lemma 5. From the analysis made in [8], [6] it follows that Step 2 is repeated $O(\log n)$ times and the number of the subarrays in each stage of Step 2 is $O(N)$. In step 2(a) we partition every column of M into four subarrays of equal size. In step 2(b) we form two lists consisting of the minimal and maximal elements of all the subarrays of M. Corollary 6 implies that Step 2(a) can be performed in $O(N)$ time. Indeed, as was shown in Lemma 2, we can obtain the column c_{i+1} from the column c_i by making a single swap in the list L_i and producing the list L_{i+1}. Moreover, the selection in the current column $c \in M$ can be done in constant time as stated in Observation 3. Step 2(e) requires the same runtime. Thus we see that in Step 2 of the algorithm the maintenance of the matrix M requires $O(N)$ time. The steps 2(b)– 2(d) and 3 are the standard steps of the algorithm presented in [8], [6]. Thus our algorithm runs in time $O(T_D \log n + N \log N) = O(T_D \log n + n^2 \log n)$. Plugging in this formula the runtime of the decision algorithm $T_D = O(n^2 \log^3 n)$ [1], we obtain an $O(n^2 \log^4 n)$ algorithm for the two-line center problem. It can be easily seen that the space requirement of the algorithm is O(N). As was shown in [1] the space requirements of the decision algorithm do not exceed $O(n \log n)$. We conclude with the following theorem:

Theorem 7. *The algorithm above solves the two-line center problem in $O(n^2 \log^4 n)$ time and $O(n^2)$ space.*

3 The kth area triangle problem

The kth area triangle problem is stated as follows: Given a set S of n points in the plane, determine which three points define the triangle with the kth largest area.

Consider all triples of points of the set S. Clearly, each triple $p_1, p_2, p_3 \in S$ defines a triangle T. We can compute the area of T as the length of the segment $[p_1, p_2]$ times the distance from point p_3 to the line through p_1, p_2. Let us denote by $\mathcal{T}$ the set of all possible areas of triangles, determined by S.

Lemma 8. *The structure $\mathcal{R}$ represents implicitly the set $\mathcal{T}$.*

Proof. It follows from Lemma 4 that $\mathcal{R}$ represents implicitly the heights of all possible triangles defined on set S, The pair of points $p', p'' \in S$ which defines, say, the ith line $l_i \in \mathcal{L}$ defines the base for all triangles that have their heights determined by points in the list L_i. Again we can imagine the structure $\mathcal{R}$ as an implicit representation of the matrix M of size $n \times N$. We use the selection algorithm of Frederickson and Johnson [7], which states the following: Given a matrix M of size $m \times n$, with each column sorted in ascending order, and provided a constant time access to each element of M, one can solve the selection problem over the values of M in time $O(n \log m)$.

Our algorithm for the kth area triangle problem is almost identical to the algorithm for the two-line center algorithm. The difference is that instead of calling a decision algorithm as a subroutine it runs a linear time selection algorithm [2]. Thus we have proved the following theorem:

Theorem 9. *The kth area triangle problem can be solved in $O(n^2 \log n)$ time consuming $O(n^2)$ space.*

4 The Min-Max Two Rectangle Problem

The min-max two rectangle problem is formulated as follows: Given a set S of n points in the plane, find two axis-parallel rectangles r_1 and r_2 that together cover the set S and minimize the expression: $\max(\mu(r_1), \mu(r_2))$, where μ is a two-argument, monotone, nondecreasing in each argument, function of the height and the width of a rectangle (for example area, perimeter or diagonal length).

4.1 The decision algorithm for The Min-Max Two Rectangle Problem.

In this subsection we present an algorithm which solves the following decision problem: Given a planar set of points S, a rectangular measure μ acting on S and a value μ', does there exist a bipartition $S = S_1 \cup S_2$ satisfying $\max(\mu(S_1), \mu(S_2)) \leq \mu'$. Hershberger and Suri [11] consider such a rectangular measure $\mu(r)$ of the height and the width of a rectangle r and solve the following clustering problem: Given a planar set of points S, a *rectangular measure* μ acting on S and a pair of values μ_1 and μ_2, does there exist a bipartition $S = S_1 \cup S_2$ satisfying $\mu(S_i) \leq \mu_i$ for $i = (1, 2)$? They present an algorithm which solves this problem in $O(n \log n)$ time. First we review some notations and observations from [11]. The *bounding box* of the given point set S, denoted by ∂S, is the smallest axis-parallel rectangle that contains S. The bounding box of S is determined by the topmost, bottommost, leftmost, and rightmost points of S, which we denote by t, b, l and r (see Figure 2). We call these points *determinators* of ∂S. Clearly, the rectangles r_1 and r_2 have to cover together these four points. There are essentially three different ways to partition the determinators between sets S_1 and S_2:

1. One of the subsets gets three determinators and the other gets one determinator.
2. Each subset gets two determinators lying on opposite sides of ∂S.
3. Each subset gets two determinators lying on adjacent sides of ∂S.

According to the first case, assigning three determinators to, say S_1, fixes three of the four sides of r_1. Thus we need to find a placement of the fourth side of r_1 such that $\mu(r_1) \leq \mu'$ and $\mu(r_2) \leq \mu'$. We place the fourth side of r_1 such that $\mu(r_1) = \mu'$. In linear time we can test whether the set of points out of r_1 can be covered by a rectangle with measure $\mu \leq \mu'$ (see Figure 2.a).

For the second case our decision algorithm proceeds in a way similar to [11]. Assume wlog that r_1 is defined by the top and bottom determinators and r_2 is defined by the left and right determinators. The fixed height of r_1 determines a maximum width satisfying $\mu(r_1) = \mu'$. The algorithm slides r_1 of maximal possible size from left to right over the set S, assigning all points within r_1 to S_1 and all the points outside it to S_2. At each sliding step the algorithm checks whether $\mu(S_2) \leq \mu'$. There sre O(n) steps in this algorithm (see Figure 2.b). Clearly, the set S_2 can be partitioned into two subsets S_2^l and S_2^r lying to the left and to the right of the sliding rectangle r_1, respectively, such that the set S_2^l underegos insertions only and the set S_2^r underegos deletions only. We can obtain an extremal point $p \in S_2^l$ in a given direction in a constant time per insertion by maintaining a pointer to the extremal point p; for dealing with points in S_2^r there exist standard data structures that allow to perform deletions and extremum querys off-line in a constant time per query after $O(n \log n)$ preprocessing. Also, one can easily show that if the order of points of the set S along the x-axis (y-axis) is known then the ordered list of updates to the sets S_2^l and S_2^r can be constructed in linear time. It implies that after $O(n \log n)$ preprocessing the decision algorithm for the second case runs in $O(n)$ time.

In the third case we assign two adjacent determinators, say l and b, to r_1, and t and r to r_2. In this case the lower left corner of r_1 must coincide with the lower left corner of ∂S (let us define it by z as in [11]). Similarly, the upper right corner of r_2 must coincide with the upper right corner of ∂S. The decision algorithm for this case is based on the the same idea as in the previous case. Namely, it trys all placements of r_1 of measure μ' and checks whether the set of points out of r_1 can be covered by rectangle r_2 , such that $\mu(r_2) \leq \mu'$. As was observed in [11], all the rectangles r_1, satisfying $\mu(r_1) = \mu'$, whose lower left corner is z, have their upper right corner on particular curve Γ. If μ is the area then Γ is a hyperbola; if μ is the perimeter then Γ is a segment with slope -1; and if μ is the diagonal length then Γ is a quarter-circle of a radius μ' centered at z. Figure 2.c illustrates the case where μ is the perimeter. As seen in the figure, the set S_2 can be partitioned into three subsets S_2^{out}, S_2^a and S_2^r. The subset S_2^{out} consists of the points of S lying in ∂S to the right of Γ, out of r_1. The set S_2^a consists of the points above the sliding rectangle r_1 and the set S_2^r consists of the points to the right of r_1 and to the left of Γ. Clearly, S_2^{out} does not change during the running of the algorithm, since r_1 cannot cover any point from S_2^{out}. The set S_2^a underegos insertions only and the set S_2^r underegos deletions only. As above, if the order of the points of S along the x-axis (and y-axis) is known, then the ordered list of updates for sets S_2^a and S_2^r can be constructed in linear time. It implies that after $O(n \log n)$ preprocessing the algorithm for the third case runs in $O(n)$ time. These observations lead to the following lemma:

Lemma 10. *After $O(n \log n)$ preprocessing time, the decision algorithm for the min-max two rectangle problem runs in $O(n)$ time.*

4.2 The Optimization step.

We make the following two observations:

Observation 11 *The set of all distances measured along the x-axis (y-axis) between the points of S can be represented implicitly as a sorted matrix M of size $n \times n$ if the order of the points of S along the x-axis (y-axis) is known.*

Observation 12 *Given two sorted arrays X and Y, the values of the monotone, nondecreasing in each argument, function $F(X, Y)$, can be represented implicitly as a sorted matrix M of size $n \times n$.*

Proof. It is a straightforward extension of the case where the function F(X,Y) is a Cartesian product of two arrays X and Y [7].

Let us consider the geometry of the optimal solution for the min-max two rectangle problem and determine the potential values of μ for the optimal solution. Clearly there can be three kinds of solutions according to the three cases of positioning the determinators on the rectangles r_1 and r_2. In the first and the second cases the bigger rectangle has its height (width) fixed and thus its measure μ is defined by the second parameter - width (height). By Lemma 11 we can represent all these values as a sorted matrix M of size $n \times n$. In the third case the optimal rectangle with the larger measure μ, say r_1, has its width and height defined by two pairs of points lying on its opposite sides, where one point in each pair is a determinator of r_1. The distances from each such determinator to the other points of S, measured along the x-axis (y-axis respectively) define an array X (resp. Y) of linear size. Having the arrays X and Y available we can represent all potential values of μ in the third case as a sorted matrix M of size $n \times n$, as stated in Observation 12. These observations lead to the following lemma:

Lemma 13. *The set of potential values of μ can be represented as a constant number of sorted matrices of size $n \times n$ each.*

Taking into account Lemma 10 and Lemma 13 and applying the optimization technique of Fredrickson and Johnson [8], [6] we obtain the following result

Theorem 14. *The Min-max two rectangle problem can be solved in $O(n \log n)$ time.*

5   The kth L_∞-interdistance problem

Salowe [16] has solved the following problem: Given a set S of n points in the plane, determine which pair of points of S defines the kth distance in metric L_∞. Following the parametric search paradigm Salowe has presented a decision algorithm, which in $O(n \log n)$ time decides whether the given value d is less, equal or greater then the kth interdistance in metric L_∞. Appling the parametric search technique he was able to obtain $O(n \log^2 n)$ solution to the kth L_∞-interdistance problem.

We start with the following simple observation:

Observation 15 *The kth L_∞-interdistance is defined by the distance between a pair of points of the set S, measured along the x-axis or the y-axis.*

By combining this observation and Observation 11 with the optimization technique of Fredrickson and Johnson [6, 8] and using the same decision algorithm as in [16] we obtain the following result:

Theorem 16. *The kth L_∞-interdistance problem can be solved in $O(n \log^2 n)$ time.*

6   Summary

In this paper we solve efficiently a number of geometric selection and optimization problems by exploring the geometry of the optimal configurations. The discovering of some partial or total ordering on the set of potential solutions allows one to apply the technique of Fredrickson and Johnson for the selection or the optimization part of the problem.

References

1. P. Agarwal and M. Sharir. "Planar geometric location problems", *Algorithmica*, 11(1994), pp 185–195.
2. M. Blum, R.W. Floyd, , V.R. Pratt, R.L. Rivest and Tarjan, R.E. "Time bounds for selection", *J. Comput. Syst. Sci.*, 7(1972), pp. 448–461.
3. R. Cole. "Searching and storing similar lists", *J. Comput. Syst. Sci.*, 23(1981), pp. 166–204.
4. B. Chazelle. "New techniques for computing order statistics in Euclidean space", *Proc. 1st ACM Symp. on Computational Geometry*, 1985, pp. 125–134.
5. L. P. Chew and K. Kedem. "Improvements on Geometric Pattern Matching Problems", *SWAT, LNCS 621, Springer-Verlag*, 1992, pp. 318–325.
6. G.N. Frederickson. "Optimal algorithms for tree partitioning", *Proc. 2nd ACM-SIAM Symp. on Discrete Algorithms*, 1991, pp. 168–177.
7. G. N. Frederickson and D. B. Johnson. "The complexity of selection and ranking in X+Y and matrices with sorted columns", *J. Comput. Syst. Sci.*, 24(1982), pp. 197–208.
8. G. N. Frederickson and D. B. Johnson. "Finding k^{th} paths and p-center by generating and searching good data structures", *J. Algorithms*, 4(1983), pp. 61–80.
9. G. N. Frederickson and D. B. Johnson. "Generalized selection and ranking: sorted matrices.", *SIAM J. Computing*, 13(1984), pp. 14–30.
10. M. Houle and G. Toussaint, "Computing the width of a set", *Proc. 1st ACM Symp. on Computational Geometry*, 1985, pp. 1–7.
11. J. Hershberger and S. Suri. "Finding Tailored Partitions", *J. Algorithms*, 12(1991), pp. 431–463.
12. M.J. Katz, "Improved algorithms in geometric optimization via expanders", *Proc. 3rd Israel Symposium on Theory of Computing and Systems*, 1995, to appear.
13. D. Kravets and J. Park. "Selection and Sorting in Totally Monotone Arrays", *Proc. 2nd ACM-SIAM Symp. on Discrete Algorithms*, 1990, pp. 494–502.
14. M.J. Katz and M. Sharir, "An expander-based approach to geometric optimization", *Proc. 9th ACM Symp. on Computational Geometry*, 1993, pp. 198–207.
15. N. Megiddo. "Applying parallel computation algorithms in the design of serial algorithms.", *J. ACM*, 30(1983), pp. 852-865.
16. J. S. Salowe. "L-infinity interdistance selection by parametric search", *Inf. Proc. Lett.*, 30(1989), pp. 9–14.

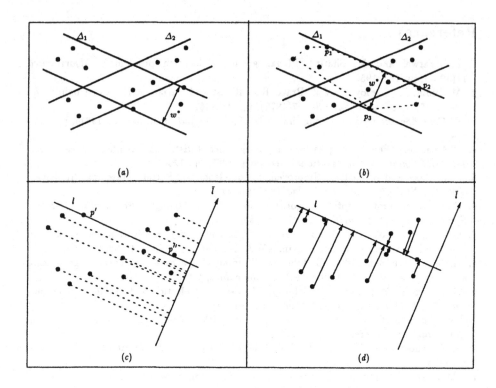

Fig. 1. Two-line center problem.

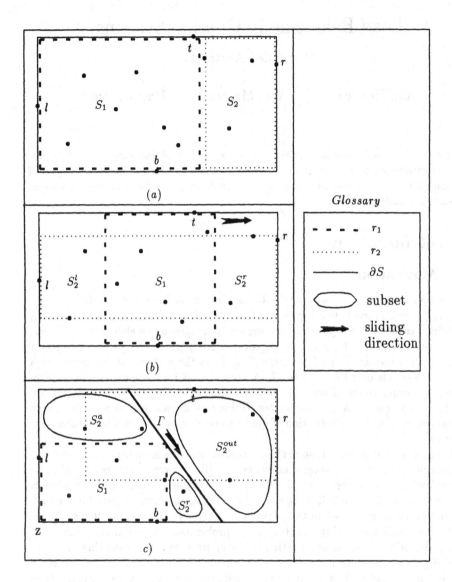

Fig. 2. The decision algorithm for min-max two rectangle problem.

Load Balancing in Quorum Systems

(Extended Abstract)

Ron Holzman [*]   Yosi Marcus [†]   David Peleg [‡]

Abstract: This paper introduces and studies the question of balancing the load on processors participating in a given quorum system. Our proposed measure for the degree of balancing is the ratio between the load on the most frequently referenced element, and on the least frequently used one.

1 Introduction

1.1 Motivation

Quorum systems serve as a basic tool providing a uniform and reliable way for achieving coordination between processes in a distributed system. Quorum systems are defined as follows. Suppose that the system is composed of n elements $u_1, \ldots, u_n$, taken from a universe U, representing sites, nodes, processors or other abstract entities. *Quorums* are sets of elements $S_i \subseteq U$ in the system. A *set system* is a collection S of sets over the universe U. A set system S is said to satisfy the *quorum intersection* requirement if for every two quorums S_i and S_j in S, the intersection $S_i \cap S_j$ is not empty. A *quorum system* (otherwise known also as an *intersecting hypergraph*, cf. [B86]) is a collection of quorums that enjoys the quorum intersection property.

Applications for quorum systems in distributed systems include control and management problems such as *mutual exclusion* (cf. [R86]), *name servers* (cf. [MV88]) and *replicated data management* (cf. [H84]). In all of these cases, the use of quorum systems is centered on the following basic idea. The application requires that certain information items be stored in the network in a reliable and consistent way. Storing the information at a single central site is problematic in case that site crashes. Storing the information at one particular *set of sites* may overcome this problem, but will prevent working in the system in case a communication failure causes a partition in the network, since if users at different parts of the network continue working separately, the information can no longer be guaranteed to be consistent.

---

[*]Department of Mathematics, Technion — Israel Institute of Technology, Haifa 32000, Israel.

[†]Department of Applied Mathematics and Computer Science, The Weizmann Institute of Science, Rehovot 76100, Israel.

[‡]Department of Applied Mathematics and Computer Science, The Weizmann Institute of Science, Rehovot 76100, Israel. peleg@wisdom.weizmann.ac.il. Supported in part by a Walter and Elise Haas Career Development Award and by a grant from the Basic Research Foundation. Part of the work was done while visiting IBM T.J. Watson Research Center.

The conceptual solution based on quorum systems is to make use of a large *collection* of possible sets of sites in the system. Each such set forms a *quorum*, in the sense that any query or update operation concerning the information at hand can be performed by accessing the elements of this single set alone, and the choice of the particular quorum to be used can be made arbitrarily (i.e., all quorums are equally adequate).

In particular, in order to perform an update to the information, the user selects one quorum S_i in the quorum system S, and records the update in every one of the elements that compose S_i. Likewise, a potential consumer of this information may choose any quorum $S_j \in S$, and query every element in S_j for the needed information. Since the intersection of every two quorums in a quorum system is not empty, the consumer is guaranteed to encounter at least one element that is able to supply the most up-to-date information.

This type of solution is capable of withstanding crashes and network partitions (up to a point), due to the greater degree of freedom in choosing the quorum by the user. In particular, in case of crashes, the consumer can choose a quorum that does not include the crashed elements, and in case of a partition, it may still be possible that one part of the network contains a complete quorum (of course, it is quite impossible that two disconnected parts of the system will both contain complete quorums!) For more on the applicability of quorum-based techniques in distributed systems, on the examples mentioned above and on the issues of fault-tolerance and availability of quorum systems, the reader is referred to [H84, GB85, PW93] and the references therein.

Considerable attention is given in the literature to a special type of quorum system called *coterie* (see [GB85] and [IK90]). A *coterie* is a quorum system in which the quorums are not allowed to fully contain each other. A subclass of special interest is that of *non-dominated coteries* (or *NDC's*), which are better than other coteries in terms of fault tolerance and communication cost. A *non-dominated coterie* is a coterie which is minimal in quorum sizes and maximal in the number of quorums, in the sense that dropping any element from any quorum or adding any quorum changes it into a set system that is not a coterie (see [GB85]). Some interesting properties of NDC's are derived in [L73, IK90], and some constructions for coterie families are discussed in [MP92].

1.2 Load balancing

When a quorum system is used in a given environment, the users employ a certain strategy for selecting the particular quorum to be used in each invocation. This strategy selects the quorums according to some distribution. This distribution, in turn, induces an access rate, or *load*, for each element, which is the sum of the access frequencies of the quorums it belongs to. The study of load issues was initiated in [M92]. In [NW94] it is shown that the maximal element load must be at least $1/\sqrt{n}$, and constructions are given for quorum systems that achieve this bound.

In this work (extending parts of [M92]) we focus on the evenness of the distribution of workload in quorum systems, and the degree of load balancing possible for various types of quorum systems. If all the users of the system prefer to use one particular quorum while possible (e.g., in a failure-free execution), then the elements participating in this quorum will be overloaded compared to others. So it makes sense to try to use a more uniform distribution for selecting the quorum to be accessed. Our proposed measure for the degree of balancing is the ratio ρ between the rate of references to the most frequently used element in the quorum system and the least frequently used one. A system is said to be *perfectly balanced* if all the elements are referenced at the same rate over time, or, $\rho = 1$.

For small systems, the effect of the particular quorum system used may be minor. However, when the systems become larger, the importance of choosing a good quorum system may significantly increase. In particular, some quorum systems may be well-adapted to the demand of load balancing, while for others, such a demand may impose heavy communication costs. Worse yet, certain types of quorum systems may be incapable of providing perfect or even partial balancing, regardless of the cost. The purpose of the current paper is to lay the grounds for a discussion of load balancing issues in the context of quorum systems.

1.3 Contributions

This paper addresses some of the basic questions related to the issue of balancing the load on processors participating in a given quorum system. The first obvious question one may ask is: how bad can the balancing ratio be for an arbitrary quorum system. We show that for any quorum system with a universe of size n, the balancing ratio is no smaller than $1/(n-1)$, and this bound is the best possible.

Since this ratio is rather poor, our next question is whether the class of non-dominated coteries (which exhibits some additional structure) enjoys better balancing ratio. This question turns out to be more challenging from a combinatorial point of view, but the answer is (almost) as disappointing: when restricting attention to NDC's, the bound becomes $2/(n - \log_2 n + o(\log n))$, and there exists an NDC with ratio $2/(n - \log_2 n - o(\log n))$. Hence in the worst case, NDC's are guaranteed to outperform ordinary quorum systems by merely a factor of about 2.

Driving this line of investigation further, we next ask whether there is some reasonably wide subclass of NDC's for which the balancing properties are better in the worst case, and ideally, whether there is such a subclass all of whose coteries are perfectly balanced. Towards this goal, we give some simple sufficient and necessary conditions for perfect balancing. We then look at the balancing properties of the common class of *voting systems* [GB85]. (A voting system is based on assigning a number of "votes" to each element of the universe; the votes induce a quorum system by taking as a quorum any collection of elements that holds a "minimal" majority of all the votes.) We prove that every voting system with odd total weight is perfectly balanced. (In fact, we prove that for the more general class of ordered NDC's.)

Given this classification of coterie classes, the next issue we address is that of the "cost" of balancing. The question is whether restricting ourselves to perfectly (or just well-) balanced quorum systems forces us to pay more in some other cost measure. Our choice of cost measure is motivated by the aforementioned distributed applications of coteries. In order for processors in a distributed system to use coteries for coordination purposes, it is necessary for a particular processor (the "user") to communicate with (at least) all the processors of a given quorum. Hence the *size* of the quorum significantly affects the *communication complexity* of the operation.

It is therefore desirable that quorums are small. Furthermore, if quorums are selected according to some weight vector, then it is desirable that the *weighted average quorum size* (WAQS) is small. Moreover, the measure of weighted average quorum size is equivalent to the notion of *(weighted) average element load* (which equals the WAQS times $1/n$).

Consequently, we study the interrelations between the two basic parameters of *load balancing* and *quorum size*, measured by either the size of the largest quorum or the *optimally weighted average quorum size* (OWAQS) of the system, to be defined precisely later on.

The results we derive reveal certain tradeoffs between the size and balancing parameters. In particular, for the class of ordered NDC's (for which perfect balancing is guaranteed), it is shown that over a universe of size n, some quorums of size $\lceil (n+1)/2 \rceil$ or more must exist (and this bound is the best possible). A similar lower bound holds for the OWAQS measure if we restrict attention to voting systems.

For non-ordered systems, perfect balancing can sometimes be achieved with much smaller quorums. A lower bound of $\Omega(\sqrt{n})$ is established for the maximal quorum size and the OWAQS of any perfectly balanced quorum system over n elements, and this bound is the best possible.

Finally, we turn to quorum systems that cannot be perfectly balanced, but have some balancing ratio $0 < \rho < 1$. For such systems we study the tradeoffs between the required balancing ratio ρ and the quorum size it admits in the best case. We derive an analogue of the result for perfect balancing, yielding a lower bound of (slightly better than) $\sqrt{n\rho}$.

As discussed earlier, the results concerning weighted average quorum size can all be translated into results on the equivalent notion of *weighted average element load*. Note that, in contrast with the $1/\sqrt{n}$ lower bound of [NW94] on the *maximal* element load, the *average* load can be made much smaller by choosing a suitable strategy. In particular, in a quorum system with a quorum of size s, a strategy using this quorum alone would enjoy an average load of s/n (hence quorum systems involving constant-size quorums could reach average load $\Theta(1/n)$). However, the price for this low average load is a high load imbalance among the elements. The last tradeoff result stated above can be reformulated as saying that as long as we restrict ourselves to strategies that insure a balancing ratio of ρ, the average load must be at least $\sqrt{\rho/n}$.

2 Basic Notions

Definition: The *quorum matrix* of a quorum system (U, S) is the $m \times n$ matrix $\hat{S} = (\hat{s}_{ij})$ obtained as follows: The elements of U are enumerated as $u_1, u_2, \ldots, u_n$, the quorums in S are enumerated as $S_1, S_2, \ldots, S_m$, and $\hat{s}_{ij} = 1$ if $u_j \in S_i$, and 0 otherwise.

In order to describe and analyze a coterie, it is often convenient to refer to the set of subsets of the universe which contain some quorum. This is facilitated by the following definition.

Definition: A *monotone quorum system* (MQS) is a quorum system $(U, \mathcal{M})$ such that $S \in \mathcal{M}$ and $S \subseteq T \subseteq U$ imply $T \in \mathcal{M}$. Given a coterie (U, S), the *MQS generated by* (U, S) is $(U, \bar{S})$, where $T \in \bar{S}$ if and only if $T \supseteq S$ for some $S \in S$. The sets in $\bar{S}$ are called the *superquorums* of the coterie (U, S). Conversely, if we are given a MQS $(U, \bar{S})$ then the coterie (U, S) is determined uniquely ($S \in S$ if and only if $S \in \bar{S}$ and no proper subset of S is in $\bar{S}$) and is called the *coterie derived from* $(U, \bar{S})$.

Example 2.1 Minimal Majority Coterie. *Let* $|U| = n$ *and let* $\bar{S} = \{S \subseteq U : |S| > \frac{n}{2}\}$, *that is, the superquorums are the sets containing a majority of elements. The coterie derived from* $(U, \bar{S})$ *is that in which the quorums are all subsets of* U *of size* $\lceil \frac{n+1}{2} \rceil$. $\square$

Notation: When $U = \{u_1, u_2, \ldots, u_n\}$ and $x_1, x_2, \ldots, x_n$ are real numbers, we let $x(S) = \sum_{u_j \in S} x_j$ for every $S \subseteq U$.

Example 2.2 Voting Coterie. *Let* $U = \{u_1, u_2, \ldots, u_n\}$ *and assume that to each* $u_j \in U$ *we assign a nonnegative integer* w_j, *called the weight of* u_j. *Then we define the MQS* $\bar{S} = \{S \subseteq U : w(S) > \frac{w(U)}{2}\}$. *The coterie derived from* $(U, \bar{S})$ *is that in which the quorums are those subsets of* U *which carry a majority of the total weight and are inclusion-minimal with respect to this property. A coterie* (U, S) *obtained in this manner is called a voting system. Observe that the Minimal Majority coterie of Example 2.1 is a special case of a voting system, in which all weights are equal.* $\square$

Example 2.3 Star Coterie. *Let* $U = \{u_1, u_2, \ldots, u_n\}$ *and let* S *consist of the* $n - 1$ *quorums* $\{u_1, u_2\}, \{u_1, u_3\}, \ldots, \{u_1, u_n\}$. *Then* (U, S) *is a coterie. We call such a coterie a star. Observe that a star is also a voting system (take* $w_1 = n - 1$, $w_2 = \cdots = w_n = 1$). $\square$

Voting systems play a distinguished role in the study of quorum systems, because of the natural and simple way in which they are specified. The defining weights also supply a ranking of the elements of U in terms of their importance for forming quorums. This notion is captured by the following definition.

Definition: Let (U, S) be a coterie. We say that (U, S) is *ordered* if it is possible to enumerate the elements of U as $u_1, u_2, \ldots, u_n$ so that the following holds: if $1 \leq i < j \leq n$ and S is a superquorum with $u_i \notin S$, $u_j \in S$, then $S_j^i = (S \setminus \{u_j\}) \cup \{u_i\}$ is also a superquorum.

Intuitively, the above property means that if $i < j$ then u_i is at least as useful as u_j for forming quorums. The reason that the definition refers to superquorums rather than quorums is that it may happen that S is a quorum but S_j^i is a non-minimal superquorum. It is straightforward to check that every voting system is ordered (enumerate the elements so that $w_1 \geq w_2 \geq \cdots \geq w_n$). The converse is known to be false, that is, there exist ordered coteries that cannot be obtained as a voting system [Os85]. There are also coteries that are not ordered, as witnessed by the following class of examples.

Example 2.4 FPP(q).   *Let U and S be the sets of points and lines respectively of a finite projective plane of order q for prime power $q \geq 2$ (see [H86]). Clearly, if (U, S) is a FPP(q), $q \geq 2$, then (U, S) is not ordered, since no point can replace another in a line.* □

A special class of coteries arises from a concept of domination among coteries (see [GB85]).

Definition: Let (U, S_1) and (U, S_2) be coteries. We say that (U, S_2) *dominates* (U, S_1) if $S_2 \neq S_1$ and for every quorum $S \in S_1$ there is a quorum $T \in S_2$ such that $T \subseteq S$. A *non-dominated coterie* (NDC) is a coterie which is not dominated by any other coterie.

Of the examples mentioned above, the Minimal Majority coterie of Example 2.1 is an NDC if and only if n is odd; a sufficient condition for a voting system (Example 2.2) to be an NDC is that the total weight be odd; a Star coterie (Example 2.3) is dominated; and FPP(q) (Example 2.4) is an NDC for $q = 2$ but is dominated for all $q > 2$.

The central concept of this research deals with load balancing.

Definition: Let (U, S) be a quorum system with quorum matrix $\hat{S} = (\hat{s}_{ij})$, $i = 1, \ldots, m$, $j = 1, \ldots, n$. A *quorum load vector* (QLV) is a vector $\mathbf{v} = (v_1, v_2, \ldots, v_m)$ whose components are real nonnegative numbers (not all zero), expressing the relative loads placed on the quorums of S. The *element load vector* (ELV) induced by the QLV $\mathbf{v}$ is the vector $\mathbf{a} = \mathbf{a}(S, \mathbf{v}) = (a_1, a_2, \ldots, a_n)$ computed by $\mathbf{a} = \mathbf{v}\hat{S}$ and expressing the relative loads placed on the elements of U when using the QLV $\mathbf{v}$.

Definition: Let (U, S) be a quorum system. Given a QLV $\mathbf{v} = (v_1, v_2, \ldots, v_m)$ which induces the ELV $\mathbf{a} = (a_1, a_2, \ldots, a_n)$, we define the *balancing ratio* for S and $\mathbf{v}$ as

$$\rho_{S, \mathbf{v}} = \frac{\min_{j=1,\ldots,n}\{a_j\}}{\max_{j=1,\ldots,n}\{a_j\}}.$$

The *balancing ratio* of (U, S) is defined as

$$\rho_S = \max\{\rho_{S, \mathbf{v}} \colon \mathbf{v} \text{ is a QLV}\}.$$

A straightforward continuity and compactness argument shows that ρ_S is well-defined. We have associated with each quorum system (U, S) a parameter $0 \leq \rho_S \leq 1$ which tells us how evenly we can spread the load among the elements of U if we are allowed to assign the relative loads to the quorums optimally. The higher ρ_S, the better behaved is our quorum system from the point of view of load balancing. Clearly, if $U \neq \cup S$ then, no matter which QLV we choose, the balancing ratio will be zero. So, in studying the balancing ratio it is natural to make the assumption that $U = \cup S$.

Definition: A quorum system (U, S) is *non-redundant* if each element appears in some quorum, i.e., $U = \cup S$.

Once this assumption holds, we have $\rho_S > 0$. The most pleasing situation is when all element loads can be made equal, that is, $\rho_S = 1$. In such a case we say that the quorum system is *perfectly balanced*.

3   The Balancing Ratio in the Worst Case

In this section we address the following question: Within the class of all non-redundant quorum systems with a universe of size n, how low can the balancing ratio be in the worst case?

Theorem 3.1 *Let (U, S) be a non-redundant quorum system with $U = \{u_1, u_2, \ldots, u_n\}$, $n \geq 2$. Then $\rho_S \geq 1/(n-1)$. This bound is the best possible.[1]*

The worst case for the balancing ratio occurs for the Star, which is a dominated coterie. What happens if we restrict attention to NDC's? The following construction, taken from [EL74], exhibits a low balancing ratio.

Example 3.2 Nucleus Coterie.   *Let $r \geq 2$ be an integer and let U be the disjoint union of the sets K and L, where $|K| = 2r - 2$ and $|L| = \binom{2r-2}{r-1}/2$. Let the elements of L be put in a one-to-one correspondence with the halvings of K, that is, to every unordered pair A, B of disjoint subsets of K of size $r - 1$ each there corresponds an element $u_{A,B}$ of L. Let S consist of all sets of the form $A \cup \{u_{A,B}\}$ and $B \cup \{u_{A,B}\}$, where A, B is a halving of K, as well as all subsets of K of size r. It is easy to verify that (U, S) is an NDC and it is non-redundant. The number of elements is $n = 2r - 2 + \binom{2r-2}{r-1}/2$. The balancing ratio is 1 when $r = 2$ and is $\rho_S = 4/\binom{2r-2}{r-1}$ when $r \geq 3$.* $\square$

We observe that for $r = 3$ the above construction gives a non-redundant NDC (U, S) with $|U| = 7$ which has balancing ratio $\rho_S = 2/3$. It is therefore an example showing that Theorem 4.3 to be presented in the next section does not remain true if the assumption of being ordered is removed. No such example with universe of size smaller than 7 exists. Indeed, for $n \leq 5$ it is known that every NDC is a voting system and hence ordered. For $n = 6$, an exhaustive search shows that all non-redundant NDC's are perfectly balanced.

For large r, the above construction gives almost the worst case:

Theorem 3.3 *For every non-redundant NDC (U, S) with $U = \{u_1, u_2, \ldots, u_n\}$, $\rho_S \geq 2/(n - \log_2 n + o(\log n))$. Furthermore, there exists such an NDC (U, S) with $\rho_S = 2/(n - \log_2 n - o(\log n))$.*

We comment that by some finer tuning of the proof it is possible to replace the $o(\log n)$ term in the lower bound by $\frac{4}{3}\sqrt{\log_2 n}$.

4   Perfect Balancing

We begin with a simple sufficient condition for perfect balancing.

Proposition 4.1 *Every regular-degree quorum system is perfectly balanced.* ∎

---

[1] Proofs are omitted throughout this abstract.

As an application of Proposition 4.1, we note that the Minimal Majority quorum systems of Example 2.1 and the FPP coterie of Example 2.4 are regular, hence perfectly balanced. The Star coterie (Example 2.3), on the other hand, is not perfectly balanced (when $n \geq 3$), since it can be seen that the load on the center of the star is the sum of the loads on the other elements.

In trying to determine when a given quorum system is perfectly balanced, the following characterization (based on Farkas' Lemma) is useful.

Proposition 4.2 *Let (U, S) be a quorum system, with $U = \{u_1, u_2, \ldots, u_n\}$. Then (U, S) is perfectly balanced if and only if there exists no $\mathbf{x} = (x_1, x_2, \ldots, x_n) \in \mathbb{P}^n$ satisfying: (C1) $x(S) \geq 0$ for all $S \in S$, and (C2) $x(U) < 0$.* ∎

Our main result in this section is concerned with ordered NDC's.

Theorem 4.3 *Every ordered non-redundant NDC is perfectly balanced.*

Corollary 4.4 *Every non-redundant voting system (Example 2.2) with odd total weight is perfectly balanced.* ∎

We remark that none of the three assumptions made in Theorem 4.3 is superfluous, as will be demonstrated in the full paper.

5 Load Balancing and Quorum Size

5.1 Measures for Quorum Size

In this section we study the extent of compatibility of two desirable goals: having a high balancing ratio and having small quorum sizes. The general theme will be that a high balancing ratio cannot be obtained with small quorum sizes.

If a quorum system is r-uniform (namely, every quorum has r elements) then clearly we should use r as the parameter describing the quorum size. But for more general quorum systems, the question arises as to which parameter should be used for evaluating quorum sizes. Two parameters turn out to be suitable for our investigation.

Definition: The *rank* of a quorum system (U, S) is defined as $r_S = \max\{|S| : S \in S\}$.

Definition: Let (U, S) be a quorum system with quorum matrix $\hat{S} = (\hat{s}_{ij})$, $i = 1, \ldots, m$, $j = 1, \ldots, n$. Let $\mathbf{v} = (v_1, v_2, \ldots, v_m)$ be a QLV. The *weighted average quorum size* (WAQS) of (U, S) corresponding to $\mathbf{v}$ is $g_{S,\mathbf{v}} = \left(\sum_{i=1}^m v_i |S_i|\right) / \left(\sum_{i=1}^m v_i\right) = \left(\sum_{j=1}^n a_j\right) / \left(\sum_{i=1}^m v_i\right)$, where $\mathbf{a} = (a_1, a_2, \ldots, a_n)$ is the ELV induced by $\mathbf{v}$, that is, $\mathbf{a} = \mathbf{v}\hat{S}$. In the case when $\mathbf{v}$ is an optimizing QLV, that is, $\rho_{S,\mathbf{v}} = \rho_S$, we refer to $g_{S,\mathbf{v}}$ as an *optimally weighted average quorum size* (OWAQS).

The *weighted average element load* of (U, S) corresponding to $\mathbf{v}$ is $g_{S,\mathbf{v}}/n = \left(\sum_{j=1}^n a_j\right) / \left(n \sum_{i=1}^m v_i\right)$, and the *optimally weighted average element load* is defined analogously.

In our context of load balancing, it seems that the notion of an OWAQS is the suitable way to measure quorum size. The rank is also interesting as a worst case measure. If the quorum system is r-uniform then all approaches give r as the answer. In general, the WAQS and even the OWAQS are not unique, as they depend on $\mathbf{v}$. Clearly, for every QLV $\mathbf{v}$ we have $g_{S,\mathbf{v}} \leq r_S$.

5.2 Quorum Size Bounds for Ordered NDC's

In the first part of our analysis we shall focus on ordered non-redundant NDC's. This is a natural class of quorum systems for which we know that perfect balancing is guaranteed (Theorem 4.3). So it is interesting to ask what quorum sizes this class admits, or more precisely, how low we can make the rank and the OWAQS within this class.

Theorem 5.1 *Let (U, S) be an ordered non-redundant NDC with universe of size n. Then $r_S \geq \lceil (n+1)/2 \rceil$. This bound is the best possible.*

We note that again, none of the assumptions of the theorem is superfluous, as will be shown in the full paper.

A similar lower bound on the OWAQS holds if we restrict attention to voting systems, a subclass of ordered coteries.

Theorem 5.2 *Let (U, S) be a perfectly balanced voting system with universe of size n. Then for every QLV $\mathbf{v}$, OWAQS is greater than $n/2$.*

Comparing the last two theorems, it is natural to ask whether the (stronger) conclusion of Theorem 5.2 holds under the conditions of Theorem 5.1. The question involves the class of ordered NDC's that are not voting systems (and therefore Theorem 5.2 does not apply to them). It is not easy to construct examples for this class, but this has been done: two such examples with universe of size 13 are given in [Os85] (in a different context). In the following theorem we show not only that there is a member of this class for which the conclusion of Theorem 5.2 fails, but that it fails for every member of this class.

Theorem 5.3 *Let (U, S) be an ordered non-redundant NDC with a universe of size n. Suppose further that (U, S) is not a voting system. Then there exists an optimizing QLV $\mathbf{v}$ whose OWAQS is equal to $n/2$.*

Theorems 5.2 and 5.3 yield the following characterization of voting systems within ordered NDC's.

Corollary 5.4 *Let (U, S) be an ordered non-redundant NDC with universe of size n. Then the following are equivalent: (a) (U, S) is a voting system. (b) Every OWAQS is greater than $n/2$. (c) No OWAQS is equal to $n/2$.*

5.3 Quorum Size Bounds for (Non-Ordered) Perfectly Balanced Quorum Systems

The foregoing theorems indicate that certain methods for constructing quorum systems or certain properties of quorum systems which guarantee perfect balancing are costly in terms of quorum size. But perfect balancing can be achieved with considerably smaller quorums. Indeed, a FPP(q) (Example 2.4) is ($q+1$)-uniform and has a universe of size $n = q^2 + q + 1$, so its rank is roughly $\sqrt{n}$. It is perfectly balanced by Proposition 4.1.

Our next goal is to prove the optimality (in terms of quorum size) of FPP(q) among all perfectly balanced quorum systems. For this purpose, we review first some known concepts and results on fractional matchings in hypergraphs, expressed using the terminology of the current paper.

Definition: Let $(U, \mathcal{S})$ be a quorum system with quorum matrix $\hat{S} = (\hat{s}_{ij})$, $i = 1, \ldots, m$, $j = 1, \ldots, n$. A *fractional matching* in $(U, \mathcal{S})$ is a QLV $\mathbf{v} = (v_1, v_2, \ldots, v_m)$ such that the induced ELV $\mathbf{a} = \mathbf{v}\hat{S} = (a_1, a_2, \ldots, a_n)$ satisfies $a_j \leq 1$, $j = 1, \ldots, n$. The *size* of a fractional matching $\mathbf{v} = (v_1, v_2, \ldots, v_m)$ is defined as $|\mathbf{v}| = \sum_{i=1}^{m} v_i$. The *fractional matching number* of $(U, \mathcal{S})$ is defined as

$$\nu_{\mathcal{S}}^* = \max\{|\mathbf{v}|: \mathbf{v} \text{ is a fractional matching in } (U, \mathcal{S})\}.$$

It is easy to deduce the following from the quorum intersection property.

Proposition 5.5 *Let $(U, \mathcal{S})$ be a quorum system. Then for every quorum $S \in \mathcal{S}$ we have $\nu_{\mathcal{S}}^* \leq |S|$. As a consequence, $\nu_{\mathcal{S}}^* \leq g_{S,\mathbf{v}}$ for every WAQS $g_{S,\mathbf{v}}$.*

The following finer estimate for $\nu_{\mathcal{S}}^*$ is due to Füredi.

Proposition 5.6 [F81]. *Let $(U, \mathcal{S})$ be a quorum system of rank $r_{\mathcal{S}} = r$. Then $\nu_{\mathcal{S}}^* \leq r - 1 + 1/r$.*

A FPP(r–1), if it exists, is a r-uniform quorum system with universe of size $r^2 - r + 1$ and fractional matching number $r - 1 + 1/r$. Thus Füredi's bound is attained for those values of r such that a FPP(r–1) exists. The following corollary of Proposition 5.6 had been proved earlier by Lovász.

Proposition 5.7 [L75]. *Let $(U, \mathcal{S})$ be a r-uniform, regular quorum system. Then $|U| \leq r^2 - r + 1$.*

Note that this bound too is attained for those values of r such that a FPP(r–1) exists.

We now return to our investigation of quorum size in perfectly balanced quorum systems.

Theorem 5.8 *Let $(U, \mathcal{S})$ be a perfectly balanced quorum system with $|U| = n$ and rank $r_{\mathcal{S}} = r$. Then (1) every OWAQS is at least $\sqrt{n}$, and (2) $n \leq r^2 - r + 1$.*

Part (2) of the theorem is seen to be a generalization of Proposition 5.7: the uniformity assumption is dispensed with, as the rank suffices, and the regularity assumption is relaxed to perfect balancing.

5.4 Size-Balancing Tradeoffs for Unbalanced Quorum Systems

We have seen that if we insist on perfect balancing then the best we can do is to use quorums of size $\sim \sqrt{n}$. What if we relax perfect balancing and are willing to accept a balancing ratio not worse than some number ρ, $0 < \rho < 1$? Is there a trade-off between the required level ρ and the quorum size it admits in the best case?

It is easy to get an analogue of Theorem 5.8 by observing that when $\rho_{S,\mathbf{v}} \geq \rho$ one obtains a bound in the form: $n\rho \leq g_{S,\mathbf{v}} \nu_S^*$. From this it follows that $g_{S,\mathbf{v}} \geq \sqrt{n\rho}$. We shall get a better estimate by a refinement of the argument.

Theorem 5.9 *Let (U, S) be a quorum system with $|U| = n$. Let $0 < \rho \leq 1$ and let $\mathbf{v}$ be a QLV such that $\rho_{S,\mathbf{v}} \geq \rho$. Then $g_{S,\mathbf{v}} \geq 2\sqrt{n\rho}/(1 + \rho)$.*

We describe now a construction showing that the bound given in Theorem 5.9 is rather tight.

Example 5.10 Ext-FPP. *Let $0 < \rho < \frac{1}{2}$ and let r be a positive integer such that a FPP(r-1) exists. Let P and $\mathcal{L}$ be the sets of points and lines respectively of a FPP(r-1). Let K be a set of size $[(1-2\rho)/\rho](r^2 - r + 1)$, disjoint from P, and let $\mathcal{M}$ be the set of all subsets of K of size $(1 - 2\rho)r$. (We ignore integrality adjustments, whose effect is negligible for large r.) Let $U = P \cup K$ and let S consist of all sets of the form $L \cup M$, where $L \in \mathcal{L}$ and $M \in \mathcal{M}$. Then (U, S) is a $2(1 - \rho)r$-uniform coterie with $|U| = n = [(1 - \rho)/\rho](r^2 - r + 1)$.* $\square$

Let $\mathbf{v}$ be a QLV assigning equal load to all the quorums in S. Then it can be verified that $\rho_{S,\mathbf{v}} = \rho$. We have to compare $g_{S,\mathbf{v}} = 2(1 - \rho)r$ with the bound of Theorem 5.9: $\frac{2\sqrt{n\rho}}{1+\rho} = \frac{2\sqrt{1-\rho}\sqrt{r^2-r+1}}{1+\rho}$. It is readily seen that the ratio between the two quantities approaches 1 as $\rho \to 0$ and $r \to \infty$. The ratio is in general less than $(1 + \rho/2)(1 + 1/(2r))$.

The theorem and the construction delineate with a good degree of precision a trade-off between the required level of balancing ρ (when $0 < \rho < \frac{1}{2}$) and the quorum size it admits in the best case.

In view of the distinguished role played by NDC's among quorum systems, it is interesting to investigate the relation between the level of balancing and the quorum size within this special class. In the full paper we show that the picture depicted by Theorems 5.8 and 5.9 (and the constructions establishing their tightness) does not change much for NDC's. This is done through showing examples of NDC's approaching these lower bounds, albeit not as tightly as the (dominated) examples FPP and Ext-FPP.

References

[B89]   Berge, C., *Hypergraphs*, North-Holland, 1989.

[B86]   Bollobás, B., *Combinatorics*, Cambridge University Press, 1986.

[EL74]   Erdős, P. and L. Lovász, Problems and results on 3-chromatic hypergraphs and some related questions, in *Infinite and Finite Sets*, Proc. Colloq. Math. Soc. J. Bolyai 10, North-Holland, 1974, pp. 609–627.

[F81]   Füredi, Z., Maximum degree and fractional matchings in uniform hypergraphs, *Combinatorica* 1 (1981) 155–162.

[GB85]   Garcia-Molina, H. and D. Barbara, How to assign votes in a distributed system, *J. ACM* 32 (1985) 841–860.

[H86]   Hall, M., *Combinatorial Theory*, John Wiley, 1986.

[H84]   Herlihy, M.P., *Replication methods for abstract data types*, Ph.D. thesis, MIT, 1984.

[IK90]   Ibaraki, T., and T. Kameda, Theory of coteries, *Tech. Report CSS/LCCR TR90-09*, Simon Fraser University, Burnaby, B.C. Canada, 1990.

[L73]   Lovàsz, L., Coverings and colorings of hypergraphs, In *Proc. 4th Southeastern Conf. on Combinatorics, Graph Theory and Computing* (Florida Atlantic University), *Utilitas Mathematica*, Winnipeg, Canada, 1973, 47–56.

[L75]   Lovász, L., On the minimax theorems of combinatorics, *Mat. Lapok* 26 (1975) 209–264 (Hungarian).

[MP92]   Y. Marcus and D. Peleg, Construction methods for quorum systems, *Tech. Report CS92-33*, the Weizmann Institute of Science, 1992.

[M92]   Y. Marcus, *Load balancing in quorum systems*, M.Sc. Thesis, the Weizmann Institute of Science, 1992.

[MV88]   Mullender, S.J., and P.M.B. Vitànyi, Distributed match-making, *Algorithmica* 3 (1988), 367–391.

[NW94]   Naor, M., and A. Wool, The load, capacity and availability of quorum systems, to appear in *Proc. FOCS'94*.

[Os85]   Ostmann, A., Decisions by players of comparable strength, *Z. für Nationalökonomie* 45 (1985) 267–284.

[Ow82]   Owen, G., *Game Theory*, Academic Press, 1982.

[PW93]   Peleg, D., and A. Wool, The availability of quorum systems, Technical Report CS93-17, The Weizmann Institute of Science, Rehovot, Israel, 1993.

[R86]   Raynal, M., *Algorithms for mutual exclusion*, MIT Press, 1986.

[T85]   Tuza, Zs., Critical hypergraphs and intersecting set-pair systems, *J. Combin. Th. (Ser. B)* 39 (1985) 134–145.

Balanced Distributed Search Trees Do Not Exist

Brigitte Kröll   Peter Widmayer

Institut für Theoretische Informatik,
ETH Zentrum, 8092 Zürich, Switzerland.
Tel.: +41/1/632 74 01, Fax: +41/1/632 11 72
e-mail: <last name>@inf.ethz.ch

Abstract. This paper is a first step towards an understanding of the inherent limitations of distributed data structures. We propose a model of distributed search trees that is based on few natural assumptions. We prove that any class of trees within our model satisfies a lower bound of $\Omega(\sqrt{m})$ on the worst case height of distributed search trees for m keys. That is, unlike in the single site case, balance in the sense that the tree height satisfies a logarithmic upper bound cannot be achieved. This is true although each node is allowed to have arbitrary degree (note that in this case, the height of a single site search tree is trivially bounded by one). By proposing a method that generates trees of height $O(\sqrt{m})$, we show the bound to be tight.

1 Introduction

Distributed data structures have attracted considerable attention in the past few years. From a practical viewpoint, this is due to the increasing availability of networks of workstations. These networks offer an enormous computing power not only for distributed algorithms, but also for efficient storage and retrieval. Since collections of data become larger and larger, and efficient access is still a bottleneck in quite a few applications, it is useful to know how to efficiently maintain data in a distributed environment. From a theoretical perspective, the appeal of this question comes from the fact that the distributed setting turns out to be substantially different from its classical (single site) counterpart, and that it poses challenging new problems.

The seminal work on distributed linear hashing (LH*, Litwin et al. [5]) has been followed by suggestions based on distributed extendible hashing (Devine [1], Vingralek et al. [7]), distributed random binary search trees (DRT, Kröll et al. [2]), and a distributed variant of B-trees (RP*, Litwin et al. [6]). In some essential aspects of the model of distributed data structures (such as scalability requirements) and of the measure of efficiency, all of this work agrees with the proposal by Litwin et al. [5]. Nevertheless, this whole research area is still far from an accepted setting that models all essential features of the distributed world well enough. In particular, it is by no means clear what performance could possibly be achieved in a particular setting.

In this paper, we are interested primarily in lower bounds on the performance of distributed data structures. We therefore ignore distributed hashing methods (Devine [1], Litwin et al. [5]), because they fail to guarantee good worst-case efficiency, and we restrict ourselves to *general* distributed search structures that are only based on key comparisons. Within this framework, we naturally limit ourselves to search trees. Up until today, two distributed search tree structures have been proposed in the literature, a distributed random tree DRT [2] and a distributed variant of a B-tree [6]. None of both is satisfactory from a theoretical point of view: The DRT is not able to narrowly bound the length of a longest search path, and the distributed B-tree variant cannot confine a search on a path from the root to a leaf — it may err and need to go back up in the tree, and therefore the logarithmic bound on its height does not imply a logarithmic bound on the search time. In order to better understand the inherent limitations of distributed search trees, we study classes of distributed leaf search trees of a certain type that can be viewed as a natural generalization of the usual single site leaf search trees. We will show that no class of trees of this type can guarantee a logarithmic bound on the path length. This puts the distributed case in contrast with the traditional single site case, where we know how to balance search trees.

More precisely, we prove that any class of trees within our model satisfies a lower bound of $\Omega(\sqrt{m})$ on the worst-case height of distributed search trees for m keys. We give a matching upper bound by sketching a method that generates trees of exactly that height.

This paper is organized as follows. Section 2 discusses the problem of scalable, distributed access structures and reports on crucial aspects of the proposals in the literature. Section 3 defines the model of distributed data structures on which we base our lower bound proof. In Section 4, we prove the lower bound; in Section 5 we propose a distributed data structure that leads to a matching upper bound. Section 6 discusses implications of our result.

2 The distributed search problem

We want to study the inherent efficiency limitations of dynamic, distributed data structures. Therefore, we ignore most of the problems that a distributed data structure might encounter in practice (such as faulty communication, for instance) and resort to a simple model. We will show that our lower bound holds already in this simple model. Like all schemes proposed recently in the literature, we assume that a given set of sites (processors) is connected by a point-to-point network. Each site in the network is either a *server* that stores data or a *client* that initiates requests. Sites communicate by sending and receiving messages. A site can send a message to any site, given the identifier of the destination site (we assume site identifiers to be unique network addresses), in a single communication step. The network communication is free of errors. Each site buffers all incoming messages and guarantees that each message is handled in finite time after its arrival. All clients together operate on a (presumably huge) common file that must be distributed over the servers dynamically. Each server can store a single block of at most b data items, for a fixed, constant number b (we will therefore not include b in the asymptotic efficiency bounds to be derived later in the paper). The maintenance of the data within each server's storage space is irrelevant; in particular, it does not matter whether the data local to a server are stored in main memory or on external storage. The distributed data structure determines the distribution of the data over the servers; there are no preconditions as to where the data can be stored. The data is viewed as a set of keys that are drawn from a linearly ordered universe, where a key represents an arbitrary object whose nature is irrelevant for access purposes. In this set, a client triggers an insert or search operation for a key by sending a message to a server. In the best case, this server can perform the operation on its local data. In general, however, it may be necessary for the server to forward the message to some other server (and so on), because the distribution of the keys among the servers changes dynamically according to the set of inserted keys. We disregard deletions, in line with the literature so far.

For the purpose of measuring efficiency, we view the given network to be a complete graph with bidirectional links. We measure the efficiency of operations solely in the number of messages exchanged between sites. That is, the length of a message and the topology of a connected network that may in reality underly the complete communication graph do not influence the cost of a message transmission (this measure of efficiency was already proposed by Litwin et al. [5]).

The distributed random tree

To illustrate some essential aspects of distributed search trees, let us now briefly discuss the distributed random tree DRT; for a full description of this method see [2].

DRT distributes data according to a virtual, global, complete binary random leaf search tree T. Each node of T is uniquely assigned to one server. The clients and servers have some possibly obsolete knowledge of some part of T. In any case, the knowledge of a server is at least sufficient for guiding a search: For an interior node assigned to a server, the server knows about the node and its children, in the sense that it can correctly forward a key in a search operation to its left or its right child (see Fig. 1). For a leaf assigned to a server, the server stores all inserted keys in the data set whose search paths end at that leaf. Only one leaf is assigned to a server at any given time. That is, a server stores the block of data items whose keys lie in the key interval of the server's leaf, plus a subtree of T to help guide a search. In order to guarantee that no server is forced to store more than b keys, the virtual, global tree T grows at the leaves, exactly like a random search tree, and the assignment of nodes to servers is adjusted as follows: Whenever a leaf is transformed into an interior node with two leaves as children, the new interior node remains assigned to its server, one of the new leaves is assigned to the same server, and the other leaf is assigned to a new server. Now, conceptually, a search for key k traverses the search path defined by k in T and ends in a leaf assigned to the server that holds the data with which the request can be answered. The traversal of the path in the virtual, global tree T is realized by forwarding the request from one server to the next on this path. While in the DRT method the knowledge that active clients and

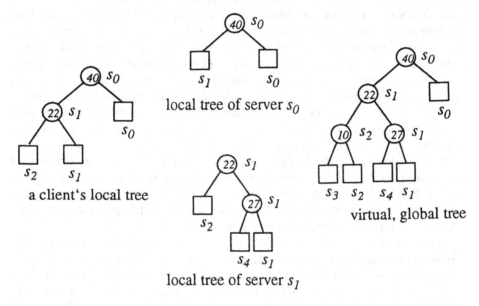

local tree of server s_0

a client's local tree

local tree of server s_1

virtual, global tree

Fig. 1. An illustration of the DRT method (it shows for each node the assigned server).

servers often have about the virtual, global tree implies that a leaf will often be reached with none or only a few forward steps, in the worst case a forward step may actually occur in each position on the search path in which the server changes. In addition, the virtual, global tree may degenerate to a single path on which different interior nodes are assigned to different servers. As a consequence, in the worst case the number of forward steps of a request is linear in the number of servers that currently participate in the method.

Distributed search trees in general

Our interest in this paper is whether we can avoid this worst case; ideally, we would like to define a class of distributed search trees with logarithmic height. To state the problem precisely, we need a suitable definition of the term *search tree* for the distributed case. Let us recall the single site case. The search tree reflects the partition of the universe into intervals according to the set of keys: Each node represents a key interval, with the root representing the universe, and the children of a node representing the intervals that partition the node's interval. A search operation maintains the invariant that a key visits a node only if it lies in the node's interval; it does so by starting the search at the root and progressing at each node to the appropriate child. Let us call this part of the search tree behavior the *straight guiding property*.

In the distributed case, however, we count the number of messages instead of counting the steps in the tree traversal as usual. That is, we want to guarantee the straight guiding property for these messages. We restrict our attention to the case in which only one server (and not more than one) is associated with a node; this is the case in all methods suggested so far in the literature. We call such a tree a *distributed search tree*. Our goal is to ensure that a key that arrives at a server belongs to the set of keys that the server represents (that is the union of the key intervals of all nodes with which the server is associated). This is not trivially satisfied in a distributed environment: The virtual, global tree changes over time, including the association of servers to nodes, and not all sites know the respective current tree. Therefore, a key may be sent to a server based on potentially obsolete information on the sender's side, and thus we need to make sure that at any time, the receiving server can straightly guide all keys that it could correctly receive (and hence guide) at some previous time. This distributed version of the straight guiding property is the key requirement that we impose on distributed search trees; it limits our freedom in modifying the search tree structure itself, and in associating servers with nodes of the search tree. Let a *stable distribution method* denote a method that guarantees that the distributed straight guiding property is satisfied.

Observe that the virtual, global tree of the DRT method possesses the distributed straight guiding property. Hence, the random search tree method naturally generalizes to a stable distribution method, namely the DRT method. Does the same hold for some class of balanced search trees, in the sense that each path has only logarithmic height? If it does not, can we still define a class of balanced, distributed search trees?

To get some insight into where the difficulties might lie, let us for a moment try to distribute a file according to a search tree that is rebalanced by means of rotations (see Fig. 2). Assume that server s_1 is assigned to v_1 and server

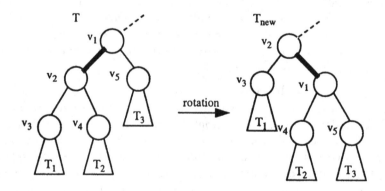

Fig. 2. The effect of a distributed rotation.

$s_2 \neq s_1$ to v_2 in T, which is transformed to T_{new} by the rotation shown in Fig. 2. Now, let us try to reassign servers to nodes in T_{new} in a way that guarantees the straight guiding property. Note that the set of keys visiting v_1 in the search tree T before the rotation is a superset of the set of keys visiting v_1 in the search tree

T_{new} after the rotation. Thus, server s_1 may receive a request with a key whose search path ends in T_1, since s_1 is assigned to v_1 in T. Now, by simply reassigning the servers s_1 and s_2 to the nodes v_1 and v_2 in T_{new}, we cannot guarantee the straight guiding property. In this case, we must assign one of the servers to a node on the path from the root to v_2 (except v_2 itself) in T_{new}. Because this affects nodes outside the scope of the rotation, this example indicates that it is impossible to directly make use of rotations for balancing a distributed search tree while guaranteeing the straight guiding property.

In the following, we will show that distributed search trees that are balanced (in the sense that the tree height satisfies a logarithmic upper bound) according to a stable distribution method do not exist. This is true although we allow each node in the tree to have arbitrary degree (note that in this case, the height of a single site search tree is trivially bounded from above by 1), and although each insert operation may change the virtual, global tree entirely (provided that the straight guiding property remains satisfied). Our results show that no stable distribution method can generate distributed search trees with a height of $o(\sqrt{m})$, where m is the number of stored keys; a bound of $O(\sqrt{m})$, however, can be achieved.

3 The model

Let us now formally describe the model that underlies our lower bound on the performance of stable distribution methods. It largely makes the preceding discussion more precise.

Let $\mathcal{K}$ be a totally ordered universe of keys with the following two properties. First, between any two different keys, there is an infinite number of other keys, and second, no minimum and no maximum key exist. Examples for $\mathcal{K}$ are the set of rational and the set of real numbers. We define $-\infty$ (resp. ∞) to be smaller (resp. bigger) than all keys in $\mathcal{K}$.

We limit our discussion to the class of leaf search trees for $\mathcal{K}$ with the following notation (for an example, see Fig. 3): Each node represents a key interval $[k_0, k_r)$ of all keys bigger than or equal to k_0 and smaller than k_r ($k_0, k_r \in \mathcal{K} \cup \{-\infty, \infty\}$) and stores the interval boundaries k_0 and k_r. For the root node, we have $k_0 = -\infty$ and $k_r = \infty$. As usual, each interior node stores the partition of its key interval $[k_0, k_r)$ represented by its children; it does so by storing $r - 1$ routers $k_1, \ldots, k_{r-1} \in \mathcal{K}$, where $r \geq 2$ and $k_0 < k_1 < \ldots < k_r$. A search in the tree starts at the root and is guided by the routers on a unique search path down the tree to a leaf: For key $k \in \mathcal{K}$, the search follows the ith pointer if $k_{i-1} \leq k < k_i$ holds. Each leaf of the tree represents the data block of all data within its key interval; that is, the tree is merely an index structure (a leaf search tree) that does not store keys in interior nodes. For brevity, from now on we use the term *search tree* to denote a tree with the properties just described. We enumerate the *levels* of nodes in a search tree from the root to the leaves: The root is at level 0, and the children of a node at level i are at level $i + 1$. The *height* $h(T)$ of a search tree T is the highest level number of a node in T. We denote with

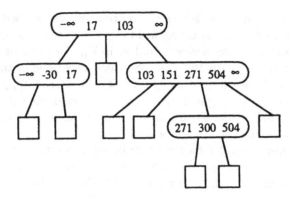

Fig. 3. An example search tree: round nodes denote interior nodes, angular nodes denote leaves.

$\mathcal{K}_T(v) \subseteq \mathcal{K}$ the key interval represented by a node v in T, that is the set of all keys in $\mathcal{K}$ whose search path passes through v. The nature of $\mathcal{K}$ and the choice of the routers in the interior nodes imply that each such set $\mathcal{K}_T(v)$ is infinite.

A search tree is called *distributed*, if each node v is associated with a positive integer $j(v)$, the *server number* of v. For a distributed search tree T and a path $p = v_0, \ldots, v_s$ from the root to a leaf, the *distributed length $dl(p)$ of the path p* is the number of changes of the servers between adjacent nodes; more formally, $dl(v_0, \ldots, v_s) = |\{0 \le i < s | j(v_i) \ne j(v_{i+1})\}|$. The *distributed height $dh(T)$* is the maximum of all distributed lengths of paths in T. Our interest in the distributed search tree height comes from the fact that in case the nodes on a path in T whose distributed length is $dh(T)$ are associated with $dh(T)$ different servers, answering a request may cost at least $dh(T)$ messages. That is, $dh(T)$ is then a lower bound on the number of messages for an operation in the worst case. The proof of Theorem 4.1 will show that in the worst case, in a distributed search tree that is generated by a stable method and stores m keys, there is a path whose distributed length is proportional to $\sqrt{m}$ and whose nodes are associated with just that many servers. Therefore, in such a distributed search tree for m keys, a request does need $\Omega(\sqrt{m})$ messages in the worst case.

Now, we formalize the idea that a sequence of insertions of keys according to a certain method creates a distributed search tree. Let $b \in \mathbf{N}$ be the block capacity, that is the maximal number of keys each server can hold (b is the same for all servers). A *distribution method M* is a process which maps each sequence $k_1, \ldots, k_m (m \in \mathbf{N})$ of pairwise different (p.d., for short) keys in $\mathcal{K}$ to a distributed search tree $T_M(k_1, \ldots, k_m)$ in such a way that for each server, the search path of at most b of the keys $k_1, \ldots, k_m$ ends at one of the leaves assigned to that server.

For a distribution method M and an integer $m \in \mathbf{N}$, let $dh_M(m)$ be the maximal distributed height of all search trees $T_M(k_1, \ldots, k_\mu)(k_1, \ldots, k_\mu \in \mathcal{K}$ p.d., $\mu \le m)$ that M can generate by inserting at most m keys (let this value denote infinity, if no finite maximum exists).

Let us now formalize the search tree concept discussed previously. We call M *stable*, if for all $m \in \mathbf{N}$, for all p.d. keys $k_1, \ldots, k_m, k_{m+1} \in \mathcal{K}$, and for each node $v \in T_M(k_1, \ldots, k_m)$, there exist nodes $v_1, \ldots, v_n \in T_M(k_1, \ldots, k_m, k_{m+1})$ with $j(v_1) = \ldots = j(v_n) = j(v)$ and $\mathcal{K}_{T_M(k_1,\ldots,k_m)}(v) \subseteq \mathcal{K}_{T_M(k_1,\ldots,k_m,k_{m+1})}(v_1) \cup \ldots \cup \mathcal{K}_{T_M(k_1,\ldots,k_m,k_{m+1})}(v_n)$.

Our interest is in the degree of balancing that distributed search trees resulting from a stable method can achieve. For a real valued function $f : \mathbf{N} \to \mathbf{R}$, we call a distribution method M *f-dh-balanced*, if there is a constant $c_M > 0$ with $dh_M(m) \leq c_M f(m)$ for all $m \in \mathbf{N}$ (that is, $dh_M \in O(f)$).

4 A lower bound

Theorem 4.1 *Let $f : \mathbf{N} \to \mathbf{R}$ be a function with $f(m) = o(\sqrt{m})$. There exists no stable, f-dh-balanced distribution method.*

Proof:

Assume to the contrary that such a method M exists. The idea is to let an adversary insert keys whose search paths end in a leaf for which the distributed path length is longest.

To do so, let $k_1 \in \mathcal{K}$ be any key and $T^0 := T_M(k_1)$ the search tree that M generates. Let l^0 be the leaf in T^0 to which the search path for k_1 is guided; that is, $k_1 \in \mathcal{K}_{T^0}(l^0)$. For an example for T^0 and some further search trees in this proof, see Fig. 4.

Now we choose b pairwise different keys $k_2, \ldots, k_{b+1} \in \mathcal{K}_{T^0}(l^0)$, all of them different from k_1 (this is possible, since $\mathcal{K}_{T^0}(l^0)$ is infinite), and consider the search tree $T^1 := T_M(k_1, k_2, \ldots, k_{b+1})$. T^1 has at least one leaf l^1 whose key set $\mathcal{K}_{T^1}(l^1)$ is not disjoint from $\mathcal{K}_{T^0}(l^0)$, and whose server number $j(l^1) \neq j(l^0)$. Since M is stable and $\mathcal{K}_{T^1}(l^1) \cap \mathcal{K}_{T^0}(l^0) \neq \emptyset$, there is a node v_1^1 in T^1 with $j(l^0) = j(v_1^1) \wedge \mathcal{K}_{T^1}(l^1) \cap \mathcal{K}_{T^1}(v_1^1) \neq \emptyset$. Because $j(l^1) \neq j(v_1^1)$, the node v_1^1 is different from l^1. Since l^1 and v_1^1 are nodes in the same search tree and l^1 is a leaf, v_1^1 must be a node on the path in T^1 from the root to l^1, that is, $\mathcal{K}_{T^1}(l^1) \subseteq \mathcal{K}_{T^1}(v_1^1)$. This implies that the distributed height $dh(T_M(k_1, k_2, \ldots, k_{b+1}))$ is at least 1.

Now we continue by choosing $2b$ keys $k_{b+2}, \ldots, k_{3b+1} \in \mathcal{K}_{T^1}(l^1)$ in such a way that the keys $k_1, k_2, \ldots, k_{3b+1}$ are pairwise different. Since M is a distribution method, the search tree $T^2 := T_M(k_1, k_2, \ldots, k_{3b+1})$ has at least one leaf l^2, for which $\mathcal{K}_{T^2}(l^2) \cap \mathcal{K}_{T^1}(l^1) \neq \emptyset$, $j(l^2) \neq j(l^1)$ and $j(l^2) \neq j(v_1^1)$. Since M is stable, $\mathcal{K}_{T^2}(l^2) \cap \mathcal{K}_{T^1}(l^1) \neq \emptyset$ and $\mathcal{K}_{T^2}(l^2) \cap \mathcal{K}_{T^1}(v_1^1) \neq \emptyset$, there are nodes $v_1^2, v_2^2 \in T^2$ with $j(l^1) = j(v_1^2) \wedge \mathcal{K}_{T^2}(l^2) \cap \mathcal{K}_{T^2}(v_1^2) \neq \emptyset$ and $j(v_1^1) = j(v_2^2) \wedge \mathcal{K}_{T^2}(l^2) \cap \mathcal{K}_{T^2}(v_2^2) \neq \emptyset$. Since $j(l^2), j(v_1^2)$ and $j(v_2^2)$ are pairwise different, v_1^2 and v_2^2 are different interior nodes on the path from the root to leaf l^2 in T^2, that is, either $\mathcal{K}_{T^2}(l^2) \subseteq \mathcal{K}_{T^2}(v_1^2) \subseteq \mathcal{K}_{T^2}(v_2^2)$ or $\mathcal{K}_{T^2}(l^2) \subseteq \mathcal{K}_{T^2}(v_2^2) \subseteq \mathcal{K}_{T^2}(v_1^2)$ holds. It follows that the distributed height $dh(T_M(k_1, k_2, \ldots, k_{3b+1}))$ is at least 2.

Now we continue by choosing $3b$ keys $k_{3b+2}, \ldots, k_{6b+1} \in \mathcal{K}_{T^2}(l^2)$ in such a way that $k_1, \ldots, k_{6b+1}$ are pairwise different; by arguments extended from those given above, we get a search tree $T^3 := T_M(k_1, k_2, \ldots, k_{6b+1})$ with a distributed height of at least 3.

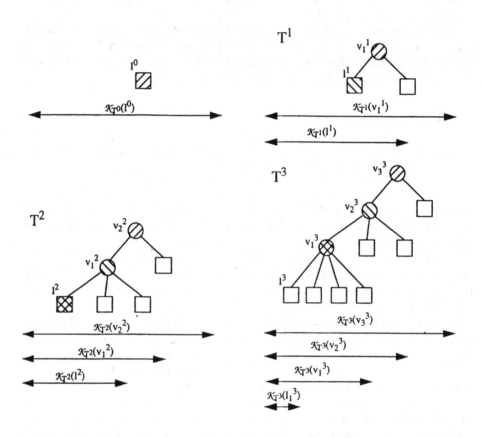

Fig. 4. An example for a splitting history: Nodes with the same shading have the same server number.

In general, in the sth step we choose sb keys in $\mathcal{K}_{T^{s-1}}(l^{s-1})$, and we get a search tree $T^s := T_M(k_1, k_2, \ldots, k_{m(s)})$ with a distributed height of at least s, where

$$m(s) = 1 + \sum_{i=1}^{s} ib = 1 + \frac{s(s+1)}{2}b.$$

That leads to

$$dh_M\left(1 + \frac{s(s+1)}{2}b\right) \geq s \text{ for all } s \in \mathbf{N}.$$

Since dh_M is monotonously increasing, and $1 + \frac{s(s+1)}{2}b \leq s^2 b$ holds for $s \geq 2$, we get

$$dh_M(s^2 b) \geq s \text{ for all } s \geq 2,$$

that is,

$$dh_M(m) \geq \sqrt{\frac{m}{b}} \text{ for an infinite number of values } m \in \mathbb{N}.$$

This contradicts the assumption that M is f-dh-balanced. $\qquad\square$

5 A method that reaches the lower bound

The purpose of the next theorem is to show that the given bound of $\sqrt{m}$ in Theorem 4.1 is tight.

Theorem 5.1 *There exists a stable, $\sqrt{m}$-dh-balanced distribution method.*

Proof:
We prove this theorem by proposing a stable, $\sqrt{m}$-dh-balanced distribution method M. Let us first describe the method.

For $k_1 \in \mathcal{K}$, let $T_M(k_1)$ consist of only one leaf with server number 1.

Now, we inductively define the search trees that method M generates. Let $k_1, \ldots, k_m, k_{m+1} \in \mathcal{K}$ be pairwise different. $T_M(k_1, \ldots, k_m, k_{m+1})$ is generated from $T_M(k_1, \ldots, k_m)$ in the following way. Let $v_0, \ldots, v_s = l$ be the nodes on the search path for the key k_{m+1} in $T_M(k_1, \ldots, k_m)$. We denote the interval boundaries and the routers stored in v_{s-1}, the father of l (if it exists), by $\bar{k}_0, \ldots, \bar{k}_{\bar{r}}$, and we assume that the ith pointer of v_{s-1} is pointing to l. Now, we distinguish the following cases.

Case 1: [For less than b of the keys $k_1, \ldots, k_m$, the search path in $T_M(k_1, \ldots, k_m)$ ends in l.]
   We define $T_M(k_1, \ldots, k_m, k_{m+1}) := T_M(k_1, \ldots, k_m)$.
Case 2: [For b of the keys $k_1, \ldots, k_m$, the search path in $T_M(k_1, \ldots, k_m)$ ends in l.[1]]
Case 2.1: [$s \geq 1$ and $j(l) = j(v_p)$ holds for some $0 \leq p \leq s - 1$.]
   We define $T_M(k_1, \ldots, k_m, k_{m+1})$ by changing $T_M(k_1, \ldots, k_m)$ in the following way. We split l into two leaves l_1 and l_2, with father v_{s-1}; that is, the ith pointer of v_{s-1} is pointing to l_1, and an additional pointer between the ith and the $(i+1)$th pointer is added, pointing to l_2. Further, an additional router k between $\bar{k}_{i-1}$ and $\bar{k}_i$ is added. We choose k as a median of the keys $\mathcal{K}(l) \cap \{k_1, \ldots, k_{m+1}\}$[2]. In addition, we change some server numbers of $T_M(k_1, \ldots, k_m)$. For doing so, we distinguish two cases.

---

[1] It is not possible that for more than b of the keys $k_1, \ldots, k_m$, the search path in $T_M(k_1, \ldots, k_m)$ ends in l, since the method M will turn out to be a distribution method.

[2] A median of r pairwise different keys $k_1, \ldots, k_r$ (w. l. o. g. given as an ordered sequence) is the key $k_{\frac{r+1}{2}}$, if r is odd, and a key bigger than $k_{\frac{r}{2}}$ and smaller than $k_{\frac{r}{2}+1}$, if r is even.

Case 2.1.1: [There is a leaf $\bar{l}$ in $T_M(k_1, \ldots, k_m)$ with the properties that
  - the level of $\bar{l}$ is smaller than the level of l,
  - there is a node $v_q \in \{v_0, \ldots, v_{s-1}\}$ with $j(v_q) = j(\bar{l})$.]
  We set $(j(\bar{l}), j(l_1), j(l_2)) := (j_{new}, j(l), j(\bar{l}))$, where j_{new} is a server number that does not occur in the search tree $T_M(k_1, \ldots, k_m)$.

Case 2.1.2: [There is no such leaf $\bar{l}$ with the properties required in case 2.1.1]
  We set $(j(l_1), j(l_2)) := (j(l), j_{new})$.

Case 2.2: [$s = 0$ or ($s \geq 1$ and $j(l) \neq j(v_p)$ holds for all $0 \leq p \leq s - 1$)]
  Here, l becomes an interior node storing the interval boundaries $\bar{\bar{k}}_0$ and $\bar{\bar{k}}_2$ and the router $\bar{\bar{k}}_1$ with $\bar{\bar{k}}_0 = -\infty, \bar{\bar{k}}_1 = k$ and $\bar{\bar{k}}_2 = \infty$, if $s = 0$, resp. $\bar{\bar{k}}_0 = \bar{k}_{i-1}, \bar{\bar{k}}_1 = k$ and $\bar{\bar{k}}_2 = \bar{k}_i$, if $s \geq 1$, where k is chosen as in Case 2.1. l has two pointers to two new leaves l_1 and l_2. As in Case 2.1, we distinguish two cases for changing some server numbers of $T_M(k_1, \ldots, k_m)$.

Case 2.2.1: [$s \geq 1$ and there is a leaf $\bar{l}$ in $T_M(k_1, \ldots, k_m)$ with the properties that
  - the level of $\bar{l}$ is smaller than or equal to the level of l,
  - there is a node $v_q \in \{v_0, \ldots, v_{s-1}\}$ with $j(v_q) = j(\bar{l})$.]
  We set $(j(\bar{l}), j(l_1), j(l_2)) := (j_{new}, j(l), j(\bar{l}))$.

Case 2.2.2: [$s = 0$ or ($s \geq 1$ and there is no such leaf $\bar{l}$ with the properties required in case 2.2.1)]
  We set $(j(l_1), j(l_2)) := (j(l), j_{new})$.

This completes the description of the method M. The proof that M is a distribution method, stable and $\sqrt{m}$-dh-balanced can be found in [3]. $\qquad \Box$

6 Discussion

We have shown that the distributed height of a distributed search tree resulting from a stable distribution method is $\Omega(\sqrt{m})$ in the worst case for m keys. In addition, we have shown that there is a stable distribution method satisfying the bound of $O(\sqrt{m})$ on the distributed height of its distributed search trees. Hence, these bounds are tight.

The method M proposed in the proof of Theorem 5.1 does not fully describe a distributed dictionary: It only describes the development of the virtual, global tree over time by describing how the tree grows and how servers are associated with nodes. This does not define which site knows which part of the virtual, global tree, which messages must be forwarded to which servers, and how we can make sure that eventually, each request arrives at the correct server. It also does not define a mechanism of correction messages that bring the obsolete knowledge of a site up to date. The full description of a suitable method is not within the focus of this paper, since we are interested here mainly in a step towards a theoretical foundation of distributed data structures. It may suffice to state that a method using no more than $O(\sqrt{m})$ messages per operation can actually be derived ([4]). On the constructive side, our result implies that we will have to drop the stability requirement in order to arrive at fast distributed search trees. Litwin et al. [6] do so for their distributed variant of a B-tree, and they indeed achieve logarithmic height. A search operation, however, does not simply follow a path from the root to a leaf; it may need to go back up in the tree to the parent of a visited node. As a consequence, Litwin et al. [6] do not give a bound on the number of messages. In addition, the loss of the straight guiding property may impede scalability: Sending messages to father nodes may distribute the message handling load over the servers more unevenly, with a disadvantage for servers whose nodes are closer to the global root.

Acknowledgement

We wish to thank Thomas Ottmann for many fruitful and inspiring discussions.

References

1. R. Devine: *Design and Implementation of DDM: A Distributed Dynamic Hashing Algorithm.* 4th Int. Conference on Foundations of Data Organization on Algorithms FODO, 1993.
2. B. Kröll, P. Widmayer: *Distributing a Search Tree among a Growing Number of Processors.* Proc. ACM SIGMOD Conference on the Management of Data, 1994, 265 – 276.
3. B. Kröll, P. Widmayer: *Balanced Distributed Search Trees Do Not Exist.* Technical Report 233, ETH Zürich, 1995.
4. B. Kröll, P. Widmayer: manuscript, in preparation, 1995.
5. W. Litwin, M.-A. Neimat, D.A. Schneider: *LH* — Linear Hashing for Distributed Files.* Proc. ACM SIGMOD Conference on the Management of Data, 1993, 327 – 336.
6. W. Litwin, M.-A. Neimat, D.A. Schneider: *RP* — A Family of Order Preserving Scalable Distributed Data Structures.* Proc. of VLDB, 1994, 342 – 353.
7. R. Vingralek, Y. Breitbart, G. Weikum: *Distributed File Organization with Scalable Cost/Performance.* Proc. ACM SIGMOD Conference on the Management of Data, 1994, 253 – 264.

Two-Floodlight Illumination of Convex Polygons

V. Estivill-Castro

Laboratorio Nacional de Informática Avanzada, Xalapa, Veracruz, México

J. Urrutia

Department of Computer Science, University of Ottawa, Ottawa, Ontario, Canada.

Abstract

A floodlight of size α is a light source that projects light in a cone of size α. In this paper we study the problem of illuminating a convex polygon using floodlights. We give an $O(n^2)$ time algorithm to find an optimal pair of floodlights to illuminate a convex polygon P with n vertices; that is a pair of floodlights to illuminate a convex polygon in such a way that the sum of their sizes is minimized. When our polygon is cocircular (i.e. all of the vertices of P lie on a circle) such a pair of floodlights can be found in linear time.

Introduction

Art Gallery problems have always been of great interest in Computational Geometry. Many articles on guarding or illumination problems dealing with numerous variations of the classical Art Gallery Theorem of Chvátal have been published [CV, FI]. Problems dealing with guarding of simple polygons, orthogonal polygons [O'R, ECU], families of convex sets on the plane [FT, UZ, CRCU1], edge guards [O'R], vertex guards etc. have received much attention. For a survey of recent results on this area, see [SHER]. In this paper we continue the study of illumination problems using floodlights.

A floodlight is a light source that illuminates the area within a cone. Floodlight illumination problems were introduced in [BGLOSU]. One of the motivations for the study of floodlight illumination problems, is that many illumination or guarding devices cannot search or illuminate all around themselves in all directions. Floodlights, for example illuminate only a circular cone. As it turns out, many communication devices used in the broadcasting of satellite and telecommunication signals can be idealized as floodlights. For example, satellites transmit signals using dishes that restrict the area of coverage to a cone.

Perhaps the main open problem in this area is that known as the *Stage Illumination Problem*. In this problem, we are given a line segment L (the stage) and a set of floodlights with fixed sizes and apexes, and we are asked to decide if we can rotate the floodlights around their apexes in such a way that L is completely illuminated.

Floodlight illumination problems can be grouped in two classes, decision type problems and optimization problems. In the decision type problems, we usually have a set of floodlights and an object, or collection of objects to be illuminated [BGLOSU, BBCUZ, SS, ECO'RUX, O'RX]. In the optimization type problems, we again have an object to be illuminated and are asked to find a set of floodlights satisfying certain restrictions that illuminate our objects subject to the condition that the sum of the sizes of our floodlights or the number of floodlights used is minimized [CRCU, ECO'RUX, ECU, O'RX].

In this paper we study the Two-Floodlight Illumination Problem, that is, the problem of finding two floodlights that illuminate a convex polygon with n vertices, in such a way that the sum of their sizes is minimized. We give an $O(n^2)$ algorithm to solve the Two-Floodlight Illumination Problem. Despite the fact that we are restricting ourselves to two floodlights and a convex polygon, our problem turns out to have a rich geometric structure which is used to derive our algorithm. We show that, when the polygon is cocircular,that is, when all its vertices lie on a circle, the Two-Floodlight Illumination Problem can be solved in linear time.We have been unable to obtain a faster algorithm to solve the Two-Floodlight Illumination Problem, but contrary to the natural intuition that $O(n\log(n))$ should be achievable, we suspect that $O(n^2)$ *is* optimal.

This paper is structured as follows: in Section 2 we develop an $O(n^2)$ algorithm to solve the Two-Floodlight Illumination Problem for convex polygons with the restriction that no four vertices of our polygon lie on a circle. In Section 3, we find a linear time algorithm for the Two-Floodlight Illumination Problem when all the vertices of a polygon lie on a circle. A solution for the general case can easily be obtained by combining the cocircular and the general position case, and will not be treated here. In Section 4, we present some open problems.

2. Optimal 2-Floodlight Illumination of Convex Polygons in General Circular Position

Some terminology and definitions will be given now. A floodlight F_i of size α is a light source that projects light in a cone of size α. F_i will be called an $\alpha - floodlight$ If the apex of an $\alpha - floodlight$ is located at a point p and p is a vertex of a polygon, we call it a *vertex* $\alpha - floodlight$.

Consider two points a and b on the boundary of a polygon P, not necessarily vertices of P. The vertex interval (a,b) of P is defined to be the set of vertices of P that we meet when we move in the clockwise direction on the boundary of P from a to b. For short, we will refer to the interval (a,b) rather than to the vertex interval (a,b). Notice that $(a,b) \neq (b,a)$. In particular, when a and b are interior points of edges of P, $(a,b) \cup (b,a)$ is the set of vertices of P.

A pair of floodlights F_1 and F_2 that illuminates a polygon P will be called a floodlight illuminating pair and will be called a FLIP of P. If F_1 and F_2 are such that the sum of their apertures is minimized, we call them an optimal FLIP. We call F_1, F_2 an *opposite* FLIP if the intersection of the regions illuminated by F_1 and F_2 is a quadrilateral with all of its vertices on the boundary of P, see Figure 1(a). If the interior of the regions illuminated by a FLIP F_1 and F_2 are disjoint, we call F_1, F_2 a dividing FLIP, see Figure 1(b). Observe that an optimal FLIP must be either an opposite FLIP or a dividing FLIP.

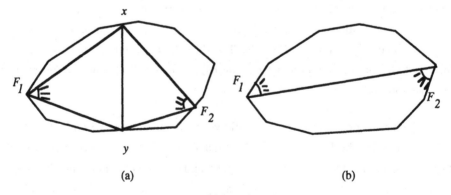

Figure 1

Lemma 1: Let F_1, F_2 be an optimal FLIP of a polygon P. Then the apexes of F_1 and F_2 are located at vertices of P.

Proof: Suppose that F_1, F_2 is an optimal FLIP of a polygon P. Two cases arise:

a) F_1 and F_2 is an opposite FLIP with apexes at q and r such that r is not a vertex of P. Let x, r, y, q be the vertices of the intersection of the area illuminated by F_1 and F_2. Consider the circle $C(x, y, p)$ that passes through x, y and a vertex p of P such that $C(x, y, p)$ contains all the vertices of the interval (x, y) of P. Notice that the angle spanned by p and the line segment $l(xy)$ is smaller than that spanned by r and $l(xy)$. Therefore if we replace F_2 by a floodlight F_3 with apex in p and illuminating the angular sector determined by x, p and y, then F_1 and F_3 also illuminate P and the sum of their sizes is smaller than that of F_1 and F_2, see Figure 2(a).

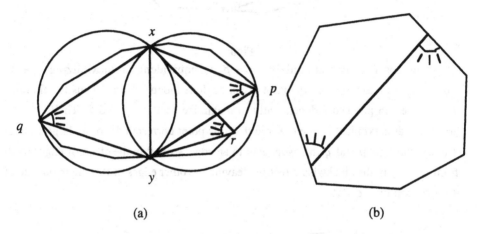

(a)   (b)

Figure 2

b) F_1 and F_2 form a *partitioning* pair of floodlights, see Figure 2(b). The reader may easily verify that in this case, we can slide the apex of F_1 and F_2 towards two vertices of P such that the sum of the sizes of F_1 and F_2 decrease.

QED.

Suppose now that we want to find a FLIP F_1 and F_2 of a polygon P in such a way that the apexes of F_1 and F_2 *must be located on two fixed vertices p and q of P* and the sum of the sizes of F_1 and F_2 are minimized. Call such a FLIP an optimal $(p, q) - FLIP$. We now show:

Lemma 2: Given two vertices p and q of a polygon P, we can find an opposite optimal $(p, q) - FLIP$ in linear time.

Proof: Our objective here is to find two points, x and y, on the boundary of P such that the sum of the angles $\alpha = ypx$ and $\beta = xqy$ is minimized. Consider the angles γ and δ formed by pxq and qyp as in Figure 3.

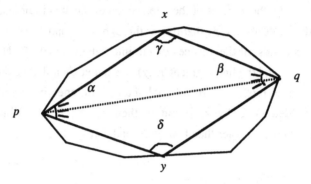

Figure 3

We now observe that minimizing $\alpha + \beta$ is equivalent to maximizing $\gamma + \delta$. However, the maximization of γ and δ can be done independently! Thus to minimize $\alpha + \beta$, we can proceed independently to maximize each of γ and δ. To locate the point x that maximizes γ we observe that this point corresponds to the largest circle $C(p,q)$ through p and q that is tangent to an edge e of P in the chain of edges of P from p to q in the clockwise direction, leaving the other edges of that chain outside of $C(p,q)$, see Figure 4(a).

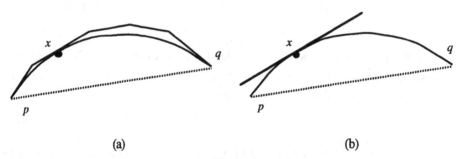

(a)   (b)

Figure 4

Thus all we need to do is to locate for each edge e of the chain of edges of P from p to q the point x on e that maximizes the angle pxq, see Figure 4(b). Clearly this can be done in constant time per edge, so x can be found in linear time. The same procedure is applied to find y. A degenerate case could happen here when $C(p,q)$ is tangent to the edge of P containing p, q or both. In the first and last cases simply take $x = p$, in the second case take $x = q$.

QED.

We now provide a criterion to reduce the number of pairs of vertices of P that can be apexes of an optimal *opposite* FLIP of P. Consider the set D of all diagonals of P joining all pairs of vertices of P with the property that there is a circle through their endpoints that contains P. Under our general circular position on the vertices of P, it is easy to see that the elements of D induce a triangulation $T(P)$ of P. Using standard techniques for calculating Voronoi Diagrams of convex polygons, D and $T(P)$ can be found in linear time [AGSS].

A subset of three vertices $\{u, v, w\}$ of the vertex set of P is called a $c-triple$ if $\{u, v, w\}$ is the set of vertices of a triangle of $T(P)$. It is well known that circle $C(u, v, w)$ determined by $\{u, v, w\}$ contains P. Under our general position assumption, the number of $c-triples$ of P is exactly $n-2$, see Figure 5. We say that two $c-triples$ $\{u, v, w\}$ and $\{x, y, z\}$ are adjacent if they share two common elements, i.e. $u = x$, $v = y$ and $w \neq z$. The vertices w and z will be called the antipodal vertices of the adjacent $c-triples$ $\{u, v, w\}$ and $\{x, y, z\}$.

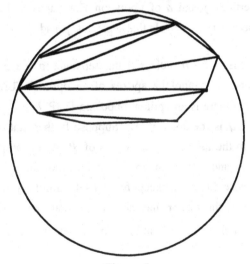

Figure 5

Given two vertices p and q of a polygon P, we say that a $c-triple$ $\{r, s, t\}$ separates p and q if p and q are both different from r, s and t and when we traverse the boundary of P from p to q (and from q to p) in the clockwise order, we meet either one of r, s or t before we meet q (resp. p), see Figure 6.

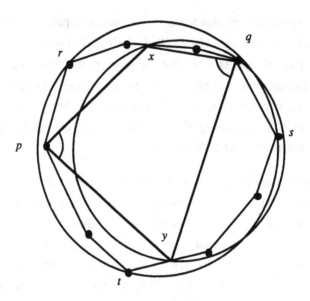

Figure 6

Lemma 3: If two vertices p and q of a polygon P are apexes of an optimal FLIP of a polygon P then there is no $c - triple$ that separates p and q.

Proof: Suppose there is a $c - triple\{r,s,t\}$ that separates p and q, see Figure 6. We now show that p and q. cannot be apexes of an optimal FLIP F_1, F_2 of P.. Suppose otherwise that there is an optimal opposing FLIP F_1, F_2 of P such that p is the apex of F_1 and q is the apex of F_2. Suppose further that F_1 and F_2 meet at two points x and y in the interior of two edges of P. As in the proof of Lemma 1, the circle through x, y and q contains in its interior all of the vertices of P between x and y in the clockwise direction, except for q itself. Similarly for the circle trough y, p and x. However, the reader may now verify that one of these circles has to intersect the circle through r, s and t at least four times, which is impossible.

QED.

From Lemma 3 the following result follows immediately:

Corollary 4: Let p and q, be the apexes of an optimal FLIP a polygon P. Then there is a circle through p and q containing P or p and q are the antipodal vertices of two adjacent $c - triples$ $\{u,v,p\}$ and $\{q,u,v\}$ of P.

We are now ready to give our algorithm O-FLIP to obtain an optimal floodlight illumination pair of a polygon P.

O-FLIP

Input a polygon P with n vertices.

Step 1:   Find the triangulation $T(P)$ of P, and all $c - triples$ of P.

Step 2:   Find all antipodal pairs of vertices for all the pairs of adjacent $c - triples$ of P.

Step 3:   For each pair of antipodal vertices p and q of a polygon P, find an optimal opposite $(p, q) - FLIP$ in linear time.

Step 4:   For each pair of vertices p and q of P find in constant time the partitioning pair of floodlights F_1, F_2 with apexes at p and q that illuminates P and minimizes the sum of the sizes of F_1 and F_2.

Output the FLIP of minimum weight identified in Steps 3 and 4.

Theorem 1:   Given a convex polygon P with n vertices in general position, O-FLIP finds an optimal FLIP of P in $O(n^2)$.

Proof: Steps 1 and 2 can be carried out in linear time. Step 3 requires $O(n^2)$ time, since there are at most n-2 antipodal pairs, and solving each of them requires $O(n)$ time. In Step 4, we need to test all pairs of vertices p and q of P. However, for every pair of vertices p and q of P, there are exactly two partitioning FLIP's of P, thus the complexity of Step 4 is $O(n^2)$.

QED.

3. Optimal 2-Floodlight Illumination of Cocircular Polygons

A polygon P is called cocircular if all of its vertices lie on a circle. In this section we will prove that finding an optimal FLIP of a cocircular polygon can be done in linear time. We start by proving the following lemma:

Lemma 4: Let P be a cocircular polygon, then any optimal FLIP of P is a dividing FLIP.

Proof: Suppose that P is cocircular and that it has an opposing optimal FLIP F_1, F_2. Let $C(P)$ be the circle containing the vertices of P. Assume that the apexes of F_1, F_2 are at two vertices p and q of P and that the vertices of the quadrilateral defined by F_1, F_2 are p, x, q, y, see Figure 7.

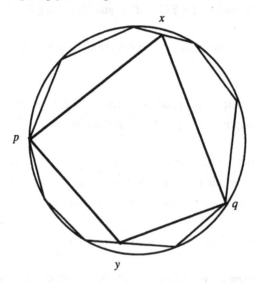

Figure 7

By Lemma 1, the circle $C(x,q,y)$ through x, q and y contains all the vertices of the interval (x, y) of P. This implies that $C(x,q,y)$ intersects $C(P)$ in at least three points, once in the middle of the arc of $C(P)$ joining the endpoints of the edge of P containing x, a second time in the middle of the arc of $C(P)$ joining the endpoints of the edge of P containing y and a third time at q. Since this is not possible our lemma follows.

QED.

By Lemma 4, all we have to do to solve the cocircular optimal FLIP problem, is to find the optimal partitioning FLIP.

Consider a cocircular polygon P and the circle $C(P)$ containing the vertices of P. Assume that $C(P)$ has radius 1 and that we measure the lenght of arcs of $C(P)$ in radians. The vertex set of P partitions the circle $C(P)$ into n arcs of sizes $\alpha_1, \ldots, \alpha_n$. The following two observations will prove useful:

Observation 1: Any FLIP F_1, F_2 of P illuminates all of $C(P)$ except two subarcs α_i and α_j of P. The sum of the sizes of F_1, F_2 is $\dfrac{2\pi - \alpha_i - \alpha_j}{2}$, see Figure 8.

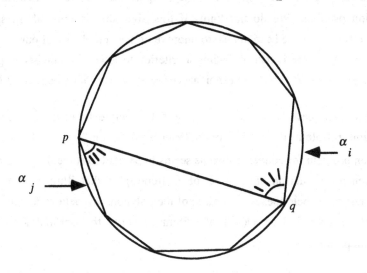

Figure 8

Observation 2: Given any two α_i and α_j of P, there is a FLIP of P that illuminates all of $C(P)$ except the arcs α_i and α_j. Notice here that if we want to avoid illuminating two consecutive arcs α_i and α_j of P, all we need to do is to illuminate P with a single floodlight placed at the vertex that separates α_i from α_j.

Theorem 2: Finding an optimal FLIP of a cocircular polygon can be done in linear time.

Proof: Choose the two largest arcs α_i and α_j of $C(P)$ and illuminate P as in Observation 2. Our result now follows.

$\hfill$ QED.

It is now easy to see that the results of Sections 2 and 3 can be used to solve the general Two Floodlight Illumination problem in $O(n^2)$ time. The details are left to the reader. Summarizing, we have:

Theorem 3: Finding an optimal FLIP for an arbitrary convex polygons can be done in $O(n^2)$ time.

4. Conclusions

In this paper we have given an $O(n^2)$ algorithm to solve the two-floodlight illumination problem. We do not know if this algorithm is optimal. In spite of numerous efforts we have been unable to improve on the complexity of our algorithm. The main problem here is that of finding a criterion to lower the number of pairs of vertices of a polygon P which are candidates to be the apexes of an optimal FLIP.

An open question is that of deciding if the complexity of the two-floodlight illumination problem is $O(n^2)$ or $O(n\log(n))$ or better. The k-floodlight illumination problem for convex polygons seems to be hard to solve. For instance, we cannot even prove that an optimal set of k floodlights that illuminate a convex polygon must have their apexes at vertices of the polygon. We believe this to be true. In general, can we find an $O(n^k)$ algorithm to solve the optimal k-floodlight illumination problem?

Another open problem is that of finding optimal floodlight illuminating sets for simple polygons.

References

[AGSS]   A. Aggarwal, L.J. Guibas, J. Saxon and P.W. Shor, "A linear time algorithm for computing the Voronoi diagram of a convex polygon", *Discrete and Computational Geometry* **4** (1989) 591-604 .

[BBCUZ]   P. Belleville, P. Bose, J. Czyzowicz, J. Urrutia and J. Zaks, "K-Guarding polygons on the plane", *Proc. 6th. Canadian Conference on Computational Geometry,* Saskatoon, Sask. Canada (1994) 381-386.

[BGLOSU]   P. Bose, L. Guibas, A. Lubiw, M. Overmars, D. Souvaine and J. Urrutia, "The floodlight illumination problem", to appear in *Int. J. on Computational Geometry.*

[CV]   V. Chvátal, "A combinatorial theorem in plane geometry", *J. Comb. Theory Ser. B,* **18** (1975) 39 - 41.

[CRCU1]   J. Czyzowicz, E. Rivera-Campo and J. Urrutia, "Illuminating rectangles and triangles on the plane", *Journal of Combinatorial Theory (B)* **57** (1993) 1-17.

[CRCU2]   J. Czyzowicz, E. Rivera-Campo and J. Urrutia, "Optimal floodlight illumination of stages", *Proc. 5th Canadian Conference on Computational Geometry,* Waterloo, Ont. Canada (1993) 393-398.

[ECO'RUX] V. Estivill-Castro, J. O'Rourke, J. Urrutia and D. Xu, "Illumination of polygons with vertex floodlights", Technical Report (TR#037) Department of Computer Science, Smith College, Northampton, MA 01063, Aug. 1994.

[ECU]   V. Estivill-Castro and J. Urrutia, "Optimal floodlight illumination of orthogonal art galleries", *Proc. 6th. Canadian Conference on Computational Geometry,* Saskatoon, Sask. Canada (1994) 81-86.

[FT]   L. Fejes Toth, "Illumination of convex discs", *Acta Math. Acad. Sci. Hung.* **29** (1977) 355-360.

[FI]   S. Fisk, "A short proof of Chvátal's watchman theorem", *J. Comb. Theory, Ser. B* **24** (1978) 374 .

[KKK]   J. Kahn, M. Klawe and D. Kleitman,"Traditional galleries require fewer watchmen", *SIAM J. Algebraic and Discrete Methods* **4** (1980) 194-206.

[O'R]   J. O'Rourke, *Art Gallery Theorems and Algorithms.* Oxford University Press, 1987.

[O'RX]   J. O"Rourke and D. Xu,"Illumination of polygons with 90° vertex lights", in *Snapshots in Comp. Geometry,* Univ. Saskatchewan, Aug. 1994 and Technical Report TR #034, Department of Computer Science, Smith College, July 1994.

[SHER]   T. Shermer, "Recent results in Art Galleries", in *Proceedings of the IEEE* **80** 1992) 1384-1399.

[SS]   W. Steiger and I. Streinu, "Positive and negative results on the floodlight problem", in *Proc. 6th. Canadian Conference on Computational Geometry,* Saskatoon, Sask. Canada, 87-92, 1994.

[UZ]   J. Urrutia and J. Zaks, "Illuminating convex sets on the plane", University of Ottawa Technical Report TR-89 (1989).

On the Complexity of Approximating and Illuminating Three-Dimensional Convex Polyhedra
(Preliminary Version)

GAUTAM DAS* MICHAEL T. GOODRICH[†]

Univ. of Memphis Johns Hopkins Univ.

Abstract

We show that several well-known computational geometry problems involving 3-dimensional convex polyhedra are NP-hard or NP-complete. One of the techniques we employ is a linear-time method for realizing a planar 3-connected triangulation as a convex polyhedron.

1 Introduction

Convex polyhedra are fundamental geometric structures (e.g., see [14]). Moreover, due to a beautiful theorem of Steinitz [14, 23], they provide a strong link between computational geometry and graph theory, for Steinitz shows that a graph forms the edge structure of a convex polyhedra if and only if it is planar and 3-connected.

Unfortunately, algorithmic problems dealing with 3-dimensional convex polyhedra seem to be much harder than their 2-dimensional counterparts. In addition, this difficulty goes beyond simple notions of running time; it also impacts our notions of efficiently-representable structures. For example, although the published proofs of Steinitz's theorem can easily be converted to algorithms running in $O(n^3)$ time in the real-RAM model, these algorithms produce polyhedra that may require an exponential number of bits to represent.

In this paper we formally establish that several natural problems on convex polyhedra are provably difficult, including several problems involving the approximation and illumination of convex polyhedra. Interestingly, a key ingredient in our proofs is a linear-time method for realizing any 3-connected planar triangulation as a convex polyhedron using a polynomial number of bits.

We describe this realization method in the section that follows. In the subsequent section we establish the NP-completeness of the problem of finding the minimum number of vertex lamps needed to illuminate a convex polyhedron, which is a problem studied by Grünbaum and O'Rourke and featured in O'Rourke's book on "art gallery" theorems [20], where they show that, for a convex polyhedron P with f faces in $\mathbb{R}^3$, $\lfloor (2f - 4)/2 \rfloor$ vertices are sometimes necessary and always sufficient to see the exterior of P. Finally, in Section 4, we show that finding an optimal decision tree in $\mathbb{R}^3$ is NP-complete, as is the problem of finding a minimum-facet convex polyhedron lying between two polyhedra in $\mathbb{R}^3$ is NP-complete, which fixes a "gap" in a proof by Das and Joseph [6, 7].

---

*This research supported in part by NSF Grant CCR-9306822. Math Sciences Dept., Univ. of Memphis, Memphis, TN 38152. E-mail: dasg@next1.msci.memst.edu.

[†]This research supported by the NSF under Grants IRI-9116843 and CCR-9300079. Department of Computer Science, Johns Hopkins University, Baltimore, MD 21218, USA. E-mail: goodrich@cs.jhu.edu

2 Realizing 3-Connected Triangulations in $\mathbb{R}^3$

In this section we show how to realize a 3-connected planar triangulation as a convex polyhedron in linear time. Our algorithm constructs a polyhedron that can be represented using a polynomial number of bits in the rational-RAM model.

Theorem 2.1 *Given a n-vertex 3-connected planar triangulation $G = (V, E)$, one can realize G as a convex polyhedron P with a bit complexity that is polynomial in n. The running time is $O(n)$ in the rational-RAM model.*

Before we prove this theorem we present the following graph-theoretic lemma, which has been proven in various forms (e.g., see [10, 17]).

Lemma 2.2 *Given a n-vertex planar graph $G = (V, E)$, one can compute in linear time an independent set with at least $n/18$ vertices such that each vertex has degree ≤ 8.*

The overall idea of our algorithm is as follows. We compute a large independent set of G, and "compress" each vertex in this set with one of its neighbors along a common incident edge. We show that one can always choose a neighbor so that this results in a smaller planar triangulation that is still 3-connected; hence, we can recursively construct an equivalent polyhedron P' for the compressed graph G'. To construct P, we then "expand" the previously compressed edges appropriately so that convexity is maintained. Although this approach seems fairly straightforward, implementing it in $O(n)$ time is not so easy.

Since we compress a constant fraction of the vertices in each level, there are $O(\log n)$ levels of recursion. Our algorithm ensures that at each level the number of bits required to represent each added vertex is within a constant multiple of the number of bits required to represent a vertex of the previous level. Thus, the total bit complexity of representing P is polynomial in n.

We now give more details of our algorithm. Let the exterior face of the input triangulation contain the vertices u, v and w. At every level of the recursion, along with other properties, we will also ensure that u, v and w are on the xy-plane ($u = (0, 0, 0)$, $v = (2, 0, 0)$ and $w = (1, 2, 0)$), and the remaining vertices are above this plane, but strictly within the vertical "tube" whose horizontal cross section is congruent to the triangle uvw.

Case 1 $(n = 4)$: Let the four vertices be u, v, w and t. In this case we construct a tetrahedron by positioning u at $(0, 0, 0)$, v at $(2, 0, 0)$, w at $(1, 2, 0)$, and t at $(1, 1, 1)$, which completes the construction.

Case 2 $(n > 4)$: Using the method of Lemma 2.2, we compute a large independent set I of G. Let $I_1 = I \setminus \{u, v, w\}$, so that I_1 contains only interior vertices. Then, we repeat the following for each vertex s in I_1. Let s be incident to the vertices $s_1, s_2, \ldots s_l$, where $l \leq 8$. We choose one of the vertices s_j and compress the edge (s, s_j), removing any parallel edges this produces. We cannot choose just any vertex, however, for compressing s with some s_j's may violate 3-connectivity of the resulting planar graph. Consider the face $f = s_1 s_2 \ldots s_l$ that would result if we were to remove the edges incident to s, and mark the edges $(s_1, s_2), (s_2, s_3), \ldots, (s_l, s_1)$ as *peripheral* edges. The vertex s_j is selected as follows. If there are no edges connecting two non-adjacent vertices of f, then any vertex of f may be selected, say s_1. If, on the other hand, there are indeed such "exterior" edges, then there has to be an edge (s_i, s_k) such that the closed region defined by (s_i, s_k) and the boundary of f does not further contain such exterior edges. Consider the relevant boundary of f between s_i and s_k. It has to contain at least one intermediate vertex, and we select this to be s_j.

Let the resultant graph after all the edge compressions are performed be G'. We recursively construct an equivalent polyhedron P' for this graph. We know that the vertices of P' other than u, v and w are strictly confined within a vertical tube with cross section congruent to uvw.

Recall that some edges of P' have been marked as peripheral. We compute for each peripheral edge e a plane $p(e)$ as follows. If $e \in \{(u, v), (v, w), (w, u)\}$, then $p(e)$ is the vertical plane tangential to P' at e, otherwise $p(e)$ is any plane tangential to P' at e. Let s' be some vertex of P' created by the compression of some s and s_j in G, and let f be the cycle of edges marked as peripheral by this compression. For each edge $e \in f$, consider the half-space defined by $p(e)$ which includes P'. The intersection of these halfspaces defines a "pyramid" over f. Next, consider the half-spaces not containing P corresponding to each face of P' within f. If we intersect these half-spaces with the above pyramid, the resulting region will be convex. We show in the full version that if we expand s' into s_j and s, where the point[1] s_j remains at s', and s is selected inside this convex region, then P (which is the convex hull of s and P') will be convex. We can find s so that its resulting bit complexity (using rational arithmetic) is at most a constant factor larger than the bit complexity needed to represent each vertex of f. Performing this edge expansion for each s' that resulted from an edge compression, then, completes the construction.

Implementing the compression algorithm

In this subsection we show how to implement a single recursive level in our edge-contraction algorithm in $O(n)$ time. Since the size of the graph decreases by a constant-factor with each recursive level, this will establish that the total running time of our drawing algorithm is $O(n)$.

The important step in our procedure is identifying, for a particular node s in our independent set I_1, an adjacent node s_j such that the edge (s, s_j) can be compressed without violating 3-connectivity. The crucial condition for this to be possible is that s and s_j cannot already be members of a separating triangle, for then merging them would create a separating pair (and the graph would no longer be 3-connected). As observed above, the set of adjacencies for s define a face f, whose edges we call the peripheral edges. Since the graph is triangulated, the crucial condition for s to to be mergeable with s_j is equivalent to the condition that s_j cannot be adjacent to another vertex of f through a non-peripheral edge (i.e., an edge external to f). We say that such an adjacency *disqualifies* the merge of s and s_j. It is not immediately clear, however, how we can efficiently test this condition for each candidate s_j around f during the compression step for s, since some of these s_j's may have a large number of adjacencies in the graph.

---

[1] We ask the readers indulgence into this abuse of notation so that s (resp., s_j) can denote a vertex in G and its corresponding point on P.

Our implementation is to break this computation into a batch component, which we perform in advance for all the s's in our independent set, and an on-line component, which we perform for each s in turn as we perform our edge compressions. Our batch computation is as follows:

1. We identify, for each s in I_1, and each vertex s_j adjacent to s, all the candidate adjacencies that would disqualify our being able to merge s and s_j. There are $d(s)(d(s)-2) = O(1)$ such adjacencies for each s in I_1, where $d(s)$ denotes the degree of s; hence, the total number of all such candidate adjacencies is $O(n)$. We label each such candidate adjacency between s_j and some s_i on f as (s_i, s_j, s) meaning "adjacency (s_i, s_j) would disqualify the merging of s_j and s."

2. We then radix sort into a list L all the labels computed in the previous step together with all the existing adjacencies in G, lexicographically. This takes $O(n)$ time.

3. For any match of a real adjacency (s_i, s_j) with a candidate disqualifying adjacency (s_i, s_j, s) we mark the edge (s_j, s) as "disqualified." We remove all the (s_i, s_j) and (s_i, s_j, s) labels from the sorted list L for each such match. This step also takes $O(n)$ time.

4. Finally, we group together in one list $L_{i,j}$ each sublist of the sorted list L that identify the same candidate disqualifying adjacency (s_i, s_j) (for several different s's in our independent set). We store a pointer to the list $L_{i,j}$ in the records of each s in I_1 that contributes an element to $L_{i,j}$. The total number of such fields is $O(1)$ for any such s and the total space needed for all the $L_{i,j}$'s is clearly $O(n)$.

The meaning for each list $L_{i,j}$ is that this is a disqualifying adjacency that currently does not exist in G, but may exist at some point during the compression phase. Thus, for the compression computation for a node s in I_1, we choose an edge (s_j, s) that is not marked "disqualified" and compress it. For each new adjacency (s_i, s_j) this creates, we consult the list $L_{i,j}$ (if it exists), and for each (s_i, s_j, s') label in $L_{i,j}$ (with $s' \neq s$) we mark the edge (s_j, s') as "disqualified." We then discard the list $L_{i,j}$.

We have already argued why there will always be some edge incident upon s that is not marked "disqualified;" hence, the above computation can always proceed to the next s in I_1. The total time needed is $O(n)$ for the preprocessing step, and then an additional $O(n)$ time during the compression step (for once an $L_{i,j}$ list is consulted it is then discarded). Therefore, we can complete a recursive step in our 3-d drawing algorithm in $O(n)$ time, as claimed.

Since we can perform each level in the recursion in $O(n)$ time, by Lemma 2.2, this results in a linear-time algorithm for drawing G as a convex polyhedron. Moreover, the fact that there are only $O(\log n)$ levels in this recursion implies that our method produces a polyhedron that can be represented using a polynomial number of bits (using rational arithmetic).

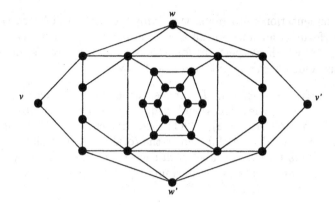

Figure 1: The cross-over gadget.

3   Polytope Illumination

In this section we prove that polyhedron illumination is NP-complete. We begin by showing that the well-known vertex cover problem remains NP-complete even for 3-connected planar graphs, and show how this can be used to further extend the NP-completeness of vertex covering to convex polyhedra in $\mathbb{R}^3$. This extends the previous results of Garey and Johnson [11] and Garey, Johnson, and Stockmeyer [13], which showed that the vertex cover problem remains NP-complete for planar graphs with degree at most three.

Vertex Cover for 3-connected planar graphs

Our reduction is actually a chain of reductions, starting from the (standard) vertex cover problem. So, let $G = (V, E)$ and k be the graph and integer parameter defining an instance of the vertex cover problem. Without loss of generality, we can assume that $|V| \geq 4$. We begin our chain of transformations by augmenting G by adding three new vertices v_1, v_2, and v_3 that we define to be adjacent to all the vertices in G. Clearly, the resulting graph G' is 3-connected.

Claim 3.1 *G has a vertex cover of size $k < n$ if and only if G' has a vertex cover of size $k + 3$.*

Proof: Omitted in this preliminary version. ■

Thus, the vertex cover problem remains NP-complete for 3-connected graphs. So, let us now use G and k to together denote an instance of vertex cover with G being 3-connected. We will reduce this version of vertex cover to the version of the problem where the graph is 3-connected and *planar*. Our reduction is an adaptation of the proof of Garey *et al.* [13], who give a reduction from general graphs to planar graphs that does not preserve 3-connectivity. We begin by drawing G in the plane so as to have $c = O(n^2)$ edge crossings (e.g., using a simple straight-line strategy). We replace each edge crossing by the "gadget" illustrated in Figure 1 as illustrated in Figure 2. Performing all these replacements results in a 3-connected planar graph G'.

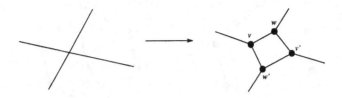

Figure 2: The way the cross-over gadget replaces an edge crossing.

Claim 3.2 *G has a vertex cover of size k if and only if G' has a vertex cover of size $16c + k$.*

Proof: A close inspection of the gadget we use to replace each edge crossing shows that the edges of the gadget can be covered with 16 nodes only if we include at most one member of $\{v, v'\}$ and at most one member of $\{w, w'\}$. Thus, if there is a vertex cover of size k in G, we can create a vertex cover of size $16c + k$ by including the 16 nodes in each crossover gadget so as to also cover each of the edges joining crossover gadgets (and original vertices of G). Suppose, conversely, that G' has a vertex cover of size $16c + k$. As we have already observed, each cross-over gadget can be covered with 16 nodes only if at most 16 nodes only if we include at most one member of $\{v, v'\}$ and at most one member of $\{w, w'\}$. That is, covering each gadget with 16 nodes establishes a "parity" along any chain of gadgets derived from a single edge in G. Thus, by a counting argument, which is similar to one given by Garey *et al.* [13], we can conclude that G must have a vertex cover of size k. ■

Therefore, the vertex cover problem remains NP-complete for 3-connected planar graphs. We can further restrict our graphs, however, and the problem still remains NP-complete.

Polytope Vertex Cover

Given an embedded 3-connected planar graph G, define the *stellation* of a face f in G as the insertion of a vertex in the interior of f that we then make adjacent to each vertex on f. Moreover, if f is a triangle, then we also allow any of edges of f to be subsequently removed, so long as we still preserve the 3-connectivity of G. (See Figure 3.) Define a *stellation* of the entire graph G to be the result of performing a collection of independent, non-interfering face stellations on a subset of the faces of G. Further define the *t-stellation* of G to be the result of performing t consecutive stellations on G.

An interesting property of stellations is that they have a natural analogue with respect to convex polyhedra. In particular, if a 3-connected planar graph G is represented as a convex polyhedron in $\mathbb{R}^3$, then the stellation of a face f of G can be accomplished geometrically by introducing a point p "above" f so that the convex full of p unioned with P results in the updated graph G'. Indeed, the proof of Steinitz's theorem (e.g., see [14]), showing that a graph can be drawn as a convex polyhedron in $\mathbb{R}^3$ if and only if it is 3-connected and planar, is essentially equivalent to showing that any 3-connected planar graph (or polyhedron) can be constructed from a planar embedding of K_4 (or tetrahedron) in a series of

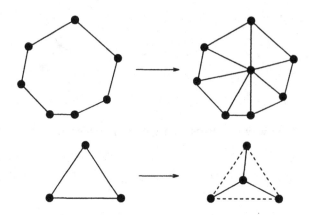

Figure 3: The stellation of a face.

$O(n^3)$ stellations or "inverse" stellations. We show that the vertex cover problem remains NP-complete for c-stellations of 3-connected 3-regular planar graphs, for any constant $c \geq 4$.

We have shown, in Section 2, that any 3-connected planar triangulation can be drawn as a convex polyhedron in $\mathbb{R}^3$ using a polynomial number of bits. By a simple duality argument, this immediately implies that any 3-connected 3-regular planar graph can also be drawn as a convex polyhedron in $\mathbb{R}^3$ using a polynomial number of bits. Since performing a stellation of a convex polyhedron in $\mathbb{R}^3$ will increase the bit complexity of its representation by at most a constant factor, this also implies that the c-stellations of a 3-connected 3-regular planar graph can be drawn as a convex polyhedron in $\mathbb{R}^3$ using a polynomial number of bits if c is a constant. Thus, by showing that vertex cover remains NP-complete for c-stellations of 3-connected 3-regular planar graphs we will establish the NP-completeness of the Polytope Vertex Cover problem, where we are given a convex polyhedron P and an integer k and asked if there is a subset V of the vertices on P such that each edge on P has at least one end in V.

Our reduction will be from the vertex cover problem for 3-connected planar graphs. So, let G be a 3-connected planar graph and let k be a given integer parameter. Our reduction is a modification of an argument of Garey and Johnson [11], who showed that vertex cover remains NP-complete for planar graphs with degree at most 3. For each vertex v in G, we replace v by a cycle C_v of size $d(v)$, where $d(v)$ denotes the degree of v, so that each vertex on C_v retains exactly one adjacency of v. Clearly, the graph that results from this transformation will be a 3-connected 3-regular graph. We stellate each face defined by the interior of a C_v by introducing a new vertex v' in its interior. We furthermore stellate each triangle T incident on v' so as to eliminate all the edges of T. (See Figure 4.) The resulting graph, G', is a c-stellation of a 3-connected 3-regular graph (the last step can be accomplished by first stellating the odd-numbered triangles around v' and then doing the even-numbered ones, with possibly one more to do after that if the number of triangles is odd).

Claim 3.3 $G = (V, E)$ *has a vertex cover of size* k *if and only if* G' *has a vertex cover of size* $k + 2|E|$.

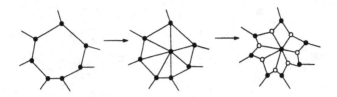

Figure 4: The stellations forming the subgraph of G' associated with a face in G.

Proof: Suppose G has a vertex cover of size k. For any v in G in this cover, we can put in a cover for G' all the vertices in the cycle C_v we created for v, together with the interior vertex v' (these vertices are shown in black in Figure 4). If v is not in the cover for G, then we can cover the subgraph of G' associated with v by using the vertices introduced in the stellation of each triangle incident on v' (these vertices are shown in white in Figure 4). The set of all such vertices will clearly form a cover of G'. We use $d(v)+1$ vertices for each vertex v in the cover for G and $d(v)$ vertices for each vertex v not in the cover, where $d(v)$ denotes the degree of v; hence, the total size of this cover is $k + \sum_{v \in G} d(v) = k + 2|E|$.

Conversely, suppose G' has a vertex cover of size $k + 2|E|$. The subgraph in G' determined by a vertex v in G can be covered with $d(v)$ vertices (using the nodes colored white in Figure 4), and $d(v)$ nodes are necessary. To cover an edge of G' outside of such a subgraph (i.e., an edge corresponding to an edge of G), however, requires that we use a vertex from some C_v (i.e., a black vertex). But if such a vertex is included in a cover for the subgraph of G' corresponding to a vertex v, then covering this subgraph now requires $d(v)+1$ vertices. But we can cover such a subgraph using $d(v)+1$ vertices using only the vertices of C_v and the new vertex v' (the black vertices). We can thus define a cover of G by including each vertex v whose corresponding subgraph in G has at least $d(v)+1$ vertices and this cover will have size at most k in G. ∎

As we mentioned above, given the result of Section 2 regarding drawing 3-connected 3-regular planar graphs as convex polyhedra, Claim 3.3 immediately applies to the Polytope Vertex Cover problem.

Theorem 3.4 *The Polytope Vertex Cover problem is NP-complete.*

Polytope Lamp Cover

We are now ready to prove our result regarding lamp placement on convex polyhedra. Specifically, in this problem we are given a convex polyhedron P in $\mathbb{R}^3$ and an integer k and asked if there are k vertices on P such that each point on the boundary of P can be connected to a vertex in this set by a line segment that does not intersect the interior of P. We show that deciding if a given k number of vertices suffice for P is NP-complete. Our proof is based upon a reduction from Polytope Vertex Cover.

So, suppose we are given a polyhedron Q and an integer k such that we would like to know if there is a k-node vertex cover on Q. Our reduction is to form a c-stellation of Q, where, for each face f on Q, we form a vertex F in its interior and form triangles with the nodes on f. We then perform two more stellations,

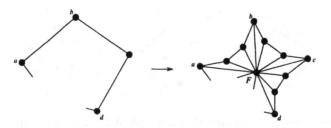

Figure 5: An example stellation used in forming P.

so as to form for each triangle $\triangle abF$ incident on F, three consecutive triangles $\triangle axF$, $\triangle xyF$, and ybF. Call this transformed polyhedron, P. (See Figure 5.)

Claim 3.5 *Q has a vertex cover of size k if and only if P has a lamp cover of size $k + \mathcal{F}$, where $\mathcal{F}$ is the number of faces on Q.*

Proof: Suppose Q has a vertex cover of size k. We can form a lamp cover for P by including each vertex in the cover for Q together with each vertex F created in the stellation of a face f of Q. This lamp cover will have size $k + \mathcal{F}$.

Conversely, suppose P has a lamp cover of size $k + \mathcal{F}$. Consider the subgraph in P associated with any face f from Q. If F is not included in a lamp cover, then illuminating this portion of P requires at least $\lceil 3e/2 \rceil$ vertices, where $e \geq 3$ is the number of edges on f. But, by including F in a lamp, we can illuminate this portion of P using just one vertex! The only other faces that are not illuminated are faces that correspond to edges of Q (that no stellation vertex F can see). Since we can assume without loss of generality that the lamp cover for P includes each stellation vertex F, we can further assume that each other vertex in the lamp cover is also a vertex in Q (for if this were not the case, we can substitute such a vertex (labeled x or y above) with a vertex that is also in Q and illuminate more faces of P). Thus, taking the vertices in the lamp cover for P that are also vertices in Q forms a vertex cover for Q of size k. ∎

This immediately implies the following:

Theorem 3.6 *The Polytope Lamp Cover problem is NP-complete.*

4   Approximating Convex Polyhedra

In this section we consider the problem of *polyhedral approximations*, where one wishes to construct a polyhedron Q from a given polyhedron P, such that Q is simpler than P and may be used to replace P. This is a very loose definition, and the exact requirements which Q should satisfy of course depends upon the particular problem. For example, there have been many results describing and analyzing various approximation schemes (e.g., see [2, 1, 6, 7, 8, 19]). We are in particular concerned with the *combinatorial* simplicity of the approximate object, e.g., it should not have too many faces.

Approximation by a Decision Tree

The first approximation problem we consider is that of defining an efficient decision tree that can be used as a discriminator for a given polyhedron (indeed, we define the problem for any point set in $\mathbb{R}^3$). It is well known, for example, that constructing a best decision tree in general settings [15, 16] or in arbitrary dimensions [3, 18] is NP-complete, but in the context of fixed-dimensional decision-tree approximations, however, each of these NP-completeness proofs fail. Still,

Theorem 4.1 *Given a set S of n points in $\mathbb{R}^3$, divided into two concept classes "red" and "blue," deciding if is there a linear decision tree T with at most k nodes that separates the red points from the blue points is NP-complete.*

Proof: First, let us observe that this problem is in NP. This is because each candidate split in a linear decision tree is determined by 3 points, hence, there are $\Theta(n^3)$ candidate splits. We can therefore guess k splits and a tree structure with one of these splits at each node, and we can then test that this decision tree separates all the red and blue points.

To prove the problem NP-hard we reduce POLYTOPE VERTEX-COVER to it. For the sake of simplicity, let us allow as input point sets where red points and blue points can "overlap". A complete classification of such a pair of points must therefore have a split that passes through this common location in space. Our reduction is based upon judiciously placing such pairs of points on the edges of Q, the Poincaré dual to P, i.e., Q is a convex polyhedron whose 1-skeleton is the graph-theoretic planar dual to the 1-skeleton of P. Thus, a *face cover* in Q corresponds immediately to a vertex cover in P. We place two red-blue pairs along each edge of Q so that the only way four such pairs can be co-planar is if they all lie on the same face of Q. Let S denote this set of red and blue points. Note that, since Q is a convex polyhedron, each face of Q contains at least six pairs of points in S.

We claim there is a k-node decision tree for S if and only if there is a k-face face-cover for Q. First, note that if there is a k-face face-cover for Q, then there must be k planes that collectively contain all the pairs in S; hence, there is a k-node decision tree for S. For the more difficult direction, suppose there is no k-face face-cover for Q; that is, any face cover requires more than k faces. This implies that any decision tree restricted to splits containing faces of P must have more than k nodes. Note, however, that each such split contains at least six pairs of points in S whereas any other type of split contains at most three pairs of points in S. Therefore, since each pair of points in S must be contained in some split, there must be more then k nodes in any decision tree that completely separates the pairs in S. ∎

Polyhedral Separability

Another well-known instance of polyhedral approximation we consider is *polyhedral separability*. In the simplest sense, given two polyhedral objects, we ask whether they are separate in space or whether they intersect. If they are indeed separate, we may want to construct a *separator* between them, such as a hyperplane, or a surface with minimum number of faces. Polyhedral separability has been the subject of extensive research, e.g., see [1, 4, 9, 19, 21].

84

The version we address is is that one is given two concentric polyhedra, and one wishes to find a separating polyhedra with minimum faces nested between the two. The nested polyhedral separability problem that we consider was first raised by Victor Klee [21], which arose during the study of *sequential stochastic automata* [22]. In two dimensions, this problem has been solved in polynomial time by Aggarwal et al [2]. Das and Joseph [6, 7] proved the interesting result that the problem is NP-hard for three dimensions, *even for convex polyhedra*. While the combinatorial and logical aspects of the proof are correct, a certain geometric part has a flaw. More precisely, a part of the reduction requires constructing a convex polyhedron from a 3-connected planar triangulation, and the version presented in [6] does not run in polynomial time. As we show below, Theorem 2.1 can be used to correct this flaw in the proof.

Since the results in [6, 7] appeared, there have been several efforts to design good approximation algorithms for the problem. In particular, Mitchell and Suri designed an efficient algorithm in [19] which achieves an approximation ratio of $O(\log n)$. This bound was matched by a simple randomized scheme of Clarkson [5], and extended to terrains by Agarwal and Suri [1]. More recently, Brönnimann and Goodrich [4] show how to achieve an approximation ratio of $O(1)$ for the convex polyhedral case.

Theorem 4.2 *The problem of fitting a polyhedron with minimum faces between two concentric convex polyhedra is NP-hard.*

Proof: The original NP-hardness proof in [6, 7] is a reduction from Planar-3SAT [12]. The first part of the reduction is graph-theoretic, where an instance of Planar-3SAT is used to construct a planar triangulation G where, (1) the exterior face may not be a triangle, (2) the interior faces are marked either *fixed* or *removable*. We modify this slightly by enclosing G in a triangle, and triangulating the region between G and the enclosing triangle such that the resulting graph G' is a 3-connected planar triangulation. Let the new faces be marked *fixed*.

The next step is geometric, where two polyhedra P' and Q are constructed such that Q is inside P'. Instead of following the procedure in [6], we use the polynomial-time procedure in Theorem 2.1 to construct Q from G'. Thus Q can be expressed in a polynomial number of bits in the rational-RAM model.

We can retain the old procedure to construct P'. Recall that a *pyramid* of a face f of Q is defined to the region above f and below the intersection of the three faces adjacent to f. We construct an intermediate P, defined to be the (non-convex) polyhedral region of the union of Q with all the pyramids of the removable faces of Q. This takes polynomial time, since each pyramid only requires the computation of intersections of planes. Next, P' is constructed to be the convex hull of P, which can be performed in polynomial time. ∎

Acknowledgements

We would like to thank Marek Chrobak for his encouragement and his diligence in pointing out places in previous versions of this paper that needed more details. The second author would also like to thank the U.S. Army Research Office for their support. The views, opinions, and/or findings contained in this document are those of the authors and should not be construed as an official Department of the Army position, policy, or decision, unless so designated by other documentation.

References

[1] P. K. Agarwal and S. Suri. Surface approximation and geometric partitions. In *Proc. Fifth Annual ACM-SIAM Symposium on Discrete Algorithms*, 1994.

[2] A. Aggarwal, H. Booth, J. O'Rourke, S. Suri, and C. K. Yap. Finding minimal convex nested polygons. *Inform. Comput.*, 83(1):98–110, October 1989.

[3] A. Blum and R. L. Rivest. Training a 3-node neural net is NP-Complete. *Neural Networks*, 5:117–127, 1992.

[4] H. Brönnimann and M. T. Goodrich. Almost optimal set covers in finite VC-dimension. In *Proc. 10th Annu. ACM Sympos. Comput. Geom.*, pages 293–302, 1994.

[5] K. L. Clarkson. Algorithms for polytope covering and approximation. In *Proc. 3rd Workshop Algorithms Data Struct.*, volume 709 of *Lecture Notes in Computer Science*, pages 246–252, 1993.

[6] G. Das. *Approximation schemes in computational geometry*. Ph.D. thesis, University of Wisconsin, 1990.

[7] G. Das and D. Joseph. The complexity of minimum convex nested polyhedra. In *Proc. 2nd Canad. Conf. Comput. Geom.*, pages 296–301, 1990.

[8] G. Das and D. Joseph. Minimum vertex hulls for polyhedral domains. *Theoret. Comput. Sci.*, 103:107–135, 1992.

[9] D. P. Dobkin and D. G. Kirkpatrick. Fast detection of polyhedral intersection. *Theoret. Comput. Sci.*, 27:241–253, 1983.

[10] H. Edelsbrunner. *Algorithms in Combinatorial Geometry*, volume 10 of *EATCS Monographs on Theoretical Computer Science*. Springer-Verlag, Heidelberg, West Germany, 1987.

[11] M. R. Garey and D. S. Johnson. The rectilinear Steiner tree problem is NP-complete. *SIAM J. Appl. Math.*, 32:826–834, 1977.

[12] M. R. Garey and D. S. Johnson. *Computers and Intractability: A Guide to the Theory of NP-Completeness*. W. H. Freeman, New York, NY, 1979.

[13] M. R. Garey, D. S. Johnson, and L. Stockmeyer. Some simplified NP-complete graph problems. *Theoretical Computer Science*, 1:237–267, 1976.

[14] B. Grünbaum. *Convex Polytopes*. Wiley, New York, NY, 1967.

[15] L. Hyafil and R. L. Rivest. Constructing optimal binary decision trees is NP-complete. *Information Processing Letters*, 5:15–17, 1976.

[16] S. Judd. On the complexity of loading shallow neural networks. *J. of Complexity*, 4:177–192, 1988.

[17] D. G. Kirkpatrick. Optimal search in planar subdivisions. *SIAM J. Comput.*, 12:28–35, 1983.

[18] N. Megiddo. On the complexity of polyhedral separability. *Discrete Comput. Geom.*, 3:325–337, 1988.

[19] J. S. B. Mitchell and S. Suri. Separation and approximation of polyhedral surfaces. In *Proc. 3rd ACM-SIAM Sympos. Discrete Algorithms*, pages 296–306, 1992.

[20] J. O'Rourke. *Art Gallery Theorems and Algorithms*. Oxford University Press, New York, NY, 1987.

[21] J. O'Rourke. Computational geometry column 4. *SIGACT News*, 19(2):22–24, 1988. Also in Computer Graphics 22(1988), 111–112.

[22] C. B. Silio, Jr. An efficient simplex coverability algorithm in E^2 with applications to stochastic sequential machines. *IEEE Trans. Comput.*, C-28:109–120, 1979.

[23] E. Steinitz and H. Rademacher. *Vorlesungen über die Theorie der Polyeder*. Julius Springer, Berlin, Germany, 1934.

Scheduling Jobs That Arrive Over Time

(Extended Abstract)

Cynthia Phillips*[1], Clifford Stein**[2] and Joel Wein ***[3]

[1] Sandia National Labs, Albuquerque, NM, USA
[2] Department of Computer Science, Dartmouth College, Hanover, NH, USA
[3] Department of Computer Science, Polytechnic University, Brooklyn, NY, USA

Abstract. A natural problem in scheduling theory is to provide good average quality of service to a stream of jobs that arrive over time. In this paper we consider the problem of scheduling n jobs that are released over time in order to minimize the average completion time of the set of jobs. In contrast to the problem of minimizing average completion time when all jobs are available at time 0, all the problems that we consider are $\mathcal{NP}$-hard, and essentially nothing was known about constructing good approximations in polynomial time.

We give the first constant-factor approximation algorithms for several variants of the single and parallel machine model. Many of the algorithms are based on interesting algorithmic and structural relationships between preemptive and nonpreemptive schedules and linear programming relaxations of both. Many of the algorithms generalize to the minimization of average *weighted* completion time as well.

1 Introduction

Two characteristics of many real-world scheduling problems are (1) tasks arrive over time and (2) the goal is to optimize some function of average performance or satisfaction. In this paper we study several scheduling models that include both of these characteristics; in particular we study minimizing the average (weighted) completion time of a set of jobs with release dates. In most of these models polynomial-time algorithms were known to minimize average completion time when all jobs are available at time 0; the introduction of release dates makes these problems $\mathcal{NP}$-hard and little was known about approximation algorithms.

We give the first constant-factor approximation algorithms for the minimization of average completion time in these models. Our performance bounds come

---

* `caphill@cs.sandia.gov`. This work was performed under U.S. Department of Energy contract number DE-AC04-76AL85000.

** `cliff@cs.dartmouth.edu`. Research partly supported by NSF Award CCR-9308701, a Walter Burke Research Initiation Award and a Dartmouth College Research Initiation Award.

*** `wein@mem.poly.edu`. Research partially supported by NSF Research Initiation Award CCR-9211494 and a grant from the New York State Science and Technology Foundation, through its Center for Advanced Technology in Telecommunications.

from the combination of two different types of results. First, we prove structural theorems about the relative quality of preemptive versus nonpreemptive schedules, and give algorithms to convert from the former to the latter with only a small degradation in schedule quality. Second, we give the first constant-approximation algorithms for preemptively scheduling parallel machines with release dates. When the machines are identical, we give a combinatorial algorithm which yields a two approximation. For unrelated machines, we give a new integer programming formulation. We then solve the linear programming relaxation and give methods to round the fractional solution to valid preemptive schedules. It is possible that these methods will be of use in other settings.

Models: We are given n jobs $J_1, \ldots, J_n$ where job J_j has processing time p_j, and release date r_j, before which it can not be processed on any machine. We are also given m machines $M_1, \ldots, M_m$. We focus both on the one machine ($m = 1$) environment and two fundamental variants of parallel machine scheduling. In the *identical parallel machine* environment, job J_j runs in time p_j on every machine [8]. In the *unrelated parallel machine scheduling* environment, we are given speeds s_{ij} which characterize how fast job J_j runs on machine M_i, and p_{ij}, the processing time of job J_j on machine M_i, is defined to be $p_{ij} = p_j/s_{ij}$ and thus depends on both the machine and the job [8]. Throughout this paper, unless specified otherwise, all jobs have release dates.

We give algorithms for both preemptive and nonpreemptive scheduling. In *nonpreemptive* scheduling, once a job begins running on a machine, it must run uninterruptedly to completion, while in *preemptive* scheduling, a job that is running can be preempted and continued later on any machine. At any time a job may run on at most one machine.

Let C_j^S denote the completion time of job J_j in schedule S. We will often drop the superscript when it is clear to which schedule we refer. Our basic optimization criterion is the *average completion time* of a set of jobs, $\frac{1}{n}\sum_j C_j$. At times we will associate with J_j a weight w_j and seek to minimize the average *weighted* completion time, $\frac{1}{n}\sum_j w_j C_j$. These optimality criteria are fundamental in scheduling theory and accordingly have received much attention, e.g. [2, 3, 5, 6, 7, 9, 10, 11, 13].

We distinguish between *off-line* and *on-line* algorithms. In an off-line algorithm, all the input data associated with jobs (r_j and p_j) is known in advance. In an *on-line* algorithm, nothing is known about a job J_j until time r_j, (at which point p_j is specified as well). The scheduling algorithm must decide what job (if any) to be scheduling at time t *with no knowledge of what jobs will arrive in the future*. In this paper, unless explicitly stated otherwise, all algorithms are off-line.

A ρ-*approximation algorithm* produces, in polynomial time, a schedule whose value is guaranteed to be at most ρ times the minimum possible value.

New Results: We first focus on *nonpreemptively* scheduling jobs on one machine to minimize average completion time. This problem is $\mathcal{NP}$-hard [9]. We give a simple 2-approximation algorithm which transforms the optimum preemptive schedule for the problem, which can be found in polynomial time [1].

The best previous approximation algorithm for this problem was an $O(\log^2 n)$-approximation algorithm [12]. Our proof demonstrates that for any set of jobs with release dates, the minimum average completion time of a preemptive one-machine schedule for these jobs is at least 1/2 the corresponding minimum average completion time of a nonpreemptive one-machine schedule. Our algorithm can be modified slightly to be on-line. We also show that any on-line scheduling algorithm for the problem must be at least a $\frac{3}{2}$-approximation algorithm.

Turning to parallel identical machines, we give a technique that converts preemptive schedules to nonpreemptive schedules while at most tripling the completion time of any job. This technique applies even when the preemptive schedule is fractional (fractional parts of different jobs are assigned simultaneously to one machine) which proves useful in rounding linear program solutions to obtain valid schedules. This technique, however, does not by itself yield nonpreemptive approximation algorithms since the corresponding preemptive problems are $\mathcal{NP}$-hard. Thus we consider preemptive scheduling of parallel machines.

For identical machines, when all release dates $r_j = 0$, McNaughton [10] showed that no preemptions are needed to minimize average completion time; therefore the polynomial-time algorithm for the nonpreemptive version of this problem [2, 5] solves it directly. When release dates are introduced, however, even the two-machine problem becomes $\mathcal{NP}$-hard [3]. When weights are added even the one-machine problem becomes $\mathcal{NP}$-hard [7]. To the best of our knowledge, nothing was known about approximation algorithms for any version of these problems.

We give a combinatorial 2-approximation algorithm for the preemptive scheduling of identical machines and a 3-approximation algorithm for the nonpreemptive problem. These techniques, however, do not apply to weighted completion times or to unrelated machines. To solve these problems, we introduce an integer program that is closely related to preemptive schedules that minimize average weighted completion time on unrelated machines. We show how to round the corresponding linear programming relaxation to a feasible, provably good, preemptive schedule. This rounding idea may be useful in other contexts. This formulation gives different approximation guarantees for different problems; Fig. 1 summarizes our results.

Environment	Nonprmpt. $\sum C_j$	Nonprmpt. $\sum w_j C_j$	Prmpt. $\sum C_j$	Prmpt. $\sum w_j C_j$
One machine	2	$16 + \epsilon$	1[1]	$16 + \epsilon$
Identical	3	$24 + \epsilon$	2	$16 + \epsilon$
unrelated	$O(\log^2 n)$[12]	$O(\log^2 n)$[12]	$24 + \epsilon$	$32 + \epsilon$

Fig. 1. Summary of results. Unreferenced results are new results found in this paper, and $\epsilon = o(1)$.

One consequence of this last result is the first constant-approximation algorithm for preemptively scheduling unrelated machines so as to minimize average completion time when all jobs are available at time 0. It is not known if this problem is $\mathcal{NP}$-hard; in [8] it states, "Very little is known about this problem ... it remains one of the more vexing questions in the area of preemptive scheduling."

Previous Work: The only work we know of that studies average completion time in these models is [12] which gives $O(\log^2 n)$-approximation algorithms for the nonpreemptive versions of the problems, as a special case of a very general theorem. There is some similarity of spirit between the algorithms there and those we give in Sec. 5 in that both solve a generalized matching problem. The generalization of matching, the rounding techniques, and the quality of approximation achieved, however, are quite different.

2   One Machine

In this section we consider the $\mathcal{NP}$-hard problem of nonpreemptively scheduling n jobs with release dates on one machine to minimize the average completion time. We first give an 2-approximation algorithm, and then discuss the consequences for the relationship between preemptive and nonpreemptive schedules. We then show how to make the algorithm on-line, and prove a lower bound on the performance of *any* on-line scheduling algorithm for this problem.

Theorem 1. *There is a polynomial-time 2-approximation algorithm for scheduling jobs with release dates on one machine so as to minimize the average completion time of the jobs.*

Proof. It is well-known that the preemptive version of this problem is solvable in polynomial time by the shortest processing time (SPT) rule: always be processing the job with the shortest remaining processing time [1]. Our algorithm for the nonpreemptive case transforms the preemptive schedule as follows.
Algorithm ONE-MACHINE:

1. Compute the optimum preemptive schedule.
2. Schedule the jobs nonpreemptively in the order of their completion time in the preemptive schedule, subject to the constraint that no job starts before its release date.

The second step of the algorithm can be visualized as follows. Let C_j^p be the completion time of J_j in the preemptive schedule. Consider the last scheduled piece of J_j, which is scheduled from time $C_j^p - k$ to C_j^p in the preemptive schedule. Insert $p_j - k$ extra units of time in the schedule at time C_j^p, and schedule J_j nonpreemptively in the resulting available block of length p_j. We remove from the schedule all pieces of J_j that were processed before $C_j^p - k$. We then push all jobs forward in time as much as possible without changing the scheduled order of the jobs or violating a release date constraint. The result is exactly the schedule computed by Algorithm ONE-MACHINE.

C_j^N, the completion time in the nonpreemptive schedule, is at most $C_j^p + \sum_{\{k:C_k^p \leq C_j^p\}} p_k$, where the second term follows from the fact that job J_j can only be moved back by processing times associated with jobs that finish earlier in the preemptive schedule. However, since all this processing did occur before time C_j^p this sum is at most C_j^p and hence $C_j^N \leq 2C_j^p$. □

Theorem 2. *Given n jobs with release dates on one machine, let C_p be the minimum possible average completion time of those jobs when preemption is allowed, and let C_N be the minimum average completion time with no preemption allowed. Then $C_N \leq 2C_p$. Furthermore, there exist instances for which $C_N/C_p = \frac{4}{3} - \epsilon$, for any $\epsilon > 0$.*

Proof. (sketch) The lower bound is realized by a two-job instance: J_0 with $p_0 = x$ and $r_0 = 0$, and J_1 with $p_1 = 1$ and $r_1 = \frac{x}{2}$. □

This theorem generalizes to average *weighted* completion time.

Corollary 3. *Given a preemptive one-machine schedule of average weighted completion time W, there exists a linear-time algorithm to find a nonpreemptive schedule for the same instance of average weighted completion time $2W$.*

There is an instance showing that our analysis of the performance guarantee of algorithm ONE-MACHINE is tight.

On-Line Scheduling Algorithm ONE-MACHINE can be easily modified to be on-line without affecting its performance. We just observe that all decisions made in the algorithm only depend on jobs that arrived previously and obtain the following corollary:

Corollary 4. *There is an on-line nonpreemptive 2-approximation algorithm for scheduling jobs with release dates on one machine to minimize average completion time.*

We can also show that no on-line nonpreemptive ρ-approximation algorithm exists for scheduling jobs with release dates on one machine so as to minimize the average completion time of the jobs with $\rho < \frac{3}{2}$. We omit the details in this extended abstract.

3 A Conversion Algorithm for Identical Parallel Machines

We now consider scheduling jobs with release dates on parallel machines, so as to optimize average completion time. The nonpreemptive versions of these problems are $\mathcal{NP}$-hard due to the $\mathcal{NP}$-hardness of the one-machine problem. When preemption is allowed the one machine problem is solvable in polynomial-time but the scheduling of even two identical machines is $\mathcal{NP}$-hard [3].

In this section we give a technique to convert from preemptive identical parallel machine schedules to nonpreemptive schedules. In the next two sections we give a combinatorial algorithm to preemptively schedule identical machines, and then a linear-programming formulation that yields a constant-approximation algorithm for average *weighted* completion time. Combining with the techniques of this section, we obtain the first constant approximation algorithms for the corresponding nonpreemptive problems.

Theorem 5. *Given a preemptive schedule S for a set of n jobs with release dates on parallel identical machines, construct a nonpreemptive schedule N for the same jobs by scheduling them nonpreemptively in order of their completion times in the nonpreemptive schedule, respecting any release date constraints. Then $C_j^N \leq 3C_j^S$.*

Proof. Consider J_j (the jth job to finish in S), which in S was released at r_j and completed at C_j^S. J_j is not started in N until $J_1, J_2, \ldots, J_{j-1}$ are started.

Let r_k be the latest release date of any job in $J_1, \ldots, J_j$, for $k \leq j$. We know that $r_k + p_k \leq C_j^N$, since $C_k^S \leq C_j^S$. By time r_k, jobs $J_1, \ldots, J_{j-1}$ have all been released. Thus, even if no processing happens before time r_k, at least one machine will have no more processing to do on any one of $J_1, \ldots, J_{j-1}$ by time $r_k + (\sum_{i=1}^{j-1} p_i)/m$, and so J_j starts in the nonpreemptive schedule by time $r_k + (\sum_{i=1}^{j-1} p_i)/m \leq r_k + C_j$. This last inequality holds because $J_1, \ldots, J_j$ all completed by time C_j^S in S. Therefore, J_j completes by time $r_k + C_j + p_j \leq 3C_j$. $\square$

Corollary 6. *Given n jobs with release dates, let C_p be the minimum possible average weighted completion time of those jobs scheduled preemptively on m identical machines and let C_N be the minimum average weighted completion time of a nonpreemptive schedule. Then $C_N \leq 3C_p$.*

Theorem 5 is essentially tight, since we have an example in which one job finishes close to three times later in the nonpreemptive schedule. Bounds for the corollary, however, can probably be improved by a cumulative argument.

Fractional Schedules Define a *fractional* preemptive schedule as one in which a job J_j can be scheduled simultaneously with several other jobs on one machine, where each job receives some fraction of the machine's resources and the sum of all the fractions assigned to a machine at any time is at most one. In other words, let $f_j^i(t)$ be the fractional amount of machine M_i assigned to J_j at time t, with time taken as continuous, and let t_f be the completion time of a schedule. A fractional schedule satisfies $\sum_j f_j^i(t) \leq 1$ for all machines i and times t; $\sum_i \int_{t=0}^{t_f} s_{ij} f_j^i(t) = p_j$ for all jobs j, and for any pair of t, j only one of the $f_j^i(t)$ is non-zero. The following corollary to Theorems 1 and 5 will be useful in rounding fractional linear program solutions to valid schedules.

Corollary 7. *Given a fractional preemptive schedule for a [one machine/parallel identical machine] problem of average weighted completion time W, there exists a nonpreemptive schedule for the problem of average weighted completion time [2W/3W].*

4 Scheduling Identical Machines

In this section we give a 2-approximation algorithm for minimizing the average completion time of a set of jobs with release dates run with preemption on a set of m identical parallel machines. We also give a 3-approximation algorithm for the nonpreemptive version. For one machine, the shortest-processing-time (SPT) algorithm is optimal. The multiple-machine generalization (always run the m jobs with the shortest remaining amount of work) does not yield the optimal preemptive schedule, even for 2 machines.

We show that a variation on SPT is a 2-approximation for this problem. Let $f_{\mathrm{OPT}}(t)$ denote the number of jobs finished in some fixed optimal schedule OPT by time t. We describe a BIN algorithm that computes a *pseudoschedule*, an assignment of sets of jobs to a block of time without explicit scheduling of times and machines for individual jobs. Let $f_{\mathrm{BIN}}(t)$ be the number of jobs finished by the pseudoschedule at time t. We show that $f_{\mathrm{BIN}}(t) \geq f_{\mathrm{OPT}}(t)$ for $1 \leq t \leq T$, where T is the length of the optimal schedule. Thus if the xth job finishes at time t in the BIN algorithm, t is a lower bound on the finish time of the xth job in the optimal schedule. We then convert this pseudoschedule BIN into an actual schedule RSPT (*revised shortest processing time*) such that $f_{\mathrm{RSPT}}(2t) \geq f_{\mathrm{BIN}}(t)$, for $1 \leq t \leq T$. That is, if the xth job finishes at time t in the BIN algorithm, then the xth job to finish in the RSPT schedule (not necessarily the same job) will finish by time $2t$. Thus we conclude that the average completion time of the RSPT schedule is at most 2 times the average completion time of the optimal schedule for the preemptive identical parallel machine problem.

We now describe how to construct the pseudoschedule BIN that yields an upper bound on the number of jobs that can be completed by time t in *any* schedule for the preemptive identical parallel machine problem. Let $r_1, r_2, \ldots, r_n$ be the release dates of the input jobs in order, and let $r_{n+1} = \infty$. We can assume that $r_1 = 0$. We construct n "bins" B_j of size $I_j = r_{j+1} - r_j$ for $j = 1, \ldots, n-1$ and the final bin B_n of size $I_n = \infty$. We consider the following greedy procedure. Sort all the jobs released at time 0 by processing time. Place the first mI_1 units of work from this list into bin B_1 with the restriction that no job can have more than I_1 units of work in the bin (but making no attempt to pack things onto m processors). Decrease all processing times of jobs in B_1 by the amount of processing they contribute to B_1. If this sets a processing time to zero, we say the job finishes in B_1. Now we repeat the process for B_2, a bin of size $r_3 - r_2$, considering all the jobs released at or before time r_2 that still have positive processing times, and continue through all bins.

We now define $F_{\mathrm{BIN}}(t)$, the set of jobs finished by the BIN pseudoschedule for any time $t \geq 0$. Suppose $r_i \leq t < r_{i+1}$. Let $F_{\mathrm{BIN}}(t)$ be the jobs finished in the first $i-1$ bins, plus the jobs that would be finished in a modified ith bin B_i' of size $I_i' = t - r_i$ which can accept only I_i' units from each job and a total of mI_i' work. That is, we consider what the procedure BIN would pack if forced to stop at time t. We have $f_{\mathrm{BIN}}(t) = |F_{\mathrm{BIN}}(t)|$ and define C_j^{BIN} to be the first t such that $J_j \in F_{\mathrm{BIN}}(t)$.

Lemma 8. $f_{\mathrm{BIN}}(t) \geq f_{\mathrm{OPT}}(t)$.

Our revised shortest-processing-time (RSPT) algorithm schedules the work assigned to bin B_j from time $2r_j$ to time $2r_{j+1}$. The RSPT algorithm takes all jobs placed in bin B_j by the BIN pseudoschedule, sorts the pieces by processing time and then list schedules the job pieces on m processors. Since we are list processing the jobs (or job pieces) within each bin, these jobs will clearly all finish by time $2r_{j+1}$. However, we can claim something slightly stronger.

Lemma 9. $f_{\text{RSPT}}(2t) \geq f_{\text{BIN}}(t)$.

Proof. We show that the RSPT algorithm finishes the set of jobs $F_{\text{BIN}}(t)$ by time $2t$. Suppose $r_i \leq t < r_{i+1}$. Consider the work (pieces of jobs) placed in bin B_j for $j \leq i$. RSPT schedules these job pieces starting at time $2r_j$. These jobs are all available at time $2r_j$ so there are no preemptions. Since at most mI_j units of work are in bin B_j, by time $2r_j + I_j$ either RSPT has finished the work or some processor has fallen idle, which can happen only if all jobs from bin B_j have started. These jobs finish (to the extent BIN finished them) by time $2r_{j+1}$, since no job had more than I_j units of processing assigned to bin B_j. Thus by time $2r_i$, RSPT has finished all the work that BIN finishes by time r_i. We now argue that over the next $2(t - r_i)$ units, RSPT finishes all the work that would be packed by BIN into a modified bin B_i' of size $t - r_i$. RSPT list schedules jobs from the original bin B_i from time $2r_i$ to $2r_{i+1}$. At time $2r_i + I_i'$ RSPT has completed the first mI_i' units of work from bin B_i, but no more than I_i' per job, unless some processor has fallen idle. In this case, all jobs in B_i (and hence B_i') have started. These jobs continue (or finish) in the next I_i' time units, finishing all work assigned to B_i'. □

Theorem 10. *There is an $O(n \lg n)$-time on-line 2-approximation algorithm for preemptively scheduling n jobs with release dates on parallel identical machines.*

We can apply the technique of Theorem 5 to the pseudoschedule to obtain a 3-approximation algorithm for the nonpreemptive problem.

Theorem 11. *There is an $O(n \lg n)$-time on-line 3-approximation algorithm for nonpreemptively scheduling n jobs with release dates on parallel identical machines.*

Proof. (sketch) We have $\frac{1}{n} \sum_j C_j^{\text{BIN}}$ as a lower bound on the average completion time of any nonpreemptive schedule for the jobs. Our algorithm list schedules jobs nonpreemptively in the order of their completion times in BIN. The proof of Theorem 5 is still valid because BIN respects release dates ($r_k \leq C_j^{\text{BIN}}$), BIN allows only mt units of processing in time t, ($\sum_{i=1}^{j-1} p_i \leq mC_j^{\text{BIN}}$ for the jth job to finish), and BIN allows only q units of a job in a bin of size q ($p_j \leq C_j^{\text{BIN}}$). □

5 Preemptive Schedules and LP Relaxations

In this section we introduce an integer program closely related to the preemptive versions of our scheduling problem. We utilize this integer program in two ways.

First, the solutions of its linear-programming relaxation can be immediately converted, using the techniques of Sec. 3, to nonpreemptive schedules for identical machines. Second, we give a method of rounding the fractional solutions generated by the linear program to valid preemptive schedules, and obtain the first constant-factor approximation algorithms for minimizing average weighted completion time on unrelated parallel machines. Unless otherwise stated, all results in this section apply to this most general case.

Our approach utilizes a generalization of bipartite matching, which we sketch here for identical parallel machines. We divide a job J_j of size p_j into p_j *units*. One side of the partition has a node for each unit of each job, and the other side of the partition has a node (m_i, t) for each unit of time t on each machine m_i, where we include every possible unit of time during which a job might need to be processed in an optimal schedule. We place an edge between the kth unit of J_j and (m_i, t) if and only if $r_j \leq t - (k-1)$, i.e. scheduling that unit at that time is feasible with respect to the release date. All edges cost 0 except those that represent the scheduling of the last unit of a job; these cost $w_j t$, the weighted completion time of J_j if its last unit is scheduled using this edge. We seek the minimum-weight matching of all job units *subject to the constraint* that for a job of size x, $x - 1$ units of it have been completed before the last unit is processed.

The resulting integer program is quite large; in fact, unless the job sizes are polynomial in n and m this formulation will not be polynomial in the input size. However, with Lemma 17 we will show how to scale the input data to be of size polynomial in n and m, and how to interpret the scaled solution as a solution for the original instance with little degradation in the quality of approximation.

This formulation models schedules in which preemptions are only allowed between units, and does not capture preemption within a unit. Its solution, however, gives a lower bound on *nonpreemptive* schedules. We will also show that its solutions are at most a constant factor worse than those of the optimal preemptive schedule, therefore yielding high-quality preemptive approximations. Although all of our algorithms are polynomial-time algorithms, the polynomials involved can be quite large. Therefore, for the rest of this section we do not discuss running times.

Polynomial Size Jobs Throughout this section we assume that no preemption is allowed within single units of a job, $m \leq n$, and $p_j \leq n^4$. We later show how to remove these assumptions. Note that although preempting an individual unit is not allowed, in the unrelated machine model, due to the speeds of the machines, units may take fractional amounts of time to complete.

We introduce the following $\{0, 1\}$-integer program $\mathcal{IP}$. The set of times a job can run is $T = \{t | \exists j \text{ s.t. } r_j \leq t \leq t + np_{\max}\}$. By the assumptions of this section, T is of polynomial size. Setting variable $x_{ijkt} = 1, 1 \leq i \leq m, 1 \leq j \leq n, 1 \leq k \leq p_j, t \in T$ represents scheduling unit k of job J_j on machine m_i at time t. Note that the range of k depends on j. Recall that s_{ij} is the speed of job J_j on machine M_i. For all k, j such that k is the last unit of J_j, the cost associated with x_{ijkt} is $w_j t$; otherwise the cost is 0. The goal is to minimize the total cost subject to the following constraints:

$$x_{ijkt} = 0 \qquad \text{if } t \leq r_j + (k-1) \qquad (1)$$

$$\sum_{i,t} x_{ijkt} = 1 \qquad j = 1, \ldots, n; \; k = 1, \ldots, p_j \qquad (2)$$

$$\sum_{i,k} x_{ijkt}/s_{ij} \leq 1 \qquad j = 1, \ldots, n; \; t \in T \qquad (3)$$

$$\sum_{j,k} x_{ijkt}/s_{ij} \leq 1 \qquad i = 1, \ldots, m; \; t \in T. \qquad (4)$$

$$x_{ijkt} \in \{0, 1\} \qquad (5)$$

In addition, for all k, j such that k is the last unit of J_j, and for all t,

$$\sum_{i,t' < t, \ell < k} x_{ij\ell t'} \geq (k-1)x_{ijkt} \qquad (6)$$

We now characterize the relationship between $\mathcal{IP}$ and optimal solutions to variants of our scheduling problems.

Lemma 12. *Given an instance of a single machine or parallel identical machines scheduling problem, and assuming preemption of a single unit is not allowed, there is a schedule of total weighted completion time Z if and only if there is a feasible solution to $\mathcal{IP}$ of cost Z.*

For unrelated machines the relationship between $\mathcal{IP}$ and optimal preemptive schedules is more complex. A unit may run for a fractional amount of time which causes two difficulties. First a job could end at a fractional time, whereas our formulation can only capture finishes at integral times. Second, a job unit can run across two units of time in the $\mathcal{IP}$ formulation.

We can remedy these problems. First, if J_j is scheduled to complete at time t in $\mathcal{IP}$, its last piece can be scheduled into the $\lceil t \rceil$ time unit and "declared" finished at time $\lceil t \rceil$, contributing at most $t + 1$ to the objective function. Secondly, $\mathcal{IP}$ can capture a schedule with "overlap" by associating the entire overlapping piece with the time unit in which it ends. This means relaxing (4) to ≤ 2 instead of 1; call this modified program $\mathcal{IP}^2$. A solution with at most 2 units of work/machine in any time unit can be converted to a solution with at most one, while at most doubling the completion time of the last piece of any job. For the rest of this section we'll focus on $\mathcal{IP}$; our results apply, paying a factor of $2 + \frac{1}{t}$ in the completion time of each job, to $\mathcal{IP}^2$ as well. To obtain schedules of good approximate quality from $\mathcal{IP}$ we relax $x_{ijkt} \in \{0, 1\}$ to $0 \leq x_{ijkt} \leq 1$ and solve the resulting linear program $\mathcal{LP}$. In the resulting fractional solution each job contributes to the objective function its *fractional weighted completion time*: the weighted sum of the fractionally scheduled pieces of the last unit.

The solution to the linear program can not immediately be interpreted as a schedule for two reasons. First, a particular unit may be fractionally assigned across several machines during the same time unit. These fractional pieces cannot run simultaneously. Secondly, the fractional weighted completion time of J_j is a weighted sum of fractional completion times of different pieces of J_j's last unit, and does not represent the actual point in the schedule at which the last fractional unit of the job finished. In fact, the weighted completion time of J_j can be much larger than the *fractional* weighted completion time.

We now show how to remove these two concerns and produce a valid schedule. We remove the first via an application of open shop scheduling theory [4, 8]. To remove the second, we introduce a new rounding idea that may have other applications.

Lemma 13. *Consider one unit of time t' in an assignment of fractional pieces of jobs to units of time. There exists a valid schedule for that unit of time in which each machine makes at most m^4 preemptions.*

Proof. Let $p'_{i'j'} = \sum_k x_{i'j'kt'}/s_{i'j'}$ denote the amount of processing time assigned to job J_j by machine M_i during time t'. Create an operation $o'_{i'j'}$ of length $p'_{i'j'}$. Using an open-shop result of [4], we can create a preemptive schedule, with at most m^4 preemptions per processor, of length
$\max\{\max_{j'} \sum_{i'} p_{i'j'}, \max_{i'} \sum_{j'} p_{i'j'}\}$, which by constraints (3) and (4) is ≤ 1.
□

Applying Lemma 13 to each time unit of the solution to $\mathcal{LP}$, we obtain:

Lemma 14. *Given a solution to $\mathcal{LP}$ in which the last fractional piece of the last unit of J_j, $j = 1,\ldots,n$ is assigned to time t_j, there exists a valid schedule in which each J_j finishes by time t_j.*

Lemma 15. *There exists a polynomial-time algorithm, which, given a solution to $\mathcal{LP}$, converted to a valid schedule S using Lemma 14, produces a schedule with average weighted completion time at most 4 times the weighted fractional completion time of S.*

Proof. Consider a job J_j of size $p_j = k$. The kth unit of J_j may be assigned fractionally on a number of machines at different times. Let time t^* be the first unit of time such that $1/2$ of this kth unit is assigned by time t^*.

By constraint (6), by time $t^* - 1$ at least half of the first $k - 1$ units of J_j have been processed. We double the time scale of the entire schedule, remove all pieces of the first $k - 1$ units of J_j that were scheduled in S after $t^* - 1$ and any pieces of the kth unit that were scheduled after time t^*, and schedule these pieces in the "doubles" of the pieces of J_j that were scheduled by $t^* - 1$ or t^*, respectively. Therefore, by time $2t^*$ all of J_j has been processed. Noting that $\frac{t^*}{2}$ is a lower bound on the fractional completion time gives the lemma.
□

Theorem 16. *Under the assumptions that $p_{\max} \leq n^4$ and that preemption is not allowed within units of a job, there exists a polynomial-time 4-approximation algorithm for preemptive scheduling of identical machines with release dates to minimize average weighted completion time, and an $(8 + \epsilon)$-approximation algorithms for the corresponding unrelated machines problem.*

Allowing Arbitrary Preemptions and Job Sizes We can prove that if preemptions are allowed only at time intervals which are integral multiples of $1/m^4$, the weighted average completion time can only increase by at most a factor of $(2 + o(1))$, and in many cases, such as the presence of large jobs, by a $1 + o(1)$ factor. One can round and scale to take care of large jobs.

Lemma 17.
(a) Let C be the weighted average completion time of the optimal schedule. A linear program of the form $\mathcal{LP}$ in which we split each job and each time slot on each machine into m^5 equal-size pieces, will have an optimal weighted average completion time of at most $(1 + 1/m)C + \frac{1}{n}\sum w_j$.
(b) Given a ρ-approximation algorithm for the preemptive scheduling of jobs on unrelated machines to minimize average weighted completion time assuming $p_{max} \leq n^4$, there exists a $(2+\epsilon)\rho$-approximation algorithm for arbitrary job sizes.

Using Lemma 17, Theorem 16 and Corollary 7 along with a bit of balancing of different cases yields the results detailed in Fig. 1.

References

1. K. R. Baker. *Introduction to Sequencing and Scheduling.* Wiley, 1974.
2. J. Bruno, E.G. Coffman Jr., and R. Sethi. Scheduling independent tasks to reduce mean finishing time. *Communications of the ACM*, 17:382–387, 1974.
3. J. Du, J.Y.-T. Leung, and G.H. Young. Minimizing mean flow time with release time constraints. Technical report, University of Texas at Dallas, 1988.
4. T. Gonzalez and S. Sahni. Open shop scheduling to minimize finish time. *Journal of the ACM*, 23:665–679, 1976.
5. W. Horn. Minimizing average flow time with parallel machines. *Operations Research*, 21:846–847, 1973.
6. T. Kawaguchi and S. Kyan. Worst case bound of an lrf schedule for the mean weighted flow-time problem. *SIAM Journal on Computing*, 15:1119–1129, 1986.
7. J. Labetoulle, E.L. Lawler, J.K. Lenstra, and A.H.G. Rinooy Kan. Preemptive scheduling of uniform machines subject to release dates. In W.R. Pulleyblank, editor, *Progress in Combinatorial Optimization*, pp. 245–261. Academic Press, 1984.
8. E.L. Lawler, J.K. Lenstra, A.H.G. Rinooy Kan, and D.B. Shmoys. Sequencing and scheduling: Algorithms and complexity. In S.C. Graves, A.H.G. Rinnooy Kan, and P.H. Zipkin, editors, *Handbooks in Operations Research and Management Science, Vol 4., Logistics of Production and Inventory*, pages pp 445–522. 1993.
9. J.K. Lenstra, A.H.G. Rinnooy Kan, and P. Brucker. Complexity of machine scheduling problems. *Annals of Discrete Mathematics*, 1:343–362, 1977.
10. R. McNaughton. Scheduling with deadlines and loss functions. *Management Science*, 6:1–12, 1959.
11. R. Motwani, S. Phillips, and E. Torng. Non-clairvoyant scheduling. In *Proceedings of the 4th ACM-SIAM Symposium on Discrete Algorithms*, pp. 422–431, Jan. 1993.
12. C. Phillips, C. Stein, and J. Wein. Task scheduling in networks. In *Proceedings of Fourth Scandinavian Workshop on Algorithm Theory*, pages 290–301, 1994.
13. W.E. Smith. Various optimizers for single-stage production. *Naval Research Logistics Quarterly*, 3:59–66, 1956.

Dynamic Algorithms for the Dyck Languages[*]

Gudmund Skovbjerg Frandsen[**], Thore Husfeldt, Peter Bro Miltersen[***],
Theis Rauhe, and Søren Skyum

BRICS,[†] Department of Computer Science, University of Aarhus,
Ny Munkegade, DK–8000 Århus C, Denmark

Abstract. We study Dynamic Membership problems for the Dyck languages, the class of strings of properly balanced parentheses. We also study the Dynamic Word problem for the free group. We present deterministic algorithms and data structures which maintain a string under replacements of symbols, insertions, and deletions of symbols, and language membership queries. Updates and queries are handled in polylogarithmic time. We also give both Las Vegas- and Monte Carlo-type randomised algorithms to achieve better running times, and present lower bounds on the complexity for variants of the problems.

1 Introduction

1.1 Dyck Languages

The language of properly balanced parentheses contains strings like ( ) and ( )(( )) but not)). The notion of balancedness also makes sense if we add more types of parentheses: ([ ])( ) balances but [ ) does not.

More formally, let $A = \{a_1, \ldots, a_k\}$ and $\bar{A} = \{\bar{a}_1, \ldots, \bar{a}_k\}$ be two disjoint sets of opening and closing symbols, respectively. For example, the pair $A = \{(, [, \mathbf{do}, \mathbf{if}\}$ and $\bar{A} = \{),], \mathbf{od}, \mathbf{fi}\}$ captures the nested structure of programming languages. The *one-sided Dyck language* D_k over $A \cup \bar{A}$ is the context-free language generated by the following grammar:

$$S \to SS \mid a_1 S \bar{a}_1 \mid \cdots \mid a_k S \bar{a}_k \mid \epsilon.$$

Closely related is the *two-sided Dyck language* D'_k over $A \cup \bar{A}$ defined by

$$S \to SS \mid a_1 S \bar{a}_1 \mid \bar{a}_1 S a_1 \mid \cdots \mid a_k S \bar{a}_k \mid \bar{a}_k S a_k \mid \epsilon.$$

---

[*] A full version of this paper with all proofs included, can be found on the BRICS World Wide Web server at URL http://www.daimi.aau.dk/BRICS/. This work was partially supported by the ESPRIT II Basic Research Actions Program of the EC under contract no. 7141 (project ALCOM II).

[**] Gudmund Frandsen was partially supported by CCI-Europe.

[***] Peter Bro Miltersen was partially supported by a grant from the Danish Natural Science Research Council, part of his research was done done at the Department of Computer Science, University of Toronto.

[†] Basic Research in Computer Science, Centre of the Danish National Research Foundation.

This corresponds to two-sided cancellation, so now also)(and (][) balance, while [) still does not.

The two-sided Dyck language has an algebraic interpretation. If we identify $\bar{a}_i$ with a_i^{-1} and view concatenation as the product operator then $x \in D'_k$ if and only if x equals the identity in the free group generated by A. For example, $\bar{a}_1 a_2 \bar{a}_2 a_1 \in D'_2$ because $a_1^{-1} a_2 a_2^{-1} a_1$ evaluates to unity.

The Dyck languages are covered in detail in Harrison's classical treatment [6].

1.2 The Dynamic Membership Problem

In this paper we consider the problem of maintaining membership in D_k or D'_k of a string from $(A \cup \bar{A})^n$ dynamically. More precisely, we want to implement a data type that contains a string $x \in (A \cup \bar{A})^n$ of even length, initially a_1^n, with the following operations:

change(i, a): change x_i to $a \in A \cup \bar{A}$,
member: return 'yes' if and only if $x \in D_k$.

The problem is well motivated: several modern editors have editing modes for specific programming languages where a rudimentary on-line syntax check is performed whenever the source is changed. We would like to know whether such a check can be performed faster than in the straightforward way. For such an application, the set of operations considered above is clearly not sufficient. At the very least, we need an operation **insert**(i, a) that inserts a symbol a between the $(i-1)$th and the ith character in the string, and an operation **delete**(i) that deletes the ith character in the string. Furthermore, the following operations would also be useful: an operation **prefix**(i) that tells whether the prefix $x_1 x_2 \cdots x_i$ is a member of the language, and, for the one-sided languages, an operation **match**(i) that given the position i of a parenthesis returns the index of its match, as well as an operation **mismatch** that returns the index of the first unmatched parenthesis. We choose the restricted set of operations above for reasons of expositional simplicity; most of our results are also valid under the extended set, we state explicitly when they are not.

Of course, the Dyck languages do not capture all aspects of the far more complicated grammar of real programming languages. Ultimately, we could wish for a fast dynamic algorithm for recognition of (a large subclass of) the deterministic context-free languages, which would allow us to implement on-line syntax checking in an editor. Hopefully, this paper is a step in the right direction. We do not expect the algorithms in this paper to be particularly useful in practice as is, however. Even though they run in polylogarithmic time (and the hidden constants are of moderate size), one should keep in mind that the original, sequential algorithm is extremely simple and probably outperforms them in normal applications. Although extremely long files do arise in practice, problems of quite a different nature—like paging, network access, etc.—would dwarf the execution time of both a dynamic and a sequential algorithm for parenthesis matching.

1.3 Results

Our main model of computation will be a unit-cost random access machine with word-size $O(\log n)$, where n is the size of the input; this model is also known as a *random access computer*. Our main result is that the Dynamic Membership problem for all Dyck languages can be solved in polylogarithmic time per operation, the exact bound is $O(\log^3 n \log^* n)$. We use a technique for maintaining dynamic sequences under equality tests by Mehlhorn, Sundar, and Uhrig [10], which also gives (Las Vegas-style) randomised algorithms that run in slightly better expected time: $O(\log^3 n)$.

We achieve better bounds for Monte Carlo-style algorithms. Using the fingerprint method of Karp and Rabin [7], where strings are represented by (non-unique) fingerprints in the form of a matrix product modulo a small randomly chosen prime, D_k can be done in time $O(\log^2 n)$ and D'_k in time $O(\log n)$. For D_1 and D'_1 we can use simpler techniques to achieve better bounds. The table below states the order of the upper bounds. Except for the $O(1)$ algorithm for D_1, all algorithms are also valid (and have the same complexity) when we extend the operations to insertion and deletion of single characters, prefix queries, and (for the one-sided case) match queries.

Table 1: Running times of algorithms with logarithmic word size.

Language	Operations	Deterministic	Las Vegas	Monte Carlo
D_1 or D'_1	all	$O(\log n)$		
D'_1	change, member	$\Theta(1)$		
D_k	all	$O(\log^3 n \log^* n)$	$O(\log^3 n)$	$O(\log^2 n)$
D'_k	all	$O(\log^3 n \log^* n)$	$O(\log^3 n)$	$O(\log n)$

We have no lower bounds for the restricted set of operations (**change, member**). However, if the **prefix**-operation is added, we can get a weak lower bound of $\Omega(\log\log n/\log\log\log n)$ using a result of Beame and Fich (personal communication, improving [11]); obviously, the same bound holds with the **mismatch** query instead. If instead we allow insertion and deletion, a lower bound of $\Omega(\log n/\log\log n)$ can be derived from a result of Fredman and Saks [4]. The same lower bound holds if we replace **member** by **match** in the restricted set of operations (for one-sided languages). The proofs of these results are omitted in this version of the paper, due to lack of space.

Table 2: Lower bounds for logarithmic word size.

Language	Operations	Lower bound
D_1 or D'_1	change, prefix	$\Omega\left(\frac{\log\log n}{\log\log\log n}\right)$
D_1 or D'_1	insert, delete, member	$\Omega\left(\frac{\log n}{\log\log n}\right)$
D_1	change, match	$\Omega\left(\frac{\log n}{\log\log n}\right)$

It is interesting that all upper bounds for the two-sided case are at least as good as the upper bounds for the one-sided case, implying that the former may be easier than the latter. In a more restricted model for dynamic algorithms, namely the cell probe model with cell size 1 (the *bit probe model*), we can indeed separate the complexity of the two problems: for D_1, we prove a lower bound of $\Omega(\log n / \log\log n)$ by a technique of Fredman [3], while we can bound the complexity of D_1' from above by $O(\log\log n)$ using a construction of [2]. The latter bound is shown to be tight by a reduction from the Dynamic Word problem for the monoid $(\{0,1\}, \vee)$, for which a lower bound is given in [2]. The upper bound for D_1 is $O(\log n \log\log n)$, not quite matching the lower bound. These results are only valid for the restricted set of operations (and are only of theoretical interest anyway). The table below summarises these results. The proofs are omitted in this version of the paper, due to lack of space.

Table 3: Bit probe complexity.

Language	Operations	Upper bound	Lower bound
D_1	change, member	$O(\log n \log\log n)$	$\Omega\left(\frac{\log n}{\log\log n}\right)$
D_1'	change, member	$\Theta(\log\log n)$	

1.4 Related Results

It is interesting that all Dyck languages seem to be equally hard in most non-dynamic computational models. Ritchie and Springsteel [14] showed that the one-sided Dyck languages are in deterministic logspace, Lipton and Zalcstein [8] extended this to the two-sided case (see also [6, Exercises 22 and 23]). One can phrase this even stronger in terms of circuit complexity: all Dyck languages are complete for TC^0 under AC^0-reductions, (this appears to be folklore).

Dynamic Word and Prefix problems for *finite* monoids are studied in [2, 11]. The free group of k generators studied in the present paper is infinite.

Turning from context-free to regular languages, it is easy to find logarithmic time algorithms for the Dynamic Membership problem for the latter class. The results from [2] give better upper bounds depending on the language's syntactic monoid $M(L)$.

One earlier paper has considered dynamic algorithms for the Dyck languages. In [13], algorithms with update and query operations in AC^0 are constructed, but no non-trivial sequential upper bounds follow from this.

1.5 Preliminaries and Notation

Strings will be denoted by lower-case letters $u, v, x, \ldots$. We let u_i denote the ith letter of string u and we write $u_{i:j}$ for $u_i \cdots u_j$. For letter a and string u, we put

$$|u|_a = |\{i \mid u_i = a\}|,$$

the number of occurrences of a in u. All logarithms are base two.

We call a string *reduced* if it contains no neighbouring pair of matching parentheses. So, for the one-sided case, ([]) is not reduced but [)(is. In the two-sided case, the latter is not reduced. To formalise this (following Harrison [6]), we introduce two mappings

$$\mu_1, \mu_2 \colon (A \cup \bar{A})^* \to (A \cup \bar{A})^*.$$

We want $\mu_1(u)$ and $\mu_2(u)$ to be the reduced form of u using one- and two-sided cancellation, respectively. To this end we define for each $1 \le i \le k$ and $j = 1, 2$:

$$\mu_1(\epsilon) = \mu_2(\epsilon) = \epsilon, \qquad \mu_1(ua_i) = \mu_1(u)a_i,$$

$$\mu_2(ua_i) = \begin{cases} \mu_2(u)a_i, & \text{if } \mu_2(u) \notin (A \cup \bar{A})^* \bar{a}_i, \\ u', & \text{if } \mu_2(u) = u'\bar{a}_i, \end{cases}$$

$$\mu_j(u\bar{a}_i) = \begin{cases} \mu_j(u)\bar{a}_i, & \text{if } \mu_j(u) \notin (A \cup \bar{A})^* a_i, \\ u', & \text{if } \mu_j(u) = u'a_i. \end{cases}$$

The functions have properties like $\mu_1(ua_i\bar{a}_i v) = \mu_1(uv)$ and $\mu_2(ua_i\bar{a}_i v) = \mu_2(u\bar{a}_i a_i v) = \mu_2(uv)$.

We formally define u^{-1} as $\bar{u}_n \cdots \bar{u}_1$ with the convention $\bar{\bar{a}} = a$ and $\epsilon^{-1} = \epsilon$.

2 Algorithms for One Pair of Parentheses

We begin with two easy upper bounds for D_1 and D_1', respectively.

Proposition 1. *The Dynamic Membership problem for D_1' can be done in constant time per operation.*

Proof. Note first that for all $x \in \{a, \bar{a}\}^*$ we have

$$x \in D_1' \quad \Longleftrightarrow \quad |x|_a = |x|_{\bar{a}}.$$

The only if direction is obvious. The other follows from the fact that a reduced string over $\{a, \bar{a}\}^*$ cannot contain both a and $\bar{a}$.

Hence we only need to count the number of occurrences of a and $\bar{a}$ in x. With unit cost operations, this is easily done in constant time per update. □

The solution does *not* apply to the extended set of operations, in fact a larger lower bound is proved below. We leave it to the reader to prove a logarithmic upper bound. Using an algorithm by Dietz [1] a solution with an $O(\log n / \log \log n)$ upper bound on the *amortised* complexity for the extended set of operations can also be found.

Proposition 2. *The Dynamic Membership problem for D_1 can be done in time $O(\log n)$ per operation.*

Proof. First note that for any $x \in \{a, \bar{a}\}^*$, the reduced string $\mu_1(x)$ is of the form $\bar{a}^r a^l$ for integers $l, r \geq 0$. We can view l and r as the number of excessive left and right parentheses, respectively.

We maintain a balanced binary tree whose ith leaf represents x_i and where each internal node represents the concatenation of its children's strings. With each node we store the tuple (r, l) describing the reduced form of the string it represents.

For the operations first note that $x \in D_1$ if and only if the root contains the tuple $(0, 0)$, corresponding to $\mu_1(x) = \epsilon$. To handle the updates it suffices to note that the value of a node can be easily derived from the values of its children, since

$$\mu_1(\bar{a}^{r_1} a^{l_1} \bar{a}^{r_2} a^{l_2}) = \begin{cases} \bar{a}^{r_1} a^{l_2 + l_1 - r_2}, & \text{if } l_1 \geq r_2, \\ \bar{a}^{r_1 + r_2 - l_1} a^{l_2}, & \text{otherwise}. \end{cases}$$

We can redo these calculations bluntly at each level and achieve a running time proportional to the height of the tree. □

The data structure is easily generalised to the extended set of operations. Most complicated are the **insert** and **delete** operations. To accommodate these, we have to maintain balance in the tree using any scheme for balancing dynamic search trees, e.g. *red–black trees* [5]. We will not comment on such extensions any further; the reader can check that they are also possible for all the algorithms in Sects. 3 and 4. The algorithm in the proof of Prop. 7 calls for the most complicated extensions, in that we also need to be able to split and merge trees.

3 Algorithms for Many Pairs of Parentheses

We move now to the main result, extending the above to larger k. The basic idea resembles very much the data structure from Prop. 2: we represent x as a balanced binary tree, where internal nodes correspond to substrings of x. At each node, we store entire sequences (rather than just a tuple as above) that are formed from the sequences stored at its children. To this end we first need a recent surprising construction for dynamically maintaining sequences.

3.1 A Data Structure for String Equality

Mehlhorn, Sundar, and Uhrig [10] present a data structure for dynamically maintaining a family of strings under equality tests. We use a slightly modified set of updates that is better suited to our problem. More precisely, we want to maintain an initially empty family S of strings from a finite alphabet Σ under the following operations:

create(σ): create a new (one-letter) string $s = \sigma \in \Sigma$ and add it to S,
destroy(s): remove s from S,
concatenate(s, s'): create a new string $s'' = ss'$ and add it to S,

split(s, i): create new strings $s' = s_1 \cdots s_i$ and $s'' = s_{i+1} \cdots s_n$, and add them to S,

equal(s, s'): return 'yes' if and only if $s = s'$,

lcp(s, s'): return the length of the longest common prefix of s and s'.

The techniques from [10] can easily be modified to cope with the above updates. The time bounds are summarised in the following lemma:

Lemma 3 [10]. *Let S_i denote the family of strings after the ith operation and define*

$$N_m = \max_{0 \le i \le m} \sum_{s \in S_i} |s|.$$

There is a data structure for the above problem such that the mth operation takes time $O(\log^2 N_m \log^* N_m)$.

3.2 The Two-Sided Case

Proposition 4. *The Dynamic Membership problem for D'_k can be done in time* $O(\log^3 n \log^* n)$ *per operation.*

Proof. We maintain a balanced binary tree whose ith leaf represents x_i and where each internal node represents the concatenation of its children's strings. With the node representing (say) y we store $\mu_2(y)$ and $\mu_2(y^{-1})$.

Let us see how we handle the operations. The query operation is easy since the root contains $\mu_2(x)$. For the change operation, we will show how to use the data structure from Sect. 3.1 to maintain the two sequences at each node. First note that the leaves of the tree are easily changed because $\mu_2(x_i) = x_i$ and $\mu_2(x_i^{-1}) = \bar{x}_i$.

From the leaf, the change propagates towards the root of the tree. To handle the changes at an internal node we exploit a useful property of the reduction function μ_2: given $u, v \in (A \cup \bar{A})^*$, write

$$\mu_2(u) = u'aw \quad \text{and} \quad \mu_2(v) = w^{-1}bv', \qquad \text{with } \bar{a} \ne b \qquad (1)$$

for some $u', v', w \in (A \cup \bar{A})^*$ and $a, b \in (A \cup \bar{A})$. Then one can show

$$\mu_2(uv) = u'abv'. \qquad (2)$$

Consider for concreteness an internal node whose children represent (say) u and v, respectively. Let w denote the longest common prefix of $\mu_2(u^{-1})$ and $\mu_2(v)$, which can be found from the information at the children of the node in time $O(\log^2 N \log^* N)$, where N denotes the total length of all sequences in the tree. Now split $\mu_2(u)$ and $\mu_2(v)$ as in (1) above and construct $\mu_2(uv)$ by (2), using a constant number of operations, each of which takes time $O(\log^2 N \log^* N)$. We remember to remove unused strings. The total number of operations for an update is then $O(\log n \log^2 N \log^* N)$. To bound N we note that at each level of the tree, the total length of all sequences maintained at that level is $2n$ and hence $N = O(n \log n)$, which gives the desired bound and completes the proof. $\quad\square$

3.3 The One-Sided Case

The proof for D_k is similar to that for D'_k but marred by the less nice algebraic properties of μ_1.

Proposition 5. *The Dynamic Membership problem for D_k can be done in time $O(\log^3 n \log^* n)$ per operation.*

Proof. As before, we maintain a balanced binary tree whose ith leaf represents x_i and where each internal node represents the concatenation of its children's strings.

We define yet another cancellation function μ, where every left paranthesis cancels every right paranthesis, regardless of its type, by

$$\mu(\epsilon) = \epsilon, \qquad \mu(ua_i) = \mu(u)a_i,$$

$$\mu(u\bar{a}_i) = \begin{cases} \mu(u)\bar{a}_i, & \text{if } \mu(u) \notin (A \cup \bar{A})^* A, \\ u', & \text{if } \mu(u) \in u'A. \end{cases}$$

For every y we can write $\mu(y)$ as $y_{\bar{A}} y_A$ for some $y_{\bar{A}} \in \bar{A}^*$ and $y_A \in A^*$. With the tree node for y we store a bit that is true if and only if $\mu_1(y) \in \bar{A}^* A^*$ (equivalently, $\mu(y) = \mu_1(y)$), as well as the strings y_A and $y_{\bar{A}}$, and their formal inverses $(y_A)^{-1}$ and $(y_{\bar{A}})^{-1}$. The intuition is that if this bit is false then x cannot balance, since

$$\mu_1(y) \in \bar{A}^* A^* \quad \text{if and only if} \quad \exists u, v\colon uyv \in D_k, \tag{3}$$

and then it suffices to store that information only. In the other case, $\mu_1(y)$ consists only of $y_{\bar{A}}$ and y_A, and these two strings (together with their formal inverses) are easily maintained, as we shall see below.

We turn to the operations. First note that membership of x in D_k can be read off the root node, since

$$x \in D_k \quad \text{if and only if} \quad \mu_1(x) \in \bar{A}^* A^* \text{ and } x_A = x_{\bar{A}} = \epsilon.$$

For the updates it suffices to explain how we can derive the information at a node from its children using a constant number of string operations. Let u and v denote the strings represented by the node's children and assume without loss of generality $|u_A| \geq |v_{\bar{A}}|$ (the other case is symmetrical). Write u_A as $u_{A,1} u_{A,2}$, where $|u_{A,2}| = |v_{\bar{A}}|$. Then $y_A = u_{A,1} v_A$ and $y_{\bar{A}} = u_{\bar{A}}$. Moreover,

$$\mu_1(y) \in \bar{A}^* A^* \quad \text{if and only if} \quad \mu_1(u), \mu_1(v) \in \bar{A}^* A^* \text{ and } u_{A,2} = (v_{\bar{A}})^{-1}.$$

The formal inverses $(y_A)^{-1}$ and $(y_{\bar{A}})^{-1}$ are easily maintained. This completes the proof. □

The upper bounds from the last two propositions can be improved to expected time $O(\log^3 n)$ by using the Las Vegas variant of the algorithm described in Sect. 3.1, see [10].

4   Monte Carlo Algorithms

4.1   The Two-Sided Case

We begin with D'_k, which is quite simple. We use the well-known *fingerprint* string matching technique of Karp and Rabin [7].

Proposition 6. *The Dynamic Membership problem for D'_k can be done in time $O(\log n)$ per operation such that the probability of an erroneous answer in any sequence of n updates is $O(\frac{1}{n})$.*

Proof. We start by considering D'_2 over the alphabet $A = \{a_1, a_2\}$ and $\bar{A} = \{\bar{a}_1, \bar{a}_2\}$. Define the congruence $\sim$ by

$$u \sim v \cdot \text{ if and only if } \quad \mu_2(u) = \mu_2(v).$$

Then the quotient $(A \cup \bar{A})^* / \sim$ is a group (*the free group over* $\{a_1, a_2\}$) with concatenation as the operator and ϵ as the identity.

Following Lipton and Zalcstein [8] (see also [9, Problem 2.3.13]), we represent $(A \cup \bar{A})^* / \sim$ as a group of 2×2 integer matrices using the group homomorphism $h: (A \cup \bar{A})^* / \sim \to M_2(Z)$ given by

$$h(a_1) = \begin{pmatrix} 1 & 2 \\ 0 & 1 \end{pmatrix} \quad \text{and} \quad h(a_2) = \begin{pmatrix} 1 & 0 \\ 2 & 1 \end{pmatrix}.$$

In this terminology, x is in D'_2 if and only if $h(x)$ is the identity matrix.

This suggests a randomised algorithm in the spirit of [7]: compute $h(x)$ modulo a randomly chosen prime p and check whether the result is the identity matrix.

For the dynamic version we need to maintain $h(x) \bmod p$ under updates to x; we write n for $|x|$. For a fixed prime $p \le n^4$ we can recompute $h(x) \bmod p$ in logarithmic time using a balanced binary tree, where the ith leaf contains $h(x_i)$ and an internal node contains the product (in $M_2(Z_p)$) of the value of its children. Thus the root contains $h(x) \bmod p$.

To bound the probability of error we note that all entries in the matrix $h(x)$ are bounded by 3^n, so there can be at most n distinct primes p such that $h(x) \equiv 1 \pmod{p}$ if in fact $h(x) \ne 1$. Choosing $p \le n^4$ randomly and choosing a new p for every n operations by the *global rebuilding* technique of Overmars [12] we guarantee that the probability of an erroneous answer in a sequence of n consecutive queries is bounded by $O(\frac{1}{n})$.

The above construction can be extended to larger k using the fact that the free group on k generators is a subgroup of the free group on two generators g_1, g_2. Indeed, if for $1 \le i \le k$ we put $c_i = g_1^i g_2^i$ then $c_1, \ldots, c_k$ generate a free group, see [9, Problem 1.4.12]. $\square$

4.2 The One-Sided Case

The algorithm for D_k is somewhat more difficult. We will combine the tree-structure we used for the deterministic algorithm for D_k (Prop. 5) with the Monte Carlo algorithm for D'_k from the last proposition. Recall that in the deterministic algorithm, we use the expensive string operations from Sect. 3.1 to test whether certain internal substrings (namely, $u_{A,2}$ and $(v_{\bar{A}})^{-1}$) constitute a match. But since $u_{A,2} \in A^*$ and $v_{\bar{A}} \in \bar{A}^*$, this is true if and only if $u_{A,2}v_{\bar{A}} \in D'_k$, so we can use the much faster Monte Carlo algorithm for D'_k instead.

Proposition 7. *The Dynamic Membership problem for D_k can be done in time $O(\log^2 n)$ per operation such that the probability of an erroneous answer in any sequence of n updates is $O(\frac{1}{n})$.*

Proof. As before, we maintain a balanced binary tree whose ith leaf represents x_i and where each internal node represents the concatenation of its children's strings.

For every y we define y_A, $y_{\bar{A}}$, u, v, $u_A = u_{A,1}u_{A,2}$, and $v_{\bar{A}}$ as in the proof of Prop. 5. In particular, we assume $|u_A| \geq |v_{\bar{A}}|$ (the other case is symmetrical). Write $w = u_{A,2}v_{\bar{A}}$. With the tree node for y (of length m, say) we maintain the following information:

1. a bit that is true if and only if $\mu_1(y) \in \bar{A}^*A^*$,
2. three balanced binary search trees whose leaves store the indices (in x) of y_A, $y_{\bar{A}}$, and w, respectively,
3. the lengths $|y_A|$, $|y_{\bar{A}}|$, and $|w|$,
4. a string $w_{\#} \in (A \cup \bar{A} \cup \{\#\})^m$ defined as follows: since w is a subsequence of y, we can write $w = y_{i_1} \ldots y_{i_l}$ for some $i_1 < \cdots < i_l$. Then we define

$$w_{\#} = \#^{i_1 - 1} y_{i_1} \#^{i_2 - i_1 - 1} y_{i_2} \#^{i_3 - i_2 - 1} y_{i_3} \cdots \#^{i_l - i_{l-1} - 1} y_{i_l} \#^{m - i_l}.$$

One can view this as a padded w of fixed length.

Note that we do not store y itself.

Turning to the operations, we first note that the query is handled as in the proof of Prop. 5. A tedious case analysis shows that when a single letter of y is changed then at most two changes are induced in each of y_A and $y_{\bar{A}}$ and at most four changes in w and $w_{\#}$. The corresponding updates at the node representing y can be done in time $O(\log n)$ given knowledge about the updates at lower levels.

To see whether $w \in D'_k$, we apply the technique from the last proposition, using $w_{\#}$ as instance; the extra letter $\#$ is handled by letting h map it to the identity matrix. Hence we can maintain the information at each level of the tree in time $O(\log n)$, from which the stated time bound follows.

To bound the error probability, note that we use $O(n)$ distinct versions of the data structure from Prop. 6. Using a prime from a larger set (say, $p \leq n^5$), we obtain the stated bound. $\qquad\square$

References

1. Paul F. Dietz. Optimal algorithms for list indexing and subset rank. In F. Dehne, J.-R. Sack, and N. Santoro, editors, *Proc. First Workshop on Algorithms and Data Structures (WADS)*, volume 382 of *Lecture Notes in Computer Science*, pages 39–46. Springer Verlag, Berlin, 1989.

2. Gudmund Skovbjerg Frandsen, Peter Bro Miltersen, and Sven Skyum. Dynamic word problems. In *Proc 34th Ann. Symp. on Foundations of Computer Science (FOCS)*, pages 470–479, 1993.

3. Michael L. Fredman. The complexity of maintaining an array and computing its partial sums. *Journal of the ACM*, 29:250–260, 1982.

4. Michael L. Fredman and Michael E. Saks. The cell probe complexity of dynamic data structures. In *Proc. 21st Ann. Symp. on Theory of Computing (STOC)*, pages 345–354, 1989.

5. Leo J. Guibas and Robert Sedgewick. A dichromatic framework for balanced trees. In *Proc. 19th Ann. Symp. on Foundations of Computer Science (FOCS)*, pages 8–21. IEEE Computer Society, 1978.

6. Michael A. Harrison. *Introduction to Formal Language Theory*. Addison-Wesley, 1978.

7. Richard M. Karp and Michael O. Rabin. Efficient randomised pattern-matching algorithms. *IBM J. Res. Develop.*, 31(2):249–260, March 1987.

8. Richard J. Lipton and Yechezkel Zalcstein. Word problems solvable in logspace. *Journal of the ACM*, 24(3):522–526, 1977.

9. Wilhelm Magnus, Abraham Karrass, and Donald Solitar. *Combinatorial Group Theory*, volume 13 of *Pure and Applied Mathematics*. Interscience Publishers, 1966.

10. K. Mehlhorn, R. Sundar, and C. Uhrig. Maintaining dynamic sequences under equality-tests in polylogarithmic time. In *Proc. 5th Ann. Symp. on Discrete Algorithms (SODA)*, pages 213–222. ACM-SIAM, 1994.

11. Peter Bro Miltersen. Lower bounds for union-split-find related problems on random access machines. In *Proc. 26th Ann. Symp. on Theory of Computing (STOC)*, pages 625–634. ACM, 1994.

12. Mark H. Overmars. *The design of dynamic data structures*, volume 156 of *Lecture Notes in Computer Science*. Springer Verlag, Berlin, 1983.

13. Sushant Patnaik and Neil Immerman. Dyn-FO: A parallel, dynamic comlexity class. In *Proc. 13th ACM Symp. on Principles of Database Systems (PODS)*, pages 210–221, 1994.

14. R. W. Ritchie and F. N. Springsteel. Language recognition by marking automata. *Information and Control*, 20:313–330, 1972.

Arrangements in Higher Dimensions: Voronoi Diagrams, Motion Planning, and Other Applications*

Micha Sharir[†]

Abstract

We review recent progress in the study of arrangements of surfaces in higher dimensions. This progress involves new and nearly tight bounds on the complexity of lower envelopes, single cells, zones, and other substructures in such arrangements, and the design of efficient algorithms (near optimal in the worst case) for constructing and manipulating these structures. We then present applications of the new results to motion planning, Voronoi diagrams, visibility, and geometric optimization.

The combinatorial, algebraic, and topological analysis of arrangements of surfaces in higher dimensions has become one of the most active areas of research in computational geometry during the past 5 years. This is partly due to the fact that many geometric problems in diverse areas can be reduced to questions involving such arrangements. A typical example is the following general *motion planning problem*. Assume that we have a robot system B with d degrees of freedom, i.e., we can represent each placement of B as a point in d-space. Suppose that the workspace of B is cluttered with obstacles, whose shapes and locations are known. For each combination of a geometric feature (vertex, edge, face) of an obstacle and a similar feature of B, define their *contact surface* as the set of all points in d-space that represent a placement of B in which contact is made between these specific features. Let Z be a point corresponding to a given initial *free* placement of B, in which it does not intersect any obstacle. Then the set of all free placements of B that can be reached from Z via a collision-free continuous motion will obviously correspond to the cell containing Z in the arrangement of the contact surfaces. Thus, the robot motion planning problem leads more or less directly to the problem of computing a single cell in an arrangement of surfaces in higher dimensions. The *combinatorial complexity* of this cell, i.e., the total number of lower-dimensional faces appearing on its boundary serves as a trivial lower bound for the running time of the motion planning problem (assuming the entire cell has to be output). It turns out that in most instances this bound can be almost matched by suitable algorithms.

Other applications that call for combinatorial analysis of arrangements involve geometric algorithms for constructing arrangements, which are based on randomized or ε-net techniques, and whose running times are usually directly influenced by the combinatorial complexity of the relevant geometric substructures of the arrangements that they manipulate; this will be explained in more detail below. We will also describe below more applications of higher-dimensional arrangements to problems in visibility, in geometric optimization, and involving generalized Voronoi diagrams. For some basic terminology related to arrangements, the reader is referred to [30, 39, 45, 65].

This survey describes many recent advances in the study of combinatorial, topological, and algorithmic problems involving arrangements of algebraic surfaces in higher dimensions. In these studies there are three main relevant parameters: the number n of surfaces, their maximum algebraic degree b, and the dimension d. In the approach taken here, we are mainly interested in a 'combinatorial' approach, in which we want to calibrate the dependence of the complexity of

*by NSF Grants CCR-91-22103 and CCR-93-11127, by a Max-Planck Research Award, and by grants from the U.S.-Israeli Binational Science Foundation, the Israel Science Fund administered by the Israeli Academy of Sciences, and the G.I.F., the German-Israeli Foundation for Scientific Research and Development.

[†]School of Mathematical Sciences, Tel Aviv University, Tel Aviv 69978, Israel, and Courant Institute of Mathematical Sciences, New York University, New York, NY 10012, USA

the various structures and algorithms on the number n of surfaces, assuming that the maximum degree, as well as any other factor that does not depend on n, is constant. In this way, all issues related to the algebraic complexity of the problem are 'swept under the rug'. These issues should be (and indeed have been) picked up in the complementary 'algebraic' mode of research, where the dependence on the maximum degree b is more relevant; see [48, 62] for studies of this kind.

We should emphasize that, although quite a few of the problems reviewed here are combinatorial in nature, most of them are motivated by algorithmic applications. As mentioned above, it is an interesting feature of the area that the complexity of efficient algorithms for constructing various substructures in arrangements depends mainly on the combinatorial complexity of these structures. This is, of course, always true in terms of lower bounds (as the algorithm must at least output the desired structure), but there is also a strong influence of the combinatorial complexity on the running time of the algorithms. A typical example involves algorithms that are based on *vertical decompositions* in arrangements—see below for details.

During the past three years, significant progress has been made on the problem of bounding the complexity of the *lower envelope* (pointwise minimum) of a collection of multivariate functions. This problem has been open since 1986, when it was shown in [46] that the combinatorial complexity of the lower envelope of n univariate continuous functions, each pair of which intersect in at most s points, is at most $\lambda_s(n)$, the maximum length of an (n, s)-*Davenport–Schinzel sequence*. This bound is slightly super-linear in n, for any fixed s (for example, it is $\Theta(n\alpha(n))$ for $s = 3$, where $\alpha(n)$ is the extremely slowly growing inverse of Ackermann's function [46]; see also [8, 65]). Since the complexity of the arrangement of such a collection of functions can be $\Theta(n^2)$ in the worst case, this result shows that the complexity of the lower envelope is smaller than the overall complexity of the arrangement by nearly a factor of n.

It was then conjectured that a similar phenomenon occurs in higher dimensions. That is, the combinatorial complexity of the lower envelope of a collection $\mathcal{F}$ of n 'well-behaved' d-variate functions should be close to $O(n^d)$ (as opposed to $\Theta(n^{d+1})$), which can be the complexity of the entire arrangement of the function graphs). More precisely, according to a stronger version of this conjecture, this quantity should be at most $O(n^{d-1}\lambda_s(n))$, for some constant s depending on the shape of the functions in $\mathcal{F}$. These conjectures have been confirmed only in some special cases, including the case in which the graphs of the functions are d-simplices in $\mathbb{R}^{d+1}$, where a tight worst-case bound, $\Theta(n^d\alpha(n))$, was established in [31, 59]. (The case $d = 1$, involving n segments in the plane, where the bound is $\Theta(n\alpha(n))$, had been analyzed earlier, in [46, 69].) There are also some even more special cases, like the case of hyperplanes, where the maximum complexity of their lower envelope is known to be $\Theta(n^{\lfloor(d+1)/2\rfloor})$, by the so-called *Upper Bound Theorem* for convex polytopes [57]. The case of balls also admits a much better bound, using a standard lifting transformation (see [30]). However, the general problem remained open.

Last year this problem was almost completely settled in [43] and [64]: Let $\mathcal{F}$ be a collection of (possibly partially-defined) d-variate functions, such that all functions in $\mathcal{F}$ are algebraic of constant maximum degree and, in case of partial functions, the domain of definition of each function is a semi-algebraic set defined by a constant number of polynomial equalities and inequalities of constant maximum degree. We refer to such a region as having *constant description complexity*. It was shown that, for any $\varepsilon > 0$, the combinatorial complexity of the lower envelope of $\mathcal{F}$ is $O(n^{d+\varepsilon})$, where the constant of proportionality depends on ε, d, and on the maximum degree of the functions and of the polynomials defining their domains. Thus, apart from a small remaining gap, the above conjecture has been settled in the affirmative.

The proof is based on the probabilistic method developed by Clarkson and Shor [25]. Informally (and not very precisely), one charges each vertex p of the envelope to a block of k 'nearby' vertices that lie along an edge leading from p away from the envelope (here k is some sufficiently large constant parameter). Each of the charged vertices lies at *level* at most k in the arrangement of the function graphs (that is, at most k graphs lie below such a vertex). The Clarkson-Shor technique allows us to bound the number of such nearby vertices by a term equal to $O(k^{d+1})$ times the number of vertices of the lower envelope of a random sample of n/k functions of $\mathcal{F}$. This implies that the number of vertices of the envelope can be bounded by roughly $O(k^d)$ times the number of vertices of the envelope of a random sample of size n/k, which leads to a recurrence, whose solution gives the asserted bounds. (We caution that this description glosses over many technical details, given in the papers cited above, and is given only as an intuitive explanation of the main idea of the proof.)

This result was then followed by several further developments. Lower envelopes (just like single cells) naturally arise in motion planning, scene analysis, Voronoi diagrams, and geometric optimization. The new results can therefore be applied to obtain improved algorithmic and combinatorial bounds for a variety of problems. Some of these applications have already appeared in the literature (and will be mentioned below), but we believe that many more await to be discovered. The above results have also opened up the door to many significant new research problems, and, in our opinion, it will take at least several years to settle most of them.

Algorithms for Lower Envelopes

Once the combinatorial complexity of lower envelopes of multivariate functions has been (more or less) resolved, the next task is to derive efficient algorithms for computing such lower envelopes. One of the strongest forms of such a computation is as follows. We are given a collection $\mathcal{F}$ of d-variate algebraic functions satisfying the above conditions. We want to compute the lower envelope $E_{\mathcal{F}}$ and store it in some data structure, so that, given a query point $p \in \mathbb{R}^d$, we can efficiently compute the value $E_{\mathcal{F}}(p)$, and the function(s) attaining $E_{\mathcal{F}}$ at p. (Of course, we need to assume here an appropriate model of computation, where various primitive operations on a constant number of functions can be each performed in constant time. There are several different models of this kind, such as the exact arithmetic model in real algebraic geometry; see, e.g., [48].)

This task has recently been accomplished for the case of bivariate functions in several papers [5, 16, 17, 27, 64]. Some of these techniques use randomized algorithms, and their expected running time is $O(n^{2+\varepsilon})$, for any $\varepsilon > 0$, which is comparable with the maximum complexity of such an envelope. The simplest algorithm is probably the one given in [5]. It is deterministic and uses divide-and-conquer. Its analysis is based on an interesting property of the *overlay* of (the xy-projections of) two lower envelopes of bivariate functions, that the complexity of such an overlay is also $O(n^{2+\varepsilon})$, where n is the total number of functions. (To appreciate this result, observe that, in general, the overlay of two planar maps of complexity N each can have $\Theta(N^2)$ complexity.)

In higher dimensions, the only result known so far is that lower envelopes of trivariate functions satisfying the above properties can be computed, in the above strong sense, in randomized expected time $O(n^{3+\varepsilon})$ [1]. For $d > 3$, it is also shown in [1] that all vertices, edges and 2-faces of the lower envelope of n d-variate functions, as above, can be computed in randomized expected time $O(n^{d+\varepsilon})$. It is still an open problem whether such a lower envelope can be computed within similar time bounds in the above stronger sense, and this problem should certainly be investigated further. Another, more difficult problem is to devise *output-sensitive* algorithms, whose complexity depends on the actual combinatorial complexity of the envelope. It would also be interesting to develop algorithms for certain special classes of functions, where better bounds are known for the complexity of the envelope, e.g., for envelopes of piecewise-linear functions (see below for more details).

Some of the applications of the algorithms produced so far are mentioned below. It can be expected that the proposed extensions of these algorithms will also find other interesting applications.

Single Cells

Lower envelopes are closely related to other substructures in arrangements, notably *single cells* and *zones*. In two dimensions, it was shown in [40] that the complexity of a single face in an arrangement of n arcs, each pair of which intersect in at most s points, is $O(\lambda_{s+2}(n))$, and so is of the same asymptotic order of magnitude as the complexity of the lower envelope of such a collection of arcs. Again, the prevailing conjecture is that the same holds in higher dimensions.

That is, the complexity of a single cell in an arrangement of n algebraic surfaces in d-space satisfying the above assumptions is close to $O(n^{d-1})$, or, in a stronger form, this complexity should be $O(n^{d-2}\lambda_s(n))$, for some appropriate constant s. The weaker version of this conjecture for the 3-dimensional case has recently been confirmed in [44]: Let $\mathcal{A}$ be an arrangement of n 2-dimensional surface patches in $\mathbb{R}^3$, all of them algebraic of constant description complexity. It was proved in [44] that, for any $\varepsilon > 0$, the complexity of a single cell in $\mathcal{A}$ is $O(n^{2+\varepsilon})$, where the constant of proportionality depends on ε and on the maximum degree of the surfaces and of their boundaries. The proof is based on an extension of the argument developed for lower envelopes, but one has to add several nontrivial ingredients, in order to handle the more complex topology of a single cell. The analysis in [44] seems to extend to higher dimensions, except for some key steps that seem to require the introduction of new algebraic geometry techniques.

The results of [44] mentioned above easily imply that, for fairly general robot systems with 3 degrees of freedom, the complexity of the space of all free placements of the system, reachable from a given initial placement, is $O(n^{2+\varepsilon})$, a significant improvement over the previous, naive bound $O(n^3)$. The corresponding algorithmic problem, of devising an efficient (near-quadratic) algorithm for computing such a cell, has very recently been solved in [63]. We will say more about this result when we discuss vertical decompositions below. Prior to this result, several other near-quadratic algorithms were proposed for some special classes of surfaces [5, 13, 41, 42]. For example, the paper [42] gives a near-quadratic algorithm for the single cell problem in the special case of arrangements that arise in the motion planning problem for a (nonconvex) polygonal robot moving (translating and rotating) in a planar polygonal region. However, this algorithm exploits the special structure of the surfaces that arise in this case, and does not extend to the general case. The algorithm given in [5] also provides a near-quadratic solution for the case that all the surfaces are graphs of totally-defined continuous algebraic bivariate functions (so that the cell in question is xy-monotone).

In higher dimensions, we mention the special case of a single cell in an arrangement of n $(d-1)$-simplices in $\mathbb{R}^d$. It was shown in [13] that the complexity of such a cell is $O(n^{d-1}\log n)$; a simplified proof was recently given in [67]. This bound is much sharper than the general bound stated above; the best lower bound known for this complexity is $\Omega(n^{d-1}\alpha(n))$, so a small gap between the upper and lower bounds still remains.

Zones

Given an arrangement $\mathcal{A}$ of surfaces in $\mathbb{R}^d$, and another surface σ_0, the *zone* of σ_0 is the collection of all cells of the arrangement $\mathcal{A}$ that σ_0 crosses, and the complexity of the zone is the sum of complexities of all these cells. The 'classical' Zone Theorem [30, 34] asserts that the maximum complexity of the zone of a hyperplane in an arrangement of n hyperplanes in $\mathbb{R}^d$ is $\Theta(n^{d-1})$, where the constant of proportionality depends on d. This has been extended in [10] to the zone of an algebraic or convex surface (of any dimension $p < d$) in an arrangement of hyperplanes. The bound on the complexity of such a zone is $O(n^{\lfloor (d+p)/2 \rfloor}\log^c n)$, and $\Omega(n^{\lfloor (d+p)/2 \rfloor})$ in the worst case, where $c = 1$ when $d - p$ is odd and $c = 0$ when $d - p$ is even. It is not clear whether the logarithmic factor is really needed, or that it is just an artifact of the proof technique.

The result of [44] can easily be extended to obtain a bound of $O(n^{2+\varepsilon})$, for any $\varepsilon > 0$, on the complexity of the zone of an algebraic surface σ_0 (of constant description complexity) in an arrangement of n algebraic surfaces in $\mathbb{R}^3$, as above. Intuitively, the proof proceeds by cutting each of the given surfaces along its intersection curve with σ_0, and by shrinking the surface away from that curve, thus leaving a 'tiny' gap there. These modifications transform the zone of σ into a single cell in the arrangement of the new surfaces, and the result of [44] can then be applied. (The same technique has been used earlier in [32], to obtain a near-linear bound on the complexity of the zone of an arc in a 2-dimensional arrangement of arcs.) Once the bound on the complexity of a single cell is extended to higher dimensions, it should lead right away to a similar bound for a zone of a surface. A similar technique implies that the complexity of the zone of an algebraic or convex surface in an arrangement of n $(d-1)$-simplices in $\mathbb{R}^d$ is $O(n^{d-1}\log n)$ [13, 67].

Generalized Voronoi Diagrams

One of the interesting applications of the new lower bounds on the complexity of lower envelopes is to generalized Voronoi diagrams in higher dimensions. Let S be a set of n 'simply-shaped' pairwise-disjoint convex objects in d-space (or in higher dimensions), and let ρ be some metric. The *Voronoi diagram* Vor(S) of S under the metric ρ is defined, as usual, as the decomposition of d-space into *Voronoi cells* $V(s)$, for $s \in S$, where

$$V(s) = \{x \in \mathbb{R}^d \mid \rho(x, s) \leq \rho(x, s') \text{ for all } s' \in S\}.$$

The problem is to study the combinatorial complexity of Vor(S), and to devise efficient algorithms for its construction. In the classical case, in which ρ is the Euclidean metric and the objects in S are singletons (points), the maximum possible complexity of Vor(S) is $\Theta(n^{\lceil d/2 \rceil})$ (see, e.g., [30]). In three dimensions, this bound is $\Theta(n^2)$. It has been a long-standing open problem whether a similar quadratic or near-quadratic bound holds in 3-space for more general objects and metrics. As is well known [33], the Voronoi diagram Vor(S) is the 'minimization diagram' (projection onto the xyz-hyperplane) of the lower envelope $\min_{s \in S} \rho(x, s)$ (in 4-space). Under reasonable assumptions on the shape of the objects in S and on the metric ρ, the resulting trivariate functions $\rho(x, s)$ can be assumed to be piecewise-algebraic of constant maximum degree, and the recent results concerning lower envelopes, as reported above, give an upper bound of $O(n^{3+\varepsilon})$, for any $\varepsilon > 0$, for the complexity of Vor(S). Thus the problem stated above calls for improving this bound by roughly another factor of n. It thus appears to be a considerably more difficult problem than that of lower envelopes, and the only hope of making progress there is to exploit the special structure of the functions $\rho(x, s)$.

Fortunately, some progress on this problem was recently done. It was shown in [23] that the complexity of the Voronoi diagram is $O(n^2 \alpha(n) \log n)$, for the case where the objects of S are lines, and the metric ρ is a convex distance function induced by a convex *polytope* with a constant number of facets. (Note that the L_1 and L_∞ metrics are special cases of such distance functions. Note also that such a distance function is not necessarily a metric, because it will fail to be symmetric if the defining polytope is not centrally symmetric.) The best known lower bound for the complexity of the diagram in this special case is $\Omega(n^2 \alpha(n))$. In another recent paper [18], it is shown that the maximum complexity of the L_1-Voronoi diagram of a set of n points in $\mathbb{R}^3$ is $\Theta(n^2)$. However, no near-quadratic bound is known for point sites and more general polyhedral convex distance functions. We hope that these results will open up this research direction, and lead to many subsequent results. The most intriguing unsolved problem is to obtain a similar bound for a set S of n lines in space but under the Euclidean distance. The proof technique of [23] breaks down in this case. Other, more tractable open problems are to extend these results to sets of more general convex objects (e.g., convex polytopes, or just singleton points) under the same polyhedral convex distance functions.

An interesting special case of these problems involves *dynamic Voronoi diagrams* for moving points in the plane. Let S be a set of n points in the plane, each moving along some line at some fixed velocity. The goal is to bound the number of combinatorial changes of Vor(S) over time. This dynamic Voronoi diagram can easily be transformed into a 3-dimensional Voronoi diagram, by adding the time t as a third coordinate. The points become lines in 3-space, and the metric is a distance function induced by a horizontal disc (that is, the distance from a point $p(x_0, y_0, t_0)$ to a line ℓ is the Euclidean distance from p to the point of intersection of ℓ with the horizontal plane $t = t_0$). Here too the open problem is to derive a near-quadratic bound on the complexity of the diagram. Cubic or near-cubic bounds are known for this problem, even under more general settings [36, 38, 64], but subcubic bounds are known only in some very special cases [22].

Next, consider the problem of bounding the complexity of generalized Voronoi diagrams in higher dimensions. As mentioned above, when the objects in S are n points in $\mathbb{R}^d$ and the metric is Euclidean, the complexity of Vor(S) is $O(n^{\lceil d/2 \rceil})$. As d increases, this becomes drastically smaller than the naive $O(n^{d+1})$ bound or the improved bound, $O(n^{d+\varepsilon})$, obtained by viewing the Voronoi diagram as a lower envelope in $\mathbb{R}^{d+1}$. The same bound of $O(n^{\lceil d/2 \rceil})$ has recently been obtained in [18] for the complexity of the L_∞-diagram of n points in d-space (it was also shown that this bound is tight in the worst case). It is thus tempting to conjecture that the maximum complexity of generalized Voronoi diagrams in higher dimensions is close to this bound. Unfortunately, this was recently shown to be false in [11], where a lower bound of $\Omega(n^{d-1})$ is given. The sites used in this construction are convex polytopes, and the distance is either Euclidean or a polyhedral convex distance function. For $d = 3$, this lower bound does not contradict the conjecture made above, that the complexity of generalized Voronoi diagrams should be at most near-quadratic in this case. Also, in higher dimensions, the conjecture mentioned above is still not refuted when the sites are singleton points. Finally, for the general case, the construction of [11] still leaves a gap of roughly a factor of n between the known upper and lower bounds.

Union of Geometric Objects

A subproblem related to generalized Voronoi diagrams is as follows. Let S and ρ be as above (say, for the 3-dimensional case). Let K denote the region consisting of all points $x \in \mathbb{R}^3$ whose smallest distance from a site in S is at most r, for some fixed parameter $r > 0$. Then $K = \bigcup_{s \in S} B(s, r)$, where $B(s, r) = \{x \in \mathbb{R}^3 \mid \rho(x, s) \le r\}$. We thus face the problem of bounding the combinatorial complexity of the union of n objects in 3-space (of some special type). For example, if S is a set of lines and ρ is the Euclidean distance, the objects are n congruent infinite cylinders in 3-space. In general, if the metric ρ is a distance function induced by some convex body P, the resulting objects are the *Minkowski sums* $s \oplus (-rP)$, for $s \in S$, where $A \oplus B = \{x + y \mid x \in A, y \in B\}$. Of course, this problem can also be stated in any higher dimension.

Since it has been conjectured that the complexity of the whole Voronoi diagram should be near-quadratic (in 3-space), the same conjecture should apply to the (simpler) structure K (whose boundary can be thought of as a 'cross-section' of the diagram at 'height' r). Recently, this conjecture has been confirmed in [14], in the special case where both P and the objects of S are convex polyhedra [14]. Let us discuss this result in more detail. An earlier paper [12] has studied the case involving the union of k arbitrary convex polyhedra in 3-space, with a total of n faces. It was shown there that the complexity of the union is $O(k^3 + nk \log^2 k)$, and can be $\Omega(k^3 + nk\alpha(k))$ in the worst case. The upper bound was subsequently improved to $O(k^3 + nk \log k)$ [15], which still leaves a small gap between the upper and lower bounds. In the subsequent paper [14], these bounds were improved in the special case where the polyhedra in question are Minkowski sums of the form $s_i \oplus P$, where the s_i's are k pairwise-disjoint convex polyhedra, P is a convex polyhedron, and the total number of faces of these Minkowski sums is n. The improved bounds are $O(nk \log k)$ and $\Omega(nk\alpha(k))$. They are indeed near-quadratic, as conjectured (in fact, they are much better than quadratic when $k \ll n$).

However, the case where P is a ball (namely, the case of the Euclidean distance) is still open. The simplest unsolved instance of this problem is to establish a near-quadratic upper bound for the complexity of the union of n congruent infinite cylinders in 3-space.

There are various extensions that are also interesting to consider. First, it would be interesting to study the problem in higher dimensions. This is likely to be much more difficult, so one should look at relatively simple cases, like the union of axis-parallel hypercubes, or of other simply-shaped objects. The case of axis-parallel hypercubes has recently been solved in [18], where it was shown that the maximum complexity of the union of n such hypercubes in d-space is $\Theta(n^{\lceil d/2 \rceil})$, and this improves to $\Theta(n^{\lfloor d/2 \rfloor})$ when all the hypercubes have the same size. Second, we can consider the case of more general objects (not necessarily Minkowski sums) which satisfy some 'fatness' properties, extending results obtained in [56] for 'fat' triangles in the plane. For example, what is the complexity of the union of n arbitrary (non-isothetic) unit cubes in $\mathbb{R}^3$?

Vertical Decomposition

In many algorithmic applications, one needs to be able to decompose a d-dimensional arrangement, or certain portions thereof, into a small number of subcells, each having constant description complexity. In a typical setup where this problem arises, we need to process in a certain manner an arrangement of n surfaces in d-space. We choose a random sample of r of the surfaces, for some sufficiently large constant r, construct the arrangement of these r surfaces, and decompose it into subcells as above. Since no such subcell is crossed by any surface in the random sample, it follows by standard ε-net theory [24, 47, 53] that, with high probability, none of these subcells is crossed by more than $O(\frac{n}{r} \log r)$ of the n given surfaces. (For this result to hold, it is essential that each of these subcells have constant description complexity.) This allows us to break the problem into recursive subproblems, one for each of these subcells, solve each subproblem separately, and then combine their outputs to obtain a solution for the original problem. The efficiency of this method crucially depends on the number of subcells. The smaller this number is, the faster is the resulting algorithm. (We note that the construction of a 'good' sample of r surfaces can also be performed deterministically, e.g., using the techniques of Matoušek [54].)

The only general-purpose known technique for decomposing an arrangement of surfaces into subcells of constant description complexity is the *vertical decomposition* technique. In this method, we erect a vertical 'wall' up and down (in the x_d-direction) from each $(d-2)$-dimensional face of the arrangement, and extend these walls until they hit another surface. This results in a decomposition of the arrangement into subcells so that each subcell has a unique top facet and a unique bottom facet, and each vertical line cuts it in a connected (possibly empty) interval. We next project each resulting subcell on the hyperplane $x_d = 0$, and apply recursively the same technique within each resulting $(d-1)$-dimensional projected cell, and then 'lift' this decomposition back into d-space, by extending each subcell c in the projection into the vertical cylinder $c \times \mathbb{R}$, and by cutting the original cell by these cylinders. We continue the recursion in this manner until we reach $d = 1$, and thereby obtain the vertical decomposition of the given arrangement. The resulting subcells have the desired properties. Furthermore, if we assume that the originally given surfaces are algebraic of constant maximum degree, then the resulting subcells are semi-algebraic and are defined by a constant number of polynomials of constant maximum degree (although the latter degree can grow quite fast with d). In what follows, we ignore the algebraic complexity of the subcells of the vertical decomposition, and will be mainly interested in bounding their number as a function of n, the number of given surfaces.

It was shown in [20] that the number of cells in such a vertical decomposition is $O(n^{2d-3}\beta(n))$, where $\beta(n)$ is a slowly growing function of n (related to the inverse Ackermann's function). However, the only known lower bound is the trivial $\Omega(n^d)$, so there is a considerable gap here, for $d > 3$; for $d = 3$ the two bounds nearly coincide. Improving the upper bound appears to be a very difficult task. This problem has been open since 1989; it seems difficult enough to preempt, at the present state of knowledge, any specific conjecture on the true maximum complexity of the vertical decomposition in $d > 3$ dimensions.

The bound stated above applies to the vertical decomposition of an entire arrangement of surfaces. In many applications, however, one is interested in the vertical decomposition of only a portion of the arrangement, e.g., a single cell, the region lying below the lower envelope of the given surfaces, the zone of some surface, a specific collection of cells of the arrangement, etc. Since, in general, the complexity of such a portion is known (or conjectured) to be smaller than the complexity of the entire arrangement, one would like to conjecture that a similar phenomenon applies to vertical decompositions. Very recently, it was shown in [63] that the complexity of the vertical decomposition of a single cell in an arrangement of n surface patches in 3-space, as above, is $O(n^{2+\varepsilon})$, for any $\varepsilon > 0$. As mentioned above, this leads to a near-quadratic algorithm for computing such a single cell, which implies that motion planning for fairly general systems with three degrees of freedom can be performed in near-quadratic time, thus settling a major open problem in the area. A challenging open problem is to obtain improved bounds for the complexity of the vertical decomposition of the region lying below the lower envelope of n d-variate functions, for $d \geq 3$.

Finally, an interesting special case is that of hyperplanes. For such arrangements, the vertical decomposition is a too cumbersome construct, because there are other easy methods for decomposing each cell into simplices, whose total number is $O(n^d)$. Still, it is probably a useful exercise to understand the complexity of the vertical decomposition of an arrangement of n hyperplanes in d-space. A recent result of [37] gives an almost tight bound of $O(n^4 \log n)$ for this problem in 4-space, but nothing significantly better than the general bound is known for $d > 4$. Another interesting special case is that of triangles in 3-space. This has been studied by [28, 67], where almost tight bounds were obtained for the case of a single cell ($O(n^2 \log^2 n)$), and for the entire arrangement ($O(n^2 \alpha(n) \log n + K)$, where K is the complexity of the undecomposed arrangement). The first bound is slightly better than the general bound of [63] mentioned above. The paper [67] also derives sharp complexity bounds for the vertical decomposition of many cells in such an arrangement, including the case of all nonconvex cells.

Other Applications

We conclude this survey by mentioning some additional applications of the new advances in the study of arrangements. We have already discussed in some detail the motion planning application, and have seen how the new results lead to a near-optimal algorithm for the general motion planning problem with three degrees of freedom. Here we discuss two other kinds of applications: to visibility problems in three dimensions, and to geometric optimization.

Visibility in Three Dimensions:

Let us consider a special case of the so-called *aspect graph* problem, which has recently attracted much attention, especially in the context of three-dimensional scene analysis and object recognition in computer vision. The aspect graph of a scene represents all topologically-different views of the scene. For background and a survey of recent research on aspect graphs, see [19]. Here we will show how the new complexity bounds for lower envelopes, with some additional machinery, can be used to derive near-tight bounds on the number of views of polyhedral terrains.

Let K be a *polyhedral terrain* in 3-space; that is, K is the graph of a continuous piecewise-linear bivariate function, so it intersects each vertical line in exactly one point. Let n denote the number of edges of K. A line ℓ is said to *lie over* K if every point on ℓ lies on or above K. Let $\mathcal{L}_K$ denote the space of all lines that lie over K. (Since lines in 3-space can be parametrized by four real parameters, we can regard $\mathcal{L}_K$ as a subset of 4-space.) The *lower envelope* of $\mathcal{L}_K$ consists of those lines in $\mathcal{L}_K$ that touch at least one edge of K. Assuming general position of the edges of K, a line in $\mathcal{L}_K$ (or any line, for that matter) can touch at most four edges of K. We estimate the combinatorial complexity of this lower envelope, in terms of the number of its *vertices*, namely those lines in $\mathcal{L}_K$ that touch four distinct edges of K. It was shown in [43] that the number of vertices of $\mathcal{L}_K$, as defined above, is $O(n^3 \cdot 2^{c\sqrt{\log n}})$, for some absolute positive constant c.

We give here a sketch of the proof. We fix an edge e_0 of K, and bound the number of lines of $\mathcal{L}_K$ that touch e_0 and three other edges of K, with the additional proviso that the three other contact points all lie on one fixed side of the vertical plane passing through e_0. We then multiply this bound by the number n of edges, to obtain a bound on the overall number of vertices of $\mathcal{L}_K$. We first rephrase this problem in terms of the lower envelope of a certain collection of surface patches in 3-space, one patch for each edge of K (other than e_0), and then exploit the results on lower envelopes reviewed above.

The space $\mathcal{L}_{e_0}$ of oriented lines that touch e_0 is 3-dimensional: each such line ℓ can be specified by a triple (t, k, ζ), where t is the point of contact with e_0 (or, more precisely, the distance of that point from one designated endpoint of e_0), and $k = \tan \theta$, $\zeta = -\cot \phi$, where (θ, ϕ) are the spherical coordinates of the direction of ℓ, that is, θ is the orientation of the xy-projection of ℓ, and ϕ is the angle between ℓ and the positive z-axis.

For each edge $e \neq e_0$ of K, let σ_e be the surface patch in $\mathcal{L}_{e_0}$ consisting of all points (t, k, ζ) representing lines that touch e and are oriented from e_0 to e. Note that if $(t, k, \zeta) \in \sigma_e$ then

$\zeta' > \zeta$ iff the line (t, k, ζ') passes below e. It thus follows that a line ℓ in $\mathcal{L}_{e_0}$ is a vertex of the lower envelope of $\mathcal{L}_K$ if and only if ℓ is a vertex of the lower envelope of the surfaces σ_e in the $tk\zeta$-space, where the height of a point is its ζ-coordinate. It is easy to show that these surfaces are algebraic of constant description complexity. Actually, it is easily seen that the number s of intersections of any triple of these surfaces is at most 2. The paper [43] studies the special case of lower envelopes of collections of such algebraic surface patches in 3-space, with the extra assumptionthat $s = 2$. It is shown there that the complexity of the lower envelope of such a collection is $O(n^2 \cdot 2^{c\sqrt{\log n}})$, for some absolute positive constant c, a bound that is slightly better than the general bound stated above. These arguments immediately complete the proof. (This bound has been independently obtained by Pellegrini [60], using a different proof technique.) Recently, de Berg [26] has given a lower bound construction, in which the lower envelope of $\mathcal{L}_K$ has complexity $\Omega(n^3)$, implying that the upper bound stated above is almost tight in the worst case.

We can extend the above result as follows. Let K be a polyhedral terrain, as above. Let $\mathcal{R}_K$ denote the space of all rays in 3-space with the property that each point on such a ray lies on or above K. We define the lower envelope of $\mathcal{R}_K$ and its vertices in complete analogy to the case of $\mathcal{L}_K$. By inspecting the proof sketched above, one easily verifies that it applies equally well to rays instead of lines. Hence we obtain that the number of vertices of $\mathcal{R}_K$, as defined above, is also $O(n^3 \cdot 2^{c\sqrt{\log n}})$.

We can apply this bound to obtain a bound of $O(n^5 \cdot 2^{c'\sqrt{\log n}})$, for any $c' > c$, on the number of topologically-different orthographic views (i.e., views from infinity) of a polyhedral terrain K with n edges. We omit here details of this analysis, which can be found in [43]. The paper [29] gives a lower bound construction that produces $\Omega(n^5\alpha(n))$ topologically-different orthographic views of a polyhedral terrain, so the above bound is almost tight in the worst case. It is also instructive to note that, if K is an arbitrary polyhedral set in 3-space with n edges, then the maximum possible number of topologically-different orthographic views of K is $\Theta(n^6)$ [61].

Consider next the extension of the above analysis to bound the number of perspective views of a terrain. As shown recently in [6], the problem can be reduced to the analysis of $O(n^3)$ lower envelopes of appropriate collections of 5-variate functions. This leads to an overall bound of $O(n^{8+\varepsilon})$, for any $\varepsilon > 0$, for the number of topologically-different perspective views of a polyhedral terrain with n edges. This bound is also known to be almost tight in the worst case, as follows from another lower bound construction given in [29]. Again, in contrast, If K is an arbitrary polyhedral set with n edges, the maximum possible number of topologically-different perspective views of K is $\Theta(n^9)$ [61].

Geometric Optimization:

In the past few years, many problems in geometric optimization have been attacked by techniques that reduce the problem to a problem involving arrangements of surfaces in higher dimensions. These reduced problems sometimes call for the construction of, and searching in lower envelopes or other substructures in such arrangements. Hence the area of geometric optimization is a natural extension, and a good application area, of the study of arrangements, as described above.

One of the basic techniques for geometric optimization is the *parametric searching* technique, originally proposed by Megiddo [58]. It has been used to solve a wide variety of geometric optimization problems, including many of those that involve arrangements. Some specific results of this kind include:

- **Selecting distances in the plane:** Given a set S of n points in $\mathbb{R}^2$ and a parameter $k \leq \binom{n}{2}$, find the k-th largest distance among the points of S [2]. Here the problem reduces to the construction and searching in 2-dimensional arrangements of congruent disks.

- **The segment center problem:** Given a set S of n points in $\mathbb{R}^2$, and a line segment e, find a placement of e that minimizes the largest distance from the points of S to e [35].

Using lower envelopes of bivariate functions, the problem can be solved in $O(n^{1+\epsilon})$ time, for any $\epsilon > 0$, improving substantially a previous near-quadratic solution given in [4].

- **Extremal polygon placement:** Given a convex polygon P and a closed polygonal environment Q, find the largest similar copy of P that is fully contained in Q [66]. This is just an extension of the corresponding motion planning problem, where the size of P is fixed. The running time of the algorithm is almost the same as that of the motion planning algorithm given in [51, 52].

- **Width in three dimensions:** Compute the width of a set S of n points in $\mathbf{R}^2$; this is the smallest distance between two parallel planes enclosing S between them. This problem has been studied in a series of papers [1, 7, 21], and the current best bound is $O(n^{3/2+\epsilon})$, for any $\epsilon > 0$ [7]. The technique used in attacking this and the two following problems reduce them to problems involving lower envelopes in 4 dimensions, where we need to construct and to search in such an envelope.

- **Biggest stick in a simple polygon:** Compute the longest line segment that can fit inside a given simple polygon with n edges. The current best solution is $O(n^{3/2+\epsilon})$, for any $\epsilon > 0$ [7] (see also [1, 9]).

- **Smallest-width annulus:** Compute the annulus of smallest width that encloses a given set of n points in the plane. Again, the current best solution is $O(n^{3/2+\epsilon})$, for any $\epsilon > 0$ [7] (see also [1, 9]).

- **Geometric matching:** Consider the problem where we are given two sets S_1, S_2 of n points in the plane, and we wish to compute a minimum-weight matching in the complete bipartite graph $S_1 \times S_2$, where the weight of an edge (p, q) is the Euclidean distance between p and q. One can also consider the analogous nonbipartite version of the problem, which involves just one set S of $2n$ points, and the complete graph on S. The goal is to explore the underlying geometric structure of these graphs, to obtain faster algorithms than those available for general abstract graphs.

  It was shown in [68] that both the bipartite and the nonbipartite versions of the problem can be solved in time close to $n^{2.5}$. Recently, a fairly sophisticated application of vertical decomposition in 3-dimensional arrangements, given in [3], has improved the running time for the bipartite case to $O(n^{2+\epsilon})$, for any $\epsilon > 0$. This technique does not yet extend to the nonbipartite case, which remains an interesting open problem.

This list is by no means exhaustive.

A final comment is that, although the parametric searching technique yields algorithms that are efficient theoretically, they are usually quite difficult to implement, or even just to describe, because an efficient implementation of algorithms based on parametric searching requires the existence of a fast parallel algorithm for some related problem. Moreover, in most of the applications, one needs to compute the roots of high-degree polynomials, which, if done exactly, slows down the algorithm considerably.

Some effort was made recently to replace parametric searching by alternative, simpler, and more geometric-oriented techniques. The alternative methods that have been used for problems involving arrangements include randomization [7, 55], and expander graphs [49, 50]. However, these techniques work so far only in some special cases, and no general technique is known.

References

[1] P.K. Agarwal, B. Aronov and M. Sharir, Computing envelopes in four dimensions with applications, *Proc. 10th ACM Symp. on Computational Geometry* (1994), 348–358.

[2] P.K. Agarwal, B. Aronov, M. Sharir and S. Suri, Selecting distances in the plane, *Algorithmica* 9 (1993), 495–514.

[3] P.K. Agarwal, A. Efrat and M. Sharir, Vertical decompositions of shallow levels in arrangements and their applications, *Proc. 11th ACM Symp. on Computational Geometry* (1995).

[4] P.K. Agarwal, A. Efrat, M. Sharir and S. Toledo, Computing a segment-center for a planar point set, *J. Algorithms* 15 (1993), 314–323.

[5] P.K. Agarwal, O. Schwarzkopf and M. Sharir, The overlay of lower envelopes in 3-space and its applications, to appear in *Discrete Comput. Geom.*

[6] P.K. Agarwal and M. Sharir, On the number of views of polyhedral terrains, *Discrete Comput. Geom.* 12 (1994), 177–182.

[7] P.K. Agarwal and M. Sharir, Efficient randomized algorithms for some geometric optimization problems, *Proc. 11th ACM Symp. on Computational Geometry*, 1995.

[8] P. Agarwal, M. Sharir and P. Shor, Sharp upper and lower bounds for the length of general Davenport Schinzel sequences, *J. Combin. Theory, Ser. A* 52 (1989), 228–274.

[9] P.K. Agarwal, M. Sharir and S. Toledo, New applications of parametric searching in computational geometry. *J. Algorithms* 17 (1994), 292–318.

[10] B. Aronov, M. Pellegrini and M. Sharir, On the zone of a surface in a hyperplane arrangement, *Discrete Comput. Geom.* 9 (1993), 177–186.

[11] B. Aronov, personal communication, 1995.

[12] B. Aronov and M. Sharir, The union of convex polyhedra in three dimensions, *Proc. 34th IEEE Symp. on Foundations of Computer Science* (1993), 518–527.

[13] B. Aronov and M. Sharir, Castles in the air revisited, *Discrete Comput. Geom.* 12 (1994), 119–150.

[14] B. Aronov and M. Sharir, On translational motion planning in three dimensions, *Proc. 10th ACM Symp. on Computationl Geometry* (1994), 21–30.

[15] B. Aronov, M. Sharir and B. Tagansky, The union of convex polyhedra in three dimensions, to appear in *SIAM J. Comput.* (a revised version of [12]).

[16] J.D. Boissonnat and K. Dobrindt, Randomized construction of the upper envelope of triangles in $\mathbb{R}^3$, *Proc. 4th Canadian Conf. on Computational Geometry* (1992), 311–315.

[17] J.D. Boissonnat and K. Dobrindt, On-line randomized construction of the upper envelope of triangles and surface patches in $\mathbb{R}^3$, to appear in *Comp. Geom. Theory Appls.*

[18] J.D. Boissonnat, M. Sharir, B. Tagansky and M. Yvinec, Voronoi diagrams in higher dimensions under certain polyhedral convex distance functions, *Proc. 11th ACM Symp. on Computational Geometry* (1995).

[19] K.W. Bowyer and C.R. Dyer, Aspect graphs: An introduction and survey of recent results, *Int. J. of Imaging Systems and Technology* 2 (1990), 315–328.

[20] B. Chazelle, H. Edelsbrunner, L. Guibas and M. Sharir, A singly exponential stratification scheme for real semi-algebraic varieties and its applications, *Proc. 16th Int. Colloq. on Automata, Languages and Programming* (1989), 179–193.

[21] B. Chazelle, H. Edelsbrunner, L. Guibas and M. Sharir, Diameter, width, closest line pair, and parametric searching, *Discrete Comput. Geom.* 10 (1993), 183–196.

[22] L.P. Chew, Near-quadratic bounds for the L_1 Voronoi diagram of moving points, *Proc. 5th Canadian Conf. on Computational Geometry* (1993), 364–369.

[23] L.P. Chew, K. Kedem, M. Sharir, B. Tagansky and E. Welzl, Voronoi diagrams of lines in three dimensions under a polyhedral convex distance function, *Proc. 6th ACM-SIAM Symp. on Discrete Algorithms* (1995), 197–204.

[24] K.L. Clarkson, New applications of random sampling in computational geometry, *Discrete Comput. Geom.* 2 (1987), 195–222.

[25] K.L. Clarkson and P.W. Shor, Applications of random sampling in computational geometry, II, *Discrete Comput. Geom.* 4 (1989), 387–421.

[26] M. de Berg, personal communication, 1993.

[27] M. de Berg, K. Dobrindt and O. Schwarzkopf, On lazy randomized incremental construction, *Proc. 26th ACM Symp. on Theory of Computing* (1994), 105–114.

[28] M. de Berg, L. Guibas and D. Halperin, Vertical decomposition for triangles in 3-space, *Proc. 10th ACM Symp. on Computational Geometry* (1994), 1–10.

[29] M. de Berg, D. Halperin, M. Overmars and M. van Kreveld, Sparse arrangements and the number of views of polyhedral scenes, Manuscript, 1991.

[30] H. Edelsbrunner, *Algorithms in Combinatorial Geometry*, Springer-Verlag, Heidelberg 1987.

[31] H. Edelsbrunner, The upper envelope of piecewise linear functions: Tight complexity bounds in higher dimensions, *Discrete Comput. Geom.* 4 (1989), 337–343.

[32] H. Edelsbrunner, L. Guibas, J. Pach, R. Pollack, R. Seidel and M. Sharir, Arrangements of curves in the plane: topology, combinatorics, and algorithms, *Theoret. Comput. Sci.* 92 (1992), 319–336.

[33] H. Edelsbrunner and R. Seidel, Voronoi diagrams and arrangements, *Discrete Comput. Geom.* 1 (1986), 25–44.

[34] H. Edelsbrunner, R. Seidel and M. Sharir, On the zone theorem for hyperplane arrangements, *SIAM J. Comput.* 22 (1993), 418–429.

[35] A. Efrat and M. Sharir, A near-linear algorithm for the planar segment center problem, to appear in *Discrete Comput. Geom.*

[36] J.-J. Fu and R.C.T. Lee, Voronoi diagrams of moving points in the plane, *Internat. J. Comput. Geom. Appl.* 1 (1994), 23–32.

[37] L. Guibas, D. Halperin, J. Matoušek and M. Sharir, On vertical decomposition of arrangements of hyperplanes in four dimensions, *Discrete Comput. Geom.* 14 (1995) (in press).

[38] L. Guibas, J. Mitchell and T. Roos, Voronoi diagrams of moving points in the plane, *Proc. 17th Internat. Workshop Graph-Theoret. Concepts Computer Science*, Lecture Notes in Comp. Sci., vol. 570, Springer-Verlag, pp. 113–125.

[39] L. Guibas and M. Sharir, Combinatorics and algorithms of arrangements, in *New Trends in Discrete and Computational Geometry*, (J. Pach, Ed.), Springer-Verlag, 1993, 9–36.

[40] L. Guibas, M. Sharir and S. Sifrony, On the general motion planning problem with two degrees of freedom, *Discrete Comput. Geom.* 4 (1989), 491–521.

[41] D. Halperin, On the complexity of a single cell in certain arrangements of surfaces in 3-space, *Discrete Comput. Geom.* 11 (1994), 1–33.

[42] D. Halperin and M. Sharir, Near-quadratic bounds for the motion planning problem for a polygon in a polygonal environment, *Proc. 34th IEEE Symp. on Foundations of Computer Science* (1993), 382–391.

[43] D. Halperin and M. Sharir, New bounds for lower envelopes in three dimensions with applications to visibility of terrains, *Discrete Comput. Geom.* 12 (1994), 313–326.

[44] D. Halperin and M. Sharir, Almost tight upper bounds for the single cell and zone problems in three dimensions, *Proc. 10th ACM Symp. on Computational Geometry* (1994), 11–20.

[45] D. Halperin and M. Sharir, Arrangements and their applications in robotics: Recent developments, in *The Algorithmic Foundations of Robotics*, K. Goldberg, D. Halperin, J.C. Latombe and R. Wilson, Eds., A.K. Peters, Boston, MA, 1995, 495–511.

[46] S. Hart and M. Sharir, Nonlinearity of Davenport–Schinzel sequences and of generalized path compression schemes, *Combinatorica* 6 (1986), 151–177.

[47] D. Haussler and E. Welzl, ε-nets and simplex range queries, *Discrete Comput. Geom.* 2 (1987), 127–151.

[48] J. Heintz, T. Recio and M.F. Roy, Algorithms in real algebraic geometry and applications to computational geometry, in *Discrete and Computational Geometry: Papers from DIMACS Special Year*, (J. Goodman, R. Pollack, and W. Steiger, Eds.), American Mathematical Society, Providence, RI, 137–163.

[49] M. Katz and M. Sharir, Optimal slope selection via expanders, *Inform. Process. Lett.* 47 (1993), 115–122.

[50] M. Katz and M. Sharir, An expander-based approach to geometric optimization, *Proc. 9th ACM Symp. on Computational Geometry* (1993), 198–207.

[51] K. Kedem and M. Sharir, An efficient motion planning algorithm for a convex rigid polygonal object in 2–dimensional polygonal space, *Discrete Comput. Geom.* 5 (1990), 43–75.

[52] K. Kedem, M. Sharir and S. Toledo, On critical orientations in the Kedem-Sharir motion planning algorithm for a convex polygon in the plane, *Proc. 5th Canadian Conference on Computational Geometry* (1993), 204–209.

[53] J. Komlós, J. Pach and G. Woeginger, Almost tight bound on epsilon–nets, *Discrete and Computational Geometry* 7 (1992), 163–173.

[54] J. Matoušek, Approximations and optimal geometric divide-and-conquer, *Proc. 23rd ACM Symp. on Theory of Computing* (1991), 506–511.

[55] J. Matoušek, Randomized optimal algorithm for slope selection, *Inform. Process. Lett.* 39 (1991), 183–187.

[56] J. Matoušek, J. Pach, M. Sharir, S. Sifrony and E. Welzl, Fat triangles determine linearly many holes, *SIAM J. Comput.* 23 (1994), 154–169.

[57] P. McMullen and G. C. Shephard, *Convex Polytopes and the Upper Bound Conjecture*, Lecture Notes Ser. 3, Cambridge University Press, Cambridge, England, 1971.

[58] N. Megiddo, Applying parallel computation algorithms in the design of serial algorithms, *J. ACM* 30, 852–865.

[59] J. Pach and M. Sharir, The upper envelope of piecewise linear functions and the boundary of a region enclosed by convex plates: Combinatorial analysis, *Discrete Comput. Geom.* 4 (1989), 291–309.

[60] M. Pellegrini, On lines missing polyhedral sets in 3-space, *Proc. 9th ACM Symp. on Computational Geometry* (1993), 19–28.

[61] H. Plantinga and C. Dyer, Visibility, occlusion, and the aspect graph, *International J. Computer Vision*, 5 (1990), 137–160.

[62] J.T. Schwartz and M. Sharir, On the Piano Movers' problem: II. General techniques for computing topological properties of real algebraic manifolds, *Advances in Appl. Math.* 4 (1983), 298–351.

[63] O. Schwarzkopf and M. Sharir, Vertical decomposition of a single cell in 3-dimensional arrangements and its applications, in preparation.

[64] M. Sharir, Almost tight upper bounds for lower envelopes in higher dimensions, *Discrete Comput. Geom.* 12 (1994), 327–345.

[65] M. Sharir and P.K. Agarwal, *Davenport-Schinzel Sequences and Their Geometric Applications*, Cambridge University Press, New York, 1995.

[66] M. Sharir and S. Toledo, Extremal polygon containment problems, *Comput. Geom. Theory Appls.* 4 (1994), 99–118.

[67] B. Tagansky, A new technique for analyzing substructures in arrangements, *Proc. 11th ACM Symp. on Computational Geometry* (1995).

[68] P.M. Vaidya, Geometry helps in matching, *SIAM J. Comput.* 18 (1989), 1201–1225.

[69] A. Wiernik and M. Sharir, Planar realization of nonlinear Davenport–Schinzel sequences by segments, *Discrete Comput. Geom.* 3 (1988), 15–47.

Computing a Shortest Watchman Path in a Simple Polygon in Polynomial-Time

Svante Carlsson*   Håkan Jonsson*

Abstract. In this paper we present the first polynomial-time algorithm for finding the shortest polygonal chain in a simple polygon such that each point of the polygon is visible from some point on the chain. This chain is called the shortest watchman path, or equivalently, the shortest weakly visible curve of the polygon. In proving this result we also give polynomial time algorithms for finding the shortest aquarium-keeper's path that visits all edges of the polygon, and for finding the shortest postman path that visits all vertices of a polygon.

1 Introduction

It has been known for a long time that the so called art gallery problem is NP-hard [1, 16, 18]. This is the problem of finding the smallest set of guards within a simple polygon such that each point of the polygon is visible from at least one guard. At the same time there are many examples of optimization problems and in particular shortest route problems (for instance the Travelling Salesperson Problem) that are NP-hard. The combined problem, to find the shortest closed curve (watchman route) inside a simple polygon such that each point of the polygon is visible to at least one point from the curve seems to be at least as hard as the two above. Therefore, it was quite surprising when Chin and Ntafos showed that it was possible to find, in $O(n^4)$ time, the shortest watchman route that is forced to pass a given point (a *door*) on the boundary of the polygon [6]. This was later improved by Tan *et al.* to $O(n^2)$ time, and also used to solve some related problems [21, 22]. Just recently, Carlsson *et al.* showed that the general problem of finding an overall shortest watchman route *without a given door* can also be solved in polynomial time($O(n^4)$) [3, 17]. Some of the techniques used to solve these problems have also been used to find efficient solutions to some restricted versions of the watchman route problem, such as the Zoo-keeper's and the Aquarium keeper's problem [5, 7, 13, 8].

All the above mentioned problems have the property that the computed curve has to be a route (i.e. closed), since the order it has to visit some given objects in the polygon must be in the same order as they appear along the boundary. For the corresponding and more general *path* problems, where the start and end

---

* Division of Computer Science, Luleå University of Technology, S-971 87 LULEÅ, Sweden. Correspondence (e-mail): `Svante.Carlsson@sm.luth.se` and `Hakan.Jonsson@sm.luth.se` This paper has been supported by a grant from the Swedish Research Council for Engineering Sciences (Teknikvetenskapliga forskningsrådet).

points do not necessarily coincide (at a given door, for instance), this order is not given. Therefore, it has been conjectured that several of these path problems are NP-hard [20].

In this paper we present the first polynomial-time algorithm for finding the shortest polygonal chain in a simple polygon such that each point of the polygon is visible from some point on the chain. This chain is called the shortest watchman path, or equivalently, the shortest weakly visible curve of the polygon. To show how to compute a shortest watchman path, we start by designing an algorithm that computes a shortest postman path, i.e. the shortest path that visits all the vertices of a simple polygon, in $O(n^3)$ time. We then extend this algorithm to solve the somewhat harder Aquarium-keeper's path problem, where the shortest path visits all the edges of a simple polygon, in $O(n^4)$ time. Finally, we show that these ideas can also be extended further to solve the even harder shortest watchman path problem in polynimial time.

Our motivation for this problem comes from applied robotics, where one want to design a rescuing robot that should search a burning building for persons or objects [15, 11]. This result also generalize some illumination problems concerning weak visibility [10, 9, 2, 19].

2   The Shortest Postman Path

To be able to find a shortest watchman path one has to solve the subproblem of determining the order a special set of line segments in a polygon should be visited in to minimize the length of the visiting path. As a first step, we show how to solve the problem of computing a shortest postman path, i.e. a shortest path in a simple polygon that visits all the vertices.

First, we show how to compute a shortest postman path S_{st} forced to start at a given start vertex v_s and end at a given end vertex v_t in a simple polygon **P** containing n vertices. After that, we show how to find the shortest path S_s from a given start vertex on the boundary that visits all other vertices of **P** within the same time and space bounds. Last, we point out how to compute the overall shortest path that visits all vertices of a simple polygon **P**, without any restriction on start or end points.

We start by showing that a shortest path that is required to visit all vertices of a simple polygon does not intersect itself.

Lemma 1. *A shortest postman path S_{st} in a simple polygon* **P** *does not intersect itself.*

Proof Sketch: Each crossing can be removed by performing a local change to the path. The pair of intersecting edges can be substituted by the shortest paths from w_i to w_j and from w_{i+1} to w_{j+1} (dotted lines in the figure) to obtain a shorter path which still visits all vertices of the polygon.   □

If the given start and end vertex are the same, the shortest path S_{st} will be closed and follow the boundary of the polygon. If they are not, we divide the boundary in two directed polygonal chains R and L between v_t and v_s. Let R, the *right* chain, be the counter-clockwise directed polygonal chain of vertices $r_0, r_1, \ldots, r_{\text{rmax}}$ from v_t to v_s and let the *left* directed polygonal chain L be the counter-clockwise chain $l_0, l_1, \ldots, l_{\text{lmax}}$ from v_t to v_s. Note that the polygonal chains R and L are directed from v_t to v_s although we seek a shortest path from v_s to v_t. This reversal of the chains is done to ease the forthcoming presentation (Figure 3).

By using Lemma 1 we can show:

Lemma 2. *A shortest path S_{st} from vertex v_s (i.e. r_{rmax}) to v_t (i.e. r_0) that visits all vertices of a simple polygon $\mathbf{P}$, visits the vertices of R in reversed order so that vertex r_i is visited prior to r_{i-1}, and similar for vertices of L.*

In what follows, we use Lemma 2 together with dynamic programming to show how to find a shortest postman path between two given vertices on the boundary of a polygon $\mathbf{P}$ in $O(n^2)$ time and space.

Consider a shortest path S_{st} that has visited vertex r_i in the right chain and vertex l_j of the left chain on its way from v_s to v_t. Then, by Lemma 2, the next vertex S_{st} visits has to be either r_{i-1} in R or l_{j-1} in L. If the lengths of the shortest paths from r_{i-1} and l_{j-1} that visits the remaining vertices of the polygon are known, we can choose the next vertex of S_{st} in constant time.

Definition 3. $S_{i,j}^L(t)$ is the shortest path starting at l_j and visiting all vertices from r_i to r_1 and l_{j-1} to l_1 before ending at v_t (i.e. r_0 or l_0). Similarly, $S_{i,j}^R(t)$ is the shortest path starting at r_i and visiting all vertices from r_{i-1} to r_1 and l_j to l_1 before ending at v_t. We call the shortest paths $S_{i,j}^L(t)$ and $S_{i,j}^R(t)$ **partial** since they might be a part of the shortest path S_{st}.

We can compute $S_{i,j}^R(t)$ and $S_{i,j}^L(t)$ from the recursive formula

$$\begin{cases} |S_{i,j}^R(t)| = \min(d(r_i, r_{i-1}) + |S_{i-1,j}^R(t)|, d(r_i, l_j) + |S_{i-1,j}^L(t)|) \\ |S_{i,j}^L(t)| = \min(d(l_j, l_{j-1}) + |S_{i,j-1}^L(t)|, d(l_j, r_i) + |S_{i,j-1}^R(t)|) \end{cases} \qquad (1)$$

where $d(p, q)$ is the length of the shortest path between two points p and q inside the polygon. This corresponds to computing the shortest distance to the next vertex on the right chain plus the length of the partial shortest path from that vertex, and similar for the left chain, and then taking the minimum of the two. The lengths of all shortest paths $d(\cdot, \cdot)$ can be computed in $O(n^2)$ time by using a *shortest path tree* [12] for each vertex of $\mathbf{P}$.

By using a dynamic programming scheme, all $|S_{i,j}^R(t)|$ and $|S_{i,j}^L(t)|$ can be computed in $\Theta(n^2)$ time using equation Eq. 1. Using the stored lengths, the shortest path S_{st} from v_s to v_t can be constructed in linear time from v_s using a greedy strategy. We summarize this in the following lemma.

Lemma 4. *The shortest path between two given vertices on the boundary of a simple polygon that visits all other vertices of the polygon can be computed in $O(n^2)$ time and space.*

Using the result in Lemma 4, the overall shortest path that visits all vertices of **P** from a given start vertex v_s on the boundary can be found in $O(n^3)$ time. This complexity can be decreased by observing that there are great similarities between the partial shortest paths used to compute shortest postman paths S_{st} and $S_{s't}$ for adjacent vertices v_s and $v_{s'}$.

Since there are n vertices at which the overall shortest path could end, we need a total of $\Theta(n^2)$ time to find the overall shortest path from a given start point, which we state as a theorem:

Theorem 5. *The shortest path from a given vertex on the boundary of a polygon that visits every other polygon vertex can be found in $O(n^2)$ time and space.*

We also immediately conclude that

Corollary 6. *The overall shortest path in a simple polygon that visits all vertices can be computed in $O(n^3)$ time.*

3 The Shortest Aquarium-Keeper's Path

As a second step towards the solution to the shortest watchman path problem we show a polynomial-time solution to the somewhat easier problem of computing a shortest aquarium-keeper's path , i.e. the shortest path that visits all edges of a simple polygon. The shortest aquarium-keeper's paths resembles shortest watchman paths as where the former visits edges of **P** the later visits specific line segments in **P** as will be described in the next section.

The problem of computing a shortest mailman path that was considered in the previous section could be solved since the vertices of **P** had to be visited in order, as the shortest mailman path could be shown not to intersect itself. By an analogous argument we have

Lemma 7. *A shortest aquarium-keeper's path from point p to point q on the boundary of a simple polygon **P** visits the edges of the clockwise (counter-clockwise) part of the boundary between p and q in order from p to q.*

By Lemma 7 we can understand why the ideas of the solutions to the problems in Section 2 can also be used to find a shortest aquarium-keeper's path. First, we will show how to find a shortest aquarium-keeper's path from a given edge on the boundary of a simple polygon **P** that is forced to end at some other given edge of **P**. To do this we use a dynamic programming scheme similar to the one presented in the previous section, to compute a compact representation of shortest aquarium-keeper's paths from the start edge to all points on the ending edge. Then we show how to obtain a shortest aquarium-keeper's path from a given start edge without any restriction on where to start or to end.

Given the order in which the edges of the polygon **P** should be visited, a shortest aquarium-keeper's path A_{pq} between two points p and q on the boundary can be computed in linear time using the polygon folding technique by Chin and Ntafos. Their technique make use of the *reflection principle*, which is due to Heron in 100 AD and will be discussed further later on. The polygon **P** is first triangulated and then *unfolded* into a polygonal region called an *hourglass* [4, 5, 6] in linear time using the edges of **P** as mirrors. In this hourglass, the shortest path from p to the mirror image q' of q corresponds directly to A_{pq}. The seemingly hard problem of finding a shortest aquarium-keeper's path that is forced to visit the edges of **P** in a given order can thus be transformed into the problem of computing a shortest path in an hourglass, a problem which can be solved in linear time [12].

Let e_t be a given edge of the polygon **P** on which a shortest aquarium-keeper's path from a given start edge e_s is forced to end. To find a point p_t on e_t where the shortest aquarium-keeper's path ends and the order in which the edges of the polygon **P** is visited in, we compute *folding intervals* on the edges of **P**.

Definition 8. Let $\mathcal{B}$ be a set of chords and edges of a simple polygon **P**. Also let S_p denote a shortest path in **P** from a point p that ends on a given line segment and which is required to visit the elements of $\mathcal{B}$. Then a **folding interval** is a line segment in **P** such that the shortest paths S_{p_1} and S_{p_2} from any pair of points p_1 and p_2 in the folding interval reflect on and visit end points of the elements of $\mathcal{B}$ in the same order, and the length of a shortest path S_p from a point p in the folding interval is a monotone function in the monotone movement of p.

There is a linear number of *sets* of folding intervals on each edge e. Each set contains folding intervals with respect to a unique set of edges the shortest aquarium-keeper's paths starting from e have to visit.

Below, we prove that all points on an edge e such that the order the edges of **P** are visited in by shortest aquarium-keeper's paths from the points to e_s is the same, form an interval on e. Hence, it is meaningful to speak of folding intervals. First we present a fundamental lemma that relates shortest aquarium-keeper's paths to each other.

Lemma 9. *Let p_1 and p_2 be two unique points on a chord c and consider two shortest paths S_1 and S_2 from p_1 and p_2 respectively that reflects on the same set of chords and that start by visiting points x_1 and x_2 on some chords. Then the first part of S_1 from p_1 to x_1 does not intersect with the first part of S_2 from p_2 to x_2.*

Proof Sketch: At least one of the shortest aquarium-keeper's paths can be shortened by instead visiting the first reflection point of the other path. □

Finally, we show the existence of folding intervals.

Lemma 10. *Let q_1 and q_2 be two unique points on a chord c of a simple polygon **P** and let e_s be a given edge on the boundary. Let S_{q_1} and S_{q_2} be shortest paths from q_1 and q_2 to e_s respectively that reflects on a subset $\mathcal{B}$ of chords of the polygon **P** in the same order.*

Then for all points p between q_1 and q_2 there is a shortest path S_p from e_s that visits the subset $\mathcal{B}$ of chords in the same order as S_{q_1} and S_{q_2}.

Proof Sketch: Follows from Lemma 9 and induction over the subset $\mathcal{B}$. □

From this we now get

Corollary 11. *The subset of points on an edge that share the same order in which a shortest aquarium-keeper's path from a point in the subset visits a set of edges, is connected.*

3.1 An Algorithm for Computing a Shortest Aquarium-Keeper's Path

In this section, we show how to compute the shortest aquarium-keeper's path from a given edge e_s by computing sets of folding intervals on the edges of the polygon. We begin by discussing an algorithm for computing a shortest aquarium-keeper's path from e_s forced to end on an edge e_t. Since the lengths of shortest aquarium-keeper's paths from points within a folding interval changes monotonically, this approach guarantees that once a set of folding intervals on an edge e has been computed, the overall shortest aquarium-keeper's path from e_s forced to end on e will end at an end point of a folding interval. By computing the shortest aquarium-keeper's path forced to end on each of the edges of the polygon, we get the overall shortest aquarium-keeper's path by simply comparing their lengths.

Divide the boundary of $\mathbf{P}$ between the edge e_s and the edge e_t in two directed polygonal chains $R = r_0, r_1, \ldots, r_{rmax}$ and $L = l_0, l_1, \ldots, l_{lmax}$, where R is orientated counter-clockwise and L clockwise. By Lemma 7, a shortest aquarium-keeper's path from e_s to some point on e has to visit the edges $er_i = \overline{r_i r_{i-1}}$ of R and $el_j = \overline{l_j l_{j-1}}$ of L in order. For each pair of edges er_i of R and el_j of L there is a set of folding intervals $\mathcal{E}_{i,j}^R$ on er_i and a set of folding intervals $\mathcal{E}_{i,j}^L$ on el_j. Note that the set of folding intervals $\mathcal{E}_{i,j}^R$ ($\mathcal{E}_{i,j}^L$) contain a compact representation of all shortest aquarium-keeper's path that starts by visiting the edge er_i (el_j) and than visits the edges $er_{i-1}, \ldots, er_1$ of R and $el_j, \ldots, el_1$ of L ($er_i, \ldots, er_1$ and $el_{i-1}, \ldots, el_1$) before ending at e_s. For clarity, we also point out that $\mathcal{E}_{i,j}^R$ is computed using $\mathcal{E}_{i-1,j}^R$ on er_{i-1} and $\mathcal{E}_{i-1,j}^L$ on el_j, and that $\mathcal{E}_{i,j}^L$ is computed using $\mathcal{E}_{i,j-1}^R$ on er_i and $\mathcal{E}_{i,j-1}^L$ on el_{j-1}. To compute the folding intervals we use a dynamic programming technique similar to that in Section 2.

As for the shortest mailman path problem we have to decide for each point on an edge el_j (or er_i) if we should go to the next edge on the right chain or on the left chain to get the shortest path to e_t, visiting all remaining edges. Due to Corollary 11 and the definition of folding interval, we only need to compute the end points of the folding intervals on the edge, given the edges remaining to visit.

To compute the folding intervals on an edge, e, when we have left to visit all edges on the right chain up to er_i and all edges up to el_j on the left chain, we first compute the folding intervals on e if we are forced to visit el_j first, and then we compute the same if we are forced to visit er_i first. Finally, we merge the two sets of folding intervals in linear time by computing which set of folding intervals is relevant, for each point on e.

We will start by describing how we can compute the set of folding intervals on e when forced to start by visiting el_j. We do this by a sliding operation on el_j using both end points of each folding interval, in $\mathcal{E}_{i,j}^L$, as event points for the sliding. During the sliding we maintain the following invariant: When all folding intervals g_m for $m \leq k$ have been considered, a set of folding intervals on e has been computed that contains a compact representation of all shortest aquarium-keeper's paths from e that are forced to first visit el_j at some of the folding intervals $g_0, \ldots, g_m$, where g_k is the k:th folding interval of $\mathcal{E}_{i,j}^L$.

Assume that we slide on el_j from right to left. Also assume that we have computed the invariant up to g_m. If the next event point in the sliding is a left end point of a folding interval we can compute a new tentative endpoint of a folding interval on e. This can be done since we know the last segment of the partial shortest aquarium-keeper's path at the end point, and the total length of the path. By making a perfect reflection on el_j we get the position of the tentative interval end point on e.

We then reach the right end point of the folding interval g_{m+1} directly to the left of the previous one. In the same way as above we can compute a new tentative interval end point on e. If this new tentative interval end point comes before the latest tentative interval endpoint so far computed, we know that somewhere in between them is a point, on e, from which the length of a shortest aquarium-keeper's path is the same no matter whether it pass trough one or the other folding interval. This point can be computed in constant time, with the information stored for each folding interval. Let this new point be the new tentative interval end point, and let it replace the two latest. If this new tentative interval end point still comes before another tentative interval end point computed earlier, we repeat this procedure until it is not. The reason for us being able to do this relies heavily on the fact that two shortest aquarium-keepers paths can not intersect (Lemma 10).

After the sweep of el_j we also add the end points of e as interval end points to a set $\mathcal{E}_l$ of tentative interval end points thus formed. We also perform a symmetrical sweep on er_i to get another set of tentative end points $\mathcal{E}_r$ on e. We then scan the interval end points of the two tentative sets $\mathcal{E}_l$ and $\mathcal{E}_r$ from left to right on e to see which folding intervals gives the shortest aquarium-keeper's paths. The folding intervals that remain after this sweep, form the resulting set of folding intervals on e. Note that due to Lemma 10, this last sweep may introduce at most one new folding interval end point where it is equally far to start by going to el_j or er_i first.

After having computed the event set for the last edge, e_t, we also have to check if there is a path with the first segment perpendicular to e_t that is shorter than all the other paths.

The complexity of the sliding operation depends essentially on the number of folding intervals, or event points, considered. A *new* event point is a point on an edge such that the shortest aquarium-keeper's path from the point does not pass through any other event point (in a set of folding intervals on some edge). Other event points are called *inherited*. We have:

Lemma 12. *An event point q of an event set E is directly inherited by at most one event set.*

Proof Sketch: At q we have a shortest path visiting the edges given by E. From Heron's reflection principle we know that for any point that will have a shortest path trough q the path has to make a perfect reflection at q. So, there is only one point, p, on the boundary where the shortest path from p to e_s that makes a perfect reflection at q and visit the set of edges given by E. □

We can also show by using Lemma 10 and the definition of folding intervals that the number of new event points is also bounded.

Lemma 13. *In each event set computed, a constant number of event points are new.*

Lemma 14. *The total number of event points in all sets of folding intervals is $O(n^3)$.*

Proof Sketch: By Lemma 12, event points are directly inherited by at most one event set. In each step during the process of computing sets of folding intervals, an event point can be inherited by at most one of two sets of folding intervals. At most it can be re-inherited a linear number of times. Since there are $O(n^2)$ number of sets of folding intervals containing a constant number of new event points each, it follows that there are $O(n^3)$ event points in total. □

We can now state the main theorem of this section:

Theorem 15. *A shortest aquarium-keeper's path of a simple polygon can be computed in $O(n^4)$ time and $O(n^3)$ space.*

Proof Sketch: The time to compute the shortest aquarium-keeper's path between two given edges can easily be shown to be proportional to the total number of folding intervals. By a similar technique as for the shortest mailman path we can compute the shortest aquarium-keeper's path from a given edge to any other edge in the polygon. Even though the technique is similar the proof is much more complicated, and is omitted due to space restrictions.

By computing the shortest aquarium-keeper's path from all possible start edges we get the claimed time and space bound. □

4 Computing a Shortest Watchman Path

In this section we will present the main contribution of this paper, a polynomial time algorithm that solves the problem of finding a shortest path in a simple polygon such that each point of the polygon is visible from some point on the path. As will be shown, the computation of a shortest watchman path has some resemblance that of computing the shortest aquarium-keeper's path. These similarities enables us to use the dynamic programming scheme presented in previous sections of this paper in order to build an algorithm, although in a much more intricate way.

The most crucial difference between the two kinds of paths, is that the line segments a shortest watchman path is forced to visit are located inside the polygon and that these segments might intersect each other. Whereas a shortest aquarium-keeper's path always reflects on the edges of the polygon, a shortest watchman path might also make crossing contacts (to be defined later on) with the intersecting line segments.

In a simple polygon without holes, only reflex vertices might block the view. This means that to guard the entire polygon $\mathbf{P}$, a watchman has to at least look around every reflex vertex that obstructs the view. An edge e at a reflex vertex v can be extended inside $\mathbf{P}$ from v until the extension reach the boundary at a point q. The line segment (actually a chord) $\overline{vq}$ thus constructed is called an *essential cut*, since a watchman that visits the cut will also by definition see the edge e. To visit the essential cuts implies seeing the edges incident to the reflex vertices of the polygon.

We say that a point lies to the right (left) of a cut, if the point lies locally to the right (left) in the sub-polygon separated by the cut. An essential cut c is a *forward essential cut with respect to a point* p if p lies to the right of c. An essential cut c *dominates* an other essential cut c' if all points in $\mathbf{P}$ to the left of c are also to the left of c'. An essential cut not dominated by any other essential cut is called *proper*. By definition, visiting the proper forward essential cuts implies visiting all dominated essential cuts (Figure 5). This gives us:

Lemma 16. *It is sufficient and necessary for a shortest watchman path to visit all proper backward essential cuts.*

A shortest watchman path ends on a forward proper essential cut. Hence, it suffices to choose the ending point of a shortest watchman path from points on the proper forward essential cuts in order to get the optimum path. Our way to do this selection of an end point is by sliding along the proper forward essential cuts.

The set of proper forward essential cuts can be computed in $O(n \log n)$ time. To do this we use a ray shooting data structure as presented by Guibas *et al.* [12] and Hershberger and Suri [14].

The fact that the proper forward essential cuts might intersect implies that a shortest watchman path can visit all these cuts while only reflecting on a small subset of them.

We can view the proper forward essential cuts with respect to some point p as having a cyclic ordering specified by the start points of the cuts as they are encountered during a counterclockwise scan of the polygon boundary. In this way each cut has a predecessor and a successor.

There can be $O(n)$ proper forward essential cuts in $\mathbf{P}$. If k is the actual number of proper forward essential cuts, each cut is intersected by at most $n-1$ other cuts. Each cut is subdivided into at most k line segments called *fragments* between the intersection points. In total there are $O(n^2)$ fragments. A shortest watchman path has to, visit all proper forward essential cuts, and therefore at least one fragment of each essential cut. As for shortest aquarium-keeper's path we also have the important property of one shortest watchman route that it is not self-intersecting.

4.1 The Algorithm

The algorithm is based on the observation that a shortest watchman path has to pass via a key point or to share its hourglass with a shortest watchman path forced through a point on a fragment in an immediate surrounding of a key point. A *key point* is either a fragment end point or an order changing event point on a fragment as defined in Section 3. Note that a key point on an essential cut is defined with respect to the end cut and the set of essential cuts the shortest watchman paths from the start cut visit.

For all pairs of essential cuts, we compute shortest watchman paths between the cuts through all key points and then find the shortest watchman path by applying the sliding technique of the previous section. To do this, we need shortest watchman paths between key points.

Shortest Watchman Paths Between Key Points In this section, we show how to compute shortest watchman paths between all pairs of key points. To do this we use dynamic programming in several ways. The main one, however, is similar to the one used in the previous section.

Let C_s and C_e be the given start and end cuts between which shortest watchman paths will eventually be computed. As in Section 3, we first partition the essential cuts of $\mathbf{P}$ into a right and a left set of essential cuts between C_s and C_e. Although a shortest watchman path might jump back-and-forth across the polygon from one chain to the other, the cuts in each set will still be reflected on in order.

In our dynamic programming scheme each entry of $\mathcal{M}^R$ and $\mathcal{M}^L$ contain the shortest path from each fragment end point of the corresponding cut to all key points in the current set of cuts to visit in all possible partitions of such cuts in cuts visited before or after this key point. Furthermore, we have the shortest path from all order changing event points to all key points except from the one ones on the cut just computed.

To maintain the invariant, we use a subroutine, SWP-P1, that relies on a dynamic programming solution itself. In this "second-level" dynamic programming scheme, another subroutine SWP-P2 computes shortest watchman paths from fragment end points on the current cut to key points on cuts already considered. To compute a shortest watchman path from a fragment end point t on SWP-P2 proceeds as follows: For each key point, s', on a cut the shortest watchman path will visit and given which cuts has to be visited before and after s', shortest watchman paths from t to s' and from s' to s are concatenated into a shortest watchman path from t to s forced to reflect on a fragment at s'. The reflection point is then subject to a sliding process until the shortest watchman path coincides with a key point y. Should the two edges of the path joined at the sliding point become collinear during the sliding, we have reached a point where the length of the shortest watchman path has a local minimum and has to be considered. A sliding operation can be performed in linear time.

To determine the time complexities of our subroutines, we first prove a bound on the number of key points:

Lemma 17. *Given the start cut and the set of essential cut shortest watchman paths from the start cut has to visit, there is at most one order changing key point on a fragment.*

Proof. Follows from Lemma 9.

Since there are $O(n^2)$ entries in the matrices, each containing a linear number of fragment end points of an essential cut, we conclude that:

Lemma 18. *There are $O(n^3)$ key points in the matrices $\mathcal{M}^R$ and $\mathcal{M}^L$.*

Lemma 19. SWP-P2 *computes a shortest watchman path between a fragment end point and a key point in $O(n^4)$ time.*

Proof. Since there, by Lemma 18, are at most $O(n^3)$ key points s', and each concatenation of a path followed by a constant number of sliding operations can be performed in linear time, the lemma follows.

By Lemma 18 and Lemma 19, we also have:

Lemma 20. SWP-P1 *computes shortest watchman paths from a point on a fragment to all key points in $O(n^7)$ time during the dynamic programming scheme.*

Corollary 21. *Both matrices $\mathcal{M}_{i,j}^R$ and $\mathcal{M}_{i,j}^L$ can be computed in $O(n^{10})$ time.*

The subroutine SWP-P1 also compute order changing key points on the fragments. In each step in the dynamic programming scheme, $O(n^4)$ shortest watchman paths from fragment end points on the current essential cut are computed. By inspecting the order in which these paths visit the essential cuts and where they reflect with respect to each other, we can find the order changing key points.

Lemma 22. *All order changing key points and the partial shortest watchman paths from these to other key points can be computed in $O(n^{10})$ time.*

Shortest Watchman Paths from Key Points to a Cut In the second step of the algorithm, to find a shortest watchman path in **P**, we use shortest watchman paths between key points to find shortest watchman paths from the key points to the end cut. To do this, we use a subroutine SWP-P3 almost the same as the subroutine SWP-P1 from the end cut. During this dynamic programming scheme, a shortest watchman path from the end cut to a key point s is computed by concatenating subpaths between s and all possible key points s' between s and the end cut, with subpaths from s' to the end cut, and we perform a sliding.

Lemma 23. *Computing shortest watchman paths from all the key points to an essential cut can be done in $O(n^8)$ time given the key points.*

Computing a Shortest Watchman Path In the third and final step, we find a shortest watchman path in **P** by computing shortest watchman paths from the given start cut to the end cut and also in the opposite direction (i.e. from the end cut to the start cut). In this way we get shortest watchman paths from key points to the end cut *as well as* shortest watchman paths from key points to the start cut. In addition to these paths, we also compute partial shortest watchman paths from order changing key points belonging to the set of shortest watchman paths of the other cut. In that way, for each key point s' in any of the sets of key points, we have shortest watchman paths to both cuts.

For each key point s', we concatenate shortest watchman paths from s' to the end cut with shortest watchman paths from s' to the start cut, and perform a sliding operation at s' very similar to the one in **SWP-P3**. In this way we will end up with the shortest watchman path between the cuts.

Lemma 24. *Computing a shortest watchman path between two essential cuts can be done in $O(n^{10})$ time.*

By computing shortest watchman paths between every pair of proper essential cuts, we get the shortest watchman path in **P**.

Theorem 25. *A shortest watchman path in a simple polygon can be computed in $O(n^{12})$ time.*

Proof. By computing shortest watchman paths between each of the $O(n^2)$ pairs of proper essential cuts in **P** in, by Lemma 24, $O(n^{10})$ time each and choosing the shortest one, we get the shortest watchman path in **P** in $O(n^{12})$ time.

References

1. A. Aggarwal. *The Art Gallery Theorem: Its variations, applications and algorithmic aspects.* PhD thesis, John Hopkins University, 1984.
2. B. K. Bhattacharya, A. Mukhopadhyay, and G. T. Toussaint. A linear time alogorithm for computing the shortest line segment from which a polygon is weakly externally visible. In *Proceedings of 2nd WADS*, pages 412–424. Springer-Verlag, 1991.
3. S. Carlsson, H. Jonsson, and B. J. Nilsson. Finding the shortest watchman route in a simple polygon. In *Proceedings of ISAAC'93*, pages 58–67. Springer-Verlag, 1993. LNCS 762.
4. B. Chazelle. Triangulating a simple polygon in linear time. In *Proceedings of the 31th Symposium on Foundations of Computer Science*, pages 220–230, 1990.
5. W. Chin and S. Ntafos. Optimum watchman routes. *Inform. Process. Lett.*, 28:39–44, 1988.
6. W. Chin and S. Ntafos. Shortest watchman routes in simple polygons. *Disc. Comp. Geometry*, 6:9–31, 1991.

7. W. Chin and S. Ntafos. The zookeeper route problem. *Inform. Sci.*, 63:245–259, 1992.

8. J. Czyzowicz, P. Egyed, H. Everett, D. Rappaport, T. Shermer, D. Souvaine, G. Toussaint, and J. Urrutia. The aquarium keeper's problem. In *Proceedings of the 2nd ACM-SIAM Symposium on Discrete Algorithms*, pages 459–464, 1991.

9. G. Das, P. J. Heffernan, and G. Narasimhan. Finding all weakly-visible chords of a polygon in linear time. In *Proceedings of the 4th Scandinavian Workshop on Algorithm Theory (SWAT'94)*, pages 119–130. Springer-Verlag, 1994. LNCS 824.

10. G. Das and G. Narasimhan. Optimal linear-time algorithm for the shortest illuminating line segment in a polygon. In *Proceedings of the 10th Annual Symposium on Computational Geometry*, pages 259–266, 1994.

11. J. Forsberg, U. Larsson, and Å. Wernersson. On mobile robot navigation in cluttered rooms using the range weighted hough transform. *IEEE Robotics and Automation Society Magazine*, 1995. Department of Computer Science and Electrical Engineering, Luleå University of Technology. Accepted for publication in the special issue on mobile robots.

12. L. Guibas, J. Hersberger, D. Leven, M. Sharir, and R. Tarjan. Linear time algorithms for visibility and shortest path problems inside triangulated simple polygons. *Algorithmica*, 2:209–233, 1987.

13. J. Hersberger and J. Snoeyink. An efficient solution to the zookeeper's problem. In *Proceedings of the 6th Canadian Conference on Computational Geometry*, pages 104–109, 1994. U. of Saskatchewan, Saskatoon, Ontario.

14. J. Hersberger and S. Suri. A pedestrian approach to ray shooting: Shoot a ray, take a walk. In *Proceedings of the 4th ACM-SIAM Symposium on Discrete Algorithms*, pages 54–63, 1993.

15. J.-C. Latombe, editor. *Robot Motion Planning*. Kluwer Academic Publishers, Norwell, MA, 1991.

16. D.T. Lee and A.K. Lin. Computational complexity of art gallery problems. *IEEE Trans. Info. Theory*, 32(2):276–282, 1986.

17. B. Nilsson. *Guarding Art Galleries; Methods for Mobile Guards*. PhD thesis, Lund University, Sweden, 1995.

18. J. O'Rourke. *Art Gallery Theorems and Algorithms*. Oxford univ. press, 1987. ISBN 0-19-503965-3.

19. J.-R. Sack and S. Suri. An optimal algorithm for detecting weak visibility. *IEEE Trans. Comput.*, 39:1213–1219, 1990.

20. T. Shermer. Recent results in art galleries. In *Proceedings of the IEEE*, pages 1384–1399, September 1992.

21. X.-H. Tan, T. Hirata, and Y. Inagaki. An incremental algorithm for constructing shortest watchman routes. In *Proceedings of ISA'91*, pages 163–175. Springer-Verlag, 1991. LNCS 557.

22. X.-H. Tan, T. Hirata, and Y. Inagaki. Constructing shortest watchman routes by divide–and–conquer. In *Proceedings of ISAAC'93*, pages 68–77. Springer-Verlag, 1993. LNCS 762.

Going Home Through an Unknown Street*

Alejandro López-Ortiz[1] and Sven Schuierer[2]

[1] Department of Computer Science, University of Waterloo, Waterloo, Ontario CANADA N2L
3G1,
e-mail: alopez-o@neumann.UWaterloo.ca
[2] Department of Computer Science, University of Western Ontario, London, Ont., Canada N6A
5B7, and Institut für Informatik, Universität Freiburg, Am Flughafen 17, D-79110 Freiburg, FRG,
e-mail: schuiere@informatik.uni-freiburg.de

Abstract. We consider the problem of a robot traversing an unknown polygon with
the aid of standard visibility. The robot has to find a path from a starting point s
to a target point t. We provide upper and lower bounds on the ratio of the distance
traveled by the robot in comparison to the length of a shortest path.
We consider two problems in this context. First we assume that the location of the
target t is known to the robot. We prove a lower bound of $\sqrt{2}$ on the competitive
ratio of any deterministic algorithm that solves this problem. This bound matches the
competitive ratio for searches in a rectilinear streets with an unknown target point
which implies that, for rectilinear streets, such knowledge provides no advantage for
the robot. In addition, we obtain a lower bound of 9 for the competitive ratio of
searching in generalised streets with known target which closely matches the upper
bound for an unknown target. Secondly, we consider a new strategy for searching in
an arbitrarily oriented street where the location of t is unknown. We show that our
strategy achieves a competitive ratio of $\sqrt{1 + (1 + \pi/4)^2}$ (~ 2.05) which significantly
improves the best previously known ratio of $2\sqrt{1 + 1/\sqrt{2}}$ (~ 2.61).

1 Introduction

One of the main problems in robotics is to find a path from the current location of the robot
to a given target. While most of the work in this area has focussed on efficient algorithms for
path planning if the robot is given a map of its environment in advance, a more natural and
realistic setting is to assume that the robot has only a partial knowledge of its surroundings.

In this paper we assume that the robot is equipped with a vision system that provides
a visibility map of its *local* environment. Based on this information the robot has to find a
path to a given target that is located somewhere within the scene. The search of the robot
can be viewed as an on-line problem since it discovers its surroundings as it travels. Hence,
one way to analyze the quality of a search strategy is to use the framework of competitive
analysis as introduced by Sleator and Tarjan [12]. A search strategy is called *c-competitive*
if the path traveled by the robot to find the target is at most c times longer than a shortest
path. c is called the *competitive ratio* of the strategy.

Since there is no strategy with a competitive ratio of $o(n)$ for scenes with arbitrary obstacles having a total of n vertices [2], the on-line search problem has been studied previously
in various contexts where the geometry of the obstacles is restricted. Papadimitrou and Yannakakis were the first to consider the case of traversing an unknown scene with rectangular
obstacles in search of a target whose location is known [11]. They show a lower bound of
$\Omega(\sqrt{n})$ for the competitive ratio of any strategy. Later Blum, Raghavan, and Schieber provided a strategy that achieves this bound [2]. If the aspect ratio or the length of the longest
side of the rectangles are bounded, better strategies are possible [3, 10].

* This research is partially supported by the DFG-Project "Diskrete Probleme", No. Ot 64/8-1.

Kleinberg studies the problem of a robot searching inside a simple polygon for an unknown target located on the boundary of the polygon [8]. He introduces the notion of *essential cuts* inside a polygon of which there may be considerably fewer than polygon vertices and gives an $O(m)$-competitive strategy for orthogonal polygons with m essential cuts.

Klein introduced the notion of a *street* which allowed for the first time a search strategy with a constant competitive ratio even though the location of the target is unknown [7]. In a street the starting point s and the target t are located on the boundary of the polygon and the two polygonal chains from s to t are mutually weakly visible. Klein presents a strategy for searching in streets and gives an upper bound on its competitive ratio of $1 + 3/2\pi$ (~ 5.71). The analysis was recently improved to $\pi/2 + \sqrt{1 + \pi^2/4}$ (~ 4.44) by Icking [6]. Though Klein's strategy performs well in practice—he reports that no example had been found for which his strategy performs worse than 1.8—the strategy and its analysis are both quite involved and no better competitive ratio could be shown until recently when Kleinberg presented a new approach. His strategy for searching in streets allows to prove a competitive ratio of $2\sqrt{2}$ with a very simple analysis [8]. Moreover, for rectilinear streets Kleinberg shows that his strategy achieves a competitive ratio of $\sqrt{2}$ which is optimal due to the trivial example shown in Figure 1. Assume the goal is located in either one of the left or right "ears" of the rectangle. Here, if a strategy moves to the left or right before seeing t, then t can be placed on the opposite side, thus forcing the robot to travel more than $\sqrt{2}$ times the diagonal. Curiously enough, this is the only known lower bound even for arbitrarily oriented streets. Finally, a more general class of polygons, called $\mathcal{G}$-streets, has been introduced by Datta and Icking that allows search strategies with a competitive ratio of 9.06 [4]. All the these strategies fall into the category of Unknown Destination Searches (UDS) in which the location of the target point is unknown.

One natural source of information for the robot are the coordinates of the target . The first problem we consider is a lower bound for strategies for Known Destination Searches (KDS) in a street where the location of the target is given in advance to the robot. In this case the example of Figure 1 obviously no longer provides a lower bound. We prove that even in orthogonal streets a $\sqrt{2}$-competitive ratio is optimal as well, thus providing the first non-trivial lower bound for searching in streets. This result is different from the general search problem as considered by Papadimitrou and Yannakakis in which knowledge of the destination improves the competitive ratio.

Secondly we consider a new strategy for searching in arbitrarily oriented streets. We achieve a competitive ratio of $\sqrt{1 + (1 + \pi/4)^2}$ (~ 2.05), providing a significant improvement over previous strategies and the best performance guarantee for searching strategies in streets known so far.

The paper is organized as follows. In Section 2 we introduce the basic geometric concepts necessary for the rest of the paper. In particular, we give a precise definition of a street. In Section 3 we show that any deterministic search algorithm for orthogonal streets that knows the location of the target can be forced to travel $\sqrt{2} - O(1/\sqrt{n})$ times the distance of a shortest path to the target where n is the number of vertices of the polygon. Finally, Section 4 deals with a new strategy to search in streets and its analysis.

2 Definitions and Assumptions

We consider a simple polygon P in the plane with n vertices and a robot inside P which is located at a start point s on the boundary of P. The robot has to find a path from s to the target point t. The search of the robot is aided by simple vision (i.e. we assume that the robot knows the visibility polygon of its current location). Furthermore, the robot retains all the information seen so far (in memory) and knows its starting and current position. We are, in particular, concerned with a special class of polygons called *streets* first introduced by Klein [7].

Definition 1. [7] Let P be a simple polygon with two distinguished vertices, s and t, and let L and R denote the clockwise and counterclockwise, resp., oriented boundary chains leading from s to t. If L and R are mutually weakly visible, i.e. if each point of L sees at least one point of R and vice versa, then (P, s, t) is called a *street*.

Definition 2. In the class of Known Destination Search (KDS) problems, a robot searches a simple rectilinear polygon, starting from s on the boundary of the polygon, for a target point t on the boundary of P with known location.

We denote the L_2-distance between two points p_1 and p_2 by $d(p_1, p_2)$ and the L_2-norm of a point p by $\|p\|$.

Let P be a street with start point s and target t. If p is a point of P, then the *visibility polygon* of p is the set of all points in P that are seen by p. It is denoted by $V(p)$. A *window* of $V(p)$ is an edge of $V(p)$ that does not belong to the boundary of P.

A window w splits P into a number of subpolygons $P_1, \ldots, P_k$ one of which contains $V(p)$. We denote the union of the subpolygons that do not contain $V(p)$ by P_w.

3 A $\sqrt{2}$-competitive lower bound

We construct a family of polygons which are $(\sqrt{2} - \epsilon)$-competitive for KDS, for any $\epsilon > 0$. First, we define some widgets which will be used in the general construction.

Definition 3. An *eared rectangle* is a rectangle two units wide and one unit tall. The center of the base is the *entry point* and on the top left and right corners there are two small alleys (ears) attached to it (see Figure 1). One of the alleys is *connecting*, the other is *a dead alley*.

Definition 4. The *aspect ratio* A of a general polygon is defined as the ratio between the smallest and the longest edge of the polygon. Thus $A \leq 1$.

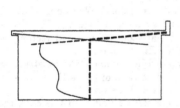 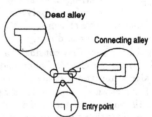

Fig. 1. Eared Rectangle, with walk inside. **Fig. 2.** Interconnecting Eared Rectangles.

Lemma 5. *An eared rectangle may be traversed from the entry point to the connecting alley at a $(\sqrt{2} - \epsilon)$-competitive ratio, with $\epsilon = O(A)$, which is optimal.*

Proof. First we show that a $\sqrt{2}$-competitive ratio is attainable. The robot walks up the middle of the rectangle, until it sees the top boundaries of both alleys. At this time the robot can see into either alley and determine which one is open, and proceed to walk in this direction (see bold dashed lines in Figure 1). The length of the trajectory is $1 - \tan\theta + 1/\cos\theta$, where θ is the angle of the line between the extreme upper and the closer lower end point of the alleys. Notice that θ can be made arbitrarily small by means of reducing the height of the alley. Thus, this strategy gives a walk of length arbitrarily close to $\sup_{\theta \to 0}\{1 + 1/\cos\theta - \tan\theta\} = 2$. The optimal walk is of length $\sqrt{2}$ for a competitive ratio of $\sqrt{2} - \epsilon$ where $\epsilon = (1/\sqrt{2})(1 + \tan\theta - 1/\cos\theta) = O(A)$.

This strategy is optimal as well. We use an adversary argument to show this. The adversary simply opens the first alley to be looked into by the robot, and closes the other alley. Clearly the alley opened is always in the opposite half of the rectangle in which the robot is currently located. (see curvy path plus dashed line in Figure 1). A simple application of the triangle inequality shows that the path in bold is shorter, and thus has a better competitive ratio.

138

Eared rectangles can be interconnected to create paths. Figure 2 shows the details of such rectangles.

Theorem 1 *There exists a street with n vertices which can be searched with an optimal competitive ratio of $\sqrt{2} - O(1/\sqrt{n})$.*

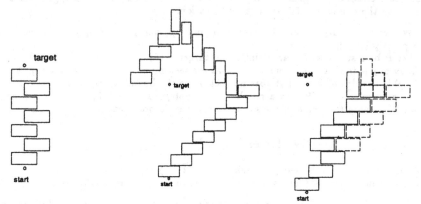

Fig. 3. Walk the Middle Policy

Fig. 4. Always to the Right Policy

Fig. 5. Wavering Policy

Proof. As proved by Kleinberg [8], there exists a $\sqrt{2}$-competitive strategy for UDS which can be applied in a straightforward way to the KDS problem and gives a strategy of the same competitive ratio for all polygons in the KDS problem.

What remains to be shown is that this competitive ratio is optimal. We assume that the target is at some distance directly above the start point as shown in Figure 3. To prove a lower bound of $\sqrt{2}$ we first consider two extreme cases of interconnecting eared rectangles, namely the *Walk the Middle Policy* and the *Always to the Right Policy*.

If the algorithm uses a strategy such as the one proposed in Lemma 5, the construction of Figure 3 shows an example of a polygon with a competitive ratio of $(2n + 1)/(\sqrt{2}n + 1)$, where n is the number of rectangles between the start point and the target.

Thus, an algorithm needs to deviate from the *Walk the Middle Policy*. In this case, the adversary presents the algorithm with an eared rectangle and it opens and closes the alleys according to the strategy proposed in Lemma 5. If we assume that the algorithm always meets the line of sight in the left half, then the adversary consistently opens the right alley (see Figure 4). This creates a staircase moving to the right. Notice that the L_1 distance from the current robot position to the target is always within one unit of the L_1 distance from the start point to the target. That is, the adversary has forced the algorithm to move at a worse than $\sqrt{2}$ competitive ratio, but the target is no closer than before.

When the current connecting alley is now horizontally aligned with the target, the adversary moves one unit closer to the target (we assume that the algorithm also moves optimally in this part, since it knows the position of the target) and proceeds to construct a new staircase. This results in a spiraling set of staircases converging to the start point. The spiral is of length quadratic in n (see [1]) and, thus, the competitive ratio is $O((2n^2 + n)/(\sqrt{2}n^2 + n))$ which goes to $\sqrt{2}$ as n goes to infinity.

Having analyzed these extreme cases, we now consider a *Wavering Policy* in which the algorithm neither walks up the middle, nor consistently slants either way (see Figure 5). The *Walk the Middle Policy* and *Always to the Right Policy* can be viewed as extreme instances of the *Wavering Policy*. In the case of a wavering algorithm, the adversary maintains the strategy described above. Every time the algorithm deviates from the *Always to the Right Policy*, the adversary moves to the left. As a consequence, the L_1 distance to the target is reduced by two units, while the competitive ratio remains above $\sqrt{2}$.

From the point of view of the algorithm a left turn, is equivalent to a "jump" from one level of the spiral to a level on the spiral associated to a start point two units closer to the target (see Figure 5, with the polygon in solid lines, and the older staircase in dashed lines).

Assume $n = 2m$ is even. Let k be the number of turns to the left deviating from the *Always to the Right Policy*. Without loss of generality let $k \leq m$, since the the case $k > m$ can be seen as a deviation from the symmetric *Always to the Left Policy*. Furthermore, assume that the algorithm jumps at staircases $a_1, a_2, \ldots, a_k$, where the staircases are numbered, starting from 1, in the order they are traversed. Then, the total length of the path traversed by the algorithm is

$$2 \sum_{0 \leq j < a_1} (n - 2j) + 2 + 2 \sum_{a_1 \leq j < a_2} (n - 2a_1 - 2j) + 2 + 2 \sum_{a_2 \leq j < a_3} (n - 2a_1 - 2a_2 - 2j) + 2 + \cdots$$

where each sum represents the length of a segment of a spiral staircase in between jumps.

Lemma 6. *Consider two strategies for walking up the staircase. Strategy A turns left in staircases $\{a_i\}_{1 \leq i \leq k}$, and Strategy B turns left in the staircases $\{b_i\}_{1 \leq i \leq k}$, such that $b_i = a_i - 1$, for all i with $a_i > 1$, and $b_i = 1$ otherwise. Then strategy B has a better competitive ratio than strategy A.*

Proof. Since $a_i \geq b_i$ it follows that the summation above is, term by term, larger for strategy A than for strategy B, from which the claim follows.

Thus, setting $a_i = 1$, for all i, is optimal. Let $n = 2m$. If the algorithm jumps or turns left k times, then we have

Length of shortened spiral $= n + \sum_{i=0}^{m-k} (n - 2k - 2i) = n + (m - k)(m - k + 1)$

Length of optimal walk $= \sqrt{2}\,(n + (m - k)(m - k + 1)) + n - 2k$

Distance traversed by the algorithm $= 2\,(n + (m - k)(m - k + 1)) + n - 2k$

Competitive ratio $= \sqrt{2} - \xi$ where $\xi = \dfrac{2(m - k)(\sqrt{2} - 1)}{\sqrt{2}\,(n + (m - k)(m - k + 1)) + n - 2k}$.

To improve its competitive ratio, the algorithm can select the optimal value of k for all given m that maximizes ξ. It can be shown that $k = m - \sqrt{2m}$ maximizes ξ to $O(1/\sqrt{m})$. Since each eared rectangle is traversed at a $\sqrt{2} - O(A)$ competitive ratio, we have that the adversary strategy described above forces any algorithm into a $\sqrt{2} - O(A) - O(1/\sqrt{n})$ competitive ratio, which in the limit is $\sqrt{2}$.

As it can be seen, regardless of the policy, a $\sqrt{2}$ inefficiency factor is necessarily introduced, even in the case where the robot knows where it is going, but is ignorant of the terrain in which is moving.

Datta and Icking [4] introduced the notion of $\mathcal{G}$-streets and showed for the UDS problem a competitive ratio of 9.06.

Definition 7 [4]. A simple polygon in the plane is called a *generalized street* if for every boundary point $p \in L \cup R$, there exists a horizontal chord with end points in L and R and from which p is weakly visible.

Datta and Icking proved a lower bound by building a "rake" polygon which is traversed at a 9-competitive ratio on the limit (see Figure 6).

For the KDS problem, as in the case of eared rectangles, a single rake polygon does not suffice to obtain a lower bound on the competitive ratio of 9.

A similar strategy to the one presented results in a 9-competitive ratio for this problem.

Corollary 1 *There exists a family of orthogonal $\mathcal{G}$-streets with 9-competitive ratio, which is close to optimal.*

Proof. Consider a target at a distance n of the start point, and placed directly above it on the vertical direction. Then a set of n^2 rakes placed one above the other, each of height $1/n$, gives the desired lower bound.

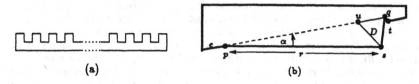

Fig. 6. (a) A "rake" polygon. (b) A lower bound example for Kleinberg's strategy.

4 Traversing a Street

In this section we present a new strategy to traverse a street from the starting point s to the target point t. Our strategy closely follows the approach of Kleinberg [8] in order to deal with the simple cases which his strategy handles optimally but deviates in the more complicated cases.

The competitive ratio of Kleinberg's strategy is shown to be $2\sqrt{2}$ (~ 2.83) in his paper but a tighter analysis—also mentioned in his paper—yields an upper bound of $2\sqrt{1 + 1/\sqrt{2}}$ (~ 2.61). Before we describe our approach we show that this bound is tight for his strategy. Figure 6 shows an example of a polygon where his bound is achieved asymptotically.

Here Kleinberg's strategy follows the diagonal D to point u where the chain to the left of point p is visible to the robot and then moves to the right to point q. In order to see that a competitive ratio of $2\sqrt{1 + 1/\sqrt{2}}$ is achieved let $d = \sqrt{2} + 1$ and q be chosen to have the coordinates $(q_1, q_2) = (1/\sqrt{d^2 + 1}, d/\sqrt{d^2 + 1})$ where we assume s to be the origin. If p has distance r to s and we observe that $\sin \alpha = q_1/(r + q_2)$, then $u = (u_1, u_2) = (r \sin \alpha/(\sin \alpha - 1), r \sin \alpha/(\sin \alpha - 1))$. Hence, the total distance traveled by a robot following Kleinberg's strategy is $\geq \sqrt{2}u_2 + u_1 + q_1$. If we take into account that $u_1 = u_2 = q_2 - O(1/r)$, then the distance traveled by the robot is $q_1 + (\sqrt{2} + 1)q_2 - O(1/r) = 1/\sqrt{d^2 + 1} + d^2/\sqrt{d^2 + 1} - O(1/r) = \sqrt{d^2 + 1} - O(1/r)$ which tends to $2\sqrt{1 + 1/\sqrt{2}}$ as r approaches $+\infty$. By keeping edge e collinear with q and moving t closer and closer to q it can be seen that the claimed ratio can be achieved arbitrarily closely.

Our strategy has a competitive ratio of at most $\sqrt{1 + (1 + \pi/4)^2}$ (~ 2.05) but in contrast to Kleinberg's analysis, the analysis of our strategy is not tight. Before we describe the strategy we need a few definitions and observations.

As observed by Kleinberg the shortest path $\mathcal{P}_{st}$ from s to t consists of a number of line segments that touch reflex vertices of P. The general strategy we follow is to start at a reflex vertex v of P that belongs to $\mathcal{P}_{st}$ and to identify another reflex vertex v' of $\mathcal{P}_{st}$ that is closer to t by traveling further on. If the robot has identified v', then it moves to it and starts the search anew. A move from one reflex vertex of P on $\mathcal{P}_{st}$ to another closer to t is called a *step*. Recall that a window is an edge of the boundary of the visibility polygon $V(p)$ of p that does not belong to the boundary of P.

All windows are collinear with p. The end point of a window w that is closer to p is called the *entrance point* of w. We assume that a window w has the orientation of the ray from p to entrance point of w. We say a window w is a *left window* if P_w is locally to the left of w w.r.t. the given orientation of w. A *right window* is defined similarly.

If the robot has traveled along the path $\mathcal{P}$, then we assume that the robot knows the part of P that can be seen from $\mathcal{P}$, i.e. the robot maintains the polygon $V(\mathcal{P}) = \bigcup_{p \in \mathcal{P}} V(p)$. We say a window w of $V(p)$ is a *true window* w.r.t. $\mathcal{P}$ if it is also a window of $V(\mathcal{P})$.

We have the following lemma about true windows.

Lemma 8. *If w is a right (left) window of $V(p)$ and the boundary of P_w belongs to L (R), then w is not a true window.*

We say two windows w_1 and w_2 are *clockwise consecutive* if the clockwise oriented polygonal chain of $V(p)$ between w_1 and w_2 does not contain a window different from w_1 and w_2. *Counterclockwise consecutive* is defined analogously.

Lemma 9. *All windows that belong to L (R) are clockwise (counterclockwise) consecutive in $V(p)$.*

True windows are called *consecutive* if there is no true window that is between them. An immediate corollary of Lemmas 8 and 9 is that true left and true right windows are consecutive.

Corollary 10. *If w_0 is the window that is intersected by $\mathcal{P}$ the first time, then all true left (right) windows are clockwise (counterclockwise) consecutive from w_0 in $V(p)$.*

Because of Corollary 10 there is a clockwise-most true left entrance point from w_0 which we denote by p^+ and a counterclockwise-most true right entrance point of $V(p)$ which we denote by p^- if $V(p)$ contains both true left and right windows. The point p^+ is called the *left extreme entrance point* and p^- the *right extreme entrance point* of $V(p)$.

Now assume the robot starts at s and travels towards its target. We consider five cases:

Case 1 t is visible to the robot.
The robot moves to t on a straight line.

Case 2 There is no true left window (right window).
The robot moves to p^- (p^+).

Case 3 The angle at the location of the robot between p^+ and p^- is greater than or equal to $\pi/2$.
We apply Algorithm *Move-in-Quadrant* as described below until we are able to decide which of p^+ and p^- is part of a shortest path from s to t.

If none of the above cases apply, then p^+ and p^- are defined and the angle at p between p^+ and p^- is less than $\pi/2$. The robot chooses a direction such that p^+ is to the left of the direction and p^- to the right. It travels following the direction until one of the above or one of the following two cases occurs.

Case 4 A new point p^+ or p^- appears and p, p^+ and p^- are collinear.
The robot moves along the line through p, p^+, and p^- to the closer point of p^+ and p^-.

Case 5 The angle at the location of the robot between p^+ and p^- equals $\pi/2$.
We apply Algorithm *Move-in-Quadrant* as described below until we are able to decide which of p^+ and p^- is part of a shortest path from s to t.

The *orthogonal projection* p' of a point p onto a line segment l is defined as the point of l that is closest to p. If the line segment joining p with p' is orthogonal to l, then p' is a *non-degenerate* orthogonal projection.

> **Algorithm Move-in-Quadrant**
> **Input:** A point p_0 in P such that the angle at p_0 of p_0^+ and p_0^- of $V(p_0)$ is $\geq \pi/2$;
> $i := 0$;
> **while** p_i^+ and p_i^- of $V(p_i)$ are defined **do**
> (1) Move to the orthogonal projection p_{i+1} of p_0 onto the line segment l_i;
>   Compute the points p_{i+1}^+ and p_{i+1}^- of $V(p_{i+1})$;
> $i := i + 1$;
> **end while**;

The correctness of the algorithm follows from the following lemma.

Lemma 11. *If the robot has reached the line segment l_i, then one of p_i^+ or p_i^- is not an extreme entrance point of $V(p_{i+1})$ anymore.*

For the analysis consider the Cases 1, 2, and 4 first. In the Cases 1 and 2 the robot moves directly to the next point on a shortest path from s to t, hence, the competitive ratio is 1. If Case 4 occurs before Algorithm *Move-in-Quadrant* is invoked, then the angle between the line segment from the robot to p_i^+ or p_i^- and the traveling direction is less or equal $\pi/2$ which implies that if the robot moves directly to p_i^+ or p_i^-, then the competitive ratio is bounded by $\sqrt{2}$.

4.1 Analysis of the Algorithm *Move-in-Quadrant*

If during the movement in Step (1) one of the Cases 1 or 4 occurs, then the robot moves immediately to t or the closer of the points p^+ or p^-. Nevertheless, for the analysis we assume that the robot first moves to the line segment determined by the old points p^+ and p^- and then to the closer one of the two. In the following we assume that the Algorithm *Move-in-Quadrant* has stopped after k iterations.

Lemma 12. *During the Algorithm Move-in-Quadrant the shortest path from s to t goes through either p_i^+ or p_i^-, for all $0 \leq i \leq k$.*

Because of Lemma 12 it suffices to bound the ratio of the length of the path traveled by the robot to the distance between p_0 and p_k^+ or p_k^-—whichever is detected as a part of the shortest path from s to t.

We introduce a coordinate system where p_0 is the origin and the x-axis passes through p_0^-. Note that since the angle at p_0 between between p_0^+ and p_0^- is greater than or equal to $\pi/2$, there is no reflex vertex of P in the first quadrant of the introduced coordinate system that is visible to p_0. Assume that we have arrived at point p_i and move to point p_{i+1} in the next iteration. We make a few simple observations about the locations of p_i^+, p_i^-, and the line segment l_i from p_i^+ to p_i^-.

Lemma 13. *The point p_i^+ belongs to the second quadrant and the point p_i^- belongs to the fourth quadrant, for all $0 \leq i \leq k$.*

Lemma 14. *The line segments l_i and l_{i+1} do not intersect in the first quadrant.*

Since the line segment l_i intersects the first, second, and fourth quadrant, the orthogonal projection of p_0 onto l_i is non-degenerate.

In order to simplify the analysis we consider the line segment l_i' from the intersection point of l_i with the y-axis to the intersection point of l_{i+1} with the x-axis. The line segment l_i' is located between l_i and l_{i+1}. If we consider the path $\mathcal{P}_i'$ from p_0 to p_i that visits the orthogonal projections of p_0 onto the line segments l_j and l_j' in order, for $0 \leq j \leq i$, then the length of $\mathcal{P}_i'$ is obviously greater than or equal to the length of $\mathcal{P}_i$. Furthermore, $\mathcal{P}_i$ and $\mathcal{P}_i'$ share the same start and end point. Hence, for the simplicity of exposition we assume in the following that p_i^+ is located on the y-axis, p_i^- on the x-axis, and either $p_i^+ = p_{i+1}^+$ or $p_i^- = p_{i+1}^-$.

Let L_i be the length of the path $\mathcal{P}_i$ traveled by the robot to reach p_i; let α_i^- be the angle between the line segment $\overline{p_0 p_i}$ from p_0 to p_i and the x-axis and d_i^- the distance between p_0 and p_i^-. Similarly, let α_i^+ be the angle between $\overline{p_0 p_i}$ and the y-axis and d_i^+ the distance between p_0 and p_i^+. We define the angle α_i as $\min\{\alpha_i^+, \alpha_i^-\}$ and the distance d_i as $\min\{d_i^+, d_i^-\}$.

Our approach to analyze our strategy is based on the idea of a potential function. Each point p_i is assigned a potential Q_i which is defined as $Q_i = \alpha_i d_i$. It is our aim to show that $L_i + Q_i \leq (1 + \pi/4)d_i$, for all $0 \leq i \leq k$.

So suppose the robot has reached the point p_i and d_i is equal to the distance between p_0 and p_i^- and $L_i \leq (1 + \pi/4 - \alpha_i)d_i$. Note that since $d_i = d(p_0, p_i^-)$, the line segment l_i has a slope greater than or equal to $\pi/4$ and p_i is below the diagonal of the first quadrant. Hence, α_i is the angle between the line segment $\overline{p_0 p_i}$ and the x-axis. For simplicity of description we assume that the distance from p_0 to p_i^+ is 1 and, therefore, $d_i = \tan \alpha_i$. The robot moves now from p_i to p_{i+1}. We distinguish three cases.

Case 1 The line segment l_{i+1} is steeper than the line segment l_i.
Hence, $d_{i+1} = d_i$. Note that p_{i+1} is on the circle C_i with center at $c_i = (d_i/2, 0)$ and radius $d_i/2$ (see Figure 7a). The arc a_i of C_i from p_i to p_{i+1} has length $2(\alpha_i - \alpha_{i+1})d_i/2 =$

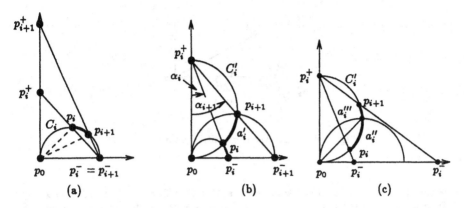

Fig. 7. Cases 1, 2, and 3 if the robot moves from p_i to p_{i+}.

$(\alpha_i - \alpha_{i+1})d_i$ since the angle between p_i and p_{i+1} at c_i is $2(\alpha_i - \alpha_{i+1})$. Clearly, the line segment $\overline{p_i p_{i+1}}$ is shorter than the arc a_i. Hence,

$$L_{i+1} = L_i + d(p_i, p_{i+1}) \leq (1 + \frac{\pi}{4} - \alpha_i)d_i + (\alpha_i - \alpha_{i+1})d_i = (1 + \frac{\pi}{4} - \alpha_{i+1})d_{i+1}$$

Case 2 The line segment l_{i+1} is steeper than $\pi/4$ but less steep than the line segment l_i (see Figure 7b).
Hence, $d_{i+1} = \tan \alpha_{i+1}$. Note that p_{i+1} is on the circle C_i' with center at $c_i' = (0, 1/2)$ and radius $1/2$. The arc a_i' of C_i' from p_i to p_{i+1} has length $2(\alpha_{i+1} - \alpha_i)1/2 = \alpha_{i+1} - \alpha_i$ since the angle between p_i and p_{i+1} at c_i' is $2(\alpha_i - \alpha_{i+1})$. Clearly, the line segment $\overline{p_i p_{i+1}}$ is shorter than the arc a_i. Hence, $L_{i+1} = L_i + d(p_i, p_{i+1}) \leq (1 + \frac{\pi}{4} - \alpha_i)d_i + (\alpha_{i+1} - \alpha_i)$

We want to show that $\quad (1 + \frac{\pi}{4} - \alpha_i)d_i + (\alpha_{i+1} - \alpha_i) \leq (1 + \frac{\pi}{4} - \alpha_{i+1})d_{i+1} \quad$ (1) or

$$1 + \frac{\pi}{4} \geq \frac{\alpha_{i+1}d_{i+1} - \alpha_i d_i + \alpha_{i+1} - \alpha_i}{d_{i+1} - d_i} = \frac{\alpha_{i+1}(1 + \tan\alpha_{i+1}) - \alpha_i(1 + \tan\alpha_i)}{\tan\alpha_{i+1} - \tan\alpha_i} \text{ with } 0 \leq \alpha_i \leq$$

$\alpha_{i+1} \leq \pi/4$. If define $\beta_i = \alpha_{i+1} - \alpha_i$ and $f(\alpha_i, \beta_i) = (\beta_i + (\alpha_i + \beta_i)\tan(\alpha_i + \beta_i) - \alpha_i \tan\alpha_i)/(\tan(\alpha_i + \beta_i) - \tan\alpha_i)$, then we want to prove that $f(\alpha, \beta) \leq \pi/4$, for all $(\alpha, \beta) \in \Delta = \{(x, y) \mid x \geq 0, y \geq 0, x + y \leq \pi/4\}$. As a first step we notice that $\frac{\partial f}{\partial \alpha}(\alpha, \beta) \geq 0$, for all $(\alpha, \beta) \in \Delta$. Hence,

$$\min_{(\alpha,\beta)\in\Delta} \frac{\partial f}{\partial \alpha}(\alpha, \beta) = \min_{\beta\in[0,\pi/4]} \frac{\partial f}{\partial \alpha}\left(\frac{\pi}{4} - \beta, \beta\right) = \min_{\beta\in[0,\pi/4]} \frac{\sin\beta + \beta(\sin\beta - \cos\beta)}{\sin\beta} \geq 0.$$

Therefore, f is monotone in α and $\max_{(\alpha,\beta)\in\Delta} f(\alpha, \beta) = \max_{\beta\in[0,\pi/4]} f(\pi/4 - \beta, \beta)$. If $g(\beta) = f(\pi/4 - \beta, \beta)$, then $dg/d\beta = (2\beta - \sin\beta)/(\cos 2\beta - 1) \leq 0$ and, therefore,

$$\max_{(\alpha,\beta)\in\Delta} f(\alpha, \beta) = \max_{\beta\in[0,\pi/4]} g(\beta) = \lim_{\beta\to 0} \frac{\beta + \frac{\pi}{4}\tan(\frac{\pi}{4}) - (\frac{\pi}{4} - \beta)\tan(\frac{\pi}{4} - \beta)}{\tan(\frac{\pi}{4}) - \tan(\frac{\pi}{4} - \beta)}$$

$$= \lim_{\beta\to 0} \frac{\beta}{\sin(2\beta)}(1 + \cos(2\beta)) + \frac{\pi}{4} = 1 + \frac{\pi}{4}$$

Case 3 The line segment l_{i+1} is less steep than $\pi/4$ (see Figure 7c).
Hence, d_{i+1} is now the distance from p_0 to $p_{i+1}^+ = p_i^+$ which is 1 by our assumption. Furthermore, α_{i+1} is the angle between $\overline{p_0 p_{i+1}}$ and the y-axis. If α_{i+1}' is the angle between $\overline{p_0 p_{i+1}}$ and the x-axis, then $\alpha_{i+1} + \alpha_{i+1}' = \pi/2$.

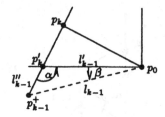

Fig. 8. Bounding the competitive ratio in Case 3.

Note that p_{i+1} is on the circle C_i' with center at $c_i' = (0, 1/2)$ and radius $1/2$. The arc a_i' of C_i from p_i to p_{i+1} has length $2(\alpha_{i+1}' - \alpha_i)1/2 = \alpha_{i+1}' - \alpha_i$. Again, the line segment $\overline{p_i p_{i+1}}$ is shorter than the arc a_i'. And as above we obtain

$$L_{i+1} = L_i + d(p_i, p_{i+1}) \leq (1 + \frac{\pi}{4} - \alpha_i)d_i + (\alpha_{i+1}' - \alpha_i)$$

We split a_i' into two arcs a_i'' and a_i''' where a_i'' is the arc from p_i to the diagonal of the first quadrant and a_i''' is the arc from the diagonal of the first quadrant to p_{i+1}. The arc a_i'' is paid for by the increase $d_{i+1} - d_i$ while the arc a_i''' just reduces the potential. More precisely, we have

$$(1 + \frac{\pi}{4} - \alpha_i)d_i + (\alpha_{i+1}' - \alpha_i) = (1 + \frac{\pi}{4} - \alpha_i)d_i + (\frac{\pi}{4} - \alpha_i) + (\alpha_{i+1}' - \frac{\pi}{4})$$

$$\leq (1 + \frac{\pi}{4} - \frac{\pi}{4}) \cdot 1 + (\frac{\pi}{4} - \alpha_{i+1})$$

$$= (1 + \frac{\pi}{4} - \alpha_{i+1})d_{i+1}$$

where the last inequality follows from Inequality (2) if we set $\alpha_{i+1} = \pi/4$. This proves the claim.

In fact we have shown the following lemma.

Lemma 15. *For all* $0 \leq i \leq k$, $\qquad 1 + \frac{\pi}{4} \geq \max\left\{ \dfrac{L_i + d(p_i, p_i^+)}{d(p_0, p_i^+)}, \dfrac{L_i + d(p_i, p_i^-)}{d(p_0, p_i^-)} \right\}$

4.2 Analysis of Cases 3 and 5

In order to obtain the final competitive ratio for one step we have to take into account that the robot has to move to either p_{k-1}^+ or p_{k-1}^-. First consider Case 3. If p_k^- is undefined, then p_{k-1}^+ belongs to the shortest path from s to t. Lemma 15 gives a tight bound on the maximum distance the robot travels in order to reach p_k' in Figure 8.

Let l_{k-1}'' be the line segment between p_{k-1}^+ and p_k' and α the angle between l_{k-1}' and l_{k-1}''. The length of l_{k-1} grows monotonously with α if the lengths of l_{k-1}' of l_{k-1}'' are fixed. Hence, the maximum ratio is assumed for the minimum angle α which is $\alpha = \pi/2$. If we set l_{k-1} to have length 1, then the length of l_{k-1}' is $\cos\beta$ and the length of l_{k-1}'' is $\sin\beta$. Hence, the maximum distance traveled by the robot from p_0 to p_{k-1}^+ is bounded by

$$\max_{0 \leq \beta \leq \pi/2} \sin\beta + c\cos\beta \qquad \text{or} \qquad \max_{0 \leq x \leq 1} \sqrt{1 - x^2} + cx.$$

where $c = 1 + \pi/4$. This maximum is achieved for $z = c/\sqrt{c^2 + 1}$ and yields a value of $\sqrt{c^2 + 1}$. The same analysis applies if p_k^+ is undefined.

Now we consider Case 5. This case turns out to be somewhat more complicated than the previous one. Let p be the point where the robot started its search. We denote the position of the robot at time t by $p(t)$ with left entrance point $p^+(t)$ and right entrance point $p^-(t)$. After traveling some distance d the robot encounters a point $p_0 = p(t_0)$ where the angle between $p^+(t_0)$ and $p^-(t_0)$ is exactly $\pi/2$. Note that the angle between $p^+(t)$ and $p^-(t)$ at the robot position is a continuous, monotonously increasing function if the robot moves on a ray. At p_0 the robot invokes the Algorithm *Move-in-Quadrant*. Let S be the coordinate system with origin p_0 and p_0^+ on the y-axis and p_0^- on the x-axis both in the first quadrant. Note that the x- and the y-coordinate of p in S are non-positive.

Suppose that p_k^- is undefined. Then, a shortest path from s to t visits p (by the induction hypothesis), p_0^+, and p_{k-1}^+. Hence, we have the situation displayed in Figure 9a.

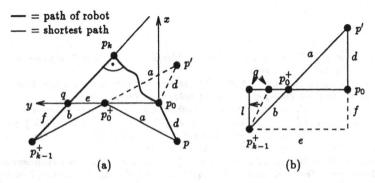

Fig. 9. (a): Computing the competitive ratio in Case 5. (b): A triangle with a right angle can be formed.

The length of the shortest path from p to p_{k-1}^+ is at least the sum of the distance a from p to p_0^+ and the distance b from p_0^+ to p_{k-1}^+. We first consider for which point p_0^+ the sum $a + b$ is minimized given p, p_0, and p_{k-1}^+. In order to compute this point p_0^+ we reflect p at the y-axis to a point p' and note that the distance between p' and p_0^+ equals a (see Figure 9). Hence, $a + b$ is minimized if p_0^+ is located on the line from p_{k-1}^+ to p'. Furthermore, the distance d from p to p_0 which is traveled by the robot is maximized if p is located on the x-axis given fixed p_0, p_0^+, and a.

Now we consider the maximum of $e + f$ given p_{k-1}^+ where the line segment l from q to p_{k-1}^+ must form an angle of less or equal $3\pi/2$ with the y-axis. As can be seen by applying the triangle inequality it is obtained if l is orthogonal to the y-axis (see Figure 9b).

So assume q has the same y-coordinate as p_{k-1}^+. If we translate the line segment l such that q coincides with p_0 and also translate the line segment from p_0 to q such that q coincides with p_{k-1}^+ (see Figure 9b), then we obtain a triangle whose sides have length e, $d + f$ and $a + b$ with a right angle in its right hand corner. The previous analysis applies and

$$\sqrt{1 + c^2} \geq \frac{d + f + ce}{a + b}$$

with $c = 1 + \pi/4$ as claimed. We have shown the following theorem.

Theorem 2 *If P is a street with start point s and target point t, then there is a strategy for a robot with access to the local visibility map of its surroundings to travel from s to t on a path that is at most $\sqrt{1 + (1 + \pi/4)^2}$ times longer than the shortest possible route.*

5   Conclusions

We consider two problems in this paper. First we provide a lower bound of $\sqrt{2} - O(1/\sqrt{n})$ for the competitive ratio of any deterministic strategy that a robot may use to search in a rectilinear street if the coordinates of the target are given in advance to the robot. This implies that knowledge of the location of the target does not provide any advantage even for searching in rectilinear streets. We further show a similar result for $\mathcal{G}$-streets.

Secondly, we present a new strategy to search in arbitrarily oriented streets. We show a performance guarantee of $\sqrt{1 + (1 + \pi/4)^2}$ (~ 2.05) for our strategy.

Unfortunately, the gap between the upper and lower bounds for searching in streets is still quite large and it seems that new ideas are needed to narrow it down.

References

1. R. Baeza-Yates, J. Culberson and G. Rawlins. "Searching in the plane", *Information and Computation*, Vol. 106, (1993), pp. 234-252.
2. A. Blum, P. Raghavan and B. Schieber. "Navigating in unfamiliar geometric terrain", *Proc. of 23rd ACM Symp. on Theory of Computing*, (1991), pp. 494-504.
3. K-F. Chan and T. W. Lam. "An on-line algorithm for navigating in an unknown environment", *International Journal of Computational Geometry & Applications*, Vol. 3, (1993), pp. 227-244.
4. A. Datta and Ch. Icking. "Competitive searching in a generalized street", *Proc. of 10th ACM Sypm. on Computational Geometry*, (1994), pp. 175-182.
5. X. Deng, T. Kameda and C. Papadimitriou. "How to learn an unknown environment I : The rectilinear case", *Technical Report CS-93-04*, Department of Computer Science, York University, 1993. A preliminary version appeared in *Proc. 32nd IEEE Symp. on Foundations of Computer Science*, (1991), pp. 298-303.
6. Ch. Icking. Ph. D. Thesis, Fernuniversität Hagen, 1994.
7. R. Klein. "Walking an unknown street with bounded detour", *Computational Geometry: Theory and Applications* 1, (1992), pp. 325-351.
8. J. Kleinberg. "On-line search in a simple polygon", *Proc. of 5th ACM-SIAM Symp. on Discrete Algorithms*, (1994), pp. 8-15.
9. A. López-Ortiz and S. Schuierer. Simple, Efficient and Robust Strategies to Traverse Streets. Manuscript. 1995.
10. A. Mei and Y. Igarashi. "Efficient strategies for robot navigation in unknown environment" *Proc. of 21st International Colloquium on Automata, Languages and Programming*, (1994), to appear.
11. C. H. Papadimitriou and M. Yannakakis. "Shortest paths without a map", *Theoretical Computer Science* 84, (1991), pp. 127-150.
12. D. D. Sleator and R. E. Tarjan. "Amortized efficiency of list update and paging rules", *Communications of the ACM* 28, (1985), pp. 202-208.

Page Migration with Limited Local Memory Capacity

Susanne Albers*   Hisashi Koga**

Abstract. Most previous work on page migration assumes that each processor, in the given distributed environment, has infinite local memory capacity. In this paper we study the migration problem under the realistic assumption that the local memories have limited capacities. We assume that the memories are *direct-mapped*, i.e., the processors use a hash function in order to locate pages in their memory. We show that, for a number of important network topologies, on-line algorithms with a constant competitive ratio can be developed in this model. We also study distributed paging. We examine the *migration version* of this problem in which there exists only one copy of each page. We develop efficient deterministic and randomized on-line algorithms for this problem.

1 Introduction

Many on-line problems of practical significance arise in distributed data management. As a result, there has recently been a lot of research interests in problems such as page migration, page replication and distributed paging, see e.g. [1, 2, 3, 5, 6, 8, 10, 12]. In page migration and replication problems, a set of memory pages must be distributed in a network of processors, each of which has its local memory, so that a sequence of memory accesses can be processed efficiently. Specifically, the goal is to minimize the communication cost. If a processor p wants to read a memory address from a page b that is not in its local memory, then p must send a request to a processor q holding b and the desired information is transmitted from q to p. The communication cost incurred thereby is equal to the distance between q and p. It is also possible to move or copy a page from one local memory to another. However, such a transaction incurs a high communication cost proportional to the page size times the distance between the involved processors.

In the *migration problem* it is assumed that there exists only one copy of each page in the entire distributed system. This model is particularly useful when we deal with writable pages because we do not have to consider the problem of keeping multiple copies of a page consistent. The migration problem is to decide which local memory should contain the single copy of a given page. In the *replication problem*, multiple copies of a page may exist. Hence this model is suitable when we deal with read-only pages. The decision whether a given page should be migrated or replicated from one local memory to another must typically be made *on-line*,

* International Computer Science Institute, Berkeley; and Max-Planck-Institut für Informatik, Saarbrücken, Germany. Supported in part by an Otto Hahn Medal Award of the Max Planck Society and by the ESPRIT Basic Research Actions Program of the EU under contract No. 7141 (ALCOM II). E-mail: albers@icsi.berkeley.edu

** Department of Information Science, The University of Tokyo, Tokyo 113, Japan. Part of this work was done while the author was visiting the Max-Planck-Institut für Informatik. E-mail: nwa@is.s.u-tokyo.ac.jp

i.e., the memory management algorithm does not know which processors will have to access a page in the future. Because of this on-line nature, the performance of migration and replication algorithms is usually evaluated using competitive analysis.

Page migration and replication are extensively studied problems. However, almost all of the research results are developed under the assumption that the capacities of the local memories are infinite: Whenever we want to move or copy a page into the local memory of a processor p, there is room for it; no other page needs to be dropped from p's memory. Assuming infinite local capacity, on-line migration and replication algorithms with a constant competitive ratio can be developed [1, 3, 6, 8, 10, 12]. For example, Black and Sleator [6] presented a deterministic 3-competitive migration algorithm when the network topology is a tree or a complete uniform network. In practice, however, the local capacities are of course not unlimited. Basically the only work that considers local memories with finite capacity is the paper by Bartal *et al.* [5]. They investigate a combination of the migration and replication problem and present an $O(m)$-competitive on-line algorithm for complete uniform networks. Here m is total number of pages that can be stored in the entire network. Unfortunately, this competitive ratio is too high to be meaningful in practice.

In this paper we study the migration problem under the assumption that every local memory has a fixed finite capacity. More precisely, every local memory consists of k block $[1], [2], \ldots, [k]$, each of which can hold one page. We assume that the local memories are *direct-mapped*, i.e., each processor uses a hash function in order to locate pages in its local memory. Specifically, all processors use the same hash function h. This implies that whichever local memory a page b belongs to, it is always stored in block $[h(b)_{\mathrm{mod}k} + 1]$. Direct-mapped memories constitute an important memory class in practice. From a theoretical point of view they were studied only once before in [9]. We call the migration problem in direct-mapped memories of limited capacity the *direct-mapped constrained migration problem*. We will show that for this problem, we can develop simple on-line algorithms with a constant competitive ratio. Hence this is essentially the first work on page migration that makes realistic assumptions as far as memory is concerned and develops results that are meaningful in practice.

In Section 3 we investigate lower bounds on the competitiveness that can be achieved by deterministic on-line algorithms for the direct-mapped constrained migration problem. We show that, given any network topology, no deterministic on-line algorithm can be better than 3-competitive. We also prove that there are specific network topologies for which no deterministic on-line algorithm can be better than $\Omega(n)$-competitive; n denotes the number of processors in the network. In Section 4 we develop upper bounds. First, we present an optimal 3-competitive deterministic algorithm for networks consisting of two nodes. Next we develop an 8-competitive deterministic algorithm for complete uniform networks. This algorithm achieves a competitiveness of 16 on uniform stars. Finally, we give a 5-competitive randomized and memoryless on-line algorithm for complete uniform networks against adaptive on-line adversaries.

We also study the *distributed paging problem*. In distributed paging, each time a processor p wants to access a page, this page must be brought into p's local memory, provided the page is not yet present at p. Loosely speaking, the goal is to minimize the number of times at which the requested page is not present in the corresponding local memory. For the *allocation version* of this problem, when multiple copies of a page may exist, Bartal *et al.* [5] presented a deterministic $O(m)$-competitive on-line algorithm; Awerbuch *et al.* [2] developed a randomized $O(\max\{\log(m - l), \log k\})$-competitive algorithm against the oblivious adversary. Again, m is the total number of pages that can be stored in the system, and l is the number of different pages in the system. In this paper we examine the *migration version* of the distributed paging problem; i.e., only one copy of each page may exist. In Section 5 we present an $O(k)$-competitive deterministic and an $O(\log k)$-competitive randomized on-line algorithm (k is the number of pages that each processor can hold). Our randomized algorithm is simpler than that of Awerbuch *et al.* for $l \geq m - k$.

2 Problem definition

We define the direct-mapped constrained migration problem and the distributed paging problem. We also review the notion of competitiveness.

In the *direct-mapped constrained migration problem* we are given an undirected graph $G = (V, E)$. Each node in G corresponds to a processor, and the edges represent the interconnection network. Let $|V| = n$. Associated with each edge is a *length* that is equal to the distance between the connected nodes. Let δ_{uv} denote the length of the shortest path between node u and node v. Each node has its own local memory. Every local memory is divided into k *blocks* $[1], [2], \cdots, [k]$, each of which can hold exactly one page. All nodes use the same hash function $h(b)$ to determine the unique block in which page b will reside. At any time, a node cannot simultaneously hold pages b and c with $h(b)_{\bmod k} = h(c)_{\bmod k}$. On the other hand, there is never a conflict between two pages e and f with $h(e)_{\bmod k} \neq h(f)_{\bmod k}$. Thus we can divide the direct-mapped constrained migration problem into k separate subproblems according to the block number. In the following, we concentrate on one particular block number i $(1 \leq i \leq k)$. Let B be the number of pages b such that $h(b)_{\bmod k} + 1 = i$, and let $b_1, b_2, \cdots, b_B$ be the pages whose hash value is equal to i. We always assume $B \leq n$, which is easily realized by a proper choice of h.

We say that *a node v has a page b* if b is contained in block $[i]$ of v's memory. A node v is said to be *empty* if v does not hold a page in block $[i]$. A *request to page b at a node v* occurs if v wants to read or write b. The request can be satisfied at zero cost if v has b. Otherwise the request incurs a cost equal to the distance from v to the node u holding b (i.e. the cost is δ_{uv}). After a request to page b at a node v, b may be migrated into v's local memory. If v is empty, the cost incurred by this migration is $d \cdot \delta_{uv}$. Here d denotes the page size factor. In case v has another page c, we may swap b and c, incurring a cost of $2d \cdot \delta_{uv}$. (Of course, it is also possible to move c to another node, but we will never make use of this possibility.) A direct-mapped constrained migration algorithm is usually presented with an entire sequence of requests that must be served with low total cost. The algorithm is *on-line* if it serves every request without knowledge of any future requests.

Next we define the *distributed paging problem*. Again, we consider a network consisting of n nodes, each of which can store up to k pages. We only distinguish between local and remote data accesses: A request to page b at node v can be satisfied at zero cost if v has b. Otherwise the request is satisfied by fetching b into v's local memory, which may accompany other page configuration changes. The cost incurred is equal to the number of transferred pages because each page transfer requires exactly one remote access. The goal is to reduce the total number of page transfers. The distributed paging problem is named the *migration version* if the number of copies for any page is restricted to 1.

We analyze the performance of on-line algorithms using *competitive analysis* [11]. That is, the cost incurred by an on-line algorithm is compared to the cost of an *optimal off-line algorithm*. An optimal off-line algorithm knows the entire request sequence in advance and can serve it with minimum cost. Given a request sequence σ, let $C_A(\sigma)$ and $C_{OPT}(\sigma)$ denote the cost of the on-line algorithm A and the optimal off-line algorithm OPT in serving σ. A deterministic on-line algorithm A is c-competitive if there exists a constant a such that for every request sequence $C_A(\sigma) \leq c \cdot C_{OPT}(\sigma) + a$. In case A is a randomized algorithm, the on-line setting is viewed as a request-answer game in which an adversary generates a request sequence σ, see [4]. The expected cost incurred by A is then compared to the cost paid by the adversary. The *oblivious adversary* constructs σ in advance before any actions of A are made; the adversary may serve σ off-line. The *adaptive on-line adversary* constructs σ on-line, knowing the responses of A to previous requests; the adversary also has to serve σ on-line.

3 Lower bounds

Theorem 1 shows that the power of on-line algorithms is limited, no matter how simple the underlying graph structure may be.

Theorem 1. *Let A be a deterministic on-line algorithm for the direct-mapped constrained migration problem. Then A cannot be better than 3-competitive, even on a graph consisting of only two nodes.*

Proof. Consider a 2-node network and let b_1 and b_2 be two pages whose location needs to be managed. Consider request sequences consisting of requests to b_1 only. To process such sequences, A can concentrate on the location of b_1. However, to change the location of b_1, b_2 must also be moved as the result of a swap. Thus, this situation can be regarded as a migration problem with page size factor $2d$. Therefore, the lower bound of 3-competitiveness presented by Black and Sleator [6] for the migration problem also holds for the direct-mapped constrained migration problem. □

Next we prove the existence of specific topologies for which no deterministic on-line algorithm is better than $(n-2)$-competitive. The following star H is an example. Let $v_1, v_2, \cdots, v_n$ be the nodes in H, with v_1 being the center node. The edge lengths are defined as $\delta_{v_1 v_i} = 1$ for $i = 2, \ldots, n-1$ and $\delta_{v_1 v_n} = n-2$.

Theorem 2. *Let A be a deterministic on-line algorithm for the direct-mapped constrained migration problem working on the star H. Then A cannot be better than $(n-2)$-competitive.*

This theorem certifies that there is a difference between the migration problem (when the local memories are infinite) and the direct-mapped constrained migration problem. Recall that, for the migration problem, Black and Sleator [6] developed a deterministic on-line algorithm that is 3-competitive for trees including all stars.

Proof of Theorem 2: We will construct a request sequence σ so that $C_A(\sigma)$ is at least $(n-2)$ times the cost incurred by some off-line algorithm OFF. We assume that initially, both A and OFF have the same page at v_n. The request sequence σ is constructed as follows. An adversary always generates a request at v_1; it asks for the page that A stores in v_n. Therefore, A incurs a cost of $\delta_{v_1 v_n} = n - 2$ at each request. We partition σ into phases. The first phase starts with the first request. It ends after $n-1$ distinct pages were requested during the phase and just before the remaining nth page b_r is requested. The second phase begins with the request to b_r and ends in the same way as the end of the first phase. The subsequent phases are determined similarly.

We show that in any phase, the cost incurred by A is at least $(n-2)$ times the cost incurred by OFF. Let σ' be a subsequence of σ that corresponds to a phase, and let l be the length of σ'. A incurs $n-1$ swaps in σ', each of which costs $2(n-2)d$. Thus the total cost for swaps is $2(n-1)(n-2)d$. In addition, A pays a cost of $(n-2)l$ to satisfy the requests. Therefore, $C_A(\sigma') \geq 2(n-1)(n-2)d + (n-2)l$. The following off-line algorithm OFF can serve σ' at a cost of $2(n-1)d+l$. At the beginning of σ', before the first request, OFF swaps the page located at v_n and the page b_r which is requested at the beginning of the next phase. After this swap, OFF does not change the locations of pages throughout the phase. Note that b_r is never requested in σ'. OFF incurs a cost of at most $2(n-1)d$ for the swap, and a cost of at most l to satisfy the requests in σ' because every page requested in σ' is located at one of the nodes $v_1, \ldots, v_{n-1}$. Thus $C_{OFF}(\sigma') \leq 2(n-1)d + l$. By comparing $C_A(\sigma')$ and $C_{OFF}(\sigma')$ we conclude $C_A(\sigma') \geq (n-2)C_{OFF}(\sigma')$. At the beginning of each phase, node v_n has the same page both in A's and OFF's configuration. This implies that we can extend σ arbitrarily by repeating the above construction. $\square$

4 Upper bounds

We develop on-line algorithms for the direct-mapped constrained migration problem. First we present a 3-competitive deterministic algorithm for the case that the network consists of only two nodes. This topology is of course very special, but we have an optimal algorithm for this case. Most of this section deals with important network topologies such as complete uniform graphs and uniform stars. We give $O(1)$-competitive algorithms for these networks.

First consider a 2-node network consisting of nodes u and v. A direct-mapped constrained migration algorithm has to manage the location of two pages b_1 and

b_2. Note that there are only two possible page configurations: u has b_1 and v has b_2; or u has b_2 and v has b_1. Our algorithm TN for 2-node networks is given below. The proof of Theorem 3 is omitted in this extended abstract.

Algorithm TN: The algorithm maintains one global counter that is initialized to 0. Whenever a node requests a page that is not in its local memory, the counter is incremented by 1. When the counter reaches $4d$, the page configuration changes, i.e. the pages are swapped, and the counter is reset to 0.

Theorem 3. *TN is 3-competitive for graphs consisting of two nodes.*

In the remainder of this section we study on-line algorithms for uniform graphs. First we present a deterministic algorithm for complete uniform graphs. We assume w.l.o.g. that all edges in the network have length 1. As the name suggests, our algorithm is thought of as a concurrent version of algorithm M presented by Black and Sleator [6] for the migration problem.

Algorithm Concurrent-M: Each node v has B counters $c_v^{b_i}$ ($1 \leq i \leq B$). All counters are initialized to 0. Concurrent-M processes a request at node v to page b_i as follows. If v has b_i already, then the request is free and nothing happens. If v does not have b_i, then the algorithm increments $c_v^{b_i}$, and chooses some other non-zero counter among $\{c_w^{b_i} | w \in V\}$, if there is one, and decrements it. When $c_v^{b_i}$ reaches $2d$, one of the following two steps is executed. If v is empty, then b_i is migrated to v and $c_v^{b_i}$ is reset to 0. Otherwise b_i is swapped with the page $b_j (i \neq j)$ that v currently holds, and $c_v^{b_i}$ and $c_u^{b_j}$ are reset to 0. Here u denotes the node that stored b_i before the swap.

In the above swap, we say that b_i is swapped *actively* and that b_j is swapped *passively*.

Theorem 4. *Concurrent-M is 8-competitive for complete uniform graphs.*

The next lemma is crucial for the analysis of Concurrent-M. A similar lemma was shown in [6].

Lemma 5. *For every page b, $\sum_{v \in V} c_v^b \leq 2d$.*

Proof. We prove the lemma by induction. Initially $\sum_{v \in V} c_v^b = 0$. The sum $\sum_{v \in V} c_v^b$ only increases when one counter is incremented and all other counter values are 0. Since the description of the algorithm implies that a counter value cannot exceed $2d$, the sum $\sum_{v \in V} c_v^b$ cannot be larger than $2d$. □

This lemma leads to an important fact: Just before a page b is swapped actively to node v, $c_v^b = 2d$ and all other counters associated with b are 0. After the swap, all counters associated with b are 0.

Proof of Theorem 4: We analyze the algorithm for the case $B = n$. The analysis is easily extended to $B \leq n$. Let $C_{CM}(\sigma)$ be the cost paid by Concurrent-M. We shall show that, for any (on-line and off-line) algorithm A and any request sequence σ, $C_{CM}(\sigma) \leq 8C_A(\sigma)$. Our proof uses the standard technique of comparing simultaneous runs of Concurrent-M and A on σ by merging the actions generated by Concurrent-M and A into a single sequence of events. This sequence contains three types of events: (Type I) Concurrent-M swaps pages, (Type II)

A swaps pages, and (Type III) both A and Concurrent-M satisfy a request. We shall give a non-negative potential function Φ (initially 0) such that the following inequality holds for all kinds of events.

$$\Delta C_{CM} + \Delta \Phi \leq 8\Delta C_A, \tag{1}$$

where Δ indicates the change of the values as the result of the event. If the potential function satisfies the above property for all events, summing up (1) for all events results in $C_{CM}(\sigma) + \Phi_{end} - \Phi_{start} \leq 8C_A(\sigma)$, where Φ_{start} denotes the initial value of Φ and Φ_{end} denotes the value of Φ after Concurrent-M and A finish processing σ. Since $\Phi_{start} = 0$ and $\Phi_{end} \geq 0$ from the definition of the potential function, we have $C_{CM}(\sigma) \leq 8C_A(\sigma)$, and the proof is complete. It remains to specify the potential function and verify (1) for all events.

The potential function Φ is defined as follows. Let s^b be the node that has page b in Concurrent-M and t^b be the node that has b in A.

$$\Phi = \sum_b \Phi_b, \quad \Phi_b = \begin{cases} 5\sum_{v \in V} c_v^b & \text{if } s^b = t^b. \\[2ex] 4d - c_t^b + 3\sum_{\substack{v \in V \\ v \neq t}} c_v^b & \text{if } s^b \neq t^b \end{cases}$$

In the following we prove (1) for all kinds of events. In the subsequent proof we omit the specification of the page in the counter variables when it is obvious.

(Type I): Concurrent-M swaps pages.

Suppose that page b_1 is swapped actively from s to s' and page b_2 is swapped passively from s' to s. As the result of this swap, $c_{s'}^{b_1}$ is reset from $2d$ to 0 and $c_s^{b_2}$ is reset from some non-negative value l to 0. Let t be the location of b_1 and let u be the location of b_2 in A. Then $\Delta C_{CM} = 2d$ and $\Delta C_A = 0$. So we must show that $\Delta \Phi \leq -2d$. Trivially, $\Delta \Phi = \Delta \Phi_{b_1} + \Delta \Phi_{b_2}$. First consider $\Delta \Phi_{b_1}$. There are three cases depending on whether s, s' coincide with t. Lemma 5 and the fact obtained from the lemma make the calculation of $\Delta \Phi_{b_1}$ very simple.

$$s' = t : \Delta \Phi_{b_1} = 5\sum 0 - (4d - 2d + \sum 0) = -2d$$

$$s = t : \Delta \Phi_{b_1} = (4d - 0 - 3\sum 0) - 5 \cdot 2d = -6d$$

$$s, s' \neq t : \Delta \Phi_{b_1} = (4d - 0 - 3\sum 0) - (4d - 0 - 3 \cdot 2d) = -6d$$

Next we calculate $\Delta \Phi_{b_2}$. For clearness, we express the counter value of c_s before the swap simply by $c_s(=l)$ and that after the swap by $c_s'(=0)$.

$$s = u : \Delta \Phi_{b_2} = 5\sum_{v \in V} c_v - (4d - c_u + 3\sum_{\substack{v \in V \\ v \neq u}} c_v) = 2\sum_{\substack{v \in V \\ v \neq s}} c_v + 5c_s' + c_s - 4d$$

$$= 2\sum_{\substack{v \in V \\ v \neq s}} c_v + c_s - 4d \leq 2\sum_{v \in V} c_v - 4d \leq 0.$$

$$s' = u : \Delta \Phi_{b_2} = (4d - c_u + 3\sum_{\substack{v \in V \\ v \neq u}} c_v) - 5\sum_{v \in V} c_v \leq (4d + 3\sum_{\substack{v \in V \\ v \neq s'}} c_v) - 5\sum_{\substack{v \in V \\ v \neq s'}} c_v$$

$$\leq 4d + 3c'_s - 5c_s - 2 \sum_{\substack{v \in V \\ v \neq s, s'}} c_v \leq 4d$$

$$s, s' \neq u : \Delta\Phi_{b_2} = (4d - c_u + 3 \sum_{\substack{v \in V \\ v \neq u}} c_v) - (4d - c_u + 3 \sum_{\substack{v \in V \\ v \neq u}} c_v)$$

$$= 3(c'_s - c_s) = -3l \leq 0.$$

Adding $\Delta\Phi_{b_1}$ and $\Delta\Phi_{b_2}$ we can calculate $\Delta\Phi$. For example, if $s = t$ and $s' = u$, then $\Delta\Phi = \Delta\Phi_{b_1} + \Delta\Phi_{b_2} \leq -6d + 4d = -2d$. The sum $\Delta\Phi_{b_1} + \Delta\Phi_{b_2}$ can only be greater than $-2d$ if $s' = t$ and $s' = u$. However, this case is impossible because a node cannot have both b_1 and b_2 at the same time, and hence t and u cannot be identical. Thus, in all cases $\Delta\Phi \leq -2d$ and (1) holds for (Type I).

(Type II): A swaps pages.

Suppose that page b_1 is swapped from t to t' and that page b_2 is swapped from t' to t. Then $\Delta C_{CM} = 0$ and $\Delta C_A = 2d$. We must show that $\Delta\Phi \leq 16d$. Again we calculate $\Delta\Phi_{b_1}$ and $\Delta\Phi_{b_2}$ separately and then compute $\Delta\Phi$. Let s be the location of b_1 and w be the location of b_2 in Concurrent-M. First consider $\Delta\Phi_{b_1}$.

$$t' = s : \Delta\Phi_{b_1} = 5 \sum_{v \in V} c_v - (4d - c_t + 3 \sum_{\substack{v \in V \\ v \neq t}} c_v) \leq 6 \sum_{v \in V} c_v - 4d \leq 12d - 4d = 8d$$

$$t = s : \Delta\Phi_{b_1} = (4d - c_{t'} + 3 \sum_{\substack{v \in V \\ v \neq t'}} c_v) - 5 \sum_{v \in V} c_v = 4d - 6c_{t'} - 2 \sum_{\substack{v \in V \\ v \neq t'}} c_v \leq 4d$$

$$t, t' \neq s : \Delta\Phi_{b_1} = (4d - c_{t'} + 3 \sum_{\substack{v \in V \\ v \neq t'}} c_v) - (4d - c_t + 3 \sum_{\substack{v \in V \\ v \neq t}} c_v) = 4(c_t - c_{t'}) \leq 8d$$

We conclude $\Delta\Phi_{b_1} \leq 8d$. Next consider $\Delta\Phi_{b_2}$. Since there is no distinction between b_1 and b_2, the same analysis as above gives $\Delta\Phi_{b_2} \leq 8d$. Thus, the total change in potential is $\Delta\Phi = \Delta\Phi_{b_1} + \Delta\Phi_{b_2} \leq 16d$, and (1) holds for (Type II).

(Type III) A request is satisfied by both A and Concurrent-M.

Suppose there is a request at node v to page b. Let s be the node at which Concurrent-M stores b, and let t be the node at which A holds b.

Case 1: $v = s$. $\Delta C_{CM} = 0$. $\Delta C_A \geq 0$. $\Delta\Phi = 0$. Thus (1) is satisfied.

Case 2: $v \neq s$.   In this case $\Delta C_{CM} = 1$ because v does not have b in Concurrent-M. The counter c_v^b is incremented by 1. We need to consider three cases.

Case (a): Suppose that $v = t$. $\Delta C_A = 0$. So we have to show that $\Delta\Phi \leq -1$. Note that $s \neq t$. The increment of c_t^b decreases Φ by 1. In case another counter is decremented, then Φ decreases further by 3. Thus $\Delta\Phi \in \{-4, -1\} \leq -1$.

Case (b): Suppose that $v \neq t = s$. $\Delta C_A = 1$. So we must show that $\Delta\Phi \leq 7$. The increment of c_v^b increases Φ by 5. If another counter is decremented, then Φ decreases by 5. Thus $\Delta\Phi \in \{0, 5\} \leq 7$.

Case (c) Suppose that $v \neq t \neq s$. $\Delta C_A = 1$ and we must show that $\Delta\Phi \leq 7$. The increment of c_v^b increases Φ by 3. If no decrement takes place, $\Delta\Phi = 3$. Else if another counter except c_t^b is decremented, Φ decreases by 3 and totally $\Delta\Phi = 0$. If c_t^b is decremented, Φ increases by 1, and in total $\Delta\Phi = 4$. $\square$

We can treat Concurrent-M as an on-line algorithm for uniform stars (stars in which all edges have length 1).

Theorem 6. *Concurrent-M is 16-competitive for uniform stars.*

Proof. Let US be the uniform star consisting of n nodes $v_1, v_2, \cdots, v_n$, with v_1 being the center node. All edges have length 1. Let K_1 and K_2 be two complete uniform graphs consisting of n nodes each; in K_1 all edges have length 1 and in K_2 all edges have length 2. Let $u_1, u_2, \cdots, u_n$ and $w_1, w_2, \cdots, w_n$ be the nodes in K_1 and K_2, respectively. Our analysis maps an arbitrary request sequence σ on US onto two request sequences σ' on K_1 and σ'' on K_2, and then compares simultaneous runs of Concurrent-M on σ, σ' and σ''. Assume that initially, nodes v_i, u_i and w_i have the same page in their memory, for all i ($1 \leq i \leq n$).

We construct σ' from σ by replacing each request to a page b at node v_i in σ by a request to b at node u_i in σ'. σ'' is derived from σ similarly. If we simultaneously run Concurrent-M on σ, σ' and σ'', the (fixed) counter decrement strategy implies that whenever Concurrent-M moves a page from v_i to v_j in US, the same page is moved from u_i to u_j in K_1 and from w_i to w_j in K_2. Hence, at any time, the page stored at v_i is identical to the page stored at u_i and w_i. Since for any pair of indexes i and j, $\delta_{u_i u_j} \leq \delta_{v_i v_j} \leq \delta_{w_i w_j}$, we have $C_{CM}(\sigma') \leq C_{CM}(\sigma) \leq C_{CM}(\sigma'')$. Similarly, $C_{OPT}(\sigma') \leq C_{OPT}(\sigma) \leq C_{OPT}(\sigma'')$. We have $C_{CM}(\sigma'') \leq 8C_{OPT}(\sigma'')$ because, by Theorem 4, Concurrent-M is 8-competitive for complete uniform graphs. Also, $C_{OPT}(\sigma'') = 2C_{OPT}(\sigma')$ because of the relation between K_1 and K_2. The above formulae give $C_{CM}(\sigma) \leq C_{CM}(\sigma'') \leq 8C_{OPT}(\sigma'') = 16C_{OPT}(\sigma') \leq 16C_{OPT}(\sigma)$ □

Next we present a randomized on-line algorithm for complete uniform graphs. The algorithm is *memoryless*, i.e. it does not need any memory (e.g. for counters) in order to determine when a migration or a swap should take place.

Algorithm COINFLIP: Suppose that there is a request at node v to page b. If v has b, COINFLIP performs no action. If v does not have b, the algorithm serves the request by accessing to the node u that has b. Then with probability $\frac{1}{3d}$, the algorithm migrates b from u to v if v is empty, and moves b from u to v by a swapping operation if v is not empty.

Theorem 7. *COINFLIP is 5-competitive against adaptive on-line adversaries.*

Proof. A detailed proof is omitted; we just give the main idea. Let $\Phi = 5d \cdot |S|$, where S is the set of nodes at which COINFLIP and the adversary A have different pages. Using this potential function we can show $E[C_{CF}(\sigma)] \leq 5C_A(\sigma)$. □

5   On-line algorithms for distributed paging

We present a deterministic on-line algorithm for the migration version of the distributed paging problem. Let B be the number of different pages in the system.

Algorithm DLRU: Each processor v has B counters $c_v[b_i]$ ($1 \leq i \leq B$). All counters are initialized to 0. The algorithm maintains the invariant that $c_v[b_i] = 0$ if (but not only if) b_i does not belong to v's memory. DLRU serves a request at node v to page b_i as follows. If v has b_i, then the request is free and the algorithm sets $c_v[b_i]$ to k, while all counters whose values were strictly larger than $c_v[b_i]$

before the request are decremented by 1. If v does not have b_i, then b_i is fetched into v from the node u holding b_i, and a number of counters are changed. In node v, $c_v[b_i]$ is set to k and all positive counters are decremented by 1. In node u, $c_u[b_i]$ is reset to 0 and all positive counters whose values were smaller than $c_u[b_i]$ before the request are incremented by 1. In particular, when v is full, a page b_j such that $b_j \in v$ and $c_v[b_j] = 0$ is chosen arbitrarily and is swapped out to u. Such a page b_j can always be found after the counter manipulation.

We mention a simple fact that we will use in the proof of Theorem 8. When a node v has l positive counters, these counters take distinct values in $[k - l + 1, k]$.

Theorem 8. *DLRU is $2k$-competitive.*

Proof. We assume $B = kn$. The analysis can be extended to $B < kn$ with only small changes. Let S^v_{opt} be the set of pages stored at v in OPT. We define

$$\Phi = \sum_{v \in V} \sum_{b \in S^v_{opt}} 2(k - c_v[b])$$

as our non-negative potential function. It suffices to prove that, for an arbitrary request sequence σ, $\Delta C_{DL} + \Delta \Phi \leq 2k \Delta C_{OPT}$, for all events contained in the simultaneous run of DLRU and OPT on σ. Here ΔC_{DL} denotes the cost incurred by DLRU during the event. We assume w.l.o.g. that when there is a request, first OPT transfers pages to serve the request and then DLRU starts satisfying it. So when DLRU is serving, the requested page belongs to S^v_{opt}. We have to consider two types of events: (Type I) OPT swaps two pages; (Type II) DLRU satisfies the request. Due to space limitations we prove $\Delta C_{DL} + \Delta \Phi \leq 2k \Delta C_{OPT}$ only for (Type II). Suppose that there is a request to page b_i at node v.

Case 1: DLRU already has b_i at node v.

In this case $\Delta C_{DL} = \Delta C_{OPT} = 0$ and $c_v[b_i]$ is augmented from some non-negative integer $l(\leq k)$ to k. In addition, at most $k - l$ counters in v decrease their values by 1. Since $b_i \in S^v_{opt}$, the change of Φ is smaller than $-2(k - l) + (k - l) \cdot 2 = 0$. Thus we obtain $\Delta C_{DL} + \Delta \Phi \leq 0 + 0 = 0 = 2k \Delta C_{OPT}$.

Case 2: DLRU does not have b_i at node v yet.

Again $\Delta C_{OPT} = 0$. $\Delta C_{DL} = 2$ because DLRU loads b_i into v's local memory, which requires one swap. Let u be the node that stored b_i before the request and let b_j be the page brought from v to u to make room at v for b_i. In v, $c_v[b_i]$ is set from 0 to k, and in the worst case k positive counters are decremented. Since $b_i \in S^v_{opt}$, at least one of the decreased k counters is not in S^v_{opt}, and the change of Φ with respect to v is less than $-2k + (k - 1) \cdot 2 = -2$. In node u, $c_u[b_i]$ is reset to 0 and several counters may be incremented. The change of Φ corresponding to u is less than or equal to 0, because the counter increments lower Φ and $b_i \notin S^u_{opt}$. The total change of Φ is the sum of the change at u and v. Hence $\Delta \Phi \leq -2 + 0 = -2$ and $\Delta C_{DL} + \Delta \Phi \leq 2 + (-2) = 0 = 2k \Delta C_{OPT}$. $\square$

Finally, we investigate randomized distributed paging. For uni-processor paging, a well-known randomized on-line algorithm called Marking attains $(2 \log k)$-competitiveness against the oblivious adversary [7]. We can generalize Marking to the migration version of the distributed paging problem.

Algorithm VMARK: The algorithm is defined for each node v separately. Each of the k blocks in node v has a marker bit and a page field associated with it. The marker bit and the page field are called the *attribute* of a block. The page field is used to specify the name of a page; the page stored in a block can be different from that specified in the page field, though. Roughly speaking, a page field memorizes the page which would occupy the corresponding block if there were no requests at any nodes except v. The algorithm works in a series of phases. Like Marking, at the beginning of every phase, all marker bits are reset to 0. As the phase proceeds, the number of marker bits that take the value 1 monotonically increases. After all bits have been marked, the phase is over at the next request to an item not contained in the set of pages written on the k page fields in v. Marker bits and page fields can be modified only if there is a request at v or a page is swapped out to v from other nodes. The details of the algorithm are given in the program style. At a page collision, VMARK moves the evicted page to the block that the incoming page occupied before.

```
type block = record
    mark : 0 or 1
    page : name of the page
end
```

Procedure Fetchblock /* there is a request at v to b_i */
if b_i belongs to v's local memory **then**
    let BL_i be the block holding b_i.
    if $BL_i.page = b_i$ then set $BL_i.mark$ to 1 and exit.
    else choose randomly one block BL_j s.t. $BL_j.mark = 0$.
        copy BL_i's attribute to BL_j's attribute.
        $BL_i.mark \leftarrow 1. \; BL_i.page \leftarrow b_i.$
else /* b_i does not belong to v's local memory */
    if there is a block BL s.t. $BL.page = b_i$ **then**
        swap out a page from BL if BL is not empty. /* page collision */
        fetch b_i to BL. $\;\; BL.mark \leftarrow 1.$
    else choose randomly one block BL' s.t. $BL'.mark = 0$.
        swap out a page from BL' if BL' is not empty. /* page collision */
        fetch b_i to BL'. $\;\; BL'.mark \leftarrow 1. \;\; BL'.page \leftarrow b_i.$

Procedure Dropped /* page b_i stored at v is fetched by node u
and b_j is brought into v instead because of a page collision at u */
let BL be the block that b_i occupied before leaving v.
bring b_j to BL.
if there is a block BL' s.t. $BL'.page = b_j$ **then**
    exchange the attributes of BL and BL'.

The program is composed of two procedures, Fetchpage and Dropped. Fetchpage explains the action when there is a request at v. Dropped is called when a page is discarded into v because of a page collision in another node u. Note that if requests are generated at only one node v, the algorithm performs in exactly the same way as Marking. VMARK preserves the following crucial properties. (1) During a phase, exactly k different pages are requested at v. (2) There never exist two blocks BL_1 and BL_2 in a node v so that BL_1 stores a page b and at the same time b is specified in the page field of BL_2. (3) If the page stored in block BL

158

at v is different from the page b memorized in the page field of BL, then b left v because some other node generated a request to b.

Theorem 9. *VMARK is $(8 \log k)$-competitive against the oblivious adversary.*

Proof (Sketch). Let $C_{VM}(\sigma)$ be the cost incurred by VMARK. We analyze the cost by dividing $C_{VM}(\sigma)$ and $C_{OPT}(\sigma)$ among all nodes. Then, for each node v, we compare VMARK's and OPT's cost. The cost $C_{VM}(\sigma)$ is divided as follows. Suppose that there is a request at node v to page b and that VMARK does not have b in v's local memory. Then we charge a cost of 2 to v, even if v is empty and the actual cost would only be 1. This can only overestimate $C_{VM}(\sigma)$. As for OPT, whenever OPT moves a page from u to v, we assign a cost of $\frac{1}{2}$ to both v and u. Using this cost-assignment, when we pay attention to a particular node v, the influence from other nodes (e.g. other nodes generate requests to pages stored in v or drop pages to v as the result of a page collision) does not increase the cost ratio of VMARK to OPT on v. Thus we can assume that requests only occur at node v and can apply the analysis for Marking [7] to v. □

References

1. B. Awerbuch, Y. Bartal and A. Fiat. Competitive distributed file allocation. In *Proc. 25th Annual ACM Symposium on Theory of Computing*, pages 164-173, 1993.
2. B. Awerbuch, Y. Bartal and A. Fiat. Heat & Dump: Competitive Distributed Paging. In *Proc. 34th Annual IEEE Symposium on Foundations of Computer Science*, pages 22-32, 1993.
3. S. Albers and H. Koga. New on-line algorithms for the page replication problem. In *Proc. 4th Scandinavian Workshop on Algorithm Theory*, pages 25-36, 1994.
4. S. Ben-David, A. Borodin, R.M. Karp, G. Tardos and A. Wigderson. On the power of randomization in on-line algorithms. *Algorithmica*, 11:2-14,1994.
5. Y. Bartal, A. Fiat and Y. Rabani. Competitive algorithms for distributed data management. In *Proc. 24th Annual ACM Symposium on Theory of Computing*, pages 39-50, 1992.
6. D.L. Black and D.D. Sleator. Competitive algorithms for replication and migration problems. Technical Report Carnegie Mellon University, CMU-CS-89-201, 1989.
7. A. Fiat, R.M. Karp, M. Luby, L.A. McGeoch, D.D. Sleator and N.E. Young. Competitive paging algorithm. *Journal of Algorithm*, 12:685-699, 1991.
8. H. Koga. Randomized on-line algorithms for the page replication problem. In *Proc. 4th International Annual Symposium on Algorithms and Computation*, pages 436-445, 1993.
9. A.R. Karlin, M.S. Manasse, L. Rudolph and D.D. Sleator. Competitive snoopy caching. *Algorithmica*, 3:79–119, 1988.
10. C. Lund, N. Reingold, J. Westbrook and D. Yan. On-line distributed data management. In *Proc. 2nd Annual European Symposium on Algorithms*, pages 202-214, 1994.
11. D.D. Sleator and R.E. Tarjan. Amortized efficiency of list update and paging rules. *Communication of the ACM*, 28:202-208, 1985.
12. J. Westbrook. Randomized Algorithms for the multiprocessor page migration. In *Proc. of the DIMACS Workshop on On-Line Algorithms*, pages 135-149, 1992.

Randomized Algorithms for Metrical Task Systems

Sandy Irani* and Steve Seiden

Department of Information and Computer Science
University of California
Irvine, CA 92717

Abstract. Borodin, Linial, and Saks introduce a general model for on-line systems in [BLS92] called *task systems* and show a deterministic algorithm which achieves a competitive ratio of $2n-1$ for any metrical task system with n states. We present a randomized algorithm which achieves a competitive ratio of $e/(e-1)n - 1/(e-1) \approx 1.5820n - 0.5820$ for any metrical task system of n states. For the uniform metric space, Borodin, Linial, and Saks present an algorithm which achieves a competitive ratio of $2H_n$, and they show a lower bound of H_n for any randomized algorithm. We improve their upper bound for the uniform metric space by showing a randomized algorithm which is $(H_n/\ln 2 + 1 \approx 1.4427H_n + 1)$-competitive.

1 Introduction

In computer systems, it is often necessary to solve problems with incomplete information. The input evolves with time, and incremental computational decisions must be made based on only part of the input. A typical situation is where a sequence of tasks must be performed. How past tasks are performed effects the cost of future tasks. Examples include managing a two level store of memory, performing a sequence of operations on a dynamic data structure, and maintaining data in a multiprocessing environment [KMMO94, MMS90, ST85b, Wes92]. An algorithm that decides how to perform an operation based only on past requests with no knowledge of the future is said to be an *online algorithm*. In contrast, we refer to an algorithm which has complete information about the tasks to be performed before making any decisions as an *offline algorithm*.

Much progress has been made in the study of particular online problems. However, much of the work that has been done in on-line algorithms is ad-hoc in nature, both the assortment of problems studied and the techniques that have been developed to address them. In order to develop a more uniform approach to the study of online algorithms, Borodin, Linial and Saks introduced *task systems* in [BLS92]. A task system is defined as a pair (S, d), where $S = \{s_1, \ldots, s_n\}$ is a set of n states, and d, the *distance matrix*, is an $n \times n$ non-negative matrix. $d_{s,t}$ is the distance from s to t. The input is a sequence of *tasks*, $\sigma = T^1, T^2, \ldots, T^\ell$.

---

* Research supported in part by NSF grant number CCR-9309456.

A task is a vector with n entries, where $T^i(s_j)$ is the cost of processing task i in state s_j. The algorithm starts in state s_1 and the objective is to determine a state in which to process each task, balancing the cost of moving with the cost of processing the tasks. An algorithm receives a sequence σ of ℓ requests and produces a schedule π, a function from $[1, \ldots, \ell]$ to S. $\pi(i)$ is the state in which task i is processed. If the algorithm is online, then $\pi(i)$ is a function only of $T^1, \ldots, T^i$. The cost of a schedule π on σ is the sum of the cost of moving from state to state (the *moving costs*) and the cost of processing the tasks (the *stationary costs*):

$$\text{cost}(\pi, \sigma) = \sum_{i=1}^{\ell} d_{\pi(i-1), \pi(i)} + \sum_{i=1}^{\ell} T^i(\pi(i)) .$$

We denote by $A(\sigma)$ the schedule produced by algorithm A on input σ. The *cost of algorithm A on σ* denoted $\text{cost}_A(\sigma)$ is $\text{cost}(A(\sigma), \sigma)$. The cost of the optimal offline algorithm for the sequence π is

$$\text{cost}(\sigma) = \min_{\pi} \text{cost}(\pi, \sigma) .$$

A simple dynamic programming approach suffices to determine the optimal schedule for a sequence.

We evaluate an online algorithm by comparing its performance to that of the optimal offline algorithm. An online algorithm A is said to be c-competitive if there is a constant d such that for all σ,

$$\text{cost}(\sigma) \leq c \cdot \text{cost}_A(\sigma) + d .$$

If the algorithm A is randomized, then its cost on a given sequence $c_A(\sigma)$ is a random variable. We compare the expectation of this cost to the cost of the optimal algorithm on σ: A is said to be c-competitive if there is a constant d such that for all σ,

$$\text{cost}(\sigma) \leq c \cdot \text{E}[\text{cost}_A(\sigma)] + d .$$

The *competitive ratio* of A is the infimum over all c such that A is c-competitive. This approach to analyzing online problems called *competitive analysis* was initiated by Sleator and Tarjan, who used it to analyze the List Update problem [ST85a]. The term *competitive analysis* was coined in [KMMO94]. The goal for a given task system (d, S) is to determine the best competitive ratio achievable on task system, $c(d, S)$, and to determine the algorithm that achieves it.

In the case of deterministic algorithms, Borodin, Linial, and Saks show in [BLS92] that for every task system (d, S) with n states where the distance matrix is metrical (symmetric and obeys the triangle inequality), $c(d, S) = 2n - 1$. For randomized algorithms, less is known. Borodin et al. have shown a lower bound of H_n and an upper bound of $2H_n$, for the uniform distance matrix on n states ($d_{s,t} = 1$ for all $s \neq t$). We call such tasks systems *uniform task systems*.

In this work, we present two results. We present a randomized algorithm for uniform task systems, the THRESHOLD OFFSET algorithm, which achieves a competitive ratio of $\frac{H_n}{\ln 2} + 1 \approx 1.4427 H_n + 1$ against an oblivious adversary. We also present the first randomized algorithm for the general distance metric, the THRESHOLD WORK FUNCTION algorithm. We show that the THRESHOLD WORK FUNCTION algorithm is $\left(\frac{e}{e-1}\right) n - \frac{1}{e-1}$ competitive against an oblivious adversary.

In Sect. 2 we describe the THRESHOLD OFFSET algorithm. In Sect. 2.1 we present a proof of Theorem 2 which is the upper bound for the algorithm. In Sect. 3 we describe the THRESHOLD WORK FUNCTION algorithm. In Sect. 3.1 we present an upper bound on the competitiveness of this algorithm. We have shown that our analysis is tight for both the THRESHOLD OFFSET and the THRESHOLD WORK FUNCTION algorithms by showing a lower bounds for both algorithms. However, the proofs are omitted here.

2 The THRESHOLD OFFSET Algorithm

For convenience, we adopt a continuous time model also used in [BLS92] where state transitions can be made in the middle of the discrete time intervals. A *continuous time schedule* for ℓ tasks is a function from the continuous interval $[1, \ell + 1)$ to S such that for any state $x \in S$, $\pi^{-1}(x)$ is the finite disjoint union of half open intervals $[t, t')$. There are a finite number of transition times $t_1 < t_2, \ldots, t_k$. Denote the state to which the algorithm moves at time t_i by x_i. The cost for the schedule is then

$$\text{cost}(\pi, \sigma) = \sum_{i=1}^{k} d_{x_{i-1}, x_i} + \sum_{i=1}^{\ell} \int_{i}^{i+1} T^i(\pi(t)) dt \ .$$

Allowing an algorithm the freedom to move any time in a continuous time interval does not supply any additional power. Borodin et al. prove the following lemma:

Lemma 1. *For any online continuous time algorithm A, there is an online discrete time algorithm A' that performs at least as well on any sequence of tasks.*

In order to describe the algorithm, we require one more definition: the *work function* for a sequence of tasks. The work function w maps states onto the non-negative real numbers. Intuitively, at any point in time, the work function on state s is the minimum cost required to process the tasks seen so far and end up in state s. The idea of work functions was first introduced in [BLS92]. Initially, for all x, $w(x) = d_{x, x_0}$. After the next task T arrives, the work function is updated as follows:

$$w(x) \leftarrow \min_{x'} w(x') + T(x') + d_{x, x'} \ .$$

$\min_x w(x)$ is a lower bound on the adversary cost. Also note that for any two states x_i and x_j, $w(x_i) \leq w(x_j) + d_{i,j}$. Since we assume the distance matrix is uniform, no work function value is more than one plus the minimum work function value.

We can similarly extend the definition of the work function to the continuous time interval. Let w be the work function at some integer time t, let T be the next task and let λ be a real number such that $0 \leq \lambda < 1$. The work function at time $t + \lambda$ is

$$w(x) \leftarrow \min_{x'} w(x') + \lambda T(x') + d_{x,x'} \ .$$

We are now ready to describe the algorithm. Consider the algorithm in Fig. 1 with parameter m. We refer to a as the *threshold constant* and a/m as the *threshold*. Similarly, b is the *offset constant* and b/m the *offset*. We prove the following theorem:

Theorem 2. $P_1, \ldots, P_m$ *can be chosen so that algorithm* THRESHOLD OFFSET *is* $[H_n/(H_{2m} - H_m) + 1]$-*competitive for uniform task systems on n states.*

$H_{2m} - H_m$ converges to $\ln 2$ as m gets large. The constant m can be chosen to be arbitrarily large.

The $2H_n$-competitive algorithm of Borodin et al. is essentially the algorithm above with the threshold deterministically set to 1 and the offset deterministically set to 0. Their algorithm can be forced to incur a cost of 2 every time it moves: one for the stationary costs and one for the moving costs. Our algorithm avoids some of the stationary costs by randomizing over the values of the threshold and the offset.

Algorithm THRESHOLD OFFSET

1. Pick a randomly from $1, \ldots, m$ with distribution $\Pr[a = i] = P_i$.
2. Pick b randomly from $0, \ldots, a - 1$ uniformly.
3. Stay in the initial state until its work function reaches 1.
4. While there is some state with work function value less than $1 + b/m$:
   (a) Move to a random state with work function value less than $1 + b/m$, and stay there until its work function reaches $1 + b/m$.
5. Assign $i \leftarrow 1 + b/m$.
6. Loop until the end of the request sequence:
   (a) While there is some state with work function value less than $i + a/m$:
      i. Move to a random state with work function value less than $i + a/m$, and stay there until its work function reaches $i + a/m$.
   (b) Assign $i \leftarrow i + a/m$.

Fig. 1. A description of the THRESHOLD OFFSET algorithm.

2.1 Upper Bound for the Algorithm

The cost incurred in Step 3 can be upper bounded by a constant which is independent of the sequence. Thus, we only bound the cost incurred in Steps 4 through 6. Fix a sequence. Divide the sequence into subphases where subphase l ends the moment all states have reached a work function value of l/m. If there are l subphases completed, then l/m is a lower bound on the adversary cost. At the beginning of each subphase, normalize the work function by subtracting off $\min_x w(x)$. Then the minimum value is 0 at the start of each subphase. The subphase ends as soon as all states have reached a work function value of $1/m$. We then renormalize so that the minimum value is 0 at the start of the new subphase.

Pick an arbitrary subphase. With probability p_i, where $p_i = \sum_{j=i}^{m} \frac{P_j}{j}$, the algorithm will changes states when the work function value of the current state reaches i/m. Notice that the distribution is the same regardless of which subphase is chosen. Thus, we only have to bound the expected cost to the algorithm for each phase. Notice also that for any distribution $(p_1, \ldots, p_m)$ such that $p_i \geq p_{i+1}$ for all $1 \leq i \leq m$, we can pick the P_j's to achieve this distribution: simply let $P_j = j(p_j - p_{j+1})$ and $p_{m+1} = 0$.

For $1 \leq i \leq m$, we define S_i to be the set of states which have a work function value strictly less than i/m at the beginning of the subphase. We define S_i' to be to be the number of states which have a work function value strictly less than i/m at the beginning of the next subphase. Note that at the beginning of the next subphase, the offset has increased by $1/m$, so we have that $S_i' \subseteq S_{i+1}$. Denote $|S_i|$ and $|S_i'|$ by s_i and s_i', respectively. Define $S_0 = \emptyset$, $s_0 = 0$, and $H_{s_0} = 0$.

The value of the work function on state x is $w(x)$ before the subphase and $w'(x)$ after the subphase.

Claim 3. *The expected cost to the algorithm during the subphase is at most*

$$\sum_{i=1}^{m} p_i \left\{ \left(1 + \frac{i}{m}\right) \left[H_{s_i} - H_{s_{i-1}'}\right] - \sum_{x \in S_i} \frac{w(x)}{s_i} + \sum_{x \in S_{i-1}'} \frac{w'(x)}{s_{i-1}'} + \frac{1}{m} \right\} .$$

Proof. Consider the case where the threshold and offset are chosen so that the algorithm changes state when the work function value of the current state reaches i/m. This happens with probability p_i. We will account for the cost incurred by the algorithm due to increases in the work function for states in S_{i-1}', $S_i - S_{i-1}'$ and the complement of S_i separately.

Any increase in the work function for states not in S_i cost the algorithm nothing. For any state in S_{i-1}', the work function value never reaches the threshold, so if the algorithm is in one of these states, it won't change state for the rest of the subphase. Furthermore, if the algorithm is in some state in S_{i-1}', it is in a random state from this set. Thus, the total expected cost incurred due to charges to states in S_{i-1}' is the total increase in the work function for these states divided by s_{i-1}'. The increase in the work function for states in S_{i-1}' is

$$\sum_{x \in S_{i-1}'} \frac{1}{m} + w'(x) - w(x) .$$

The first term takes account for the fact that the offset increases by $1/m$ for each state at the end of the subphase.

Name the rest of the states in $S_i - S'_{i-1}$ according to the order in which they reach the threshold i/m in the subphase: $x_1, x_2, \ldots, x_k$, where $k = s_i - s'_{i-1}$. The probability that the algorithm is in state x_j when x_j reaches the threshold is $1/(s_i - j + 1)$. The cost incurred by the algorithm in this case is at most $i/m - w(x_j)$ in stationary costs and at most 1 in moving costs. Thus, the expected cost incurred by the algorithm due to the charges to state x_j is at most

$$\left(1 + \frac{i}{m} - w(x_j)\right)\left(\frac{1}{s_i - j + 1}\right) \leq \left(1 + \frac{i}{m}\right)\left(\frac{1}{s_i - j + 1}\right) - \left(\frac{w(x_j)}{s_i}\right) .$$

Summing up over all x_j for $1 \leq j \leq k$,

$$\sum_{j=1}^{k}\left[\left(1 + \frac{i}{m}\right)\left(\frac{1}{s_i - j + 1}\right) - \left(\frac{w(x_j)}{s_i}\right)\right]$$

$$\leq \left(1 + \frac{i}{m}\right)\sum_{j=1}^{k}\frac{1}{s_i - j + 1} - \sum_{x \in S_i - S'_{i-1}}\frac{w(x_j)}{s_i}$$

$$= \left(1 + \frac{i}{m}\right)\left[H_{s_i} - H_{s'_{i-1}}\right] - \sum_{x \in S_i - S'_{i-1}}\frac{w(x_j)}{s_i} .$$

Taking the expectation over all i:

$$\sum_{i=1}^{m} p_i \left\{\left(1 + \frac{i}{m}\right)\left[H_{s_i} - H_{s'_{i-1}}\right] - \sum_{x \in S_i - S'_{i-1}}\frac{w(x)}{s_i} + \sum_{x \in S'_{i-1}}\frac{\frac{1}{m} + w'(x) - w(x)}{s'_{i-1}}\right\}$$

$$\leq \sum_{i=1}^{m} p_i \left\{\left(1 + \frac{i}{m}\right)\left[H_{s_i} - H_{s'_{i-1}}\right] - \sum_{x \in S_i}\frac{w(x)}{s_i} + \sum_{x \in S'_{i-1}}\frac{w'(x)}{s'_{i-1}} + \frac{1}{m}\right\} .$$

$\square$

We would like to choose the p_i's so that for all i and j,

$$p_i\left(1 + \frac{i}{m}\right) = p_j\left(1 + \frac{j}{m}\right) .$$

In that case, $p_i = p_1(m+1)/(m+i)$. Note that our condition that $p_i \geq p_{i+1}$ for all $1 \leq i \leq m$ is satisfied. To solve for p_1,

$$1 = p_1(m+1)\sum_{i=1}^{m}\frac{1}{m+i} = p_1(m+1)(H_{2m} - H_m) .$$

Denote $H_{2m} - H_m$ by c. Then $p_i = 1/c(m+i)$ and $p_i(1+\frac{i}{m}) = \frac{1}{cm}$. Thus, the expected cost for the subphase is at most

$$\sum_{i=1}^{m} \left\{ \frac{1}{cm} \left[H_{s_i} - H_{s'_{i-1}} \right] - \sum_{x \in S_i} \frac{p_i w(x)}{s_i} + \sum_{x \in S'_{i-1}} \frac{p_i w'(x)}{s'_{i-1}} + \frac{p_i}{m} \right\} .$$

Define the functions Ψ_i and Ψ'_i as follows:

$$\Psi_i = \sum_{x \in S_i} \frac{w(x)}{s_i}, \qquad \Psi'_i = \sum_{x \in S'_i} \frac{w'(x)}{s'_i} .$$

Note that since $S_0 = S'_0 = \emptyset$, $\Psi_0 = \Psi'_0 = 0$, the bound on the expected cost of the algorithm in the subphase can be written:

$$\sum_{i=1}^{m} \left\{ \frac{1}{cm} \left[H_{s_i} - H_{s'_{i-1}} \right] - p_i \Psi_i + p_i \Psi'_{i-1} + \frac{p_i}{m} \right\}$$

$$\le \frac{1}{m} + \sum_{i=1}^{m} \frac{1}{cm} \left[H_{s_i} - H_{s'_{i-1}} \right] - \sum_{i=1}^{m} p_i \Psi_i + \sum_{i=1}^{m} p_{i-1} \Psi'_{i-1}$$

$$\le \frac{1}{m} + \sum_{i=1}^{m} \frac{1}{cm} \left[H_{s_i} - H_{s'_{i-1}} \right] + \sum_{i=1}^{m-1} p_i (\Psi'_i - \Psi_i) .$$

The first inequality holds because $p_{i-1} \ge p_i$. Now define a potential function:

$$\Phi = \frac{1}{cm} \sum_{i=1}^{m-1} H_{s_i} - \sum_{i=1}^{m-1} p_i \Psi_i .$$

Φ is the value of the potential function at the beginning of the current subphase, while Φ' is the value at the beginning of the next subphase. Since the value of the potential function is bounded by a constant independent of the request sequence at the beginning of the sequence, we simply have to upper bound the amortized cost for the subphase:

$$\frac{1}{m} + \sum_{i=1}^{m} \frac{1}{cm} \left[H_{s_i} - H_{s'_{i-1}} \right] - \sum_{i=1}^{m-1} p_i (\Psi_i - \Psi'_i) + \Phi' - \Phi$$

$$= \frac{1}{m} + \frac{1}{cm} \left[\sum_{i=1}^{m} (H_{s_i} - H_{s'_{i-1}}) + \sum_{i=1}^{m-1} H_{s'_i} - \sum_{i=1}^{m-1} H_{s_i} \right]$$

$$+ \sum_{i=1}^{m-1} p_i (\Psi'_i - \Psi_i) - \sum_{i=1}^{m-1} p_i \Psi'_i + \sum_{i=1}^{m-1} p_i \Psi_i$$

$$= \frac{1}{m} + \frac{1}{cm} (H_{s_m} - H_{s'_0}) \le \frac{1}{m} + \frac{1}{cm} H_n .$$

Thus the expected cost to the algorithm in the subphase is $[1 + H_n(H_{2m} - H_m)]/m$ and the cost to the optimal algorithm is $1/m$. The competitive ratio is $H_n/(H_{2m} - H_m) + 1$ which goes to $H_n/\ln 2 + 1$ as m gets large.

3 The THRESHOLD WORK FUNCTION Algorithm

To design a randomized algorithm which is competitive for any metric space, we begin with a deterministic algorithm which know to be competitive, and apply the techniques used in the design of the previous algorithm. The algorithm which we randomize is a variant of the WORK FUNCTION algorithm, introduced by Borodin, Linial and Saks [BLS92]. The basic idea of the (continuous time) WORK FUNCTION algorithm is as follows: When the work function of the current state s reaches a value where $w(s) = w(t) + d_{s,t}$ for some other state t, the algorithm moves to the state t. A simple variant of this is as follows: For some real number $\alpha \in (0,1]$, when the work function of the current state s reaches a value where $w(s) = w(t) + \alpha \cdot d_{s,t}$ for some other state t, the algorithm moves to the state t. We call this generalized version the ALPHA WORK FUNCTION algorithm, after an algorithm of the same name for the k-server and layered graph traversal problems [CL91, Bur93]. Borodin, Linial and Saks have shown that the WORK FUNCTION algorithm is $(2n - 1)$-competitive [BLS92]. Further, they show that the WORK FUNCTION algorithm is optimal; any deterministic algorithm for metrical task systems must have a competitive ratio of at least $2n - 1$. It is not hard to extend their proof to show that the ALPHA WORK FUNCTION algorithm is $(\frac{\alpha+1}{\alpha}n - \frac{1}{\alpha})$-competitive.

By utilizing randomization, we hope to achieve a lower competitive ratio. We investigate the algorithm which chooses α randomly, according to a distribution $\mathcal{D}$. The algorithm has a parameter m which is a positive integer. The algorithm chooses α from $(0,1]$ as follows: The probability that $\alpha \in \left(\frac{i-1}{m}, \frac{i}{m}\right]$ is p_i. If $\alpha \in \left(\frac{i-1}{m}, \frac{i}{m}\right]$ then it is uniformly chosen from this interval. We derive $p_1, \ldots, p_m$ in Sect. 3.1. We refer to the randomly chosen α as the *threshold*; it plays the same role as the threshold of the previous algorithm. We call this randomized algorithm the THRESHOLD WORK FUNCTION algorithm.

For convenience, we again adopt a continuous time model. A formal description of the THRESHOLD WORK FUNCTION algorithm appears in Fig. 2.

Algorithm THRESHOLD WORK FUNCTION

1. $a \leftarrow 1, \ldots, m$ randomly with distribution $\Pr[a = i] = p_i$.
2. $b \leftarrow (0, \frac{1}{m}]$ uniformly.
3. $\alpha \leftarrow \frac{a}{m} + b$.
4. $u \leftarrow s_1$.
5. Loop until end of task sequence:
   (a) While $w(u) < w(s) + \alpha \cdot d_{u,s}$ for all s
      i. Stay in u.
   (b) $u \leftarrow s$. If several states s exist such that $w(u) \geq w(s) + \alpha \cdot d_{u,s}$, pick the least indexed state s_i such that $w(s_i) < w(s') + \alpha \cdot d_{s_i,s'}$ for all s'.
   (c) Move to s.

Fig. 2. A description of the THRESHOLD WORK FUNCTION algorithm.

3.1 Upper Bound for the Algorithm

We require a few definitions. Let $P_{i,j} = \sum_{k=i}^{j} p_k$. We define

$$\phi_s(t) = \frac{w(s) - w(t)}{d_{s,t}}, \quad \text{if } t \neq s, \qquad \phi_s(s) = 0 \ .$$

We define $\Phi_s = \max_t \phi_s$. Let $T_s = \{t \in S | \phi_s(t) = \alpha\}$. T_s describes the states to which the algorithm might move to if it were in s and α is Φ_s. If $|T_s| = 1$ the algorithm only has one choice of states to move to, and we let $\eta(s)$ be the single member of T_s. Otherwise, we break ties as the algorithm does, $t = \eta(s)$ is the least indexed state with $\Phi_t < \alpha$. That we can always do this is shown in the following lemma.

Lemma 4. *There exists a $t \in T_s$ such that $\Phi_t < \alpha$.*

The proof is omitted

Corollary 5. *The algorithm is never in a state s with $\Phi_s \geq \alpha$.*

Note that $0 \leq \Phi_s \leq 1$. The lower bound $0 \leq \Phi_s$ is due to the fact that $\phi_s(s) = 0$, and so $\max_{t \in S} \phi_s(t)$ is at least 0. The upper bound is due to the fact that the work function of a state s is no more that $d_{s,t}$ greater than the work function of any other state t. Also note that since all work functions change continuously with time, Φ_s also changes continuously, because when $\eta(s)$ changes from t to t' we have that $\phi_s(t) = \phi_s(t')$.

We define the *useful work* of a task T^i to be the amount by which T^i increases work functions. Formally, the useful work u_i of T^i is $u_i = \sum_{s \in S} w_i(s) - w_{i-1}(s)$.

Lemma 6. *For a sequence of tasks σ let u_i be the useful work of task T^i and let $U_\ell = \sum_{i=1}^{\ell} u_i$. Then the optimal cost is at least $\frac{U_\ell}{n} - d_{\max}$, where $d_{\max} = \max_{s,t \in S} d_{s,t}$.*

Proof. The total increase of all work functions is the total useful work. There is at least one state s whose work function value is at least $\sum u_i/n$. For all t we have $w_\ell(t) \geq w_\ell(s) - d_{s,t}$. And so, for all t we have $w_\ell(t) \geq w_\ell(s) - d_{\max}$. Note that the optimal cost is $\min_{s \in S} w_\ell(s)$. $\qquad \square$

A *period* with respect to a state s is a continuous time interval during which:

1. $\Phi_s < 1$.
2. $\eta(s)$ remains fixed.
3. Φ_s is either monotonically increasing (in which case the period is an *increasing period*), or monotonically non-increasing (in which case the period is an *non-increasing period*), but not both.

A *sub-period* with respect to s is a continuous sub-interval of a period with respect to s.

A *maximal period* with respect to s is a period which is not a sub-period of any other period with respect to s.

A *minimum period* with respect to s is a period with respect to s during which $w(s) \leq w(t)$ for all states t. Note that during a minimum period $\Phi_s = 0$, and so necessarily a minimum period is a non-increasing period.

We analyze the competitiveness of the algorithm against an oblivious adversary. We bound the expected cost by summing over all states s, the expected stationary cost incurred while in state s and the expected moving cost incurred in leaving state s. Note that, when $\Phi_s = 1$, the algorithm cannot be in s and therefore we need only consider possible costs incurred by the algorithm during each period. Thus, we divide the time line of each state s into maximal periods. We upper-bound the costs incurred by the algorithm due to each of these periods, and then bound the overall cost by summing over all periods.

Consider a single period of state s. We show that:

Lemma 7. *For any non-increasing period with respect to a state s, the ratio of the expected cost incurred by the* THRESHOLD WORK FUNCTION *algorithm while in state s or leaving state s to the increase in useful work is at most 1.*

Lemma 8. *There exists a distribution $\mathcal{D}$ such that, for any increasing period with respect to a state s, the ratio of the expected cost incurred by the* THRESHOLD WORK FUNCTION *algorithm to the increase in useful work is at most c, for some constant c.*

From these lemmas we derive an upper bound on the competitive ratio.

Proof of Lemma 7. Let w be the work function at the beginning of the period, and w' be the work function at the end. Suppose that the work function of s increases from $x = w(s)$ to $x' = w'(s)$ during the period. If the period is a non-increasing period with respect to s and the algorithm is in s, it incurs a cost of at most $x' - x$, since it will not move from s. The useful work increases by $x' - x$, and the ratio of expected cost to increase in useful work is 1. □

Proof of Lemma 8. We begin by noting that during any increasing period with respect to a state s, the algorithm will leave s at most once during the period. To see this, note that the algorithm never visits any state s with $\Phi_s \geq \alpha$. If the algorithm is in s and Φ_s reaches α the algorithm will leave and not return. The value of Φ_s achieves a value of α at most once during the period.

Let $t = \eta(s)$. Let w be the work function at the beginning of the period, and w' be the work function at the end. Let i be the least integer for which $\frac{i}{m}d_{s,t} \geq w(s)-w(t)$, and j be the greatest integer such that $\frac{i}{m}d_{s,t} \leq w'(s)-w'(t)$. Let $k = j - i + 1$. Define:

$$y_0 = w(s) - w(t),$$
$$y_1 = \tfrac{i}{m}d_{s,t},$$
$$y_2 = \tfrac{i+1}{m}d_{s,t},$$
$$\vdots \quad \vdots \quad \vdots$$
$$y_k = \tfrac{i}{m}d_{s,t},$$
$$y_{k+1} = w'(s) - w'(t) \ .$$

Let t_i be the point in time, after the beginning of the period, at which $w(s) - w(t) = y_i$. Since the period is increasing, these times are unique. The given period is broken into sub-periods, each of which is itself a period. The first sub-period starts at t_0 and ends at t_1, the second sub-period starts at t_1 and ends at t_2, etc. ... . If the hypothesis is true for each of these sub-periods, then it will be true for the period.

Let $x = w(s)$ and $x' = w'(s)$. We define $y = w(s) - w(t)$ and $y' = w'(s) - w'(t)$. Note that since the period is increasing $y' - y < x' - x$. The useful work increases by $x' - x$. By the conclusion of the previous paragraph, it is sufficient to show the hypothesis for the case where

1. At the start of the period, we have that $y \geq \frac{i}{m} d_{s,t}$.
2. At the end of the period, we have $y' \leq \frac{i+1}{m} d_{s,t}$.

The probability that the algorithm is in s is at most $1 - P_{1,i-1}$ at the beginning of the period, and decreases during the period. Given that the algorithm is in s, it incurs a stationary cost of at most $x' - x$. The probability that the algorithm moves to t at cost $d_{s,t}$ during the interval $(\frac{i}{m}, \frac{i+1}{m}]$ is $p_i / P_{i,m}$. Note that the distribution of α within $(\frac{i}{m}, \frac{i+1}{m}]$ is uniform, and so the expected cost to the algorithm is at most

$$(1 - P_{1,i-1}) \left(x' - x + \frac{y' - y}{\frac{1}{m} d_{s,t}} \cdot \frac{p_i}{P_{i,m}} d_{s,t} \right) \leq P_{i,m} \left(x' - x + \frac{x' - x}{\frac{1}{m} d_{s,t}} \cdot \frac{p_i}{P_{i,m}} d_{s,t} \right)$$

$$= m(x' - x)(1 - P_{1,i-1}) \left(\frac{1}{m} + \frac{p_i}{P_{i,m}} \right) = m(x' - x) \left((1 - P_{1,i-1}) \frac{1}{m} + p_i \right) .$$

Let $z_i = (1 - P_{1,i-1}) \frac{1}{m} + p_i$. We choose the distribution $p_1, \ldots, p_m$ so that $z_1 = z_2 = \cdots = z_m$. Consider z_i and z_{i+1}

$$z_i = (1 - P_{1,i-1}) \frac{1}{m} + p_i, \qquad z_{i+1} = (1 - P_{1,i}) \frac{1}{m} + p_{i+1} .$$

Assuming that $z_i = z_{i+1}$, the difference of these two equations is $p_i + p_i \frac{1}{m} - p_{i+1} = 0$. And so $p_{i+1} = (1 + \frac{1}{m}) p_i$. This recurrence has solution $p_{i+1} = (1 + \frac{1}{m})^i p_1$. To find p_1, we note that

$$1 = \sum_{i=1}^{m} p_i = p_1 \sum_{i=1}^{m} (1 + \tfrac{1}{m})^{i-1} = p_1 \sum_{i=0}^{m-1} (1 + \tfrac{1}{m})^i = p_1 \left(m(1 + \tfrac{1}{m})^m - m \right) .$$

And so $p_1 = 1/(m(1 + \frac{1}{m})^m - m)$. Since z_i is independent of i, we abbreviate z_i by z. We have

$$z = z_1 = \frac{1}{m} + \frac{1}{m(1 + \frac{1}{m})^m - m} .$$

The increase in useful work is $x' - x$ and so, the ratio of expected cost to increase in useful work is at most

$$\frac{mz(x' - x)}{x' - x} = 1 + \frac{1}{(1 + \frac{1}{m})^m - 1} .$$

$\square$

Theorem 9. *Let $c = 1 + 1/((1 + \frac{1}{m})^m - 1)$. Then algorithm* THRESHOLD WORK FUNCTION *is $(c \cdot n - c + 1)$-competitive.*

Proof. Let A_ℓ be the total useful work incurred during minimum periods. Since, at the end of the request sequence, the minimum work function value is at least $U_\ell/n - d_{\max}$, we have that $A_\ell \geq U_\ell/n - d_{\max}$. The total expected cost to the algorithm is at most $c(U_\ell - A_\ell) + A_\ell$. By Lemma 6, the cost to the optimal algorithm at least $U_\ell/n - d_{\max}$. For the algorithm to be $(c \cdot n - c + 1)$-competitive we must have for some constant k that $\text{cost}_{\text{twf}}(\sigma) \leq (c \cdot n - c + 1)\text{cost}(\sigma) + k$, for all task sequences σ. Let $k = c \cdot n \cdot d_{\max} - 2c \cdot d_{\max}$. Then we have

$$\text{cost}_{\text{twf}}(\sigma) \leq c(U_\ell - A_\ell) + A_\ell \leq c\left(U_\ell - \frac{U_\ell}{n} - d_{\max}\right) + \frac{U_\ell}{n} - d_{\max}$$

$$= c \cdot U_\ell - c\frac{U_\ell}{n} - c \cdot d_{\max} + \frac{U_\ell}{n} - d_{\max}$$

$$= \left(c - \frac{c}{n} + \frac{1}{n}\right)U_\ell - c \cdot d_{\max} - d_{\max}$$

$$\leq (c \cdot n - c + 1)\text{cost}(\sigma) + k \ .$$

$\square$

Is this better than $2n - 1$? The competitive ratio of the algorithm is

$$\left(1 + \frac{1}{(1 + \frac{1}{m})^m - 1}\right)n - \frac{1}{(1 + \frac{1}{m})^m - 1} \ .$$

Note that $\lim_{m \to \infty}(1 + \frac{1}{m})^m = e$. The competitive ratio can therefore be made arbitrarily close to $(\frac{e}{e-1})n - \frac{1}{e-1}$, by choosing sufficiently large m. For large m the competitive ratio is approximately $1.581977n - 0.581977$.

References

[BLS92]   A. Borodin, N. Linial, and M. E. Saks. An optimal on-line algorithm for metrical task systems. *Journal of the ACM*, 39(4):745–763, Oct 1992.

[Bur93]   W. R. Burley. Traversing layered graphs using the work function algorithm. Technical Report CS93-319, University of California, San Diego, Sep 1993.

[CL91]   M. Chrobak and L. L. Larmore. Server problems and on-line games. In *Proc. DIMACS Workshop on On-line Algorithms*, Feb 1991.

[KMMO94] A. R. Karlin, M. S. Manasse, L. A. McGeoch, and S. Owicki. Competitive randomized algorithms for non-uniform problems. *Algorithmica*, 11(6):542–571, Jun 1994.

[MMS90]   M. S. Manasse, L. A. McGeoch, and D. D. Sleator. Competitive algorithms for server problems. *Journal of Algorithms*, 11:208–230, 1990.

[ST85a]   D.D. Sleator and R.E. Tarjan. Amortized efficiency of list update and paging rules. *Communications of the ACM*, 28(2):202–208, Feb 1985.

[ST85b]   D.D. Sleator and R.E. Tarjan. Self adjusting binary search trees. *Journal of the ACM*, 32(3):652–686, Jul 1985.

[Wes92]   J. Westbrook. Randomized algorithms for multiprocessor page migration. In *Proc. DIMACS Workshop on On-line Algorithms*, 1992.

Efficient Geometric Algorithms for Workpiece Orientation in 4- and 5-Axis NC-Machining

Prosenjit Gupta[1]   Ravi Janardan[1]   Jayanth Majhi[1]
Tony Woo[2]

Abstract

In 4- and 5-axis NC machines, the time to dismount, recalibrate, and remount the workpiece after each set of accessible faces has been machined can be considerable in comparison to the actual machining time. The problem of minimizing the number of setups is NP-hard. Efficient algorithms are given for a greedy heuristic which finds an orientation maximizing the number of faces that can be machined in a single setup. These results are based on geometric duality, topological sweep, interesting new properties concerning intersection and covering on the unit-sphere, and on techniques for efficiently constructing and searching an arrangement of polygons on the unit-sphere.

1   Introduction

The mass-production of parts of complex shape to close tolerances often requires highly-sophisticated, numerically-controlled (NC) machines. NC-machines are typically classified as 3-, 4-, or 5-axis machines, depending on the (effective) number of degrees of freedom (DOF) enjoyed by the cutter. In a *3-axis machine*, the cutter can translate up and down in the z direction, while the work-table can be translated back and forth in the x and y directions. In a *4-axis machine*, the work-table can additionally rotate a full 360° about the z-axis. In a *5-axis machine*, the cutter can also swivel partially about a second axis, say, the x-axis. Clearly, the versatility of these machines increases with the DOF; unfortunately, so does the cost of acquiring and maintaining them.

The ability of a cutter to access a workpiece surface depends not only on the DOF but on the nature of the cutter itself. Cutters are classified as flat-end,

---

[1]Department of Computer Science, University of Minnesota, Minneapolis, MN 55455, U.S.A. E-mail: {pgupta,janardan,majhi}@cs.umn.edu. The research of these authors was supported in part by NSF grant CCR–9200270.

[2]Presently: Dept. of Industrial and Operations Engg., University of Michigan Ann Arbor, MI 48109. Email: tony.woo@um.cc.umich.edu. After July 1: Dept. of Industrial Engineering, FU-20, University of Washington, Seattle, WA 98195. Email: twoo@u.washington.edu

fillet-end, and ball-end cutters, depending on the maximum angle, θ, that the cutter's axis can be tilted from the normal to the surface at a given point. In a *flat-end* cutter, $\theta = 0°$; in a *fillet-end* cutter, $\theta < 90°$; and in a *ball-end* cutter, $\theta = 90°$. Clearly, ball-end cutters offer the greatest range of movement; they are often used for finishing operations. Flat-end and fillet-end cutters are usually used for larger-scale material removal [1].

However, even with a 4- or 5-axis machine equipped with a ball-end cutter, it may not be possible for the cutter to access all the surfaces of the workpiece in a single setup. The process of dismounting the workpiece and remounting and recalibrating it can be very time-consuming in comparison to the actual machining time (often, hours versus minutes). This can result in low machine availability and may not justify the high capital cost associated with such a machine. Moreover, frequent setups can lead to loss of dimensional accuracy.

This motivates the problem of finding a sequence of workpiece orientations such that the number of setups is minimized. This problem has been considered previously in [1, 8], and, as noted there, is known to be NP-hard. The natural approach then is to find an efficient strategy which approximates closely the minimum number of setups. In [1, 8], an efficient, "greedy" approach is presented to this problem for a 4-axis machine equipped with a ball-end cutter. The algorithm finds a workpiece orientation that allows the maximum number of surfaces to be machined in a single setup. Then a second such orientation is found for the as-yet-unmachined surfaces, and so on. We state the running time and approximation ratio of this approach after formalizing the problem below. (The *approximation ratio* is the maximum value of the ratio of the number of setups needed by the greedy method to the minimum number of setups.)

1.1 Formalization of the problem

Hereafter, until the end of Section 4, we will primarily consider a ball-end cutter. We discuss fillet-end cutters in Section 5. We follow the approach in [1, 8]. The key idea is to capture the notion of the cutter's accessibility to a workpiece surface by means of a visibility map. The *visibility map* (or VMap, for short) of a surface is the set of all directions along which an unobstructed line-of-sight can be established from the cutter (which is treated as a point) to every point on the surface. For a ball-end cutter, the VMap of a surface can be represented on the unit sphere $\mathbf{S}^2$ as a *spherical polygon*, i.e., a closed region on $\mathbf{S}^2$ bounded by arcs of great circles.

As in [1, 8], we assume that we are given N VMaps with a total of V vertices, representing all the directions along which the cutter can access different surfaces of the workpiece. (We do not address here the issue of how these VMaps are computed; we assume they are given. See [5] for details about their construction.) In a 4-axis machine, the directions along which the cutter can access the workpiece in a single setup can be represented by a great circle on $\mathbf{S}^2$. In a 5-axis machine where the cutter can partially swivel by an angle of $\pm b$ radians, the directions along which the cutter can access the workpiece can be represented by a spherical band of width $2b$. (A *spherical band* of width $2b$ is the region of

S^2 consisting of points that are at a distance of at most b on either side of a great circle, where the distance is measured along the surface of the sphere.)

We can now formulate as follows the problem of orienting the workpiece on a 4- or 5-axis machine so that the maximum number of its surfaces can be accessed in a single setup:

Problem 1.1 (FOUR_AXIS) *"Given N spherical polygons with a total of V vertices, find a great circle which intersects the maximum number of polygons."*

Problem 1.2 (FIVE_AXIS) *"Given N spherical polygons with a total of V vertices, and a real number b, where $0 \leq b < \pi/2$, find a spherical band of width $2b$ which intersects the maximum number of polygons."*

1.2 Summary of results and contributions

In [1], an $O(VN \log N)$-time and $O(VN)$-space algorithm is presented for Problem FOUR_AXIS. Moreover, it is noted that if this algorithm is applied repeatedly to the polygons not yet intersected, then the approximation ratio for the workpiece setup problem is only $O(\log N)$.

In the worst case, N can be $\Theta(V)$, so that the above algorithm runs in $O(V^2 \log V)$ time and $O(V^2)$ space. (This worst case can occur often; for instance, if the workpiece is a non-convex polyhedron and if each of its "pockets" has a small number of faces.) We present a completely different algorithm which runs in $O(V^2)$ time. The algorithm uses $O(VN)$ space, which is $O(V^2)$ in the worst-case. Our approach is based on geometric duality and on topological sweep [2] applied to a set of colored lines.

To our knowledge, Problem FIVE_AXIS has not been solved before. In [8], it is suggested that one could solve the workpiece setup problem for 5-axis machines by repeatedly using the solution to Problem FOUR_AXIS (rather than Problem FIVE_AXIS). While this is true, the approximation ratio can be $\Theta(N)$.

Our second result is an $O(VN \log N)$-time and $O(VN)$-space algorithm for Problem FIVE_AXIS. This immediately implies an $O(\log N)$ approximation ratio for the workpiece setup problem on a 5-axis machine. This result is based on several interesting new results that we establish about intersections and coverings on S^2 and on techniques for efficiently constructing and searching an arrangement of polygons on the unit-sphere.

Our third result is an $O(V^2 + VN \log N)$-time and $O(V^2)$ space algorithm for a 4- or 5-axis machine equipped with a fillet-end cutter. We note that this problem poses significant new challenges since the VMaps for a fillet-end cutter are defined by arcs of small circles on S^2 rather than arcs of great circles. Our result is based on further new results on S^2 that we establish for such VMaps.

As discussed in the full paper [6], recent results in computational geometry [4] suggest strongly that the problems that we consider may require quadratic time in the worst case. Thus, it is unlikely that the bounds above can be improved substantially.

2 Preliminaries

Formally, we define the *unit sphere* as $\mathbf{S}^2 = \{P \in \mathbb{R}^3 |\ |P| = 1\}$. A point P in $\mathbf{S}^2$ is a unit vector in $\mathbb{R}^3$ and is represented by the three-tuple (P_1, P_2, P_3). Two points P and Q of $\mathbf{S}^2$ are *antipodal* if $P = -Q$. For point $P \in \mathbf{S}^2$, we define a *great circle* $G(P)$ with pole P as $G(P) = \{x \in \mathbf{S}^2 |\ P \cdot x = 0\}$. Note that $G(P) = G(-P)$. We use $int(\cdot)$ and $bd(\cdot)$ to denote the interior and boundary of a region respectively. We define the *distance* $d(P, Q)$ between two points P and Q of $\mathbf{S}^2$ as the length of the shorter of the two great arcs joining P and Q, i.e., $d(P, Q) = \cos^{-1}(P \cdot Q)$. A *spherical disk* $D(P, r)$ with pole P and radius r, where $0 \le r \le \pi/2$ is defined as $D(P, r) = \{X \in \mathbf{S}^2 |\ d(P, X) \le r\}$. Throughout, we shall refer to a spherical disk simply as a *disk*. Note that the circle $bd(D(P, r))$ is a great circle if $r = \pi/2$; otherwise it is a *small circle*. Also note that $D(P, \pi/2)$ is a hemisphere with pole P.

Given any two distinct nonantipodal points P and Q in $\mathbf{S}^2$, there is a unique great circle passing through P and Q denoted as $circ(P, Q)$. We define the shorter of the two arcs of $circ(P, Q)$ joining P and Q as *segment* $\overline{PQ}$. A *spherical polygon* $\mathcal{P}$ on $\mathbf{S}^2$ (or *polygon*, for short) is defined as the closed region bounded by a path of segments $\overline{P_1 P_2}$, $\overline{P_2 P_3}$, ..., $\overline{P_n P_1}$, where P_i, $i = 1 \ldots n$, are the vertices of $\mathcal{P}$. The *opposite* of a polygon $\mathcal{P}$ is the polygon $opp(\mathcal{P})$ formed by the antipodes of the vertices of $\mathcal{P}$. An *arc* $\overset{\smile}{PQ}$ is the arc of a small circle. For an arc γ, $radius(\gamma)$ (resp. $pole(\gamma)$) is the radius (resp. pole) of its supporting circle $C(\gamma)$. A *minor arc* is one which is no larger than a semicircle. An *arc polygon* $\check{\mathcal{P}}$ is the closed region bounded by a path of arcs $\overset{\smile}{P_1 P_2}$, $\overset{\smile}{P_2 P_3}$, ..., $\overset{\smile}{P_n P_1}$, where P_i, $i = 1 \ldots n$, are the vertices of $\check{\mathcal{P}}$. A set of points S in $\mathbf{S}^2$ is *quasiconvex*, if, for any pair of nonantipodal points p and q in S, $\overline{pq}$ is also in S. A set is *convex* if it is quasiconvex and has no antipodal pairs of points.

A point P on a surface is (locally) visible to a *ball-end cutter* if the tool axis deviates from the surface unit normal n_P at P by an angle no greater than $\pi/2$ radians. The *visibility map* or *VMap of point P* is defined as $\{X \in \mathbf{S}^2 |\ (X \cdot n_P) \ge 0\}$, and is a hemisphere on $\mathbf{S}^2$. The *VMap of a surface* is the intersection of hemispheres on $\mathbf{S}^2$, i.e. it is a polygon.

A point P on a surface is (locally) visible to a *fillet-end cutter* if the tool axis deviates from the surface unit normal n_P at P by an angle no greater than θ, where $0 < \theta < \pi/2$ [1]. The VMap of point P is defined as $\{X \in \mathbf{S}^2 |\ \cos^{-1}(X \cdot n_P) \le \theta\}$ which is a region on $\mathbf{S}^2$ bounded by a small circle. Then the VMap of a surface is the intersection of spherical disks of radius θ on $\mathbf{S}^2$ i.e. an arc polygon.

3 The algorithm for Problem FOUR_AXIS

Tang *et al* [8] show how to map Problem FOUR_AXIS to the plane using *central projection*: Each spherical polygon is mapped to up to two (linear) simple polygons in the plane. (If a spherical polygon does not cross the equator of $\mathbf{S}^2$, then it is mapped to a single polygon in the plane; otherwise, it is mapped to two unbounded polygons.) Thus we get $O(N)$ polygons of total size $O(V)$. Any great circle maps to a straight line. Moreover, the mapping preserves incidences in $\mathbf{S}^2$ on the plane as well and vice versa. Thus, Problem FOUR_AXIS is equivalent to the following problem (called MIPP[3] in [8]):

Problem 3.1 (MIPP) *"Given $O(N)$ simple polygons in the plane (where the polygons may be unbounded and overlapping) with a total of $O(V)$ vertices, find a straight line which intersects the maximum number of polygons."*

3.1 An $O(V^2)$-time algorithm for MIPP

We color each of the given polygons with a different color; two unbounded polygons that result from the same spherical polygon get the same color. Then, using the well-known point-line duality transform, we dualize each edge of each polygon to a doublewedge of the same color. In this way, we get $O(V)$ doublewedges. The arrangement of these doublewedges has $O(V^2)$ vertices, edges, and faces; also each face is convex. MIPP is now equivalent to finding in $\mathcal{A}$ a face which is covered by the maximum number of distinctly-colored doublewedges. We show below how to find this face in $O(V^2 \log V)$ time. Then we apply topological sweep to improve the time to $O(V^2)$. (Our approach is similar to the one in [2] for the uncolored problem).

Using the algorithm of [3] we compute $\mathcal{A}$ in $O(V^2)$ time. Then we sort its vertices by decreasing x-coordinates in $O(V^2 \log V)$ time. We sweep $\mathcal{A}$ with a vertical line L from $x = -\infty$ to $x = \infty$, stopping at the vertices and doing the processing described in Cases (a) to (d) below. Call a face f *active* if it is currently cut by L. Clearly there are $O(V)$ active faces. For each active face f, we store an array $A_f[1 : N]$ and an integer k_f: $A_f[i]$ is the number of doublewedges of color i that cover f and k_f is the number of distinct colors among the doublewedges covering f.

Suppose that the sweep reaches a vertex v. Let f and g be the faces to the left and right of L at v. Note that, by convexity, v is the rightmost vertex of f and the leftmost vertex of g. Therefore, f ceases to be active and g becomes active at v. We first rename A_f as A_g and k_f as k_g. Next, we need to update A_g and k_g. There are four cases to consider:

(a) v is the articulation point of a doublewedge of color p, i.e., the intersection point of the bounding lines of a doublewedge. (Fig. 1(a).) In this case, A_f and A_g (hence k_f and k_g) are identical, since the color p lost due to f no longer being active is regained because g becomes active.

If v is not an articulation point, then it is the intersection point of bounding lines from two distinct doublewedges, one of color p and the other of color q (where it is possible that $p = q$). There are three possibilities, as discussed below. Note that in each case, f and g are covered by the same set of doublewedges, except for the two doublewedges in question. Hence we need to consider only these two doublewedges in updating A_g and k_g.

---

[3]For "Maximal Intersection of Polygons in the Plane".

(b) See Fig. 1(b). We decrement $A_g[q]$ and if $A_g[q] = 0$ now, then we decrement k_g. Also, we increment $A_g[p]$ and if $A_g[p] = 1$ now, then we increment k_g.

(c) See Fig. 1(c). We increment $A_g[p]$ and $A_g[q]$. Suppose $p = q$. Then if $A_g[p] = 2$, we increment k_g. Suppose $p \neq q$. Then if $A_g[p] = 1$, we increment k_g, and if $A_g[q] = 1$, we increment k_g.

(d) See Fig. 1(d). We decrement $A_g[p]$ and $A_g[q]$. If $A_g[p] = 0$ then we decrement k_g. If $A_g[q] = 0$ and $p \neq q$ then we decrement k_g.

The dominant costs above are the $O(V^2 \log V)$ time to sort and the $O(V^2)$ space to store the entire arrangement. *Topological sweep* [2] is a variant of the standard sweep paradigm designed to eliminate these two bottlenecks. Replacing the straight-line sweep described above by topological sweep, we conclude:

Theorem 3.1 *Problem* MIPP *(hence Problem* FOUR_AXIS*) can be solved in* $O(V^2)$ *time and* $O(VN)$ *space.* $\square$

4 The algorithm for Problem FIVE_AXIS

Note that we cannot apply central projection to map this problem to the plane (as we did for Problem FOUR_AXIS) because central projection does not map the small circles that bound a band to straight lines.

Let B be a band of width $2b$ and let $G(P)$ be the great circle defining B. The *complement* of B is the region $\overline{B} = int(D(P, \pi/2 - b)) \cup int(D(-P, \pi/2 - b))$. We make the following easy observations: (i) a polygon $\mathcal{P}$ is not intersected by B iff $\mathcal{P}$ is completely within $\overline{B}$; (ii) $\mathcal{P}$ is completely within $int(D(P, \pi/2 - b))$ (resp. $int(D(-P, \pi/2 - b))$) iff $opp(\mathcal{P})$ is completely within $int(D(-P, \pi/2 - b))$ (resp. $int(D(P, \pi/2 - b))$). It now follows that if we reflect each VMap to its opposite polygon, then we can reformulate problem FIVE_AXIS as follows:

Problem 4.1 (FIVE_AXIS') *"Given* $2N$ *spherical polygons with a total of* $2V$ *vertices, and a real number* b, *where* $0 \leq b \leq \pi/2$, *find a point* X_{opt} *on* $\mathbf{S}^2$ *such that the number of polygons completely contained in* $int(D(X_{opt}, \pi/2 - b))$ *is minimum."*

Observation 4.1 *For* $X \in \mathbf{S}^2$, *a disk* $D(X, r)$, $0 \leq r < \pi/2$ *is convex.*

Lemma 4.1 *Let* X, P *and* Q *be points on* $\mathbf{S}^2$ *and let* $0 \leq r < \pi/2$. *Then* $X \in int(D(P, r) \cap D(Q, r))$ *iff* $\forall Y \in \overline{PQ}$, $Y \in int(D(X, r))$. $\square$

Theorem 4.1 *Let* $\mathcal{P}$ *be a spherically convex polygon with vertices* $P_1, P_2, \ldots P_k$, *taken in clockwise order around* $\mathcal{P}$. *Let* X *be a point on* $\mathbf{S}^2$. *Let* $\mathcal{R}(\mathcal{P}) = \cap_{i=1}^{k} D(P_i, r)$. *Then* $X \in int(\mathcal{R}(\mathcal{P}))$ *iff* $\mathcal{P} \subseteq int(D(X, r))$. $\square$

4.1 Solving problem FIVE_AXIS'

By Theorem 4.1 , we want to find a point X_{opt} which is contained in the interior of the minimum number of regions $\mathcal{R}(\mathcal{P})$. For each $\mathcal{P} \in \mathbf{S}$, with vertices $P_1, P_2, \ldots, P_k$, we construct $\mathcal{R}(\mathcal{P}) = \cap_{i=1}^{k} D(P_i, r)$. Then we construct the arrangement $\mathcal{A}$ of these regions $\mathcal{R}(\mathcal{P})$. $\mathcal{A}$ is a "planar" graph on $\mathbf{S}^2$ and it partitions $\mathbf{S}^2$ into three types of elements: faces, edges and vertices.

Each *face* f of $\mathcal{A}$ is the intersection of zero or more regions $\mathcal{R}(\mathcal{P})$. Therefore, any point $X \in int(f)$ is in the interior of the same set of regions $\mathcal{R}(\mathcal{P})$ as any other point $X' \in int(f)$. Let $count(f)$ be the number of such regions $\mathcal{R}(\mathcal{P})$.

Each *edge* e of $\mathcal{A}$ is an arc belonging to $bd(\mathcal{R}(\mathcal{P}))$ for some region $\mathcal{R}(\mathcal{P})$. Any point $X \in int(e)$ is in the interior of zero or more other regions $\mathcal{R}(\mathcal{P}')$. Therefore any point $X \in int(e)$ is in the interior of the same set of regions $\mathcal{R}(\mathcal{P}')$ as any other point $X' \in int(e)$. Let $count(e)$ be the number of such regions $\mathcal{R}(\mathcal{P}')$.

Finally each *vertex* v of $\mathcal{A}$ is either a vertex of some $\mathcal{R}(\mathcal{P})$ or the intersection of two or more edges of $\mathcal{A}$ and is contained in the interior of zero or more other regions $\mathcal{R}(\mathcal{P}')$. Let $count(v)$ be the number of such regions $\mathcal{R}(\mathcal{P}')$.

It now follows by Theorem 4.1, that finding X_{opt} is equivalent to finding that element h (face, edge, or vertex) of $\mathcal{A}$ such that $count(h)$ is minimum. If h is a face or edge, X_{opt} is any point in $int(h)$. Otherwise, X_{opt} is the vertex h.

4.2 Constructing $\mathcal{A}$ efficiently

The construction of $\mathcal{A}$ involves computing the regions $\mathcal{R}(\mathcal{P})$ and the intersection of these regions. In Section 4.2.1 below, we give several properties of disk intersections on $\mathbf{S}^2$ (Lemmas 4.2–4.4) and show how to use these to compute intersections of several disks quickly (Theorem 4.2). These results are similar to those of Hershberger and Suri [7] for a different problem in the plane, except for minor modifications to make them applicable on $\mathbf{S}^2$. (See [6].)

4.2.1 Properties of disk intersections on $\mathbf{S}^2$

Let $P_1, P_2, \ldots, P_j, P_{j+1}$ be distinct points on $\mathbf{S}^2$, where $j \geq 1$, and let r be a real number satisfying $0 \leq r < \pi/2$. Let $\mathcal{R}_j = \cap_{i=1}^{j} D(P_i, r)$ and let $D_{j+1} = D(P_{j+1}, r)$.

Lemma 4.2 *If $bd(\mathcal{R}_j)$ and $bd(D_{j+1})$ intersect, then they do so at one point (tangential intersection) or two points (proper intersection).* □

Lemma 4.2 implies that $\mathcal{R}_j$ has $h = O(j)$ vertices. Next we consider how to compute the (at most two) points in $bd(\mathcal{R}_j) \cap bd(D_{j+1})$. The method uses a certain pair v_i, v_ℓ of vertices of $\mathcal{R}_j$ to split $bd(\mathcal{R}_j)$ into two chains. Clearly, one of the following cases holds: (i) $v_i \in D_{j+1}$ and $v_\ell \notin D_{j+1}$ or vice versa, (ii) $v_i, v_\ell \in D_{j+1}$, or (iii) $v_i, v_\ell \notin D_{j+1}$. Lemmas 4.3 and 4.4 consider these cases. Theorem 4.2 follows from Lemmas 4.3 and 4.4. Let $v_0, v_1, \ldots, v_{h-1}$ be these vertices of $\mathcal{R}_j$ in clockwise order.

Lemma 4.3 *Given vertices v_i and v_ℓ of $\mathcal{R}_j$, where $v_i \in D_{j+1}$ and $v_\ell \notin D_{j+1}$, the points in $bd(\mathcal{R}_j) \cap bd(D_{j+1})$ can be computed in $O(\log j)$ time.* □

Lemma 4.4 *Let v_i, v_ℓ be vertices of $\mathcal{R}_j$ such that either $v_i, v_\ell \in D_{j+1}$ or $v_i, v_\ell \notin D_{j+1}$, but neither v_i nor v_ℓ lies on $bd(D_{j+1})$. Let C_1 (resp. C_2) be the chain $(v_i, v_{i+1}, \ldots, v_\ell)$ (resp. $(v_\ell, v_{\ell+1}, \ldots, v_i)$). Then at least one of C_1 and C_2 is not intersected by $bd(D_{j+1})$ and this chain can be identified in $O(1)$ time.* □

Theorem 4.2 *The (at most two) points in $bd(\mathcal{R}_j) \cap bd(D_{j+1})$ can be found in $O(\log j)$ time.*

Proof (sketch) We store $bd(\mathcal{R}_j)$ as two chains $(v_i, \ldots, v_\ell)$ and $(v_\ell, \ldots, v_i)$ in balanced search trees and search each separately. The desired intersections are found by checking the position of v_i, v_ℓ w.r.t. D_{j+1} and either (a) applying Lemma 4.3 or (b) recursively applying Lemma 4.4 $O(\log n)$ times (within the framework of binary search), followed by any one application of Lemma 4.3. □

4.2.2   Constructing $\mathcal{A}$

We first incrementally compute $\mathcal{R}(\mathcal{P})$ for a spherical polygon $\mathcal{P}$ with vertices $P_1, P_2, \ldots, P_k$, as follows: Let $\mathcal{R}_j = \cap_{i=1}^{j} D(P_i, r)$; thus $\mathcal{R}(\mathcal{P}) = \mathcal{R}_k$. Inductively, assume that $\mathcal{R}_j$ has been computed and its vertices are stored in order in a balanced binary tree T_j. We then apply Theorem 4.2 to find the (at most two) intersection points between $bd(\mathcal{R}_j)$ and $bd(D_{j+1})$. We then discard the portion of $bd(\mathcal{R}_j)$ lying outside D_{j+1}. This involves doing $O(1)$ split and join operations on T_j and yields a balanced tree T_{j+1} for $\mathcal{R}_{j+1} = \mathcal{R}_j \cap D_{j+1}$. Therefore $\mathcal{R}(\mathcal{P})$ can be computed in time $O(\sum_{i=1}^{k} \log j) = O(k \log k)$ and all $\mathcal{R}(\mathcal{P})$'s can be computed in $O(V \log V)$ time.

Next we compute the arrangement $\mathcal{A}$ of the regions $\mathcal{R}(\mathcal{P})$. We use the algorithm of Chen *et al.* [1], with one crucial change: An important step in their algorithm is finding the intersections of pairs of polygons on $\mathbf{S}^2$. In our case, we need to find intersections of pairs of regions $\mathcal{R}(\mathcal{P})$. To find the intersections of two such regions $\mathcal{R}' = \mathcal{R}(\mathcal{P}')$ and $\mathcal{R}'' = \mathcal{R}(\mathcal{P}'')$, we simply intersect each arc a of $\mathcal{R}'$ with $\mathcal{R}''$ using Theorem 4.2. This takes $O(|\mathcal{R}'| \log |\mathcal{R}''|)$ time. Summing over all other regions, keeping $\mathcal{R}''$ fixed, gives a time bound of $O(V \log |\mathcal{R}''|)$. Thus the overall time taken is $O(V N \log V)$. The rest of the algorithm is similar to that of [1] and takes $O(V N \log N)$ time. Thus $\mathcal{A}$ can be built in time $O(V N \log V)$. The construction yields a representation of $\mathcal{A}$ in which the edges incident at each vertex are in sorted order around the vertex consistent with the embedding of $\mathcal{A}$ on $\mathbf{S}^2$. Note that $\mathcal{A}$ has $O(V N)$ vertices, edges and faces.

4.3   Searching $\mathcal{A}$

Recall from Section 4.1 that with each vertex v (resp, edge e, face f) we store an integer $count(v)$ (resp. $count(e)$, $count(f)$). We need to search $\mathcal{A}$ and compute the minimum value of these counts to solve the 5-axis problem.

4.3.1 Classifying the two faces of $\mathcal{A}$ incident with each edge

Let e be any edge of $\mathcal{A}$. Let e belong to the boundary of some region $\mathcal{R}(\mathcal{P})$ and some disk D. Of the two faces of $\mathcal{A}$ that share e, exactly one of them is contained in $\mathcal{R}(\mathcal{P})$. Moreover, this face is also contained in D (since $\mathcal{R}(\mathcal{P})$ is the intersection of disks). We call this face the *inside face of* e and denote it by $in(e)$. We call the other face the *outside face of* e and denote it by $out(e)$. Thus, the face on the concave side of e is $in(e)$ and the face on the convex side of e is $out(e)$. We can determine this information for each edge as follows: For each face f of $\mathcal{A}$, we pick an interior point X and for each edge e of f, we check (in constant time) if X is in the interior of the disk whose boundary contains e. If so, then we set $in(e)$ equal to f; otherwise, we set $out(e)$ equal to f. (The other piece of information for e is computed when the face sharing e with f is processed similarly.) It follows that the desired information for all edges can be computed in $O(VN)$ time and space.

4.3.2 Computing $count(\cdot)$ for each face f and edge e

We first build the dual graph $\mathcal{A}'$ of $\mathcal{A}$ as follows: For each face f of $\mathcal{A}$, we pick an interior point f' of f as a vertex of $\mathcal{A}'$. We join two vertices of $\mathcal{A}'$ by an edge e' if the corresponding faces of $\mathcal{A}$ share an edge e. This takes $O(VN)$ time and space. $\mathcal{A}'$ has $O(VN)$ vertices, edges, and faces.

We then do a depth-first search of $\mathcal{A}'$. Suppose that the search visits a vertex h' from a vertex g'. In other words, we move from a face g to a face h of $\mathcal{A}$, crossing the edge, e shared by these faces. Let $e \in bd(\mathcal{R}(\mathcal{P}))$ for some region $\mathcal{R}(\mathcal{P})$. If $g = in(e)$, then this implies that we are leaving $\mathcal{R}(\mathcal{P})$. Therefore, we set $count(h) = count(g) - 1$. If $g = out(e)$, this implies that we are entering $\mathcal{R}(\mathcal{P})$. Therefore, we set $count(h) = count(g) + 1$. It follows that the minimum count for faces can be found in $O(VN)$ time.

Let e be the edge above. We can compute $count(e)$ during the depth-first search. If $g = in(e)$ then we set $count(e) = count(g) - 1$; if $g = out(e)$, then we set $count(e) = count(g)$.

4.3.3 Computing $count(v)$ for each vertex v

We do a depth-first search of $\mathcal{A}$ (not $\mathcal{A}'$) and for each vertex v of $\mathcal{A}$, we compute $count(v)$ the first time we visit v. Let e be the edge along which we visit v for the first time. Let $\mathcal{I}$ be the set of regions $\mathcal{R}(\mathcal{P})$ such that $v \in int(\mathcal{R}(\mathcal{P}))$; thus $count(v) = |\mathcal{I}|$. Let $X \in int(e)$ and let $\mathcal{I}'$ be the set of regions $\mathcal{R}(\mathcal{P})$ such that $X \in int(\mathcal{R}(\mathcal{P}))$; thus $count(e) = |\mathcal{I}'|$. Since X and v both belong to e, we must have $\mathcal{I} \subseteq \mathcal{I}'$. Thus, $count(v) = count(e) - k$, where k is the number of regions $\mathcal{R}(\mathcal{P})$ that intersect at v and contain e in their interior. Let $e = e_1, e_2, \ldots, e_t$ be the clockwise sequence of the edges incident at v. Let $e_j \in bd(\mathcal{R}(\mathcal{P}_{i_j}))$, $1 \le j \le t$. Note that for each edge e_j there is another edge e_ℓ in the sequence such that $i_j = i_\ell$; i.e., each region intersecting at v contributes two edges. We will compute k by scanning the sequence $e_1, e_2, \ldots, e_t$. Clearly, each region $\mathcal{R}(\mathcal{P}_{i_j})$ which satisfies the following property should be included in k: "As we scan, we first exit $\mathcal{R}(\mathcal{P}_{i_j})$ and then re-enter it later." We use an N-bit vector $SEEN[1:N]$, where $SEEN[i_j] = 1$ implies that we have so far seen one edge of $\mathcal{R}(\mathcal{P}_{i_j})$ and $SEEN[i_j] = 0$ implies that we have seen neither edge or both edges of $\mathcal{R}(\mathcal{P}_{i_j})$. Initially, when the depth-first search begins, $SEEN[1:N]$ is initialized to all-zero. The algorithm executed at v is shown below.

Algorithm *Vertex_Count*

$SEEN[i_1] \leftarrow 1;\; k \leftarrow 0$
for $j \leftarrow 2$ **to** t **do**
$\quad f_j \leftarrow$ face shared by e_{j-1} and e_j.
$\quad (f_j$ can be computed as $\{in(e_{j-1}), out(e_{j-1})\} \cap \{in(e_j), out(e_j)\})$.
$\quad$ **if** $(f_j = in(e_j)$ and $\neg SEEN[i_j])$ **then** $k \leftarrow k+1$
$\quad SEEN[i_j] \leftarrow \neg SEEN[i_j]$
$count(v) \leftarrow count(e_1) - k$

Note that because each region contributes exactly two edges at v, at the end of the algorithm at v, $SEEN[1:N]$ is all-zero again and available for use at the next vertex visited. Thus, we do not have to spend $\Theta(N)$ time reinitializing it at each vertex. Since $count(v)$ can be computed in time $O(degree(v))$ and $\mathcal{A}$ has $O(VN)$ edges, the counts for all vertices can be computed in in $O(VN)$ time.

Theorem 4.3 *Problem* FIVE_AXIS' *(hence Problem* FIVE_AXIS*) can be solved in* $O(VN \log V)$ *time and* $O(VN)$ *space.* $\square$

5 The algorithm for a fillet-end cutter

Since our solutions to the 4- and 5-axis problems are the same, we will focus on the 5-axis problem described below. As discussed in Section 2, for a fillet-end cutter, each VMap is an arc polygon, i.e., either a small circle or the intersection of two or more small circles. All small circles are of the same radius θ.

Problem 5.1 (FIVE_AXIS_FILLET) *"Given N arc polygons on $\mathbf{S}^2$, with a total of V vertices, and a real number b, where $0 \leq b < \pi/2$, find a spherical band of width $2b$ which intersects the maximum number of polygons."*

Our aim is to construct for each arc polygon $\breve{\mathcal{P}}$, representing some VMap, the region $\mathcal{R}(\breve{\mathcal{P}}) \subseteq \mathbf{S}^2$ such that for any point $X \in \mathcal{R}(\breve{\mathcal{P}})$, $\breve{\mathcal{P}} \subseteq int(D(X, r))$.

An arc polygon is either a small circle of radius θ or the intersection of two or more such circles. Let γ denote a minor arc of a small circle or a small circle. We let $pole(\gamma) = P$ and $radius(\gamma) = \theta$. When γ is a minor arc, we let A, B be the endpoints of γ. Let H_A^+ (resp. H_A^-) be the closed hemisphere bounded by $circ(P, A)$ whose intersection with $int(\gamma)$ is non-null (resp. null). Similarly we define H_B^+ (resp. H_B^-). When γ is a small circle, we let $H_A^- = H_B^- = \mathbf{S}^2$.

Theorem 5.1 establishes the possible locations of the center X of a disk $D(X, r)$ such that arc γ of some arc polygon $\breve{\mathcal{P}}$ is in $int(D(X, r))$. We call the locus of such points X, the *feasible region* $f(\gamma)$ of γ. See Fig. 2.

Theorem 5.1 *For any* r, $\gamma \subseteq int(D(X, r))$ *iff* $X \in f(\gamma)$ *where* $f(\gamma) = int(((H_A^- \cap H_B^-) \cap D(P, r-\theta)) \cup ((H_A^- \cap H_B^-)^c \cap D(A, r) \cap D(B, r))))$. *(Here we take* $D(P, r) = \emptyset$ *for* $r < \theta$.)* $\square$

Theorem 5.2 *Let* $\breve{\mathcal{P}}$ *be an arc polygon with small arcs* $\gamma_1, \ldots, \gamma_k$. *Let* $\mathcal{R}(\breve{\mathcal{P}}) = \cap_{i=1}^k f(\gamma_i)$. *Then* $X \in int(\mathcal{R}(\breve{\mathcal{P}}))$ *iff* $\breve{\mathcal{P}} \subseteq int(D(X, r))$. $\square$

Thus for a fillet-end cutter, the feasible region $f(\gamma)$ for an arc γ is bounded by three small arcs. Let arc polygon $\breve{\mathcal{P}}$ be represented by (small) arcs $\gamma_1, \gamma_2, \cdots \gamma_k$. We first compute $f(\gamma_i)$ for all i, $1 \leq i \leq k$. Then the region $\mathcal{R}(\breve{\mathcal{P}}) = \cap_{i=1}^{i=k} f(\gamma_i)$ is computed incrementally. This can be done in $O(|\mathcal{R}(\breve{\mathcal{P}})|^2)$ time and hence $O(V^2)$ for all $\mathcal{R}(\breve{\mathcal{P}})$. Next we compute the arrangement $\mathcal{A}$ of the regions $\mathcal{R}(\mathcal{P})$. We use the algorithm of [1] with one crucial change: to find the intersection of two such regions $\mathcal{R}' = \mathcal{R}(\mathcal{P}')$ and $\mathcal{R}'' = \mathcal{R}(\mathcal{P}'')$, we simply intersect each arc a of $\mathcal{R}'$ with $\mathcal{R}''$. It can be shown that the total time to construct $\mathcal{A}$ is $O(V^2 + VN \log N)$. Next we compute the minimum $count(\cdot)$ for faces, edges, and vertices by searching $\mathcal{A}$. Except for a few changes (described in [6]), the approach is similar to that in Section 4 and takes $O(VN)$ time.

Theorem 5.3 *Problem* FIVE_AXIS_FILLET *can be solved in* $O(V^2 + VN \log N)$ *time and* $O(VN)$ *space.* $\square$

References

[1] L. Chen, S. Chou and T. Woo. Separating and intersecting spherical polygons: computing machinability on three-, four-, and five-axis numerically controlled machines. *ACM Trans. on Graphics*, 12(4):305–326, 1993.

[2] H. Edelsbrunner and L.J. Guibas. Topologically sweeping an arrangement. *J. Comput. Syst. Sci.*, Vol. 38, pages 165–194, 1989.

[3] H. Edelsbrunner, J. O'Rourke and R. Seidel. Constructing arrangements of lines and hyperplanes with applications. *SIAM J. on Computing*, Vol. 15, pages 341–363, 1986.

[4] A. Gajentaan and M.H. Overmars On a class of $O(n^2)$ problems in computational geometry. RUUCS-93-15, Dept. of Computer Sc., Utrecht University.

[5] J.G. Gan, T.C. Woo and K. Tang. Spherical maps: their construction, properties, and approximation. *J. of Mech. Design*, 116:357–363, 1994.

[6] P. Gupta, R. Janardan, J. Majhi and T. Woo. Efficient geometric algorithms for workpiece orientation in 4-axis and 5-axis NC-machining. Technical Report, TR-95-015, Dept. of Computer Science, University of Minnesota.

[7] J. Hershberger and S. Suri. Finding tailored partitions. *Journal of Algorithms*, Vol. 12, pages 431–463, 1991.

[8] K. Tang, T. Woo and J. Gan. Maximum intersection of spherical polygons and workpiece orientation for 4- and 5-Axis Machining. *Journal of Mechanical Design*, Vol. 114, pp. 477–485, 1992.

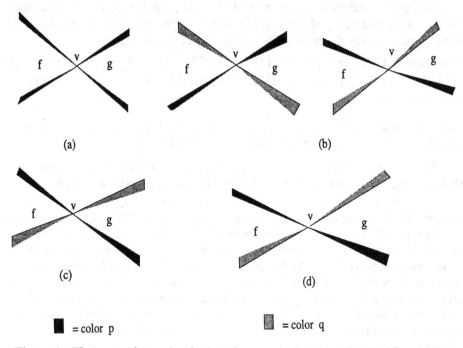

Figure 1: The cases that arise during the sweep algorithm for Problem MIPP.

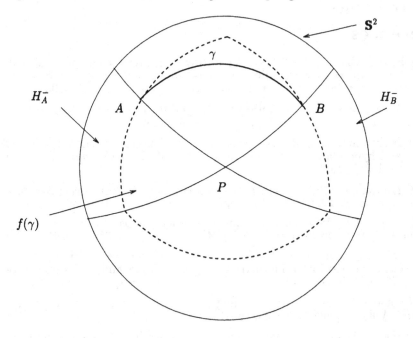

Figure 2: The feasible region $f(\gamma)$ (shown bounded by dashed lines) for a small arc γ, for a fillet-end cutter.

Computing Common Tangents
Without a Separating Line*

David Kirkpatrick   Jack Snoeyink

Department of Computer Science, University of British Columbia
201-2366 Main Mall, Vancouver, BC V6T 1Z4 Canada

Abstract

Given two disjoint convex polygons in standard representations, one can compute outer common tangents in logarithmic time without first obtaining a separating line. If the polygons are not disjoint, there is an additional factor of the logarithm of the intersection or convex hull, whichever is smaller.

1 Introduction

In this paper, we revisit an old problem: computing a tangent line common to two disjoint polygons, P and Q, that are represented by ordered lists of n vertices stored in arrays or balanced binary trees.

Because a tangent to a polygon P through a given point q can be found in $\Theta(\log n)$ time by binary search, there is an easy $O(\log^2 n)$ time algorithm for finding a tangent common to P and Q that uses nested binary search. Overmars and van Leeuwen [9], as part of a data structure for dynamic convex hulls, gave a logarithmic-time algorithm for the special case in which P and Q have a known vertical separating line. Because one can compute a separating line for disjoint polygons in logarithmic time—by finding the shortest segment joining them [4] or using hierarchical representations [3, 8]—the Overmars/van Leeuwen algorithm gives a complete solution.

This method of solution by reduction to a previously solved problem makes for elegant mathematics, but can complicate the task of implementing the resultant algorithm in the computer. One needs algorithms for each subproblem, and one must correctly handle the special cases that arise in each. Inspired by Gries and Stojmenović's note on Graham Scan [6], we decided to start from invariants to derive a short algorithm that could compute a common tangent without first computing a separator or even putting the polygons into a special position.

In the next section, we show that tangents for disjoint convex polygons can be computed in logarithmic time by using a tentative prune-and-search tech-

---

*Both authors supported in part by NSERC Research Grants. The second was also supported by a fellowship from the B.C. Advanced Systems Institute.

nique [8]. C code is given in an appendix. The approach is much like Overmars and van Leeuwen's [9]—starting with lists of vertices for P and for Q that are known to contain the tangent vertices, attempt to discard half of some list by doing a constant-time local test. Without a separating line, however, some tests do not give sufficient information. One can proceed by making tentative discards that are later certified or revoked; the analysis uses a potential function to show that the amount of work done is still logarithmic.

There are two additional benefits to computing a common tangent without the knowledge of the separator. First, the data structure of Overmars and van Leeuwen has been adapted for other purposes that do not have a vertical bias— including implicit storage of arrangements [5, 7], ray shooting [1, 2], etc. Using our tangent-finding algorithm simplifies and speeds up these applications by a constant factor. Second, one can adapt the algorithm to look for common tangents in situations where no separating line exists. Guibas et al. [7] have shown that to compute an outer common tangent to intersecting polygons P and Q requires $\Omega(\log^2 n)$ time, even if points in $P - Q$ and $Q - P$ are given. Our algorithm can run in $O(\log n \log N)$ time, where N is the minimum of the sizes of the intersection $P \cap Q$ and the size of the convex hull of $P \cup Q$. Thus, both of these quantities must be large for the lower bound to apply.

2 The algorithm

Our algorithm $\text{Tang}(P, Q)$ takes as input two disjoint convex polygons whose vertices are stored in arrays in counter-clockwise (ccw) order. It finds vertices $p_i \in P$ and $q_j \in Q$ such that no vertex of P or Q lies to the right of the oriented line $\overrightarrow{p_i q_j}$. In case of degeneracy, p_i is chosen as the furthest such cw and q_j as the furthest ccw. Thus, $\text{Tang}(P, Q)$ produces an outer common tangent that leaves P ccw and goes to Q. The call $\text{Tang}(Q, P)$ produces the other outer tangent.

We describe state variables and the invariants that the algorithm maintains. Then we initialize the variables and show how the $\textbf{Refine}()$ procedure preserves the invariants while refining intervals that contain the common tangent vertices.

2.1 State information and invariants

The algorithm maintains several pieces of state information for each polygon. For P, we store the vertices p_0 to p_{n-1} in ccw order, and their number $P.n = n$ so that all access can be performed modulo $P.n$. For each vertex $p_k \in P$, we choose a canonical tangent τ_k to be the oriented tangent line at p_k that is furthest ccw: $\tau_k = \overrightarrow{p_k p_{k+1}}$. (We can use the orientation to speak about the right and left sides of τ_k and to order points along τ_k.) We also store three indices, $0 \le P.st \le P.tent < P.end \le 2P.n$, that satisfy two invariants below. Finally, we store a boolean variable $P.wrap$ that is defined in section 2.3.

For Q, the vertices are also stored in ccw order, but the tangent σ_k is chosen furthest cw: $\sigma_k = \overrightarrow{q_{k-1} q_k}$. The indices for Q have their order reversed, $0 \le Q.end < Q.tent \le Q.st \le 2Q.n$.

We would like to break P's circular list of vertices into a linear list on which we can perform binary search. No assumptions are made about the location of p_0; if one knew that p_0 would be inside the convex hull of $P \cup Q$, then this would be trivial.

Define interval I_P to be the indices of vertices of P that lie on the convex hull of $P \cup \{q_0\}$. As in figure 1, if no point of P is right of the oriented line $\overrightarrow{q_0 p_m}$ for $0 < m \leq P.n$ and no point of P is right of $\overrightarrow{p_{m'} q_0}$ for $m \leq m' < m + P.n$, then $I_P = [m, m']$. Notice that as index l runs over the interval $[m, m']$, we may encounter tangents τ_l that intersect Q before p_l, then those that do not intersect Q, and then tangents τ_l that inter-

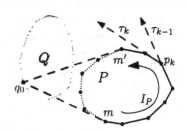

Fig. 1: Defining, but not computing, I_P

sect Q (equivalently, that intersect $\overrightarrow{q_0 q_j}$) after p_l. (The final tangent $\tau_{m'}$ should be limited so that q_0 does not appear to its right.) Define the interval I_Q similarly to contain indices of Q's vertices on the convex hull of $Q \cup \{p_0\}$. We never explicitly compute I_P or I_Q but we use them in the invariants.

Let $\overrightarrow{p_i q_j}$ be the common tangent that $\text{Tang}(P, Q)$ seeks—that is, no point of P or Q is right of $\overrightarrow{p_i q_j}$. The invariants for P are:

1. The desired tangent index i is in the interval $(P.st, P.end] \cap I_P$.
2. If $P.tent \neq P.st$ then $P.tent \in (P.st, P.end] \cap I_P$ and points $q_{Q.tent}$ and $q_{Q.end}$ are left of tangent $\tau_{P.tent}$.

The invariants for Q are essentially the same:

1. The desired tangent index j is in the interval $(Q.st, Q.end] \cap I_Q$.
2. If $Q.tent \neq Q.st$ then $Q.tent \in (Q.st, Q.end] \cap I_Q$ and points $p_{P.tent}$ and $p_{P.end}$ are left of tangent $\sigma_{Q.tent}$.

2.2 Tentative prune and search

Using the invariants of the previous section we can outline the tentative prune-and-search method to compute the common tangent and prove it correct.

If *tent* $\neq$ *st* for a polygon, then we say that that polygon is *tentatively refined* or simply *refined*. We say that indices in $(tent, end]$ are *remaining* and those in $(st, tent]$, if any, have been *tentatively discarded*. If both polygons are tentatively refined and the invariants hold, then the index of the common tangent on at least one of the polygons is among those remaining. In other words, at most one tentative discard can be mistaken.

Lemma 1 *Suppose that the invariants hold for disjoint polygons P and Q. If $\overrightarrow{p_i q_j}$ is the desired common tangent, then either $i \in (P.tent, P.end]$ or $j \in (Q.tent, Q.end]$.*

Proof: If one of the polygons is not refined, then $tent = st$ and the lemma follows from invariant 1. Therefore, suppose that both polygons are refined. Further suppose, for the sake of deriving a contradiction, that both tentative discards are mistaken: that is, $i \notin (P.tent, P.end]$ and $j \notin (Q.tent, Q.end]$ as illustrated in figure 2. We make three observations.

First, $p_{P.tent}$ is in $\triangle p_i q_j q_0$: Since $P.tent \in [i, P.end] \cap I_P$, point $p_{P.tent}$ lies on a convex curve from p_i to q_0. This curve cannot crosssegment $\overline{q_j q_0}$ because P and Q are disjoint, nor can it cross the common tangent $\overline{p_i q_j}$.

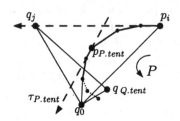

Fig. 2: At most one mistaken tentative discard

Second, $p_{P.tent}$ is in $\triangle p_i q_j q_{Q.tent}$: By invariant 2, q_0 and $q_{Q.tent}$ are both left of the tangent $\tau_{P.tent}$. By disjointness, $p_{P.tent}$ is not in $\triangle q_j q_0 q_{Q.tent}$. By the first observation, and the fact that $q_{Q.tent}$ is left of the common tangent, we know that $p_{P.tent}$ is in $\triangle p_i q_j q_{Q.tent}$.

Third, $q_{Q.tent}$ is not in the triangle $\triangle p_i q_j p_{P.tent}$: This is immediate from the second observation.

The situations of P and Q are completely symmetric, however. We can derive observations that assert that $q_{P.tent}$ is in $\triangle p_i q_j p_{P.tent}$ by interchanging the roles of P and Q. This contradiction establishes the theorem. ∎

As a corollary, when only one candidate is remaining on each polygon, then we have found the common tangent.

Corollary 2 *If the invariants for P and Q hold and intervals $(Q.tent, Q.end]$ and $(P.tent, P.end]$ contain one candidate each, then $q_{Q.end}$ and $p_{P.end}$ are the points of tangency desired.*

Proof: By lemma 1, we know that one of the intervals is correct: Say that $q_{Q.end}$ is one point of tangency. If P is not refined, then invariant 1 says that $p_{P.end}$ is the other. If P is refined, then invariant 2 says that $q_{Q.end}$ is left of $\tau_{P.tent}$, so the point of tangency must be after (ccw of) $p_{P.tent}$. Invariant 1 says that $p_{P.end}$ is the only candidate. ∎

Our algorithm discards indices from initial lists containing $O(n)$ indices using *refinement operations* A–C. We shall see in section 2.4 that $\mathtt{Refine}(P, Q)$ implements these refinement operations.

A. The interval $(P.tent, P.end]$ is halved by setting $P.tent$ or $P.end$ or both $P.tent$ and $P.st$ to be the midpoint of $(P.tent, P.end]$.

B. Possibly Q is *certified*—made unrefined by setting $Q.st = Q.tent$.

C. Possibly a mistake is found on Q. Then we revoke the tentative discard by $Q.end = Q.tent$, $Q.tent = Q.st$, and certify P by $P.st = P.tent$, because lemma 1 implies that the discards to P were correct.

The call **Refine**(Q, P) will handle the intervals for Q in a similar manner. We can perform a refine unless the $(tent, end]$ intervals on both polygons contain only a single index. If we alternately call **Refine**(P, Q) and **Refine**(Q, P), then we find the common tangent in logarithmic time.

Lemma 3 *If* **Refine**() *correctly implements the refinement operations A–C, then* **Tang**(P, Q) *terminates after* $O(\log |P| + \log |Q|)$ *steps.*

Proof: We can define a potential for a polygon in terms of its indices st, $tent$, and end:

$$\Phi(P) = \log |P.end - P.st| + 2\log |P.end - P.tent| + (P.tent \neq P.st).$$

All logarithms are base 2 and the expression $(P.tent \neq P.st)$ equals 1 if the boolean test is true and 0 otherwise. The total potential is $\Phi = \Phi(P) + \Phi(Q)$.

To make analysis easier, we simplify the algorithm in a way that can only make the running time worse. We call **Refine**() on any unrefined polygon until both polygons are refined. Thus, an "unsuccessful" refine decreases Φ by 4; a successful one decreases Φ by 1. Then we call **Refine**(P, Q) and **Refine**(Q, P) alternately and either certify all tentative discards on one polygon and revoke those on the other or else extend the tentative discard (as if the index changes were always $P.tent$). Extending the tentative discard decreases Φ by 2. Certifying P after i refine steps decreases $\Phi(P)$ by $2i + 1$ and revoking Q after j steps increases $\Phi(Q)$ by at most $2j - 1$. Because of the alternation, $j \leq i + 1$ so the net change in Φ is at most zero. Note that certification can happen only after two successful refines, so every three steps Φ decreases by at least 2.

Since the initial potential $\Phi = O(\log P.n + \log Q.n)$ and Φ cannot be negative, the lemma is established. ∎

2.3 Initialization

To initialize P, if q_0 is not left of tangent τ_0, then we know that the interior of $\overline{p_0 p_1}$ is inside the convex hull of $P \cup \{q_0\}$. We break P at p_0 by setting $st = tent = 0$, $end = n$, and $wrap = F$. Otherwise, we start at p_0 and wrap around P twice, as illustrated in figure 3, by setting $st = 0$, $tent = n$, $end = 2n$, and $wrap = T$.

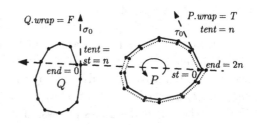

Fig. 3: Initializing P, with $P.wrap = T$, and Q, with $Q.wrap = F$.

We initialize Q in a similar manner: if p_0 is not left of tangent σ_0, set $st = tent = n$, $end = 0$, and $wrap = F$. Otherwise, we start at q_0 and wrap around Q twice by setting $st = 2n$, $tent = n$, $end = 0$, and $wrap = T$.

Lemma 4 *Initially, the two invariants hold for P and Q.*

    Proof: We prove this for P. If $P.wrap$ is false, then $I_P \subset (0, P.n]$ and invariants 1 and 2 are trivial.

    If $P.wrap$ is true, then the base segment $\overline{q_0 p_0}$ intersects some edge $\overline{p_k p_{k+1}}$ of P where q_0 is not left of τ_k and $0 \leq k < P.n$. The index of the common tangent vertex p_i can be chosen from $I_P \subset (k, k + P.n]$ to satisfy part of invariant 1. The remaining conditions of invariants 1 and 2 are trivial. ∎

2.4 Refining the intervals

Finally, we show that `Refine()` implements the refinement operations A–C listed in section 2.2.

    Our most basic test determines whether a point (X, Y) is right or left of an oriented line $\overrightarrow{pq}$ by evaluating sign of the determinant

$$\begin{vmatrix} px & py & 1 \\ qx & qy & 1 \\ X & Y & 1 \end{vmatrix} = X(py - qy) - Y(px - qx) + (px\,qy - qx\,py).$$

Points to the left of $\overrightarrow{pq}$ make this determinant positive; those to the right make it negative. For a detailed treatment of signed homogeneous coordinates see Stolfi [10].

    Suppose that there are candidates remaining on P: that $(P.tent, P.end]$ contains more than one index. Choose mid to be a median index in $(P.tent, P.end]$.

We are going to consider making $P.end = mid$ or $P.tent = mid$. Thus, if Q is refined, we test if p_{mid} is left of $\sigma_{Q.tent}$ to preserve invariant 2 for Q. If the oriented tangent line $\sigma_{Q.tent}$ intersects segment $\overline{p_0 p_{mid}}$ after $q_{Q.tent}$, then the point of tangency cannot be ccw of $q_{Q.tent}$.

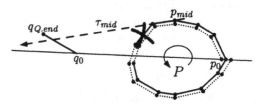

Fig. 4: A situation causing $P.end = mid$

We can certify the tentative discard to Q by $Q.st = Q.tent$. If $\sigma_{Q.tent}$ intersects $\overline{p_0 p_{mid}}$ before $q_{Q.tent}$, then the point of tangency cannot be cw of $q_{Q.tent}$. We can revoke tentative discards on Q by the assignments $Q.end = Q.tent$ and $Q.tent = Q.st$ and certify those on P by $P.st = P.tent$.

    Next we check if $mid \in I_P$ as follows: If τ_{mid} intersects $\overline{q_0 p_0}$ after p_{mid} or if $P.wrap$ and $mid > P.n$ and p_{mid} is not right of the base line $\overline{q_0 p_0}$, then nothing ccw of p_{mid} is in I_P. We can set $P.end = mid$. If τ_{mid} intersects $\overline{q_0 p_0}$ before p_{mid} or if $P.wrap$ and $mid < P.n$ and p_{mid} is right of the base line $\overline{q_0 p_0}$, then nothing cw of p_{mid} is in I_P. We can set $P.st = mid$ and $P.tent = mid$.

    In a similar way, if τ_{mid} intersects $\overline{q_0 q_{Q.end}}$ or $\overline{q_0 q_{Q.tent}}$ after p_{mid}, as in figure 4, then the point of tangency cannot be ccw of p_{mid} and we set $P.end =$

mid. If τ_{mid} intersects $\overline{q_0 q_{Q.end}}$ or $\overline{q_0 q_{Q.tent}}$ before p_{mid} then we set $P.st = mid$ and $P.tent = mid$. Finally, if none of these actions occur, we set $P.tent = mid$. This preserves the invariants for P.

Therefore, **Refine**() implements the refinement operations needed for lemma 3. Since we can also initialize by lemma 4, we conclude with theorem 5.

Theorem 5 *The algorithm* Tang(P, Q) *computes a common tangent to disjoint convex polygons P and Q in $O(\log |P| + \log |Q|)$ time.*

3   Intersecting polygons

One can extend this analysis to intersecting polygons and obtain a theorem that covers the gap between the logarithmic-time algorithm for disjoint polygons and the $\Omega(\log^2 n)$ worst-case bound for intersecting polygons. We consider the case where polygons P and Q have at most two common tangents and where *helper points* in their differences are given: $p_0 \in P \setminus Q$ and $q_0 \in Q \setminus P$. Notice that these helper points certify that there is a common tangent; without them it would take $\Omega(n)$ time to determine if one polygon contained the other.

Theorem 6 *Let P and Q be two convex polygons whose boundaries intersect at most twice and let $p_0 \in P \setminus Q$ and $q_0 \in Q \setminus P$. One can compute the common tangent from P to Q in $O(\log(|P| + |Q|) \log K)$ time, where $K = \min\{|P \cap Q|, |CH(P \cup Q)|\}$.*

Proof: We sketch the proof for $O(\log(|P| + |Q|) \log |P \cap Q|)$ and leave many details to the reader. Begin by using the helper points to define the intervals I_P and I_Q as before and, in addition, compute these intervals in logarithmic time. One can check whether the tangents to p_0 and q_0 that define these intervals are the desired common tangent. We assume that they are not.

Even if P and Q intersect, if some point of Q is found to the right of tangent τ_{mid}, the tangent to P at p_{mid}, then by tests similar to that shown in figure 4, we can discard a portion of P so as to preserve the common tangent. Only when the inspected points of Q are left of τ_{mid} and the inspected points of P are left of $\sigma_{mid'}$ does local information fail to eliminate half of one of the polygons. Then there are the two cases, depicted in figure 5a and 5b, to consider: either the segments $\overline{p_0 p_{mid}}$ and $\overline{q_0 q_{mid'}}$ are disjoint, or they intersect.

If they are disjoint, then lemma 1 implies that we can tentatively discard the indicated "outer" portions of P and Q. If they intersect, then we can prove that tentatively discarding the "inner" portions leads to at most one mistake. In either case, we can continue the computation in tentative mode until both "inner" and "outer" discards have been applied, as in figure 5c. In the illustrated case P is refined twice, at p_{m_1} and p_{m_2}, and all of Q has been tentatively discarded. There is a symmetric case in which Q is refined twice and all of P is discarded.

We can determine whether $q_{mid'}$ is inside or outside of P by searching between p_{m_1} and p_{m_2} for the edge of P that intersects the ray $\overrightarrow{q_0 q_{mid'}}$. Finding

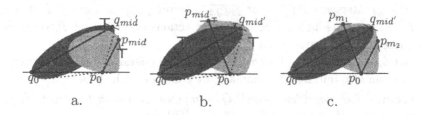

Fig. 5: Two tentative discard cases and their combination

$q_{mid'}$ outside P allows the deletion of the portions of P and Q that are left of $\overrightarrow{q_0 q_{mid'}}$, because P is inside Q to the left of this ray. Finding $q_{mid'}$ inside P allows the deletion of the portions of P and Q that are right of $\overrightarrow{q_0 q_{mid'}}$, because cutting both polygons along $\overrightarrow{q_0 q_{mid'}}$ leaves a tangent from P to Q that is to the left of this ray. We can use similar analyses on the ray $\overrightarrow{p_0 p_{m_1}}$.

If edge $\overline{p_j p_{j+1}}$ is the edge of P that intersects $\overrightarrow{q_0 q_{mid'}}$ with $j \in [m_1, m_2)$, then we can find this edge in $O(\log(m_2 - j))$ steps by using an increasing-increment search from p_{m_2}—testing the 1st, 2nd, 4th, etc. vertex from p_{m_2} until a vertex passes the ray $\overrightarrow{q_0 q_{mid'}}$, then applying binary search. We can use a simultaneous increasing-increment searches from an end of I_Q clockwise towards $q_{mid'}$ for the edge of Q that intersects $\overrightarrow{p_0 p_{m_1}}$. When one of these searches succeeds, we delete portions of P and Q and escape this mode.

If p_{m_1} is found to be outside of Q or if $q_{mid'}$ is found outside of P, then the searches on Q or on P, respectively, walked only on portions on the boundary of $P \cap Q$. On the other hand, if the search on Q found that p_{m_1} was inside Q, then the unsuccessful search on P walked on $P \cap Q$. Similarly, if the search on P found $q_{mid'}$ inside P, then the search on Q walked on $P \cap Q$. Thus, one of the two searches succeeds in $O(\log |P \cap Q|)$ steps. (For the lemma, we simultaneously search from p_{m_1} and q_0; one of these succeeds in $O(\log |CH(P \cup Q)|)$ steps.)

A potential function analysis similar to that of lemma 3 shows that we perform $O(\log(|P| + |Q|))$ steps, each costing $O(\log \min\{|P \cap Q|, |CH(P \cup Q)|\})$. This completes our sketch of the proof. ∎

References

[1] Pankaj K. Agarwal. *Intersection and decomposition algorithms for planar arrangements*. Cambridge University Press, 1991.

[2] Bernard Chazelle and Leonidas J. Guibas. Visibility and intersection problems in plane geometry. *Discrete & Computational Geometry*, 4:551–581, 1989.

[3] David P. Dobkin and David G. Kirkpatrick. Determining the separation of preprocessed polyhedra: A unified approach. In *Seventeenth International Colloquium on Automata, Languages and Programming*, number 443 in Lecture Notes in Computer Science, pages 400–413. Springer-Verlag, 1990.

[4] H. Edelsbrunner. Computing the extreme distances between two convex polygons. *Journal of Algorithms*, 6:213–224, 1985.

[5] Herbert Edelsbrunner, Leonidas Guibas, John Hershberger, Raimund Seidel, Micha Sharir, Jack Snoeyink, and Emo Welzl. Implicitly representing arrangements of lines or segments. *Discrete & Computational Geometry*, 4:433–466, 1989.

[6] D. Gries and I. Stojmenović. A note on Graham's convex hull algorithm. *Information Processing Letters*, 25:323–327, 1987.

[7] Leo Guibas, John Hershberger, and Jack Snoeyink. Compact interval trees: A data structure for convex hulls. *International Journal of Computational Geometry & Applications*, 1(1):1–22, 1991.

[8] David Kirkpatrick and Jack Snoeyink. Tentative prune-and-search for computing Voronoi vertices. In *Proceedings of the Ninth Annual ACM Symposium on Computational Geometry*, pages 133–142, 1993.

[9] M. Overmars and J. van Leeuwen. Maintenance of configurations in the plane. *Journal of Computer and System Sciences*, 23:166–204, 1981.

[10] Jorge Stolfi. *Oriented projective geometry: A framework for geometric computations*. Academic Press, 1991.

Appendix A: C code for computing a common tangent to disjoint polygons

This code implements the common tangent algorithm described in the text. It is available on the Web, with a short test program for using the Silicon Graphics GL graphics library: `http://www.cs.ubc.ca/spider/snoeyink/nosep.html`

```c
/* main.h    Jack Snoeyink    Common tangent without a separating line
 */


#pragma once
#include <stdio.h>
#include <math.h>

#define MAXPTS 2000          /* Maximum number of points per polyline */
#define EPSILON 1.0e-12      /* Approximation of zero                 */

typedef double COORD;
typedef COORD POINT[2];      /* Most data is Cartesian points         */
typedef COORD HOMOG[3];      /* Some partial calc'ns use homogeneous  */
#define XX 0
#define YY 1
#define WW 2

typedef struct Polygon {
  int n,                     /* Number of vertices in polygon         */
  ccw,                       /* 1 = ccw -1 = cw                       */
  st, end,                   /* Tangent is in (st, end]               */
  tent,                      /* Index of tentative refinement if tent != st */
  wrap;                      /* Boolean indicates wraparound          */
  HOMOG tang;                /* Tangent τ_tent when refined (tent != st) */
  POINT v[MAXPTS];
} Polygon;
```

```
#define DET2(p, q) DET2x2(p,q, XX,YY)      /* Determinants                     */
#define DET2x2(p, q, i, j) ((p)[i]*(q)[j] - (p)[j]*(q)[i])
#define DET3C(p, q, r) DET2(q,r) - DET2(p,r) + DET2(p,q)
#define DOTPROD_2CH(p, q)                  /* 2-d Cartesian to Homog dot product  */
    ((q)[WW] + (p)[XX]*(q)[XX] + (p)[YY]*(q)[YY])
#define CROSSPROD_2SCCH(s, p, q, r)        /* 2-d Cart to Homog cross prod w/ sign */
    (r)[XX] = s * (- (q)[YY] + (p)[YY]);\
    (r)[YY] = s * (  (q)[XX] - (p)[XX]);\
    (r)[WW] = s * ((p)[XX] * (q)[YY] - (p)[YY] * (q)[XX]);\
#define ASSIGN_H(p, op, q)                 /* Homogeneous assignment            */
    (p)[WW] op (q)[WW];  (p)[XX] op (q)[XX];  (p)[YY] op (q)[YY];

#define LEFT(x) (x > EPSILON)              /* Sidedness tests                   */
#define RIGHT(x) (x < -EPSILON)
#define LEFT_PL(p, l) LEFT(DOTPROD_2CH(p, l))
#define RIGHT_PL(p, l) RIGHT(DOTPROD_2CH(p, l))
#define LEFT_PPP(p, q, r) LEFT(DET3C(p, q, r))
#define RIGHT_PPP(p, q, r) RIGHT(DET3C(p, q, r))



/* nosep.c   Jack Snoeyink     Common tangent without a separating line
 */
#include "main.h"

#define Pv(m) P->v[(m) % P->n]             /* Indexing into polygon vertices mod n  */
#define Qv(m) Q->v[(m) % Q->n]

#define CCW(x) (x->ccw == 1)               /* Is x oriented counterclockwise?    */
#define DONE(x)
        ((x->end-x->tent) == x->ccw)       /* Any candidates left?              */
#define REFINED(x) (x->st != x->tent)      /* Is x refined?                     */

#define DISC_START   0                     /* Actions in Refine()               */
#define DISC_END     1
#define NO_DISC      2


void Refine(P, Q)
    Polygon *P, *Q;                        /* We refine polygon P checking against Q. We
{                                             can assume that more than one candidate exists
  HOMOG q0pm, mtang;                          in (P.tent, P.end] and the invariants hold.  */
  register int mid, left_base, action = NO_DISC;
  register COORD *pm, *pm1, *qend, *qt;

  mid = P->tent + (P->end-P->tent) / 2;  /* Check mid point. Round towards P.tent */
  pm = Pv(mid); pm1 = Pv(mid + P->ccw);
  CROSSPROD_2SCCH(P->ccw,pm,pm1,mtang);  /* Generate τmid                     */
  CROSSPROD_2SCCH(1, Qv(0), pm, q0pm);
  left_base = RIGHT_PL(Pv(0), q0pm);
```

```
  if (REFINED(Q) && !LEFT_PL(pm, Q->tang)) {
    qt = Qv(Q->tent);
    if (CCW(Q) ^ LEFT_PPP(Pv(0),qt,pm))  /* Check σ_Q.tent               */
      Q->st = Q->tent;                    /* Certify tentative to Q       */
    else {
      Q->end = Q->tent;
      Q->tent = Q->st;                    /* Revoke tentative to Q        */
      P->st = P->tent;                    /* Certify tentatve on P (if refined)  */
    }
  }


  qend = Qv(Q->end);  qt = Qv(Q->tent);

  if (P->wrap && (left_base ^ (mid > P->n)))
    action = !left_base;                  /* Handle P wrapped around.     */
  else if (!LEFT_PL(Qv(0), mtang))
    action = left_base;                   /* Can not be tangent w.r.t q0.  */
  else if (!LEFT_PL(qend, mtang))
    action = LEFT_PL(qend, q0pm);         /* Can not be tangent w.r.t q_Q.end.  */
  else if (REFINED(Q) && !LEFT_PL(qt, mtang))
    action = LEFT_PL(qt, q0pm);           /* Can not be tangent w.r.t q_Q.tent.  */

  if (action == NO_DISC)                  /* We tentatively refine at mid  */
    { P->tent = mid; ASSIGN_H(P->tang, =, mtang) }
  else if (CCW(P) ^ action)               /* A discard at P.st occurred    */
    P->st = P->tent = mid;                /* A discard at P.end occurred   */
  else P->end = mid;
}




void Tang(P, Q)
     Polygon *P, *Q;
{                                         /* Initialize P and Q and call Refine() to com-
  register int n1 = Q->n - 1;                pute a tangent from P to Q    */

  P->ccw = 1; P->st = P->tent = 0; P->end = P->n;
  CROSSPROD_2SCCH(1, Pv(0), Pv(1), P->tang);
  if (P->wrap = LEFT_PL(Qv(0), P->tang))
    { P->tent = P->n; P->end += P->n; } /* Wrap P initially               */

  Q->ccw = -1; Q->st = Q->tent = Q->n; Q->end = 0;
  CROSSPROD_2SCCH(1, Qv(n1), Qv(0), Q->tang);
  if (Q->wrap = LEFT_PL(Pv(0), Q->tang))
    Q->st += Q->n;                        /* Wrap Q initially             */

  while (!DONE(P) || !DONE(Q)) {
    if (!DONE(P)) Refine(P, Q);
    if (!DONE(Q)) Refine(Q, P);
  }                                       /* Q.end and P.end indicate tangent  */
}
```

Online Perfect Matching and Mobile Computing

Edward F. Grove*, Ming-Yang Kao**, P. Krishnan***, and Jeffrey Scott Vitter[†]

Department of Computer Science, Duke University, Durham NC 27708, USA
Email:{efg,kao,pk,jsv}@cs.duke.edu

Abstract. We present a natural online perfect matching problem motivated by problems in mobile computing. A total of n customers connect and disconnect sequentially, and each customer has an associated set of stations to which it may connect. Each station has a capacity limit. We allow the network to preemptively switch a customer between allowed stations to make room for a new arrival. We wish to minimize the total number of switches required to provide service to every customer. Equivalently, we wish to maintain a perfect matching between customers and stations and minimize the lengths of the augmenting paths. We measure performance by the worst case ratio of the number of switches made to the minimum number required.

When each customer can be connected to at most two stations:
- Some intuitive algorithms have lower bounds of $\Omega(n)$ and $\Omega(n/\log n)$.
- When the station capacities are 1, there is an upper bound of $O(\sqrt{n})$.
- When customers do not disconnect and the station capacity is 1, we achieve a competitive ratio of $O(\log n)$.
- There is a lower bound of $\Omega(\sqrt{n})$ when the station capacities are 2.
- We present optimal algorithms when the station capacity is arbitrary in special cases.

1 Introduction

We present an online problem related to the emerging field of *mobile computing* [AwP, DKM, IDJ, USE, Wei]. Current trends suggest that in the near future there will be many customers with portable computing boxes, trying to connect to a huge network of services. The most probable way this will happen will be for the customers to connect to a local "station" through a cellular connection or a wireless LAN, using infrared technology or radio frequency [Dav], and then access the sites of their choice via wired links, e.g., the Internet.

---

[*] Support was provided in part by Army Research Office grant DAAH04–93–G–0076.
[**] Support was provided in part by NSF grant CCR-9101385.
[***] Support was provided in part by an IBM Fellowship, by NSF research grant CCR–9007851, by Army Research Office grant DAAH04-93-G-0076, and by Air Force Office of Scientific Research grant F49620–94–1–0217. The author is currently visiting Duke University from Brown University.
[†] Support was provided in part by NSF research grant CCR–9007851 and by Army Research Office grant DAAH04–93–G–0076.

The bottleneck in the mobile interconnection process is the wireless link connecting a customer to a *mobile support station* (MSS). As customers come into the system, the decision of which station they should connect to must be made online. A customer who wants to leave the system *disconnects* from the system. The physical moving of a customer in the world can be modeled by a disconnection at its present site followed by a connection at its new location. As more customers get connected to a station, the response-time performance of the system degrades.

In this paper, we use the standard definition of *competitiveness* to analyze online algorithms. An algorithm A is said to be C-competitive if there exists a constant b such that for every sequence σ of customer connects and disconnects,

$$Cost_A(\sigma) \leq C \cdot Cost_{OPT}(\sigma) + b,$$

where OPT is the optimal offline algorithm, and $Cost_X(\sigma)$ is the expected cost of running X on σ.

Azar et al. [ABK, AKP, ANR] studied the problem of load balancing, motivated by the cellular phone system. They place no limit on the maximum number of customers that can be connected to a station and try to minimize the maximum number of customers connected to any station. In [ANR], the authors assume that customers do not disconnect, and show that the greedy algorithm is strongly competitive with a competitive ratio of $\Theta(\log n)$. In [ABK], customers are allowed to disconnect, and the greedy algorithm is shown to be $\Theta(n^{2/3})$ competitive, with a lowerbound of $\Omega(\sqrt{n})$ on the competitive ratio for the problem. This gap is closed in [AKP] by an algorithm that is $O(\sqrt{n})$ competitive. In [ABK, AKP, ANR], a customer, once connected to a station, cannot be preempted.

Should preemptive scheduling be allowed? It is clear that in some cases it would be advantageous for the system to move a customer from a heavily loaded MSS to another MSS with a lighter load. Preemption adds overhead and makes the system more complicated. We would like to know whether the gains of preemptive scheduling are substantial enough to make it worthwhile. In this paper we fix the maximum number of customers that can be connected to a station. We focus our attention on the problem of online perfect matching, where we maintain a perfect matching of customers to stations, and the cost of connecting a customer is the number of customers that are switched to make room for the new customer (in essence, the length of the augmenting path). In order to get results, we make strong simplifying assumptions. We hope to generate interest in this version of online matching. Deep results will be required to answer the basic questions of mobile computing that motivate the problems.

Consider the case in which each customer can be connected to at most two stations. When the station capacities are 1, we achieve a competitive ratio of $O(\sqrt{n})$. We show that intuitive algorithms have lower bounds of $\Omega(n)$ and $\Omega(n/\log n)$. If, in addition, we do not allow customers to disconnect, we achieve a competitive ratio of $O(\log n)$. We can derive a lower bound of $\Omega(\sqrt{n})$ when the station capacities are 2. We also present algorithms with optimal competitive factors when station capacity is arbitrary in some special cases.

2 Preemptive Scheduling: Model and Algorithms

Model: Each station has a *capacity*, which is the maximum number of customers that can be connected to the station. Customers arrive and depart sequentially. When a customer enters the system, it announces a set of stations to which it may be connected. While the customer remains in the system, it must be connected to one of those stations, but the system has the power to *switch* the customer from of these stations to another. A station is called *full* if the number of customers connected to it is equal to its capacity. A customer is denied service if and only if the stations to which it may connect remain full no matter how customers presently in the system are switched around. Connected customers cannot be disconnected to make room for new customers. A connection costs 1, a disconnection costs 1, a switch costs 1, and there is no cost for denying service.

Our goal is to develop algorithms which do not need to do too much switching in order to connect the incoming customers.

This paper concentrates on the case when each customer can be connected to at most two stations. For this case, there is a graph-based representation that is simpler than the definition above.

Simplified Model: The stations and customers are represented by a graph. We denote by $G = (S, E)$ the graph on the set of stations S. Let $n = |S|$ be the number of stations. The customers appear on the edges or on the nodes of G. A customer appearing on edge $(v_i, v_j) \in E$ can be connected either to station v_i or to station v_j. A customer appearing at node v_i can be connected only to station v_i. A customer on edge (v_i, v_j) who is connected to station v_i can be *switched* at a cost of 1 to be connected to station v_j.

If the capacity of every station is 1, there can be at most two customers on each edge (v_i, v_j). Let the capacity of each station be 1. An edge (v_i, v_j) is said to *point towards* station v_i if there is one customer on edge (v_i, v_j) and it is connected to station v_i. We say that an edge (v_i, v_j) is *unaligned* for algorithms A and B, if edge (v_i, v_j) points towards station v_i for algorithm A, and towards station v_j for algorithm B. An edge (v_i, v_j) is *aligned* for algorithms A and B, if edge (v_i, v_j) points towards the same station for both A and B. An edge that is neither aligned nor unaligned is *irrelevant*. A maximal path $(v_{i_1}, v_{i_2}, \ldots, v_{i_k})$ in G is called a directed *chain* if for all $1 \le j \le k - 1$, edge $(v_{i_j}, v_{i_{j+1}})$ points towards station $v_{i_{j+1}}$; station v_{i_k} is called the *head* of the chain, and station v_{i_1} is the *tail* of the chain. Two chains are said to be (un)aligned for algorithms A and B if all the edges on the chain are (un)aligned for algorithms A and B. A directed chain $(v_{i_1}, v_{i_2}, \ldots, v_{i_k})$ can be *switched* to get the directed chain $(v_{i_k}, v_{i_{k-1}}, \ldots, v_{i_1})$. A switch that is not required to provide connection to a new customer is called a *useless* switch.

Algorithm GREEDY: Assigns a new customer to a station that minimizes the number of switches, choosing arbitrarily if there is a tie.

Algorithm ASSIGNLEFT: (valid for trees, and circles of stations) Define a uniform preferred direction "left" on the edges of the graph of stations (e.g., anti-clockwise on a circle, and towards the root for a tree). Assign the new customer on edge (v_1, v_2) to the station along the preferred direction (switching existing customers, if necessary) unless that is impossible.

Algorithm RAND: When switches have to be made to connect an incoming customer, switch a chain with a probability inversely proportional to the length of the chain.

3 When Customers Never Disconnect

When the station capacities are all 1, the "pointing" of edges essentially defines a matching of edges to vertices. Also, each edge is in at most one chain. If a new customer appears on edge (v_i, v_j) and stations v_i, v_j are full, there are at most two possible chains (the chains with v_i and v_j as their heads) that can be switched to accommodate the new customer, assuming no useless switches are made. Irrelevant edges are those with 0 or 2 customers.

Theorem 1. *There is a a lower bound of $\Omega(\log n)$ on the competitive ratio of any deterministic algorithm when there are no disconnections. A graph with $O(n \log n)$ edges achieves this lower bound.*

Proof. (Sketch) The lower bound is achieved on a complete graph where each station has a capacity of 1. The lower bound holds when stations have finite capacities greater than 1, since for each station v of capacity $cap(v)$ we can force $cap(v) - 1$ customers to connect to station v, leaving a graph where each station has capacity 1 to play our game.

Given two complete subgraphs on 2^k stations each, we can "combine" these two subgraphs while maintaining the following invariants: On each subgraph with 2^k stations:

1. The adversary forces the online configuration to be a chain.
2. The adversary can have its chain either aligned or unaligned with the online's.
3. The adversary incurs a cost of at most $2^k - 1$, while the online incurs a cost of at least $k2^{k-2}$.

Condition 3 of the invariant implies that a complete graph on n nodes will force a competitive ratio of $\Omega(\log n)$ between the costs of the online algorithm and the adversary. The construction can be improved to use only $O(n \log n)$ edges (details omitted from this abstract). □

Theorem 2. *When the capacity of every station is 1 and there are no disconnections,* GREEDY *is $O(\log n)$-competitive.*

Proof. (Sketch) Let us define a *component* to be the set of nodes connected by edges on which there are customers. Initially, each node is a component by itself. As connection requests arrive, two things can happen:

1. A component becomes "dead" when a cycle is formed (i.e., a chain $(v_{i_1}, \ldots, v_{i_1})$), or when a customer appears at a station (rather than an edge adjacent to the station). Once this happens, the nodes of the component don't affect anything in the future.
2. Two components C_1 and C_2 join. In this case, there are two chains $c_1 \in C_1$ and $c_2 \in C_2$ that can be switched. GREEDY switches the smaller of the two chains. We charge the cost of switching the smaller chain uniformly to the edges of the chain of the smaller component. (This implies that each edge is assigned a cost of at most 1.)

Any edge (v_i, v_j) is charged a total cost of at most $O(\log n)$, since the size of the component to which (v_i, v_j) belongs at least doubles each time it is charged. The adversary incurs $\Omega(n)$ cost for the connections. GREEDY is therefore $O(\log n)$ competitive. $\qquad\qquad\square$

The proof of Theorem 2 does not hold when the capacities of the stations are arbitrary since Item 1 above is not true when station capacities are greater than 1. However, we show that ASSIGNLEFT is 2-competitive when the graph is a tree and or a cycle of stations even when the capacities on the nodes are arbitrary.

Theorem 3. *When disconnections are not allowed, ASSIGNLEFT is 2-competitive against trees and circles of stations with arbitrary capacities.*

Proof. (Sketch) If a customer is assigned or switched to a station against the preferred direction, it will not be switched again. Assigning or switching to a station against a preferred direction can happen only because the station in the preferred direction is full. Since there are no disconnections, full stations remain full. The algorithm first tries to assign a customer to the preferred direction. It follows that any customer can be switched at most once. Notice that the proof is valid for any graph with exactly one path between any two nodes.

The lower bound of 2 is obtained easily when the capacity on every station is 1 by forcing a chain for the online algorithm and forcing a switch of the chain by placing a connect request at the head of the chain. $\qquad\qquad\square$

4 When Customers Disconnect

The lower bounds are achieved by a circle of stations with capacity 1. Theorem 1 implies the following lemma.

Lemma 4. *There is a lower bound of $\Omega(\log n)$ on the competitive ratio of any deterministic algorithm even when there are disconnections.*

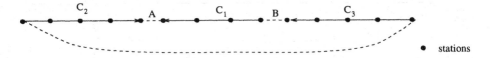

Fig. 1. Proof of Theorem 6. Lower bound of GREEDY.

A *lazy* algorithm does not perform switches if it can connect the customer without making any switches. For the lower bounds we will discuss in this section, we need to let the adversary set a specific initial configuration for use against lazy online algorithms. The following simple observation says that any desired configuration can be obtained at nominal costs.

Lemma 5. *Given a lazy algorithm, an adversary can achieve any desired legal assignment of customers to stations with $O(n)$ cost, when the capacity of each station is constant.*

We now show that some intuitive algorithms have high lower bounds on the competitive ratio. It is interesting that we do not need complicated graphs to prove these lower bounds. All of the lower bounds can be obtained using circles of stations or path-graphs with capacity 1 on the stations.

Theorem 6. GREEDY *has a lower bound of $\Omega(n)$ on its competitive ratio. This lower bound is achieved on a circle of stations with capacity 1 each.*

Proof. We first force the configuration shown in Figure 1 for both the online and the adversary. Let $|C_1| < |C_2| = |C_3|$. We repeat the following sequence: connect at A, disconnect at A, connect at B, disconnect at B. On the first connect at A, the online switches chain C_1 but the adversary switches chain C_2. On the first request at B, the online switches chain C_1 while the adversary switches chain C_3. In every future request, the online switches chain C_2 back and forth, while the adversary satisfies the requests without any switches. The competitive ratio is asymptotically $|C_1| \approx n/3$. □

Theorem 7. ASSIGNLEFT *has a lower bound of $\Omega(n)$ on its competitive ratio. This lower bound is achieved on a circle of stations with capacity 1 each.*

Notice that Theorem 7 taken in conjunction with Theorem 3 gives a clear indication of the power of allowing disconnections in the model. The ASSIGNLEFT algorithm, which is 2-competitive without disconnections on a circle of stations, has a lower bound of $\Omega(n)$ on a circle of stations when deletions are allowed.

GREEDY and ASSIGNLEFT have bad competitive ratios because the adversary makes them repeatedly switch the same chain. Does it help to try to avoid this behavior?

Algorithm WEIGHTEDGREEDY: Amongst all chains along which to switch customers to accommodate a new request, choose the one along which the total number of switches already made is minimum.

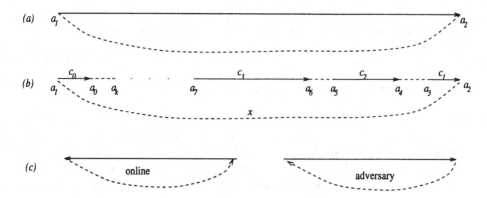

Fig. 2. Proof of Lemma 8. Lower bound of the weighted greedy algorithm.

Unfortunately, WEIGHTEDGREEDY also has a high lower bound on its competitive ratio.

Lemma 8. *There is a lower bound of $\Omega(n/\log n)$ on the competitive ratio for* WEIGHTEDGREEDY. *This lower bound is achieved on a circle of stations with capacity 1 each.*

Proof. We first force the configuration shown in Figure 2a for the online and the adversary (without switching any customers). By Lemma 5, this set-up phase costs $O(n)$ for both the online and the adversary. Now repeat the following "routine:" disconnect the customer between a_0 and a_k, a_3 and a_4, a_5 and a_6, ..., where, $|c_1| = |c_0|, |c_2| = 2|c_1| - 1, |c_3| = 2|c_2| - 1, \ldots$. The situation is as shown in Figure 2b. Make a request at a_0. Both the online and the adversary switch chain c_0. Delete the customer at a_0 and make a request at x. The weighted greedy algorithm will switch chain c_1 (since the customers on chain c_0 have been switched more times than the ones on chain c_1), while the adversary switches chain c_0. For every subsequent request at (a_{2i-1}, a_{2i}) the online switches chain c_i, while the offline does $O(1)$ work. (The length of the chains have been adjusted to make this happen.) Now the chains look as in Figure 2c. Disconnect the customer at x and force the online to switch and get aligned on all edges with the offline.

For the requests made in the "routine," the adversary does $O(\log n)$ work while the online does $O(n)$ work. Asymptotically, this implies a lower bound of $\Omega(n/\log n)$ on the competitive ratio. □

We have seen that intuitive deterministic algorithms have a bad competitive ratio. We can do better if we use randomization. We will now analyze RAND.

Theorem 9. *There is a lower bound of $\Omega(\sqrt{n})$ on the competitive ratio of* RAND *against an adaptive adversary, and a lower bound of $\Omega(n^{1/3})$ on the competitive ratio of* RAND *against an oblivious adversary. These lower bounds are achieved on a circle of stations of capacity 1.*

Proof. (Sketch) We first get the configuration for the online and the adaptive adversary as in Figure 3a with $\Theta(n)$ cost (see Lemma 5). Delete the customers

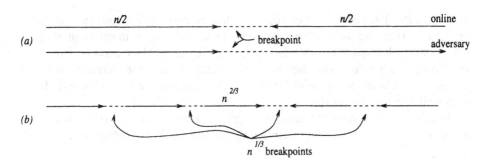

Fig. 3. Proof of Theorem 9. Lower bound of RAND.

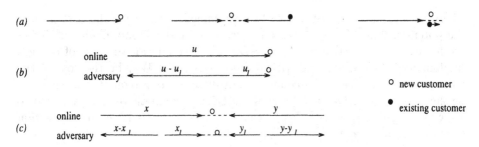

Fig. 4. Proof of competitiveness of RAND. (a) Ways in which forced moves happen. (b) Forced move scenario. (c) Unforced move scenario.

that are at distance $\sqrt{n}$ to the left and right of the "break point" and make a request at the break point. The adversary incurs a cost of 1 and the online incurs a cost of $\sqrt{n}$ to connect this new customer, and the break point moves. Repeat this process until the break point reaches one of the ends. By the theory of random walks, the break point takes an expected $\Theta(n)$ times before it reaches one of the ends.

The expected cost of the online algorithm is $\Theta(n)$ (for the setup) + $\Theta(n\sqrt{n})$, while the adversary's cost is $O(n)$ (for the setup) + $\Theta(n)$, giving a lower bound of $\Omega(\sqrt{n})$ on the competitive ratio.

Against an oblivious adversary, we do not know where the break point is. We divide the chain into $n^{1/3}$ sub-chains of length $n^{2/3}$ each thereby defining $n^{1/3}$ breakpoints as shown in Figure 3b. We place a request at each of these $n^{1/3}$ breakpoints and repeat this $n^{2/3}$ times (the expected time for RAND to align with the adversary). The online does a total of $\Omega(n^{4/3})$ work, while the adversary does $O(n)$ work, giving a lower bound of $\Omega(n^{1/3})$ for the competitive ratio. □

We are now ready to upper bound RAND. The proof uses an interesting potential function derived from the random walk idea used in the lower bound proof of Theorem 9.

Theorem 10. *For any graph with station capacity 1, RAND is $O(\sqrt{n})$-competitive.*

Proof. (Sketch) A customer can appear either on an edge between two stations, or at a station. An adversary can generate a customer connect request at a station which forces a lot of switches and then disconnect the customer. However, intuitively, such forced switches make the online paths more aligned with the adversary's. We use a potential function that accurately captures the gain from such switches for the future.

Let D be the number of unaligned edges between RAND and OPT, and let S be the number of aligned edges between RAND and OPT. We define our potential function as

$$\Phi = k_1 D\sqrt{n} + \frac{k_2 DS}{\sqrt{n}}, \qquad (1)$$

where k_1 and k_2 are constants to be determined. Intuitively, the first part of the potential function, $\Phi_1 = k_1 D\sqrt{n}$, accounts for the situation when switches are forced. The second part, $\Phi_2 = k_2 DS/\sqrt{n}$ accounts for the cost of doing a random walk before aligning with the adversary. Let W_{on} be the cost of the online algorithm to service a connection or disconnection request, and let W_{adv} be the cost for the adversary. To show an $O(\sqrt{n})$ competitive ratio, we need to show that $\sum W_{on} \leq c\sqrt{n} \sum W_{adv}$. It suffices to show that for each (connection or disconnection) request,

$$W_{on} + \Delta\Phi \leq c\sqrt{n} \times W_{adv}, \qquad (2)$$

since summing (2) over all requests will give us our result.

It is easy to see that for a disconnection, the potential always drops (i.e., $\Delta\Phi < 0$) and so (2) is satisfied. The case when a connection can be satisfied without any switches is also easily verified. The hard part is when a connection forces switches. We divide our analysis into two cases.

1. In *forced moves*, the online algorithm does not have a choice of which chain of customers to switch. Forced moves happen because of the situations given in Figure 4a. The forced move scenario is given in Figure 4b. In this case, $W_{on} = u$, and u_1 edges along the chain are aligned between the online algorithm and the adversary, $0 \leq u_1 \leq u$. We have $W_{adv} \geq u_1$. Clearly, $\Delta D = -(u - u_1)$, and $\Delta S = u - u_1$. Hence, $\Delta\Phi = -k_1\sqrt{n}(u - u_1) + k_2(u - u_1)(D - S - u + u_1)/\sqrt{n}$. Since $(D - S - u + u_1) \leq n$, it can be verified that (2) holds as long as $k_1 \geq k_2$.

2. In *unforced moves*, the online algorithm has a choice between two chains of customers to switch. The situation is as depicted in Figure 4c, where $0 \leq y_1 \leq y$, and $0 \leq x_1 \leq x$. In this case, the online algorithm switches the chain of length x with a probability of $y/(x + y)$, and the chain of length y with a probability of $x/(x + y)$ incurring an expected cost of $2xy/(x + y)$. Without loss of generality, assume that the adversary switches the chain of length y_1; hence $W_{adv} = y_1 + 1$. We need to verify that (2) holds. If the online algorithm switches the chain of length y, $\Delta D = -(y - y_1)$, and $\Delta S = y - y_1 + 1$. If the online algorithm switches the chain of length x,

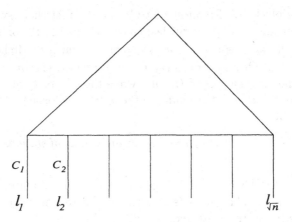

Fig. 5. Lower bound of $\Omega(\sqrt{n})$ for a tree.

$\Delta D = 2x_1 - x + y_1 + 1$, and $\Delta S = x - 2x_1 - y_1$. Substituting and simplifying, we get

$$\Delta\Phi_1 \approx \frac{2k_1\sqrt{n}y(x_1 - x)}{x + y}; \tag{3}$$

$$\Delta\Phi_2 \approx \frac{k_2y(x - x_1)(2D + 4x_1)}{\sqrt{n}(x + y)} + \frac{2k_2yS(x_1 - x)}{(x + y)\sqrt{n}} - \frac{k_2xy}{\sqrt{n}}. \tag{4}$$

In simplifying to get the above expressions, we ignored terms of value less than or equal to $c_3\sqrt{n}(y_1 + 1)$. For an appropriately large c, terms of value $\leq c_3\sqrt{n}(y_1+1)$ appearing on the lhs of (2) will be "paid for" by W_{adv} on the rhs of (2). The constant c_3 is independent of c. Note that $\Delta\Phi_1 \leq 0$. Since $2D + 4x_1 = O(n)$ and $x \geq 0$, the first term of $\Delta\Phi_2$ is non-negative but is "paid for" by $\Delta\Phi_1$, if $k_1 \geq 3k_2$. The second term of $\Delta\Phi_2$ is negative and can be ignored. The third term of $\Delta\Phi_2$ (i.e., $-k_2xy/\sqrt{n}$) "pays" for the online cost of $2xy/(x+y)$, if $k_2 > 2$ and $x+y \geq \sqrt{n}$. If $x+y < \sqrt{n}$, the adversary's cost pays for the online cost.

$\square$

Theorem 11. *There is a lower bound of $\Omega(\sqrt{n})$ on the competitive ratio of any algorithm (if randomized, against an adaptive adversary) when the capacities of the stations are 2. This lower bound is achieved by a tree of stations.*

Proof. (Sketch) Consider the tree of stations in Figure 5. The capacity on each station is 2. The idea of the proof is to force an initial configuration with all chains pointing towards the root. The adversary then places a connect request at the root, and the online switches a chain C_i with some leaf l_i as the tail of the chain. It then disconnects the new customer and forces the online to switch the chain C_i again by placing a request at l_i. Divide the request sequence into minimal blocks, such that for every block the online switches all the $\sqrt{n}$

chains. For the block B_j of requests, let $C_{j,1}$ be the first chain switched by the online algorithm and let $C_{j,m}$ be the last chain switched by the online algorithm, $m \geq \sqrt{n}$. For the first request in block B_j, the adversary switches chain $C_{j,m}$ incurring a cost of $O(\sqrt{n})$. For every connect request except the first in the block, the online incurs a cost of $\Omega(\sqrt{n})$, while the adversary incurs a cost of 1. The net ratio of the cost of the online to the adversary for any block of connect requests is $\Omega(\sqrt{n})$. $\qquad\qquad\square$

Theorem 12. RAND *is* $O(\sqrt{n})$-*competitive on a circle of stations with arbitrary capacities.*

Like the proof of Theorem 10, this proof is based on a potential function that measures a random walk, but it is of a rather different form. For brevity, the proof is omitted from this abstract.

5 Conclusions

We have presented in this paper a model of mobile connectivity. There are some very challenging questions that arise from our model. The most obvious open question is: Is there an $O(\sqrt{n})$-competitive algorithm for general graphs when disconnections are allowed, and the capacities are arbitrary? We have a generalization of RAND that we believe is $O(\sqrt{n})$-competitive. When the capacities are arbitrary, the main difficulty is that there can be many non-disjoint augmenting paths for a new connect request. Our generalization of RAND defines a resistive network [CDR] of the augmenting paths and switches a path proportional to the current that would flow through it when a unit voltage is placed at the new connect request point. We expect that the online algorithms discussed in this paper will do better when the capacities of the stations are larger, and the degree of each customer is greater than 2, because intuitively, more paths help the algorithm more than adversary.

References

[AwP] B. Awerbuch and D. Peleg, "Concurrent Online Tracking of Mobile Users," *Proceedings of SIGCOMM 1991*.

[ABK] Y. Azar, A. Y. Broder, and A. R. Karlin, "On-line Load Balancing," *Proceedings of the 33rd Symposium on Foundations of Computer Science* (October 1993), 218–225.

[AKP] Y. Azar, B. Kalyanasundaram, S. Plotkin, K. R. Pruhs, and O. Waarts, "Online Load Balancing of Temporary Tasks," *Proceedings of the 1993 Workshop on Algorithms and Data Structures* (August 1993).

[ANR] Y. Azar, J. Naor, and R. Rom, "The Competitiveness of On-Line Assignments," *Proceedings of the 3rd Annual ACM-SIAM Symposium on Discrete Algorithms* (January 1992).

[CDR] D. Coppersmith, P. Doyle, P. Raghavan, M. Snir, "Random Walks on Weighted Graphs and Applications to On-line Algorithms," *Proceedings of the 22nd Annual ACM Symposium on Theory of Computing* (May 1990, and 369–378), Also appears as IBM Research Report RC 15840.

[Dav] D. W. Davis, "Wirless LANs broadcast their benefits over cable," Electronic Business, May 1991.

[DKM] F. Douglis, P. Krishnan, and B. Marsh, "Thwarting the Power Hungry Disk," *Proceedings of the 1994 Winter USENIX Conference* (January 1994).

[IDJ] J. Ioannidis, D. Duchamp, and G. Macquire, Jr., "IP-based Protocols for Mobile Internetworking," *Proceedings of SIGCOMM '91* (September 1991), 235–245.

[USE] USENIX, "Proceedings of the USENIX Mobile and Location-Independent Computing Symposium," Cambridge, MA, August 1993.

[Wei] M. Weiser, "The Computer for the 21st Century," *Scientific American* (September 1991), 94–104.

Competitive Algorithms for the On-line Traveling Salesman*

Giorgio Ausiello[1], Esteban Feuerstein[1]**, Stefano Leonardi[1], Leen Stougie[2] and Maurizio Talamo[1]

[1] Dipartimento di Informatica e Sistemistica, Università di Roma "La Sapienza", via Salaria 113, 00198-Roma, Italia.
e-mail: {ausiello,esteban,leonardi,talamo}@dis.uniroma1.it.
[2] Department of Operations Research, University of Amsterdam, Roetersstraat 11, 1018WB Amsterdam, The Netherlands.
e-mail: leen@sara.nl.

Abstract. In this paper the problem of efficiently serving a sequence of requests that are presented in a metric space in an on-line fashion and then returning back to the departure point is considered. The problem is the on-line version of a variant of the Traveling Salesman Problem (namely the Vehicle Routing Problem with release times), and we call it the On-Line Traveling Salesman Problem (OLTSP). It has a variety of relevant applications in logistics and robotics.

After proving a ≈ 1.64 lower bound on the competitive ratio that can be achieved by on-line algorithms for OLTSP, two competitive algorithms are shown, one of which is 2-competitive and works for any metric space. The second one allows to achieve a nearly optimal competitive ratio of 1.75 on the real line.

1 Introduction

The Traveling Salesman Problem (TSP) and in general vehicle routing and scheduling problems have been widely studied for more than three decades. A common characteristic of almost all this research effort is the off-line point of view. The whole instance of the problem is known before an algorithm computes a route that visits a set of locations in a space (possibly subject to various constraints) with the goal of minimizing the distance traveled or the completion time.

However, in many routing and scheduling applications the instance is only known in an on-line fashion. In other words, the input of the problem is communicated in successive steps, and moreover, in general it is not possible to determine which is the last request, i.e. when the instance is completely known.

---

* This work was partly supported by ESPRIT BRA Alcom II under contract No.7141, by Italian Ministry of Scientific Research Project 40% "Algoritmi, Modelli di Calcolo e Strutture Informative", and by a grant from the SCIENCE project "Algorithmic Approaches to Large and Complex Combinatorial Optimization Problems".
** New address: Departamento de Computación, Facultad de Ciencias Exactas y Naturales, Universidad de Buenos Aires. Pabellón I, Ciudad Universitaria, Buenos Aires, Argentina.

In this paper we consider the following on-line variation of TSP in a metric space: while the salesman is traveling, new sites to visit may be communicated to him. His goal is to visit all the sites and turn back to the departure point, minimizing the completion time.

This setting models many natural applications. Think for example of a salesman or of a repairman with a cellular phone, of a robot that has to service locations of its working space (for example in the Euclidean plane) and of many other routing and scheduling problems on a transportation network modeled with a graph. We will refer to this problem as the *On-line Traveling Salesman Problem* (OLTSP).

As the input to the salesman (from now on we will refer to him as the *server*) is communicated in an on-line way, the scheduled route will have to be updated also in an on-line way during the trip. Therefore, the final solution will not be optimal in general. The fact of dealing with incomplete information introduces an additional source of difficulty unrelated to that of computational complexity. In other words, in general it is not possible to compute the optimal solution on all instances even using non polynomial time algorithms.

The most widely accepted way of measuring the performance of on-line algorithms is *competitive analysis*. The quality of a certain on-line strategy is measured by the worst-case ratio between the time needed by the on-line algorithm for a sequence of requests and the optimal time needed to serve it by an algorithm who knows the entire sequence in advance. This ratio is called the *competitive ratio* of the on-line algorithm. Therefore, an algorithm is ρ-competitive if for every input its completion time is at most ρ times the optimal completion time for the same input. Competitive analysis has been introduced in [10], and since then has been used for analyzing the performance of on-line strategies for a great variety of on-line problems, ranging from scheduling to financial decision making, and for many data structure problems (among the wide literature on the subject, see for example [3, 7, 10, 9]).

We will therefore compare the performance of on-line algorithms with the optimal solution of the corresponding off-line problem, namely the Vehicle Routing Problem with release times [8]. In that problem, each site must be visited at or after a given release time. The release time of a request corresponds to the time in which the request is communicated to the on-line server. This problem is part of a family of off-line variants of TSP generally called *routing and scheduling with time window constraints* [5, 8, 11], that may associate to each request also a deadline or a handling time.

A similar problem has already been studied by the authors in [2]. In that work the case in which the server has to visit the requested sites following a path rather than a tour was considered. The added constraint of ending the trip at the departure point changes the nature of the problem (and henceforth the kind of applications). Besides, lower bounds and algorithms for the two problems are qualitatively and quantitatively different.

Another related work [6] considers the problem of visiting the whole set of vertices of an unknown graph, when the set of edges leaving a node is revealed only once the node is visited. In our case, the metric space is completely known from the beginning, but what is revealed in an on-line way is the set of locations that must be visited.

It is important to note that OLTSP is different from the famous *k-server problem* [7]. In that problem the requests have to be served in the order in which they are presented, with the goal of minimizing the total distance traveled by the k servers. On the contrary, in OLTSP the task is precisely to decide the order in which the requests will be served.

In this work we propose competitive on-line algorithms for OLTSP. In particular, we give:

- a lower bound of $\frac{9+\sqrt{17}}{8} \approx 1.64$ on the competitive ratio achievable by any on-line algorithm (Section 3);
- a 2-competitive algorithm for any metric space (Section 4);
- a 7/4-competitive algorithm for the case in which the metric space is isomorphic to the real line (Section 5).

The lower bound is obtained on the real line, and hence the existing gap is particularly small in that case (≈ 1.64 *vs* 1.75).

Our 2-competitive algorithm for arbitrary metric spaces is not polynomial, but we also show how to obtain a 3-competitive polynomial time algorithm. As we mentioned before, the on-line nature of the problem is a source of difficulty independent of its computational complexity, and therefore on-line algorithms achieving good competitive ratios are of interest also if their time or space requirements are not polynomially bounded.

Our setting can be naturally applied to situations in which the server moves along the edges of a graph, and serves requests that are presented on the nodes. If a distance or a *traversing time* is associated to each edge of the graph, the notions of distance and path can be extended to pairs of points that lie on the edges. This allows us to model also transportation problems on road networks (for some of our algorithms, U-turns must be always allowed). It is important to note that the on-line server does not need to know the whole metric space. However, an oracle is available to answer questions on the distances and paths between any known pair of points in the space.

2 Preliminaries

In this paper we consider the on-line traveling salesman problem (OLTSP). The input of OLTSP consists in a metric space M with a distinguished point o (the origin), and a sequence of pairs $< t_i, p_i >$ where p_i is a point of M and t_i is a real number, $0 \leq t_i \leq t_j$ for every $i < j$. t_i represents the moment in which the request is known. A server located at point o at time 0 that moves not faster than unit speed must serve all the requests and go back to o with the goal of minimizing the total completion time.

An on-line algorithm for OLTSP determines the behavior of the server in a certain moment t as a function of all requests $< t_i, p_i >$ such that $t_i \leq t$.

We will denote the completion time of the solution produced by an on-line algorithm OL by Z^{OL} and that of the optimal (off-line) solution by Z^*. An on-line algorithm for OLTSP is ρ-competitive if for any sequence of requests $Z^{OL} \leq \rho Z^*$. With $p^{OL}(t)$ and $p^*(t)$ we denote respectively the position of OL's server and the optimal off-line server at time t.

For every pair of points x, y in the metric space M, $d(x, y)$ indicates the distance between x and y in M. Let T be a path in the metric space; with $|T|$ we will denote the length of T.

3 A lower bound

First of all let us prove a lower bound on the competitive ratio ρ for any on-line algorithm for OLTSP. In the proof an adversary will play the advocate of the devil, by providing, given a ρ-competitive on-line algorithm, a sequence of requests for which ρ must be at least the claimed value.

The proof is constructed on a particular metric space, namely the real line with the origin o at point 0.

Theorem 3.1 *If an on-line algorithm is ρ-competitive, then $\rho \geq (9 + \sqrt{17})/8$.*

Proof: Both the adversary and the on-line algorithm OL start at 0 at time $t = 0$. Thus, $p^{OL}(0) = p^*(0) = 0$.

Before time $t = 1$ no requests are presented. At that moment, the position $p^{OL}(1)$ of the server of any ρ-competitive on-line algorithm must be inside the interval $[-(2\rho - 3), (2\rho - 3)]$. In fact, if $p^{OL}(1) > (2\rho - 3)$ the first (and unique) request of the sequence could be at point -1, giving $Z^{OL} > 1 + (2\rho - 3) + 2 = 2\rho$, because OL has to travel from its current position to -1 and back to 0. On the other hand, for this sequence $Z^* = 2$, and therefore the algorithm would not be ρ-competitive. The case in which $p^{OL}(1) < -(2\rho - 3)$ is symmetric.

Then, $p^{OL}(1) \in [-(2\rho - 3), (2\rho - 3)]$. Now the adversary presents two simultaneous requests at points -1 and 1 at time $t = 1$. At time $t = 3$, the on-line server can not have served *both* requests. Suppose, without loss of generality, that it has not served the request in -1. If it has served the request in 1 it must be to the right of $-(2\rho - 3)$ since it has started to move towards +1 after time 1 from a position not to the right of $(2\rho - 3)$.

We now show that if $-(7 - 4\rho) < p^{OL}(3) < (7 - 4\rho)$ then OL can not be ρ-competitive. In this case the adversary could be in $p^*(3) = 1$, present a new request in +1 and go back to the origin with a total cost $Z^* = 4$. OL, however, would still have to serve requests in both extremes, and hence $Z^{OL} > 3 + 1 - (7 - 4\rho) + 3 = 4\rho$, since starting at time $t = 3$ it would have to go to one of the extremes and then to the other and back to 0.

Note that if $\rho \geq (9 + \sqrt{17})/8$ the thesis follows, otherwise if $\rho < (9 + \sqrt{17})/8$ the interval $[-(7 - 4\rho), (7 - 4\rho)]$ strictly contains the interval $[-(2\rho - 3), (2\rho - 3)]$.

Thus, we are left with two cases to be considered.

1. At time $t = 3$ the on-line server has not served +1, and $-1 \leq p^{OL}(3) \leq -(7-4\rho)$ or $(7 - 4\rho) \leq p^{OL}(3) \leq 1$.
2. At time $t = 3$ the on-line server has served +1. Hence $(7 - 4\rho) \leq p^{OL}(3) \leq 1$, because we have already shown that $-(2\rho - 3) \leq p^{OL}(3)$.

We notice that in both cases the following situation occurs: the on-line server is within distance $1 - (7 - 4\rho)$ of the extreme on one side and has not served the extreme on the other side. This property is sufficient for the rest of the proof, where we will suppose that the on-line server is near 1 and has not served the request in -1 (the other case is symmetric).

In this case the optimal algorithm on the requests presented so far has served -1, is at position $p^*(3) = +1$ and finishes with $Z^* = 4$. Then, any ρ-competitive on-line algorithm has to pass point 0 at some time within $4\rho - 2$. Let's denote the time at which the on-line server crosses the origin as $3 + q$. Therefore we have

$$q \leq 4\rho - 5. \tag{1}$$

At time $(3 + q)$ the adversary can be in position $(1 + q)$ and it can then place one request at that point and go back to 0. For this sequence we have that $Z^{OL} = 7 + 3q$ and $Z^* = 4 + 2q$, and therefore $\frac{Z^{OL}}{Z^*} = \frac{7+3q}{4+2q}$. By hypothesis OL is ρ-competitive, then

$$\rho \geq \frac{7 + 3q}{4 + 2q}.$$

This is a monotonically decreasing function of the value q, and by equation (1) we get

$$\rho \geq \frac{7 + 3(4\rho - 5)}{4 + 2(4\rho - 5)}. \tag{2}$$

The least value of ρ that satisfies inequality (2) is the value that achieves equality, that is $\rho = \frac{9+\sqrt{17}}{8}$.

□

4 A 2-competitive algorithm

Let us now turn to the search of a competitive algorithm for OLTSP. The most intuitive algorithm one can think of is the "greedy" algorithm that follows at every time the shortest path that starts in its current position, visits all the points that still have to be served, and ends at the origin. It is easy to see that this strategy is 2.5-competitive. In this section we will show that it is possible to do better. We present an algorithm that achieves a competitive ratio of 2 for any metric space. We call the algorithm PAH (for Plan-At-Home). We abbreviate with p the position $p^{PAH}(t)$. PAH works as follows:

1. At any time t the server is at the origin, it starts to follow an optimal route that serves all the requests and goes back to the origin.
2. At any time t a new request is presented at some point x, it takes one of two actions depending on its current position p:
   2a. If $d(x, o) > d(p, o)$, then the server goes back to the origin (following the shortest path) where it appears in Case 1.
   2b. If $d(x, o) \leq d(p, o)$ then the server ignores it until it arrives at the origin, where again it reenters Case 1.

Note that requests that are presented between an occurrence of case 2a and the arrival to the origin do not make PAH deviate from its current route.

Theorem 4.1 *PAH is 2-competitive.*

Proof: Assume that at time t a new request is presented at position x. We show that in each of the three cases 1, 2a and 2b, PAH is 2-competitive.

Let T^* be the optimal tour that starts at the origin, serves all the requests presented so far, and ends at the origin. Clearly $Z^* \geq t$ since no algorithm can finish before the last request is presented, and $Z^* \geq |T^*|$.

In case ,1 PAH's server is at the origin at time t. Then it starts an optimal tour that serves all the unserved requests and goes back to the origin. The time needed by PAH is $Z^{PAH} \leq t + |T^*| \leq 2\,Z^*$.

If, when the new request arrives, PAH's server is not at the origin, we can distinguish two cases, corresponding to cases 2a and 2b.

2a. $d(o, x) > d(o, p)$. Then the server goes back to o, where it will arrive before time $t + d(o, x)$. At that moment, we read from the description of the algorithm, that PAH will compute and follow an optimal tour through all the unserved requests. Therefore, $Z^{PAH} < t + d(o, x) + |T^*|$.

Notice first that $Z^* \geq t + d(o, x)$, since from the time t the request is presented every algorithm has to travel at least the distance from the request to the origin, and secondly that, as before, $Z^* \geq |T^*|$. Thus, $Z^{PAH} < 2\,Z^*$.

2b. $d(o, x) \leq d(o, p)$. We have two cases:

- PAH's server is going back to o due to a previous occurrence of case 2a. As in case 2a, PAH will arrive to the origin before the adversary can finish and hence it is 2-competitive.
- PAH is following a route R that has been computed the last time the server was at the origin. Let S be the set of requests that have been temporarily ignored since the last time the server left the origin. Let s be the location of the first request in S served by the adversary, and t_s the time at which s was presented. Let P_S^* be the shortest *path* that starts at s, visits all the points in S and ends at o. Clearly, $Z^* \geq t_s + |P_S^*|$.

  At time t_s, the distance that the server still has to travel on the route R before arriving at o is at most $|R| - d(o, s)$. In fact $d(o, p(t_s)) \geq d(o, s)$ implies that PAH has traveled on the route R a distance not less than $d(o, p(t_s))$. Therefore, it will arrive to o before time $t_s + |R| - d(o, s)$. After that it will follow an optimal tour T_S^* that covers the set of yet unserved requests that is S. Therefore the total time for completion will be $Z^{PAH} \leq t_s + |R| - d(o, s) + |T_S^*|$. Because $|T_S^*| \leq d(o, s) + |P_S^*|$, we have $Z^{PAH} \leq t_s + |R| - d(o, s) + d(o, s) + |P_S^*| = t_s + |R| + |P_S^*|$. Since, obviously, $Z^* \geq |R|$ and, as established before, $Z^* \geq t_s + |P_S^*|$, we have that $Z^{PAH} \leq 2\,Z^*$.

□

Note that we could have added another condition to the algorithm stating that whenever the new request would not have changed the tour followed so far by the on-line server, then it is included in the current tour. However, this extra condition would not decrease the competitive ratio achieved by the algorithm, as is shown in the following example, which proves tightness of the worst-case bound.

For this we consider an instance in which the metric space is the real line with the origin o at point 0.

The sequence of requests starts with a request at time 1 at position $+1$. PAH remains at the origin until time 1 when it leaves towards 1. Each time the on-line server arrives to point $+\epsilon$, a new request is presented "slightly" to the left of $-\epsilon$, in such a way that the server always turns back to 0. The optimal strategy consists in serving first the request in $+1$ and then all the requests to the left of 0 with a total cost arbitrarily close to $2 + 2\epsilon$, while the on-line algorithm will be to the left of $+\epsilon$ at least until time $2 + \epsilon$, with a total cost of at least 4. Making ϵ arbitrarily small yields a ratio of 2.

Step 1 of PAH requires to solve an NP-hard problem. A polynomial time competitive algorithm can be obtained from PAH by replacing the optimal tour with a 3/2-approximate tour calculated using Christofides' polynomial algorithm [4] for TSP on metric spaces. This algorithm is 3-competitive as can be proved with arguments similar to those of the previous proof.

5   A 7/4-competitive algorithm on the line

Both the greedy algorithm described at the beginning of the previous section and PAH can be applied in the particular case in which the metric space is the real line. However, even on the line, none of these two algorithms achieves a ratio better than 2. In this section we present an algorithm whose competitive ratio is 7/4, which is fairly close to the lower bound presented in section 3 that has been achieved precisely on the real line. We call this algorithm PWT (for Plan-While-Traveling).

PWT works in phases. The first phase starts with the first request, and each successive phase starts when a new request that is not on the currently scheduled tour and whose abscissa's absolute value is bigger than that of any other unserved request is presented.

At the beginning of a phase, say at time t, PWT schedules the shortest route that, starting from the current position $p^{PWT}(t)$ of the server, serves all the unserved requests and goes back to the origin. Requests may be presented *during* the phase. Some of them may call for computation of a new tour, while others are ignored temporarily and served after the server has returned to the origin.

Let us first define some auxiliary notation and definitions. At any moment in time we define R as the *current route* followed by PWT, i.e., the *part* of the most recently computed route that is still to be traversed. We call *greedy route* the shortest route that starts at the current position of the on-line server, serves all the unserved requests and goes back to the origin.

During a phase, we refer to the *long side* as the half line from 0 on which the (furthest) request is located, whose presentation caused the start of the phase. The other side is then referred to as the *short side*.

Let Q be the set of temporarily ignored requests. When a phase starts the set Q is empty, while during a phase it contains only requests on the short side. Requests are removed from Q when served. The current route will consist in general of a greedy route concatenated with a tour that serves all the requests in Q and goes back to the origin.

PWT is described completely by its behavior at the moment a new request is presented, say time t:

1. If the new request is on the current route R then just proceed following R and serve the request when it is passed; else
2. If the new request is the furthest request from the origin among the requests not yet served then start a new phase, empty the set Q and let the current route be the greedy route; else
3. If the new request is on the long side then empty the set Q and let the current route be the greedy route; else
4. If the new request is on the short side then insert it in Q and let the current route be the remainder of the last computed greedy route concatenated with the route that, starting at the origin, serves all the requests in Q and returns to the origin.

The current route will consist in general of a greedy route concatenated with a tour that serves all the requests in Q and goes back to the origin.

Intuitively, to be 7/4-competitive it is sufficient to start following a shortest tour before the optimal algorithm leaves the furthest extreme towards the origin, after having visited the requests on the short side. It is with this goal that PWT temporarily ignores the requests on the short side that are relatively close to the origin.

Without loss of generality, we will suppose that the long side is the right side, and the short side is the left side. Therefore, we will denote the requests on the long side by positive numbers and those on the short side by negative numbers. Let $-x$ and X be respectively the leftmost and rightmost requests not yet served at the beginning of the current phase, so that $X \geq x$. If there is no unserved request to the left of the origin then we set $x = 0$.

Let $-x'$ and X' be respectively the leftmost and the rightmost points not yet served by PWT when the greedy route was computed for the last time (i.e. after an occurrence of case 2 or 3 of the algorithm), and let $I = [-x', X']$.

Finally, let $-\mathcal{Y}$ and $\mathcal{X}$ be, respectively, the leftmost and the rightmost requests *ever* presented.

We state four lemmas preliminary to the competitiveness proof, that are trivial or almost trivial to prove.

Lemma 5.1 *The position of PWT is always inside the interval* $[-\mathcal{Y}, \mathcal{X}]$.

Lemma 5.2 *The distance to the origin of any request presented in a phase is at most* X.

Lemma 5.3 *If a request leads to the occurrence of Case 3 then it is the rightmost request not yet served.*

Proof: Case 3 occurs if the request presented is on the right (long) side and it is not on the current route. $\qquad\square$

Lemma 5.4 *If Case 3 occurs then the request is on the long side at position* X', *and* $x' \geq X'$.

Proof: When the new request at position X' is presented, by Lemma 5.3 it is the rightmost request not yet served. Therefore, as it does not initiate a new phase, the leftmost request not yet served has distance from the origin greater or equal than X'. □

Theorem 5.5 *PWT is 7/4-competitive.*

Proof: We prove the claim by showing that if the algorithm is 7/4-competitive before a new request is presented at time t, which is obviously true for $t = 0$, then the algorithm has the same competitive ratio after it has taken any of the actions described upon presentation of the new request. We prove it for each of the four cases that have been specified. When the time t is clear from the context we abbreviate $p^{PWT}(t)$ with p.

1. In the first case, the new request is on the current route and the route is not changed. Since Z^{PWT} does not increase and the algorithm was 7/4 competitive before the request is presented, the claim still holds.

2. In the second case a new phase starts. Then the presented request is at position X. p can not be to the right of X, otherwise X would have been on the current route. Two cases are distinguished:

   - p is within the interval I at time t. Since the on-line algorithm follows the newly computed current route starting at time t ¿ from p, we have that $Z^{OL} \leq t + 2x + 2X$. For the optimal algorithm it holds $Z^* \geq t + X$ because the request in X has been presented at time t and after that the algorithm has to reach the origin. Also $Z^* \geq 2x + 2X$. Thus, since $x \leq X$,

   $$\frac{Z^{PWT}}{Z^*} \leq \frac{t + 2x + 2X}{Z^*} = \frac{t + X}{Z^*} + \frac{2x + X}{Z^*} \leq 1 + \frac{2x + X}{2x + 2X} \leq \frac{7}{4}.$$

   - p is outside the interval I at time t. Then p must be to the left of $-x$. By Lemma 5.1 $|p| \leq \mathcal{Y}$. The time needed by PWT to serve all the requests is then $Z^{PWT} \leq t + |p| + 2X$ while for the optimal solution $Z^* \geq t + X$ and $Z^* \geq 2|p| + 2X$. Then, the ratio between the on-line and the optimal solution is

   $$\frac{Z^{PWT}}{Z^*} \leq \frac{t + |p| + 2X}{Z^*} = \frac{t + X}{Z^*} + \frac{|p| + X}{Z^*} \leq 1 + \frac{|p| + X}{2|p| + 2X} \leq \frac{3}{2}.$$

3. X' is the position of the new request on the long side. By Lemma 5.2 $X' \leq X$ and $x' \leq X$; and by Lemma 5.4 $X' \leq x'$. For the same reason as in case 2, if p is outside I then it must be to the left of $-x'$. Also in this case we consider two subcases:

   - p is within the interval I at time t. For the on-line algorithm we have $Z^{PWT} \leq t + 2x' + 2X'$, while for the optimal solution we have $Z^* \geq t + X'$ and $Z^* \geq 2x' + 2X \geq 4x'$. Hence the ratio is

   $$\frac{Z^{PWT}}{Z^*} \leq \frac{t + 2x' + 2X'}{Z^*} = \frac{t + X'}{Z^*} + \frac{2x' + X'}{Z^*}$$

   $$\leq 1 + \frac{2x' + X'}{2x' + 2X} \leq 1 + \frac{3x'}{4x'} = \frac{7}{4}.$$

- p is outside the interval I, and hence to the left of $-x'$. By Lemma 5.1 $|p| \leq \mathcal{Y}$. The time needed by the on-line algorithm to serve all the requests is therefore $Z^{OL} \leq t + |p| + 2X'$ while for the optimal solution $Z^* \geq t + X'$ and $Z^* \geq 2|p| + 2X'$. Then, the ratio between the on-line and the optimal solution is

$$\frac{Z^{PWT}}{Z^*} \leq \frac{t + |p| + 2X'}{Z^*} = \frac{t + X'}{Z^*} + \frac{|p| + X'}{Z^*} \leq 1 + \frac{|p| + X'}{2|p| + 2X'} \leq \frac{3}{2}.$$

4. Let $-x''$ be the position of the new request that is inserted in Q. Clearly the new request is the leftmost request in Q since otherwise it falls inside the current route. We consider two subcases:

- The optimal solution serves X' before $-x''$. Let t' be the time at which the request in X' was presented, that is the time at which the current greedy route was computed. For the optimal solution we get $Z^* \geq t' + X' + 2x''$. Again, two subcases are distinguished, depending on the position $p^{PWT}(t')$ of PWT's server at time t', relative to the interval $I = [-x', X']$:

  • The on-line server was inside I at time t'. Then $Z^{PWT} \leq t' + 2x' + 2X' + 2x''$ while for the adversary $Z^* \geq 2x' + 2X$. In this case the ratio is

$$\frac{Z^{PWT}}{Z^*} \leq \frac{t' + 2x' + 2X' + 2x''}{Z^*} = \frac{t' + X' + 2x''}{Z^*} + \frac{2x' + X'}{Z^*}$$
$$\leq 1 + \frac{2x' + X'}{2x' + 2X} \leq \frac{7}{4},$$

  since either $X' = X$, in which case by Lemmas 5.2 and 5.4 $x' = x \leq X$, or $X' < X$, which implies by Lemma 5.4 that $X' \leq x'$.

  • PWT was outside I at time t'. Since the request in X' was not on the previous route, PWT's server was to the left of $-x'$ at some position $p^{PWT}(t')$. By Lemma 5.1, $|p^{PWT}(t')| \leq |\mathcal{Y}|$. This implies that $Z^{PWT} \leq t' + |p^{PWT}(t')| + 2X' + 2x''$. On the other hand, $Z^* \geq 2|p^{PWT}(t')| + 2X$, and then

$$\frac{Z^{PWT}}{Z^*} \leq \frac{t' + |p^{PWT}(t')| + 2X' + 2x''}{Z^*}$$
$$= \frac{t' + X' + 2x''}{Z^*} + \frac{|p^{PWT}(t')| + X'}{Z^*} \leq 1 + \frac{|p^{PWT}(t')| + X'}{2|p^{PWT}(t')| + 2X} \leq \frac{3}{2}.$$

- The optimal algorithm serves $-x''$ before X'. Then, for the optimal solution we have $Z^* \geq t + x'' + 2X'$. Again, two more subcases:

  • PWT is within the interval I at time t. We consider two more subcases:
    ∗ $x' < x''$. Then $Z^{PWT} \leq t + 2x' + 2X' + 2x''$ while for the adversary we have $Z^* \geq 2x'' + 2X$. In this case the ratio is

$$\frac{Z^{PWT}}{Z^*} \leq \frac{t + 2x' + 2X' + 2x''}{Z^*} = \frac{t + 2X' + x''}{Z^*} + \frac{2x' + x''}{Z^*}$$
$$\leq 1 + \frac{2x' + x''}{2x'' + 2X} \leq \frac{7}{4},$$

    since by Lemma 5.2 $x'' \leq X$.

$*$ $x' \geq x''$. Since the request in $-x''$ is not visited with the current route, the on-line server has already visited x' at time t and $p > -x''$. Then, $Z^{PWT} < t + x'' + 2X' + 2x''$ while for the optimal solution it holds $Z^* \geq 2x'' + 2X$. The ratio is

$$\frac{Z^{PWT}}{Z^*} \leq \frac{t + x'' + 2X' + 2x''}{Z^*} = \frac{t + 2X' + x''}{Z^*} + \frac{2x''}{Z^*}$$

$$\leq 1 + \frac{2x''}{2x'' + 2X} \leq 3/2,$$

since $x' \leq X$.

- PWT is outside the interval I at time t. This can happen either because i) it is to the right of X' or ii) it is to the left of $-x'$. We first show that i) is impossible: if PWT had been to the right of X' when X' was presented, then that request would have not produced the re-computation of a greedy route, and if PWT was to the left of X' at that moment, then it had no reason to go to the right of it. It remains to show what happens in case ii). p can not be also to the left of $-x''$ because in that case $-x''$ would be on the current route, and therefore we have that $x' < x''$ and p is inside the interval $[-x'', -x']$. For the optimal solution it holds $Z^* \geq t + x'' + 2X'$ and $Z^* \geq 2x'' + 2X$, while $Z^{PWT} \leq t + x'' + 2X' + 2x''$. Then

$$\frac{Z^{PWT}}{Z^*} \leq \frac{t + x'' + 2X' + 2x''}{Z^*} = \frac{t + 2X' + x''}{Z^*} + \frac{2x''}{Z^*} \leq \frac{3}{2},$$

since, by Lemma 5.2, $x'' \leq X$.

□

The competitive ratio of 7/4 is tight for PWT. This is proved by providing a sequence that achieves the ratio indeed. At time 1 two requests are presented in $+1$ and -1. PWT is at the origin until time 1, when it starts a greedy tour that without loss of generality serves $+1$ at time 2, -1 at time 4 and returns at the origin at time 5. At time 3, when the on-line server crosses the origin, a new request is presented at position $1 + \epsilon$. This new request starts a new phase since it is the furthest request not yet served. Then a new greedy route is computed that starts from the origin at time 3, serves the two requests in -1 and $1 + \epsilon$ and goes back to the origin at time $7 + 2\epsilon$. For the optimal, it serves -1 at time 1, $+1$ at time 3, $1 + \epsilon$ at time $3 + \epsilon$ and returns to the origin at time $4 + 2\epsilon$. Making ϵ arbitrarily small, the ratio is arbitrarily close to 7/4.

6 Conclusions and open problems

The obvious open problem is to close the gaps between lower and upper bounds. It would be also interesting to study other particular metric spaces (such as trees, cycles, half-lines, etc.) to see if better bounds can be obtained (as we did for the real line). An interesting question is what happens if more than one server are used. In that case, it is easy to obtain a 2.5 competitive ratio, but improvements should be possible.

217

References

1. M. Atallah and S. Kosaraju, "Efficient solutions for some transportation problems with application to minimizing robot arm travel", *SIAM J. on Computing*, 17 (1988), pp. 849-869.
2. G. Ausiello, E. Feuerstein, S. Leonardi, L. Stougie, M. Talamo, "Serving requests with on-line routing", *Proc. of the 4th Scandinavian Workshop on Algorithm Theory*, LNCS 824.
3. R. El-Yaniv, A. Fiat, R.M. Karp and G. Turpin, "Competitive analysis of financial games", *Proc. 33rd Annual Symposium on Foundations of Computer Science* (1992), pp. 327-333.
4. M. Garey, and D. Johnson, *Computers and intractability: a guide to the theory of NP-completeness*, Freeman, San Francisco (1979).
5. Y. Karuno, H. Nagamochi and T. Ibaraki, "Vehicle scheduling on a tree with release times and handling times", *Proc. 4th. International Symposium on Algorithms and Computation ISAAC'93*, LNCS 762 (1993), Springer-Verlag, pp. 486-495.
6. B. Kalyanasundaram and K.R. Pruhs, "Constructing competitive tours from local information", *Proc. 20th International Colloquium on Automata, Languages and Programming*, LNCS 700 (1993), Springer-Verlag.
7. M. Manasse, L.A. McGeoch and D. Sleator, "Competitive algorithms for server problems", *Journal of Algorithms* 11 (1990), pp. 208-230.
8. H. Psaraftis, M. Solomon, T. Magnanti and T. Kim, "Routing and scheduling on a shoreline with release times", *Management Science* 36-2 (1990), pp. 212-223.
9. D.B. Shmoys, J. Wein, D.P. Williamson, "Scheduling parallel machines on-line", *Proc. of the 32nd Annual Symposium on Foundations of Computer Science*, 1991.
10. D. Sleator, R. Tarjan, "Amortized efficiency of list update and paging rules", *Comm. ACM* 28 (1985), pp. 202-208.
11. M. Solomon and J. Desrosiers, "Time window constrained routing and scheduling problems: a survey", *Transportation Science*, 22 (1988), pp. 1-13.

Quadrangulations of Planar Sets

Godfried Toussaint

School of Computer Science
McGill University
Montreal, CANADA

ABSTRACT

Given a set S such as a polygon or a set of points, a quadrangulation of S is a partition of the interior of S, if S is a polygon, or the interior of the convex hull of S, if S is a set of points, into quadrangles (quadrilaterals) obtained by inserting edges between pairs of points (diagonals between vertices of the polygon) such that the edges intersect each other only at their end points. Not all polygons or sets of points admit quadrangulations, even when the quadrangles are not required to be convex (convex quadrangulations). In this paper we briefly survey some recent results concerning the characterization of those planar sets that always admit quadrangulations (convex and non-convex) as well as some related computational problems.

1. Introduction

In the field of computational geometry a *triangulation* of a finite planar set such as a set of points, line segments or polygon, is a well studied structure [O'R94], [PS85]. For one thing, a triangulation always exists and for another, triangulations have a wide variety of applications in practice. Two of the most important applications in engineering are (1) mesh generation for finite element methods [SNTM], [ZT89], [Ho88], [SP89], [BE92] and (2) scattered data interpolation [QS90], [LS94]. Triangulations have also been heavily applied to other application areas such as pattern recognition, computer graphics, solid modelling and geographic information systems [AHMS], [BS94], [OBS92], [SS88], [To86], [Wa92], [WA86], [Yo75]. However, in the study of finite element methods and scattered data interpolation, it has recently been shown that quadrangulations of point sets may be more desirable objects than triangulations. A quadrangulation of a set of points S is a planar subdivision whose vertices are the points of S, whose outer face is the convex hull of S, and every face of the subdivision (except possibly the outer face) is a quadrilateral. Compared to triangulations, quadrangulations have received scant attention in the computational geometry literature.

The classical problem in scattered bivariate data interpolation can be stated as follows. Given a set $V = (v_1, v_2,..., v_n)$ of n points in the plane along with an elevation z_i, $i = 1,2,..., n$ associated with each point v_i, determine a function f such that $f(v_i) = z_i$, for all i. There is a large body of literature on this subject describing a variety of methods that yield functions with different properties. Most of these methods start with a triangulation of V which is subsequently refined in some way [Wa92]. Since a triangulation of a point set always exists there is no problem starting in this way. Recently Lai [La94] and Lai & Schumaker [LS94] showed that there are certain advantages that can be obtained by starting with a quadrangulation rather than a triangulation. They also gave algorithms for computing such interpolation functions starting from quadrangulations.

The above applications provide motivation for the study of quadrangulations of point sets from the computational geometry point of view. We remark that quadrangulations of *polygons*, on the other hand, have been investigated in the computational geometry literature for some time, mostly in the context of guarding or illumination problems. In this paper we briefly survey some known results concerning the characterization of those planar sets that always admit quadrangulations (convex and non-convex) as well as some related computational problems. Furthermore we concentrate on the recent results on (1) quadrangulating sets of points rather than polygons and (2) "converting" triangulations to quadrangulations.

2. Quadrangulating Orthogonal Polygons

One of the earliest results on quadrangulations concerns orthogonal polygons, i.e., polygons whose sides are parallel to two orthogonal axes. The motivation here was not the quadrangulation itself but rather its application to locating $n/4$ guards (lights) to cover (illuminate) the interior of the polygon. Sack and Toussaint [ST81] showed that a star-shaped orthogonal polygon of n vertices can always be decomposed into *convex* quadrangles in $O(n)$ time. Kahn, Klawe and Kleitman [KKK83] proved this result for arbitrary simple orthogonal polygons. However, their existential proof did not lead to an algorithm for quadrangulating the polygon. Later, Sack and Toussaint [Sa82], [ST88] and independently Lubiw [Lu85] obtained constructive proofs of the [KKK83] result that led to an $O(n \log n)$ time algorithm. Lubiw [Lu85] also showed under a fairly general computational model that $\Omega(n \log n)$ time is a lower bound on the complexity of this problem. Some work has also been done on computing minimum "ink" quadrangulations of simple orthogonal polygons. In this setting one is interested in the convex quadrangulation whose total length (sum of diagonal lengths) is a minimum. Independently, Keil & Sack [KS85] and Lubiw [Lu85] showed this could be done in $O(n^4)$ time and $O(n^2)$ space. A very special case of convex quadrangulations, of great interest in VLSI, is that of decomposing an orthogonal polygon into *rectangles*. For example, Lipski et al. [LLLMP79] and Ohtsuki [Oh82] give polynomial-time algorithms for partitioning orthogonal polygonal regions into the minimum number of rectangles.

3. Quadrangulating Simple Polygons

Whereas an orthogonal polygon always admits a *convex* quadrangulation, an arbitrary simple polygon does not necessarily admit a quadrangulation, even if convexity of the resulting quadrangles is not a requirement. In fact, Lubiw [Lu85] has shown that the problem of deciding whether a polygon with holes admits a quadrangulation is *NP*-complete. On the other hand, if we are allowed to add new points that act as vertices (usually called Steiner points) then, depending on how many such points we are allowed to add, we may always obtain even convex quadrangulations. However, it is not difficult to construct polygons that require $\Omega(n)$ Steiner points in order to complete a quadrangulation. A transparently simple proof and algorithm for obtaining a convex quadrangulation of a simple polygon is due to Mark de Berg [ELOSU] His algorithm first triangulates the polygon and is illustrated in Figure 1, which is self-explanatory. This method however uses many Stainer points to yield many quadrilaterals. Inspired by de Berg's method Everett et al. [ELOSU] have shown that a simple polygon can always be quadrangulated into $5(n-2)/3$ strictly convex quadrangles and that $n-2$ quadrangles are sometimes necessary. For polygons with holes, they showed that a polygon on n vertices with h holes can always be decomposed into $8(n+2h-2)/3$ strictly convex quadrangles.

Some work has also been done on computing minimum "ink" quadrangulations of simple polygons. Conn & O'Rourke [CO90] showed this could be done in $O(n^3 \log n)$ time and $O(n^3)$ space. To close this section we mention a special case of convex quadrangulations of polygons that has also been studied before and this concerns the problem of decomposing a polygon into *trapezoids*. In fact, many polygon triangulation algorithms start out by first obtaining a trapezoidization of the polygon and subsequently converting this trapezoidization

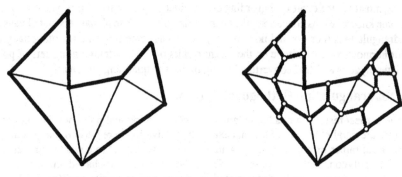

Fig. 1 Example of de Berg's construction of a convex quadrangulation from an arbitrary triangulation of a polygon.

into a triangulation [FM84]. Here the trapezoidization is merely a step towards another goal.
Furthermore, we should point out that in the work on trapezoids, triangles are allowed as degenerate trapezoids. On the other hand, trapezoidizations are used as the main goal in electron-
beam lithography systems [SS79] where subsequent processing time is proportional to the
number of trapezoids in the decomposition. Asano, Asano and Imai [AAI86] have shown that
a partition of a polygonal region into the minimum number of trapezoids can be obtained in
$O(n^2)$ time.

4. Quadrangulating Point Sets

One characterization of those sets of points that admit a quadrangulation is via *matchings*
[RRT95]. A set S of points (not all on a line) admits a quadrangulation if, and only if, there
exists a triangulation of S such that its dual graph contains a *perfect* matching. Of course this
characterization is not useful for obtaining algorithms to quadrangulate S because there are too
many triangulations to enumerate. On the other hand, for the problem of converting triangulations to quadrangulations by only deleting edges in the triangulation, this characterization is
most useful as it allows us to apply the known results on matchings to solve a variety of optimization problems concerning quadrangulations [RRT95].

A much more useful characterization of those sets of points that admit a
quadrangulation was obtained by Bose & Toussaint [BT95]. They show that S admits a
quadrangulation if and only if S does not have an odd number of extreme points (vertices on
the convex hull of S). If S admits a quadrangulation, they present an algorithm that computes
a quadrangulation of S in $O(n \log n)$ time. Furthermore, their algorithm can handle the
presence of collinear points with trivial modifications. If S does *not* admit a quadrangulation,
then their algorithm can quadrangulate S with the addition of no more than *one* Steiner point,
which is optimal. Their algorithm is conceptually simple, but to achieve the $O(n \log n)$ time
complexity, they need to use some complicated data structures. However, from the conceptual
description of the algorithm, a very simple $O(n^2)$ time algorithm is implied which may be more
desirable from a practical point of view than the $O(n \log n)$ algorithm. They also point out an
$\Omega(n \log n)$ time lower bound for the problem. Finally, their results imply that a set of points S
admits a k-angulation for any k with the addition of at most k-3 Steiner points. A k-angulation
of a set of points S is a planar subdivision whose vertices are the points of S, whose outer face
is the convex hull of S, and every face of the subdivision (except possibly the outer face) is a
simple polygon with k vertices. Below we give a brief description of their method.

Their existence proof immediately implies the following Sequential Insertion (SI) Algorithm. Compute the convex hull of S in $O(n \log n)$ time with any of several algorithms available (see [O'R94]). If the number of convex hull vertices is even, partition the convex hull into quadrilaterals in $O(n)$ time by joining one vertex to every other vertex of the polygon in a clockwise fashion. Subsequently, the remaining points are inserted one at a time. The insertion stage of the algorithm is the crucial part of the entire procedure. The obvious method of inserting the points results in an $O(n^2)$ time algorithm. However, a variety of algorithms are available in the literature for point insertion [BJM94]. The main difficulty in obtaining efficient implementations of the SI algorithm is determined by the fact that the data structure that supports fast point location must be dynamic so that subsequent point locations after an insertion remain efficient. If the quadrangulation is maintained as a triangulation one can exploit the additional structure over arbitrary planar subdivisions. Furthermore in our context we do not need fully dynamic algorithms since we are not interested in deletions. If we demand $O(n)$ storage space then the best relevant algorithms available, from the worst-case complexity point of view, are the algorithms of Preparata & Tamassia [PT89] and Cheng & Janardan [CJ92]. The former algorithm has both a point location query time and an insertion (update) time of $O(\log^2 n)$. The latter algorithm is slightly better because it has a point location query time of $O(\log^2 n)$ but only an $O(\log n)$ insertion time. However, in the present context every point location query is followed by an insertion and hence the worst-case complexities of both algorithms are the same. Therefore the Sequential Insertion (SI) Algorithm for quadrangulating S runs in worst-case time $O(n \log^2 n)$ and uses $O(n)$ storage space when implemented in this manner. This approach yields a rather complicated algorithm which also has $O(n \log^2 n)$ expected time complexity. However, by embedding the quadrangulation in a triangulation (as above) but using a very simple randomized triangulation algorithm [AHMS], one can obtain a very simple quadrangulation algorithm with $O(n^2)$ worst-case and $O(n \log n)$ expected time complexities.

Another implementation of the SI Algorithm is to use a sweep-line approach (see [O'R94] or [PS85] for examples of sweep-line algorithms). Once the convex hull has been partitioned into quadrilaterals (say $Q_1, ..., Q_j$), determine into which quadrilaterals Q_i, the remaining points fall. A simple sweep-line can be used to quadrangulate the set of points lying inside each Q_i, $i = 1, ..., j$ in $O(n_i \log n_i)$ time where n_i is the number of points inside Q_i. Therefore the total complexity of the SI algorithm implemented in this way is $O(n \log n)$.

From a theoretical computational complexity point of view, the SI algorithm is optimal. However it has its drawbacks. For one thing, the SI algorithm with random insertion of the points, fails if points are not in general position, although Joe Mitchell has shown that inserting the points using a sweep-line approach, allows a non-trivial modification of the algorithm that can handle collinearities. The main drawback however, as Figure 2 illustrates, of the sequential insertion algorithm is that it yields quadrangulations that are not desirable in practice since they tend to yield long non-convex quadrangles when fat convex quadrangles are desired. For this reason, Bose & Toussaint [BT95] propose another algorithm which yields much nicer quadrangles, and easily accommodates points in general position.

Their second approach is to show that a set of points S always admits a simple spanning polygonal chain (whose vertex set is precisely the set of points in S) that in turn always admits a *serpentine* triangulation. In such a triangulation the diagonals (and hence triangles) are ordered in accordance to the ordering of the vertices of the dual chain. By removing every other diagonal starting at one end of the chain, they obtain the desired quadrangulation except perhaps a single triangle at the end. In such an eventuality they add one Steiner point outside the convex hull of S to convert the final triangle to a quadrangle. Then they show that the

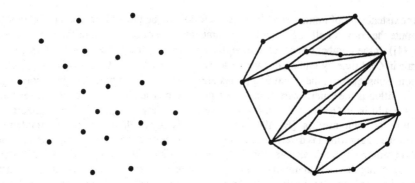

Fig. 2 A set of points S and the quadrangulation obtained with a
variant of the Sequential Insertion Algorithm.

Steiner point is necessary if, and only if, the number of points h on the convex hull of S is odd.

In a different context concerned with fast rendering in computer graphics, Arkin et al. [AHMS] proposed an $O(n \log n)$ time algorithm for obtaining a serpentine triangulation (Hamiltonian in their terminology) of a set of points. However, their algorithm is based on sequentially inserting triangles in a triangulation of the points and hence, like the SI algorithm described above, its application to the quadrangulation problem leads to poor quadrangles similar to those in Figure 2. The serpentine triangulation algorithm of Bose & Toussaint [BT95] promisees to yield very nice and usually convex quadrilaterals.

A simple spanning polygonal chain most convenient for this purpose is the convex spiral of S. For the set of points in Figure 2 the resulting convex spiral is illustrated in Figure 3. This structure has appeared in the literature for some time and is closely related to the *onion peeling* of a set or the *convex layers* [Ch85], [To86], [Wi80]. In fact one can compute the spiral and the convex layers, one from the other, in $O(n)$ time [PS85] with a trivial scan of either structure. Bose & Toussaint [BT95] show that the convex spiral of a set S admits a serpentine triangulation. They then triangulate the spiral polygonal region with a variant of the *rotating calipers* [To83].

The Spiraling Rotating Caliper (SRC) Algorithm produces a serpentine triangulation. Therefore the diagonals and triangles of $T(P)$ are ordered according to the order of the vertices comprising the dual chain of $T(P)$. Let $D = (d_1, d_2,..., d_m)$ denote the diagonals in this order. If m is even, then if we delete from the triangulation every other diagonal $d_2, d_4,...$ and so on, we obtain a quadrangulation. If m is odd we may delete every other diagonal starting from the last diagonal d_m. This will quadrangulate P except for the presence of one triangle on the boundary of the convex hull. Finally, by inserting one Steiner point just outside the convex hull of S near this triangle we may convert the triangle to a quadrangle.

Consider now the complexity of the SRC algorithm. The first step of the algorithm is to compute the convex spiral of the given set of points. This can be done via the convex layers of S in $O(n \log n)$ time using the algorithm of Chazelle [Ch85] or the algorithm of Hershberger and Suri [HS90]. This is the most difficult step in the algorithm, as both these algorithms are fairly involved. From the convex layers, we can compute a convex spiral P of S in $O(n)$ time with the procedure of Preparata and Shamos [PS85]. The spiraling rotating caliper algorithm for obtaining a serpentine triangulation of P runs in $O(n)$ time since no backtracking is involved. Therefore the entire algorithm runs in $O(n \log n)$ time.

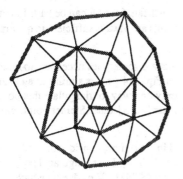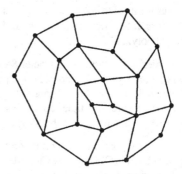

Fig. 3 Illustrating the convex spiral, serpentine triangulation and resulting quadrangulation of the set of points in Figure 2.

5. Converting Triangulations to Quadrangulations

Since little is known about computing quadrangulations, whereas triangulations have been well studied for a long time [Be92], engineers have devoted some attention to the problem of converting quadrangulations to triangulations [He83], [JSK91]. These methods are heuristic, conceptually cumbersome and require many Steiner points. For example, Johnston et al. integrate several heuristics into a system that automatically converts a triangular mesh into a quadrangular mesh which runs in $O(n^2)$ time and adds $O(n)$ Steiner points in the process. The problem of converting triangulations to quadrangulations has recently been investigated formally from graph-theoretic and computational geometric points of view by Ramos, Ramaswami & Toussaint [RRT95]. They have obtained a variety of characterizations for when a triangulation (of some structure such a polygon, set of points, line segments or planar subdivision) admits a quadrangulation without using Steiner points (or with a bounded number of Steiner points). They also propose efficient algorithms for accomplishing these tasks. For example, they point out (as mentioned earlier) that a triangulated polygon admits (contains) a quadrangulation *without* adding Steiner points if and only if the dual tree admits a *perfect matching*. They can also obtain quadrangulations with certain properties by applying *maximum weighted* matching algorithms on the dual graphs of the given triangulations. They also have several results on obtaining quadrangulations with bounded numbers of Steiner points. For example they show that a triangulated polygon can always be quadrangulated by adding at most $\lfloor n/3 \rfloor$ Steiner points *external* to the polygon and that there exist polygons that require this many *external* Steiner points. Furthermore, these Steiner points can be located in $O(n)$ time. The sufficiency of $\lfloor n/3 \rfloor$ Steiner points follows immediately from Fisk's proof [Fi78] for Chvátal's art gallery theorem [Chv75]. In his proof, Fisk showed that every triangulation of an n-gon P can be partitioned into $\leq \lfloor n/3 \rfloor$ *fans* (a *fan* is a triangulation where one vertex, called the *fan center*, is shared by all the triangles). Note that these fans start and end at edges of the polygon.

Consider now a vertex v of P that is a fan center. Vertex v defines a sequence of triangles in the triangulation. These triangles can be paired up to form quadrilaterals. If the number of such quadrilaterals is odd, we will be left with one triangle, one of whose edges is an edge of the polygon. One of the end-points of e is v; let the other be v'. We can convert this to a quadrilateral by adding a Steiner point p outside e, deleting the edge e and connecting p to the two vertices v and v'.

Thus we need to add at most one Steiner point per fan. Since P can be partitioned into $\leq \lfloor n/3 \rfloor$ fans, it follows that $\lfloor n/3 \rfloor$ outer Steiner points are always sufficient to quadrangulate a simple polygon.

In order to see that $\lfloor n/3 \rfloor$ outer Steiner points are sometimes necessary to quadrangulate a polygon it suffices to consider the polygon in Figure 4 (this is similar to an example of a polygon that requires $\lfloor n/3 \rfloor$ guards). There is only one way to triangulate this polygon, as shown in the figure. A simple case analysis shows that $\lfloor n/3 \rfloor$ outer Steiner points are necessary in order to quadrangulate the polygon.

To see that these Steiner points can be located in $O(n)$ time, consider the following: P can be triangulated in $O(n)$ time by Chazelle's algorithm [Ch91]. The triangulated polygon can then be three-colored in linear time (Kooshesh and Moret [KS92]). The edge on which a guard is placed gives us the fan-arm e outside which we place the Steiner point. To find an appropriate placement of the Steiner point, we may triangulate the simple polygon(s) that lie outside P and within the convex hull of P, which can also be done in linear time. The Steiner point for e can be placed anywhere inside the triangle incident on e (and outside P). If e is an edge of the convex hull, then it is not difficult to find a placement for the Steiner point. It follows therefore that all Steiner points can be located in $O(n)$ time. ∎

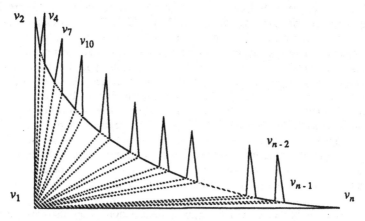

Fig. 4 A quadrangulation of this polygon requires $\lfloor n/3 \rfloor$ outer Steiner points. This polygon admits only one triangulation (as shown).

6. Open Problems

It is easy to see that a set of points does not always yield a quadrangulation where every quadrangle is convex. This observation leads to the following interesting open questions. Can one decide if a set of points admits a quadrangulation where every quadrangle is convex? This question was raised by Joe Mitchell at the MSI Workshop in Stonybrook in 1993. Can one compute the quadrangulation of a set of points that has the maximum number of convex quadrilaterals? Since Lubiw [Lu85] has shown that the decision problem is *NP*-complete for polygons that allow holes, it seems reasonable to believe that the same might hold for point sets. There is an intriguing open question concerning the SI (Sequential Insertion) algorithm for quadrangulating point sets when collinearities are allowed. Joe Mitchell has shown that the SI algorithm can be modified so that it works in spite of collinearities if we insert the points in order, say, sorted by x-coordinate. Does an optimal algorithm exist for points inserted in arbitrary order? Finally, we mention that paper-and-pencil examples suggest that the rotating-caliper algorithm gives significantly nicer quadrangulations than the SI algorithm. It would be interesting to compare these two algorithms both quantitatively and experimentally to determine the extent of the improvement afforded by the rotating-caliper algorithm for different measures of the quality of a quadrangulation.

7.   Acknowledgments

The author is grateful to Larry Schumaker for introducing him to quadrangulations, and to Prosenjit Bose, Francisco Gomez, Joe Mitchell, Suneeta Ramaswami, Pedro Ramos and Xun Xue for interesting discussions on the topic.

8.   References

[AAI86]   Takao Asano, Tetsuo Asano and H. Imai, "Partitioning a polygonal region into trapezoids," *Journal of the A.C.M.*, vol. 33, No. 2, April 1986, pp. 290-312.

[AHMS]   Arkin, E., M. Held, J. Mitchell, and S. Skiena, "Hamiltonian triangulations for fast rendering," *Algorithms-ESA'94*, J. van Leeuwen, ed., Utrecht, NL, LNCS 855, pp. 36-47, September 1994.

[BE92]   Bern, M. and Eppstein, D., "Mesh generation and optimal triangulation," in *Computing in Euclidean Geometry*, F. K. Hwang and D.-Z. Du, eds., World Scientific 1992.

[BJM94]   Baumgarten, H., Jung, H. and Mehlhorn, K., "Dynamic point location in general subdivisions," *Journal of Algorithms*, vol. 17, 1994, pp. 342-380.

[BS94]   Barequet, G., and M. Sharir, "Piecewise-linear interpolation between polygonal slices," *Proceedings of the 10th Annual Symposium on Computational Geometry*, pp. 93-102, 1994.

[BT95a]   Bose, P., and G. Toussaint, "No Quadrangulation is Extremely Odd," technical report #95-03, Dept. of Computer Science, University of British Columbia, January 1995.

[BT95b]   P. Bose and G. T. Toussaint, "On computing quadrangulations of planar point sets," *10th Colloquium on Graph Theory, Combinatorics and Applications*, Feb. 27 - March 3, 1995, Xalapa, Mexico.

[BT95c]   P. Bose and G. T. Toussaint, "Generating quadrangulations of planar point sets," accepted for publication in *Computer Aided Geometric Design*.

[Ch85]   Chazelle, B., "On the convex layers of a convex set," *IEEE Transactions on Information Theory*, vol. IT-31, 1985, pp. 509-517.

[Ch91]   B. Chazelle, "Triangulating a simple polygon in linear time," *Discrete Comput. Geom.*, vol. 6, 1991, pp. 485-524.

[Chv75]   V. Chvátal, "A combinatorial theorem in plane geometry," *J. Combin. Theory Ser. B*, vol. 18, 1975, pp. 39-41.

[CJ92]   Cheng, S. W. and Janardan, R., "New results on dynamic planar point location," *SIAM Journal on Computing*, vol. 21, 1992, pp. 972-999.

[CO90]   H. E. Conn and J. O'Rourke, "Minimum weight quadrilateralization in O(n^3 log n) time," *Proc. of the 28th Allerton Conference on Comm. Control and Computing*, October 1990, pp. 788-797.

[ELOSU] Everett, H., W. Lenhart, M. Overmars, T. Shermer, and J. Urrutia, "Strictly convex quadrilateralizations of polygons," in *Proceedings of the 4th Canadian Conference on Computational Geometry*, pp. 77-83, 1992.

[Fi78]   S. Fisk, "A short proof of Chvátal's watchman theorem," *J. Combin. Theory Ser. B*, vol. 24, 1978, pp. 374.

[FM84]   A. Fournier and D. Y. Montuno, "Triangulating simple polygons and equivalent problems," *ACM Transactions on Graphics*, vol. 3, No. 2, 1984, pp. 153-175.

[He83]   Heighway, E., "A mesh generator for automatically subdividing irregular polygons into quadrilaterals," *IEEE Transactions on Magnetics*, 19, 6, pp. 2535-2538, 1983.

[Ho88]   Ho-Le, K., "Finite element mesh generation methods: A review and classification," *Computer Aided Design*, 20, pp. 27-38, 1988.

[HS90]   Hershberger, J., and S. Suri, "Applications of a semi-dynamic convex hull algorithm," *Proceedings of the second S.W.A.T., Lecture Notes in Computer Science 447*, Bergen, Sweden, pp. 380-392, 1990.

[JSK91] Johnston, B. P., Sullivan, J. M. and Kwasnik, A., "Automatic conversion of triangular finite meshes to quadrilateral elements," *International Journal of Numerical Methods in Engineering*, vol. 31, No. 1, 1991, pp. 67-84.

[KKK83] Kahn, J., M. Klawe, D. Kleitman, "Traditional galleries require fewer watchmen," *SIAM J. Algebraic Discrete Methods*, 4, pp. 194-206, 1983.

[KM91]   A. A. Kooshesh and B. M. E. Moret, "Three-coloring the vertices of a triangulated simple polygon," *Pattern Recognition*, vol. 25, 1992.

[KS85]   J. M. Keil and J.-R. Sack, "Minimum decompositions of polygonal objects," in *Computational Geometry*, Ed., G. T. Toussaint, North-Holland, Amsterdam, pp. 197-216.

[La94]   Lai, M. J., "Scattered data interpolation and approximation by using C^1 piecewise cubic polynomials," submitted for publication.

[LLLMP79] W. Lipski, Jr., E. Lodr, F. Luccio, C. Mugnal and L. Pagli, "On two dimensional data organization II, *Fundanmenta Informaticae*, vol. 2, 1979, pp. 245-260.

[LS94]   Lai, M. J. and Schumaker, L. L., "Scattered data interpolation using C^2 piecewise polynomials of degree six," *Third Workshop on Proximity Graphs*, Mississippi State University, Starkville, Mississippi, December 1-3, 1994.

[Lu85]   Lubiw, A., "Decomposing polygonal regions into convex quadrilaterals," *Proc. Symposium on Computational Geometry*, 1985, pp. 97-106.

[OBS92] Okabe, A., B. Boots, and K. Sugihara, *Spatial Tessellations: Concepts and Applications of Voronoi Diagrams*, John Wiley & Sons, Chichester, England, 1992.

[Oh82]   T. Ohtsuki, "Minimum dissection of rectilinear regions," in *Proc. IEEE International Symposium on Circuits and Systems*, Rome, 1982, pp. 1210-1213.

[O'R94] O'Rourke, J., *Computational Geometry in C*, Cambridge University Press, 1994.

[PS85]   Preparata, F. P. and Shamos, M. I., *Computational Geometry: An Introduction*, Springer-Verlag, New York, 1985.

[PT89]   Preparata, F. P. and Tamassia, R., "Fully dynamic point location in a monotone subdivision," *SIAM Journal on Computing*, vol. 18, 1989, pp. 811-830.

[QS90]   Quak, E. and Schumaker, L. L., "Cubic spline fitting using data dependent triangulations." *Computer-Aided Geometric Design*, vol. 7, 1990, pp. 293-301.

[RRT95] Ramaswami, S., Ramos, P. and G. T. Toussaint, "Converting triangulations to quadrangulations," manuscript in preparation.

[Sa82]   Sack, J. R., "An $O(n \log n)$ algorithm for decomposing simple rectilinear polygons into convex quadrilaterals," *Proc. 20th Annual Conf. on Communications, Control and Computing*, Allerton, 1982, pp. 64-74.

[SNTM]   Srinivasan, V., Nackman, L. R., Tang, J.-M. and Meshkat, S. N., "Automatic mesh generation using the symmetric axis transformation of polygonal domains," *Proceedings of the IEEE*, vol. 80, No. 9, September 1992, pp. 1485-1501.

[SP89]   Sapidis, N. and Perucchio, R., "Advanced techniques for automatic finite element meshing from solid models," *Computer Aided Design*, vol. 21, No. 4, May 1989, pp. 248-253.

[SS79]   N. Sugiyama and K. Saitoh, "Electron-beam exposure system AMDES," *Computer Aided Design*, vol. 11, 1979, pp. 59-65.

[SS88]   Schroeder, W., and M. Shephard, "Geometry-based fully automatic mesh generation and the Delaunay triangulation," *International Journal for Numerical Methods in Engineering*, 24, pp. 2503-2515, 1988.

[ST81]   Sack, J.-R. and Toussaint, G. T., "A linear-time algorithm for decomposing rectilinear star-shaped polygons into convex quadrilaterals," *Proc. 19th Annual Conf. on Communications, Control and Computing*, Allerton, 1981, pp. 21-30.

[ST88]   Sack, J.-R. and Toussaint, G. T., "Guard placement in rectilinear polygons," in *Computational Morphology*, Ed., G. T. Toussaint, North-Holland, 1988, pp. 153-175.

[To83]   Toussaint, G. T., "Solving geometric problems with the *rotating calipers*," *Proc. IEEE MELECON 83*, Athens, Greece, 1983, pp. A10002/1-4.

[To86]   Toussaint, G. T., "New results in computational geometry relevant to pattern recognition in practice," in *Pattern Recognition in Practice II*, E. S. Gelsema and L. N. Kanal, Eds., North-Holland, 1986, pp. 135-146.

[Wa92]   Wang, T., "A C^2-quintic spline interpolation scheme on triangulation," *Computer Aided Geometric Design*, vol. 9, 1992, pp. 379-386.

[WA86]   Wang, Y., and J. Aggarwal, "Surface reconstruction and representation of 3-d scenes," *Pattern Recognition*, 19, pp. 197-207, 1986.

[Wi80]   Wismath, S. K., "Triangulations: An algorithmic study," Tech. Report 80-106, Queens University, Kingston, Canada, July 1980.

[Yo75]   Yoeli, P., "Compilation of data for computer-assisted relief cartography," in *Display and Analysis of Spatial Data*, J. Davis, and M. McCullagh, eds., John Wiley & Sons, New York, 1975.

[ZT89]   Zienkiewicz, O. C. and Taylor, R. L., *The Finite Element Method*, vol. I, McGraw-Hill, London, 1989.

A Linear-time Construction of the Relative Neighborhood Graph within a Histogram

Andrzej Lingas [*]   Asish Mukhopadhyay [†]
Lund University   IIT Kanpur

Abstract

A linear-time algorithm for constructing the constrained relative neighborhood graph or the constrained Gabriel graph of a histogram is presented.

1 Introduction

Planar triangulations belong to the most useful structures in computational geometry. Among them, the Delaunay triangulation seems to be the most known and useful [3, 18, 20]. A triangulation of a planar point set, in particular its Delaunay triangulation, is an example of the so called planar straight-line graph [20]. There are known several useful subgraphs of the Delaunay triangulation, the Euclidean minimum spanning tree being a finest example [20]. Another example is the Gabriel graph introduced by Gabriel and Sokal for the purpose of geographic pattern analysis [6]. Also the relative neighborhood graph, introduced and shown useful in pattern recognition by Toussaint [21], is well known. Several other authors studied the problem of efficiently constructing these subgraphs, and their generalizations [2, 9, 10, 11, 16, 19, 20, 24].

The relative neighborhood graph is a subgraph of the Gabriel graph by the definitions (see next section). Also, the two subgraphs of the Delaunay triangulation are known to include the Euclidean minimum spanning tree [20, 24] (see Fig. 1). They also admit a linear-time construction from the Delaunay triangulation [10, 16] (see also [24]). It is an interesting open problem whether these subgraphs as well as the Delaunay triangulation could be deterministically constructed from the Euclidean minimum spanning tree in linear time.

The above geometric structures have been generalized to take a planar straight-line graph as input instead of a planar point set. In geographical applications, the edges of the graph may represent terrain barriers in addition to the given

---

[*]Department of Computer Science, Lund University, Box 117, S-221 00 Lund, Sweden, e-mail: Andrzej.Lingas@dna.lth.se

[†]Computer Science and Engineering, Indian Institute of Technology, Kanpur, INDIA-208016, e-mail: am@iitk.ernet.in

sites. These edges are of importance and in general need to be preserved during the computation of various structures within the graph. For this reason several constrained geometric structures such as the constrained relative neighborhood graph, constrained Gabriel graph, and constrained Delaunay triangulation were introduced [4, 17, 23].

The constrained relative neighborhood graph is a subgraph of the constrained Gabriel graph which in turn is a subgraph of the constrained Delaunay triangulation [23, 8]. Also, it is known that these three structures can be computed in time $O(n \log n)$ [8, 22, 25].

When the input straight-line graph is a simple polygon, its constrained Delaunay triangulation can be computed in expected linear time by a randomized algorithm [13]. It is a major open problem whether the constrained Delaunay triangulation of a simple polygon could be deterministically computed in linear time. As it is shown in [13], this problem is equivalent to the problem of computing in linear time the constrained Delaunay triangulation of a special case of a simple polygon called histogram. Currently, only sophisticated linear-time deterministic algorithms for the constrained Delaunay triangulation of a histogram (and consequently of a simple polygon) in L_1 metric [12], and for the Delaunay triangulation of a convex polygon are known [1].

It has been also observed in [14] that the linear-time randomized algorithm for the constrained Delaunay triangulation of a histogram yields a linear-time randomized algorithm for computing the Delaunay triangulation of a planar point set from its minimum spanning tree. Similarly, a linear-time deterministic algorithm for the former problem would yield a linear-time deterministic algorithm for the latter problem.

In this paper, we make a substantial progress on the aforementioned open problems. We show that the constrained relative neighborhood graph and the constrained Gabriel graph of a histogram can be computed deterministically in linear time. In the literature, only in the case of a convex polygon a deterministic linear-time algorithm for the relative neighborhood graph is known [24]. A crucial step in our linear-time method is the construction of a triangulation of a histogram including all edges of its constrained Gabriel graph (Section 3). The triangulation is pruned to the constrained relative neighborhood graph by using a method similar to that for pruning Delaunay triangulation given in [16] (Section 4). Analogous method works for the generalizations of the constrained relative neighborhood graph called constrained β-skeletons ($1 \leq \beta \leq 2$), in particular for the constrained Gabriel graph (Section 5).

2 Definitions

A *triangulation* of a planar, finite point set V is a maximal set of non-intersecting segments with endpoints in V. The Delaunay triangulation of the set V, $DT(V)$, is a triangulation of V where the circumcirle of each (empty) triangle is free from the points in V different from the corners of the triangle.

A planar triangulation, in particular $DT(V)$, may be regarded as the so called *planar straight-line graph*, PSLG for short [20]. Generally, a PSLG G is a pair (V, E) such that V is a set of points in the plane and E is a set of nonintersecting, open straight-line segments whose endpoints are in V. The points in V are called vertices of G, whereas the segments in E are called edges of G. If G is a simple cycle, it is a (simple) polygon. If G has no edges, it is a planar point set.

The *Euclidean minimum spanning tree* of V, $MST(V)$, the *relative neighborhood graph* of V, $RNG(V)$, and the *Gabriel graph* of V, $GG(V)$, are examples of PSLG. $MST(V)$ is a connected PSLG (V, E) achieving the smallest possible total edge length (known to be a subgraph of $DT(V)$). For a, b in V, let $lune(a, b)$ be the set of points in the plane whose Euclidean distance to each of a and b is less than the Euclidean distance between a and b. Similarly, let $disk(a, b)$ be the set of points in the plane whose Euclidean distance to the middle of (a, b) is not greater than half the length of (a, b). The segment (a, b) is an edge of $RNG(V)$ if and only if $lune(a, b)$ is free from points in V. Analogously, the segment (a, b) is an edge of $GG(V)$ if and only if $disk(a, b)$ is free from points in V different from a and b.

A *diagonal* of a PSLG $G = (V, E)$ is an open straight-line segment with endpoints in V neither intersecting any edge of G nor including any vertex of G. A triangulation of G is a maximal set of nonintersecting diagonals of G.

In the definitions of the constrained versions of $RNG()$, $GG()$ and $DT()$, the notion of visibility plays crucial role. Two vertices of a PSLG G are *visible* from each other if the straight-line segment connecting them is either an edge or a diagonal of G.

The *constrainded Delaunay triangulation* of G, $DT(G)$, is a triangulation of G such that circumcirle of each empty triangle formed by the edges of G and $DT(G)$ doesn't contain any vertex of G different and visible from the three corners of the triangle.

For a diagonal (a, b) of G, let $clune(a, b)$ be the set of points in $lune(a, b)$ that are visible both from a and b. Similarly, let $cdisk(a, b)$ be the set of all points in $disk(a, b)$ that are visible both from a and b. The segment (a, b) is an edge of $CRNG(G)$ if and only if $clune(a, b)$ is free from points in V. Analogously, (a, b) is an edge of $CGG(G)$ if and only if $cdisk(a, b)$ is free from points in V different from a and b.

3 RNG and GG within a histogram

3.1 A nice triangulation of a histogram

In this section, we provide a linear-time algorithm for constructing a special triangulation of a histogram. We also show that the triangulation includes all edges of the constrained Gabriel graph or the constrained relative neighborhood graph of the input histogram.

Definition 3.1 A simple polygon H given by the vertex sequence $q_0, q_1, \ldots, q_{n+1}$ is called a *normal histogram* if the q_i have ascending X-coordinates, if q_0 and

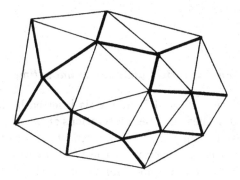

Figure 1: $RNG(V)$ (fat lines) is a subgraph of $DT(V)$.

q_{n+1} have the same Y-coordinates, and if all other vertices have larger Y-values. We call q_0 and q_{n+1} the *base vertices* of H. A non-base vertex q is a *local maximum* if none of the two vertices adjacent to q has greater Y-coordinate than q. A triangulation of H is *nice* if the middle (with respect to X-coordinates) corner of each triangular face has its Y-coordinate not smaller than the Y-coordinates of the two remaining corners.

In the algorithm, for a vertex w, $Y(w)$ denotes its Y-coordinate.

Algorithm 1

Input: A normal histogram H.
Output: A nice triangulation of T.

1. $T \leftarrow \emptyset$;

2. $F \leftarrow H$;

3. for each vertex v set $l(v)$, $r(v)$ respectively to the left and right neighbor of v on the perimeter of H;

4. $LM \leftarrow$ the set of all local maxima of H;

5. **while** LM is not empty **do**

   begin

   remove a vertex v from LM;

   augment T with $(l(v), r(v))$;

   cut off the triangle $(v, l(v), r(v))$ from F;

   set $l(r(v))$ to $l(v)$ and $r(l(v))$ to $r(v)$;

   if $l(v)$ or $r(v)$ respectively is a local maximum in F not in LM

       then insert it into LM

end

6. output T

Lemma 3.2 *Algorithm 1 is correct and runs in linear time.*

Proof: Since no vertex removed from LM is inserted back into LM, Algorithm 1 terminates after linear number of iterations of the block under the while statement. The steps preceding the while statement can be easily implemented in linear time. Also, each instruction in the block takes constant time. For example, to check whether $l(v)$ is a local maximum in the updated F we simply compare the Y-coordinates of $l(l(v))$, $l(v)$, $r(l(v))$. Thus, Algorithm 1 runs in linear time.

When Algorithm 1 terminates, the sub-histogram F has no local maximum, i.e., F is simply collapsed to the base of H. Each triangle $(l(v), v, r(v))$ cut off from F satisfies the requirement for a triangular face in a nice triangulation. $\square$

The following lemma is useful in proving properties of nice triangulations of histograms.

Lemma 3.3 *For a normal histogram F, no diagonal incident to a local maximum of F is in $CGG(F)$.*

Proof: Let v be a local maximum in F. Consider a diagonal (v, w) of F. We may assume w.l.o.g that w doesn't lie to the left of v. It follows that w cannot lie to the left of the right neighbor $r(v)$ of v. Consequently, the angle $(v, r(v), w)$ has more than 90 degrees. It follows that the $disc(v, w)$ contains $r(v)$. Consequently, (v, w) cannot be in $CGG(F)$. $\square$

Theorem 3.4 *For each nice triangulation T of a normal histogram H, $CGG(H)$ is a subgraph of T.*

Proof: Reduce H to a sub-histogram F by cutting off triangles in T until a diagonal (v, w) of F in $CGG(H) \setminus T$ with v incident to two edges of F is encountered. Since (v, w) is not in T it has to cross the triangle of T within F cornered by v. It follows from the nicety of T that v is a local maximum in F. Hence, (v, w) cannot be in $CGG(F)$ by Lemma 3.3. Consequently, (v, w) cannot be in $CGG(F)$. $\square$

The following property of a nice triangulation of a histogram will be used in the next section.

Lemma 3.5 *Let T be a nice triangulation of a normal histogram H. For each diagonal (a, b) in T, all vertices in the pocket of H cut off by e have their Y-coordinates not smaller than that of a and b.*

Proof: Suppose otherwise. Let d be the vertex in the pocket different from a and b with the minimum Y-coordinate. There must be a triangle (f, d, h) in T such that (f, d) is an edge of H lying below d. It follows that d is the middle corner of the triangle, and as such, it has its Y-coordinate not smaller than that of f, h. Since f and h are also in the pocket we obtain a contradiction with our supposition by the choice of d. $\qquad\square$

3.2   RNG within a histogram

In [16], a subroutine for testing the Delaunay edges within a simple polygon (bounded by RNG edges) for membership in RNG has been among others presented. The correctness of the subroutine relies on two basic lemmata. Roughly, the first lemma due to Supowit (Lemma 3 in [24]) states that for each diagonal $d \notin$ RNG there is a vertex v in the input set that belongs to $lune(d)$ as well as to the lunes of all diagonals that "block" p from d. The other lemma due to Jaromczyk et $al.$ [10] says that if two vertices on a side of a Delaunay triangle are in the lune of the corresponding side then they can belong to the lune of at most one of the two remaing triangle sides.

Our algorithm for CRNG of a (normal) histogram H is similar to that aforementioned subroutine from [16]. Instead of the Delaunay triangulation the nice triangulation produced by Algorithm 1 is used. The two aforementioned lemmata are replaced by their generalizations/modifications to include input edges and the nice triangulation. For a diagonal d and a vertex v of the input histogram, testing whether $v \in clune(d)$ might be costly. Therefore, in our lemmata we require vertices to be only in $lune(d)$ and see it in at least one of six fixed directions in order to witness $d \notin CRNG(H)$. Clearly, we show the sufficiency of the weaker requirement.

To present our lemmata we need the following notation.

Definition 3.6 The ray starting at a point p in direction k will be denoted by $ray(p, k)$. We shall distinguish the six directions forming respectively the angle of $l \times 60$ degrees with the X-axis. Let v be a vertex of a PSLG G, and let e and e_1 be two diagonals of G disjoint from v. We say that e_1 *blocks* e from v in direction k if $ray(v, k)$ intersects the interior of e after intersecting the interior of e_1 and before intersecting any edge of G. Also, we say that v *eliminates* e in direction k if $v \in lune(e)$ and $ray(v, k)$ intersects the interior of e before intersecting any edge of G.

The following lemma shows that any vertex that eliminates a diagonal e of G in one of the six directions is indeed a witness of $e \notin CRNG(G)$.

Lemma 3.7 *A diagonal e of a PSLG G is not in $CRNG(G)$ if and only if there is a vertex v and one of the six directions k such that v eliminates e in the direction k.*

Proof: If e is not in $CRNG(G)$ then there is at least one vertex v in $clune(e)$ different from the endpoints of e. By the definition of $clune(e)$, such a vertex v eliminates e in any direction that passes through v and the inside of e. Since the angle formed by v with the two endpoints of e is of at least sixty degrees, v eliminates e in one of the six directions.

Suppose in turn that there is a vertex $v \in lune(e)$ and direction k such that v eliminates e in this direction. Let $e = (w_1, w_2)$. It follows that some vertex of G lying in $lune(e)$ is visible to w_1 since otherwise all vertices of G in $lune(e)$ would lie behind edges of G totally crossing $lune(e)$. Let u be the closest to e among the vertices in $lune(e)$ visible to w_1. Suppose that u is not visible to the other endpoint w_2 of e. Then, there is an edge of G that crosses (u, w_2) and has one endpoint inside the triangle (w_1, u, w_2). Let z be the vertex inside the triangle that is closest to (w_1, u). Clearly, z is visible from w_1 and its distance to e is smaller than that of u. We obtain a contradiction with the definition of u. □

The following lemma is not a full generalization of Supowit's lemma since in the definition of the elimination of a diagonal e by a vertex, the vertex is not required to be in $clune(e)$, only to be in $lune(e)$ and to see a point inside e. Nevertheless, by Lemma 3.7 it is totally sufficient.

Lemma 3.8 *Let E_1 be a triangulation of a PLSG $G = (V, E)$. For $e \in E_1 \setminus CRNG(G)$, let v be a vertex of G in $clune(e)$ closests to e. For each diagonal $e_1 \in E$, if e_1 blocks v from e in direction k then v eliminates e_1 in direction k.*

Proof: By arguing analogously as in the proof of Lemma 3 in [24], we infer that v is in $lune(e_1)$. Also, $ray(v, k)$ intersects the inside of e_1 before intersecting any edge of G. We conclude that v eliminates e_1 in direction k. □

Our algorithm for RNG within a histogram computes sets of potential witnesses of $e \notin CRNG(H)$ for all diagonals e of a normal histogram $H = (V, E)$. We begin with defining their subsets $w_1(e)$, $w_2(e)$ consisting of true witnesses.

Definition 3.9 Let $H_1(e)$, $H_2(e)$ be the subpolygons the edge e splits H into such that the base of H lies within $H_2(e)$. For $i = 1, 2$, let $w_i(e)$ be the set of vertices v of $H_i(e)$ in $lune(e)$ such that there is one of the six direction k in which $ray(v, k)$ intersects e and lies inside $H_i(e)$ at least to the intersection point.

By Lemma 3.7, the above definition and the definition of $CRNG(H)$, we obtain the following lemma immediately.

Lemma 3.10 *A diagonal e of a normal histogram H is in $CRNG(H)$ if and only if $w_1(e) \cup w_2(e) = \emptyset$.*

We may consider the union $w_1(e) \cup w_2(e)$ as exactly the set of witnesses of $e \notin CRNG(H)$. For $i = 1, 2$, our algorithm will compute a set $pw_i(e)$ of vertices of $H_i(e)$ such that $pw_i(e) = \emptyset$ if and only if $w_i(e) = \emptyset$. The computation of the sets pw_i relies on a lemma characterizing propagation of witnesses of $e \notin CRNG(H)$ for diagonals e in a nice triangulation of H. The latter lemma can be regarded as a modification of the aforementioned lemma for Delaunay triangulation given by Jaromczyk et al. in [10]. To present our lemma we need the following notation.

Consider a triangle (a, b, c) lying within H where a, b, c are vertices of H. We say that v is *external* to (a, b, c) with respect to (a, b) if and only if c and v are separated by the straight-line passing through (a, b).

Lemma 3.11 *Let T be a nice triangulation of a normal histogram $H = (V, E)$. Suppose that v, $w \in V$ eliminate an edge (a, b) of a triangle (a, b, c) in T. If v and w are external to (a, b, c) with respect to (a, b) then (a, c) and (b, c) cannot be both eliminated by v or w.*

Proof: Suppose first that c is the midle corner of the triangle lying over (a, b). We may assume w.l.o.g that a lies to the left of b and the straight-line induced by (a, b) doesn't intersect that induced by the base of H to the right of a. It follows that both v and w lie to the right of and below b. Since the Y-coordinate of c is not smaller than those of a and b, the lune of (c, b) below (c, b) lies to the left of b. Thus, neither v nor w is in $lune(c, b)$.

It remains to consider the case where b is the middle corner lying over (a, c). By Lemma 3.5, the vertices v and w have their Y-coordinates not smaller than that of b. Hence, they cannot lie in $lune(b, c)$. $\qquad\square$

The following immediate corollary will be especially useful.

Corollary 3.12 *Let (a, b, c) be a triangle in a nice triangulation of a normal histogram $H = (V, E)$, and let W be a set of vertices in V which eliminate (a, b) and are external to (a, b, c) with respect to (a, b). Then either no vertex in W eliminates (a, c) or no vertex in W eliminates (b, c).*

Now, we are ready to derive our main result in this section.

Theorem 3.13 *For a histogram H on n vertices, the constrained relative neighborhood graph $CRNG(H)$ of H can be constructed deterministically in time $O(n)$.*

Proof: We may assume w.l.o.g that H is a normal histogram. Run Algorithm 1 to construct a nice triangulation T of H. By Theorem 3.4, T includes $CRNG(H)$. Preprocess H by solving the problem of vertex-edge visibility (see [5]) in the six distinguished directions within H. Top-down and bottom-up traverse the tree dual to T computing the sets $pw_i(e)$, $e \in T$, analogously as in [16], relying on Lemma 3.8 and Corollary 3.12 instead of Lemma 2.3 and Corollary 2.6 from [16]. During the traversals, extend the tests of containment of a vertex in a $lune(e)$ to the test of whether the vertex eliminates e by finding the six projections of the vertex on the perimeter of the histogram. Using the vertex-edge visibility information it can be done in constant time. Delete all diagonals e in T for which $pw_1(e) \cup pw_2(e) \neq \emptyset$.

By Lemma 3.2, the construction of the nice triangulation takes linear time. By [5], the six vertex-edge visibility problems can be solved in linear time using the simple algorithm for triangulating monotone polygons due to Garey et al. [7] (a normal histogram is a special case of a monotone polygon). □

4 Extensions

We can generalize our linear-time algorithm for the relative neighborhood graph within a histogram to include the construction of the so called β-skeleton within the histogram (see [10, 15]).

Definition 4.1 Let $G = (V, E)$ be a PSLG. For $1 \leq \beta \leq 2$, and a, b in V, $lune_\beta(a, b)$ is the interior of the intersection of the two circles, with radii equal to $\frac{\beta}{2} \mid a, b \mid$, centered on (a, b) in the distance $\left(\frac{\beta}{2}\right) \mid a, b \mid$ from a or b respectively. Analogously, $clune_\beta(a, b)$ is the set of all points in $lune_\beta(a, b)$ that are visible from both a and b. Now, the edge (a, b) is in the constrained β-skeleton $CS_\beta(G)$ if and only if $clune_\beta(a, b)$ is free from vertices in V.

Note that $CS_2(G) = CRNG(G)$. Also, $disk(a, b)$ is the closure of $lune_1(a, b)$. Hence, for $1 < \beta \leq 2$, $CS_\beta(G)$ is a subgraph of $CGG(G)$, and $CGG(G)$ is a subgraph of $CS_1(G)$.

Theorem 3.4 can be easily generalized to include $CS_\beta(H)$ for $1 \leq \beta \leq 2$. If we substitute $CS_\beta(H)$ and $clune_\beta()$, where $1 \leq \beta \leq 2$, or $CGG(H)$ and $cdisk()$ respectively for $CRNG(H)$ and $clune()$ then Lemma 3.10 and Corollary 3.12 will still hold. Therefore, we analogously obtain:

Theorem 4.2 Let $1 \leq \beta \leq 2$. For a histogram H on n vertices, the constrained β-skeleton $CS_\beta(H)$ of H can be constructed deterministically in time $O(n)$.

Theorem 4.3 For a histogram H on n vertices, the constrained Gabriel graph $CGG(H)$ of H can be constructed deterministically in time $O(n)$.

5 Final Remarks

It is an interesting open problem whether the constrained Gabriel graph of a histogram could be extended to the constrained Delaunay triangulation of the histogram deterministically in linear time. If so, the constrained Delaunay triangulation of a simple polygon could be deterministically computed in linear time by Theorem 4.3 and [13]. Hence, also the Delaunay triangulation of a planar point set V, as well as $RNG(V)$ and $GG(V)$, could be deterministically constructed from $MST(V)$ in linear time (see [14, 16]).

Another approach would be to combine the known method of partitioning a simple polygon into pseudo-histograms [12, 13] with our method for the constrained β-skeleton of a histogram to obtain a linear-time method for the constrained β-skeleton of a simple polygon. This approach avoiding constructing the constrained Delaunay triangulation requires developing new merging techniques for constrained β-skeletons (in particular CRNG or CGG).

6 Acknowledgements

The authors are very grateful to Dr. Bengt Nilsson for his careful reading and insightful comments on this work.

References

[1] A. Aggarwal, L.J. Guibas, J. Saxe, and P.W. Shor, A Linear-Time Algorithm for Computing the Voronoi Diagram of a Convex Polygon. *Discrete and Computational Geometry 4*, 1987.

[2] P.K. Agarwal and J. Matousek, Relative Neighborhood Graphs in Three Dimensions, *Computational Geometry: Theory and Applications 2(1)*, pp. 1-14 (1992).

[3] F. Aurenhammer, Voronoi Diagrams - A Survey of a Fundamental Geometric Data Structure, *ACM Computing Surveys*, Vol. 23, No. 3, September 1991, pp.345-406.

[4] L. P. Chew, Constrained Delaunay Triangulations, *Algorithmica 4* (1989), pp. 97-108.

[5] A. Fournier and D. Y. Montuno, Triangulating Simple Polygons and Equivalent Problems, *ACM Transactions on Graphics 3(2)*, pp. 153-174, 1984.

[6] K. R. Gabriel and R. R. Sokal, A New Statistical Approach to Geographic Variation Analysis, *Systematic Zoology 18* (1969), pp. 259-278.

[7] M.R. Garey, D.S. Johnson, F.P. Preparata and R.E. Tarjan, Triangulating a simple polygon, *IPL 7(4)*, pp. 175-179, 1978.

[8] E. Jennings and A. Lingas, Relationships between Constrained Geometric Structures, *Proc. ISAAC'92*, Nagoya, LNCS 650, pp. 165-176, Springer Verlag.

[9] J.W. Jaromczyk and M. Kowaluk, A note on relative neighborhood graphs, *Proc. 3rd ACM Symp. on Computational Geometry*, pp. 233-241 (1987).

[10] J.W. Jaromczyk and M. Kowaluk and F.F. Yao, An Optimal Algorithm for Constructing β-skeletons in L_p metric , to appear in *SIAM J. Computing*.

[11] J. W. Jaromczyk and G. T. Toussaint, Relative Neighborhood Graphs and Their Relatives, *Proceedings of the IEEE 80(9)*, pp.1502-1516 (1992).

[12] R. Klein and A. Lingas, Manhattonian Proximity in a Simple Polygon, *Proc. 8th ACM Symposium on Computational Geometry*, Berlin, 1992, pp. 312-319. To appear in Int. J. Comput. Geom. & Applications.

[13] R. Klein and A. Lingas, A Linear-time Randomized Algorithm for the Bounded Voronoi Diagram of a Simple Polygon, *Proc. ACM Symposium on Computational Geometry*, San Diego, 1993.

[14] R. Klein and A. Lingas, Fast Skeleton Construction, manuscript 1994.

[15] D.G. Kirkpatrick and J.D. Radke, A Framework for Computational Morphology, in *Computational Geometry*, edited by G. Toussaint, pp. 217-248, North-Holland, 1985.

[16] A. Lingas, A linear-time construction of the relative neighborhood graph from the Delaunay triangulation, *Computational Geometry: Theory and Applications* 4, pp. 199-208 (1994).

[17] D. T. Lee and A. K. Lin, Generalized Delaunay Triangulation for Planar Graphs, *Discrete and Computational Geometry*, 1 (1986), pp. 201-217.

[18] D.T. Lee and B. Schachter, Two algorithms for constructing Delaunay triangulations, *Int. J. Comput. and Info. Sci. 9(3)*, pp. 219-242 (1980).

[19] D.W. Matula and R.R. Sokal, Properties of Gabriel graphs relevant to geographic variation search and the clustering of points in the plane, *Geogr. Analysis 12*, pp. 205-222 (1980).

[20] F.P. Preparata and M.I. Shamos, Computational Geometry: An Introduction, *Texts and Monographs in Theoretical Computer Science*, Springer Verlag, New York, 1985.

[21] G.T. Toussaint, The relative neighbourhood graph of a finite planar set, *Pattern Recognition 12*, pp. 261-268 (1980).

[22] R. Seidel, Constrained Delaunay Triangulations and Voronoi Diagrams with Obstacles, In Rep. 260, IIG-TU, Graz, Australia, 1988, pp. 178-191.

[23] T.H. Su and R.C. Chang, Computing the constrained relative neighborhood graphs and constrained Gabriel graphs in Euclidean plane, *Pattern Recognition 24*, pp. 221-230 (1991).

[24] K.J. Supowit, The relative neighborhood graph with an application to minimum spanning trees, *J. Assoc. Comput. Mach. 30*, pp. 428-448 (1983).

[25] C. A. Wang and L. Schubert, An Optimal Algorithm for Constructing the Delaunay Triangulation of a Set of Line Segments, *Proc. 3rd Annual Symposium on Computational Geometry*, June 8-10, 1987, Waterloo, Ontario, Canada, pp. 223-232.

Computing Proximity Drawings of Trees in the 3-Dimensional Space*

G. Liotta[1], G. Di Battista[2]

[1] Dipartimento di Informatica e Sistemistica, Università di Roma 'La Sapienza', via Salaria 113, I-00198 Roma, Italia. liotta@infokit.dis.uniroma1.it
[2] D.I.F.A., Università della Basilicata, via della Tecnica 3, 85100 Potenza, Italia. dibattista@iasi.rm.cnr.it

Abstract. Representing a graph in the 3-dimensional space is one of the most recent and challenging research issues for the graph drawing community. We deal with 3-dimensional proximity drawings of trees. We provide combinatorial characterizations of the classes of representable graphs and present several drawing algorithms.

1 Introduction and Overview

The availability of cheap workstations and of of cheap 3D-software is making feasible the development of applications that use as interfaces 3-dimensional graph drawing packages (see, e.g., [17, 1]). On the other hand, the 3-dimensional space promises to contain the solution to the increasing demand of more and more sophisticated graph drawing features.

Unfortunately, in spite of the growing maturity of the graph drawing theory (more than 300 papers in the last ten years that solve several open problems in the area [6]), only a few researchers have addressed the problem of devising 3-dimensional graph drawing algorithms (see, e.g. [4, 17]). Thus, there is a lack of general methodologies that software developers can use to draw graphs in the 3-dimensional space.

In this paper we tackle the problem of constructing proximity drawings of trees in the 3-dimensional space. Our work has the following theoretical and practical motivations. Trees are a classical field of investigations in graph drawing; the need of drawing trees arises in several application areas, including software visualization, project management, and organization analysis. Increasing attention has been recently given to proximity drawings [7]. In a proximity drawing a proximity region is usually associated to any pair of vertices in the graph. A proximity drawing is such that the proximity regions associated to adjacent vertices are empty (do not contain any other vertex) and the proximity regions associated to nonadjacent vertices are not empty (contain at least one other vertex). Proximity drawings have been deeply investigated in the 2-dimensional space because of their interesting graphical features (see, e.g. [15, 3, 8, 9, 2]):

---

* Research supported in part by Progetto Finalizzato Sistemi Informatici e Calcolo Parallelo of the Italian National Research Council (CNR).

edges are represented as straight lines, consecutive edges have a large angle be-
tweeen them, and vertices not incident to a certain edge are drawn far apart
from that edge. Furthermore, in a proximity drawing groups of adjacent vertices
tend to cluster together.

Our main contributions are the following. (1) We study in the 3-dimensional
space the concept of β-drawing ($0 \leq \beta \leq \infty$). β-drawings are a widely accepted
family of proximity drawings of the 2-dimensional space. A β-drawable graph
is a graph that admits a β-drawing. Each value of β defines a proximity region and a type of proximity drawing. The proximity regions can be open or
closed. (2) We give a method for determining, for any given value of β, an upper
bound to the maximum vertex degree of β-drawable trees. (3) We present several efficient algorithms for computing β-drawings in the 3-dimensional space.
(4) Based upon the above algorithms and the above methodology we systemati-
cally explore the capability of the 3-dimensional space in supporting β-drawings
of trees. Table 1 summarizes our results and compares them with previous results in the 2-dimensional space, showing how the set of drawable trees changes
from the 2-dimensions to the 3-dimensions as β changes. Namely, let $\mathcal{T}_{(\beta)}$ ($\mathcal{T}_{[\beta]}$)
be the class of trees that have a proximity drawing where the proximity region
is the open (closed) β-region. We denote with $\mathcal{T}_k$ the set of all finite trees of
maximum vertex degree at most k. Class $\mathcal{T}'$ is defined as the class of trees that
have at least two adjacent vertices of degree three. The class $\overline{\mathcal{T}}$ are the so-called
"forbidden" trees defined in [3]. Observe that for several values of β our study
is tight since we characterize the classes $\mathcal{T}_{(\beta)}$ and $\mathcal{T}_{[\beta]}$ while for other values of β
we restrict the classes of trees to investigate. (5) As a side effect, we show that in
the 3-dimensional space all trees with vertex degree at most 9 can be drawn as
minimum spanning trees. Notice that in the 2-dimensional space all trees with
vertex degree at most 5 can be drawn as minimum spanning trees and that no
tree with maximum vertex degree greater than 7 can be a minimum spanning
tree [16, 8].

The paper is organized as follows. Preliminaries are in Section 2. Section 3 describes the method for computing an upper bound to the maximum vertex degree
of β-drawable trees. Efficient drawing algorithms for computing 3-dimensional
proximity drawings of trees are sketched in Section 4. Finally, open problems
and further directions of research are discussed in Section 5. Because of space
limitations we omit most of the proofs.

2 Preliminaries

We study the problem of computing proximity drawings when a certain type of
proximity region is given. We consider an infinite family of parametrized proximity regions, first introduced by [11] for the 2-dimensional space, that covers
the most well-known proximity regions on the plane presented in the literature
(for an extensive survey on the different types of proximity regions see [10]). The
extension of the definition to the 3-dimensional space is straightforward. Namely,
the definition on the plane is based on intersecting disks. In the 3-dimensional
space it is based on intersecting spheres.

	β	$\mathcal{T}_{(\beta)}$ 2-D [3, 2, 14]	$\mathcal{T}_{(\beta)}$ 3-D	$\mathcal{T}_{[\beta]}$ 3-D
1	$\beta = 0$	$\mathcal{T}_{(\beta)} = \{K_1, K_2\}$	$\mathcal{T}_{(\beta)} = \{K_1, K_2\}$	$\mathcal{T}_{[\beta]} = \mathcal{T}_2$
2	$0 < \beta < \frac{2}{3}$	$\mathcal{T}_{(\beta)} = \mathcal{T}_2$	$\mathcal{T}_{(\beta)} = \mathcal{T}_2$	$\mathcal{T}_{[\beta]} = \mathcal{T}_2$
3	$\beta = \frac{1}{2\sin^2(\frac{\pi}{3})} = \frac{2}{3}$	$\mathcal{T}_{(\beta)} = \mathcal{T}_2$	$\mathcal{T}_{(\beta)} = \mathcal{T}_2$	$\mathcal{T}_{[\beta]} = \mathcal{T}_3 - \mathcal{T}'$
4	$\frac{2}{3} < \beta < \frac{1}{2\sin^2(\arcsin\sqrt{\frac{2}{3}})}$	$\mathcal{T}_{(\beta)} = \mathcal{T}_3$	$\mathcal{T}_{(\beta)} = \mathcal{T}_3$	$\mathcal{T}_{[\beta]} = \mathcal{T}_3$
5	$\beta = 0.75$	$\mathcal{T}_{(\beta)} = \mathcal{T}_3$	$\mathcal{T}_{(\beta)} = \mathcal{T}_3$	$\mathcal{T}_3 \subset \mathcal{T}_{[\beta]} \subseteq \mathcal{T}_4$
6	$\frac{3}{4} < \beta < \frac{1}{2\sin^2(\frac{\pi}{4})} = 1$	$\mathcal{T}_{(\beta)} = \mathcal{T}_3$	$\mathcal{T}_{(\beta)} = \mathcal{T}_4$	$\mathcal{T}_{[\beta]} = \mathcal{T}_4$
7	$\beta = 1$	$\mathcal{T}_{(\beta)} = \mathcal{T}_3$	$\mathcal{T}_{(\beta)} = \mathcal{T}_4$	$\mathcal{T}_4 \subset \mathcal{T}_{[\beta]} \subset \mathcal{T}_6$
8	$1 < \beta < \frac{1}{2\sin^2(\frac{7\pi}{30})}$	$\mathcal{T}_{(\beta)} = \mathcal{T}_4$	$\mathcal{T}_{(\beta)} = \mathcal{T}_6$	$\mathcal{T}_{[\beta]} = \mathcal{T}_6$
9	$\frac{1}{2\sin^2(\frac{7\pi}{30})} \le \beta < \frac{1}{2\sin^2(\frac{13\pi}{60})}$	$\mathcal{T}_{(\beta)} = \mathcal{T}_4$	$\mathcal{T}_6 \subseteq \mathcal{T}_{(\beta)} \subseteq \mathcal{T}_7$	$\mathcal{T}_6 \subseteq \mathcal{T}_{[\beta]} \subseteq \mathcal{T}_7$
10	$\frac{1}{2\sin^2(\frac{13\pi}{60})} \le \beta < \frac{1}{2\sin^2(\frac{37\pi}{180})}$	$\mathcal{T}_{(\beta)} = \mathcal{T}_4$	$\mathcal{T}_6 \subseteq \mathcal{T}_{(\beta)} \subseteq \mathcal{T}_8$	$\mathcal{T}_6 \subseteq \mathcal{T}_{[\beta]} \subseteq \mathcal{T}_8$
11	$\frac{1}{2\sin^2(\frac{37\pi}{180})} \le \beta < \frac{1}{2\sin^2(\frac{\pi}{5})}$	$\mathcal{T}_{(\beta)} = \mathcal{T}_4$	$\mathcal{T}_6 \subseteq \mathcal{T}_{(\beta)} \subseteq \mathcal{T}_9$	$\mathcal{T}_6 \subseteq \mathcal{T}_{[\beta]} \subseteq \mathcal{T}_9$
12	$\beta = \frac{1}{2\sin^2(\frac{\pi}{5})}$	$\mathcal{T}_{(\beta)} = \mathcal{T}_4$	$\mathcal{T}_6 \subseteq \mathcal{T}_{(\beta)} \subseteq \mathcal{T}_9$	$\mathcal{T}_6 \subseteq \mathcal{T}_{[\beta]} \subseteq \mathcal{T}_9$
13	$\frac{1}{2\sin^2(\frac{\pi}{5})} < \beta \le \frac{1}{2\sin^2(\frac{7\pi}{36})}$	$\mathcal{T}_4 \subset \mathcal{T}_{(\beta)} \subseteq \mathcal{T}_5$	$\mathcal{T}_7 \subseteq \mathcal{T}_{(\beta)} \subseteq \mathcal{T}_9$	$\mathcal{T}_7 \subseteq \mathcal{T}_{[\beta]} \subseteq \mathcal{T}_9$
14	$\frac{1}{2\sin^2(\frac{7\pi}{36})} < \beta \le \frac{1}{2\sin^2(\frac{67\pi}{360})}$	$\mathcal{T}_4 \subset \mathcal{T}_{(\beta)} \subseteq \mathcal{T}_5$	$\mathcal{T}_7 \subseteq \mathcal{T}_{(\beta)} \subseteq \mathcal{T}_{10}$	$\mathcal{T}_7 \subseteq \mathcal{T}_{[\beta]} \subseteq \mathcal{T}_{10}$
15	$\frac{1}{2\sin^2(\frac{67\pi}{360})} < \beta \le \frac{1}{2\sin^2(\frac{16\pi}{90})}$	$\mathcal{T}_4 \subset \mathcal{T}_{(\beta)} \subseteq \mathcal{T}_5$	$\mathcal{T}_7 \subseteq \mathcal{T}_{(\beta)} \subseteq \mathcal{T}_{11}$	$\mathcal{T}_7 \subseteq \mathcal{T}_{[\beta]} \subseteq \mathcal{T}_{11}$
16	$\frac{1}{2\sin^2(\frac{16\pi}{90})} < \beta \le \frac{1}{2\sin^2(\frac{61\pi}{360})}$	$\mathcal{T}_4 \subset \mathcal{T}_{(\beta)} \subseteq \mathcal{T}_5$	$\mathcal{T}_7 \subseteq \mathcal{T}_{(\beta)} \subseteq \mathcal{T}_{12}$	$\mathcal{T}_7 \subseteq \mathcal{T}_{[\beta]} \subseteq \mathcal{T}_{12}$
17	$\frac{1}{2\sin^2(\frac{61\pi}{360})} < \beta < \frac{1}{2\sin^2(\frac{\pi}{6})}$	$\mathcal{T}_4 \subset \mathcal{T}_{(\beta)} \subseteq \mathcal{T}_5$	$\mathcal{T}_7 \subseteq \mathcal{T}_{(\beta)} \subseteq \mathcal{T}_{13}$	$\mathcal{T}_7 \subseteq \mathcal{T}_{[\beta]} \subseteq \mathcal{T}_{13}$
18	$\beta = 2$	$\mathcal{T}_{(\beta)} = \mathcal{T}_5$	$\mathcal{T}_9 \subseteq \mathcal{T}_{(\beta)} \subseteq \mathcal{T}_{13}$	$\mathcal{T}_9 \subseteq \mathcal{T}_{[\beta]} \subseteq \mathcal{T}_{13}$
19	$2 < \beta < \frac{1}{\cos(\frac{61\pi}{180})}$	$\mathcal{T}_4 \subset \mathcal{T}_{(\beta)} \subseteq \mathcal{T}_5$	$\mathcal{T}_7 \subseteq \mathcal{T}_{(\beta)} \subseteq \mathcal{T}_{13}$	$\mathcal{T}_7 \subseteq \mathcal{T}_{[\beta]} \subseteq \mathcal{T}_{13}$
20	$\frac{1}{\cos(\frac{61\pi}{180})} \le \beta < \frac{1}{\cos(\frac{16\pi}{45})}$	$\mathcal{T}_4 \subset \mathcal{T}_{(\beta)} \subseteq \mathcal{T}_5$	$\mathcal{T}_7 \subseteq \mathcal{T}_{(\beta)} \subseteq \mathcal{T}_{12}$	$\mathcal{T}_7 \subseteq \mathcal{T}_{[\beta]} \subseteq \mathcal{T}_{12}$
21	$\frac{1}{\cos(\frac{16\pi}{45})} \le \beta < \frac{1}{\cos(\frac{67\pi}{180})}$	$\mathcal{T}_4 \subset \mathcal{T}_{(\beta)} \subseteq \mathcal{T}_5$	$\mathcal{T}_7 \subseteq \mathcal{T}_{(\beta)} \subseteq \mathcal{T}_{11}$	$\mathcal{T}_7 \subseteq \mathcal{T}_{[\beta]} \subseteq \mathcal{T}_{11}$
22	$\frac{1}{\cos(\frac{67\pi}{180})} \le \beta < \frac{1}{\cos(\frac{7\pi}{18})}$	$\mathcal{T}_4 \subset \mathcal{T}_{(\beta)} \subseteq \mathcal{T}_5$	$\mathcal{T}_7 \subseteq \mathcal{T}_{(\beta)} \subseteq \mathcal{T}_{10}$	$\mathcal{T}_7 \subseteq \mathcal{T}_{[\beta]} \subseteq \mathcal{T}_{10}$
23	$\frac{1}{\cos(\frac{7\pi}{18})} \le \beta < \frac{1}{\cos(\frac{2\pi}{5})}$	$\mathcal{T}_4 \subset \mathcal{T}_{(\beta)} \subseteq \mathcal{T}_5$	$\mathcal{T}_7 \subseteq \mathcal{T}_{(\beta)} \subseteq \mathcal{T}_9$	$\mathcal{T}_7 \subseteq \mathcal{T}_{[\beta]} \subseteq \mathcal{T}_9$
24	$\beta = \frac{1}{\cos(\frac{2\pi}{5})}$	$\mathcal{T}_4 \subset \mathcal{T}_{(\beta)} \subset \mathcal{T}_5$	$\mathcal{T}_6 \subseteq \mathcal{T}_{(\beta)} \subseteq \mathcal{T}_9$	$\mathcal{T}_6 \subseteq \mathcal{T}_{[\beta]} \subseteq \mathcal{T}_9$
25	$\frac{1}{\cos(\frac{2\pi}{5})} < \beta < \frac{1}{\cos(\frac{37\pi}{90})}$	$\mathcal{T}_{(\beta)} = \mathcal{T}_4$	$\mathcal{T}_6 \subseteq \mathcal{T}_{(\beta)} \subseteq \mathcal{T}_9$	$\mathcal{T}_6 \subseteq \mathcal{T}_{[\beta]} \subseteq \mathcal{T}_9$
26	$\frac{1}{\cos(\frac{37\pi}{90})} \le \beta < \frac{1}{\cos(\frac{13\pi}{30})}$	$\mathcal{T}_{(\beta)} = \mathcal{T}_4$	$\mathcal{T}_6 \subseteq \mathcal{T}_{(\beta)} \subseteq \mathcal{T}_8$	$\mathcal{T}_6 \subseteq \mathcal{T}_{[\beta]} \subseteq \mathcal{T}_8$
27	$\frac{1}{\cos(\frac{13\pi}{30})} \le \beta < \frac{1}{\cos(\frac{7\pi}{15})}$	$\mathcal{T}_{(\beta)} = \mathcal{T}_4$	$\mathcal{T}_6 \subseteq \mathcal{T}_{(\beta)} \subseteq \mathcal{T}_7$	$\mathcal{T}_6 \subseteq \mathcal{T}_{[\beta]} \subseteq \mathcal{T}_7$
28	$\frac{1}{\cos(\frac{7\pi}{15})} < \beta < \infty$	$\mathcal{T}_{(\beta)} = \mathcal{T}_4$	$\mathcal{T}_{(\beta)} = \mathcal{T}_6$	$\mathcal{T}_{[\beta]} = \mathcal{T}_6$
29	$\beta = \infty$	$\mathcal{T}_3 \subset \mathcal{T}_{(\beta)} \subset \mathcal{T}_4$	$\mathcal{T}_4 \subset \mathcal{T}_{(\beta)} \subset \mathcal{T}_6$	$\mathcal{T}_{[\beta]} = \mathcal{T}_4$

Table 1. Comparing 2-D and 3-D spaces.

Given a pair x, y of points in the 3-dimensional space, the *open β-region of influence of x and y*, and the *closed β-region of influence of x and y*, denoted by $R(x, y, \beta)$ and $R[x, y, \beta]$ respectively, are defined as follows. For $0 < \beta < 1$, $R(x, y, \beta)$ is the intersection of the two open spheres of radius $d(x,y)/(2\beta)$ passing through both x and y. $R[x, y, \beta]$ is the intersection of the two corresponding closed spheres. For $1 \leq \beta < \infty$, $R(x, y, \beta)$ is the intersection of the two open spheres of radius $\beta d(x, y)/2$ and centered at the points $(1 - \beta/2)x + (\beta/2)y$ and $(\beta/2)x + (1 - \beta/2)y$. $R[x, y, \beta]$ is the intersection of the two corresponding closed spheres. $R(x, y, \infty)$ is the open infinite corridor perpendicular to the line segment $\overline{xy}$ and $R[x, y, \infty]$ is the closed infinite corridor perpendicular to the line segment $\overline{xy}$. Finally, $R(x, y, 0)$ is the empty set and $R[x, y, 0]$ is the line segment connecting x and y.

Let G be a graph. A *(β)-drawing* of G is a proximity drawing of G such that for each pair of points x, y the proximity region is $R(x, y, \beta)$. So, in a (β)-drawing of G for each pair of x, y of adjacent vertices $R(x, y, \beta)$ does not contain any other vertex of the drawing; conversely, for each pair z, w of nonadjacent vertices $R(z, w, \beta)$ does contain at least on vertex of the drawing. Analogously, a *[β]-drawing* of G is a proximity drawing of G such that for each pair of points x, y the proximity region is $R[x, y, \beta]$. A graph is *(β)-drawable* if it has a (β)-drawing. Analogously, a graph is *[β]-drawable* if it has a [β]-drawing. (β)- and [β]-drawable graphs are also called (β)- and [β]-graphs, respectively. A class of graphs is (β)-drawable (resp. [β]-drawable) if all its graphs are (β)-drawable (resp. [β]-drawable). A class of graphs is not (β)-drawable (resp. [β]-drawable) if it contains at least one graph that is not (β)-drawable (resp. [β]-drawable). When it is clear from the context or when it is not necessary to distinguish between open and closed proximity regions, we will often simplify the notation by talking about *β-drawings* and *β-drawable* graphs (classes).

One of the quantities which is frequently used in analyzing β-drawings is the angle $\alpha(\beta) = \inf\{\angle xzy | z \in R(x, y, \beta)\}$. Clearly if x and y are not adjacent in $G(P, \beta)$ ($G[P, \beta]$), then there is a point $z \in P$ such that $\angle xzy > \alpha(\beta)$ ($\angle xzy \geq \alpha(\beta)$). The converse, however, does not always hold. Note $\alpha(0) = \pi$ and $\alpha(\infty) = 0$.

A related quantity is the angle $\gamma(\beta)$, which is defined, for $\beta \geq 2$, as follows. Consider the region $R(x, y, \beta)$ for two points x, y. Let z be a point on the boundary of $R(x, y, \beta)$ such that $d(x, y) = d(x, z)$. Then $\gamma(\beta) = \angle zxy$. Note that $\gamma(\infty) = \pi/2$, $\gamma(2) = \alpha(2) = \pi/3$, and, for $\beta > 2$, $\gamma(\beta) > \alpha(\beta)$.

Property 1. *β is related to $\alpha(\beta)$ and $\gamma(\beta)$ by the following equation:* $\beta = \frac{1}{2 \sin^2(\frac{\alpha(\beta)}{2})} = \frac{1}{\cos \gamma(\beta)}$.

Given a set P of distinct points of the 3-dimensional space we denote by $G(P, \beta)$ the graph whose vertices correspond to the points of P and such that there is an edge (x, y) between two vertices corresponding to points x and y iff $R(x, y, \beta) \cap P = \emptyset$. It is easy to see that $G(P, \beta)$ has a (β)-drawing that is obtained by connecting with straight-line segments the points of P that correspond to adjacent vertices of $G(P, \beta)$. Hence, $G(P, \beta)$ is a (β)-graph. For simplifying the notation we denote, where this does not cause ambiguity, by $G(P, \beta)$ both the graph and its (β)-drawing and by P both the set of vertices and the points representing them in the drawing. Analogously, we denote by $G[P, \beta]$ the graph whose vertices correspond to the points of P and such that there is an edge between two vertices x and y iff $R[x, y, \beta] \cap (P - \{x, y\}) = \emptyset$.

In [2] it is proved the following.

Property 2. *[2] If β_1 and β_2 are such that $0 \leq \beta_1 < \beta_2 \leq \infty$ then $G[P, \beta_2] \subseteq G(P, \beta_2) \subseteq G[P, \beta_1] \subseteq G(P, \beta_1)$.*

Given a set P of points, consider a connected straight-line graph G on P, that is, a graph having as its edge set E a collection of line segments connecting pairs of vertices of P. Define the *weight* of G to be the sum of all of the edge lengths of G. Such a graph is called a *minimum spanning tree of P*, denoted by $MST(P)$, if its weight is no greater than the weight of any other connected straight-line graph on P. (It is easy to see that such a graph must be a tree.) In general, a set P may have many minimum spanning trees (for example, if P consists of the vertices of a regular polygon).

Lemma 3. *[2] If $0 \leq \beta < 2$, then $MST(P) \subseteq G(P, \beta)$ and $MST(P) \subseteq G[P, \beta]$. Furthermore, $MST(P) \subseteq G(P, 2)$.*

The relationship between β-drawings and minimum spanning trees allows to determine the minimum angle between any two edges of a β-drawing, that are incident on the same vertex. The following lemma is proved with a technique similar to the one shown in [2].

Lemma 4. *Let $G(P, \beta)$ be a tree. If $0 \leq \beta \leq 2$, the angle between any two edges of $G(P, \beta)$ incident on a common vertex is greater than $\alpha(\beta)$. The angle between any two edges of $G[P, \beta]$ incident on a common vertex is at least $\alpha(\beta)$. If $2 < \beta \leq \infty$, the angle between any two edges of $G(P, \beta)$ incident on a common vertex is at least $\gamma(\beta)$. The angle between any two edges of $G[P, \beta]$ incident on a common vertex is greater than $\alpha(\beta)$.*

Finally, an induced subgraph of a graph G which is obtained by repeated removal of leaves is called a *pruning* of G. Let G be a graph which admits a (β)-drawing ($[\beta]$-drawing) Γ and let G' be a pruning of G obtained by removing the set of vertices V'. Let Γ' be obtained from Γ by removing the points corresponding to the set V'. If for all prunings G' of G, Γ' is a (β)-drawing of G', then G is called a (β)- ($[\beta]$-stable) graph and Γ is a *(β)-stable ($[\beta]$-stable)* drawing of G. Observe that if Γ is a (β)-stable (or $[\beta]$-stable) drawing of a tree T, then for any pair of non-adjacent vertices x and y in T, there is a vertex v on the (unique) path between x and y such that, in Γ, v is contained in the proximity region of x and y.

3 Exploring the Capability of the 3-dimensional Space in Supporting Proximity Drawability

Aim of this section is to present a methodology for finding an upper bound to the maximum vertex degree of β-drawable trees in the 3-dimensional space, for any fixed $\beta > 1$. The methodology is based on: (i) studying the geometry of the arrangement of k edges around a common vertex in the 3-dimensional space with the constraint that the minimum angle between any two edges is at least $max\{\alpha(\beta), \gamma(\beta)\}$; (ii) incrementally constructing an upper bound for the maximum vertex degree of β-drawable trees with the following strategy. Start with a β-drawable tree composed by one vertex adjacent to k leaves and test the β-drawability of the tree when incrementing the number of its leaves to $k + 1$. If the tree is not β-drawable, then k is the wanted upper bound; otherwise, increase the number of vertices adjacent to v by one unit and repeat the procedure. In what follows we assume that points, segments and drawings are in the 3-dimensional space.

In order to understand how many edges can be drawn around one vertex, because of Lemma 4, we study here the following geometric problem. Let θ be an angle such that $\pi/3 \le \theta < \pi/2$, and let v be a point. How many half-lines (*spokes*) can originate from v such that the (acute) angle between any two spokes is at least θ? Observe that, since $\theta < \pi/2$, the question is interesting for $k > 6$ (it is always possible to arrange six spokes around v so that the minimum angle between any two spokes is exactly $\pi/2$). A multi-dimensional version of the above problem has been studied in the sphere-packing context; several references can be found in [5]. However, the computed approximations are usually affected by the more general context. We propose a simple and practical method.

Suppose that v originates $k > 6$ spokes $r_1 \cdots r_k$ and consider a unit sphere S of center v. Let p_i be the intersection point between S and r_i. For each p_i consider its *spherical Voronoi region* $V(p_i)$, i.e. the set of points on the surface of S that are closer to p_i than to any other p_j with $i \ne j$, where the distance between two points on the surface of S is measured as the length of the shortest arc on the surface of S between the points. Observe that such distance between p_i and p_j coincides with the angle between r_i and r_j. Let $\Omega(p_i)$ be the solid angle that is seen in $V(p_i)$ looking from v. Observe that $\Omega(p_i)$ is the portion of the surface of S occupied by $V(p_i)$.

A first rough lower bound for $\Omega(p_i)$ can be found as follows. Consider a cone $C(r_i)$ with apex v, axis r_i and angle θ, and let $D(p_i)$ be the intersection between $C(p_i)$ and the surface of S. Since the the angle between r_i and r_j is at least θ, we have.

Property 5. *Given any pair p_i, p_j, with $i \ne j$, $D(p_i) \cap D(p_j)$ consists of at most one point. Given any p_i, $D(p_i) \subseteq V(p_i)$.*

By Property 5 one can think of approximating each $\Omega(p_i)$ with the solid angle $\Gamma(P_i)$ defined by $C(r_i)$. Now, fixed θ, an upper bound to the maximum number of spokes incident on v can be found by computing the minimum k for which $\sum_1^k \Gamma(P_i) > 4\pi$ (the solid angle of a sphere is 4π). As an example, this procedure allows to say that $k \le 14$ when $\theta = \pi/3$ and that $k < 14$ for all other possible values $\pi/3 < \theta < \pi/2$. However, a much tighter approximation for $\Omega(p_i)$ can be found by carefully exploiting the following property, that can be proved with basic spherical trigonometry.

Property 6. *Let x_i be the number of edges of $V(p_i)$. Consider a regular spherical x_i-gon X circumscribed to $D(p_i)$ and let $\Phi(p_i)$ be the solid angle that is seen in X looking from v. Then, $\Phi(p_i) \leq \Omega(p_i)$.*

The following lemma is proved with spherical trigonometry and with convexity arguments.

Lemma 7.

$$\frac{\Phi(p_i)}{\pi} = 2 - x_i + \frac{x_i}{90} \cdot \arccos(\cos\frac{\theta}{2} \cdot \sin\frac{\pi}{x_i}).$$

Also, $\Phi(p_i)$ is a convex decreasing function of x_i for $3 \leq x_i \leq 14$.

By Property 6 and Lemma 7, if we know the number x_i of edges of a certain Voronoi region $V(p_i)$, then we also know how to approximate its solid angle. Unfortunately, we do not have any information about x_i. Thus, instead of searching how to approximate the single $\Omega(p_i)$, we will look for a lower bound of the whole summation $\sum_1^k \Omega(P_i)$. Suppose, we will remove this assumption later (in Theorem 10), that no four points of $p_1, \cdots, p_k$ are co-circular. This implies that the overall number of edges of Voronoi regions is equal to $3k - 6$ (number of edges of the corresponding Delaunay triangulation). We have $\sum_1^k \Omega(P_i) \geq \sum_1^k \Phi(P_i)$. But, $\Phi(P_i)$ depends only on x_i, so it is possible to write: $\sum_1^k \Phi(P_i) = \sum_1^k \Phi(x_i) \geq \min_{x_1, \cdot, x_k} \sum_1^k \Phi(x_i)$.

Where the minimum function is subject to the constraints: (i) $\sum_1^k x_i = 6k - 12$ and (ii) $3 \leq x_i \leq k$, since each Voronoi region has at least 3 and at most k edges. Also, such a minimum can be determined by observing that its computation is in one-to-one correspondence to a minimum cost-flow problem on the following network N. Nodes: there is a node for each p_i; also there is a source node s and a sink node t. Arcs: there is an arc from s to each node p_i, with lower capacity 3, upper capacity k and cost function $\Phi(x_i)$. There is an arc from each node p_i to the sink node and a return arc from t to s; such arcs have infinite capacity and zero cost. The flow outgoing from s is equal to $6k - 12$.

Each unit of flow in N from s to p_i corresponds to one edge of the Voronoi region $V(p_i)$. The flow of minimum cost corresponds to the assignment of edges to the Voronoi regions that minimizes the $\sum_1^k \Phi(x_i)$. By exploiting (Lemma 7) the convexity and the decreasing behaviour of the cost functions on the arcs of N it can be proved that the overall cost on N is minimized by minimizing the difference between the flows in any two distinct arcs (s, p_i), (s, p_j) (see, e.g. [12]). This directly implies the following.

Lemma 8. *The cost of the flow on N is minimized by minimizing the variation of the flow in the arcs $(s, p_1), \cdots, (s, p_k)$.*

By the previous lemma and since $6 < k \leq 14$, it follows that $\min_{x_1, \cdot, x_k} \sum_1^k \Phi(x_i)$ can be expressed in a very compact way.

Lemma 9. *If $6 < k \leq 12$, then $\min_{x_1, \cdot, x_k} \sum_1^k \Phi(x_i) = (2k - 12) \cdot \Phi(5) + (12 - k) \cdot \Phi(4)$. If $12 < k \leq 14$, then $\min_{x_1, \cdot, x_k} \sum_1^k \Phi(x_i) = (k - 12) \cdot \Phi(6) + 12 \cdot \Phi(5)$.*

Proof. We prove the first statement. The argument for the second statement is analogous. If $6 < k \leq 12$ then $\lfloor \frac{6k-12}{k} \rfloor = 4$, because of Lemma 8, the min-cost-flow problem on N is solved by distributing the flow on the arcs of N as much evenly as possible. Hence, a flow of minimum cost for N can be computed with the following two steps procedure. Assign four units of flow to each of the arcs $(s, p_1), \cdots, (s, p_k)$. Evenly distribute the remaining $6k - 12 - 4k = 2k - 12$ units of flow by adding one unit of flow to each of the arcs $(s, p_1), \cdots, (s, p_{k-12})$.

Observe that, because of Lemma 9, the distribution of the points $p_i, \cdots, p_k$ with $6 < k \leq 12$ that has the minimum cost is such that $2k - 12$ spherical Voronoi regions have five edges and the remaining $12 - k$ have four edges.

The results of this subsection are summarized in the following theorem.

Theorem 10. *Let v be a point, S a unit sphere of center v, and θ an angle such that $\pi/3 \leq \theta < \pi/2$. If $6 < k \leq 14$ spokes originate from v such that the angle between any two spokes is at least θ, then*

$$((6k-12) \bmod k) \cdot \Phi(\lfloor \frac{6k-12}{k} \rfloor + 1) + (k - ((6k-12) \bmod k)) \cdot \Phi(\lfloor \frac{6k-12}{k} \rfloor)) \leq 4\pi,$$

where $\Phi(x)$ is the portion of the surface of S occupied by a regular spherical x-gon circumscribed to a circumference of spherical radius $\theta/2$.

Proof. If no four intersection points $p_i, \cdots, p_k$ between the k spokes $r_1, \cdots, r_k$ and the sphere S are co-circular, the theorem is straightforward from what above. Suppose now that at least four of the points $p_i, \cdots, p_k$ are co-circular. It follows that the overall number of edges of the spherical Voronoi regions decreases. Hence, the minimum computed in Lemma 9 is still a valid approximation.

The result of Theorem 10, along with Lemma 4 allow to give a general methodology for computing an upper bound to the maximum vertex degree of β-drawable trees when β ranges from 1 to ∞. Namely, fixed a value of β such that $1 < \beta < \infty$, suppose a β-drawing of a tree has a vertex v with $deg(v)$ incident edges. For Lemma 4 the minimum angle δ between any two edges incident on v is at least $\delta_0 = \max\{\alpha(\beta), \gamma(\beta)\}$. Observe that $\pi/3 \leq \delta_0 < \pi/2$ for $1 < \beta < \infty$. Consider a sphere S of center v intersecting all the $deg(v)$ edges (since β-drawings are not affected by a change in scale, we may assume that S has unit radius). Also we can associate to each edge e incident on v a spoke incident on the same point and with the same slope of e. Thus, an upper bound for $deg(v)$ can be found by computing the maximum number of spokes incident on v that satisfy the condition stated by Theorem 10. Such methodology gives rise to the following.

Theorem 11. *As β ranges in the interval $(1, \infty)$, the relations of the type $T_{(\beta)} \subseteq T_k$ and $T_{[\beta]} \subseteq T_k$ $(6 < k < 13)$ shown in the third and fourth column of Table 1 are correct.*

Observe that for $\beta = 2$ a better bound can be achieved by applying the construction of Leech [13] for showing $k \leq 12$.

4 Proximity Drawings of Trees in the Air

We refer to statements in the Table as follows: $S(k)$ refers to the statement of row k and column $\mathcal{T}_{(\beta)}$ 3-D; similarly, $S[k]$ refers to the statement of row k and column $\mathcal{T}_{[\beta]}$ 3-D. The notation $S(k), \cdots S[j]$, with $k < j$ refers to all the statements of the third and fourth column of Table 1 from row k included to row j included.

We start with a property stating the angular resolution of vertices of degree four in the 3-dimensional space. The property can be easily proved by considering the angle between any two segments connecting the center of a regular tetrahedron to a distinct pair of the vertices of the tetrahedron.

Property 12. *Let v be an edge of degree four. There always exist two edges incident on v forming an angle which is at most $2 \cdot \arcsin(\sqrt{\frac{2}{3}})$.*

Property 12, along with Property 1 and Lemma 4 immediately imply the following.

Lemma 13. *Both (β)- and $[\beta]$-drawable trees have no vertices of degree four when $\beta < \dfrac{1}{2 \sin^2 (\arcsin \sqrt{\frac{2}{3}})} = \frac{3}{4}$.*

Lemma 14. *Given any β such that $0 \le \beta < \frac{3}{4}$ and a tree T, T is β-drawable in the 3-dimensional space if and only if it is β-drawable in the 2-dimensional space. Furthermore, T is $(\frac{3}{4})$-drawable in the 3-dimensional space if and only if it is $(\frac{3}{4})$-drawable in the 2-dimensional space.*

Theorem 15. *Statements $S(1), \cdots, S[5]$ are correct. Furthermore, a β-drawing of any of the β-drawable trees in such statements can be computed in linear time in the real RAM model.*

Proof. The truth of Statements $S(1), \cdots, S[4]$, plus Statement $S(5)$ descends from Lemma 14. Statement $S[5]$ is proved by observing that a tree consisting of a vertex v of degree four adjacent to four leaves has a $[\frac{3}{4}]$-drawing where v is the center of a regular tetrahedron and the leaves are the vertices of the tetrahedron. Because of Lemma 14, both the drawing algorithms and the bounds on the time complexity are the same shown in [2, 14].

Motivated by Theorem 15 we concentrate on computing β-drawings of trees with maximum vertex degree greater than three, for $\beta > \frac{3}{4}$.

We extend the ideas underlying the computation of proximity drawings of binary trees in the plane of [14, 2] to represent trees with maximum vertex degree at most four in the 3-dimensional space.

Lemma 16. *For each $T \in \mathcal{T}_4$ and for any given β' such that $\frac{3}{4} < \beta' \le \infty$ there exists a set P of points of the 3-dimensional space such that: (1) for each $\beta' \le \beta \le \infty$, $G(P, \beta)$ is a (β)-stable drawing of T, and (2) for each $\beta' \le \beta \le \infty$, $G[P, \beta]$ is a $[\beta]$-stable drawing of T.*

Theorem 17. *Class $\mathcal{T}_4$ is (β)-drawable and [β]-drawable for all values of β such that $\frac{3}{4} < \beta \leq \infty$. Furthermore, given a $T \in \mathcal{T}_3$ and a β such that $\frac{3}{4} < \beta \leq \infty$, a ($\beta$)-drawing and a [$\beta$]-drawing of T can be computed in linear time in the real RAM model.*

Proof. The first part of the theorem follows immediately from Lemma 16. The drawing algorithm implicit in Lemma 16 can be produced in linear time since the spheres S_1 and S_2 can each be computed in linear time.

Besides the above theorem, in order to prove the correctness of statements on Table 1 for $\frac{3}{4} < \beta \leq 1$ we need the following property on arrangements of edges around a vertex in any 3-dimensional drawing.

Property 18. *Let v be an edge of degree five. There always exist two edges incident on v forming an angle which is at most $\pi/2$.*

Property 18, along with Property 1 and Lemma 4 immediately imply the following.

Lemma 19. *Both (β)- and [β]-drawable trees have no vertices of degree five when $\beta < 1$. Furthermore, (1)-drawable trees have no vertices of degree five.*

Theorem 20. *Statements $S(6), \cdots, S[7]$, Statement $S(29)$, and Statement $S[29]$ are correct.*

Proof. The correctness of Statements $S(6)$, $S[6]$, and $S(7)$ follows from Lemma 19. To prove the correctness of Statements $S[7]$ and $S(29)$, observe that, because of Lemma 16 every $T \in \mathcal{T}_4$ admits both a [1]- and an (∞)-drawing. Also observe that a tree consisting of one vertex v of degree six and six leaves has both a [1]- and an (∞)-drawing by orthogonally connecting v to its neighbors.

Lemma 21. *For each $T \in \mathcal{T}_6$ and for any given β' and β'' such that $1 < \beta' < \beta'' < \infty$ there exists a set P of points in the 3-dimensional space such that: (1) for each $\beta' \leq \beta \leq \beta''$, $G(P, \beta)$ is a (β)-stable drawing of T, and (2) for each $\beta' \leq \beta \leq \beta''$, $G[P, \beta]$ is a [β]-stable drawing of T.*

Theorem 22. *Class $\mathcal{T}_6$ is (β)-drawable and [β]-drawable for all values of β such that $1 < \beta < \infty$. Furthermore, given a $T \in \mathcal{T}_6$ and a β such that $1 < \beta < \infty$, a (β)-drawing and a [β]-drawing of T can be computed in linear time in the real RAM model.*

Proof. The first statement follows from Lemma 21; the second from the observation that spheres S_1 and S_2 as in the proof of the lemma can be found in linear time.

Theorem 22 along with Theorem 10 imply the following.

Theorem 23. *Statements $S(8), \cdots, S[12]$ and Statements $S(24), \cdots, S[28]$ are correct.*

Lemma 24. *For each $T \in \mathcal{T}_7$ and for any given β' and β'' such that $\frac{1}{2\sin^2(\frac{\pi}{5})} < \beta' < \beta'' < \frac{1}{\cos(\frac{2\pi}{5})}$ there exists a set P of points of the 3-dimensional space such that: (1) for each $\beta' \le \beta \le \beta''$, $G(P, \beta)$ is a (β)-stable drawing of T, and (2) for each $\beta' \le \beta \le \beta''$, $G[P, \beta]$ is a $[\beta]$-stable drawing of T.*

Theorem 25. *Class $\mathcal{T}_7$ is (β)-drawable and $[\beta]$-drawable for all values of β such that $\frac{1}{2\sin^2(\frac{\pi}{5})} < \beta < \frac{1}{\cos(\frac{2\pi}{5})}$. Furthermore, given a $T \in \mathcal{T}_7$ and a β such that $\frac{1}{2\sin^2(\frac{\pi}{5})} < \beta \le \frac{1}{\cos(\frac{2\pi}{5})}$, a (β)-drawing and a $[\beta]$-drawing of T can be computed in linear time in the real RAM model.*

Theorem 22 along with Theorem 10 imply the following.

Theorem 26. *Statements $S(13), \cdots, S[117]$ and Statements $S(19), \cdots, S[23]$ are correct.*

Lemma 27. *For each $T \in \mathcal{T}_9$ there exists a set P of points of the 3-dimensional space such that: (1) $G(P, 2)$ is a (2)-stable drawing of T, and (2) $G[P, 2]$ is a $[2]$-stable drawing of T.*

Theorem 28. *Class $\mathcal{T}_9$ is (2)-drawable and $[2]$-drawable. Furthermore, given a $T \in \mathcal{T}_9$, a (2)-drawing and a $[2]$-drawing of T can be computed in linear time in the real RAM model.*

Theorem 29. *Statements $S(18)$ and $S[18]$ are correct.*

An immediate consequence of Theorem 29, Theorem 10 and Lemma 3 concerns the drawability of trees as minimum spanning trees in the 3-dimensional space.

Corollary 30. *In the 3-dimensional space every tree with maximum vertex degree at most 9 can be drawn as a minimum spanning tre.*

5 Open Problems

Several problems on 3-D proximity drawings remain open. (1) Are all trees in class $\mathcal{T}_{12}$ 3-D β-drawable for $\beta = 2$? (2) Extending the drawing algorithm for $\mathcal{T}_7$. For example given any $T \in \mathcal{T}_7$ it is not hard to modify the drawing algorithm implicit in the proof of Lemma 24 in order to construct both a $[\frac{1}{2\sin^2(\frac{\pi}{5})}]$- and a $(\frac{1}{2\sin^2(\frac{\pi}{5})})$-drawing of T by slightly moving three of the five co-planar points below plane Π. However it would be interesting to study whether there exist values for β such that the class of β-drawable trees coincides with $\mathcal{T}_7$. (3) Study other families of β-drawable graphs in the 3-dimensional space, like outerplanar graphs and planar triangulations. (4) Exploring other types of proximity drawings [7] in the 3-dimensional space.

Acknowledgements

We are extremely grateful to Bill Lenhart, Henk Meijer, and David Rappaport for their encouragement, the many comments and the useful discussions.

References

1. Advanced Visual Interfaces, Proccedings of the Workshop AVI'92, edited by T. Catarci, M.F. Costabile, and S. Levialdi, *World Scientific series in Computer Science*, Vol. 36, 1992.
2. P. Bose, G. Di Battista, W. Lenhart, and G. Liotta. Proximity Constraints and Representable Trees. *Proc. Graph Drawing'94*, LNCS, pp. 340–351, Princeton, NJ, 1994.
3. P. Bose, W. Lenhart, and G. Liotta. Characterizing Proximity Trees. To appear in *Algorithmica: Special Issue on Graph Drawing*.
4. R. Cohen, P. Eades, T. Lin, and F. Ruskey. Three-Dimensional Graph Drawing. *Proc. Graph Drawing'94*, LNCS, pp. 1–1, Princeton, NJ, 1994.
5. J.H. Conway, N.J.A. Sloane. *Sphere Packings, Lattices, and Groups*, Springer Verlag, 1993.
6. G. Di Battista, P. Eades, R. Tamassia and I.G. Tollis. Algorithms for Automatic Graph Drawing: An Annotated Bibliography. *Computational Geometry: Theory and Applications*, **4, 5**, 1994, pp. 235–282.
7. G. Di Battista, W. Lenhart, and G. Liotta. Proximity Drawability: a Survey. *Proc. Graph Drawing'94*, LNCS, pp. 328–339, Princeton, NJ, 1994.
8. P. Eades and S. Whitesides. The Realization Problem for Euclidean Minimum Spanning Trees is NP-hard. *Proc. ACM Symposium on Computational Geometry*, 1994, pp. 49–56.
9. H. ElGindy, G. Liotta, A. Lubiw, H. Meijer, and S.H. Whitesides. Recognizing Rectangle of Influence Drawable Graphs. *Proc. Graph Drawing'94*, LNCS, pp. 352–363, Princeton, NJ, 1994.
10. J. W. Jaromczyk and G. T. Toussaint. Relative Neighborhood Graphs and Their Relatives. *Proceedings of the IEEE*, **80**, 1992, pp. 1502–1517.
11. D. G. Kirkpatrick and J. D. Radke. A Framework for Computational Morphology. *Computational Geometry*, G. T. Toussaint, Elsevier, Amsterdam, 1985, pp. 217–248.
12. E. L. Lawler. *Combinatorial Optimization: Networks and Matroids*, Holt, Rinehart and Winston, New York, 1976.
13. J. Leech. The Problem of the Thirteen Spheres. *The Mathematical Gazette*, **40**, 1956, pp. 22-23.
14. G. Liotta. Computing Proximity Drawings of Graphs. Ph.D Thesis, University of Rome "La Sapienza", 1995.
15. A. Lubiw, and N. Sleumer, All Maximal Outerplanar Graphs are Relative Neighborhood Graphs. *Proc. CCCG '93*, 1993, pp. 198–203.
16. C. Monma and S. Suri. Transitions in Geometric Minimum Spanning Trees. *Proc. ACM Symposium on Computational Geometry*, 1991, pp. 239–249.
17. S. P. Reiss. 3-D Visualization of Program Information. *Proc. Graph Drawing'94*, LNCS, pp. 12–24, Princeton, NJ, 1994

Routing on Trees via Matchings[*]

ALAN ROBERTS[1], ANTONIS SYMVONIS[1] and LOUXIN ZHANG[2]

[1] Department of Computer Science, University of Sydney, N.S.W. 2006, Australia
[2] Department of Computer Science, University of Waterloo, Canada, N2L 3G1

Abstract. In this paper we consider the routing number of trees, denoted by $rt()$, with respect to the matching routing model. The only known result is that $rt(T) \leq 3n$ for an arbitrary tree T of n nodes [2, 3]. By providing off-line permutation routing algorithms we prove that: i) $rt(T) \leq n + o(n)$ for a complete d-ary tree T of n nodes, ii) $rt(T) \leq 2n + o(n)$ for an arbitrary bounded degree tree T of n nodes, iii) $rt(T) \leq 2n$ for a maximum degree 3 tree T of n nodes, iv) $rt(T) \leq \frac{13}{5}n$ for an arbitrary tree T of n nodes.

1 Introduction

The *permutation packet routing problem* on a connected undirected graph is the following: We are given a graph $G = (V, E)$ and a permutation π of the vertices of G. Every vertex v of G contains a packet destined for $\pi(v)$. Our task is to route all packets to their destinations.

During the routing, the movement of the packets follows a set of rules. These rules specify the *routing model*. Let $rt_M(G, \pi)$ be the number of steps required to route permutation π on graph G by using routing model M. The routing number of graph G with respect to routing model M, $rt_M(G)$, is defined to be $rt_M(G) = \max_\pi rt_M(G, \pi)$ over all permutations π of the vertex set V of G.

The routing number of a graph was first defined by Alon, Chung and Graham in [2, 3]. In their routing model, the only operation allowed during the routing is the exchange of the packets at the endpoints of an edge of graph G. The exchange of the packets at the endpoints of a set of disjoint edges (a matching on G) can occur in one routing step. We refer to this model as the *matching routing model* and, for a graph G, we refer to the routing number of G with respect to the matching routing model, simply as the routing number of G, denoted by $rt(G)$. It was shown in [2, 3] that $rt(T) < 3n$ for any tree T of n vertices. As a consequence, $rt(G) < 3n$ for any graph G of n vertices. To the best of our knowledge, this is the only known work on routing on trees under the matching model. Algorithms for routing permutations on trees under different routing models have been presented by Borodin, Rabani and Schieber [4] (hot-potato routing model) and Symvonis [9] (simplified routing model).

In our attempt to obtain an upper bound on the routing number of complete d-ary trees, we run into a problem of independent interest. This is the problem of *heap construction*. Consider a rooted tree T and let each of its nodes have a *key-value* associated with it. We say that T is *heap ordered* if each non-leaf node satisfies the *heap invariant*: "the key-value of the node is not larger than the key-values of its

---
[*] The work of Dr Symvonis is supported by an ARC Institutional Grant.
Email: {alanr,symvonis}@cs.su.oz.au, lzhang@neumann.uwaterloo.ca.

children". When the key-value at each node is carried (or associated with) the packet currently in the node, the problem of heap construction is simply to route the packets on the tree in a way that guarantees that at the end of the routing the packets are heap-ordered based on the key-values they carry. Needless to say, we are interested in forming the heap in the smallest number of parallel routing steps when routing is performed according to the matching routing model. Heaps are also discussed in the context of the PRAM model [5, 7, 10]. Rao and W. Zhang [7] and W. Zhang and Korf [10] described how to construct a heap (implemented as a complete binary tree) of n elements within $2 \log_2 n$ steps.

1.1 Our Results

In this paper, we consider the routing number of several classes of trees with respect to the matching routing model. We present an off-line algorithm which routes any permutation on a complete d-ary tree within $n + o(n)$ steps. Firstly we describe how to route a permutation on an n-node complete binary tree in $\frac{4}{3}n + o(n)$ routing steps. Then, we extend the algorithm to route a permutation on an n-node complete d-ary tree in $(1 + \frac{1}{d^2-1})n + o(n)$, and finally we extend the later algorithm to achieve a routing time of $n + o(n)$ steps.

We also present an algorithm that routes a permutation on a bounded-degree tree of n nodes within $2n + o(n)$ routing steps. For trees of maximum-degree 3, the algorithm requires at most $2n$ routing steps. Our algorithm can be considered to be an extension of the algorithm of Alon, Chung and Graham [2, 3]. We manage to show that it is possible to partially overlap the first two major steps of their algorithm. For arbitrary trees of n nodes, application of this idea results in an algorithm that routes any permutation within $\frac{13}{5}n$ steps.

During the course of our off-line tree routing algorithms, we need to have the tree heap-ordered with respect to key-values assigned to the packets at its nodes. For this reason, we use an algorithm that can be considered to be an extension of the odd-even transposition method. The same algorithm was used for building a heap priority queue (i.e., a complete binary tree) in an EREW-PRAM environment [7, 10]. We show that an arbitrary rooted tree of height h can be heap-ordered within $2h$ routing steps. While the proof originally reported in [7] appears to generalise to arbitrary trees, we provide an analysis based on potential functions.

The paper is organised as follows: In Section 2, we present definitions used throughout the paper. In Section 3, we present the heap construction algorithm. Sections 4 and 5 are devoted to routing on complete trees. In Section 6, we consider routing on bounded degree trees and arbitrary trees. Space limitations force us to omit a large amount of technical details, including almost all proofs. These details can be found in [8].

2 Preliminaries

A *tree* $T = (V, E)$ is an undirected acyclic graph with node set V and edge set E. Throughout the paper we use standard graph theoretic terminology and we assume n-node trees, i.e., $|V| = n$. The *depth* $d_T(v)$ of node v is defined to be the distance from the root r to v. The *height* of tree T, denoted by $h(T)$, is defined to be $h(T) = max_{v \in V(T)} d_T(v)$. We say that node v is a *level-i node* (or, at *depth-level i*) if $d_T(v) = i$. The root of the tree is a level-0 node. We say that edge e is a *level-i edge* if it connects a level-i node with a level-$(i+1)$ node. All edges connected to the root r are level-0 edges. We denote by $lca(v,u)$ the *lowest common ancestor* of nodes v and u.

To comply with the usual drawing of rooted trees in which the root of a subtree is the topmost node of its drawing, we give some additional definitions. We say that a level-i node u is *below* a level-j node v if v is an ancestor of u (it is also implied that $i \leq j+1$). Equivalently, we say that node v is *above* node u. When v is the parent of u we use the terms *immediately above* and *immediately below*. Similar terminology is used for edges with respect to other edges/nodes.

A *subtree rooted at v*, denoted by T_v, consists of v, all descendants of v and the edges between them. A *partial tree* is a connected subgraph of a tree. (Note the difference between a subtree and a partial tree.) By T^i we denote the partial tree of T which is rooted at r and contains all level-j nodes, $0 \leq j \leq i$.

A *d-ary tree*, $d \geq 2$ is defined to be a rooted tree of which all internal nodes have exactly d children. A d-ary tree T is said to be *complete* if all of its leaves are level-$h(T)$ nodes. A complete d-ary tree has exactly d^i level-i nodes and its height is $h(T) = \lfloor \log_d n \rfloor$, where n is the number of nodes of the tree. We use a special naming convention for the nodes of complete d-ary tree T; the root r of the tree is denoted by $r_{(0,1)}$, and the children of the internal node $r_{(i,j)}$, $0 \leq i < h(T)$, $1 \leq j \leq d^i$ are $\{r_{(i+1,k)} \mid d(j-1)+1 \leq k \leq dj\}$. When we draw a complete d-ary tree we position node $r_{(i,j)}$ above node $r_{(k,l)}$ if $i < k$. We position node $r_{(i,j)}$ to the left of node $r_{(i,k)}$ if $j < k$. Figure 1 shows a complete ternary tree using the introduced naming and layout conventions.

Most of the work available on the routing number of trees is based on off-line recursive routing algorithms. In order to be able to apply recursion, we must identify subtrees in which all packets destined for nodes each subtree have arrived in it. We say that, for a given packet, a subtree is a *destination subtree* if it contains the node the packet is destined for. The following lemma considers the situation where we want to route packets to their destination subtree.

Lemma 1. *Consider a tree T (rooted at r) and a permutation to be routed. Let m be the number of packets that have to cross the root r in order to reach their destination and assume that these packets form partial trees rooted at the children of r. Then these m packets can be routed into their destination subtrees (rooted at children of r) within at most $m + d - 1$ steps, where d is the degree of r.*

3 Heap Construction on Rooted Trees

Consider a rooted tree T and let each node of T initially contain a packet. Moreover, let each packet have a *key-value* associated with it, with all key-values drawn from a totally ordered set. Our objective is to route the packets in such a way that, at the end of the routing, the tree is heap-ordered with respect to the key-values at its nodes.

We describe an algorithm that completes the task within $2h(T)$ routing steps. The algorithm works for arbitrary rooted trees and is a generalisation of the odd-even transposition sorting method [6, 1].

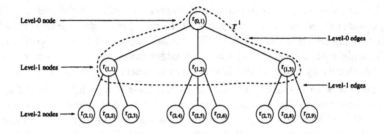

Fig. 1. A complete ternary tree.

Algorithm *Odd-Even_Heap_Construction(T)*
/* W.l.o.g., we assume that all key-values associated with the packets are distinct */

1. Assign label $h(T) - (i + 1)$ to each level-i edge, $0 \leq i < h(T)$.

2. $t = 0$

3. **While $t \leq 2h(T)$ do**

   (a) For any node u with edges connecting to its children labelled congruent to $t \bmod 2$, select out of the children of u the child, say v, that contains the packet of the smallest key-value. Order for a comparison between the key-values of the packets at u and v to take place at time t. If the key-value of the packet at v is smaller than the key value of the packet at u, a swap of the packets takes place.

   (b) $t = t + 1$

See [8] for a proof (based on a potential function) of the following theorem:

Theorem 2. *Algorithm* Odd-Even_Heap_Construction() *heap-orders any tree T in at most $2h(T)$ steps, where $h(T)$ is the height of the tree T.*

4 Routing on Complete Binary Trees

Consider the complete binary tree T of n nodes (Figure 2). Recall that a subtree rooted at node x is denoted by T_x and that by T^i we denote the complete partial tree of T of depth i.

Algorithm *Route_on_Complete_Binary_Trees*   /* RCBT, for short. */

1. Assign to every packet destined for a node in T^1 a class-value of 0. The remaining packets are assigned a class-value of 1.

2. Heap-order T with respect to the class-values of its packets.

3. Route the class-0 packets into the subtrees rooted at level-2 nodes such that each such subtree contains at most 1 class-0 packet.

4. Partition the packets into classes. A class-value is assigned to every packet based on its current position and its destination as follows:

Current node	Destination	Class-value	
$T_{r_{(1,1)}}$	$T_{r_{(2,3)}} \cup T_{r_{(2,4)}}$	0	
$T_{r_{(1,2)}}$	$T_{r_{(2,1)}} \cup T_{r_{(2,2)}}$	0	
r	$T_{r_{(2,1)}} \cup T_{r_{(2,2)}} \cup T_{r_{(2,3)}} \cup T_{r_{(2,4)}}$	0	
$T_{r_{(2,1)}}$	$T_{r_{(2,2)}}$	1	
$T_{r_{(2,2)}}$	$T_{r_{(2,1)}}$	1	
$T_{r_{(2,3)}}$	$T_{r_{(2,4)}}$	1	
$T_{r_{(2,4)}}$	$T_{r_{(2,3)}}$	1	
T	$\{r, r_{(1,1)}, r_{(1,2)}\}$	2	
$T_{r_{(2,i)}}$	$T_{r_{(2,i)}}$	3	$i = 1, 2, 3, 4$
$r_{(1,1)}$	$T_{r_{(2,1)}} \cup T_{r_{(2,2)}}$	2^*	
$r_{(1,2)}$	$T_{r_{(2,3)}} \cup T_{r_{(2,4)}}$	2^*	

5. Heap-order tree T with respect to the class-values of their packets. During the heap construction, update the class-values of packets as follows:

   - When a class-1 packet reaches the root of T, the packet immediately becomes a class-0 packet.
   - When a class-2^* packet enters its destination subtree, it immediately becomes a class-3 packet.
   - When a class-2^* packet enters a subtree that does not contain its destination, it immediately becomes a class-1 packet.
   - If at the end of the heap construction a class-2^* packet is still at a level-1 node, it becomes a class-1 packet.

6. Route the packets to their destination subtrees (T^1, and $T_{r_{(2,i)}}$, $i = 1, 2, 3, 4$).

7. Recursively route the packets in T^1, and $T_{r_{(2,i)}}$, $i = 1, 2, 3, 4$.

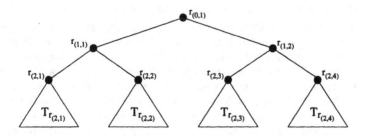

Fig. 2. A complete binary tree.

The first 5 steps are executed in order to ensure that the positions of the packets after Step 5 allow for the mplementation of Step 6 within at most $n + 2$ steps.

Some explanations are necessary regarding Steps 4 and 5 and the class updates that happen for some packets. According to the algorithm, if during the heap construction a class-1 packet reaches the root of T, then that packet becomes a class-0 packet. The reason for doing that is to stop packets from crossing the root to the other side of the tree. The class update does not affect the analysis of the heap construction algorithm since the packet will remain at the root till the end of the heap construction. Another possible class update is that of class-2* packets which become either class-1 or class-3 packets. Recall that a class-2* packet is initially located at a level-1 node and is destined for one of the subtrees rooted at its children. Firstly observe that during the heap-construction at Step 5, it is not possible for a class-2* packet to move to the root of T. This is because it will require that the class-2* packet is swapped with a class-3 packet which was at the root, a situation which cannot occur. Thus, the class-2* packets will either move to a node towards the leaves of the tree or they will remain in their current positions. In the case where a class-2* packet enters its destination subtree, we update it to a class-3 packet. Note that this update will not cause any problems to the heap construction algorithm, because the packet never moved upwards in the tree. If the class-2* packet enters the subtree which does not contain its destination, it becomes a class-1 packet. Again this class change does not cause any problems to the heap construction algorithm.

If during the heap construction a class-2* packet does not move, i.e., it remains at a level-1 node, it is updated to a class-1 packet. This update happens at the end of the heap construction algorithm and certainly does not affect its complexity.

A final comment regarding the first three steps of the algorithm. The purpose of these steps is to distribute the class-2 packets in a balanced way among subtrees $T_{r_{(1,1)}}$ and $T_{r_{(1,2)}}$. These steps are not really necessary. If we omit them we can still perform the routing on a complete binary tree in $\frac{4}{3}n + o(n)$ steps with the algorithm of this section but, the refinement of Step 6 that follows would be more complicated.

4.1   Refinement of Step 6

During the routing of Step 6, packets that enter their correct subtree continue to move towards the bottom of the subtree. Their movements stops when they reach a node such that all descendent nodes of it hold class-3 packets. This movement of packets towards the bottom of their destination subtree guarantees that the packets that have to leave the subtree will always be close to the root of the subtree.

Also note that no problems occur during the movement of a packet towards the leaves of the tree if the packet is swapped with another packet that wants to move upwards. This is because both packets move towards their destination subtree and that movement can be easily accommodated. The problems start when a packet that moved upwards because of a swap with another packet, reaches the node (other than the root) where it has to switch direction and start moving towards the leaves of the tree. In Step 6, this can only happen at the 2 level-1 nodes. This is because we are only interested in routing the packets to their destination subtree, not to their destination node. The reason that we would like the packets to switch the direction of their movement is because we do not want them to cross from one side of the tree to

5 Routing on Complete d-ary Trees

The algorithm is a generalisation of algorithm *Route_on_Complete_Binary_Trees*.

Algorithm *Route_on_Complete_d-ary_Trees*   /* $RCdT$, for short. */

1. Identical to Step 1 of Algorithm $RCBT$.

2. Identical to Step 2 of Algorithm $RCBT$.

3. Identical to Step 3 of Algorithm $RCBT$.

4. Partition the packets into classes. A class-value is assigned to packet p, currently at node *curr* and destined for node *dest*, as follows:

   - Let l be the level of the lowest common ancestor of nodes *curr* and *dest*, i.e., $l = d_T(lca(curr, dest))$.
   - **If** *dest* is in T^1 **then** p is a class-2 packet
     else if *curr* is a level-1 node and *dest* is in T_{curr} **then** p is a class-2* packet
     else if $l > 1$ **then** p is a class-3 packet
     else p is a class-l packet[3].

5. Identical to Step 5 of Algorithm $RCBT$.

6. Route the packets to their destination subtrees (T^1, and $T_{r_{(2,i)}}$, $1 \le i \le d^2$).

7. Recursively route the packets in T^1, and $T_{r_{(2,i)}}$, $1 \le i \le d^2$.

Lemma 5. *The routing that occurs during Step 6 of Algorithm RCdT terminates after at most $n + d^2 - 1$ routing steps.*

Proof. To prove the lemma we have to describe the details of the routing in Step 6. We can distinguish cases as we did for algorithm $RCBT$ but this will be a tedious repetition. Thus, we only describe what are the differences between the routing that takes place at Step 6 of algorithm $RBCT$ and that of algorithm $RBdT$.

Since in algorithm $RCBT$ we concerned with binary trees, in all sub-cases of parts 2 and 3 of the refinement of Step 6 there was only one sibling of node $T_{r_{2,1}}$ to consider. When routing in complete d-ary trees with algorithm $RCdT$, all sub-cases must be updated to account for the fact that each level-2 node has exactly $d - 1$ siblings. So, in the refinement of Step 6 of algorithm $RCdT$ case 2(a) is changed to: "$RBdT : 6.2(a)$ *There exists a sibling node of $T_{r_{2,1}}$ which contains a class-0 packet*", case 2(b) is changed to: "$RBdT : 6.2(b)$ *There exists a sibling node of $T_{r_{2,1}}$ which contains a class-1 packet*", and so on. Most importantly, these sub-cases are organised in an "if ... then ... else if ... else ..." statement. We only proceed to case 2(b) if we fail to locate a node satisfying case 2(a).

As in the analysis of algorithm $RCBT$ (Lemma 3, [8]), we can account for all "frozen steps" which involve class-1 packets. However, we have to pay the extra cost for the cases that a class-2 packet (located at a level-1 node) is swapped with a class-0

---

[3] Note that for complete binary trees the class assigned to each packet is identical with the class assigned by algorithm *Route_on_Complete_Binary_Trees*.

packet (located at a level-2 node). In this case, no class-2 packet will enter the same subtree (rooted at a level-2 node) twice. Because of the initial balancing, at most 2 class-2 packets are in each subtree rooted at a level-1 node. This implies that the extra number of routing steps for a given subtree rooted at a level-1 node is at most $2(d-1)$. This situation can occur at every subtree rooted at a level-1 node. Because of the initial balancing, in one subtree we can have at most $2(d-1)$ extra steps while in all of the remaining ones we can have a total of at most $(d-1)^2$ extra steps. We conclude that the total number of extra routing steps due to class-2 packets is $d^2 - 1$. Thus, the routing of Step 6 will terminate within $n + d^2 - 1$ steps. ∎

Note. See [8] for a more careful refinement of Step 6 of algorithm RCdT that requires $n + 2d$ steps.

Theorem 6. *Algorithm RCdT routes in an off-line fashion a permutation on an n-node complete binary tree of in at most $(1 + \frac{1}{d^2-1})n + o(n)$ steps.*

In [8], we stretch the method to its limits by firstly routing packets into their destination subtrees of $O(\sqrt{n})$ nodes. Algorithm *Fast_RCdT* is developed and we prove that:

Theorem 7. *Algorithm Fast_RCdT routes in an off-line fashion a permutation on a complete n-node d-ary tree in at most $n + o(n)$ steps.*

6 Routing on Arbitrary Trees

The design of recursive algorithms for a complete d-ary tree was facilitated by its property that the subtrees rooted at the children of its root have the same number of nodes. This property does not hold for arbitrary trees but, fortunately, we can identify a node which possesses a similar property that makes the design of recursive algorithms possible. The following theorem is considered to be part of the folklore in graph theory.

Theorem 8. *In any n-node tree T there exists a node r such that each tree in the forest resulting by removing r (and its adjacent edges) from T has at most $\lfloor \frac{n}{2} \rfloor$ nodes.*

Given the above theorem, it is quite easy to describe the algorithm of Alon, Chung and Graham [2, 3]. In their algorithm, they firstly locate a node r satisfying the property of Theorem 8 and then they assume that the tree, say T, is rooted at r. Let r have l children, denoted by r_i, $1 \le i \le l$, and let T_{r_i}, $1 \le i \le l$, be the subtrees rooted at children of r. We introduce some new notation here. Consider a packet that is currently at a node in subtree T_{r_i}, $1 \le i \le l$. If the destination of the packets does not belong to T_{r_i}, we say that the packet is an *improper* packet. Otherwise, we say that it is a *proper* packet. By $I(T_{r_i})$ and $P(T_{r_i})$ we denote the set of improper and proper packets at the beginning of the routing, respectively, in subtree T_{r_i}, $1 \le i \le l$. The algorithm of Alon, Chung and Graham contains three phases of routing. During the first phase they route the packets such that the improper packets in each subtree form a partial tree rooted at the root of the subtree. During the second phase the route all improper packets to their destination subtrees. The routing is then completed recursively.

Given a subtree T', Alon, Chung and Graham describe a greedy method to construct a partial tree rooted at its root within $|T'|$ steps (see [2, 3] for details). By realizing that the heap-ordering algorithm described in this paper can be also used to achieve the same goal, we conclude that the routing of the first phase on subtree T' can be completed within $\min(|T'|, 2h(T'))$ routing steps. The routing of the second phase is described in the proof of Theorem 1. Given the above, it is not difficult to show that the routing can be completed within $3n$ routing steps for an n-node tree (see [2, 3] for details). In this section, we show that it is possible to (partially) overlap in time the first two phases of their algorithm. By modifying their algorithm in this way, we first improve the upper bound for the routing number of an arbitrary bounded-degree tree from $rt(T) = 3n$ to $2n + o(n)$.

In the description of the algorithm we assume that a node r satisfying the property described in Theorem 8 has been already located and that tree T has been partitioned in subtrees T_{r_i} rooted at r_i, $1 \leq i \leq l$ (Figure 3).

Algorithm *Bounded_Degree_Tree_Routing*(T) /* *BDTR* for short */

1. $m = \max_{1 \leq i \leq l} |P(T_{r_i})|$

2. **Repeat** for m routing steps:
   > For each subtree T_{r_i}, $1 \leq i \leq l$, **do in parallel**
   >> move improper packets in T_{r_i} toward the root r_i;

3. **While** there still exist improper packets **do**
   begin

   (a) **If** the packet p currently at r has r as its destination **then**
      > let T' be a subtree containing improper packets

      else
      > let T' be the subtree containing the destination of the packet currently at r.

   (b) **For each** subtree T_{r_i}, $1 \leq i \leq l$, **do in parallel**
      if $T_{r_i} = T'$ **then**
      > swap the packet at r with the packet at the root of T_{r_i}

      else
      > move improper packets in T_{r_i} toward its root r_i. If the packet with destination r is in T_{r_i} ensure that it is the last one to be moved out of the subtree.

   end

4. **For each** subtree T_{r_i} **do in parallel**
   > *Bounded_Degree_Tree_Routing*(T_{r_i});

Theorem 9. *Algorithm* BDTR *routes in an off-line fashion any permutation on an n-node bounded-degree tree in at most $2n + o(n)$ steps.*

Theorem 10. *Algorithm* BDTR *(with a slight modification) routes in an off-line fashion any permutation on an n-node, maximum degree 3, tree in at most $2n$ steps.*

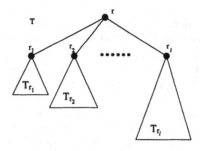

Fig. 3. Decomposing a tree T.

By incorporating the idea of partially overlapping the first two routing phases in the analysis of the algorithm of Alon, Chung and Graham [2, 3] we are also able to improve the upper bound for the routing numbers of arbitrary trees.

Theorem 11. *Any permutation on a tree with n nodes can be routed in at most $\frac{13}{5}n$ steps.*

References

1. S. Akl. *Parallel Sorting Algorithms.* Academic Press, 1985.

2. Alon, Chung, and Graham. Routing permutations on graphs via matchings. *SIAM Journal on Discrete Mathematics*, 7, 1994.

3. N. Alon, F. R. K. Chung, and R. L. Graham. Routing permutations on graphs via matchings (extended abstract). In *Proceedings of the 25th Annual ACM Symposium on Theory of Computing (San Diego, California, May 16–18, 1993)*, pages 583–591, New York, 1993. ACM SIGACT, ACM Press.

4. A. Borodin, Y. Rabani, and B. Schieber. Deterministic many-to-many hot potato routing, 1994. Unpublished manuscript.

5. N. Deo and S. Prasad. Parallel heap: An optimal parallel priority queue. *The Journal of Supercomputing*, 6(1):87–98, March 1992.

6. N. Haberman. Parallel neighbor-sort (or the glory of the induction principle). Technical Report AD-759 248, National Technical Information Service, US Department of Commerce, 5285 Port Royal Road, Springfieldn VA 22151, 1972.

7. N. Rao and W. Zhang. Building heaps in parallel. *Information Processing Letters*, 37:355–358, March 1991.

8. A. Roberts, A. Symvonis, and L. Zhang. Routing on trees via matchings. Technical Report TR-494, Basser Dept of Computer Science, University of Sydney, January 1995. Available from ftp://ftp.cs.su.oz.au/pub/tr/TR95_494.ps.Z.

9. A. Symvonis. Optimal algorithms for packet routing on trees. In *Proceedings of the 6th International Conference on Computing and Information (ICCI'94), Peterborough, Ontario, Canada*, pages 144–161, May 1994. Also TR 471, Basser Dept of Computer Science, University of Sydney, September 1993.

10. W. Zhang and R.E. Korf. Parallel heap operations on an EREW PRAM. *Journal of Parallel and Distributed Computing*, 20(2):248–255, February 1994.

A Ranking Algorithm for Hamilton Paths in Shuffle-Exchange Graphs*

Fred S. Annexstein and Eugene A. Kuchko

Department of ECECS
University of Cincinnati
Cincinnati, OH, USA 45221-0008

Abstract. In previous work, Feldmann and Mysliwietz [3] showed that every shuffle-exchange graph contains a Hamilton path. In this paper, we show that there is a linear time ranking algorithm associated with that Hamilton path. The ranking algorithm returns the rank-position of each node of the graph with respect to the order given by the Hamilton path. Ranking algorithms are important for they can be applied to yield efficient implementations of certain network emulations using SIMD-style parallel algorithms for translating node labels.

1 Introduction

In this paper we focus on the problem of logical reconfigurations involving the use of long embedded paths, in particular, Hamilton paths in shuffle-exchange graphs. The existence of Hamilton paths in shuffle-exchange graphs was shown in [3]. However, the existence of such paths does not imply that they may be used effectively in parallel computations on networks based on the shuffle-exchange graph. For example, some algorithms require that the rank position (in a linear ordering) of each node be predetermined [5].

In determining the rank position, we seek to avoid the sequential listing of all the nodes in the Hamilton path; a method that runs in time exponential in the size of the node labels. We show that such a listing is not required, for there exists an algorithm for ranking the nodes of the shuffle-exchange graph that runs in time linear in the length of a node label, i.e., logarithmic in the size of the graph. This algorithm can be applied to efficiently embed paths when run as a SIMD-style program. Hence, the ranking algorithm can be considered an efficient parallel implementation of a graph embedding [2].

Formally speaking, given a vertex-labeled graph equipped with a Hamilton path, a *ranking algorithm* takes as input the label of a node w and returns Rank(w) the rank of that node in that Hamilton path. The ranking algorithm we describe in this paper runs in time $O(|w|)$ linear in the length of the node label; we measure time by the number of bit operations. Our ranking algorithm is based in part on the linear time ranking algorithm for the standard Gray

---

* This research has been supported in part by NSF Grant CCR–93–09470. E-mail: fred annexstein@uc.edu, kuchkoe@ucunix.san.uc.edu

code [1, 6, 7]; also, we apply a result on computing prefix sums of the Gray code transition sequence, which may be of independent interest.

2 The Hamilton Path

In this section we review a construction, presented in [3], for a Hamilton path P in the shuffle-exchange graph. We show how to decompose the structure of P so that a ranking function for the path can be determined.

The order-n *shuffle-exchange graph* is the graph whose node-set is all n-bit strings. The edges (considered as opposing directed arcs) are defined as follows: given $a \in \{0,1\}$ and $w \in \{0,1\}^{n-1}$,

$$aw \leftrightarrows wa \leftrightarrows w\bar{a}$$

In this paper, we will consider only the case of order-n shuffle-exchange graphs where $n \geq 5$ and n is odd; the case where n is even is handled by similar techniques.

For $j \leq n-4$ odd, $\alpha \in \{0,1\}$, let $S_{\alpha,j}$ denote the set of all 2^{n-j-2} nodes of the form $\alpha 0^j 1 w$. In the path P, the nodes of $S_{\alpha,j}$ are visited in a certain natural order, beginning at node labeled $\alpha 0^j 101^{n-j-3}$ and terminating at the node labeled $\alpha 0^j 1^{n-j-1}$. The subpath connecting all the nodes of $S_{\alpha,j}$ is such that the subpath contains no nodes from any other distinct $S_{\alpha',j'}$; let $S^*_{\alpha,j}$ denote this subpath. These subpaths themselves are connected in a natural order, and are hooked together by *transitional paths*. The path P is determined as follows:

$$0^n \overset{\bullet}{\rightsquigarrow} S^*_{0,n-4} \overset{1}{\rightsquigarrow} S^*_{1,n-4} \overset{0}{\rightsquigarrow} S^*_{0,n-6} \overset{1}{\rightsquigarrow} S^*_{1,n-6} \overset{0}{\rightsquigarrow} \cdots S^*_{0,1} \overset{1}{\rightsquigarrow} S^*_{1,1} \overset{\bullet\bullet}{\rightsquigarrow} 1^n$$

Our strategy for deriving a ranking algorithm is as follows: we first analyze the structure of the transitional paths $\overset{0}{\rightsquigarrow}, \overset{1}{\rightsquigarrow}$, and then the structure of each subpath $S^*_{\alpha,j}$. This will allow us to determine a relatively simple function **RankS()** that can be applied to each node of $S_{\alpha,j}$. Since it follows that all other nodes are within a distance $O(n)$ of one such node, we are able to efficiently rank them as well.

The structure of transitional paths

Table 1. below illustrates the structure of each of the transitional paths $\overset{0}{\rightsquigarrow}, \overset{1}{\rightsquigarrow}$ (cf. [3], pg. 253). Note that in the table we assume that $j + k + 3 = n$.

The lengths of each transitional path can be easily determined as follows. For each j, the transitional path $\overset{1}{\rightsquigarrow}$ that terminates at $S^*_{1,j}$ has length $2(n-j-3)+4$, and the transitional path $\overset{0}{\rightsquigarrow}$ that terminates at $S^*_{0,j}$ has length $2(n-j-3)+2$. The initial path $\overset{\bullet}{\rightsquigarrow}$ (including $S^*_{0,n-4}$) has length 12, and is a special case. Another special case is the final path $\overset{\bullet\bullet}{\rightsquigarrow}$ that has length $n+2$.

Table 1. Transitional paths structure

$\overset{0}{\rightsquigarrow}$	$\overset{1}{\rightsquigarrow}$
$10^{j+2}1^k \in S_{1,j+2}$	$0^{j+1}1^{k+2} \in S_{0,j}$
$110^{j+2}1^{k-1}$	$10^{j+1}1^{k+1}$
...	...
$1^k0^{j+2}1$	$1^{k+1}0^{j+1}1$
1^k0^{j+3}	$1^{k+1}0^{j+2}$
01^k0^{j+2}	01^k10^j0
01^k00^j1	01^k10^j1
1^k00^j10	1^k10^j10
...	...
100^j101^{k-1}	110^j101^{k-1}
$00^j101^k \in S_{0,j}$	$10^j101^k \in S_{1,j}$

The structure of subpath $S_{\alpha,j}^*$

For each string $\alpha 0^j 1w \in S_{\alpha,j}$, we let $w = u\beta$, where $\beta \in \{0,1\}$. Within the subpath, the nodes of $S_{\alpha,j}$ are ordered such that the respective u strings are ordered consistent with a (translated) standard Gray code ordering. Let $G(u)$ represent the rank-order of the string u in the Gray code ordering. We use the notation $S_{\alpha,j}(G(u), \beta)$ to denote the node $\alpha 0^j 1 u\beta \in S_{\alpha,j}$. The subpath $S_{\alpha,j}^*$ is determined by progressing through the listing of all $2^{n-j-3} = \ell$ pairs of nodes in $S_{\alpha,j}$ (consistent with the Gray code ordering of the associated u strings); and these node pairs are joined together by $\ell - 1$ *connecting paths*, illustrated as follows:

$$
\begin{aligned}
S_{\alpha,j}^* = \; & S_{\alpha,j}(0,1), S_{\alpha,j}(0,0) \\
& \overset{1-path}{\rightsquigarrow} S_{\alpha,j}(1,0), S_{\alpha,j}(1,1) \\
& \overset{2-path}{\rightsquigarrow} S_{\alpha,j}(2,1), S_{\alpha,j}(2,0) \\
& \overset{3-path}{\rightsquigarrow} \\
& \quad \cdots \\
& \overset{\ell-1-path}{\rightsquigarrow} S_{\alpha,j}(\ell-1,0), S_{\alpha,j}(\ell-1,1)
\end{aligned}
$$

We note two properties of the subpath $S_{\alpha,j}^*$ that are important for the ranking algorithm: first, all pairs of nodes $S_{\alpha,j}(k, \beta)$, for fixed k and $\beta \in \{0,1\}$, appear consecutively, and second, the order of each such pair alternates, i.e., for each $1 \le k \le \ell - 1$ each connecting path $\overset{k-path}{\rightsquigarrow}$ terminates at $S_{\alpha,j}(k, (k+1) \bmod 2)$.

Each connecting path $\overset{k-path}{\rightsquigarrow}$ has a form as illustrated in Table 2. below (cf. [3], pg. 252). Note that in the table $S_{\alpha,j}(k-1)$ denotes the pair of nodes $\alpha 0^j 1 u\beta$, where $G(u) = k$. The length of the connecting path $\overset{k-path}{\rightsquigarrow}$ is determined by twice t_k, that is the kth value in the Gray code transition sequence. To compute the total length of the collection of connecting paths leading up to a

Table 2. Connecting path structure

$$
\left.
\begin{array}{l}
\alpha 0^j 1 u \beta \\
\alpha 0^j 1 u \bar\beta
\end{array}
\right\} S_{a,j}(k-1)
$$

$$
\left.
\begin{array}{l}
\bar\beta\, \alpha\, 0^j 1 u_l \cdots u_{t_k} \cdots u_1 \\
\cdots \\
u_{t_k-1}\cdots u_1\bar\beta\,\alpha\,0^j1u_l\cdots u_{t_k} \\
u_{t_k-1}\cdots u_1\bar\beta\,\alpha\,0^j1u_l\cdots \bar u_{t_k} \\
\cdots \\
\bar\beta\,\alpha\,0^j1u_l\cdots \bar u_{t_k}\cdots u_1
\end{array}
\right\} k\text{-path}
$$

$$
\left.
\begin{array}{l}
\alpha 0^j 1 u_l\cdots \bar u_{t_k}\cdots u_1\beta \\
\alpha 0^j 1 u_l\cdots \bar u_{t_k}\cdots u_1\bar\beta
\end{array}
\right\} S_{a,j}(k)
$$

node, we need to look closer at the transition sequence, and prove some results about its partial sums.

3 The Gray code transition sequence

The Gray code transition sequence (GCTS) is the infinite sequence $\{t_i\} = \{12131214\ldots\}$, and can be defined recursively as follows: for each $i \geq 0$, $t_{2^i} = i+1$, and for each $1 \leq j < 2^i$, $t_j = t_{2^i+j}$. It is well known that if you take any n-bit string and flip bits corresponding to the first $2^n - 1$ elements of GCTS, that you will produce a listing of every n-bit string. There corresponds to this listing a simple ranking algorithm [1], described as follows.

Gray code ranking algorithm

Given an n-bit string $w = w_n \cdots w_1$, the rank of this string in the listing corresponding to GCTS (with starting string $a_n \cdots a_1$) we denote by **RankG**(w). The value of **RankG**(w) can be expressed in binary as $r_n \cdots r_1$, where for each $0 \leq \ell \leq n-1$,

$$
r_\ell = \left(\sum_{i=\ell}^{n} w_i + a_i\right) \mod 2.
$$

In other words, the rank number (in binary) is an xor-scan of the (bit-wise) sum of the node-label and the initial node.

Prefix sums of GCTS

The following result is easily derived from structure of the GCTS.

Proposition 1. *The sum of the first $2^k - 1$ numbers in the Gray code transition sequence is*

$$\sum_{i=1}^{2^k-1} t_i = \sum_{i=1}^{k} i2^{k-i} = 2^{k+1} - k - 2.$$

□

We now prove a proposition that shows that each prefix sum of the GCTS is easily computable, i.e., it can be calculated in time logarithmic in the number of terms in the sum. For the following, let $k > 0$, and let k_i be the ith bit in the binary representation of k; also, let $\#(k)$ denote $\sum k_i$ the number of one bits in the binary representation of k.

Proposition 2. *The sum of the first k numbers in the Gray code transition sequence is*

$$\sum_{i=1}^{k} t_i = \sum_{i=1}^{q} k_i(2^{i+1} - 1) = 2k - \#(k)$$

Proof. From Proposition 1, it follows that the sum for values of $k = 2^q$ that are powers of 2 is $\sum_{i=1}^{2^q} t_i = 2^{q+1} - 1$, since the last term of sum is $q + 1$. Hence, the proposition holds for this case. For values of k not a power of 2, notice that any length-k prefix of the GCTS is simply the concatenation of prefixes that are each of length a (decreasing) power of 2. Hence, by considering k in its binary representation of $k_q k_{q-1} \cdots k_1$ we can apply the previous derived sum over each bit k_i, and the result follows. □

4   Computing the rank on $S_{\alpha,j}$

We can calculate the total length of the subpath $S^*_{\alpha,j}$ by summing the number of nodes in $S_{\alpha,j}$ and the lengths of each of the intermediate connecting paths $\overset{k-path}{\leadsto}$ as given by Proposition 1.

$$|S^*_{\alpha,j}| = 2^{n-j-2} + \sum_{i=1}^{2^{n-j-2}-1} 2t_i = 3 \cdot 2^{n-j-2} - 2(n - j - 1).$$

We can now rank the initial nodes of each $S^*_{\alpha,j}$ by summing up the lengths of the $S^*_{\alpha,j}$ subpaths and the intermediate connecting paths. Simple arithmetic yields the following.

Proposition 3. *For each $j \leq n-6$, the rank of the initial nodes of each set $S_{\alpha,j}$ is given as follows*

$\text{Rank}(S_{0,j}(0,1)) = 2^{n-j-1} + n - j - 6$
$\text{Rank}(S_{1,j}(0,1)) = 5 \cdot 2^{n-j-2} + n - j - 6.$

□

These results lead us to a linear time function to rank all nodes $w \in S_{\alpha,j}$. Our strategy is as follows: we first find the rank of the first node in the path $S_{\alpha,j}^*$ as determined by Proposition 3. Next we determine the distance of w from this initial node by summing the number of nodes of $S_{\alpha,j}$ preceding w and the total length of the preceding connecting paths $\overset{k-path}{\rightsquigarrow}$ (as follows from Proposition 2). This offset from the initial node in the subpath is found by applying the Gray code ranking algorithm. Finally we may need to adjust by one, according to the last bit β. The correctness of the ranking function RankS follows from our previous discussion of the structure of the path.

The following algorithm will rank all nodes of $S_{\alpha,j}$ where $j \leq n-6$; the other case ($j = n - 4$) can be done by table lookup.

function **RankS**$(\alpha 0^j 1 u \beta) =$
1. Compute $first := \text{Rank}(S_{\alpha,j}(0,1))$ // see Proposition 3.
2. Compute $k := \text{RankG}(u)$
   // apply the Gray code ranking algorithm with initial string $011 \cdots 1$.
3. If k is odd then let $b := \beta$ else let $b := 1 - \beta$
   // make adjustment based on last bit and parity of k
4. Return $first + 2k + 2(2k - \#(k)) + b$

5 The Main Ranking Algorithm

We are now ready to describe the full ranking algorithm to rank any node in the shuffle-exchange graph. Our strategy is as follows: given an n-bit string w we first determine the subpath $S_{\alpha,j}^*$ or transitional path that w is contained in. This is accomplished by scanning from the left end of w for the first match of a pattern $\alpha 0^j 1$ where $j \leq n - 4$ is odd. If such a pattern is found then we know that w is either a node of $S_{\alpha,j}^*$ or on an adjacent transitional path. If the pattern is not matched, then it is still possible for w to lie on a transitional path $\overset{0}{\rightsquigarrow}$ (see middle of Table 1). By flipping the last bit and again scanning for the pattern, we can then determine the nearest $S_{\alpha,j}$ node. In our ranking algorithm we set a bit $exflag$ to record whether this action was taken. If we fail to match the pattern this second time, we then know that w must lie on one of the special case paths, and we go to a table lookup. Finally, we can use our previously defined RankS function to determine the rank of w by adding (or subtracting) the number of shuffles to reach the nearest $S_{\alpha,j}$ node; this nearest $S_{\alpha,j}$ node can be found by shuffling in a direction determined by the parity of the Gray code ranking of the substring u and the bit β.

The correctness of the algorithm follows from the previous analysis of the structure of the Hamilton path P.

function **Rank**$(w)=$
1. Scan the string w from the left for the first occurrence of the pattern $\alpha 0^j 1$,
   where $j \leq n - 4$ is odd, and $\alpha \in \{0, 1\}$.
2. If pattern is found, set $exflag := 0$

Else flip the last bit, and scan again.

If the pattern is found, then set $exflag := 1$

Else goto tablelookup /* the node is in a special case path (i.e., $\leadsto$ or $\overset{\bullet\bullet}{\leadsto}$) */

3. Let $pos :=$ position from the left where the pattern starts.

4. Assign $\beta :=$ bit preceding α, and $u :=$ the remaining (wrapped) bit-string.

5. If $((G(u)$ is odd) and $(\beta = 0))$ or $((G(u)$ is even) and $(\beta = 1))$

then return Rank $= \text{RankS}(\alpha 0^j 1 u \beta) - pos - exflag$

else return Rank $= \text{RankS}(\alpha 0^j 1 u \beta) + pos + exflag$

6 Conclusion

We have described a linear time ranking algorithm for the Hamilton path of the shuffle-exchange graph described in [3]. Although the algorithm is asymptotically optimal, clearly a simpler Hamilton path and ranking algorithm would be preferable. In contrast, there is a simple (recursive) ranking algorithm for a Hamilton path in the related (undirected) De Bruijn graph [1]. However, this ranking algorithm runs in $O(n^2)$ time. By a simple transformation of node labels it can be seen that the shuffle-exchange graph is a subgraph of the De Bruijn graph [4]. Hence, from the results in this paper it follows that there is a linear time ranking algorithm for the (undirected) De Bruijn graph. It remains an open problem whether there is a similarly efficient ranking algorithm for a Hamilton circuit in the directed De Bruijn graph.

Finally, an *unranking algorithm* takes as input an integer r and returns the label of the rth-ranked node in the Hamilton path. It is not difficult to apply the results in this paper to produce a linear time unranking algorithm for the shuffle-exchange (based on the unranking of Gray codes).

References

1. F.S. Annexstein (1994): Ranking algorithms for hamiltonian paths in hypercubic networks, to appear in AMS DIMACS series, Proceedings of the DIMACS Workshop on Interconnection Networks and Mapping and Scheduling Parallel Computations.

2. F.S. Annexstein (1993): Parallel implementations of graph embeddings, in *Parallel Architectures and Their Efficient Use*, Lecture Notes in Computer Science 678, Springer Verlag, 207–217.

3. R. Feldmann and P. Mysliwietz (1992): The shuffle exchange network has a Hamiltonian path, Proceedings of 17th Mathematical Foundations of Computer Science (MFCS '92), Lecture Notes in Computer Science 629, Springer Verlag, 246–254.

4. R. Feldmann and W. Unger (1992): The cube-connected cycles network is a subgraph of the butterfly network. *Parallel Processing Letters (2)*, 1, 13–19.

5. D.M. Gordon (1991): Parallel sorting on Cayley graphs. *Algorithmica (6)*, 554–564.

6. F. Gray (1953): Pulse code communication, U.S. Patent Number 2,632,058.

7. H.S. Wilf (1989): Combinatorial algorithms: an update, CBMS-55, SIAM.

Amortization Results for Chromatic Search Trees, with an Application to Priority Queues

Joan Boyar, Rolf Fagerberg, Kim S. Larsen

Odense University

Abstract. The intention in designing data structures with relaxed balance, such as chromatic search trees, is to facilitate fast updating on shared-memory asynchronous parallel architectures. To obtain this, the updating and rebalancing have been uncoupled, so extensive locking in connection with updates is avoided.

In this paper, we prove that only an amortized constant amount of rebalancing is necessary after an update in a chromatic search tree. We also prove that the amount of rebalancing done at any particular level decreases exponentially, going from the leaves towards the root. These results imply that, in principle, a linear number of processes can access the tree simultaneously.

We have included one interesting application of chromatic trees. Based on these trees, a priority queue with possibilities for a greater degree of parallelism than in previous proposals can be implemented.

1 Introduction

A chromatic search tree [15, 7] is a binary search tree for shared-memory asynchronous parallel architectures. It was introduced with the aim of allowing processes to lock nodes, in order to avoid inconsistencies from updates and rebalancing operations, without decreasing the degree of parallelism too much. The means for obtaining this was a new balance criteria, referred to as relaxed balance, along with new uncoupled operations for updating and rebalancing.

The rebalancing is taken care of by background processes in small independent steps; the processes do only a constant amount of work before they release locks and move on to another problem. This means that the traditional exclusive locking of whole paths or step-wise exclusive locking down paths, which would limit the amount of parallelism possible to the height of the tree, does not take place. Another advantage of the uncoupling of the rebalancing from the updating is that all or parts of the rebalancing can be postponed until after peak working hours. The disadvantage, of course, is that the tree can become very unbalanced if there are not enough background processes doing the rebalancing.

Since the rebalancing is done in small independent steps, which can be interspersed with other updating and rebalancing operations, an actual proof of complexity is not straight-forward, and the original proposal in [15] did not contain any such proof. In [7], the proposal of [15] was analyzed, and it was proven that some updating could give rise to a super-logarithmic number of rebalancing operations. A modified set of rebalancing operations was proposed, and it was proven that the new set of rebalancing operations give rise to at most $\lfloor \log_2(n+i) \rfloor$ rebalancing operations per insertion and at most $\lfloor \log_2(n + i) \rfloor - 1$ rebalancing operations per deletion, if i insertions are performed on a tree which initially contains n leaves. Furthermore, the number of operations which actually change the structure of the tree is at most one per update. Compared to [15], a small constant number of extra locks per rebalancing operation are necessary in [7].

Having obtained logarithmic worst-case bounds, the next result to hope and search for when dealing with trees is an amortized constant number of rebalancing operations. It turns out that the proposal from [7] has these properties, though in order to get the best possible constant, one operation should be modified slightly. In this paper, we prove that, starting with an empty tree, i insertions and d deletions give rise to at most $3i + d - 2$ rebalancing operations. We also show that the number of rebalancing operations which can occur at weighted height h is at most $3i/2^{h-1}$. The latter result is especially important in a parallel environment, since many of the rebalancing operations require exclusive locks on the nodes they are accessing. The higher up in the tree a lock occurs, the larger the subtree which cannot be accessed by other operations. Our results imply that, in principle, $\Theta(n)$ processors can simultaneously access the tree, since searching does not require exclusive locking. The results are obtained assuming, as is standard in amortized analyses, that the structure is initially empty, though we also have results for the case where the structure is initially non-empty.

In the last part of the paper, we discuss one particularly interesting application of chromatic trees in greater detail. From the sequential case, it is known that in some cases search tree implementations of priority queues give better performance than heap implementations [11]. In our setting of a shared-memory architecture, it turns out that a variation of a chromatic search tree, used as a priority queue, allows for a greater degree of parallelism than in previous proposals for priority queues. The priority queue is suited for branch and bound and similar applications.

Our results supplement previous work on relaxed search trees. The chromatic search tree is a relaxed version of red-black trees [3, 8]. This structure was introduced in [15] and analyzed in [7]. A relaxed version of (a, b)-trees [10] was analyzed in [14]. Both of the common B-trees [4], 2-3 trees [2, 9], and 2-3-4 trees [8] have relaxed versions, the properties of which are also discussed in [14]. The first relaxed version of a B-tree is from [16]. The analysis of the behavior of a relaxed version of AVL trees [1] introduced in [16] was given in [13].

2 Chromatic Search Trees

In this section, we describe chromatic search trees, noting a couple of minor changes from earlier definitions [15, 7]. Chromatic trees are *leaf-oriented* binary search trees, so the keys are stored in the leaves and the internal nodes only contain *routers* which guide the search through the tree. The router stored in a node v is greater than or equal to any key in the left subtree and less than any key in the right subtree. The routers are not necessarily keys which are present in the tree, since the node containing the corresponding key may have been deleted. The tree is a *full* binary tree, so each node has either zero or two children.

Since chromatic trees are a relaxation of red-black trees, the nodes have weights[1], which are restricted to being only zero or one in a red-black tree, but can be greater than one in a chromatic tree. This relaxation means that the data structure can simply be left as it is after an update; the rebalancing is taken care of by other processes. Each node v in the tree has an associated nonnegative integer weight $w(v)$. If $w(v) = 0$, we call the node *red*; if $w(v) = 1$, we say the node is *black*; and if $w(v) > 1$, we say the node is *overweighted*. The *weight* of a path is the sum of the weights of its nodes, and the *weighted level* of a node is the weight of the path from the root to that node.

For completeness, we give definitions for both red-black trees and chromatic trees.

Definition 1. A *red-black tree* is a full binary search tree T with the following balance conditions:

B1: The leaves of T are black.
B2: All leaves of T have the same weighted level.
B3: No path from T's root to a leaf contains two consecutive red nodes.
B4: T has only red and black nodes.

Definition 2. A *chromatic tree* is a full binary search tree T with the following conditions:

C1: The leaves of T are not red.
C2: All leaves of T have the same weighted level.

The insertion and deletion operations are depicted in the appendix, along with the rebalancing operations. Squares denote leaves, circles denote general nodes (either internal nodes or leaves), and the labels denote weights. For the sake of intelligibility, the subtrees of internal nodes are not shown. An operation can be applied in any circumstances that match the left-hand side depicted, except for the blacking operation, which has one more restriction: it can only be applied if at least one of the two lower nodes has a child of weight zero. Note that we do not list symmetric cases. We also omit showing separately the special cases which apply at the root. Whenever an operation changes the weight of the root, as part of the operation, the weight of the root is set to one (thus, the weight of the root is always one). The order in which operations are applied is unrestricted. All results stated in this paper are independent of the order in which operations are carried out. Note that the third weight decreasing operation from [7] has been modified slightly in order to obtain the results in this paper. The results of [7] still hold with this modification.

---

[1] In earlier definitions of chromatic trees, the weights were associated with the edges, but here we place them on the nodes to conform with standard usage. The results in this paper and [7] hold in either formulation.

The proper location for an insertion or deletion is found by searching, as in any binary search tree. Thus, an insertion will take $O(\log n)$ time, where n is the size of the chromatic tree at that time, if the structure is still reasonably close to being a red-black tree. The actual update, however, only requires constant time.

The rebalancing operations are defined so that if, at any point, no further updates occur, but rebalancing occurs as long as any operation is applicable, then the chromatic tree will eventually become red-black [7]. The rebalancing operations are employed as follows. If a chromatic tree is not a red-black tree, it must have either two consecutive red nodes on some root-to-leaf path (a *red-red conflict*) or a node with weight greater than one (an *overweighted node*). These problems are easily identified when they are created. When a problem is identified, a pointer to the lowest node involved is placed in a problem queue for the rebalancing processes. (We do not address the problem of maintaining a "problem queue" in this paper.) If a rebalancing process creates another red-red conflict or another overweighted node, it can also easily recognize this and put a pointer to it in the problem queue. A process performing a rebalancing operation will need to find the parent of the node it finds through the problem queue. For this purpose, it is necessary for each node to have a parent pointer, in addition to left and right child pointers. In addition, a locking scheme is necessary. One possible scheme is described in detail in [6].

The red-red conflicts result in blacking operations or red-balancing operations. The latter are referred to as (rb1) and (rb2) in the appendix. Overweighted nodes result in push operations or weight decreasing operations. The latter are referred to as (w1) through (w7) in the appendix.

3 Complexity

In this section, we give new bounds on the worst case number of rebalancing operations necessary in order to restore balance after updates. Our main result is that, starting with an empty chromatic tree, a very small constant number of rebalancing operations per update are needed to keep the structure balanced. We also define the weighted height of an operation, which is closely related to the actual height at which it is taking place in the structure, and show that, in chromatic trees, the number of rebalancing operations of weighted height h is an exponentially decreasing function of h. Results for $(2, 4)$-trees, similar to the ones presented in this section, can be found in [10], which has given inspiration for the proofs presented here.

In chromatic trees, all paths starting at the same node and ending at a leaf will have the same weight. We define the *weighted height* of a node to be the weight of any path from that node to a leaf.

Definition 3. The *weighted height of an operation* in a chromatic tree is the weighted height, before the operation occurs, of the children of the top node of the operation, except for insertions, where it is the weighted height of the single leaf present before the operation.

Thus, the weighted height of a weight decreasing or push operation is at least two, and the rest of the operations have weighted height at least one. If the chromatic tree is close to being red-black, the weighted height is closely related to the actual height at which the operation takes place. Thus, if the necessary rebalancing operations are carried out concurrently with the updates, our definition is a good measure of the actual height of the operation. We can now state our main theorem:

Theorem 4. *If $i > 0$ insertions and d deletions are performed on an initially empty chromatic tree, then at most $3i + d - 2$ rebalancing operations can occur. Furthermore, the number of rebalancing operations of weighted height h that can occur is bounded by $3i/2^{h-1}$ for $h \geq 2$, and by i for $h = 1$.*

The theorem will follow from the lemmas below. These all apply to the situation where i insertions, d deletions, and some rebalancing operations have taken place on an initially empty chromatic tree. This will not be repeated in the statements of the lemmas. We let $d_h, b_h, r_h, w1_h, \ldots, w7_h$ and p_h denote the number of deletions, blacking operations, red-balancing operations, weight decreasing operations $1, \ldots, 7$ and push operations, respectively, of weighted height h that have occurred. To simplify the statements of the lemmas, we also define $b_0, w1_1, w2_1, w7_1$, and p_1 (these would otherwise be undefined) as follows: $b_0 = i$ and $w1_1 = w2_1 = w7_1 = p_1 = 0$.

Lemma 5. *For $h \geq 1$, $b_h \leq i/2^h$.*

Proof. Let T denote a chromatic tree. Call the edges above red nodes *red edges*. By the *red connected components* in T, we mean the connected components of the subgraph induced by the red edges. All red nodes in such a component have the same weighted height. By the *height of a red connected component*, we mean the weighted height of any of its red nodes. We let $C_h(T)$ denote the set of red connected components of height h in T and define a sequence, $\Phi_h(T)$, $h \in \{1, 2, 3, \ldots\}$, of potential functions on T, by $\Phi_h(T) = \sum_{r \in C_h(T)}(|r| - 1)$. Here, $|r|$ means the number of red nodes in r. An operation of weighted height k can change $\Phi_h(T)$ for some h's. Denoting this change by $\Delta\Phi_h(T)$, we note:

- For any *insertion*, $\Delta\Phi_1(T) \leq 1$ and $\Delta\Phi_h(T) = 0$, for $h \neq 1$.
- For a *blacking operation* of weighted height k, $\Delta\Phi_k(T) \leq -2$, $\Delta\Phi_{k+1}(T) \leq 1$, and otherwise $\Delta\Phi_h(T) = 0$, for $h \notin \{k, k+1\}$.
- For any other operation, $\Delta\Phi_h(T) \leq 0$, for all h.

These facts can be verified by a tedious inspection of the operations in the appendix. For an empty chromatic tree, T_0, $\Phi_h(T_0) = 0$ for all h, so by the facts above, $\Phi_1(T) \leq i - 2b_1$ and $\Phi_h(T) \leq b_{h-1} - 2b_h$, for $h \geq 2$. As $\Phi_h(T)$ is never negative, this implies that $b_1 \leq i/2$ and $b_h \leq b_{h-1}/2$ for $h \geq 2$, from which the lemma follows. $\square$

Lemma 6. *For $h \geq 1$, $b_h + r_h \leq b_{h-1}$.*

Proof. The two nodes in a red-red conflict have the same weighted height, which we call the height of the red-red conflict. Denote by $\mathcal{R}_h(T)$ the number of red-red conflicts of height h in T. The following facts can be verified by inspection of the operations:

- For any *insertion*, $\Delta\mathcal{R}_1(T) \leq 1$ and $\Delta\mathcal{R}_h(T) = 0$, for $h \neq 1$.
- For a *blacking operation* of weighted height k, $\Delta\mathcal{R}_k(T) \leq -1$, $\Delta\mathcal{R}_{k+1}(T) \leq 1$, and $\Delta\mathcal{R}_h(T) = 0$, for $h \notin \{k, k+1\}$.
- For a *red-balancing operation* of weighted height k, $\Delta\mathcal{R}_k(T) = -1$ and $\Delta\mathcal{R}_h(T) = 0$, for $h \neq k$.
- For any other operation, $\Delta\mathcal{R}_h(T) \leq 0$, for all h.

For an empty chromatic tree, T_0, $\mathcal{R}_h(T_0) = 0$ for all h, so by the facts above, $\mathcal{R}_1(T) \leq i - (r_1 + b_1)$ and $\mathcal{R}_h(T) \leq b_{h-1} - (r_h + b_h)$, for $h \geq 2$. As $\mathcal{R}_h(T)$ is never negative, the lemma follows. □

For the proofs of the next two lemmas, we need the following definition. For any chromatic tree T, we define an *expanded tree*, T', containing only nodes of weight 0 and 1. T' is constructed from T by replacing each overweighted node by a path, the length of which is equal to the weight of the original node minus one. All nodes on the path have weight 1. We call all nodes on the path, except the one closest to the leaves, *heavy*. Red and black nodes in T are left unchanged in T', except for the root, which is replaced by a path of nodes of weight 1 extending infinitely upwards. In the following example, heavy nodes are marked by an asterisk.

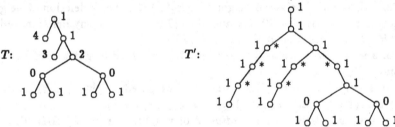

The expanded tree T_0' for the empty tree T_0 is defined as a path containing nodes of weight 1 extending infinitely upwards. As before, the weighted height of a node in T' is defined as the weight of any path from the node to a leaf. One can think of T' as a way of assigning appropriate weighted heights to the overweight in T.

Lemma 7. *For $h \geq 1$, $d_h + w1_h + w2_h + w7_h + p_h \leq b_{h-1}$.*

Proof. For a chromatic tree, T, we define a sequence $\Psi_h(T)$, $h \in \{1, 2, 3, \ldots\}$, of potential functions on T, letting $\Psi_h(T)$ denote the number of non-red nodes of weighted height h in the expanded tree T'. An operation of weighted height k can change T and thereby T', resulting in a change in $\Psi_h(T)$ for some h's. We denote this change by $\Delta\Psi_h(T)$. The following facts can be verified by inspecting the operations on T and drawing the expanded tree T' before, as well as after,

- For any *insertion*, $\Delta\Psi_1(T) \le 1$ and $\Delta\Psi_h(T) = 0$, for $h \ne 1$.
- For a *blacking operation* of weighted height k, $\Delta\Psi_{k+1}(T) = 1$ and $\Delta\Psi_h(T) = 0$, for $h \ne k+1$.
- For any other operation, $\Delta\Psi_h(T) \le 0$, for all h. In particular, for a *deletion* not resulting in an empty tree, a *weight decreasing operation 1, 2 or 7* or a *push operation* of weighted height k, $\Delta\Psi_k(T) = -1$.

For sequences of operations where there is always at least one node in the tree, except initially, the lemma is proven as follows. For an empty chromatic tree T_0, $\Psi_h(T_0) = 1$ for all h, so by the facts above, $\Psi_1(T) \le 1 + i - d_1$ and $\Psi_h(T) \le 1 + b_{h-1} - (d_h + w1_h + w2_h + w7_h + p_h)$, for $h \ge 2$. As $\Psi_h(T) \ge 1$ for all h and T, the desired inequality is proven. For more general sequences during which empty trees are encountered, the inequality will hold between any two consecutive empty trees. As no rebalancing occurs on an empty structure, the inequality holds for the entire sequence. □

Lemma 8. *For* $h \ge 2$, $z_h \le d_{h-1} + w7_{h-1} + p_{h-1}$, *where* $z_h = d_h + w1_h + w2_h + w3_h + w4_h + w5_h + w6_h + 2w7_h + p_h$.

Proof. In a chromatic tree, T, denote by $\mathcal{H}_h(T)$ the number of heavy nodes of weighted height h in the expanded tree T'. Note that $h \ge 2$, as there are no heavy nodes of weighted height 1 in T'. The following facts can be verified by inspection of the operations:

- For a *deletion* of weighted height 1, $\Delta\mathcal{H}_2(T) \le 1$. For a deletion of weighted height $k > 1$, $\Delta\mathcal{H}_{k+1}(T) \le 1$ and $\Delta\mathcal{H}_k(T) = -1$. For any deletion and any $\Delta\mathcal{H}_h(T)$ not mentioned above, $\Delta\mathcal{H}_h(T) \le 0$.
- For a *weight decreasing operation 1 to 6* of weighted height k, $\Delta\mathcal{H}_k(T) \le -1$ and $\Delta\mathcal{H}_h(T) = 0$, for $h \ne k$.
- For a *weight decreasing operation 7* of weighted height k, $\Delta\mathcal{H}_k(T) = -2$, $\Delta\mathcal{H}_{k+1}(T) \le 1$, and $\Delta\mathcal{H}_h(T) \le 0$, for $h \notin \{k, k+1\}$.
- For a *weight decreasing operation 7* of weighted height k, $\Delta\mathcal{H}_k(T) = -2$, $\Delta\mathcal{H}_{k+1}(T) \le 1$, and $\Delta\mathcal{H}_h(T) \le 0$, for $h \notin \{k, k+1\}$.
- For a *push* operation of weighted height k, $\Delta\mathcal{H}_k(T) = -1$, $\Delta\mathcal{H}_{k+1}(T) \le 1$, and $\Delta\mathcal{H}_h(T) = 0$, for $h \notin \{k, k+1\}$.
- For any other operation, $\Delta\mathcal{H}_h(T) \le 0$, for all h.

By the facts above, $\mathcal{H}_2(T) \le d_1 - z_2$ and $\mathcal{H}_h(T) \le d_{h-1} + w7_{h-1} + p_{h-1} - z_h$, for $h \ge 3$. The result follows. □

Proof of Theorem 4. The last part of Theorem 4 follows by adding the results of Lemmas 6 and 8 and using the two remaining lemmas. The first part of the theorem is proven as follows. Lemmas 5 and 6 imply that the total number of blacking and red-balancing operations cannot exceed $\lfloor \sum_{h=1}^{t} \frac{i}{2^{h-1}} \rfloor$, which is bounded by $2i - 1$ for all finite weighted heights t. In the same way, Lemmas 5 and 7 imply that the total number of push operations cannot exceed $i - 1$ (remember that a push operations has weighted height at least two). Overweight can only be introduced by deletions, each of which increases the total amount of overweight in the structure by at most one. Since each weight decreasing operation removes at least one unit of overweight, the number of weight decreasing operations is bounded by d. Adding these three bounds gives the first part of Theorem 4. $\square$

The first part of Theorem 4 can be improved to $\frac{5}{2}i + \frac{3}{2}d + \frac{1}{2}$ (see [6]). In addition, a version of Theorem 4 for the situation starting with a chromatic tree which is non-empty and red-black can also be proven, giving bounds on the number of rebalancing operations that can occur before the tree is again in balance. In the proofs of Lemmas 5 to 8, the value of the potential function of the initial tree should now appear in the inequalities at the end of the proofs, but it is not too difficult to give bounds on these values when the tree is red-black (details and proofs can be found in [6]). It turns out that if i insertions and d deletions are performed on an initially red-black tree containing $n > 0$ items, then at most $\frac{5}{2}i + \frac{3}{2}d + \frac{1}{2}(n-1)$ rebalancing operations can occur before the chromatic tree is again red-black. Furthermore, the number of rebalancing operations of weighted height $h > 1$ that can occur is bounded by $\frac{3}{2^{h-1}}i + \frac{3h-5}{2^{h+1}}n + \max\{1, \frac{n}{2^{h-3}}\} - \frac{1}{4^{h-3}}(n+i-d)$. Thus, when the number of updates is $\Omega(n)$, there are only $O(1)$ rebalancing operations per update. If the number of updates is much smaller than n, then the above bounds are not tight, but from [7] it is known that no more than $\lfloor \log_2(n+i) \rfloor$ rebalancing operations per update are ever needed.

4 Parallel Priority Queues

The problems with using priority queues in a parallel environment have been investigated extensively. Two different, largely incomparable, models for parallelism are used. One model deals with synchronous parallel processors, and the other model, which we use here, deals with asynchronous parallel processors which have access to a shared memory. In designing pointer-based priority queues to be used in such an environment, the problem of allowing processes to lock nodes, in order to avoid inconsistencies from updates and rebalancing operations, without decreasing the degree of parallelism too much, is even more serious than it is in the design of search trees, since small values are accessed frequently. Clearly, using a standard heap organization and locking the root before all updates creates a congestion problem at that node and forces sequentiality in the access to the data structure.

Previous work on priority queues in an environment with asynchronous parallel processes [5, 12, 17] all use some form of a heap [18]. Thus, the root has to be locked at the beginning of each deletemin operation, thereby preventing other processes from accessing the data structure during that time. In fact, [5] also locks the last node at the beginning of a deletemin. In [12, 17], the root is also locked at the beginning of an insertion, and step-wise locking down the update path is always used, thus further restricting the possibilities for parallelism. Additionally, since they all work on heap structures, insert as well as deletemin are $\Omega(\log n)$ in the worst case and this many locks are necessary, though not necessarily at the same time. In fact, even if data is drawn from a uniform distribution, the expected complexities for insert and deletemin are still $\Theta(\log n)$.

As already stated, binary search trees can sometimes be successfully used as priority queues. We present a quite competitive priority queue for a parallel asynchronous environment; it is based on chromatic search trees, with some modifications. The idea of uncoupling updating and rebalancing in a priority queue has also been considered in [5], but much more rebalancing is necessary there than in our proposal.

Since serializability cannot be guaranteed, our priority queue should be used when fast access is the key issue and the actual correctness of the algorithm in question does not depend on serializability (this includes the large class of problems solved using branch and bound techniques).

Our structure differs from previous work in that the processes doing updates need not have an exclusive lock on the root, so the number of processes which can work on the structure at any one time is not limited by the height of the tree: parallelism of the order the size of the tree is possible. The congestion problem is further reduced by the fact that our deletemin is constant time and the inserts (except for inserting a minimal element) proceed independently from deletemins.

4.1 Chromatic Priority Queues

Modifications of red-black and chromatic trees give us red-black and chromatic priority queues. These structures are also full binary leaf-oriented search trees, so the minimum element is the left-most leaf. Overweight is allowed on the left-most path, to decrease the amount of rebalancing necessary there and thus the probability of contention there. The operations used are those described in Sect. 2 for chromatic trees, so the updating is still uncoupled from the rebalancing.

Definition 9. A *red-black priority queue* is a red-black tree with a pointer to the element with minimum key and all of the leaves kept in a doubly linked list, except that conditions B1 and B4 from definition 1 are replaced with:

B1: The left-most leaf may be overweighted; all other leaves must be black.
B4: T has only red and black nodes, except on the left-most path.

Definition 10. A *chromatic priority queue* is a chromatic tree with a pointer to the element with minimum key and all of the leaves kept in a doubly linked list.

The pointer to the element with minimum key is used for the findmin and the deletemin operations. The doubly linked list of leaves facilitates updating this pointer after a deletemin, making the deletemin operation constant time. It is doubly linked, rather than singly linked, so that insertions can be done more efficiently; after the proper location is found by searching, as in a binary search tree, the actual update is constant time. Clearly, the findmin operation is also constant time, and so is creation of an empty queue.

Notice that allowing overweight on the left-most path does not change the fact that the length of any path in a red-black priority queue is $O(\log n)$. It does, however, decrease the amount of rebalancing necessary near the minimum element. If the only deletions allowed are deletemins, then the weight decreasing and push operations are unnecessary, as overweight can only move upwards and thus would remain on the left-most path.

In some applications of priority queues, it is useful to allow arbitrary deletions, in addition to the deletemin operation. Since chromatic trees have an arbitrary deletion operation and the necessary rebalancing operations, we can also allow these deletions in chromatic priority queues. Note that, as opposed to most other implementations of priority queues, searches for elements are supported and it is therefore not necessary to have a pointer to the element to be deleted. Introducing this deletion operation, however, creates the possibility of overweight nodes off the left-most path. The weight decreasing and push rebalancing operations can be used here, though we still never use them for the purpose of reducing overweight on the left-most path if that overweight is solely due to a deletemin operation.

It is clear that the chromatic priority queue can be made double-ended, simply by keeping a pointer to the maximum element, also, and allowing overweight on the right-most path. Results similar to those presented in the next section hold for double-ended priority queues.

4.2 Complexity

The complexity of chromatic priority queues is essentially the same as the complexity of the chromatic trees on which they are built, except that if deletemin operations are the only deletions made, then we can improve on the constants in the bounds, as we do not need to rebalance any overweight.

The results from [7] also apply to chromatic priority queues, though in a slightly modified version.

Theorem 11. *If i insertions and any number of deletemins are performed on a chromatic priority queue T, which initially is red-black and has n items (leaves), then at most $i(\lfloor \log_2(n + i - 1) \rfloor + 1)$ rebalancing operations can occur. In addition, the number of rebalancing operations which actually change the structure of the tree is at most i. If i insertions and d arbitrary deletions (excluding any deletemins) are performed, the result is $(i + d)(\lfloor \log_2(n + i - 1) \rfloor + 1) - d$, with at most $i + d$ rebalancing operations changing the structure of the tree.*

In the proofs of Lemmas 5 through 8, there is no assumption that the final tree is red-black. Thus, these lemmas still apply to chromatic priority queues, and we get the following results.

Theorem 12. *If $i > 0$ insertions and any number of deletemins are performed on an initially empty chromatic priority queue, then at most $2i - 1$ rebalancing operations can occur. Furthermore, the number of rebalancing operations of weighted height h that can occur is bounded by $i/2^{h-1}$. If $i > 0$ insertions and d arbitrary deletions (including deletemins) are performed on an initially empty* *chromatic priority queue with arbitrary deletions, then at most $3i + d - 2$ rebalancing operations can occur. Furthermore, the number of rebalancing operations of weighted height h that can occur is bounded by $3i/2^{h-1}$ for $h \geq 2$, and by i for $h = 1$.*

Proof. The last part is just a restatement of Theorem 4. The first part follows the proof of the same theorem, except that only Lemmas 5 and 6 are used, since blacking and red-balancing are the only rebalancing operations used. □

Extensions, similar to those mentioned for Theorem 4 at the end of Sect. 3, can also be made to Theorem 12. We refer the reader to [6] for this.

References

1. Adel'son-Vel'skiĭ, G. M., Landis, E. M.: An Algorithm for the Organisation of Information. Dokl. Akad. Nauk SSSR **146** (1962) 263–266 (In Russian. English translation in Soviet Math. Dokl. **3** (1962) 1259–1263)
2. Aho, A. V., Hopcroft, J. E., Ullman, J. D.: Data Structures and Algorithms. Addison-Wesley (1983)
3. Bayer, R.: Symmetric Binary B-Trees: Data Structure and Maintenance Algorithms. Acta Inform. **1** (1972) 290–306
4. Bayer, R., McCreight, E.: Organization and Maintenance of Large Ordered Indexes. Acta Inform. **1** (1972) 173–189
5. Biswas, J., Browne, J. C.: Simultaneous Update of Priority Structures. Proc. 1987 Intl. Conf. on Parallel Processing (1987) 124–131
6. Boyar, J., Fagerberg, R., Larsen, K. S.: Chromatic Priority Queues. Department of Mathematics and Computer Science, Odense University. Preprint 15 (1994)
7. Boyar, J. F., Larsen, K. S.: Efficient Rebalancing of Chromatic Search Trees. Journal of Computer and System Sciences **49** (1994) 667–682
8. Guibas, L. J., Sedgewick, R.: A Dichromatic Framework for Balanced Trees. 19th IEEE FOCS (1978) 8–21
9. Hopcroft, J. E.: Unpublished work on 2-3 trees. (1970)
10. Huddleston, S., Mehlhorn, K.: A New Data Structure for Representing Sorted Lists. Acta Inform. **17** (1982) 157–184
11. Jones, D. W.: An Empirical Comparison of Priority-Queue and Event-Set Implementations. Comm. ACM **29** (1986) 300–311
12. Jones, D. W.: Concurrent Operations on Priority Queues. Comm. ACM **32** (1989) 132–137
13. Larsen, K. S.: AVL Trees with Relaxed Balance. Proc. 8th Intl. Parallel Processing Symposium. IEEE Computer Society Press (1994) 888–893
14. Larsen, K. S., Fagerberg, R.: B-Trees with Relaxed Balance. (To appear in the proceedings of the 9th International Parallel Processing Symposium 1995)
15. Nurmi, O., Soisalon-Soininen, E.: Uncoupling Updating and Rebalancing in Chromatic Binary Search Trees. ACM PODS (1991) 192–198
16. Nurmi, O., Soisalon-Soininen, E., Wood, D.: Concurrency Control in Database Structures with Relaxed Balance. ACM PODS (1987) 170–176
17. Rao, V. N., Kumar, V.: Concurrent Access of Priority Queues. IEEE Trans. Computers **37** (1988) 1657–1665
18. Williams, J. W. J.: Algorithm 232: Heapsort. Comm. ACM **7** (1964) 347–348

Appendix: The Operations

Note that the blacking operation has one more restriction, which is not shown: it can only be applied if at least one of the two lower nodes has a child of weight zero.

Update Operations

$$\square \; w_1 \geq 1 \;\rightarrow\; {}_1 \quad {}^{w_1-1} \quad {}_1$$

(insert)

$$w_2 \quad {}^{w_1} \quad w_3 \;\rightarrow\; \bigcirc \; w_1 + w_3$$

(deletemin/delete)

Rebalancing Operations

$$0 \quad {}^{w_1 \geq 1} \quad 0 \;\rightarrow\; 1 \quad {}^{w_1-1} \quad 1$$

(blacking)

$$0 \quad {}^{w_1 \geq 1}, \; w_2 \geq 1, \; 0 \;\rightarrow\; 0 \quad {}^{w_1}, \; 0, \; w_2$$

(rb1)

$$0 \quad {}^{w_1 \geq 1}, \; w_2 \geq 1, \; 0 \;\rightarrow\; 0 \quad {}^{w_1}, \; 0, \; w_2$$

(rb2)

$$w_1 > 1, \; {}^{w_0}, \; 0, \; w_2 > 1 \;\rightarrow\; {}^{w_0}, \; 1, \; w_1-1, \; w_2-1$$

(w1)

$$w_1 > 1, \; {}^{w_0}, \; 0, \; w_2 > 0, \; w_3 > 0 \;\rightarrow\; {}^{w_0}, \; w_1-1, \; 1, \; 0, \; w_2, \; w_3$$

(w2)

$$w_1 > 1, \; {}^{w_0}, \; 0, \; 1, \; 0, \; w_2 > 0 \;\rightarrow\; {}^{w_0}, \; 0, \; 1, \; w_1-1, \; 1, \; w_2$$

(w3)

$$w_1 > 1, \; {}^{w_0}, \; 0, \; 1, \; w_2, \; 0 \;\rightarrow\; {}^{w_0}, \; 1, \; 0, \; w_1-1, \; w_2, \; 1$$

(w4)

$$w_2 > 1, \; {}^{w_1}, \; 1, \; w_3, \; 0 \;\rightarrow\; {}^{w_1}, \; 1, \; 1, \; w_2-1, \; w_3$$

(w5)

$$w_2 > 1, \; {}^{w_1}, \; 1, \; 0, \; w_3 > 0 \;\rightarrow\; {}^{w_1}, \; 1, \; 1, \; w_2-1, \; w_3$$

(w6)

$$w_2 > 1, \; {}^{w_1}, \; w_3 > 1 \;\rightarrow\; {}^{w_1+1}, \; w_2-1, \; w_3-1$$

(w7)

$$w_2 > 1, \; {}^{w_1}, \; 1, \; w_3 > 0, \; w_4 > 0 \;\rightarrow\; {}^{w_1+1}, \; w_2-1, \; 0, \; w_3, \; w_4$$

(push)

Fast Meldable Priority Queues

Gerth Stølting Brodal*

BRICS**
Department of Computer Science, University of Aarhus
Ny Munkegade, DK-8000 Århus C, Denmark

Abstract. We present priority queues that support the operations FIND-MIN, INSERT, MAKEQUEUE and MELD in worst case time O(1) and DELETE and DELETEMIN in worst case time O(log n). They can be implemented on the pointer machine and require linear space. The time bounds are optimal for all implementations where MELD takes worst case time o(n).

To our knowledge this is the first priority queue implementation that supports MELD in worst case constant time and DELETEMIN in logarithmic time.

Introduction

We consider the problem of implementing meldable priority queues. The operations that should be supported are:

MAKEQUEUE   Creates a new empty priority queue.

FINDMIN(Q)   Returns the minimum element contained in priority queue Q.

INSERT(Q, e)   Inserts element e into priority queue Q.

MELD(Q_1, Q_2)   Melds the priority queues Q_1 and Q_2 to one priority queue and returns the new priority queue.

DELETEMIN(Q) Deletes the minimum element of Q and returns the element.

DELETE(Q, e)   Deletes element e from priority queue Q provided that it is known where e is stored in Q (priority queues *do not* support the searching for an element).

The implementation of priority queues is a classical problem in data structures. A few references are [14, 13, 8, 7, 5, 6, 10].

---

* This work was partially supported by the ESPRIT II Basic Research Actions Program of the EC under contract no. 7141 (project ALCOM II) and by the Danish Natural Science Research Council (Grant No. 9400044).

** Basic Research in Computer Science, Centre of the Danish National Research Foundation.

In the amortised sense, [11], the best performance is achieved by binomial heaps [13]. They support DELETE and DELETEMIN in amortised time $O(\log n)$ and all other operations in amortised constant time. If we want to perform INSERT in worst case constant time a few efficient data structures exist. The priority queue of van Leeuwen [12], the implicit priority queues of Carlsson and Munro [2] and the relaxed heaps of Driscoll *et al.* [5], but neither of these support MELD efficiently. However the last two do support MAKEQUEUE, FINDMIN and INSERT in worst case constant time and DELETE and DELETEMIN in worst case time $O(\log n)$.

Our implementation beats the above by supporting MAKEQUEUE, FINDMIN, INSERT and MELD in worst case time $O(1)$ and DELETE and DELETEMIN in worst case time $O(\log n)$. The computational model is the pointer machine and the space requirement is linear in the number of elements contained in the priority queues.

We assume that the priority queues contain elements from a totally ordered universe. The only allowed operation on the elements is the comparisons of two elements. We assume that comparisons can be performed in worst case constant time. For simplicity we assume that all priority queues are nonempty. For a given operation we let n denote the size of the priority queue of maximum size involved in the operation.

In Sect. 1 we describe the data structure and in Sect. 2 we show how to implement the operations. In Sect. 3 we show that our construction is optimal. Section 4 contains some final remarks.

1   The Data Structure

Our basic representation of a priority queue is a heap ordered tree where each node contains one element. This is slightly different from binomial heaps [13] and Fibonacci heaps [8] where the representation is a forest of heap ordered trees.

With each node we associate a rank and we partition the sons of a node into two types, type I and type II. The heap ordered tree must satisfy the following structural constraints.

a) A node has at most one son of type I. This son may be of arbitrary rank.
b) The sons of type II of a node of rank r have all rank less than r.
c) For a fixed node or rank r, let n_i denote the number of sons of type II that have rank i. We maintain the regularity constraint that
   i) $\forall i : (0 \leq i < r \Rightarrow 1 \leq n_i \leq 3)$,
   ii) $\forall i, j : (i < j \wedge n_i = n_j = 3 \Rightarrow \exists k : i < k < j \wedge n_k = 1)$,
   iii) $\forall i : (n_i = 3 \Rightarrow \exists k : k < i \wedge n_k = 1)$.
d) The root has rank zero.

The heap order implies that the minimum element is at the root. Properties a), b) and c) bound the degree of a node by three times the rank of the node plus one. The size of the subtree rooted at a node is controlled by property c). Lemma 1 shows that the size is at least exponential in the rank. The last two properties are essential to achieve MELD in worst case constant time. The regularity constraint c) is a variation of the regularity constraint that Guibas *et al.* [9] used in their construction of finger search trees. The idea is that between two ranks where three sons have equal rank there is a rank of which there only is one son. Figure 1 shows a heap ordered tree that satisfies the requirements a) to d) (the elements contained in the tree are omitted).

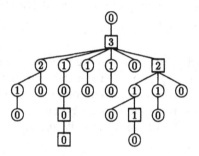

Fig. 1. A heap ordered tree satisfying the properties a) to d). A box denotes a son of type I, a circle denotes a son of type II, and the numbers are the ranks of the nodes.

Lemma 1. *Any subtree rooted at a node of rank r has size $\geq 2^r$.*

Proof. The proof is a simple induction in the structure of the tree. By c.i) leaves have rank zero and the lemma is true. For a node of rank r property c.i) implies that the node has at least one son of each rank less than r. By induction we get that the size is at least $1 + \sum_{i=0}^{r-1} 2^i = 2^r$.

Corollary 2. *The only son of the root of a tree containing n elements has rank at most $\lfloor \log(n-1) \rfloor$.*

We now describe the details of how to represent a heap ordered tree. A son of type I is always the rightmost son. The sons of type II appear in increasing rank order from right to left. See Fig. 1 and Fig. 2 for examples.

A node consists of the following seven fields: 1) the element associated with the node, 2) the rank of the node, 3) the type of the node, 4) a pointer to the father node, 5) a pointer to the leftmost son and 6) a pointer to the next sibling to the left. The next sibling pointer of the leftmost son points to the rightmost son in

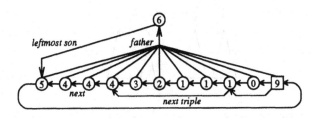

Fig. 2. The arrangement of the sons of a node.

the list. This enables the access to the rightmost son of a node in constant time too. Field 7) is used to maintain a single linked list of triples of sons of type II that have equal rank (see Fig. 2). The nodes appear in increasing rank order. We only maintain these pointers for the rightmost son and for the rightmost son in a triple of sons of equal rank. Figure 2 shows an example of how the sons of a node are arranged.

In the next section we describe how to implement the operations. There are two essential transformations. The first transformation is to add a son of rank r to a node of rank r. Because we have a pointer to the leftmost son of a node (that has rank $r - 1$ when $r > 0$) this can be done in constant time. Notice that this transformation cannot create three sons of equal rank. The second transformation is to find the smallest rank i where three sons have equal rank. Two of the sons are replaced by a son of rank $i + 1$. Because we maintain a single linked list of triples of nodes of equal rank we can also do this in constant time.

2 Operations

In this section we describe how to implement the different operations. The basic operation we use is to link two nodes of equal rank r. This is done by comparing the elements associated with the two nodes and making the node with the largest element a son of the other node. By increasing the rank of the node with the smallest element to $r + 1$ the properties a) to d) are satisfied. The operation is illustrated in Fig. 3. This is similar to the linking of trees in binomial heaps and Fibonacci heaps [13, 8].

We now describe how to implement the operations.

- MAKEQUEUE is trivial. We just return the NULL pointer.
- FINDMIN(Q) returns the element located at the root of the tree representing Q.
- INSERT(Q, e) is equal to MELD Q with a priority queue only consisting of a rank zero node containing e.

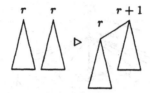

Fig. 3. The linking of two nodes of equal rank.

- MELD(Q_1, Q_2) can be implemented in two steps. In the first we insert one of the heap ordered trees into the other heap ordered tree. This can violate property c) at one node because the node gets one additional son of rank zero. In the second step we reestablish property c) at the node. Figure 4 shows an example of the first step.

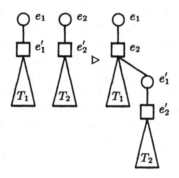

Fig. 4. The first step of a MELD operation (the case $e_1 \leq e_2 < e_1' \leq e_2'$).

Let e_1 and e_2 denote the roots of the trees representing Q_1 and Q_2 and let e_1' and e_2' denote the only sons of e_1 and e_2. Assume w.l.o.g. that e_1 is the smallest element. If $e_2 \geq e_1'$ we let e_2 become a rank zero son of e_1', otherwise $e_2 < e_1'$. If $e_2' < e_1'$ we can interchange the subtrees rooted at e_2' and e_1', so w.l.o.g. we assume $e_1 \leq e_2 < e_1' \leq e_2'$. In this case we make e_2 a rank zero son of e_1' and swap the elements e_1' and e_2 (see Fig. 4). We have assumed that the sizes of Q_1 and Q_2 are at least two, but the other cases are just simplified cases of the general case.

The only invariants that can be violated now are the invariants b) and c) at the son of the root because it has got one additional rank zero son. Let v denote the son of the root. If v had rank zero we can satisfy the invariants by setting the rank of v to one. Otherwise only c) can be violated at v. Let n_i denote the number of sons of v that have rank i. By linking two nodes of rank i where i is the smallest rank where $n_i = 3$ it is easy to verify that c) can be reestablished. The linking reduces n_i by two and increments n_{i+1} by one.

If we let $(n_{r-1}, \ldots, n_0)$ be a string in $\{1, 2, 3\}^*$ the following table shows that c) is reestablished after the above described transformations. We let x denote a string in $\{1, 2, 3\}^*$ and y_i strings in $\{1, 2\}^*$. The table shows all the possible cases. Recall that c) states that between every two $n_i = 3$ there is at least one $n_i = 1$. The different cases are also considered in [9].

$$y_1 1 \ \triangleright\ y_1 2$$
$$y_2 1 3 y_1 1 \ \triangleright\ y_2 2 1 y_1 2$$
$$y_2 2 3 y_1 1 \ \triangleright\ y_2 3 1 y_1 2$$
$$x 3 y_2 1 3 y_1 1 \ \triangleright\ x 3 y_2 2 1 y_1 2$$
$$x 3 y_3 1 y_2 2 3 y_1 1 \ \triangleright\ x 3 y_3 1 y_2 3 1 y_1 2$$
$$y_1 1 2 \ \triangleright\ y_1 2 1$$
$$y_1 2 2 \ \triangleright\ y_1 3 1$$
$$x 3 y_1 1 2 \ \triangleright\ x 3 y_1 2 1$$
$$x 3 y_2 1 y_1 2 2 \ \triangleright\ x 3 y_2 1 y_1 3 1$$

After the linking only b) can be violated at v because a son of rank r has been created. This problem can be solved by increasing the rank of v by one. Because of the given representation MELD can be performed in worst case time $O(1)$.

- DELETEMIN(Q) removes the root e_1 of the tree representing Q. The problem is that now property d) can be violated because the new root e_2 can have arbitrary rank. This problem is solved by the following transformations. First we remove the root e_2. This element later on becomes the new root of rank zero. At most $O(\log n)$ trees can be created by removing the root. Among these trees the root that contains the minimum element e_3 is found and removed. This again creates at most $O(\log n)$ trees. We now find the root e_4 of maximum rank among all the trees and replaces it by the element e_3. A rank zero node containing e_4 is created.

  The tree of maximum rank and with root e_3 is made the only son of e_2. All other trees are made sons of the node containing e_3. Notice that all the new sons of e_3 have rank less than the rank of e_3. By iterated linking of sons of equal rank where there are three sons with equal rank, we can guarantee that $n_i \in \{1, 2\}$ for all i less than the rank of e_3. Possibly, we have to increase the rank of e_3.

  Finally, we return the element e_1.

  Because the number of trees is at most $O(\log n)$ DELETEMIN can be performed in worst case time $O(\log n)$. Figure 5 illustrates how DELETEMIN is performed.

- DELETE(Q, e) can be implemented similar to DELETEMIN. If e is the root we just perform DELETEMIN. Otherwise we start by bubbling e upwards in the tree. We replace e with its father until the father of e has rank less than or equal to the rank of e. Now, e is the arbitrarily ranked son of its

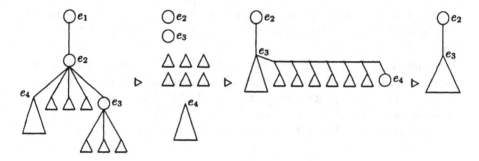

Fig. 5. The implementation of DELETEMIN.

father. This allows us to replace e with an arbitrary ranked node, provided that the heap order is still satisfied. Because the rank of e increases for each bubble step, and the rank of a node is bounded by $\lfloor \log(n-1) \rfloor$, this can be performed in time $O(\log n)$.

We can now replace e with the meld of the sons of e as described in the implementation of DELETEMIN. This again can be performed in worst case time $O(\log n)$.

To summarise, we have the theorem:

Theorem 3. *There exists an implementation of priority queues that supports* DELETE *and* DELETEMIN *in worst case time* $O(\log n)$ *and* MAKEQUEUE, FIND-MIN, INSERT *and* MELD *in worst case time* $O(1)$. *The implementation requires linear space and can be implemented on the pointer machine.*

3   Optimality

The following theorem shows that if MELD is required to be nontrivial, i.e. to take worst case sublinear time, then DELETEMIN must take worst case logarithmic time. This shows that the construction described in the previous sections is optimal among all implementations where MELD takes sublinear time.

If MELD is allowed to take linear time it is possible to support DELETEMIN in worst case constant time by using the finger search trees of Dietz and Raman [3]. By using their data structure MAKEQUEUE, FINDMIN, DELETEMIN, DELETE can be supported in worst case time $O(1)$, INSERT in worst case time $O(\log n)$ and MELD in worst case time $O(n)$.

Theorem 4. *If* MELD *can be performed in worst case time* $o(n)$ *then* DELETE-MIN *cannot be performed in worst case time* $o(\log n)$.

Proof. The proof is by contradiction. Assume MELD takes worst case time o(n) and DELETEMIN takes worst cast time o(log n). We show that this implies a contradiction with the $\Omega(n \log n)$ lower bound on comparison based sorting.

Assume we have n elements that we want to sort. Assume w.l.o.g. that n is a power of 2, $n = 2^k$. We can sort the elements by the following list of priority queue operations. First, create n priority queues each containing one of the n elements (each creation takes worst case time O(1)). Then join the n priority queues to one priority queue by $n-1$ MELD operations. The MELD operations are done bottom-up by always melding two priority queues of smallest size. Finally, perform n DELETEMIN operations. The elements are now sorted.

The total time for this sequence of operations is:

$$n\mathrm{T}_{\mathrm{MakeQueue}} + \sum_{i=0}^{k-1} 2^{k-1-i} \mathrm{T}_{\mathrm{Meld}}(2^i) + \sum_{i=1}^{n} \mathrm{T}_{\mathrm{DeleteMin}}(i) = \mathrm{o}(n \log n).$$

This contradicts the lower bound on comparison based sorting.

4 Conclusion

We have presented an implementation of meldable priority queues where MELD takes worst case time O(1) and DELETEMIN worst case time O(log n).

Another interesting operation to consider is DECREASEKEY. Our data structure supports DECREASEKEY in worst case time O(log n), because DECREASEKEY can be implemented in terms of a DELETE operation followed by an INSERT operation. Relaxed heaps [5] support DECREASEKEY in worst case time O(1) but do not support MELD. But it is easy to see that relaxed heaps can be extended to support MELD in worst case time O(log n). The problem to consider is if it is possible to support both DECREASEKEY and MELD simultaneously in worst case constant time.

As a simple consequence of our construction we get a new implementation of meldable double ended priority queues, which is a data type that allows both FINDMIN/FINDMAX and DELETEMIN/DELETEMAX [1, 4]. For each queue we just have to maintain two heap ordered trees as described in section 1. One tree ordered with respect to minimum and the other with respect to maximum. If we let both trees contain all elements and the elements know their positions in both trees we get the following corollary.

Corollary 5. *An implementation of meldable double ended priority queues exists that supports* MAKEQUEUE, FINDMIN, FINDMAX, INSERT *and* MELD *in worst case time* O(1) *and* DELETEMIN, DELETEMAX, DELETE, DECREASEKEY *and* INCREASEKEY *in worst case time* O(log n).

References

1. M. D. Atkinson, J.-R. Sack, N. Santoro, and T. Strothotte. Min-max heaps and generalized priority queues. *Communications of the ACM*, 29(10):996–1000, 1986.
2. Svante Carlsson, Patricio V. Poblete, and J. Ian Munro. An implicit binomial queue with constant insertion time. In *Proc. 1st Scandinavian Workshop on Algorithm Theory (SWAT)*, volume 318 of *Lecture Notes in Computer Science*, pages 1–13. Springer Verlag, Berlin, 1988.
3. Paul F. Dietz and Rajeev Raman. A constant update time finger search tree. In *Advances in Computing and Information - ICCI '90*, volume 468 of *Lecture Notes in Computer Science*, pages 100–109. Springer Verlag, Berlin, 1990.
4. Yuzheng Ding and Mark Allen Weiss. The relaxed min-max heap. *ACTA Informatica*, 30:215–231, 1993.
5. James R. Driscoll, Harold N. Gabow, Ruth Shrairman, and Robert E. Tarjan. Relaxed heaps: An alternative to fibonacci heaps with applications to parallel computation. *Communications of the ACM*, 31(11):1343–1354, 1988.
6. Michael J. Fischer and Michael S. Paterson. Fishspear: A priority queue algorithm. *Journal of the ACM*, 41(1):3–30, 1994.
7. Michael L. Fredman, Robert Sedgewick, Daniel D. Sleator, and Robert E. Tarjan. The pairing heap: A new form of self–adjusting heap. *Algorithmica*, 1:111–129, 1986.
8. Michael L. Fredman and Robert Endre Tarjan. Fibonacci heaps and their uses in improved network optimization algorithms. In *Proc. 25rd Ann. Symp. on Foundations of Computer Science (FOCS)*, pages 338–346, 1984.
9. Leo J. Guibas, Edward M. McCreight, Michael F. Plass, and Janet R. Roberts. A new representation for linear lists. In *Proc. 9thAnn. ACM Symp. on Theory of Computing (STOC)*, pages 49–60, 1977.
10. Peter Høyer. A general technique for implementation of efficient priority queues. Technical Report IMADA-94-33, Odense University, 1994.
11. Robert Endre Tarjan. Amortized computational complexity. *SIAM Journal on Algebraic and Discrete Methods*, 6:306–318, 1985.
12. Jan van Leeuwen. The composition of fast priority queues. Technical Report RUU-CS-78-5, Department of Computer Science, University of Utrecht, 1978.
13. Jean Vuillemin. A data structure for manipulating priority queues. *Communications of the ACM*, 21(4):309–315, 1978.
14. J. W. J. Williams. Algorithm 232: Heapsort. *Communications of the ACM*, 7(6):347–348, 1964.

On the Computation of Fast Data Transmissions in Networks with Capacities and Delays*

DIMITRIOS KAGARIS[1], GRAMMATI E. PANTZIOU[2],
SPYROS TRAGOUDAS[3] and CHRISTOS D. ZAROLIAGIS[4]

[1] Electrical Eng. Dept, Southern Illinois University, Carbondale IL 62901, USA
[2] Computer Science Dept, University of Central Florida, Orlando FL 32816, USA
[3] Computer Science Dept, Southern Illinois University, Carbondale IL 62901, USA
[4] Max-Planck-Institut für Informatik, Im Stadtwald, 66123 Saarbrücken, Germany

Abstract. We examine the problem of transmitting in minimum time a given amount of data between a source and a destination in a network with finite channel capacities and non–zero propagation delays. In the absence of delays, the problem has been shown to be solvable in polynomial time. In this paper, we show that the general problem is NP–hard. In addition, we examine transmissions along a single path, called the quickest path, and present algorithms for general and sparse networks that outperform previous approaches. The first dynamic algorithm for the quickest path problem is also given.

1 Introduction

Consider an n-node, m-edge network $N = (V, E, c, l)$, where $G = (V, E)$ is a directed graph, $c : E \to \mathbb{N}$ is a capacity function and $l : E \to \mathbb{R}^*$ is a delay function. The nodes represent transmitters/receivers without data memories and the edges represent communication channels. The capacity $c(e)$ of an edge $e \in E$ represents the amount of data that can be transmitted in a time unit through e. The delay $l(e)$ of an edge $e \in E$ represents the time required for the data to traverse edge e. If σ units of data are to be transmitted through an edge $e = (u, v)$, then the required transmission time is $l(u, v) + \frac{\sigma}{c(u,v)}$. Due to the pipelined nature of the transmission, the delay time $l(e)$ is also characterized as the *lead time* of e. Let $p = (v_1, v_2, ..., v_k)$ be a path from node v_1 to node v_k. The *capacity of p* is defined as $c(p) = \min_{1 \le i \le k-1} c(u_i, u_{i+1})$. This definition is motivated by the fact that, since the nodes have no data memories, all data that are received by a node in a time unit must be pumped out of that node in the next time unit. The *lead time of p* is defined as $l(p) = \sum_{i=1}^{k-1} l(u_i, u_{i+1})$. The *transmission time* to send σ units of data from v_1 to v_k along p is $T(\sigma, p) = l(p) + \frac{\sigma}{c(p)}$.

---

* This work was partially supported by the EU ESPRIT BRA No. 7141 (AL-COM II) and the NSF grant MIP-940990. E-mail: kagaris@zeus.c-engr2.siu.edu, pantziou@cs.ucf.edu, spyros@cs.siu.edu, zaro@mpi-sb.mpg.de.

Suppose we want to transmit σ units of data from a designated source $s \in V$ to a designated destination $t \in V$. We wish to compute a partition $\sigma_1, \cdots, \sigma_j$ of the σ units of data and a set of paths $p_1, \cdots, p_j$, from s to t (not necessarily edge or node disjoint), in order to transmit the data so that the following conditions are satisfied: (i) each σ_i, $1 \leq i \leq j$, is a positive integer; (ii) $\sum_{i=1}^{j} \sigma_i = \sigma$, where σ_i is the amount of data transmitted along path p_i; (iii) the total amount of data that passes through each edge $e \in E$ in a time unit does not exceed $c(e)$; and (iv) the transmission time $\max_{1 \leq i \leq j} T(\sigma_i, p_i)$ is minimized over all possible data partitions and groups of transmission paths. We call this problem the *Minimum Transmission Time (MTT) problem*. An example is given in Fig. 1. Note that since we have no memory at the nodes of the network, MTT needs in fact to secure each of the paths p_i from s to t beforehand and then transmit the data.

In this paper we first show (Section 2) that the MTT problem is NP-complete which, in general, precludes a polynomial solution for MTT (unless P=NP). Note that in the absence of delays (i.e., $l(e) = 0$, $\forall e \in E$), which is a special case of the problem, a polynomial time algorithm was already known [9].

An alternative approach to the MTT problem would be to partition the σ units of data as $\sigma_1, \sigma_2, ..., \sigma_k$, for some positive integer k, and then transmit (in a sequential manner) σ_i units, $1 \leq i \leq k$, along a path which minimizes the transmission time. Such a path is called the *quickest path*. The proposed partitioning scheme would consist of k stages, and at each stage i one has to find the quickest path for transmitting the σ_i units of data. We also show here (Section 2) that there is no partition of data which, when routed in this manner, yields an overall transmission time less than the time needed for transmitting all σ units of data along a single quickest path from s to t. For this reason, we also investigate in this paper the (single) quickest path problem. Note that the problem is a restricted version of the MTT one, where no partition of data is required and the transmission is done along a single path. The relation between the quickest path and the MTT problem is new, although the former problem has already been investigated [1, 10]. In particular, the best previous algorithm for the single-pair quickest path problem runs in time $O(rm + rn \log n)$ [1, 10], where r is the number of distinct edge capacities. The all-pairs quickest path problem has been solved in $O(\min\{rnm + rn^2 \log n, \ mn^2\})$ time [8].

In this paper, we give efficient algorithms for the quickest path problem in general and sparse (i.e., $m = O(n)$) networks that outperform the previous approaches. More specifically, our algorithm for the single-pair case runs in $O(r^* m + r^* n \log n)$ time, where r^* is a parameter that never exceeds the number of distinct capacities greater than the capacity of the shortest with respect to (wrt) lead time path in N (Section 3). The benefit of the proposed algorithm is that it takes advantage of the distribution of the capacity values on the network edges, which existing algorithms ignore. Depending on the capacity of the shortest wrt lead time path on the original network and moreover, on the capacity of the shortest wrt lead time paths in appropriately defined subnetworks, parameter r^* can be as low as 1, or a very small integer, even if $r = m$. Note that in the worst case $r^* = r$, but the proposed algorithm offers a substantial improvement in all cases where $r^* < r$. In addition, we present improved algorithms for the single-pair quickest path problem on sparse networks (Section 3). The complexities of the algorithms are expressed in terms of an additional parameter $\tilde{\gamma}$ which provides a measure of the topological complexity of N and ranges from 1 up to $\Theta(n)$. If N is planar, we give an $O(n \log n + n \log^3 \tilde{\gamma} + r^* \tilde{\gamma})$-time algorithm. For arbitrary non-planar sparse networks, we obtain an algorithm with time complexity varying from $O(n \log n)$ up to $O(r^* n \log n)$, depending on the particular value of $\tilde{\gamma}$. We also give efficient algorithms for the all-pairs quickest path problem. For planar networks, the problem is solved in $O(rn^2)$ time, while for arbitrary sparse networks in $O(r\tilde{\gamma}^2 \log \tilde{\gamma} + rn^2)$ time. Our results for the single-pair and the all-pairs quickest path problems compare favorably over the best previous ones and match the best previous bounds only when *both* parameters r^* and $\tilde{\gamma}$ reach their extreme values (of r and $\Theta(n)$, respectively).

All the above mentioned results, however, relate to the static version of the problem. We also consider here (Section 4) a dynamic environment, where edges can be deleted and their lead times and capacities can be modified, and also the amount of data to be transmitted can be changed. In such a case, a more efficient approach is to preprocess the input network N such that subsequently *queries*, asking for the quickest path to send σ units of data between any two given nodes, can be efficiently answered. Moreover, after a dynamic change in N, the data structures set up during preprocessing should be efficiently updated. We shall refer to this as the *dynamic quickest path problem*. To the best of our knowledge, there were no previous algorithms for this problem. We also present here the first dynamic algorithm for the case of planar and sparse networks (Section 4).

2 The intractability of the MTT problem

We show that the MTT problem is NP–hard. In particular, we show that the decision version of MTT (referred to as Bounded Transmission Time (BTT)) is NP-complete. BTT is formally defined as follows:

Problem BTT. *Input:* Network $N = (V, E, c, l)$ with integer capacities and real positive delays, a specified pair of nodes s and t, an integer amount of data σ, and a real number τ. *Question:* Is there an integer partition $\sigma_1, \cdots, \sigma_j$ of $\sigma = \sum_{i=1}^{j} \sigma_i$ and a set of not necessarily disjoint paths $p_1, \cdots, p_j$ from s to t so that the total amount of data that pass through each edge $e \in E$ in a time unit does not exceed $c(e)$, and $\max_{1 \leq i \leq j} T(\sigma_i, p_i) \leq \tau$?

We reduce from the Maximum Length-Bounded Edge-Disjoint Paths (MLEP) problem [7]. An instance of the MLEP problem consists of a directed graph $G = (V, E)$, two specified nodes s and t and two integers $J, K \leq |V|$. The question is whether G contains at least J mutually edge–disjoint paths from s to t, with every path containing at most K edges. MLEP has been shown to be NP–complete for $K \geq 5$.

Theorem 1. *The BTT problem is NP-complete.*

Proof. BTT is clearly in NP. We show a polynomial time reduction of the MLEP problem to the BTT. We transform graph $G = (V, E)$ of the given instance of MLEP to a network $N = (V, E, c, l)$ for the BTT problem by assigning a capacity $c(e) = 1$ and a lead time $l(e) = \frac{1}{K}$, $\forall e \in E$. We set $\sigma = J$ for the amount of data to be transmitted from s to t and require that the transmission be completed within time $\tau = 2$. If there is a solution to the MLEP problem then there is clearly a solution to the BTT problem by splitting σ into J parts and routing each part on a single disjoint path. Conversely, assume there is a solution to the BTT problem on the above network and the specified parameters. First we observe that each path p_j from s to t in the BTT solution must have been assigned $\sigma_j = 1$ units of data, that is there must be J paths in the BTT solution; otherwise, if some path p_i had $\sigma_i > 1 \Rightarrow \sigma_i \geq 2$ units of data, then $T(\sigma_i, p_i) = \frac{\sigma_i}{1} + l(p_i) \geq 2 + \frac{1}{K} > \tau$, which is forbidden. Secondly, each path p_j must comprise at most K edges, since otherwise a path p_i with more than K edges would have $T(\sigma_i, p_i) \geq 1 + (K+1) \cdot \frac{1}{K} > \tau$. Finally, all paths in the BTT solution must be mutually edge–disjoint. Assume that an edge (a, b) was used by two paths p_{j_1} and p_{j_2} in the BTT solution. Let l_1, l_2 be the lead times from s to a along p_{j_1} and p_{j_2}, respectively. Assume $l_1 \leq l_2$. Edge (a, b) will be occupied with the transmission of data of path p_{j_1} during time interval $[l_1, l_1 + \frac{\sigma_i}{1}] = [l_1, l_1 + 1]$. Since the capacity of (a, b) is 1, the first piece of data of path p_{j_2} must arrive at node a at a time $l_2 > l_1 + 1$. But in such a case, $T(\sigma_{j_2}, p_{j_2}) = \frac{\sigma_{j_2}}{1} + l(p_{j_2}) \geq 1 + (l_1 + 1) > \tau$. That is the J paths in the BTT solution are actually disjoint, constituting a solution for MLEP. $\square$

We have shown that it is intractable to partition the data and transmit it simultaneously from s to t so that the transmission time is minimized. An alternative approach would be to partition the σ units of data into $\sigma_1, \sigma_2, ..., \sigma_k$, for some positive integer k, and then transmit (in a sequential manner) each σ_i, $1 \leq i \leq k$, along a single path, called the *quickest path*, which minimizes the transmission time. The proposed partitioning scheme would consist of k stages, and at each stage i we would have to find the quickest path for the σ_i units of data. Lemma 2 below shows that there is no partition of data which, when routed in this manner, yields an overall transmission time less than the time needed for transmitting all σ units of data along a single quickest path from s to t. Lemma 2 together with Theorem 1, justify the importance of developing fast algorithms for the quickest path problem.

Lemma 2. *Transmitting σ units of data along a single quickest path is at least as fast as partitioning the data and transmitting sequentially each part along a single path.*

Proof. We first consider partitioning the data σ into two parts $\sigma_1 > 0$ and $\sigma_2 > 0$, $\sigma_1 + \sigma_2 = \sigma$. Let q with capacity c and lead time l be the quickest path for transmitting the σ units of data, and let p_1 and p_2 with capacities c_1 and c_2 and lead times l_1 and l_2 be any paths to transmit σ_1 and σ_2, respectively. Let $T(q, \sigma) = \frac{\sigma}{c} + l$ be the transmission time along q and $T(p_1, \sigma_1) = \frac{\sigma_1}{c_1} + l_1$, $T(p_2, \sigma_2) = \frac{\sigma_2}{c_2} + l_2$ be the transmissions times along p_1 and p_2. Since q is the quickest path, we have that $T(q, \sigma) \leq T(p_1, \sigma)$ as well as $T(q, \sigma) \leq T(p_1, \sigma)$. The total time for sequentially transmitting σ_1 and σ_2 along p_1 and p_2 respectively is $T(p_1, \sigma_1) + T(p_2, \sigma_2)$. Assume that $T(p_1, \sigma_1) + T(p_2, \sigma_2) < T(q, \sigma)$.

Then we must have that $T(p_1, \sigma_1) + T(p_2, \sigma_2) < T(q, \sigma) \leq T(p_1, \sigma)$ which (after some calculations) gives $\frac{\sigma_2}{c_2} + l_2 < \frac{\sigma_2}{c_1}$, or $l_2 < \sigma_2(\frac{1}{c_1} - \frac{1}{c_2}) \Rightarrow \frac{1}{c_1} - \frac{1}{c_2} > 0$.

However, we must also have that $T(p_1, \sigma_1) + T(p_2, \sigma_2) < T(q, \sigma) \leq T(p_2, \sigma)$ which gives $\frac{\sigma_1}{c_1} + l_1 < \frac{\sigma_1}{c_2}$, or $l_1 < \sigma_1(\frac{1}{c_2} - \frac{1}{c_1}) \Rightarrow \frac{1}{c_2} - \frac{1}{c_1} > 0$, which is incompatible. Now it is a matter of a simple induction to finish the proof of the lemma. □

3 Restricting MTT: the Quickest Path problem

The quickest path problem [1] is a restricted version of MTT by requiring the transmission of data to be done along a single path from the source to the destination (i.e., no partition of data is required). This requirement makes the problem solvable in polynomial time [1, 8, 10]. The computation of a quickest path differs in many aspects from the computation of the related shortest path. First, the latter problem is defined on a network where each edge (u, v) owns only one attribute, namely, the distance from u to v. However, such a kind of network is not applicable in many practical situations, as in the case of a communication network, where the transmission time between two nodes depends not only on the distance but also on the capacity of the edges in the network. Moreover, in the quickest path problem the selection of the path depends also on the size of the data to be transmitted. In one extreme case, if the amount of data is huge, then the quickest path should be the path with largest capacity. On the other hand, if the amount of data is quite small, then the quickest path is the shortest path wrt lead time. An additional singularity of the quickest path problem is that a subpath of a quickest path is not necessarily a quickest path itself. For example, in Fig. 2, the quickest path to transmit $\sigma = 100$ units of data from a to d is (a, b, d) with transmission time $36 + \frac{100}{5} = 56$. However, subpath (a, b) is not a quickest path to transmit $\sigma = 100$ units of data from a to b, since path (a, c, b) has smaller transmission time. This fact suggests that a Dijkstra-like labeling algorithm could not be used to solve the quickest path problem and makes interesting the study of different approaches towards the design of efficient algorithms.

3.1 Single–pair quickest paths in general networks

Let $N = (V, E, c, l)$ be a network as defined in the Introduction and let $|V| = n$ and $|E| = m$. Let also $C_1 < C_2 < ... < C_r$ be the r distinct capacity values of the edges of N, $r \leq m$. We define $N^w = (V, E^w, c, l)$ to be a subnetwork of $N = (V, E, c, l)$ such that $E^w = \{e : e \in E \wedge c(e) \geq w\}$. In the following, with shortest lead time path from u to v, we will refer to the shortest path from u to v with respect to the lead time. The following observation has been made in [10].

Fact 3. *[10] If q is a quickest path, then q is a shortest lead time path in $N^{c(q)}$.*

The algorithm of [10], for computing the quickest path from s to t in N, computes the shortest lead time path p_i in each network N^{C_i}, $1 \leq i \leq r$, and outputs as the quickest path, the one that minimizes the quantity $l(p_i) + \sigma/c(p_i)$,

$1 \leq i \leq r$. Using the result of [6], which computes a shortest path in time $O(m+n \log n)$, the overall time complexity of the algorithm is $O(rm+rn \log n)$.

The algorithm in [10] can be viewed as seeding serially for the capacity of the quickest path. If a hypothetical oracle would give us the capacity w_o of the quickest path, then the actual path could be found just in time $O(m + n \log n)$ by applying the shortest path algorithm of [6] on N^{w_o}. Below, we show that the seed for the capacity of the quickest path does not have to be serial. Let s^w denote the shortest lead time path in N^w and q the quickest path in N.

Lemma 4. *If the capacity of the quickest path q is $c(q) > C_i$ for some $i < r$, then $c(q) \geq c(s^{C_{i+1}})$.*

Proof. Since $c(q) > C_i$ for some $i < r$, q is in fact a path in subnetwork $N^{C_{i+1}}$. Let $s^{C_{i+1}}$ be the shortest lead time path in $N^{C_{i+1}}$. Since q is the quickest path, $l(q) + \sigma/c(q) \leq l(s^{C_{i+1}}) + \frac{\sigma}{c(s^{C_{i+1}})}$. However, since $s^{C_{i+1}}$ is the shortest lead time path in $N^{C_{i+1}}$, $l(s^{C_{i+1}}) \leq l(q)$. Adding the two inequalities, we get $\sigma/c(q) \leq \sigma/c(s^{C_{i+1}}) \Leftrightarrow c(q) \geq c(s^{C_{i+1}})$. □

Proposition 5. *If for some i, $1 \leq i \leq r$, the capacity of the shortest lead time path s^{C_i} is $c(s^{C_i}) = C_r$, then the capacity of the quickest path q is either $c(q) < C_i$ or $c(q) = C_r$.*

Proof. Assume $c(q) \geq C_i$ and $c(q) \neq C_r$. Since $c(q) > C_{i-1}$, then by Lemma 4, $c(q) \geq c(s^{C_{i+1}}) \Rightarrow c(q) \geq C_r \Rightarrow c(q) = C_r$, a contradiction. □

We also observe that some subnetworks N^w may not be connected graphs. In the case that there is no path from s to t in network N^{C_i} for some $i < r$, then s and t will remain disconnected in any network N^{C_j}, $j \geq i$, since N^{C_j} is a subnetwork of N^{C_i}. That is:

Lemma 6. *If there is no path from s to t in N^{C_i} for some i, $1 \leq i \leq r$, then the capacity $c(q)$ of the quickest path q is $c(q) < C_i$ (if $i = 1$, no path exists).*

By convention, we assume that if there is no path from s to t in some subnetwork, then the shortest path algorithm returns a path of "infinite" length and "infinite" capacity. Initially, all we know for the capacity of the quickest path is that $c(q) \geq C_1$. According to Lemma 4, each application of the shortest path algorithm on network N^{w_i}, where $w_1 = C_1$ and $w_i = c(s^{w_{i-1}}), i > 1$, can be regarded as a query that provides us successively with more information for the range of $c(q)$ (namely, $c(q) \geq c(s^{w_i})$). If for the ith such successive query, it happens that $c(s^{w_i}) = C_r$ or $c(s^{w_i}) = \infty$, then, by Proposition 5 or Lemma 6 respectively, we are done since only $r^* = i$ queries are required to find the quickest path. On the other hand, if $\forall i, 1 \leq i < r$, $c(s^{w_i}) = w_i \Leftrightarrow c(s^{C_i}) = C_i$, then (and only then) we end up making $r^* = r$ queries. Hence, r^* is a measure of the number of steps we need to find the quickest path based on the knowledge provided by Lemmata 4, 6 and Proposition 5. It is also clear that r^* is at most the number of distinct capacities which are greater than the capacity of the shortest lead time path in N. The above discussion leads to the following:

ALGORITHM General_Single_Pair_Quickest_Path(N)
1. $w = C_1; r^* = 0;$
2. **while** $w < C_r$ **do**
3. $r^* = r^* + 1;$
4.   Find a shortest lead time path p_{r^*} in N^w;
5.   **if** $\exists i < r$ such that $c(p_{r^*}) = C_i$ **then** $w = C_{i+1}$ **else** $w = \infty$;
6. **od**
7. The quickest path is p_k, where index k minimizes $l(p_i) + \sigma/c(p_i)$, $1 \le i \le r^*$.

Lemma 7. *Algorithm General_Single_Pair_Quickest_Path correctly finds the quickest path between two given nodes of a general network in $O(r^*m + r^*n \log n)$ time.*

Proof. The while loop in Step 2 terminates whenever $w = C_r$ or $w = \infty$. This is justified by Proposition 5 and Lemma 6. The candidate set of shortest paths from which the quickest path is chosen in Step 7, is justified by Lemma 4. Since there are r^* applications of the shortest path algorithm in Step 5, we obtain, by using the algorithm of [6], an overall time complexity of $O(r^*m + r^*n \log n)$. □

An example where r^* is significantly smaller than r is given in Fig. 2. Algorithm General_Single_Pair_Quickest_Path is applied on the network N of Fig. 2 to transmit $\sigma = 100$ units of data from a to h. The algorithm is applied successively on subnetworks $N^{(4)} = N$ (finding shortest lead time path (a, e, h) with capacity 10), $N^{(15)}$ (finding shortest lead time path (a, f, h) with capacity 20) and $N^{(25)}$ (finding no path). It thus terminates in $r^* = 3$ iterations, yielding (a, f, h) as the quickest path. In contrast, the algorithm of [10] would require $r = |E| = 13$ iterations to find the quickest path.

The above algorithm can be further enhanced in practice by making sure that among the potentially many paths in N^w with the same shortest lead time, the shortest such path with the largest minimum capacity is always chosen. This can be easily done by modifying slightly the shortest path algorithm used.

3.2 Computing quickest paths in sparse networks

In the previous section, we saw that there is a kind of "information redundancy" in the approach of [10] in the sense that not all queries that are asked may in fact be necessary. However, another potential source of redundancy may be found in the repeated applications of the shortest path algorithm on network versions that, loosely speaking, do not differ too much. That is, subnetworks N^{C_i} and $N^{C_{i+1}}$ differ only in that $N^{C_{i+1}}$ has some fewer edges than N^{C_i} and therefore, the information obtained by computing the shortest lead time path in $N^{C_{i+1}}$ may be useful in the computation of the shortest lead time path in N^{C_i}. This suggests the use of a dynamic algorithm for computing shortest paths that allows edge cost updates and/or deletions of edges.

Below, we show how dynamic shortest path algorithms can be used advantageously in the quickest path context. Before proceeding to the description of our algorithms, we need the notion of a hammock decomposition.

A *hammock decomposition* is a decomposition of an n-vertex graph G into certain outerplanar digraphs called *hammocks* [4]. Hammocks satisfy certain separator conditions and the decomposition has the following properties: (i) each hammock has at most *four* vertices in common with any other hammock (and therefore with the rest of the graph), called the *attachment vertices*; (ii) each edge of the graph belongs to exactly one hammock; and (iii) the number $\tilde{\gamma}$ of hammocks is proportional to $g(G) + q$, where G is assumed to be embedded into its orientable surface of genus $g(G)$ so as to minimize the number q of faces that collectively cover all vertices [4]. If G is sparse, then $\tilde{\gamma}$ ranges from 1 up to $\Theta(n)$. (Note that if G is planar, then $g(G) = 0$ and $\tilde{\gamma} = O(q)$. Also, if G is outerplanar then $\tilde{\gamma} = 1$.) As it has been proved in [4], the hammock decomposition can be obtained in time linear to the size of G and an embedding of G into its orientable surface does not need to be provided with the input.

A dynamic shortest path algorithm that works efficiently for planar digraphs and digraphs with small genus (i.e. $\tilde{\gamma} = o(n)$), and which supports edge cost modifications and/or edge deletions is given in [2]. More precisely, the following result (partially based on the hammock decomposition) is proved in [2].

Fact 8. *[2] Given an n-vertex planar (or small genus) digraph G with real-valued edge costs but no negative cycles, there exists an algorithm for the dynamic shortest path problem on G that supports edge cost modification and edge deletion with the following performance characteristics: (i) preprocessing time and space $O(n + \tilde{\gamma} \log \tilde{\gamma})$; (ii) single-pair distance query time $O(\tilde{\gamma} + \log n)$; (iii) single-pair shortest path query time $O(L + \tilde{\gamma} + \log n)$ (where L is the number of edges in the shortest path); (iv) update time (after an edge cost modification or edge deletion) $O(\log n + \log^3 \tilde{\gamma})$.*

Single-pair quickest paths. We will first give an algorithm for the case of sparse networks which is based on the decomposition of the original network into hammocks and on the dynamic algorithm implied by Fact 8 for outerplanar digraphs ($\tilde{\gamma} = 1$). Then, we give a more efficient algorithm for the case of planar networks and networks with small genus.

Let L_i be the length of the shortest lead time path from the source s to the destination t in subnetwork $N^{C_i} = (V, E^{C_i})$. Let also E_i be the set of edges with capacity C_i, $1 \leq i \leq r$. Note that $E^{C_{i+1}} = E^{C_i} - E_i$.

The algorithm for sparse networks consists of the following steps: (1) Decompose N into hammocks. (2) Apply the outerplanar preprocessing algorithm of Fact 8 to each hammock. (3) Repeat steps (3a) through (3e) r times. Description of stage i, $1 \leq i \leq r$: (3a) Using the outerplanar query algorithm of Fact 8, compute in N^{C_i} the shortest lead time paths from s to each attachment node of H_s (where $s \in H_s$) and from each attachment node of H_t (where $t \in H_t$) to t. (3b) Substitute each hammock H, in N^{C_i}, by a constant size outerplanar network, called its *sparse representative*, that keeps shortest lead time path information among the attachments nodes of H. (This can be done in time linear in the size of H [2].) Let $N_{\tilde{\gamma}}$ be the resulting network, which is of size $O(\tilde{\gamma})$. (3c) In $N_{\tilde{\gamma}}$, compute the four shortest lead time path trees rooted at the four attachment nodes of H_s using the algorithm of [6]. (3d) Use the shortest lead time path information computed in steps (3a) and (3c) to find L_i. (3e) For each edge $e \in E_i$, delete e from N^{C_i} and update the hammock H^e containing e using the outerplanar update algorithm of Fact 8. (4) Find the index k that minimizes $L_i + \sigma/C_i, 1 \leq i \leq r$, and obtain the quickest path by applying the shortest path algorithm of [6] on N^{C_k}.

Lemma 9. *The quickest path between a given pair of nodes in an n-node sparse network can be computed in $O(n \cdot \log n + r^* \cdot (n + \tilde{\gamma} \cdot \log \tilde{\gamma}))$ time.*

Proof. Let us first discuss the correctness of the algorithm. From Fact 3, the quickest path q is a shortest lead time path in $N^{c(q)}$. Hence, it is enough to compute the length L_i of the shortest lead time path in N^{C_i}, $1 \leq i \leq r$, and then compute the minimum of $L_i + \sigma/C_i, 1 \leq i \leq r$. Since network $N^{C_{i+1}} = (V, E^{C_{i+1}})$ differs from $N^{C_i} = (V, E^{C_i})$ in that $E^{C_{i+1}} = E^{C_i} - E_i$, and since we have already computed L_i in N^{C_i}, it is clear that L_{i+1} can be computed by deleting the edges in E_i from N^{C_i}. Since each edge of the network belongs to exactly one hammock, once an edge e is deleted from the current network, exactly one hammock H^e needs to be modified and the shortest lead time path information among its attachment nodes to be updated. The updated hammock H^e is then substituted by its sparse representative that keeps the new shortest lead time path information among its four attachment nodes, and in this way, the network $N_{\tilde{\gamma}}$ is updated. At the query time, i.e., when the distance from s to t is computed in the current network, the single source algorithm of [6] finds the updated shortest lead time paths from the attachment nodes of H_s to the attachment nodes of H_t. Regarding the time complexity, Steps (1), (2), (3a) and (3b) take $O(n)$ time by Fact 8 and the results in [2, 4]. Step (3c) takes $O(\tilde{\gamma} \cdot \log \tilde{\gamma})$ time [6] and Step (3d) takes $O(1)$ time. Step (3) consists of r iterations which can be reduced to r^*, as it was discussed in the previous subsection. Hence, the overall time complexity of Step (3), excluding Step (3e), is $O(r^* \cdot (n + \tilde{\gamma} \cdot \log \tilde{\gamma}))$. Step (3e) needs, by Fact 8, $O(\log n)$ time per each deleted edge. During the execution of the algorithm, this step is called at most $m = O(n)$ times, contributing a time complexity of $O(n \log n)$ to the total execution time of the algorithm. Finally, Step (4) takes $O(n \log n)$ time [6]. The bound follows. $\square$

We give now a more efficient algorithm for finding the quickest path between two nodes s and t, in the case where the input network is planar or has small genus. We present the algorithm for the planar case. (The other case is similar.) The algorithm consists of the following steps: (1) Run the preprocessing algorithm for planar digraphs implied in Fact 8 to build the appropriate data structures on N for answering shortest lead time path queries. (2) Repeat steps (2a) and (2b) r times. Description of stage i, $1 \leq i \leq r$: (2a) Run the query algorithm for planar digraphs of Fact 8, to find the length L_i of the shortest lead time path from s to t in N^{C_i}. (2b) For each edge e in E_i run the update algorithm of Fact 8 for planar digraphs, to delete e from N^{C_i}. (3) Find the index k that minimizes $L_i + \sigma/C_i, 1 \leq i \leq r$. (4) Obtain the quickest path by applying the (shortest path) query algorithm of Fact 8 on N^{C_k}.

Using similar arguments with those in the proof of Lemma 9, we can prove:

Lemma 10. *The quickest path between two given nodes of an n-node planar network can be computed in $O(n \cdot \log n + n \cdot \log^3 \tilde{\gamma} + r^* \cdot \tilde{\gamma})$ time.*

All–pairs quickest paths. A straightforward algorithm (based on Fact 3) for computing all–pairs quickest paths in planar (resp. sparse) networks is to apply the all–pairs shortest paths algorithm of [3] (resp. [4]) for planar (resp. sparse) digraphs, on each one of the subnetworks N^{C_i}, $1 \leq i \leq r$. This, in combination with the results in [5], gives an algorithm for the all–pairs quickest paths problem which does an $O(r(n + \tilde{\gamma}^2))$ (resp. $O(r(n + \tilde{\gamma}^2 \log \tilde{\gamma}))$) preprocessing of the subnetworks, such that a shortest lead time path between any two nodes is answered in $O(L + \log n)$ time in each N^{C_i} and hence the quickest path can be found in $O(r(L + \log n))$ time. If we want an $O(rL)$ query time algorithm, or alternatively to store the quickest path information in the standard form (of rn shortest lead time path trees which requires $\Omega(rn^2)$ preprocessing), the algorithms in [3] (resp. [4]) can be easily modified to compute all–pairs quickest paths in $O(rn^2)$ (resp. $O(r(n^2 + \tilde{\gamma}^2 \log \tilde{\gamma}))$) time. In the next section we will give a more efficient approach to the all-pairs quickest paths problem.

4 Dynamic quickest paths

In this section we present our solution to the dynamic quickest path problem in the case where the input network is planar or has small genus. We will first give a dynamic algorithm for the case of edge deletions as well as edge lead time and edge capacity modifications. Then, we shall give our dynamic algorithm in the case where the amount of data, to be transmitted between two specific nodes, changes. We shall refer to this latter problem, as the *modified* version of the dynamic quickest path problem.

Before describing the dynamic algorithm, we define a variation of the input network as follows. Let $N = (V, E, c, l)$ be the input network and $C_1 < C_2 < ... < C_r$ be the r distinct capacity values of the edges of N. Let $N_\infty^w = (V, E, c, l^w)$ be a variation of N such that for each $e \in E$, $l^w(e) = l(e)$ if $c(e) \geq w$ and $l^w(e) = \infty$ otherwise. Our dynamic algorithm consists of three procedures, namely preprocessing, query and update ones.

Preprocessing procedure: Construct the networks $N_\infty^{C_i}$, $\forall 1 \leq i \leq r$. Call the preprocessing algorithm implied in Fact 8 in each $N_\infty^{C_i}$ and create the appropriate data structures for answering shortest lead time path queries.

Query procedure: Assume that the two query nodes are u and z. Call the distance query algorithm implied in Fact 8, in each one of the networks $N_\infty^{C_i}$, $i = 1, \cdots, r$, and compute the length $L_i^{u,z}$ of the shortest lead time path from u to z in $N_\infty^{C_i}$. In each $N_\infty^{C_i}$, compute the quantity $L_i^{u,z} + \sigma/C_i$. Let k be the index that minimizes $L_i^{u,z} + \sigma/C_i$, overall $1 \leq i \leq r$. Then, find the shortest lead time path from u to z in $N_\infty^{C_k}$, using the shortest path query algorithm of Fact 8.

Update procedure: There are two update procedures. The lead time update and the capacity update procedure. The first one updates the data structure in the case of a modification to the lead time of an edge, while the second one in the case of a modification to the capacity of an edge. Note that deletion of an edge e corresponds to updating the lead time of the edge with an ∞ lead time.

Lead time update: Let e be the edge whose lead time l_1 is to be modified and let $c(e)$ be its capacity. Let also l_2 be the new lead time of e. Then, the lead time update algorithm uses the update algorithm implied in Fact 8 to change the lead time of e in each network N_∞^w, with $w \le c(e)$, from l_1 to l_2.

Capacity update: Let e be the edge whose capacity C_i is to be modified and let $l(e)$ be its lead time. Suppose also that C_j is the new capacity of e. Then, the capacity update algorithm proceeds as follows: If $C_i \le C_j$, it uses the update algorithm implied in Fact 8 to change the lead time of e in each network N_∞^w, with $C_i < w \le C_j$, from ∞ to $l(e)$. Otherwise ($C_j < C_i$), it uses the update algorithm implied by Fact 8 to change the lead time of e in each network N_∞^w, with $C_j \le w < C_i$, from $l(e)$ to ∞.

The following lemma discusses the correctness and the complexity of the above algorithm.

Lemma 11. *Given an n-node planar (or small genus) network N, there exists an algorithm for the dynamic quickest path problem on N that supports edge lead time modification, edge capacity modification and edge deletion, with the following characteristics: (i) preprocessing time $O(r(n + \tilde{\gamma}\log\tilde{\gamma}))$; (ii) single-pair quickest path query time $O(r(\tilde{\gamma} + \log n) + L)$, where L is the number of edges of the quickest path; and (iii) update time $O(r(\log n + \log^3 \tilde{\gamma}))$, after any modification and/or edge deletion.*

Proof. From the definition of the network N_∞^w, each path in N_∞^w that has lead time not equal to ∞, has capacity greater than or equal to w. It is not difficult to see that if q is a quickest path in N, then q is a shortest lead time path in $N_\infty^{c(q)}$. Thus, the query procedure correctly computes the quickest path from a node u to a node z. Suppose now that the lead time of an edge e is changed. Then, we have to update all the networks where e belongs to, namely, all the networks N_∞^w with $w \le c(e)$. If the capacity of an edge e is changed, then we have to change the lead time of e in each network N_∞^w with w between the old and the new capacity of e. The time complexity of the algorithm comes easily by Fact 8. $\qquad\square$

Consider now the modified version of the dynamic quickest path problem: The source and destination nodes of the network remain unchanged, and the amount of data to be transmitted from the source to the destination changes more frequently than the network itself changes. Then, we can modify our dynamic algorithms, given above, in such a way that the computation of the shortest lead time distance is incorporated in the preprocessing and the update procedures instead of the query one. This improves considerably the query time without increasing the preprocessing bound, but with degrading the update time by an additive factor of $r\tilde{\gamma}$. More precisely we have the following lemma.

Lemma 12. *Given an n-node planar (or small genus) network N with a source s and a destination t, there exists an algorithm for the modified dynamic quickest* path problem on N that supports edge lead time modification, edge capacity modification and edge deletion, with the following characteristics: (i) preprocessing time $O(r(n+\tilde{\gamma}\log\tilde{\gamma}))$; (ii) $s-t$ quickest path query time $O(r+L)$, where L is the number of edges in the quickest path; and (iii) update time $O(r(\tilde{\gamma}+\log n+\log^3 \tilde{\gamma}))$, after any modification and/or edge deletion.

References

1. Y. L. Chen and Y. H. Chin, "The quickest path problem", *Computers and Operations Research*, 17, pp. 153–161, 1990.

2. H. N. Djidjev, G. E. Pantziou and C. D. Zaroliagis, "On-line and Dynamic Algorithms for Shortest Path Problems," *Proc. 12th Symp. on Theor. Aspects of Computer Science (STACS'95)*, LNCS 900, pp.193-204, Springer-Verlag, 1995.

3. G. N. Frederickson, "Planar Graph Decomposition and All Pairs Shortest Paths," *J. ACM*, Vol.38, No. 1, pp.162–204, 1991.

4. G. N. Frederickson, "Using Cellular Graph Embeddings in Solving All Pairs Shortest Path Problems", *Proc. 30th Annual IEEE Symp. on FOCS*, 1989, pp.448-453.

5. G.N. Frederickson, "Searching among Intervals and Compact Routing Tables", *Proc. 20th ICALP*, 1993, LNCS 700, pp.28-39, Springer-Verlag.

6. M. L. Fredman and R. E. Tarjan, "Fibonacci heaps and their uses in improved network optimization algorithms," *J. ACM*, Vol. 34, pp. 596–615, 1987.

7. M.R. Garey, and D.S. Johnson, "Computers and Intractability. A Guide to the Theory of NP-Completeness", W.H. Freeman and Company, New York, NY, 1979.

8. Y.-C. Hung and G.-H. Chen, "On the quickest path problem," *Proc. ICCI'91*, LNCS 497, Springer-Verlag, pp. 44–46, 1991.

9. A. Itai, and M. Rodeh, "Scheduling Transmissions in a Network", *Journal of Algorithms*, 6, pp. 409–429, 1985.

10. J.B. Rosen, S.Z. Sun and G.L. Xue, "Algorithms for the quickest path problem and the enumeration of quickest paths," *Comp. and O.R.*, 18, pp.579-584, 1991.

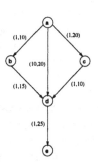

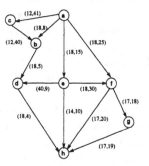

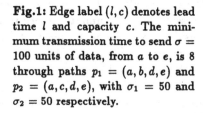

Fig.1: Edge label (l,c) denotes lead time l and capacity c. The minimum transmission time to send $\sigma = 100$ units of data, from a to e, is 8 through paths $p_1 = (a, b, d, e)$ and $p_2 = (a, c, d, e)$, with $\sigma_1 = 50$ and $\sigma_2 = 50$ respectively.

Fig.2: An example network. (Edge label (l,c) denotes edge lead time l and edge capacity c.)

Routing with Delays when Storage Is Costly

Sanjoy Baruah* and Gara Pruesse**

Dept. of Computer Science and Electrical Engineering
Dept. of Mathematics and Statistics
351 Votey Building
The University of Vermont
Burlington, VT 05401

Abstract. A model for computer networks is considered in which there is a cost associated with both the transmission of data across network links, and the storage of data at network nodes. Requests for data specify the time at which the data is to be used — early arrival therefore has no advantage, and has the disadvantage that the data must be stored at the node, accruing the related costs. A wide variety of data routing and broadcast problems are considered for this model. Efficient algorithms for solving some of these problems are presented; others are proven intractable.

1   Introduction

Otherwise very different interactive and real-time multimedia applications share some common characteristics: (1) The data involved can be very large. For example, a typical half-hour television programme, stored in the industry standard MPEG format, would require over 500 Mbytes of storage. (2) It is necessary that this data be made available in a *timely* manner — while delivering data to a site too late may not be tolerated, delivering it too early will require that this data be stored at the site (perhaps at great cost, since the volume involved is large), until needed. The traditional approach to data routing problems on computer networks has been to associate a cost with traversing each link in the network, and then determine routing strategies with the aim of meeting deadlines (or minimizing delays). The cost of storing data is usually ignored (or somehow incorporated into the transportation costs). We formalize here a model of data storage and transmission in computer networks where there is a cost associated with both transmitting data from one site to another over the network, and with storing it at a particular site.

System Model. We model a computer network as a weighted graph $G = (V, E)$, $|V| = n$, $|E| = m$, with weights on both the edges E and the vertices V of the graph. Vertices represent network nodes, and the weight $c(v)$ on a vertex v is

---

* Supported in part by NSF grants OSR-9350540 and CCR-9410752, and UVM grant PSCI94-3. Email: sanjoy@cs.uvm.edu
** Supported in part by NSF grant OSR-9350540. Email: gara@cs.uvm.edu

the cost of storing one unit of data at that node for one time unit. The edges correspond to network links; the weight $w(u, v)$ of an edge (u, v) represents the cost of transmitting a unit of data down that link (we assume that data transmission over a link takes place instantaneously). On this general model, we study the following categories of problems. In the first two categories, only one copy of the data may exist at any instant in time. The third category is essentially one of data **multicast** — the data being transmitted will not be changed at the vertices visited, and may therefore be replicated, and different copies sent to different vertices. Redundant copies may be destroyed.

Data Itinerary. Data is available at time i at vertex t_o, and needs to be made available at specified vertices $t_1, t_2, \ldots, t_r$ at specified times $i + k_1, i + (k_1 + k_2), \ldots, i + (\sum_{j=1}^{r} k_j)$ respectively. It is assumed that all the k_j's are strictly positive integers. Determine the least cost strategy that does so.

Our algorithm for solving this problem uses Dijkstra's shortest path algorithm [3] as a subroutine, and makes r calls to this subroutine on a graph $G' = (V', E')$ with $|V'| = 2n$, and $|E'| = 2m + n$. The asymptotic run-time complexity of our algorithm is thus r times that of Dijkstra's shortest-path algorithm, i.e., $O(r(n \log n + m))$.

In addition, we consider an on-line version of the problem: given any 3-tuple (i, j, k), with $i, j \in V$ and $k \in \mathbf{N}$, what is the least cost strategy for ensuring that data, currently available at vertex i, is made available at vertex j after k time units? One could, of course, use the algorithm for solving the Data Itinerary problem to determine the optimal path for each such tuple in $O(n \log n + m)$ time; if faster responses are required, however, a different approach may be necessary. We describe a method for precomputing certain data-structures in $O(n^3 \log n)$ time, and using these data structures to determine the shortest k-delay path between vertices i and j in $O(\log n)$ time, for any (i, j, k).

Delayed Tour. Data is available at time i at vertex s, and needs to visit all vertices in $U \subset V$ by time $i + k$. The data may be modified at each vertex in U; to maintain consistency, it is therefore not permissible to replicate the data and send different copies to the different vertices in U. Vertices may, however, be visited in any order. Determine the minimum-cost tour that does so.

The delayed tour problem is easily seen to be NP-hard (reduce from Traveling Salesperson Problem). We present here polynomial approximation algorithms that find delayed tours of cost no more than three-halves the cost of the minimum-cost tour.

Delayed Broadcast. Data is available at time i at all vertices in $S \subset V$, and must be made available at all vertices in V at time $i + k$. Determine the minimum-cost method of distributing the data.

We present here an algorithm of time-complexity $O(m \log n)$ that solves this problem.

Related Work. The notion of scheduling to ensure timely, rather than earliest, completion has recently been the subject of much study in Operations Research, motivated by the competitive success of the *Just-In-Time* inventory and production-control paradigm. Much of this research is, however, in the context of single machine and flowshop scheduling (see [1] for a survey).

Much previous work in time-sensitive network routing has been in the context of determining dynamic shortest paths in networks with stochastic edge-costs. For example, Psaraftis and Tsitsiklis [6] examine the shortest path problem in acyclic networks where edge costs evolve as Markov processes dependent upon certain 'environment variables,' and there are "wait costs" associated with delaying at nodes in anticipation of more favorable arc costs.

Organization of this paper. The rest of this paper is organized as follows. In Section 2, we discuss the Data Itinerary Problem. In Section 3, we present our results on Delayed Tours. We offer some efficient solutions to Delayed Broadcast in Section 4. Several of the tractable problems discussed here have natural and useful generalizations; unfortunately, most of these generalizations prove intractable. We present these intractability results in Section 5.

2 The Data Itinerary Problem

In this problem, data is initially available at vertex t_o, and must be delievered at vertex t_1 after a delay of k_1 time units, $k_1 > 0$. From t_1, the data must be delivered to vertex t_2 after a delay of k_2 time units, $k_2 > 0$. In general, data must be delivered from vertex t_{j-1} to vertex t_j after a delay of k_j ($k_j > 0$) time units, $0 < j \leq m$. Data cannot be replicated; hence there is only one copy of the data present in the network at any time, and each "leg" of the itinerary (the delivering of data from vertex t_{j-1} to vertex t_j after a delay of k_j time units) may be considered as a seperate problem instance.

Definition 1. Given a graph $G = (V, E)$, weight functions $c : V \rightarrow \mathbf{N}$ and $w : E \rightarrow \mathbf{N}$ on the vertices and edges of G respectively, vertices $s, t \in V$, and a non-negative integer k, a **k-delay s,t-path** in G is a sequence $v_1^{d_1}, v_2^{d_2}, \ldots, v_r^{d_r}$ where

- $v_1 = s$ and $v_r = t$
- $v_i \in V$, $(v_i, v_{i+1}) \in E$ for all i, $1 \leq i < r$
- $\sum_{1 \leq i \leq r} d_i = k$

The **cost** of this k-delay s,t-path is defined to be

$$\sum_{1 \leq i \leq r-1} w(v_i, v_{i+1}) + \sum_{1 \leq i \leq r} d_i \cdot c(v_i) \ .$$

□

Determining the j'th leg of the itinerary (i.e., the least-cost method of delivering the data from vertex t_j to t_{j+1} after a delay of k_j time units) thus reduces to the problem of determining the least-cost k_j-delay t_{j-i},t_j-path in G.

2.1   Least-cost k-delay s,t-paths

The following lemma plays a crucial role in our algorithm for solving the least-cost k-delay s,t-path problem:

Lemma 2. *There exists a least-cost k-delay s,t-path that has all k delays occurring at one vertex.*

Proof. Let $v_1^{d_1}, v_2^{d_2}, \ldots, v_r^{d_r}$, $v_1 \equiv s$ and $v_r \equiv t$, be a least-cost k-delay s,t-path; let c denote the cost of this path. Let vertex v_j be a vertex of minimum weight in $\{v_1, \ldots, v_r\}$. The k-delay s,t-path $v_1^{e_1}, v_2^{e_2}, \ldots, v_r^{e_r}$, where $e_j = k$ and $e_\ell = 0$ for all $\ell \neq k$, is of cost no more than c. $\square$

Given the graph $G = (V, E)$, $V = \{v_1, v_2, \ldots, v_n\}$, make another copy of G (call it G') on vertex set $\{v_1', v_2', \ldots, v_n'\}$ with the obvious isomorphism. Construct a new graph $G \times K_2$ from these two graphs by adding, for each $v \in V$, the directed edge (v, v'), with edge weight $k \cdot c(v)$. Let s, t be two vertices in V (hence s', t' are two vertices in $G \times K_2$).

Lemma 3. *The length of the shortest s, t'-path in $G \times K_2$ is the minimum cost of a k-delay s, t-path in G.*

Proof Sketch: Consider the set P of k-delay s, t-paths in G in which all the delays occur at a single node on the path. By Lemma 2, one of these is a minimum cost k-delay s, t-path.

There is a 1-1 correspondence between the elements of P and the s, t' paths in $G \times K_2$ that preserves cost. Details omitted. $\square$

It follows from this lemma that to find the least-cost k-delay s, t-path in G, it suffices to run Dijkstra's shortest path algorithm on $G \times K_2$, yielding the following theorem:

Theorem 4. *Single source least-cost k-delay paths can be computed in time $O(n \log n + m)$.*

Note: It was observed by Vazirani [7] that the restriction of the problem to single-source single-sink (i.e., from node s to node t) has a simple solution that has the same time bound: It is sufficient to determine the vertex v that minimizes the sum of length of the shortest s, v-path, the length of the shortest v, t-path, and the quantity $k \times c(v)$. This can be computed using two calls to a shortest paths algorithm (e.g., Dijkstra's algorithm) and $O(n)$ other operations.

2.2   All Pairs least-cost k-delay Paths

All pairs shortest path algorithms for graphs have been extensively studied. These algorithms typically accept as input a graph G on n vertices, and produce as output an $n \times n$ matrix A of (cost, vertex) pairs such that the (i, j)th entry $a_{i,j}$ represents the shortest path from vertex i to vertex j. Once matrix A has been computed, a shortest path from any vertex i to any vertex j can be determined by a lookup of this matrix, in cost linear in the number of edges on the path. The classical algorithm for computing the all pairs shortest path matrix is due to Floyd [4], and runs in $O(n^3)$ time.

Let G be the input graph, and let A be its all pairs shortest path matrix — A can be computed from G using, for example, Floyd's algorithm, in $O(n^3)$ time. In this section, we present an algorithm for obtaining a generalization of the all pairs shortest paths matrix A. The generalization is as follows: we wish to determine a least-cost k-delay path from vertex i to vertex j for any 3-tuple (i, j, k). Our algorithm runs in time $O(n^3 \log n)$, and produces an $n \times n$ matrix B. The elements of B are size n arrays of ordered pairs (range, vertex). Each such array is sorted by the first element – range; i.e., for each (i, j) pair, $b_{i,j}[x].\text{range} < b_{i,j}[x + 1].\text{range}$ for all x, $1 \leq x < n$. The interpretation is as follows: Let i, j be vertices in G, and let $k \in \mathbf{N}$. By Lemma 2, there exists a least-cost k-delay i,j-path in which all k delays occur at the same vertex — let this vertex be ℓ. B will be computed such that $b_{i,j}[x].\text{vertex} \equiv \ell$, where x is such that $((b_{i,j}[x].\text{range} \leq k) \land (b_{i,j}[x + 1].\text{range} > k))$. Once B has been computed, a least-cost k-delay i,j-path can be obtained in time $O(\max\{\log n, \text{the number of edges on the path}\})$, for an arbitrary tuple (i, j, k), by first determining the delay vertex ℓ — in $O(\log n)$ time, using binary search on $b_{i,j}[1], \ldots, b_{i,j}[n]$ — and then retrieving the minimum cost path from i to ℓ, and from ℓ to j, by using matrix A.

It remains to define an algorithm for computing B. Let (i, j) be a fixed pair of vertices. We describe below how $b_{i,j}[1], \ldots, b_{i,j}[n]$ may be computed in $O(n \log n)$ time. Since there are n^2 possible pairs (i, j), the overall complexity of computing B is $O(n^3 \log n)$.

Let $k \in \mathbf{N}$. Let vertex ℓ be the vertex on the least-cost k-delay i,j-path in which all delays occur. The cost of this k-delay path is

$$\text{cost}_{i,j}^{(k)}(\ell) \stackrel{\text{def}}{=} (a_{i\ell} + k \cdot c(\ell) + a_{\ell j}) . \tag{1}$$

To obtain the least-cost k-delay i,j-path, it therefore suffices to determine the vertex ℓ that minimizes the quantity (1) above, and then to determine from A the minimum path from i to ℓ, and from ℓ to j.

Let $\alpha(\ell) \stackrel{\text{def}}{=} a_{i,\ell} + a_{\ell,j}$ for all ℓ, $1 \leq \ell \leq n$. Without loss of generality, we assume that $\alpha(1) \leq \alpha(2) \leq \ldots \leq \alpha(n)$ (this can be done by sorting the $\alpha(\ell)$'s and renaming the vertices, in $O(n \log n)$ time). Observe that, if $\alpha(\ell) \leq \alpha(\ell')$, and $c(\ell) \leq c(\ell')$, then, for any k, it is not true that $\text{cost}_{i,j}^{(k)}(\ell') < \text{cost}_{i,j}^{(k)}(\ell)$, and we need not consider vertex ℓ' any further as a potential vertex entry in array $b_{i,j}$. Without loss of generality, therefore, we assume that $c(1) > c(2) > \ldots > c(n)$.

We now have (at most) n ordered pairs $(\alpha(1), c(1)), \ldots, (\alpha(n), c(n))$ with $\alpha(\ell) \leq \alpha(\ell + 1)$ and $c(\ell) > c(\ell + 1)$ for all ℓ, $1 \leq \ell < n$. For each ℓ, we wish to determine the range of values of k for which

$$(\forall \ell' :: \alpha(\ell) + k \cdot c(\ell) \leq \alpha(\ell') + k \cdot c(\ell')) . \tag{2}$$

This reduces to determining the region of intersection of n half-planes; by [5, Theorem 7.10], this can be done in $\Theta(n \log n)$ time.

3 Optimal k-Delay Tours

The Delayed Tour Problem is concerned with visiting a specified subset of the set of vertices in the graph, by a specified deadline.

Definition 5. Given a graph $G = (V, E)$, $|V| = n$, weight functions $c : V \rightarrow \mathbf{N}$ and $w : E \rightarrow \mathbf{N}$ on the vertices and edges of G respectively, vertex set $U \subset V$, and a non-negative integer k, a k-**delay tour** of U in G is a sequence $v_1^{d_1}, v_2^{d_2}, \ldots, v_r^{d_r}$ where

- $v_i \in V$, $(v_i, v_{i+1}) \in E$ for all i, $1 \leq i < r$
- $(\sum_{1 \leq i \leq r} d_i) = k$
- $U \subseteq \{v_1, \ldots, v_r\}$.

The **cost** of this k-delay tour is defined to be

$$\sum_{1 \leq i \leq r-1} w(v_i, v_{i+1}) + \sum_{1 \leq i \leq r} d_i \cdot c(v_i).$$

□

Definition 6   Delayed Tour Problems (DTP). Given a graph $G = (V, E)$, with weight functions $c : V \rightarrow \mathbf{N}$ and $w : E \rightarrow \mathbf{N}$ on the vertices and edges of G respectively.

DTP-1. Input: $U \subseteq V, k \in \mathbf{N}$. Determine a minimum-cost k-delay tour of U in G.

DTP-2. Input: $U \subseteq V, k \in \mathbf{N}$. Determine a minimum-cost k-delay tour of U in G. There must be a delay of at least one time unit between visits to any two elements of U; i.e., $d_i \geq 1$ for all i, $1 \leq i \leq r$.

□

Lemma 7. *DTP-1, DTP-2 are NP-hard.*

Proof Sketch: Reduction from the Traveling Salesperson Problem with triangle inequality[3]. Set $c(v) = 0$ for all $c \in V$, and set $k = |U|$. Details omitted.   □

Lemma 8. *There exist polynomial-time $\frac{3}{2}$-approximation algorithms for DTP-1, DTP-2.*

Proof. In [2], Christofides presented a clever polynomial-time $3/2$-approximation algorithm for the Traveling Salesperson Problem with triangle inequality. We use this algorithm in our outline, below, of polynomial-time $3/2$-approximation algorithms for both DTP-1 and DTP-2.

---

[3] A graph satisfies the triangle inequality if, for any three vertices i, j, l, $w(i, j) + w(j, l) \geq w(i, l)$.

DTP-1. To begin with, we compute all-pairs shortest paths in G (this can be done, using Floyd's algorithm, in time $O(n^3)$), and reduce G to a complete graph with all the edges equal to the shortest paths. G now satisfies the triangle inequality.

By an observation similar to Lemma 2, it may be concluded that the entire delay of k units occurs on the same vertex. Suppose that this vertex is v. The cost of the optimal k-delay tour is $f(U \cup \{v\}, G) + k \cdot c(v)$, where $f(X, G)$ is the minimum cost of a Traveling Salesperson Problem tour on G that visits all vertices in X. The Christofides algorithm returns a value within 3/2 of the optimal — i.e., for any $X \subseteq V$, $f(X, G) \leq \hat{f}(X, G) \leq \frac{3}{2} f(X, G)$, where $\hat{f}(X, G)$ is the value returned by the Christofides algorithm when asked to find a minimum-cost tour of X in G. The quantity

$$\min_{v \in V}(\hat{f}(U \cup \{v\}, G) + k \cdot c(v))$$

is therefore guaranteed to be within 3/2's of the optimal k-delay tour of U, and can be computed in time polynomial in n.

DTP-2. It is no longer true that the entire delay of k units occurs at the same node. However, by an argument similar to that used in Lemma 2, it can be shown that (at least) $(k - |U| + 1)$ units of delay occur at a single node, for some minimum cost k-delay tour.

First, as above, we compute all-pairs shortest paths in G. Next, we compute all-pairs minimum-cost 1-delay paths in G (this can be done, using an obvious variant of Floyd's algorithm, in time $O(n^3)$, or the algorithm of Section 2.2 can be used, which takes time $O(n^3 \log n)$). And finally, we compute all-pairs minimum-cost $(k - |U| + 1)$-delay paths in G, by a similar process.

If $k = |U|$, the problem now reduces to determining a minimum-cost Traveling Salesperson Problem tour $f(U, \hat{G})$, where $\hat{G}$ is the complete graph consisting of all vertices in U, with the edge costs being equal to the cost of the minimum cost 1-delay path between its end vertices. A 3/2 approximation can therefore be obtained by a single call to the Christofides algorithm $\hat{f}(U, \hat{G})$.

If $k > |U|$, let $u_0 \in U$ be the last vertex in U visited in the minimal k-delay tour before the $(k - |U| + 1)$ units delay occurs. The minimum cost of this k-delay tour is then equal to $f(U, G^{(u_0)})$ where $G^{(u_0)}$ is the complete graph consisting of all vertices in U, with all edges (u_0, u'), $u' \in U$, having cost equal to the cost of the minimum-cost $(k - |U| + 1)$-delay path between u_0 and u', and all other edges in $G^{(u_0)}$ having cost equal to the cost of the minimum cost 1-delay path between its end vertices. The quantity

$$\min_{u_0 \in U}(\hat{f}(U, G^{(u_0)}))$$

is therefore guaranteed to be within 3/2's of the optimal k-delay tour of U, and can be computed in time polynomial in n. $\square$

4   Delayed Broadcast

In delayed broadcast problems, data is available at a given time at all vertices in $S \subset V$, and must be made available at all vertices in V at some specified future time. Without loss of generality, it may be assumed that the delay is one time unit; larger – or smaller – delays can be emulated by scaling the storage costs at all vertices appropriately. We restrict our attention in this section to networks represented by undirected graphs; similar results may be obtained for directed graphs.

In the *single source* delayed broadcast problem, $|S| = 1$; i.e., data is initially available at exactly one vertex. More formally,

Definition 9. Given undirected graph $G = (V, E)$, an edge cost function $w : E \to \mathbf{N}$, node cost function $c : V \to \mathbf{N}$, and a source vertex s. A *delayed broadcast* for (G, s) is a triple (U, T, F) where

- $U \subseteq V$
- T is a subgraph of G, T is connected, and T spans $U + s$
- F is a subgraph of G, F spans V, and each component of F contains some vertex of U.

The cost of the broadcast is

$$\sum_{e \in E(T)} w(e) + \sum_{v \in U} c(v) + \sum_{e \in E(F)} w(e).$$

□

The interpretation of a delayed broadcast is as follows. Initially, G has a copy of the data at s. This data tours the subgraph T, traversing each edge exactly once, replicating itself as necessary to complete the tour. In addition, the data replicates at each vertex in U, leaving a copy there. Once this is completed, all copies of the data at vertices in $V \backslash U$ are destroyed; hence at the end of this stage, a vertex u has the data if and only if $u \in U$. The data is stored at these vertices over the delay. After the specified delay, these stored copies of the data propogate themselves around the graph F, traversing each edge exactly once and leaving exactly one copy on each vertex. Since each component T of F has $V(T) \cap U \neq 0$, this is possible; and since F spans V, every vertex gets a copy of the data.

Our results for single source delayed broadcast are generalized by the corresponding results for multiple source delayed broadcast; however, the proofs are elegant and illustrative of the methods used in the multiple source case, so we include them here.

Observation 10. *If (U, T, F) is a minimum cost delayed broadcast for (G, s), then T is a minimum cost Steiner tree for the set $U + s$, and F is a minimum among all spanning forests in G that have at least one vertex from U in each component. If the edge weights in G are all positive, then each component F_i of F has $V(F_i) \cap U = 1$.*

Lemma 11. *There is a minimum cost single source delayed broadcast that stores the data in only one vertex, i.e., where $|U| = 1$.*

Proof. We prove that, given any delayed broadcast $B = (U, T, F)$ with $|U| \geq 1$, there exists another delayed broadcast $B' = (U', T', F')$ that costs no more than B and where $|U| > |U'|$. The lemma follows.

If there exist distinct $u, v \in U$ such that u and v are connected in F, then $(U - u, T, F)$ is a broadcast with smaller U. Hence we can assume from here on that each vertex in U is in a distinct connected component of F. For all $v \in V$, let $h_F(v)$ denote the unique vertex in U that is connected to v in F. By the above stated assumption, there exists a vertex $t \in U$ such that $h_F(t) \neq h_F(s)$.

We construct B' as follows. Let $\tilde{T}$ be a spanning tree of T, rooted at s. Let a_t be the least ancestor of t in $\tilde{T}$ such that $a_t \notin h_F(t)$; by the selection of t, a_t is well defined. The child of a_t that is an ancester of t is denoted b_t.

Let T_t be the subtree of $\tilde{T}$ rooted at b_t. Let V_t be the set of vertices which are descendents of b_t, i.e., $V_t = V(T_t)$, and let E_t denote $E(T_t) \cup (a_t, b_t)$.

We prove that $(U', T', F,) = (U \setminus V_t, T - V_t, F + E_t)$ is a delayed broadcast. Any vertex v in $U \setminus V_t$ is not in the removed subtree T_t, so it's s, v-path in $\tilde{T}$ is also in $T - V_t$, and hence $T - V_t$ is connected and spans $U \setminus V_t$. We need only show that every vertex v in V is connected, in F', to some $u \in U'$. Clearly, if v is connected to a vertex in $U \setminus V_t$ in F, it is still connected to it in F'. If, on the other hand, $h_F(v) = t'$ for some $t' \in V_t$, then v is connected in F' to t (by the edges in E_t) and hence to a_t, and so also to $h_F(a_t)$; and by the selection of a_t, $h_{F'}(a_t) \in U \setminus V_t = U'$. □

Theorem 12. *Single-source minimum cost delayed broadcast can be computed in $O(m \log n)$.*

Proof. It follows from Lemma 11 and Observation 10 that there is a minimum cost delayed broadcast of the form $(\{u\}, T, F)$ where $u \in V$, T is a minimum cost s, u-path, and F is a minimum cost spanning tree. It remains only to find the vertex u. Since the cost of F is the same for any selection of u, the vertex u that minimizes the cost of the delayed broadcast is the one that minimizes the quantity $d(s, v) + c(v)$ over all $v \in V$, where $d(s, v)$ is the cost of the shortest s, v-path. Finding such a v corresponds to determining the minimum 1-delay s, v-path over all $v \in V$, and can be done in time $O(n \log n + m)$ (see Section 2.1). Finding a minimum cost spanning tree takes time $O(m \log n)$ (using, for example, Prim's algorithm). □

We now turn our attention to the case when S may contain more than one vertex.

Definition 13. Given undirected graph $G = (V, E)$, an edge cost function $w : E \to \mathbf{N}$, node cost function $c : V \to \mathbf{N}$, and a source vertex set S. A *delayed broadcast* for (G, S) is a triple (U, T, F) where

- $U \subseteq V$

- T is a subgraph of G, and each component of T contains some vertex of S. The vertices in T include all the vertices in U.
- F is a subgraph of G, F spans V, and each component of F contains some vertex of U.

The cost of the broadcast is

$$\sum_{e \in E(T)} w(e) + \sum_{v \in U} c(v) + \sum_{e \in E(F)} w(e).$$

$\square$

The following lemma can be proved by means of an argument similar to the one used in the proof of Lemma (11):

Lemma 14. *There is a minimum cost delayed broadcast* (U, T, F) *in which each component of* T *contains exactly one vertex in* U.

Theorem 15. *Minimum cost delayed broadcast can be computed in time* $O(n \log n + m)$.

Proof. We present below our algorithm for determining a delayed broadcast. The accompanying analysis assumes the network is connected, i.e., that m is in $\Omega(n)$.

Algorithm for delayed broadcast.

1. For each vertex $v \in V$ compute $\mathsf{sp}(v)$, the least cost path for getting the data to v from some vertex in S. This can be done for all vertices in V in time $O((n \log n + m))$, as follows. For each $v \in V$, compute the shortest path from S to v (i.e., the shortest path with one end in S and where the other end is v); the can be accomplished by adding a new node v_S which has a zero-weight edge to each vertex in S and no other incident edges. Executing a shortest path algorithm on the resulting graph yields the desired set of paths. Let $\hat{c}(v) \stackrel{\text{def}}{=} c(v) +$ the cost of path $\mathsf{sp}(v)$. This represents the minimum cost of getting the data to vertex v, and storing it there over the delay.

2. Construct a new graph $G' = (V', E')$, where $V' = V \cup \{u_o\}$, and $E' = E \bigcup_{v \in V} \{(u_o, v)\}$, where u_o is some new vertex not in V. Set the weight of the new edges (u_o, v) to $\hat{c}(v)$; the weights of the other edges in G' are the same as in G.

3. Construct a minimum cost spanning tree T_{mcst} of G'. A minimum cost broadcast (U, T, F) can be determined from T_{mcst}, as follows:

   (a) $U = \bigcup \{v \in V | (u_o, v)$ is an edge in $T_{\text{mcst}}\}$

   (b) $T = \bigcup \{\mathsf{sp}(u) | u \in U\}$; i.e., the components of T are exactly those shortest paths — determined above — that transport data from S to the vertices in U

   (c) $F = T_{\text{mcst}} \setminus \{u_o\}$; i.e., F is the spanning forest obtained by deleting vertex u_o and all incident edges from T_{mcst}.

The mapping between delayed braodcasts in G and spanning trees of G', given in part 3 of the algorithm, is a bijection which preserves cost. Therefore, since T_{mcst} is a minimum cost spanning tree, the resulting delayed broadcase is also minimum cost.

The algorithm runs in the time to determine Single-Source Shortest Paths and Minimum Spanning Tree. Since G is connected, this is dominated by the $O(m \log n)$ time to find the shortest paths. □

5 Conclusions

We have considered here several problems that arise during the design of data distribution strategies in arbitrary computer networks. Our attempt has been to define the most general formulation of each problem that remains tractable. We enumerate below some minor generalizations to the problems considered here, such that the modified problems are NP-hard.

- It is assumed here that data is transmitted instantaneously across an edge. A more general model may allow a *delay* $d(e)$ on each edge $e \in E$, representing the amount of time required for data to traverse the edge. Many of the tractable problems considered here, e.g., the data itinerary problem, become intractable in this more general model.
- It is assumed here that the cost of traversing an edge, or of storing data on a vertex, is time-independent. It may be more realistic to allow these rates to vary periodically; in real networks, lower night rates may render data communication cheaper, for example. However, this generalization too leads to intractable versions of the problems solved in Sections 2 and 3.
- In Section 4, data is to be broadcast to all the vertices in the graph after a specified delay. A more general problem, in which data is to be multicast to a specified subset of the vertices, is NP-hard (reduction from Steiner Tree).

Our examination of routing in the presence of delays represents progress towards (a) developing a model that more accurately represents the cost functions of real-world data routing problems, and (b) finding efficient algorithms for data routing, or proving the problem to be intractible, under this model. Additionally, the algorithms given here have wider applications to commodity routing and itinerary scheduling problems.

References

1. R. Ahmadi. Scheduling in just-in-time manufacture. Ph.D thesis. The University of Texas, Austin, TX. 1988.
2. N. Christofides. Worst-case analysis of a new heuristic for the traveling salesman problem. Technical report, GSIA, Carnegie-Mellon University, 1976.
3. E. W. Dijkstra. A note on two problems in connection with graphs. *Numer. Math.*, 1:269–271, 1959.
4. R. W. Floyd. Algorithm 97: Shortest path. *Comm. ACM*, 5:345, 1962.

5. F. Preparata and M. Shamos. *Computational Geometry: An Introduction.* Springer-Verlag, 1985.
6. H. Psaraftis and J. Tsitsiklis. Dynamic shortest paths in acyclic networks with Markovian arc costs. *Operations Research:* 14(1). 1993.
7. V. Vazirani. Personal communication. July 1994.

Algorithmic Arguments in Physics of Computation

Paul Vitányi*
CWI and University of Amsterdam

Ming Li**
University of Waterloo

Abstract. We show the usefulness of incompressibility arguments based on Kolmogorov complexity in physics of computation by several examples. These include analysis of energy parsimonious 'adiabatic' computation, and scalability of network architectures.

1 Introduction

In [Shannon, 1948] C. Shannon formulated information theory dealing with the average number of bits required to communicate a message produced by a random source from a sender to a receiver who both agree on the ensemble of possible messages. In this theory, if the universe of messages consists of a two elements, a sentence "let's go drink a beer" and Homer's Illiad, both elements equally likely, then the Illiad can be transmitted by a single bit. This illustrates that, as Shannon points out, this theory does not say anything about the information content of individual objects, but only says something about the required information exchange for communication.

In [Kolmogorov, 1965] A.N. Kolmogorov formulated a theory of information contents (Kolmogorov complexity) of individual finite objects. Since this theory deals with a stronger notion, namely information contents of *individual* objects instead of *average* information to communicate objects from *probabilistic ensembles*, it is not *a priori* obvious that properties of Shannon's notion would hold for Kolmogorov's new notion. Remarkably, it turns out that various properties, such as the 'symmetry of information' stating that the information in a random source X about another random source Y is precisely equal to the information in Y about X, holds also approximately for Kolmogorov complexity of individual objects, that is, up to a logarithmic additive term.

* Partially supported by the European Union through NeuroCOLT ESPRIT Working Group Nr. 8556, and by NWO through NFI Project ALADDIN under Contract number NF 62-376 and NSERC under International Scientific Exchange Award ISE0125663. Address: CWI, Kruislaan 413, 1098 SJ Amsterdam, The Netherlands. Email: paulv@cwi.nl

** Supported in part by NSERC operating grant OGP-046506, ITRC, and a CGAT grant. Address: Computer Science Department, University of Waterloo, Waterloo, Ontario, Canada N2L 3G1. Email: mli@math.uwaterloo.ca

Information theory à la Shannon has been shown applicable in a large range of areas ranging from combinatorics to communication and computation technologies. The special feature of Kolmogorov complexity is that it deals with individual objects. This allows topics of application were Shannon's theory is ostensibly powerless, albeit using slightly weaker laws. We and others have been able to find new simpler proofs for known results, like the Razborov – Fortnow – Laplante version of Hastad's Switching Lemma or Ian Munro's version of Russel Schaffer's exact average running time of Heapsort, to find new incompressibility arguments for combinatorial theory, a basis for inductive learning, or to resolve (formerly well known) old open problems in the theory of computation like Turing machine and PRAM time complexity. The basic theory and many of these applications are treated in our textbook [Li & Vitányi, 1993]. Recently, we have extensively used the symmetry of information law where application to individual objects seems absolutely crucial, [Jiang et al.].

Our purpose here is to point out that applicability of incompressibility arguments based on Kolmogorov complexity is not restricted to the platonic realm of mathematics and theory of computation, but can profitably be extended to the real world of physical phenomena.

1.1 Kolmogorov complexity

The Kolmogorov complexity, [Kolmogorov, 1965], of x is the length of the *shortest* effective description of x. That is, the *Kolmogorov complexity* $C(x)$ of a finite string x is simply the length of the shortest program, say in FORTRAN[3] encoded in binary, which prints x without any input. A similar definition holds conditionally, in the sense that $C(x|y)$ is the length of the shortest binary program which computes x given y as input. It can be shown that the Kolmogorov complexity is absolute in the sense of being independent of the programming language, up to a fixed additional constant term which depends on the programming language but not on x. We now fix one canonical programming language once and for all as reference and thereby $C()$.

For the theory and applications, see [Li & Vitányi, 1993]. Let $x, y, z \in \mathcal{N}$, where $\mathcal{N}$ denotes the natural numbers and we identify $\mathcal{N}$ and $\{0,1\}^*$ according to the correspondence $(0, \epsilon), (1, 0), (2, 1), (3, 00), (4, 01), \ldots$. Hence, the length $|x|$ of x is the number of bits in the binary string x. Let $T_1, T_2, \ldots$ be a standard enumeration of all Turing machines. Let $\langle \cdot, \cdot \rangle$ be a standard invertible effective bijection from $\mathcal{N} \times \mathcal{N}$ to $\mathcal{N}$. This can iterated to $\langle \langle \cdot, \cdot \rangle, \cdot \rangle$.

Definition 1. Let U be an appropriate universal Turing machine such that $U(\langle \langle i, p \rangle, y \rangle) = T_i(\langle p, y \rangle)$ for all i and $\langle p, y \rangle$. The *Kolmogorov complexity* of x given y (for free) is

$$C(x|y) = \min\{|p| : U(\langle p, y \rangle) = x, p \in \{0,1\}^*, i \in \mathcal{N}\}.$$

---

[3] Or in Turing machine codes.

2   Energy Parsimonious Computation

All computations can be performed logically reversibly, [Bennett, 1973], at the cost of eventually filling up the memory with unwanted garbage information. This means that reversible computers with bounded memories require in the long run irreversible bit operations, for example, to erase records irreversibly to create free memory space. The minimal possible number of irreversibly erased bits to do so is believed to determine the ultimate limit of heat dissipation of the computation by Landauer's principle, [Landauer, 1961, Bennett, 1973, Bennett, 1982, Proc. PhysComp, 1981, 1992, 1994]. In reference [Bennett *et al.*, 1993] we and others developed a mathematical theory for the unavoidable number of irreversible bit operations in an otherwise reversible computation. A precursor to this line of thought is [Zurek, 1989]. Here we present the operational proof in [Li & Vitányi, 1994] for the known exact expression of the number of irreversible bit operations in an otherwise reversible computation proved differently in [Bennett *et al.*, 1993].

Many currently proposed physical schemes implementing adiabatic computation reduce irreversibility by using longer switching times. This is done typically by switching over equal voltage gates after voltage has been equalized slowly. This type of switching does not dissipate energy, the only energy dissipation is incurred by pulling voltage up and down: the slower it goes the less energy is dissipated, [Proc. PhysComp, 1981, 1992, 1994]. If the computation goes infinitely slow, zero energy is dissipated. Clearly, this counteracts the purpose of low energy dissipation which is faster computation.

In [Li & Vitányi, 1994] it is demonstrated that even if adiabatic computation technology advances to switching with no time loss, a similar phenomenon arises when we try to approach the ultimate limits of minimal irreversibility of an otherwise reversible computation, and hence minimal energy dissipation. This time the effect is due to the logical method of reducing the number of irreversible bit erasures in the computation irrespective of individual switching times. By computing longer and longer (in the sense of using more computation steps), the amount of dissipated energy gets closer to ultimate limits. Moreover, one can trade-off time (number of steps) for energy: there is a new time-irreversibility (time-energy) trade-off hierarchy. The bounds we derive are also relevant for quantum computations which are reversible except for the irreversible observation steps, [Deutsch, 1985, Benioff, 1995].

2.1   Background

The ultimate limits of miniaturization of computing devices, and therefore the speed of computation, are governed by unavoidable heating up attending rising energy dissipation caused by increasing density of switching elements in the device. On a basically two dimensional device linear speed up by shortening interconnects is essentially attended by squaring the dissipated energy per area unit per second because we square the number of switching elements per area unit, [Mead & Conway, 1980].

Therefore, the question of how to reduce the energy dissipation of computation determines future advances in computing power. Around 1940 a computing device dissipated about 10^{-2} Joule per bit operation at room temperature. Since that time the dissipated energy per bit operation has roughly decreased by one order of magnitude (tenfold) every five years. Currently, a bit operation dissipates about 10^{-17} Joule.[4] Extrapolations of current trends show that the energy dissipation per binary logic operation needs to be reduced below kT (thermal noise) within 20 years. Here k is Boltzamnn's constant and T the absolute temperature in °Kelvin, so that $kT \approx 3 \times 10^{-21}$ Joule at room temperature. Even at kT level, a future laptop containing 10^{18} gates in a cubic centimeter operating at a gigahertz dissipates 3 million watts/second. For thermodynamic reasons, cooling the operating temperature of such a computing device to almost absolute zero (to get kT down) must dissipate at least as much energy in the cooling as it saves for the computing. It is unlikely that this challenge can be met by other means than the use of reversible logic.

J. von Neumann [Burks, 1966] reputedly thought that a computer operating at temperature T must dissipate at least $kT \ln 2$ Joule per elementary bit operation. Around 1960, R. Landauer [Landauer, 1961] analyzed this question and concluded that it is only 'logically irreversible' operations that dissipate energy. An operation is *logically reversible* if its inputs can always be deduced from the outputs. Erasure of information in a way such that it cannot be retrieved is not reversible. Erasing each bit costs $kT \ln 2$ energy, when computer operates at temperature T.

One should sharply distinguish between the issue of logical reversibility and the issue of energy dissipation freeness. The fact that some computer operates in a logically reversible manner says nothing about whether it dissipates heat. The only thing it says is that the laws of physics do not preclude that one can invent a technology in which to implement a logically similar computer to operate physically in a dissipationless manner. Computers built from reversible circuits, or the reversible Turing machine, [Bennett, 1973, Bennett, 1982, Fredkin & Toffoli, 1982], implemented with current technology will presumably dissipate energy but may conceivably be implemented by future technology in an adiabatic fashion. For nonreversible computers adiabatic implementation is widely considered impossible.

Thought experiments can exhibit a computer that is both logically and physically perfectly reversible and hence perfectly dissipationless. An example is the billiard ball computer, [Fredkin & Toffoli, 1982], and similarly the possibility of a coherent quantum computer, [Feynman, 1985, Deutsch, 1985].

Methods to implement (almost) reversible dissipationless computation using conventional electronic technologies appear in [Proc. PhysComp, 1981, 1992, 1994], often designated by the catch phrase 'adiabatic switching'. Our purpose is to determine the theoretical ultimate limits to which the irreversible actions in an otherwise reversible computation can be reduced.

---

[4] After R.W. Keyes, IBM Research.

2.2 Model of Computation

Energy free 'copying' of records, and cancelling of one record with respect to an identical record provided it is known that they are identical, is physically realizable (or almost realizable). This is the case when a program sets $y := x$ and later (reversibly) erases $x := 0$. We shall call reversible erasure 'cancelling'. Irrespective of the original contents of variable x we can always restore x by $x := y$. However, if the program has no copy of x which can be identified by examining the program without knowing the contents of the variables, then after (irreversibly) erasing $x := 0$ we cannot restore the original contents of x even though some variable z may have by chance the same contents. 'Copying' and 'cancelling' are logically reversible, and their energy dissipation free execution gives substance to the idea that logically reversible computations can be performed with zero energy dissipation.

We have seen that the number of irreversibly erased bits in an otherwise reversible computation which replaces input x by output y, each unit counted as $kT \ln 2$, represents energy dissipation. Complementary to this idea, if such a computation uses initially irreversibly provided bits apart from input x, then they must be accounted at the same negated cost as that for irreversible erasure. Because of the reversibility of the computation, we can argue by symmetry. Namely, suppose we run a reversible computation starting when memory contains input x and additional record p, and ending with memory containing output y and additional garbage bits q. Then p is irreversibly provided, and q is irreversibly deleted. But if we run the computation backward, then the roles of x, p and y, q are simply interchanged.

We can view any computation as consisting of a sequence of reversible and irreversible operation executions. We want the irreversibility cost to reflect all nonreversible parts of the computation. The irreversibility cost of an otherwise reversible computation is set to the *maximum* of the number of irreversibly provided and the number of irreversibly erased bits.

We consider the following axioms as a formal basis on which to develop a theory of irreversibility of computation.

Axiom 1 Reversible computations do not incur any cost.
Axiom 2 Irreversibly provided and irreversibly deleted bits in a computation incur unit cost each.
Axiom 3 In a reversible computation which replaces input x by output y, the input x is not irreversibly provided and the output y is not irreversibly deleted.
Axiom 4 All physical computations are effective.

Axiom 4 is simply an extended form of *Church's Thesis*: the notion of physical computation coincides with effective computation which coincides with the formal notion of Turing machines computation. Deutsch, [Deutsch, 1985], and others have argued the possibility that this is false. If that turns out to be the case then either our arguments are to be restricted to those physical processes for which Axiom 4 holds, or, perhaps, one can extend the notion of effective computations appropriately.

We will be talking about the ultimate limits of energy dissipation by computation. Since these limits will be expressed in the number of bits in the irreversibly erased records, we consider compactification of records. Rather as in analogy of garbage collection by a garbage truck: the cost is less if we compact the garbage before we throw it away.

The ultimate compactification which can be effectively exploited is expressed in terms of Kolmogorov complexity. This is a recursively invariant concept, and to express the ultimate limits *no other notion will do*. Consequently, this mundane matter of energy dissipation of physical computation is linked to, and expressed in, the pristine theoretical notion of Kolmogorov complexity.

2.3   Irreversibility Cost of Computation

Axioms 1—4 lead to the definition of the irreversibility cost of a computation as the number of bits we added plus the number of bits we erased in computing one string from another. Let $\mathbf{R} = R_1, R_2, \ldots$ be a standard enumeration of reversible Turing machines, [Bennett, 1973]. We define $E(\cdot, \cdot)$ as in [Bennett *et al.*, 1993] (where it is denoted as $E_3(;\cdot)$).

Definition 2. The *irreversibility cost* $E_R(x, y)$ of computing y from x by a reversible Turing machine R is is

$$E_R(x, y) = \min\{|p| + |q| : R(\langle x, p \rangle) = \langle y, q \rangle\}.$$

We denote the class of all such cost functions by $\mathcal{E}$.

We call an element E_Q of $\mathcal{E}$ a *universal irreversibility cost function*, if $Q \in \mathbf{R}$, and for all R in $\mathbf{R}$

$$E_Q(x, y) \leq E_R(x, y) + c_R,$$

for all x and y, where c_R is a constant which depends on R but not on x or y. Standard arguments from the theory of Turing machines show the following.

Lemma 3. *There is a universal irreversibility cost function in $\mathcal{E}$. Denote it by E_{UR}.*

Proof. In [Bennett, 1973] a universal reversible Turing machine UR is constructed which satisfies the optimality requirement.

Two such universal (or optimal) machines UR and UR' will assign the same irreversibility cost to a computation apart from an additive constant term c which is *independent* of x and y (but does depend on UR and UR'). We select a reference universal function UR and define the *irreversibility cost* $E(x, y)$ of computing y from x as

$$E(x, y) \equiv E_{UR}(x, y).$$

Because of the expression for $E(x,y)$ in Theorem 4 below it is called the *sum cost* measure in [Bennett *et al.*, 1993].

In physical terms this cost is in units of $kT \ln 2$, where k is Boltzmann's constant, T is the absolute temperature in degrees Kelvin, and ln is the natural logarithm.

Because the computation is reversible, this definition is *symmetric*: we have $E(x,y) = E(y,x)$.

In our definitions we have pushed all bits to be irreversibly provided to the start of the computation and all bits to be erased to the end of the computation. It is easy to see that this is no restriction. If we have a computation where irreversible acts happen throughout the computation, then we can always mark the bits to be erased, waiting with actual erasure until the end of the computation. Similarly, the bits to be provided can be provided (marked) at the start of the computation while the actual reading of them (simultaneously unmarking them) takes place throughout the computation).

Computing Between x and y Now let us consider a general computation which outputs string y from input string x. We want to know the minimum irreversibility cost for such computation. This leads to the following theorem, first proven as below and also established in [Bennett *et al.*, 1993] by a different more indirect proof, which is the basis of our theory.

Theorem 4 Fundamental theorem. *Up to an additive logarithmic term*

$$E(x,y) = C(x|y) + C(y|x).$$

Proof. We prove first an upper bound and then a lower bound.

Claim 1 $E(x,y) \le C(y|x) + C(x|y) + 2[C(C(y|x)|y) + C(C(x|y)|x)].$

Proof. We start out the computation with programs p, q, r. Program p computes y from x and $|p| = C(y|x)$. Program q computes the value $C(x|y)$ from x and $|q| = C(C(x|y)|x)$. Program r computes the value $C(y|x)$ from y and $|r| = C(C(y|x)|y)$. To separate the different binary programs we have to encode delimiters. This takes an extra additional number of bits logarithmic in the two smallest length of elements p, q, r. This extra log term is absorbed in the additive log term in the statement of the theorem. The computation is as follows. Everything is executed reversibly apart from the final irreversible erasure.

1. Use p to compute y from x producing garbage bits $g(x,y)$.
2. Copy y, and use one copy of y and $g(x,y)$ to reverse the computation to x and p. Now we have p, q, r, x, y.
3. Copy x, and use one copy of x and q to compute $C(x|y)$ plus garbage bits.
4. Use $x, y, C(x|y)$ to dovetail the running of all programs of length $C(x|y)$ to find s, a shortest program to compute x from y. Doing this, we produce more garbage bits.

5. Copy s, and reverse the computations in Steps 4, 3, canceling the extra copies and all garbage bits. Now we have p, q, r, s, x, y.
6. Copy y, and use this copy to compute the value $C(y|x)$ from r and y producing garbage bits.
7. Use $x, y, C(y|x)$, to dovetail the running of all programs of length $C(y|x)$ to obtain a copy of p, the shortest program to compute y from x, producing more garbage bits.
8. Delete a copy of p and reverse the computation of Steps 7, 6 cancelling the superfluous copy of y and all garbage bits. Now we are left with x, y, r, s, q.
9. Compute from y and s a copy of x and cancel a copy of x. Reverse the computation. Now we have y, r, s, q.
10. Erase s, r, q irreversibly.

We started out with additional shortest programs p, q, r apart from x. We have irreversibly erased the shortest programs s, q, r, where $|s| = C(x|y)$, leaving only y. This proves the claim.

Note that all bits supplied in the beginning to the computation, apart from input x, as well as all bits irreversibly erased at the end of the computation, are *random* bits. This is because we supply and delete only shortest programs, and a shortest program p satisfies $C(p) \geq |p|$, that is, it is maximally random.

Claim 2 $E(x, y) \geq C(y|x) + C(x|y)$.

Proof. To compute y from x we must be given a program to do so to start out with. By definition the shortest such program has length $C(y|x)$.

Assume the computation from x to y produces $g(x, y)$ garbage bits. Since the computation is reversible we can compute x from y and $g(x, y)$. Consequently, $|g(x, y)| \geq C(x|y)$ by definition [Zurek, 1989]. To end the computation with y alone we therefore must irreversibly erase $g(x, y)$ which is at least $C(x|y)$ bits.

Together Claims 1, 2 prove the theorem.

Corollary 5. *Erasing a record x is actually a computation from x to the empty string ϵ. Therefore, up to a logarithmic additive term, the irreversible cost (also thermodynamic cost) of erasure is $E(x, \epsilon) = C(x)$.*

2.4 Trading Time for Energy

In order to erase a record x, Corollary 5 actually requires us to have, apart from x, a program p of length $C(C(x)|x)$ for computing $C(x)$, given x. The precise bounds are $C(x) \leq E(x, \epsilon) \leq C(x) + 2C(C(x)|x)$. This optimum is not effective, it requires that p be given in some way. But we can use the same method as in the proof of Theorem 4, by compressing x using some time bound t.

First we need some definitions. Because now the time bounds are important we consider the universal Turing machine U to be the machine with two work tapes which can simulate t steps of a multitape Turing machine T in $O(t \log t)$

steps, see for example [Li & Vitányi, 1993]. If some multitape Turing machine T computes x in time t from a program p, then U computes x in time $O(t \log t)$ from p plus a description of T.

Definition 6. Let $C^t(x|y)$ be the *minimal length* of binary program (not necessarily reversibly) for the two work tape universal Turing machine U computing x given y (for free) *in time* t. Formally,

$$C^t(x|y) = \min_{p \in \mathcal{N}}\{|p| : U(\langle p, y \rangle) = x \text{ in } \leq t(|x|) \text{ steps}\}.$$

$C^t(x|y)$ is called the *t-time-limited conditional Kolmogorov complexity* of x given y. The unconditional version is defined as $C^t(x) := C^t(x, \epsilon)$. A program p such that $U(p) = x$ in $\leq t(|x|)$ steps and $|p| = C^t(x)$ is denoted as x_t^*.

Note that with $C_T^t(x|y)$ the conditional t-time-limited Kolmogorov complexity with respect to Turing machine T, for all x, y, $C^{t'}(x|y) \leq C_T^t(x|y) + c_T$, where $t' = O(t \log t)$ and c_T is a constant depending on T but not on x and y.

This $C^t(\cdot)$ is the standard definition of time-limited Kolmogorov complexity, [Li & Vitányi, 1993]. However, in the remainder of the paper we always need to use reversible computations. Fortunately, in [Bennett, 1989] the following is shown.

Lemma 7. *For any $\epsilon > 0$, ordinary multitape Turing machines using T time and S space can be simulated by reversible ones using time $O(T)$ and space $O(ST^\epsilon)$.*

To do effective erasure of compacted information, we must at the start of the computation provide a time bound t. Typically, t is a recursive function and the complexity of its description is small, say $O(1)$. However, in Theorem 8 we allow for very large running times in order to obtain smaller $C^t(\cdot)$ values. (In the theorem below t need not necessarily be a recursive function $t(|x|)$, but can also be used nonuniformly. This leads to a stronger result.)

Theorem 8 Irreversibility cost of effective erasure. *If $t(|x|) \geq |x|$ is a time bound which is provided at the start of the computation, then erasing an n bit record x by an otherwise reversible computation can be done in time (number of steps) $O(2^{|x|} t(|x|))$ at irreversibility cost (hence also thermodynamic cost) $C^t(x) + 2C^t(t|x) + 4 \log C^t(t|x)$ bits. (Typically we consider t as some standard explicit time bound and the last two terms adding up to $O(1)$.)*

Proof. Initially we have in memory input x and a program p of length $C^t(t, x)$ to compute reversibly t from x. To separate binary x and binary p we need to encode a delimiter in at most $2 \log C^t(t|x)$ bits.

1. Use x and p to reversibly compute t. Copy t and reverse the computation. Now we have x, p and t.
2. Use t to reversibly dovetail the running of all programs of length less than x to find the shortest one halting in time t with output x. This is x_t^*. The computation has produced garbage bits $g(x, x_t^*)$. Copy x_t^*, and reverse the computation to obtain x erasing all garbage bits $g(x, x_t^*)$. Now we have x, p, x_t^*, t in memory.

3. Reversibly compute t from x by p, cancel one copy of t, and reverse the computation. Now we have x, p, x_t^* in memory.

4. Reversibly cancel x using x_t^* by the standard method, and then erase x_t^* and p irreversibly.

More practical compression methods are surveyed in [Storer, 1988].

By spending more time we can reduce the thermodynamic cost of erasure of x_t^* to its absolute minimum. In the limit we spend the optimal value $C(x)$ by erasing x^*, since $\lim_{t\to\infty} x_t^* = x^*$. This suggests the existence of a trade-off hierarchy between time and energy. The longer one reversibly computes to perform final irreversible erasures, the less bits are erased and energy is dissipated. This intuitive assertion will be formally stated and rigorously proved below. We proceed through a sequence of related 'irreversibility' results.

Definition 9. Let UR be the reversible version of the two worktape universal Turing machine, simulating the latter in linear time by Lemma 7. Let $E^t(x, y)$ be the *minimum irreversibility cost* of an otherwise reversible computation from x to y *in time* t. Formally,

$$E^t(x, y) = \min_{p,q \in \mathcal{N}} \{|p| + |q| : UR(\langle x, p\rangle) = \langle y, q\rangle \text{ in } \leq t(|x|) \text{ steps}\}.$$

Since $E(x, \epsilon)$ is about $C(x)$, one is erroneously led to believe that $E^t(x, \epsilon) = C^t(x)$ up to a log additive term. However, the time-bounds introduce many differences. To reversibly compute x_t^* we may require (because of the halting problem) at least $O(2^{|x|}t(|x|))$ steps after having decoded t, as indeed is the case in the proof of Theorem 8. In contrast, $E^t(x, \epsilon)$ is about the number of bits erased in an otherwise reversible computation which uses at most t steps. It is not difficult to show that for each x and $t(|x|) \geq |x|$,

$$E^t(x, \epsilon) \geq C^t(x) \geq E^{t'}(x, \epsilon)/2, \tag{1}$$

with $t'(|x|) = O(t(|x|))$, [Li & Vitányi, 1994]. Moreover, Theorem 8 can be re-stated in terms of $E^t(\cdot)$ as

$$E^{t'}(x, \epsilon) \leq C^t(x) + 2C^t(t|x) + 4\log C^t(t|x),$$

with $t'(|x|) = O(2^{|x|}t(|x|))$. Comparing this to the righthand inequality of Equation 1 we have improved the upper bound on erasure cost at the expense of increasing erasure time. However, these bounds only suggest but do not actually prove that we can exchange irreversibility for time. But the following result, shown by incompressibility arguments in [Li & Vitányi, 1994], definitely establishes the existence of a trade-off.

Theorem 10 Irreversibility-time trade-off hierarchy. *For every large enough n there is a string x of length n and a sequence of $m = \frac{1}{2}\sqrt{n}$ time functions $t_1(n) < t_2(n) < \ldots < t_m(n)$, such that*

$$E^{t_1}(x, \epsilon) > E^{t_2}(x, \epsilon) > \ldots > E^{t_m}(x, \epsilon).$$

In the cost measures like $E^t(\cdot, \cdot)$ we have counted both the irreversibly provided and the irreversibly erased bits. But Landauer's principle only charges energy dissipation costs for irreversibly erased bits. It is conceivable that the above results would not hold if one considers as the cost of erasure of a record only the irreversibly erased bits. However, in [Li & Vitányi, 1994] it is shown that the above results hold under these considerations as well.

3 Scalability of Multiprocessor Architectures

In many areas of the theory of parallel computation we meet graph structured computational models which encourage the design of parallel algorithms where the cost of communication is largely ignored. Yet it is well known that the cost of computation - in both time and space - vanishes with respect to the cost of communication latency in parallel or distributed computing. It turns out that symmetric low diameter networks do not scale well; and random networks (and hence almost all networks) do not scale at all. This confirms that meshes are the way to go.

Models of parallel computation that allow processors to randomly access a large shared memory, such as PRAMs, or rapidly access a member of a large number of other processors, will necessarily have large latency. If we use 2^n processing elements of, say, unit size each, then the tightest they can be packed is in a 3-dimensional sphere of volume 2^n. Assuming that the units have no "funny" shapes, e.g., are spherical themselves, no unit in the enveloping sphere can be closer to all other units than a distance of radius R,

$$R = \left(\frac{3 \cdot 2^n}{4\pi}\right)^{1/3} \tag{2}$$

Because of the bounded speed of light, it is impossible to transport signals over $2^{\alpha n}$ ($\alpha > 0$) distance in polynomial $p(n)$ time. In fact, the assumption of the bounded speed of light says that the lower time bound on *any* computation using 2^n processing elements is $\Omega(2^{n/3})$ outright. Or, for the case of computations on networks which use n^α processors, $\alpha > 0$, the lower bound on the computation time is $\Omega(n^{\alpha/3})$.

In previous theoretical analysis, often a wire did not take room, did not dissipate heat, and did not cost anything - at least, not enough to worry about. This was realistic when the number of wires was low, somewhere in the hundreds. Current designs use many millions of wires (on chip), or possibly billions of wires (on wafers). In a computation of parallel nature, most of the time seems to be spent on communication - transporting signals over wires. The present analysis allows us to see that any reasonable model for multicomputer computation must charge for communication. The communication cost will impact on both physical time and physical space costs.

3.1 Regular Low Diameter Networks

At present, many popular multicomputer architectures are based on highly symmetric communication networks with small diameter. Like all networks with small diameter, such networks necessarily contain *some* long interconnects (embedded edges). We have shown in [Vitányi, 1986, Vitányi, 1988] that the desirable fast permutation properties of symmetric networks don't come free, since they require that the average of *all* interconnects is long. (Note that 'embedded edge,' 'wire,' and 'interconnect' are used synonymously.) To preclude objections that the results hold only asymptotically (and therefore can be safely ignored for practical numbers of processors), or that processors are huge and wires thin (idem), we calculated without hidden constants and assume that wires have length but no volume and can pass through everything. It is consistent with the results that wires have *zero* volume, and that *infinitely* many wires pass through a unit area. The lower bound obtained hlolds for the *average* edge length for *any* graph, in terms of certain symmetries and diameter. The lower bound deteriorates when the graph is irregular. For each regular graph topology we have examined, the resulting lower bound turned out to be sharp. It turns out that for symmetric networks like binary d-cube, cube-connected cycles, star graphs, complete graphs, the average edge length is as bad as can be. An extension of the argument shows the same for related networks like the Bruijn networks, shuffle-exchange graphs, and so on, [Koppelman, 1995].

3.2 Irregular Networks

Since low-diameter symmetric network topologies lead to high average interconnect length, it is natural to ask what happens with irregular topologies. In fact, it is sometimes proposed that since symmetric networks of low diameter lead to high interconnect length, one should use random networks where the presense or absence of a connection is determined by a coin flip. We report on some work in [Vitányi, 1994] that such networks will also have impossibly high average interconnect length.

Concretely, the problem is posed as follows. Let $G = (V, E)$ be a finite undirected graph, without loops or multiple edges, *embedded* in 3-dimensional Euclidean space. Let each embedded node have unit *volume*. For convenience of the argument, each node is embedded as a sphere, and is *represented* by the single point in the center. The *distance* between a pair of nodes is the Euclidean distance between the points representing them. The *length* of the embedding of an edge between two nodes is the distance between the nodes. How large does the *average* edge length need to be?

One way to express irregularity or *randomness* of an individual network topology is by a modern notion of randomness like Kolmogorov complexity. A simple counting argument shows that for each y in the condition and each length n there exists at least one x of length n which is *incompressible* in the sense of $C(x|y) \geq n$, 50% of all x's of length n is incompressible but for 1 bit $(C(x|y) \geq n-1)$, 75%th of all x's is incompressible but for 2 bits $(C(x|y) \geq n-2)$

and in general a fraction of $1 - 2^{-c}$ of all strings cannot be compressed by more than c bits, [Li & Vitányi, 1993].

Each graph $G = (V, E)$ on n nodes $V = \{0, \ldots, n-1\}$ can be coded (up to isomorphism) by a binary string of length $n(n-1)/2$. We enumerate the $n(n-1)/2$ possible edges in a graph on n nodes in standard order and set the ith bit in the string to 1 if the edge is present and to 0 otherwise. Conversely, each binary string of length $n(n-1)/2$ encodes a graph on n nodes. Hence we can identify each such graph with its corresponding binary string.

We shall call a graph G on n nodes *random* if it satisfies

$$C(G|n) \geq n(n-1)/2 - cn, \tag{3}$$

where c is an appropriate constant ($c = 1/16$ suffices for our purpose). Elementary counting shows that *a fraction* of at least

$$1 - 1/2^{cn}$$

of all graphs on n nodes has that high complexity.

Lemma 11. *The degree d of each node of a random graph satisfies $|d - (n-1)/2| < n/4$.*

Proof. Assume that the deviation of the degree d of a node v in G from $(n-1)/2$ is at least k. From the lower bound on $C(G|n)$ corresponding to the assumption that G is random, we can estimate an upper bound on k, as follows.

Describe G given n as follows. We can indicate which edges are incident on node v by giving the index of the connection pattern in the ensemble of

$$m = \sum_{|d-(n-1)/2| \geq k} \binom{n}{d} \leq 2^n e^{-k^2/(n-1)} \tag{4}$$

possibilities. The last inequality follows from a general estimate of the tail probability of the binomial distribution, with s_n the number of successful outcomes in n experiments with probability of success $0 < p < 1$ and $q = 1 - p$. Namely, Chernoff's bounds, [Li & Vitányi, 1993], pp. 127-130, give

$$\Pr(|s_n - np| \geq k) \leq 2e^{-k^2/4npq}. \tag{5}$$

To describe G it then suffices to modify the old code of G by prefixing it with

- the identity of the node concerned in $\lceil \log n \rceil$ bits,
- the value of d in $\lceil \log n \rceil$ bits, possibly adding nonsignificant 0's to pad up to this amount,
- the index of the interconnection pattern in $\log m + 2 \log \log m$ bits in self-delimiting form (this form requirement allows the concatenated binary sub-descriptions to be parsed and unpacked into the individual items: it encodes a separation delimiter, at the cost of adding the second term, [Li & Vitányi, 1993]),

followed by the old code for G with the bits in the code denoting the presence or absence of the possible edges which are incident on the node v deleted.

Clearly, given n we can reconstruct the graph G from the new description. The total description we have achieved is an effective program of

$$\log m + 2 \log \log m + O(\log n) + n(n-1)/2 - (n-1)$$

bits. This must be at least the length of the shortest effective binary program, which is $C(G|n)$ satisfying Equation 3. Therefore,

$$\log m + 2 \log \log m \geq n - 1 - O(\log n) - cn.$$

Since we have estimated in Equation 4 that

$$\log m \leq n - (k^2/(n-1)) \log e,$$

it follows that, with $c = 1/16$,

$$k < n/4.$$

The lemma shows that each node is connected by an edge with about 25% of all nodes in G. Hence G contains a subgraph on about 25 % of its nodes of diameter 1. This is all we need. For completeness, we derive the following lemma, using an idea due to Harry Buhrman.

Lemma 12. *Random graphs have diameter 2.*

Proof. The only graphs with diameter 1 are the complete graphs which can be described in $O(1)$ bits, given n, and hence are not random. It remains to consider G is a random graph with diameter greater than 2. Let i, j be a pair of nodes with distance greater than 2. Then we can describe G by modifying the old code for G by prefixing it with

- The identities of $i < j$ in $\lceil \log n \rceil$ bits,

followed by the old code of G with all bits representing an edge (j, k) between j and each k with (i, k) an edge of G deleted. We know that all the bits representing such edges must be 0 since the existence of any such edge shows that $(i, k), (k, j)$ is a path of length 2 between i and j contradicting the assumption that i and j have distance > 2. Since we know the identities of i and j, and the nodes adjacent to j, we can reconstruct G from this discussion and the new description, given n. Since by Lemma 11 the degree of i is at least $n/4$, the new description of G, given n, has at most

$$n(n-1)/2 + 2\lceil \log n \rceil - n/4 + O(1),$$

which contradicts Equation 3 from some n onwards.

Theorem 13. *A fraction of at least $1 - 1/2^{cn}$ $(c = 1/16)$ of all graphs on n nodes (the incompressible, random, graphs) have average interconnect length of $\Omega(n^{1/3})$ in each 3-dimensional Euclidean space embedding (or $\Omega(n^{1/2})$ in each 2-dimensional Euclidean space embedding).*

Proof. By lemma 11 we know that in a random graph G each node x is at distance 1 of $(n - 1)/2 \pm n/4$ other nodes y, and 7/8th of these nodes y (in 3 dimensions) is at distance $\Omega(n^{1/3})$ of x by Equation 2. The argument for 2 dimensions is analogous.

By Lemma 11 we know that a random graph G on n nodes has $\Omega(n^2)$ edges since each node has about $n/2$ incident edges. Therefore, we have the following.

Corollary 14. *A fraction of at least $1 - 1/2^{cn}$ ($c = 1/16$) of all graphs on n nodes (the incompressible, random, graphs) have total interconnect length of $\Omega(n^{7/3})$ in each 3-dimensional Euclidean space embedding (or $\Omega(n^{5/2})$ in each 2-dimensional Euclidean space embedding).*

Since both the very regular symmetric low diameter graphs and the random graphs have high average interconnect length which sharply rises with n, the only graphs which will scale feasibly up are symmetric fairly high diameter topologies like the mesh—which therefore will most likely be the interconnection pattern of the future massive multiprocessor systems.

3.3 Interpretation of the Results

An effect that becomes increasingly important at the present time is that most space in the device executing the computation is taken up by the wires. Let's make the very conservative estimates that the unit length of a wire has a volume which is a constant fraction of that of a component it connects.

Regular Networks. We have shown in [Vitányi, 1988] that in 3-dimensional layouts for binary d-cubes, the volume of the $n = 2^d$ components (nodes) performing the actual computation operations is an asymptotic fastly vanishing fraction of the volume of the wires needed for communication:

$$\frac{\text{volume computing components}}{\text{volume communication wires}} = o(n^{-1/3})$$

If we charge a constant fraction of the unit volume for a unit wire length, and add the volume of the wires to the volume of the nodes, then the volume necessary to embed the binary d-cube is $\Omega(n^{4/3})$. However, this lower bound ignores the fact that the added volume of the wires pushes the nodes further apart, thus necessitating longer wires again. How far does this go? A rigorous analysis is complicated, and not important here. The following intuitive argument indicates what we can expect well enough. Denote the volume taken by the nodes as V_n, and the volume taken by the wires as V_w. The total volume taken by the embedding of the cube is $V_t = V_n + V_w$. The total wire length required to lay out a binary d-cube as a function of the volume taken by the embedding is, substituting radius R obtained from $V_t = 4\pi R^3/3$ in the formula for the total wire length obtained in [Vitányi, 1988],

$$L(V_t) \geq \frac{7n}{32} \left(\frac{3V_t}{4\pi} \right)^{1/3}$$

Since $\lim_{n \to \infty} V_n/V_w \to 0$, assuming unit wire length of unit volume, we set the total interconnect length $L(V_t)$ at $L(V_t) \approx V_t$. This results in a better estimate of $\Omega(n^{3/2})$ for the volume needed to embed the binary d-cube. When we want to investigate an upper bound to embed the binary d-cube under the current assumption, we have a problem with the unbounded degree of unit volume nodes. There is no room for the wires to come together at a node. For comparison, therefore, consider the fixed degree version of the binary d-cube, the Cube Connected Cycles (CCC) topology (see [Vitányi, 1988]), with $n = d2^d$ trivalent nodes and $3n/2$ edges. The same argument yields $\Omega(n^{3/2} \log^{-3/2} n)$ for the volume required to embed CCC with unit volume per unit length wire. It is known, that every small degree n-vertex graph, e.g., CCC, can be laid out in a 3-dimensional grid with volume $O(n^{3/2})$ using a unit volume per unit wire length assumption, [Mead & Conway, 1980, Ullman, 1984]. This neatly matches the lower bound.

Because of current limitations to layered VLSI technology, previous investigations have focussed on embeddings of graphs in 2-space (with unit length wires of unit volume). We observe that the above analysis for 2 dimensions leads to $\Omega(n^2)$ and $\Omega(n^2 \log^{-2} n)$ volumes for the binary d-cube and the cube-connected cycles, respectively. These lower bounds have been obtained before using *bisection width* arguments, and are known to be optimal, [Ullman, 1984]. In [Mead & Conway, 1980] it is shown that we cannot always assume that a unit length of wire has $O(1)$ volume. (For instance, if we want to drive the signals to very high speed on chip.)

Irregular Networks. Just like for the complete graph, the situation for the random graph which we consider here, is far worse. For a random graph we have, under the assumption that the wires have unit volume per unit length, that the total wire length in 3 dimensional embeddings is $\Omega(n^{7/3})$ by Theorem 13, and that

$$\frac{\text{volume communication wires}}{\text{volume computing components}} = \Omega(n^{4/3})$$

The proof of Theorem 13 actually shows that the total interconnect length of an embedded random graph is $L(V_t) = \Omega(n^2 V_t^{1/3})$, where the radius of an as tight as possibly packed 3-dimensional sphere of the total volume V_t of nodes and wires together is $\Omega(V_t^{1/3})$. Considering that the larger volume will cause the average interconnect length to increase, as above for the binary d-cube, setting the total interconnect length $L(V_t) \approx V_t$ since the volume of the computing nodes add a negligible term, we find for a random graph that on n nodes that the total volume satisfies

$$V_t = \Omega(n^3).$$

Here we have not yet taken into account that longer wires need larger drivers and have a larger diameter, that the larger volume will again cause the average interconnect length to increase, and so on, which explosion may make embedding altogether impossible with finite length interconnects as exhibited in related contexts in [Vitányi, 1985].

The arguments we have developed are purely geometrical, apply to any graph and any technology, and give optimal lower bounds in all cases we have examined. Our observations are mathematical consequences from the noncontroversial assumptions on 3 dimensional space and the Laws of Physics.

4 Algorithmic Entropy, Chaos, Biology

Algorithmic Entropy. In [Gács, 1994, Li & Vitányi, 1993] an application of Kolmogorov complexity in statistical thermodynamics due to Péter Gács is reported. One can explain the classical theory of thermodynamics by statistical and information-theoretic analysis of an underlying deterministic model. It turns out that a complexity analysis using the powerful methods as explained in [Li & Vitányi, 1993] gives a basis of an algorithmic theory for entropy. Some applications include a proof of an 'entropy nondecrease over time' property, and 'entropy stability' property, 'entropy increase' for certain systems, and an analysis of Maxwell's demon.

Chaos and Predictability. Given sufficient information about a physical system, like the positions, masses and velocities of all particles, and a sufficiently powerful computer with enough memory and computation time, it should be possible in principle to compute all of the past and all of the future of the system. This view, eloquently propagated by P.S. Laplace, can be espoused both in classical mechanics and quantum mechanics. In classical mechanics one would talk about a single 'history', while in quantum mechanics one would talk about probability distributions over an ensemble of 'possible histories.'

Nonetheless, in practice it is impossible to obtain all parameters precisely. The finitary nature of measurement and computation requires truncation of real valued parameters; there are measuring errors; and according to basic quantum mechanics it is impossible to measure certain types of parameters simultaneously and precisely. Altogether, it is fundamental that there are minute uncertainties in our knowledge of any physical system at any time.

This effect can been combined with the consistent tradition that small causes can have large effects exemplified by the metaphor "a butterfly moving its wing in tropical Africa can eventually cause a cyclone in the Caribbean." Minute perturbations in initial conditions can cause, mediated by strictly computable functions, arbitrary large deviations in outcome. In the mathematics of nonlinear deterministic systems this phenomenon has been described by the catch term 'chaos'.

The unpredictability of this phenomenon is sometimes explained through Kolmogorov complexity. Assuming that the initial state is randomly drawn from $[0, 1)$ according to the uniform measure, [Ford, 1983] and other papers, use complexity arguments to show that the *doubling map*'s observable orbit cannot be predicted better than a coin toss. Namely, with λ-probability 1 the drawn initial state will be a Martin-Löf random infinite sequence. Such sequences by definition cannot be effectively predicted [Li & Vitányi, 1993] better than a random coin toss. But in this case we do not need to go to such trouble. The observed orbit essentially consists of the consecutive bits of the initial state. Selecting that initial state randomly from the uniform measure is isomorphic to flipping a fair coin to generate it. There emerges the question of a genuinely significant application of Kolmogorov complexity to unpredictability of chaotic trajectories.

Compression by Ants. In everyday life, we continuously compress information which is presented to us by the environment. Perhaps animals do this as well, as the following experiment reported by Zh.I. Reznikova and B.Ya. Ryabko [*Prob. Inform. Transm.*, 22:3(1986), 245-249, also reported in [Li & Vitányi, 1993]] suggests. It is claimed there that the transmission of information by ants using tactile code is a well-established fact. This led the researchers to probe both the information transmission rate and message compressing capabilities of ants. The experimental results suggest that, apparently, it takes a longer time for the scout ants to communicate 'random' sequences to the forager ants than to communicate 'regular' sequences.

References

[Benioff, 1995] P. Benioff, Review of quantum computation, Argonne National Laboratories, manuscript 1995.

[Bennett, 1973] C.H. Bennett. Logical reversibility of computation. *IBM J. Res. Develop.*, 17:525–532, 1973.

[Bennett, 1982] C.H. Bennett. The thermodynamics of computation—a review. *Int. J. Theoret. Phys.*, 21(1982), 905-940.

[Bennett, 1989] C.H. Bennett. Time-space trade-offs for reversible computation. *SIAM J. Comput.*, 18(1989), 766-776.

[Bennett et al., 1993] C.H. Bennett, P. Gács, M. Li, P.M.B. Vitányi and W.H Zurek, Thermodynamics of computation and information distance *Proc. 25th ACM Symp. Theory of Computation.* ACM Press, 1993, 21-30.

[Deutsch, 1985] D. Deutsch, Quantum theory, the Church-Turing principle and the universal quantum computer. *Proc. Royal Society London.* Vol. A400(1985), 97-117.

[Feynman, 1985] R. Feynman. Quantum mechanical computers. *Foundations of Physics*, 16(1986), 507-531. (Originally published in *Optics News*, February 1985.)

[Ford, 1983] J. Ford, 'How random is a random coin toss?', *Physics Today*, Series A, 1983.

[Gács, 1974] P. Gács. On the symmetry of algorithmic information. *Soviet Math. Dokl.*, 15:1477–1480, 1974. Correction, Ibid., 15:1480, 1974.

[Gács, 1994] P. Gács, The Boltzmann entropy and randomness tests. In: Proc. 2nd IEEE Workshop on Physics and Computation (PhysComp'94), 1994, 209-216.

[Fredkin & Toffoli, 1982] E. Fredkin and T. Toffoli. Conservative logic. *Int. J. Theoret. Phys.*, 21(1982),219-253.

[Jiang et al.] T. Jiang, J. Seiferas and P.M.B. Vitányi, Two heads are better than two tapes, In: *Proc. 26th ACM Symp. Theory of Comput.*, 1994, 668-675.

[Kolmogorov, 1965] A.N. Kolmogorov, Three approaches to the definition of the concept 'quantity of information', *Problems in Information Transmission*, 1:1(1965), 1-7.

[Koppelman, 1995] D.M. Koppelman, A lower bound on the average physical length of edges in the physical realization of graphs, Manuscript Dept ECE, Lousiana State Univ. Baton Rouge, 1995.

[Landauer, 1961] R. Landauer. Irreversibility and heat generation in the computing process. *IBM J. Res. Develop.*, 5:183–191, 1961.

[Li & Vitányi, 1993] M. Li and P.M.B. Vitányi. *An Introduction to Kolmogorov Complexity and Its Applications.* Springer-Verlag, New York, 1993.

[Li & Vitányi, 1994] M. Li and P.M.B. Vitányi. *Irreversibility and Adiabatic Computation: Trading time for energy,* submitted.

[Mead & Conway, 1980] C. Mead and L. Conway. *Introduction to VLSI Systems.* Addison-Wesley, 1980.

[Proc. PhysComp, 1981, 1992, 1994] Proc. 1981 Physics and Computation Workshop. *Int. J. Theoret. Phys.*, 21(1982). *Proc. IEEE 1992 Physics and Computation Workshop.* IEEE Computer Society Press, 1992. *Proc. IEEE 1994 Physics and Computation Workshop.* IEEE Computer Society Press, 1994.

[Shannon, 1948] C.E. Shannon, A mathematical theory of communication, *Bell System Tech. J.*, **27**(1948), 379-423, 623-656.

[Storer, 1988] J. Storer. *Data Compression: Method and Theory.* Computer Science Press, 1988.

[Ullman, 1984] J. Ullman, *Computational Aspects of VLSI*, Computer Science Press, Rockville, MD, 1984.

[Vitányi, 1985] Area penalty for sublinear signal propagation delay on chip, *Proceedings 26th Annual IEEE Symposium on Foundations of Computer Science*, 1985, 197-207.

[Vitányi, 1986] P.M.B. Vitányi, Non-sequential computation and Laws of Nature, In: VLSI Algorithms and Architectures (Proceedings Aegean Workshop on Computing, 2nd International Workshop on Parallel Processing and VLSI), *Lecture Notes In Computer Science 227*, Springer Verlag, 1986, 108-120.

[Vitányi, 1988] P.M.B. Vitányi, Locality, communication and interconnect length in multicomputers, *SIAM J. Computing,* 17 (1988), 659-672.

[Vitányi, 1994] P.M.B. Vitányi, Multiprocessor architectures and physical law. In: Proc. 2nd IEEE Workshop on Physics and Computation (PhysComp'94), 1994, 24-29.

[Burks, 1966] J. von Neumann. *Theory of Self-Reproducing Automata.* A.W. Burks, Ed., Univ. Illinois Press, Urbana, 1966.

[Zurek, 1989] W.H. Zurek. Thermodynamic cost of computation, algorithmic complexity and the information metric. *Nature*, 341:119–124, 1989.

The Buffer Tree:
A New Technique for Optimal I/O-Algorithms *

(Extended Abstract)

Lars Arge

large@daimi.aau.dk

BRICS**

Department of Computer Science, University of Aarhus, Denmark***

Abstract. In this paper we develop a technique for transforming an internal memory tree data structure into an external storage structure. We show how the technique can be used to develop a search-tree-like structure, a priority-queue, a (one-dimensional) range-tree and a segment-tree, and give examples of how these structures can be used to develop efficient I/O-algorithms. All our algorithms are either extremely simple or straightforward generalizations of known internal memory algorithms — given the developed external data structures.

1 Introduction

In the last few years, more and more attention has been given to Input/Output (I/O) complexity of existing algorithms and to the development of new I/O-efficient algorithms. This is due to the fact that communication between fast internal memory and slower external storage is the bottleneck in many large-scale computations. The significance of this bottleneck is increasing as internal computation gets faster, and especially as parallel computing gains popularity [16]. Currently, technological advances are increasing CPU speed at an annual rate of 40-60% while disk transfer rates are only increasing by 7-10% annually [18].

A lot of work has already been done on designing I/O-variants of known internal memory data structures (e.g. [10, 11, 12, 14, 15, 19]), but practically all these data structures are designed to be used in on-line settings, where queries should be answered immediately and within a good worst case number of I/O's. This effectively means that using these structures to solve off-line problems yields non-optimal algorithms, because they are not able to take full advantage of the large internal memory. Therefore a number of researchers have developed

---

* This work was partially supported by the ESPRIT II Basic Research Actions Program of the EC under contract No. 7141 (project ALCOM II) and by Aarhus University Research Foundation.

** Acronym for Basic Research in Computer Science, a Center of the Danish National Research Foundation.

*** Part of this work was done at the Department of Computer Science, Duke University.

techniques and algorithms for solving large-scale off-line problems without using external storage data structures [1, 7, 8].

In this paper we develop external storage data structures that take advantage of the large main memory. This is done by only requiring good amortized performance of the operations on the structures, and by allowing search operations to be batched. The data structures developed can then be used in simple and effective algorithms for computational geometry and graph problems. As pointed out in [7] and [8] problems from these two areas arise in many large-scale computations, e.g in object-oriented, deductive and spatial databases, VLSI design and simulation programs, geographic informations systems, constraint logic programming, statistics, virtual reality systems, and computer graphics.

1.1 I/O-Model and Previous Results

We will be working in an I/O-model introduced by Aggarwal and Vitter [1]. The I/O-model has the following parameters:

$$N = \# \text{ of elements in the problem instance}$$
$$M = \# \text{ of elements that can fit into main memory}$$
$$B = \# \text{ of elements per block}$$

An I/O-operation in the model is a swap of B elements from internal memory with B consecutive elements from external storage. The measure of performance we consider is the number of such I/Os needed to solve a given problem. Internal computation is for free. The model captures the essential parameters of many of the I/O-systems in use today.[4]

In [22] the I/O-model is extended with a parameter D. Here the secondary storage is partitioned into D distinct disk drives, and if no two blocks come from the same disk, D blocks can be transferred per I/O. Furthermore, the model can be extended such that we have more than one internal processor (see e.g. [13]), and a number of authors have considered further extended models, with so-called multilevel hierarchical memories (see e.g. [13] or [21]), which aim to capture the fact that large-scale computer systems contain many levels of memory.

Early work on I/O-algorithms concentrated on algorithms for sorting and permutation-related problems in the single disk model [1] as well as in the extended versions of the I/O-model [13, 21, 22]. External sorting requires $\Theta(n \log_m n)$ I/Os,[5] which is the external storage equivalent of the well-known $\Theta(N \log N)$ time bound for sorting in internal memory. Note that this means that $O(\frac{\log_m n}{B})$ is the I/O-bound corresponding to the $O(\log N)$ bound on the operations on many internal memory data structures. More recently researchers have designed

---

[4] The quotients N/B (the number of blocks in the problem) and M/B (the number of blocks that fit into internal memory) play an important role in the study of I/O-complexity. Therefore, we will use n as shorthand for N/B and m for M/B. Furthermore, we will say that an algorithm uses a linear number of I/O-operations if it uses at most $O(n)$ I/Os to solve a problem of size N.

[5] We define for convenience $\log_m n = \max\{1, (\log n)/(\log m)\}$.

external memory algorithms for a number of problems in different areas. Most notably I/O-efficient algorithms have been developed for a large number of computational geometry [4, 8] and graph problems [7]. In [3] a general connection between the comparison-complexity and the I/O-complexity of a given problem is shown.

1.2 Our Results

In this paper we develop a technique for transforming an internal memory tree data structure into an external storage data structure. We use our technique to develop a number of external storage data structures, which in turn can be used to develop optimal algorithms for problems from all the different areas previously considered with respect to I/O-complexity. All these algorithms are either extremely simple or straightforward generalizations of known internal memory algorithms — given the developed external storage data structures. This is in contrast to the I/O-algorithms developed so far, as they are all very I/O-specific. Using our technique we on the other hand manage to isolate all the I/O-specific parts of the algorithms in the data structures, which is nice from a software engineering point of view. Ultimately, one would like to give the task of transforming an ordinary internal memory algorithm into a good external storage one to the compiler. More specifically, the results in this paper are the following:

Sorting: We develop a simple dynamic tree structure (*The Buffer Tree*) with operations *insert, delete* and *write*. We prove amortized I/O-bounds of $O(\frac{\log_m n}{B})$ on the first two operations and $O(n)$ on the last. Using the structure we can sort N elements with the standard tree-sort algorithm in the optimal number of I/Os. This algorithm is then an alternative to the sorting algorithms developed so far. Apart from being simple, the algorithm is the first I/O-algorithm that does not need all the elements to be present at the start of the algorithm.

Graph-algorithms: We extend the buffer tree with a *deletemin* operation in order to obtain an external storage *priority-queue*. We prove an $O(\frac{\log_m n}{B})$ amortized bound on the number of I/Os used by this operation. Using the structure it is straightforward to develop an extremely simple algorithm for "circuit-like" computations as defined in [7]. This algorithm is then an alternative to the "time-forward processing technique" developed in the same paper. The time-forward processing technique only works for large values of m, while our algorithm works for all m. In [7] the time-forward processing technique is used to develop an efficient I/O-algorithm for external-memory list-ranking, which in turn is used to develop efficient algorithms for a large number of graph-problems. All these algorithms thus inherit the constraint on m and our new algorithm removes it from all of them.

Computational Geometry: We also extend the buffer tree with a *batched rangesearch* operation in order to obtain an external (one-dimensional) *range tree* structure. We prove an $O(\frac{\log_m n}{B} + r)$ amortized bound on the number of I/Os used by the operation. Here r is the number of *blocks* reported. Furthermore, we use our technique to develop an external version of the *segment tree* with operations *insert/delete* and *batched stabbing queries* with the same I/O-bounds as the corresponding operations on the range-tree structure. The two structures enable us to solve the orthogonal segment intersection, the batched range searching, and the isothetic rectangle intersection problems in the optimal number of I/O-operations. We can solve these problems with exactly the same plane-sweep algorithms as are used in internal memory. Optimal — and efficient in practice [6] — algorithms for the three problems are also developed in [8], but as noted earlier, these algorithms are very I/O-specific. A note should also be made on the fact that the search operations are *batched*. Batched here means that we will not immediately get the result of a search operation. Furthermore, parts of the result will be reported at different times. This suffices in the plane-sweep algorithms we are considering, as the sequence of operations done on the data structure during the algorithms does not depend on the results of the queries in the sequence.

Even though we will not go into the details in this extended abstract we can also prove, using a technique similar to the one used in [13], that all the developed structures can be modified to work in the D-disk model — that is, the I/O-bounds can be divided by D. Furthermore, the structures are also internal-memory optimal in the sense that we can prove an amortized $O(\log N)$ bound on the number of comparisons used by the (update and search) operations. This means that the developed sorting algorithm, as well as the three computational geometry algorithms, are all internal memory optimal. We believe that our technique and the developed structures will be useful in the development of further external-memory algorithms. In [4] an extension of the external segment tree is used to develop efficient new external algorithms for a number of important problems involving segments in the plane. Finally, we believe that algorithms relying on our structures will be effective in practice due to relatively small constants in the asymptotic bounds. We plan to implement some of the structures in the transparent parallel I/O environment (TPIE) developed by Vengroff [20].

The main organization of the rest of this paper is the following: In the next section we sketch our general technique. In section 3 we then develop the basic buffer tree structure which can be use to sort, and in section 4 and 5 we extend this structure with a *deletemin* and *batched rangesearch* operation, respectively. The external version of the segment tree is developed in section 6.[6]

2 A Sketch of the Technique

In this section, we will sketch the main ideas in our transformation technique. When we want to transform an internal memory tree data structure into an

---

[6] Due to limited space we will not discuss the applications of the developed structures further. The reader is referred to [5] for a precise definition of the three computational geometry problems and their plane-sweep solutions. Time-forward processing, the technique for doing "circuit-like" computations, is developed in [7] and it is straightforward to design an alternative algorithm using our external priority-queue. The present paper is an improved version of [2]. Some of the details on the buffer-tree and the computational geometry problems appears in [2]. Further details will appear in the full version of the present paper.

external version of the structure, we start by grouping the (binary) nodes in the structure into "super-nodes" with fan-out $\Theta(m)$ — that is, fan-out equal to the number of blocks that fit into internal memory. We furthermore group the leaves together into blocks getting a $O(\log_m n)$ "super-node height". To each of the super-nodes we then assign a "buffer" of size $\Theta(m)$ blocks. Note that no buffers are assigned to the leaves. As the number of super-nodes on the level right above the leaves is $O(n/m)$, this means that the total number of buffers in the structure is $O(n/m)$. Note also that a similar idea is used in [11].

Operations on the structure — updates as well as queries — are then done in a "lazy" fashion. If we for example are working on a search-tree structure and want to insert an element among the leaves, we do not right away search all the way down the tree to find the place among the leaves to insert the element. Instead, we wait until we have collected a block of insertions (or other operations), and then we insert this block in the buffer of the root. When a buffer "runs full" the elements in the buffer are "pushed" one level down to buffers on the next level. We call this a *buffer-emptying process*. Deletions or other and perhaps more complicated updates, as well as queries, are basically done in the same way as insertions. This means that we can have several insertions and deletions of the same element in the tree, and we therefore time-stamp the elements when we insert them in the top buffer. It also means that the queries get batched in the sense that the result of a query may be generated (and reported) in a lazy fashion by several buffer-emptying processes.

The main requirement needed to show the I/O-bounds mentioned in the introduction is that we should be able to empty a buffer in $O(m + r)$ I/O-operations. Here r is the number of blocks reported by query-operations in the emptied buffer. If this is the case, we can do an amortization argument by associating a number of credits to each block of elements in the tree. More precisely each block in the buffer of node x must hold O(the height of the tree rooted at x) credits. As we only do a buffer-emptying process when the buffer runs full, that is, when it contains $\Theta(m)$ blocks, and as we can charge the r-term to the queries that cause the reports, the blocks in the buffer can pay for the emptying-process as they all get pushed one level down. On insertion in the root buffer we then have to give each update-element $O(\frac{\log_m n}{B})$ credits and each query-element $O(\frac{\log_m n}{B} + r)$ credits, and this gives us the desired bounds. Of course we also need to consider e.g. rebalancing of the transformed structure. We will return to this, as well as the details in other operations, in later sections. Note however already now that the amortization argument holds as long as the fan-out of the super-nodes is $\Theta(m^c)$ for $0 < c \leq 1$. We will use this fact in the development of the external segment tree.

3 The Buffer Tree

In this section we will develop the basic structure — *the buffer tree* — and only consider the operations needed in order to use the structure in a simple sorting algorithm. In later sections we will then extend this basic structure in order to obtain an external priority-queue and an external (one-dimensional) range tree.

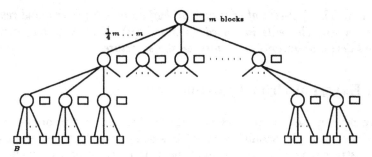

Fig. 1. The buffer tree.

The buffer tree is an (a, b)-tree [9] (with $a = m/4$ and $b = m$), extended with a buffer of m blocks in each node. The buffer tree is pictured in figure 1 (See [2] for a precise definition). As discussed in section 2, we do the following when we want to do an update on the buffer tree; we construct a new element consisting of the element to be inserted or deleted, a time stamp, and an indication of whether the element is to be inserted or deleted. When we have collected B such elements in internal memory, we insert the block in the buffer of the root. If the buffer of the root still contains less than $m/2$ blocks we stop. Otherwise, we empty the buffer. The buffer-emptying process is simple. We just load the buffer and the super-node (the partitioning/routing elements) into internal memory — this costs $O(m)$ I/Os. We then remove insert-delete "matches" between the elements from the buffer, and partition them according to the partitioning elements. Finally, we output them to the appropriate buffers. This again uses $O(m)$ I/Os. If the buffer of any super-node now contains more than $m/2$ blocks the emptying-process is recursively applied on these nodes.

We will not go into details about the balancing algorithm, that is, what happens when an update-element reaches a leaf. Basically the I/O-balancing algorithm works like the internal memory algorithm. Details are contained in [2]. Using a result due to Huddleston and Mehlhorn [9] we can prove an amortized rebalancing cost of $O(1/B)$ for each update operation. In [9] it is proven that using a particular balancing algorithm, the number of rebalance-operations in an (a, b)-tree is linear in the number of update-operations divided by the hysteresis $(b+1-2a)$ of the tree. In the full paper we prove that one rebalancing operation costs $O(m)$ I/Os, which leads to the amortized rebalancing cost of $O(1/B)$ for each operation. From the discussion in section 2 we then have:

Theorem 1. *The amortized I/O-cost of an insert or delete operation in an arbitrary sequence of N intermixed such operations on an initially empty buffer tree is $O(\frac{\log_m n}{B})$.*

In order to use the transformed structure in a simple sorting algorithm, we also need a empty/write-operation that empties all the buffers, and then reports the elements in the leaves in sorted order. The emptying of all buffers can easily be done just by performing a buffer-emptying process on all super-nodes in the tree — from the top. As emptying one buffer need $O(m)$ I/Os and as the total number of buffers in the tree is $O(n/m)$, we have the following:

Theorem 2. *The I/O-cost of emptying all buffers of a buffer tree and reporting all the remaining elements in sorted order is $O(n)$. Here N is the number of insert and delete operations performed on the structure.*

4 An External Priority-queue

Normally, we can use a search-tree structure to implement a priority-queue because we know that the smallest element in a search-tree is in the leftmost leaf. The same strategy can be used to implement an external priority-queue based on the buffer tree. There are a couple of problems though, because using the buffer tree we cannot be sure that the smallest element is in the leftmost leaf, as there can be smaller elements in the buffers of the super-nodes on the leftmost path. There is, however, a simple strategy for doing a *deletemin* operation in the desired amortized I/O-bound. When we want to perform a *deletemin* operation on the buffer tree, we simply do a buffer-emptying process on all super-nodes on the path from the root to the leftmost leaf. To do this we use $O(m \cdot \log_m n)$ I/Os. Hereafter we can be sure not only that the leftmost leaf consists of the B smallest elements, but that (at least) the $\frac{1}{4}m \cdot B$ smallest elements in the tree are in the sons (leaves) of the leftmost super-node. If we delete these elements and holds them in internal memory, we can answer the next $\frac{1}{4}m \cdot B$ *deletemin* operations without doing any I/Os. Of course we then also have to check insertions against the minimal elements in internal memory. This can be done in a straightforward way and a simple amortization argument gives us the following:

Theorem 3. *The amortized I/O-cost of an insert or deletemin operation in an arbitrary sequence of N intermixed such operations in an initially empty buffer tree is $O(\frac{\log_m n}{B})$.*

5 An External (One-Dimensional) Range-tree Structure

In this section we will extend the buffer tree with a range-search operation in order to obtain an external (one-dimensional) range-tree structure. In subsection 5.1 we discuss an alternative to the report algorithm we developed in section 3 which we need in order to develop the actual range search algorithm in subsection 5.2.

5.1 A *Report* Operation

As discussed in section 3 we can report all elements in a (sub—) buffer tree just by emptying all the buffers of the tree and report all the elements in the leaves of the resulting tree. This algorithm uses $O(n)$ I/Os, if n is the number of blocks in the leaves of the original tree. We would however like the algorithm to use $O(n_a)$ I/Os — where n_a is the actual number of blocks reported. This number could be as small as zero, as a lot of elements could be deleted by delete-elements in the buffers. But if n_d is the number of blocks occupied by delete-elements in

1. Make two sorted lists for each level of the tree (i_j and d_j) in the following way: For each level do the following for all buffers, starting from the leftmost buffer:
   - Load the buffer and remove "matching" insert- and delete-elements.
   - Output the insert- and the delete-elements again in two different lists in sorted order.
2. Push the elements downwards by doing the following for all levels j from the top:
   - "Merge" d_j with i_{j+1} removing insert/delete matches.
   - Merge d_j and d_{j+1} into d_{j+1}.
   - Merge i_j and i_{j+1} into i_{j+1}.
3. Merge the two lists and do the following for all super-nodes on the last level, starting from the leftmost super-node:
   - While more than $m/2$ blocks from the list go to the same super-node, put $m/2$ blocks in the buffer and do a buffer-emptying process on it.
   - Put the remaining blocks in the buffer and continue with the next buffer.

   Finally, do a buffer-emptying process on all super-nodes on the last level.

Fig. 2. The empty algorithm.

the tree, we have that $n = n_a + n_d$. This means that we can charge the n_d part to the delete-elements (adding $O(1/B)$ to the number of I/Os used by a *delete* operation), and get that each report-operation costs $O(n_a)$ I/Os amortized. Note that it is crucial that the delete elements are removed form the tree. For reasons that will become clear in the next subsection, we would also like to be able to report the elements in a (sub—) buffer tree without doing buffer-emptying processes on anything else than the super-nodes on the last level of the tree. In figure 2 we present such an algorithm for emptying all buffers in a buffer tree. In *step one* we make two sorted list for each level of the tree we want empty. These lists contain insert- and delete-elements, respectively. For level j, the insertion list i_j contains insertion-elements that do not have a matching delete-element on level j. Similar for the delete list d_j. It should be clear that the number of I/O-operations used to make all these lists is proportional to the number of blocks in the buffers of the tree — that is, $m \cdot O(n/m) = O(n)$. In *step two* we then "push" the elements downwards, ending up with a list of (undeleted) insert-elements and a list of (unused) delete-elements. That the merging process overall uses $O(n)$ I/Os follows from the following argument: Every level in the tree contains more super-nodes than all the levels above it together. This means that the number of I/Os used to "merge" for example d_j and i_{j+1} is bounded by a constant times the maximal number of blocks on level $j + 1$. The bound then follows from the fact that the total number of blocks in the tree is bounded by $O(n)$. Finally, in *step three* we process the leaves. By observing that the number of I/Os used to do buffer-emptying processes on full buffers must be $O(n)$ — as this is a bound on the number of blocks in the lists — and that the number of buffer-emptying processes performed on non-full buffers is bounded by the number of buffers on the last level, it follows that also this step uses $O(n)$ I/Os. By the discussion in the start of this subsection we then have the following:

Lemma 4. *The elements in a buffer tree with n leaves containing only update elements can be reported in $O(n_a)$ I/Os. After the report process all buffers of the tree are empty.*

5.2 The *Rangesearch* Operation

The *rangesearch(x_1, x_2)* operation on a buffer tree should report all the (non-deleted) elements in the tree between element x_1 and element x_2. When we perform a *rangesearch*, we make a new element that contain the interval $[x_1, x_2]$ and a time stamp, and insert it in the tree. We then have to modify our buffer-emptying process in order to deal with the new rangesearch-elements. When we meet a rangesearch-element in a buffer-emptying process, we first determine whether x_1 and x_2 are contained in the same sub-tree among the sub-trees rooted at the sons of the super-node in question. If this is the case we insert the rangesearch-element in the corresponding buffer. Otherwise we "split" the element in two — one for x_1 and one for x_2 — and report the elements in the sub-trees that are completely contained in the interval. The splitting only occurs once and hereafter the rangesearch-elements are pushed downwards in the buffer-emptying processes like the insert-elements, while elements in the trees completely contained in the interval are reported. This means that our *rangesearch* operation gets batched. Assuming that we have a report-algorithm that reports the elements in a buffer tree in $O(n_a)$ I/Os amortized, the following theorem follows by the standard credit argument:

Theorem 5. *A rangesearch(x_1, x_2) in a buffer tree with n leaves uses $O(\frac{\log_m n}{B} + r)$ I/O-operations amortized. Here $r \cdot B$ is the number of elements reported by the operation.*

However, the report-algorithm presented in the last section has to be modified when we have rangesearch-elements in the tree. As the modification is technically complicated we will not go into the details in this abstract but just refer to [2]. The main problem is that one should remember to report "matches" between insert- and rangesearch-elements in the buffers of the tree that is emptied. This is also the reason why just doing buffer-emptying processes on all the nodes will not work. The idea in the algorithm — that is, the idea of making a sorted lists for each element-type on each level and then merging them from the top — is nevertheless the same.

6 An External Segment Tree

In this section we will sketch how our technique can be used to develop an external version of the segment tree. The segment tree is a well-known data structure used to maintain a dynamically changing set of segments whose endpoints belongs to a fixed set. Given a query point, the structure returns all segments that contains the point. Such queries are called stabbing queries. Basically the internal memory segment tree is a binary tree on top of the sorted set of endpoints,

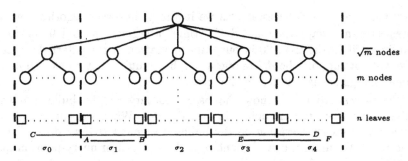

Fig. 3. An external segment tree based on a set of N segments, three of which, $\overline{AB}$, $\overline{EF}$ and $\overline{EF}$, are shown.

where a list of segments is associated with each internal node. Each segment is stored in $O(\log N)$ such lists. See e.g. [5, 17] for a definition of the segment tree and the operations on it. Because a segment can be stored in $O(\log N)$ nodes, the technique sketched in section 2, where we just group the nodes in an internal version of the structure into super-nodes, does not apply directly. Instead we need to change the definition of the segment tree slightly.

An external segment tree is shown in figure 3. The base structure is a perfectly balanced tree (buffer tree) over the set of endpoints with branching factor $\sqrt{m}$. A buffer and $O(m)$ lists of segments are associated with each super-node. A list of segments is also associated with each leaf. A set of segments are stored in this structure as follows: The first level of the tree (the root) partitions the data into $\sqrt{m}$ slabs σ_i, separated by dotted lines in figure 3. The *multi-slabs* for the root super-node are then defined as contiguous ranges of slabs, such as for example $[\sigma_1, \sigma_4]$. There are $O(m)$ multi-slabs and the $O(m)$ lists associated with a super-node is a list for each of the multi-slabs. Segments such as $\overline{CD}$ that completely span one or more slabs are then called *long segments*. A copy of each long segment is stored in a list associated with the largest multi-slab it spans. Thus, $\overline{CD}$ is stored in the list associated with the multi-slab $[\sigma_1, \sigma_3]$. All segments that are not long are called *short segments* and are not stored in any multi-slab list. Instead, they are passed down to lower levels of the tree where they may span recursively defined slabs and be stored. $\overline{AB}$ and $\overline{EF}$ are examples of short segments. Additionally, the portions of long segments that do not completely span slabs are treated as small segments. There are at most two such synthetically generated short segments for each long segment. Its easy to realize that total space utilization is $O(n \log_m n)$ blocks, because a segment is stored in at most 2 super-nodes on each level.

Given an external segment tree a stabbing query can be answered simply by proceeding down a path in the tree searching for the query value, and at each super-node encountered report all the long segments associated with each of the multi-slabs that span the query value.

6.1 Operations on the External Segment Tree

Usually, when we use a segment tree to solve e.g. the batched range searching problem, we use the operations *insert, delete* and *query*. However, a *delete* operation is really not necessary, as we in the plane-sweep algorithm we use the structure in always know at which "time" a segment should be deleted when we insert it in the tree. So in our implementation of the external segment tree we will not support the *delete* operation, but require that a delete-time is given when a segment is inserted in the tree.

It is easy to realize how the base structure can be build in $O(n)$ I/O-operations given the endpoints in sorted order. When we want to perform an *insert* or a *query* operation on the buffered segment tree we do as sketched in section 2. We make a new element with the segment or query-point in question, a time-stamp, and — if the element is an insert-element — a delete-time. When we have collected a block of such elements, we insert them in the buffer of the root. If the buffer of the root now contains more than $m/2$ elements, we perform a buffer-emptying process on it.

The buffer-emptying process is like in the buffer tree case. We simply load the elements in the buffer and report the appropriate "intersection" between query points and segments from the buffer, and between query points and segments in the relevant multi-slab lists. Then segments from the buffer that spans one or more slabs are stored in the relevant multi-slab list. Finally, the elements from the buffer, along with new short segments, are partitioned and send one level down to the relevant buffers on the next level. Because the number of multi-slab lists is $O(m)$ its easy to realize that the buffer-emptying process use $O(m + r)$ I/Os. Details are contained in the full version of the paper. The following Theorem then follows from the amortization argument presented in section 2:

Theorem 6. *The amortized number of I/O-operations used by an insert or query operation on an external segment tree in a sequence of N such operations is $O(\frac{\log_m n}{B})$ and $O(\frac{\log_m n}{B} + r)$, respectively.*

As before we also need to be able to empty all the buffers while reporting the appropriate segments in $O(n + r)$ I/Os. To do so the empty algorithm sketched in section 3 almost applies, that is, in order to empty the tree we essentially just have to do a buffer-emptying process on all buffers. Details will appear in the full paper.

Acknowledgments

I would like to thank all the people in the algorithmic groups at University of Aarhus and Duke University for valuable help and inspiration. Special thanks also go to Mikael Knudsen for the discussions that lead to many of the results in this paper, to Sven Skyum for many computational geometry discussions, and to Peter Bro Miltersen, Erik Meineche Schmidt and Darren Erik Vengroff for help on the presentation of the results in this paper. Finally, I would like to thank Jeff Vitter for allowing me to be a part of the inspiring atmosphere at Duke University.

References

1. A. Aggarwal, J.S. Vitter: The I/O Complexity of Sorting and Related Problems. In Proc. of 14th ICALP (1987), LNCS 267, 467-478, and: The Input/Output Complexity of Sorting and Related Problems. Communications of the ACM, Vol 31 (9) (1988), 1116-1127.
2. L. Arge: External-Storage Data Structures for Plane-Sweep Algorithms. BRICS Report Series RS-94-16, University of Aarhus, June 1994.
3. L. Arge, M. Knudsen, K. Larsen: A General Lower Bound on the I/O-Complexity of Comparison-based Algorithms. In Proc. of 3rd WADS (1993), LNCS 709, 83-94.
4. L. Arge, D.E. Vengroff, J.S. Vitter: External-Memory Algorithms for Processing Line Segments in Geographic Information Systems. Manuscript.
5. J.L. Bentley, D. Wood: An Optimal Worst Case Algorithm for Reporting Intersections of Rectangles. IEEE Transactions on Computers 29 (1980), 571-577.
6. Y-J. Chiang: Experiments on the Practical I/O Efficiency of Geometric Algorithms: Distribution Sweep vs. Plane Sweep. These Proceedings.
7. Y-J. Chiang, M.T. Goodrich, E.F. Grove, R. Tamassia, D.E. Vengroff, J.S. Vitter: External-Memory Graph Algorithms. In Proc. of 6th ACM-SIAM SODA (1995), 139-149.
8. M.T. Goodrich, J. Tsay, D.E. Vengroff, J.S. Vitter: External-Memory Computational Geometry. In Proc. of 34th IEEE FOCS (1993), 714-723.
9. S. Huddleston, K. Mehlhorn: A New Data Structure for Representing Sorted Lists. Acta Informatica 17 (1982), 157-184.
10. Ch. Icking, R. Klein, Th. Ottmann: Priority Search Trees in Secondary Memory. In Proc. of 1987 Graph-Theoretic Concepts in Computer Science, LNCS 314, 84-93.
11. P.C. Kanellakis, S. Ramaswamy, D.E. Vengroff, J.S. Vitter: Indexing for Data Models with Constraints and Classes. In Proc. 12th ACM PODS (1993), 233-243.
12. D.E. Knuth: The Art of Computer Programming, Vol 3: Sorting and Searching, Addison-Wesley (1973).
13. M.H. Nodine, J.S. Vitter: Deterministic Distribution Sort in Shared and Distributed Memory Multiprocessors. In Proc. of 5th ACM SPAA (1993).
14. S. Ramaswamy, S. Subramanian: Path Caching: A Technique for Optimal External Searching. In Proc. 13th ACM PODS (1994), 25-35.
15. S. Subramanian, S. Ramaswamy: The P-range Tree: A New Data Structure for Range Searching in Secondary Memory. In Proc. 6th ACM-SIAM SODA (1995), 378-387.
16. N.P. Yale: The I/O Subsystem - A Candidate for Improvement. Guest Editor's Introduction in IEEE Computer 27 (3) (1994), 15-16.
17. F. Preparata, M. Shamos: Computational Geometry, An Introduction. Text and Monographs in Computer Science, Springer-Verlag 1985.
18. C. Ruemmler, J. Wilkes: An Introduction to Disk Drive Modeling. IEEE Computer 27 (3) (1994).
19. M. Smid: Dynamic Data Structures on Multiple Storage Media. Ph.D thesis University of Amsterdam 1989.
20. D.E. Vengroff: A Transparent Parallel I/O Environment. In Proc. of 1994 DAGS Symposium on Parallel Computation.
21. J.S. Vitter: Efficient Memory Access in Large-Scale Computation (invited paper). In Proc. of 8th STACS (1991), LNCS 480, 26-41.
22. J.S. Vitter, E.A.M. Shriver: Algorithms for Parallel Memory I: Two-Level Memories. Algorithmica, 12 (2) (1994).

Experiments on the Practical I/O Efficiency of Geometric Algorithms: Distribution Sweep vs. Plane Sweep *

(Extended Abstract)

Yi-Jen Chiang

Department of Computer Science
Brown University
Providence, R. I. 02912–1910
yjc@cs.brown.edu

Abstract. We present an extensive experimental study comparing the performance of four algorithms for the orthogonal segment intersection problem. The algorithms under evaluation are distribution sweep, which has optimal I/O cost, and three variations of plane sweep, which is optimal in terms of internal computation. We generate the test data by using a random number generator while producing some interesting properties that are predicted by our theoretical analysis. The sizes of the test data range from 250 thousand segments to 2.5 million segments. The experiments provide detailed quantitative evaluation of the performance of the four algorithms. This is the first experimental work comparing the practical performance between external-memory algorithms and conventional algorithms with large-scale test data.

1   Introduction

Input/Output (I/O) communication between fast internal memory and slower external memory is the major bottleneck in many large-scale applications. The significance of this bottleneck is increasing as internal computation gets faster, and especially as parallel computing gains popularity. Due to this important fact, more and more attention has been given to the development of I/O-efficient algorithms in recent years. Most of the developed algorithms, however, are shown to be efficient only *in theory*, and their performance *in practice* is yet to be evaluated. In particular, all such algorithms assume that the internal computation is free compared to the I/O cost, which also has to be justified. In this paper, we establish the practical efficiency of one such algorithm by an extensive experimental study.

Previous Related Work. As mentioned above, most of the previous work on I/O-efficient computation is theoretical. Early work concentrates largely on sorting, matrix multiplication, and FFT [1, 17, 24]. More recently, graph and

---

* Research supported in part by the National Science Foundation, by the U.S. Army Research Office, and by the Office of Naval Research and the Advanced Research Projects Agency.

geometric problems have also been studied. Work on graph problems includes transitive closure [21], graph traversal [13], and connectivity information [10]. Also, Chiang *et al.* [7] present a collection of new techniques for designing and analyzing a wide variety of I/O-efficient graph algorithms. For geometric problems, Goodrich *et al.* [14] study a number of problems in computational geometry and develop several I/O-optimal algorithms. Further results have been obtained in [11, 25]. Also worth noting are some efficient data structures for range searching in external memory [15, 19, 20]. Very recently, a new data structure called *buffer tree* and its applications are given in [2, 3], and an external-memory version of the directed topology tree ([12]) called *topology B-tree* is given in [5].

As for experimental work, very recently Vengroff has built an environment called TPIE for programming external-memory algorithms as proposed in [22], and also Vengroff and Vitter [23] have reported some benchmarks of TPIE on sorting and matrix multiplication. This work, however, is mainly on providing a programming environment and not on performance comparisons between external-memory algorithms and conventional algorithms. Other than this, we do not know of any previous experimental work on I/O-efficient computation.

Our Results. We present an extensive experimental study comparing the performance of four algorithms for the following *orthogonal segment intersection problem*: given a set of horizontal and vertical line segments in the plane, report all intersecting horizontal-vertical pairs. The problem has important applications in VLSI layout and graphics, which are large-scale in nature. The algorithms under evaluation are distribution sweep [14] and three variations of plane sweep [18]. Distribution sweep theoretically has optimal I/O cost [14]. Plane sweep is a well-known and powerful technique in computational geometry, and is optimal for this particular problem in terms of internal computation [18]. The three variations of plane sweep differ by the sorting methods (external merge sort [1] vs. internal merge sort) used in the preprocessing phase and the dynamic data structures (B tree [4, 8, 9] vs. 2-3-4 tree [9]) used in the sweeping phase. We generate the test data by using a random number generator while producing some interesting properties that are predicted by our theoretical analysis. The sizes of the test data range from 250 thousand segments to 2.5 million segments. The experiments provide detailed quantitative evaluation of the performance of the four algorithms, and the observed behavior of the algorithms is consistent with their theoretical properties.

The contribution of this work can be summarized as follows: **(i)** We have presented the first experimental work comparing the practical performance between external-memory algorithms and conventional algorithms with large-scale test data. **(ii)** We have generated test data with interesting properties that are predicted by our theoretical analysis. In particular, we give techniques for analyzing the expected number of intersections and the average number of vertical overlaps among vertical segments in the data sets generated, which may be of independent interest. **(iii)** We have implemented distribution sweep, three variations of plane sweep and external merge sort under a uniform experimental framework. The implementations handle all degeneracies and are robust. **(iv)**

We have presented the first experimental study on the four algorithms for the important orthogonal segment intersection problem with large-scale test data, and established the practical efficiency of distribution sweep.

In this extended abstract the probabilistic analyses and some other details are omitted. They can be found in the full version [6].[2]

2   The Algorithms Under Evaluation

The four algorithms considered are distribution sweep, denoted `Distribution`, and three variations of plane sweep, denoted `B-Tree`, `234-Tree`, and `234-Tree-Core`. To discuss the time complexity, let N be the total number of segments in the given input, K the number of intersecting pairs that must be reported, and M and B the numbers of segments that can fit into the main memory and into a page, respectively. Each I/O operation transfers one page of data.

We implement plane sweep by using a horizontal sweep line to move bottom up. The three variations differ by the sorting methods used in the preprocessing phase and the dynamic data structures used in the sweeping phase. The first variation, `B-Tree`, uses external merge sort [1] and a B tree [4, 8, 9]; this is a direct way to implement plane sweep in secondary memory. The number of I/O operations performed in the first phase is optimal $O(\frac{N}{B} \log_M \frac{N}{B})$ [1], and in the second phase is $O(N \log_B \frac{N}{B} + \frac{K}{B})$. The second variation, `234-Tree`, uses external merge sort and a 2-3-4 tree [9], viewing the internal memory as virtually having an infinite size and letting the OS handle page faults during the second phase. It has the same I/O cost in the first phase and $O(N \log N + \frac{K}{B})$ in the second phase. Finally, the third variation, `234-Tree-Core`, uses internal merge sort and a 2-3-4 tree, letting the OS handle page faults all the time. The I/O costs in the first and second phases are $O(N \log N)$ and $O(N \log N + \frac{K}{B})$, respectively. Assuming an infinite-size virtual memory is conceptually the simplest, and is the most commonly used strategy today in practice.

Distribution sweep [14] is an external-memory version of plane sweep. We use external merge sort to perform the two sortings in the preprocessing phase, and implement the recursive sweeping process by letting a horizontal sweep line l moving bottom up. In each recursion, the input is split into vertical strips, and an *active list* associated with each vertical strip γ is used to maintain the vertical segments in γ that intersect l. Details are omitted here and can be found in [6, 14]. The total I/O cost is optimal $O(\frac{N}{B} \log_M \frac{N}{B} + \frac{K}{B})$. Note that distribution sweep needs two sortings as opposed to just one in plane sweep.

3   Experimental Setting

Generation and Analysis of the Test Data

We use three programs to generate our test data; all of them use a random number generator that gives a uniform distribution. The programs randomly generate several attributes of a segment such as its length, position, and type

---

[2] It is also available at `http://www.cs.brown.edu/people/yjc/`.

(horizontal/vertical). Observe that if we just randomly generate segments with lengths uniformly distributed over $[0, N]$, place them randomly and uniformly in an $N \times N$ square, and make the two types equally likely to occur, then the number K of intersections is $\Theta(N^2)$ (obtained by the analysis below). In this case, any algorithm has $\Omega(\frac{N^2}{B})$ reporting I/O cost, which dominates the searching I/O costs in all four algorithms. In fact, the following brute-force algorithm performs equally well: for each segment, check all the other $N - 1$ segments for intersections; the I/O cost is $O(N \cdot \frac{N}{B}) = O(\frac{N^2}{B})$. Certainly this kind of test data is undesirable.

Our three programs are denoted **gen-short**, **gen-long**, and **gen-rect**, and the data sets generated are correspondingly denoted **data-short**, **data-long** and **data-rect**. We try to generate test data with small number of intersections so that the searching I/O cost dominates the reporting cost. Also, the number of vertical overlaps among vertical segments at a given time decides the tree size and the total size of the active lists in that moment of plane sweep and of distribution sweep, respectively. Thus the number of vertical overlaps may affect the performance of the four algorithms. Our three programs generate test data with distinct structures regarding the number of intersections and the number of vertical overlaps. Also, all three programs decide the type (horizontal/vertical) of the current segment being generated by tossing a fair coin.

Program **gen-short** generates short segments whose lengths are uniformly distributed over $[0, \sqrt{N}]$. The segments are randomly placed in an $N \times N$ square Q. More specifically, for the left endpoints of horizontal segments, the distances to the left and bottom sides of Q are uniformly distributed over $[0, N - \sqrt{N}]$ and over $[0, N]$, respectively. Similarly, for the bottom endpoints of vertical segments, the distances to the left and bottom sides of Q are uniformly distributed over $[0, N]$ and over $[0, N - \sqrt{N}]$, respectively.

Theorem 1. *Let K be a random variable for the number of horizontal-vertical intersecting pairs in* **data-short**. *Then $E[K] = \frac{1}{16}(N - 1)$.*

Figure 1 shows the actual numbers of intersections with respect to data size N, for all three data sets generated. The observed K values are indeed $\frac{1}{16}N$ for **data-short**.

Now we proceed to analyze for **data-short** the average number of vertical overlaps among vertical segments, that is, the average number of vertical segments "cut" by the horizontal sweep line l *when l is passing through an event (i.e., an endpoint of a segment)*. The average is taken over all sweeping events. Notice that this average number is exactly the average number of vertical segments stored in the data structure when an update/query operation is performed during plane sweep. A related problem has been studied in [16].

Theorem 2. *Let V be a random variable for the number of vertical segments in* **data-short** *cut by the sweep line l for an event. Then $E[V] = \frac{1}{4}\sqrt{N} + O(1) \sim \frac{1}{4}\sqrt{N}$.*

Figure 2 shows the actual values of the average number of vertical overlaps with respect to data size N, for all three data sets generated. We also compare for

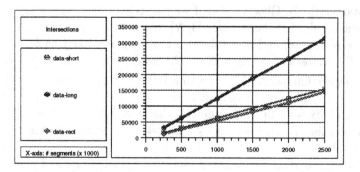

Fig. 1. The actual numbers of intersections with respect to the number of segments in data sets **data-short**, **data-long** and **data-rect**.

data-short the actual values and the analyzed values in Table 1, which shows that the observed values are indeed $\frac{1}{4}\sqrt{N}$.

N : # segments ($\times 10^3$)	250	500	1000	1500	2000	2500
Actual value	125.23	176.74	249.98	306.40	353.58	395.60
$\frac{1}{4}\sqrt{N}$ ($\sim E[V]$)	125	176.78	250	306.19	353.55	395.28

Table 1. The actual and analyzed values of the average number of vertical overlaps in data set **data-short**.

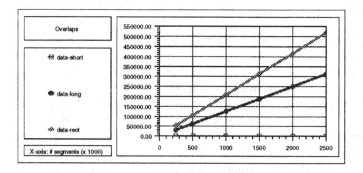

Fig. 2. The actual values of the average number of vertical overlaps with respect to the number of segments in data sets **data-short**, **data-long** and **data-rect**.

Program **gen-long** generates short as well as long segments while keeping the number of intersections small. For a horizontal segment, the length is assigned $\sqrt{N}$ (short segment); for a vertical segment, the program tosses a coin, giving length $\sqrt{N}$ (short segment) if the outcome is a head and N (long segment) otherwise. The horizontal and vertical short segments are randomly placed in the $N \times N$ sqaure Q in the same way as described in **gen-short**. As for vertical long segments, the bottom endpoints are placed randomly in an $N \times N$ square Q' whose lower-right corner coincides with the lower-left corner of Q, such that the distances from the bottom endpoints to the left and bottom sides of Q' are both uniformly distributed over $[0, N]$. Thus we have about $\frac{1}{2}N$ short horizontal segments, $\frac{1}{4}N$ short vertical segments, and $\frac{1}{4}N$ long vertical segments which cause no intersections. Using similar analysis methods as given before, we have that $E[K] = \frac{1}{8}(N-1)$ and $E[V] = \Theta(N)$. The observed K values of **data-long** are indeed $\frac{1}{8}N$ (see Fig. 1), and the observed values of the average number of vertical overlaps are also $\frac{1}{8}N$ (see Fig. 2).

In program **gen-rect**, we generate horizontal and vertical segments with lengths uniformly distributed over $[20, 60]$ and over $[0, 2N]$, respectively. The left endpoints of horizontal segments are randomly placed inside an $80N \times N$ rectangle R (with horizontal side length $80N$), such that the distances to the left and bottom sides of R are uniformly distributed over $[0, 80N]$ and over $[0, N]$, respectively. The vertical segments are placed as follows: in the x-direction, the distance between the left side of R and the i-*th vertical* segment is $(i-1) \times 160$, $i = 1, 2, \cdots$; in the y-direction, the distances from the bottom endpoints to the bottom side of R are uniformly distributed over $[0, N]$. Using similar analysis methods as given before, we have that $E[K] = \Theta(N)$ and also $E[V] = \Theta(N)$. Figures 1 and 2 show that the actual K values are $\frac{1}{18}N$, and the actual values of the average number of vertical overlaps are $\frac{1}{4.8}N$.

Computing Environment and Performance Measures

We perform the experiments on a Sun Sparc-10 workstation, which is running under Solaris 2.4 and is a multi-user distributed system. The main memory size is 32Mb and one page is of size 4Kb. Our performance measures are running time, number of I/O operations performed (i.e., number of pages read and written by the process), and number of page faults occurred.

Notice that the running time is our ultimate concern. Unlike previous experimental work, the CPU time does not correctly reflect the performance of the algorithms, since our main concern is the amount of time in which the CPU is sleeping waiting for the I/O or page faults. To overcome the difficulty, we perform all experiments by running the processes in the *real-time* class with the *highest priority* and measure the elapsed time. Also, the secondary memory used is the local disk so that the performance is not affected by the network file servers.

We are surprised to find that the system does not fully support performance statistic information. For example, it is claimed that user commands **time** and **timex** give CPU and elapsed times as well as numbers of I/O and page faults, etc., but it turns out that only the information regarding times are available. By using a system call in our program to retrieve the information in the **/proc** file system, we are able to obtain the number of page faults that require physical I/O's, yet the numbers of pages read and written by the process are still unavailable. Therefore, we also keep track of the numbers of times the **read** and **write** system calls are executed, where each time the size of the data being transferred is one page by our implementation.

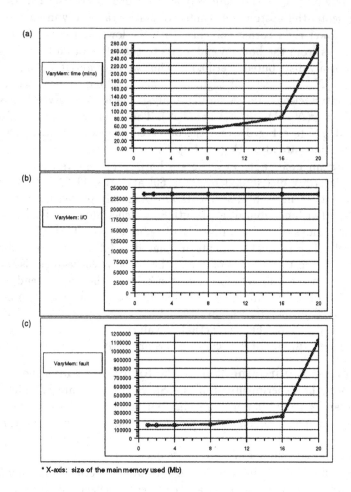

* X-axis: size of the main memory used (Mb)

Fig. 3. Running **Distribution** on data set **data-long** of 1.5×10^6 segments with various sizes of the main memory used: (a) average running times in minutes; (b) exact numbers of I/O operations; (c) average numbers of page faults.

We implement the algorithms so that the amount of main memory used can be parameterized. It is surprising that the main memory size available for use is typically much smaller than what we thought. When we run **Distribution** on **data-long** of 1.5×10^6 segments with various sizes of main memory used (see Fig. 3), in theory we would expect that using more main memory results in a better performance according to the I/O cost bound $O(\frac{N}{B} \log_{\frac{M}{B}} \frac{N}{B} + \frac{K}{B})$, but the experiments show that using 4Mb gives the best performance (average running time 47.64 minutes), and using 20Mb gives a significantly worse performance (average running time 271.97 minutes) due to a large number of page faults! This is actually a system issue. Using the `top` user command, we see that the "real" main memory size in the system configuration is only 26Mb rather than 32Mb and that processes (including their text, data, and stack portions) are never fully loaded into the main memory. The process loading behavior is decided by the OS and the user has no control over it. In the following, all the algorithms are running with the parameters of the main memory size set to 4Mb.

4 Analysis of the Experimental Results

Algorithms `Distribution`, `B-Tree`, `234-Tree`, and `234-Tree-Core` have been executed on data sets `data-short`, `data-long`, and `data-rect`, with data sizes ranging from 250 thousand segments to 2.5 million segments. While running times and numbers of page faults may differ between runs of the same example, the numbers of I/O operations are always the same. We run each example three times, and find that the variation among runs is at most 5%. More importantly, these differences among runs do not affect the performance ranking of the four algorithms. Figures 4–6 show the values of average running times, exact numbers of I/O operations, and average numbers of page faults of the four algorithms. Our experimental results show that while the performance of the three variations of plane sweep depends heavily on the average number of vertical overlaps, the performance of distribution sweep is both steady and efficient. Also, distribution sweep does not require a large amount of main memory to perform well: using 4Mb is enough. We make more detailed observations as follows:

(i) `234-Tree-Core` performs the best for small input ($N = 250 \times 10^3$) in all three data sets (see Figs. 4–6), but as input size grows, the performance becomes considerably worse, and up to $N = 10^6$ its running times are already out of comparison.

(ii) Consider data set `data-short` (see Fig. 4). Excluding `234-Tree-Core`, `234-Tree` always runs the fastest and `Distribution` always runs the slowliest. This can be explained by the small numbers of vertical overlaps which results in small tree sizes that still fit into the main memory. Also, `Distribution` performs two sortings, while all the others perform only one sorting.

(iii) For data set `data-long` (see Fig. 5), `Distribution` runs much faster than all the others for $N \geq 1.5 \times 10^6$. `234-Tree`, following `234-Tree-Core` after $N \geq 10^6$, is out of comparison for its running times and numbers of page faults after $N \geq 1.7 \times 10^6$. The running times and numbers of I/O operations of `B-Tree` are still more or less linear, and are always worse than those of `Distribution`.

(iv) For data set `data-rec` (see Fig. 6) with $N \geq 10^6$, `Distribution` performs the fastest, and the running times of the four algorithms differ significantly. For example, for $N = 1.37 \times 10^6$ and on average, `Distribution` runs for 45.29 minutes, `B-Tree` runs for 74.54 minutes, but `234-Tree` runs for more than 10.5 hours. Also, for $N = 2.5 \times 10^6$, `Distribution` always runs for less than 1.5 hours, but `B-Tree` always runs for more than 8.5 hours.

(v) Page faults seem to be more time-consuming than I/O operations (see Figs. 4–6). This is because the number of I/O operations is obtained by counting

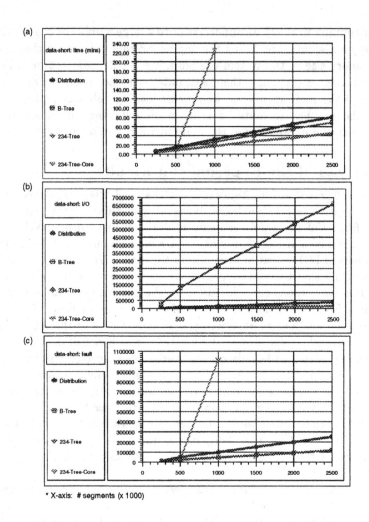

* X-axis: # segments (x 1000)

Fig. 4. The results for the algorithms running on data set **data-short**: (a) average running times in minutes; (b) exact numbers of I/O operations; (c) average numbers of page faults. We run **234-Tree-Core** only up to $N = 10^6$ since at this point it already takes time much longer than the others even at $N = 2.5 \times 10^6$.

the number of times the **read** and **write** system calls are executed, and thus some of them might be executed for pages that are still residing in main memory (i.e., in the system buffer cache), while the number of page faults only counts for those that actually require physical I/O's. We hope that the actual number of I/O operations can be available by a better system support in the future.

Acknowledgement

I would like to thank Roberto Tamassia for many stimulating discussions, and Tom Doeppner and Peter Galvin for useful information about our computing systems.

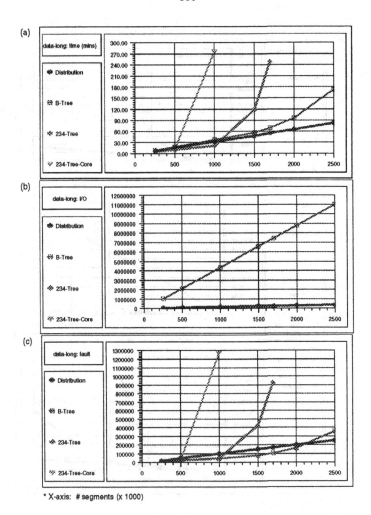

* X-axis: # segments (x 1000)

Fig. 5. The results for the algorithms running on data set **data-long**: (a) average running times in minutes; (b) exact numbers of I/O operations; (c) average numbers of page faults. We run **234-Tree-Core** only up to $N = 10^6$ and **234-Tree** only up to $N = 1.7 \times 10^6$ since at these points they already take times much longer than the others even at $N = 2.5 \times 10^6$.

References

1. A. Aggarwal and J. S. Vitter. The input/output complexity of sorting and related problems. *Communications of the ACM*, 31(9):1116–1127, 1988.

2. L. Arge. The buffer tree: A new technique for optimal I/O-algorithms. In *Proc. Workshop on Algorithms and Data Structures*, 1995.

3. L. Arge, D. E. Vengroff, and J. S. Vitter. External-memory algorithms for processing line segments in geographic information systems. Manuscript, 1995.

4. R. Bayer and E. McCreight. Organization of large ordered indexes. *Acta Inform.*, 1:173–189, 1972.

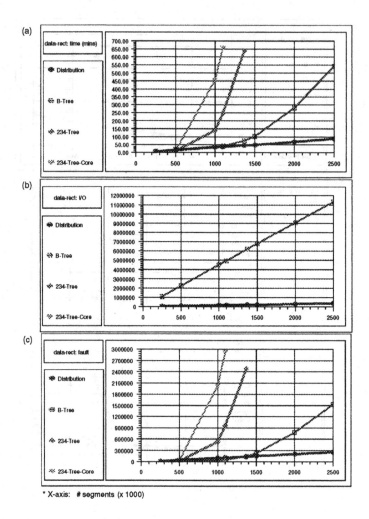

Fig. 6. The results for the algorithms running on data set **data-rect**: (a) average running times in minutes; (b) exact numbers of I/O operations; (c) average numbers of page faults. We run **234-Tree-Core** only up to $N = 1.1 \times 10^6$ and **234-Tree** only up to $N = 1.37 \times 10^6$ since at these points they already take times much longer than the others even at $N = 2.5 \times 10^6$.

5. P. Callahan, M. T. Goodrich, and K. Ramaiyer. Topology B-trees and their applications. In *Proc. Workshop on Algorithms and Data Structures*, 1995.

6. Y.-J. Chiang. Experiments on the practical I/O efficiency of geometric algorithms: Distribution sweep vs. plane sweep. Report CS-95-07, Comput. Sci. Dept., Brown Univ., 1995.

7. Y.-J. Chiang, M. T. Goodrich, E. F. Grove, R. Tamassia, D. E. Vengroff, and J. S. Vitter. External-memory graph algorithms. In *Proc. ACM-SIAM Symp. on Discrete Algorithms*, pages 139–149, 1995.

8. D. Comer. The ubiquitous B-tree. *ACM Comput. Surv.*, 11:121–137, 1979.

9. T. H. Cormen, C. E. Leiserson, and R. L. Rivest. *Introduction to Algorithms*. The MIT Press, Cambridge, Mass., 1990.

10. E. Feuerstein and A. Marchetti-Spaccamela. Memory paging for connectivity and path problems in graphs. In *Proc. Int. Symp. on Algorithms and Comp.*, 1993.

11. P. G. Franciosa and M. Talamo. Orders, implicit k-sets representation and fast halfplane searching. In *Proc. Workshop on Orders, Algorithms and Applications (ORDAL'94)*, pages 117–127, 1994.

12. G. N. Frederickson. A data structure for dynamically maintaining rooted trees. In *Proc. ACM-SIAM Symp. on Discrete Algorithms*, pages 175–184, 1993.

13. M. T. Goodrich, M. H. Nodine, and J. S. Vitter. Blocking for external graph searching. In *Proc. ACM SIGACT-SIGMOD-SIGART Symp. on Principles of Database Sys.*, pages 222–232, 1993.

14. M. T. Goodrich, J.-J. Tsay, D. E. Vengroff, and J. S. Vitter. External-memory computational geometry. In *IEEE Foundations of Comp. Sci.*, pages 714–723, 1993.

15. P. C. Kanellakis, S. Ramaswamy, D. E. Vengroff, and J. S. Vitter. Indexing for data models with constraints and classes. In *Proc. ACM Symp. on Principles of Database Sys.*, pages 233–243, 1993.

16. C. M. Kenyon-Mathieu and J. S. Vitter. The maximum size of dynamic data structures. *SIAM J. Comput.*, 20:807–823, 1991.

17. M. H. Nodine and J. S. Vitter. Paradigms for optimal sorting with multiple disks. In *Proc. of the 26th Hawaii Int. Conf. on Systems Sciences*, January 1993.

18. F. P. Preparata and M. I. Shamos. *Computational Geometry: an Introduction*. Springer-Verlag, New York, NY, 1985.

19. S. Ramaswamy and S. Subramanian. Path caching: A technique for optimal external searching. In *Proc. ACM Symp. on Principles of Database Sys.*, pages 25–35, 1994.

20. S. Subramanian and S. Ramaswamy. The P-range tree: A new data structure for range searching in secondary memory. In *Proc. ACM-SIAM Symp. on Discrete Algorithms*, pages 378–387, 1995.

21. J. D. Ullman and M. Yannakakis. The input/output complexity of transitive closure. *Annals of Mathematics and Artificial Intellegence*, 3:331–360, 1991.

22. D. E. Vengroff. A transparent parallel I/O environment. In *Proc. 1994 DAGS Symposium on Parallel Computation*, July 1994.

23. D. E. Vengroff and J. S. Vitter. I/O-efficient scientific computation using TPIE. Manuscript, 1995.

24. J. S. Vitter and E. A. M. Shriver. Algorithms for parallel memory I: Two-level memories. *Algorithmica*, 12(2), 1994.

25. B. Zhu. Further computational geometry in secondary memory. In *Proc. Int. Symp. on Algorithms and Computation*, 1994.

Computing a Dominating Pair in an Asteroidal Triple-free Graph in Linear Time

Derek G. Corneil[1], Stephan Olariu[2], Lorna Stewart[3]

[1] Department of Computer Science, University of Toronto
Toronto, Ontario, Canada M5S 1A4
[2] Department of Computer Science, Old Dominion University
Norfolk, VA 23529-0162, USA
[3] Department of Computing Science, University of Alberta
Edmonton, Alberta, Canada T6G 2H1

Abstract. An independent set of three of vertices is called an *asteroidal triple* if between each pair in the triple there exists a path that avoids the neighborhood of the third. A graph is asteroidal triple-free (AT-free, for short) if it contains no asteroidal triple. The motivation for this work is provided, in part, by the fact that AT-free graphs offer a common generalization of interval, permutation, trapezoid, and cocomparability graphs. Previously, the authors have given an existential proof of the fact that every connected AT-free graph contains a dominating pair, that is, a pair of vertices such that every path joining them is a dominating set in the graph. The main contribution of this paper is a constructive proof of the existence of dominating pairs in connected AT-free graphs. The resulting simple algorithm can be implemented to run in time linear in the size of the input, whereas the best algorithm previously known for this problem has complexity $O(|V|^3)$ for input graph $G = (V, E)$.

1 Introduction

Considerable attention has been paid to exploiting algorithmically different aspects of the linear structure exhibited by various families of graphs. Examples of such families include interval graphs [18], permutation graphs [14], trapezoid graphs [8, 7, 13], and cocomparability graphs [16].

Somewhat surprisingly, the linearity of these four classes is described in terms of ad-hoc properties of each of these classes of graphs. For example, in the case of interval graphs, the linearity property is traditionally expressed in terms of a linear order on the set of maximal cliques [5, 6]. For permutation graphs the linear behavior is explained in terms of the underlying partial order of dimension two [2], for cocomparability graphs the linear behavior is expressed in terms of the well-known linear structure of comparability graphs [17], and so on.

As it turns out, the classes mentioned above are all subfamilies of a class of graphs called the asteroidal triple-free graphs (AT-free graphs, for short). An independent triple of vertices is called an *asteroidal triple* if between every pair in the triple there exists a path that avoids the neighborhood of the third. AT-free graphs were introduced over three decades ago by Lekkerkerker and Boland

[18], who showed that a graph is an interval graph if and only if it is chordal and AT-free. Thus, Lekkerkerker and Boland's result may be viewed as showing that the absence of asteroidal triples imposes the linear structure on chordal graphs that results in interval graphs. Recently, the authors [9, 11] have studied AT-free graphs with the stated goal of identifying the "agent" responsible for the linear behavior observed in the four subfamilies. Specifically, in [9, 11] we have presented evidence that the property of being asteroidal triple-free is what is enforcing the linear behavior of these classes.

One strong "certificate" of linearity is provided by the existence of a *dominating pair* – a pair of vertices with the property that every path connecting them is a dominating set. The authors have proved [9] that every connected AT-free graph contains a dominating pair. However, the proof in [9] is existential only and rather involved.

The main contribution of the present paper is to provide a constructive proof of the existence of dominating pairs in connected AT-free graphs. A remarkable feature of our approach is that the resulting algorithm is quite simple and can easily be implemented to run in time linear in the size of the input. For each of the four families mentioned above, vertices that occupy the extreme positions in the corresponding intersection model [15] constitute a dominating pair. It is interesting to note, however, that a linear time algorithm for this problem was not known even for cocomparability graphs, a strict subclass of AT-free graphs.

To put our result in perspective, we note that previously, the most efficient algorithm for finding a dominating pair in a graph $G = (V, E)$ was the straightforward $O(|V|^3)$ algorithm described in [3]. Our result shows that the task of finding a dominating pair can be solved optimally. An important spinoff of our algorithm is that it reveals a great deal of intriguing structural properties of asteroidal triple-free graphs. It is quite conceivable that this will lead to the discovery of linear-time algorithms for a number of computational problems for this class of graphs.

The remainder of this paper is organized as follows: Section 2 surveys relevant terminology and background material; Section 3 presents the details of our linear-time algorithm; Sections 4 and 5 argue about the correctness and establish the complexity of the algorithm. Finally, Section 6 offers concluding remarks and poses some open problems.

2 Background and Terminology

All the graphs in this paper and finite with no loops nor multiple edges. In addition to standard graph theoretic terminology compatible with [4], we shall define some new terms. Given a graph $G = (V, E)$ and a set $A \subseteq V$, we let $G[A]$ denote the subgraph of G induced by A. For a vertex x, $N(x)$ denotes the set of vertices of G adjacent to x; $N'(x)$ denotes the set of vertices adjacent to x in the complement $\overline{G}$ of G.

All the paths in this work are assumed to be induced. We say that a vertex u *intercepts* a path π if u is adjacent to at least one vertex on π; otherwise, u is said to *miss* π. The *distance* between vertices u and v in a graph is the number of edges on a shortest path joining u and v.

For a connected AT-free graph with a pair of vertices x, y we let $D(x, y)$ denote the set of vertices that intercept all x, y-paths. Note that (x, y) is a dominating pair if and only if $D(x, y) = V$. In [9] the authors proved the following technical result that will be needed later in the paper.

Proposition 2.1. Let G be an asteroidal triple-free graph, let x be an arbitrary vertex of G and let C be a connected component of the subgraph of G induced by $N'(x)$. If u and v are vertices in C and $v \notin D(u, x)$, then $D(u, x) \subset D(v, x)$. □

In the remainder of this work we shall often reason about properties of the subgraph $H(x, C)$ of G induced by the set $\{x\} \cup N(x) \cup C$, where x is a distinguished vertex of G and C is a component of $N'(x)$.

We say that a vertex y of C is *special* with respect to x if $D(u, x) \subseteq D(y, x)$ for all u in C. In [9] we also showed that a vertex y of C is special with respect to x if and only if for every vertex v in C, v belongs to $D(y, x)$. In other words, (x, y) is a dominating pair in $H(x, C)$.

For a connected component C of $N'(x)$ we let S_C denote the set of vertices in $N(x)$ adjacent to at least one vertex in C. A vertex y of C is called *strong* if y is adjacent to all the vertices in S_C; otherwise y is called *weak*. A component consisting entirely of strong vertices is called *strong* and is *weak* if it contains at least one weak vertex.

Since our algorithm for finding a dominating pair in AT-free graph relies heavily on Breadth First Search (BFS, for short), we shall now briefly review this well-known graph traversal discipline (see [1] for details). The essence of BFS is that the graph is searched as broadly as possible by visiting all the neighbors of the vertex currently processed. BFS relies on a queue in which the vertices are inserted as they get "visited". When the vertices are dequeued, they become "processed". Initially, all vertices are both "unvisited" and "unprocessed". In our subsequent algorithms, we assume standard queue operations ENQUEUE(a), QUEUE_EMPTY, DEQUEUE. In addition, we shall find it convenient to use a few non-standard queue operations that we describe next:

- FLUSH: removes all the items in the queue;
- LOAD_QUEUE(A): involves a FLUSH operation followed by ENQUEUE(a) for all $a \in A$;
- EXTRACT(A, B, π): performs DEQUEUE repeatedly; each time an item is removed from the queue it is inserted in A or B depending on whether or not it satisfies predicate π.

From a slightly different perspective, BFS starting from an arbitrary vertex v of a graph G, partitions the vertices of G into *layers*, where all the vertices of a layer are at the same distance from v. In this paper we let $L^i(v)$ stand for the layer consisting of vertices at distance i from v. Let w be an arbitrary vertex in some layer $L^i(v)$. Every shortest w, v-path will be termed *direct*. Note that distinct vertices on a direct path belong to distinct layers. The *down-degree* of a vertex in layer $L^i(v)$ is the number of vertices in $L^{i-1}(v)$ to which it is adjacent. When performing a Breadth First layering of graph G, we let $L^*(v)$ and $L^{*-1}(v)$ denote the last and the second last layer, respectively. To keep notation simple, the reference to v in $L^i(v)$ will be dropped whenever no confusion can arise.

3 The Dominating Pair Algorithm

Our algorithm for finding a dominating pair in an AT-free graph is centered around a variant of BFS that we shall refer to as BFS*. Just as the classic BFS, BFS* searches the graph at hand, specified as $G[P \cup Q]$, until it reaches the last layer. At that moment, the (implict) queue that governs BFS is split into two sets P and Q. Q consists of the vertices in the queue with minimum down-degree (with respect to the current call), while P consists of all the other vertices in the queue. Next, the queue is flushed and a new BFS begins with the queue loaded with P. The details of the procedure BFS* are spelled out as follows.

Procedure BFS*(P, Q);
  {Input: vertex-disjoint sets P and Q;
  Output: new sets P and Q};
      LOAD_QUEUE(P);
      {replace the contents of the queue with the vertices of P};
      mark all vertices in Q unvisited;
      current-layer $\leftarrow$ 0;
      $z \leftarrow$ DEQUEUE;
      while not QUEUE_EMPTY **and** not all vertices visited **do**
            while layer of z is current-layer **do**
                  for each vertex w adjacent to z **do**
                        if w in previous layer **then**
                              augment the down-degree of z
                        else if w unvisited **then**
                              ENQUEUE(w)
                  endfor
                  $z \leftarrow$ DEQUEUE
            endwhile
            current-layer $\leftarrow$ current-layer $+1$
      endwhile
      if QUEUE_EMPTY **then**
            $P \leftarrow \emptyset$;
            $Q \leftarrow$ unvisited vertices
      else
            {let π be the predicate "vertex has minimum down-degree"}
            EXTRACT(Q, P, π)
      endif
end BFS*;

Our dominating pair algorithm uses a function SPECIAL which, given a vertex v and graph $H(v, C)$, returns a vertex w, special with respect to v. SPECIAL calls BFS*, which performs a modified Breadth First Search on $H(v, C)$. The details follow.

Function SPECIAL($v, H(v, C)$);
   {Input: an AT-free graph $H(v, C)$ with a distinguished vertex v;
   Output: vertex w that is special in $H(v, C)$ with respect to v};
      $P \leftarrow \{v\}$;
      $Q \leftarrow H(v, C) \backslash \{v\}$;
      while $\mid P \mid > 0$ **and** $\mid Q \mid > 1$ **do**
         BFS* (P, Q)
      endwhile;
      return an arbitrary vertex w of Q
end SPECIAL;

We are now in a position to specify the details of our algorithm that finds a dominating pair in a given AT-free graph.

Algorithm DP(G);
   {Input: connected AT-free graph G;
   Output: (y, z) a dominating pair of G};
   Step 1. Choose an arbitrary vertex x of G. If $N'(x) = \emptyset$ then return (x, x);
   Step 2. For every connected component C of $N'(x)$ compute $\mid S_C \mid$
         and determine whether C is weak;
   Step 3. Select a component C that minimizes $\mid S_C \mid$,
         breaking ties in favor of weak components;
   Step 4. $y \leftarrow SPECIAL(x, H(x, C))$;
   Step 5. Determine the connected components of $N'(y)$.
         Let X be the component that contains x;
   Step 6. $z \leftarrow SPECIAL(y, H(y, X))$;
   Step 7. return (y, z).
end DP;

Throughout the rest of the paper we use the following notation: L_i^j denotes the jth layer in the ith iteration; L_i^* and L_i^{*-1} denote the last and the second last layer, respectively, in the ith iteration; Q_i represents the vertices of L_i^* of minimum down-degree into L_i^{*-1} and P_i represents the rest of L_i^*. In general, $L_{i+1}^0 = P_i$ and initially $P_0 = \{v\}$, $Q_0 = N(v) \cup N'(v)$.

As an example, consider the AT-free graph $G = (V, E)$ of Figure 1, where $V = \{v, a, b, c, d, e, f, g, h, i, j, k, l, m, n, o\}$. Here, $L_1^0 = P_0 = \{v\}$, $L_1^1 = \{a\}$, $L_1^2 = L_1^{*-1} = \{b, c\}$, $L_1^3 = L_1^* = V \setminus \{v, a, b, c\}$, $L_2^0 = P_1 = \{d\}$, $L_2^1 = \{e\}$, $L_2^2 = L_2^{*-1} = \{f, g\}$, $L_2^3 = L_2^* = V \setminus \{v, a, b, c, d, e, f, g\}$, $L_3^0 = P_2 = \{h\}$, $L_3^1 = \{i\}$, $L_3^2 = L_2^{*-1} = \{j, k\}$, $L_3^3 = L_3^* = \{l, m, n, o\}$, $L_4^0 = P_3 = \{l\}$, $L_4^1 = \{m\}$, $L_4^2 = L_4^{*-1} = \{n\}$, and $L_4^3 = L_4^* = \{o\}$.

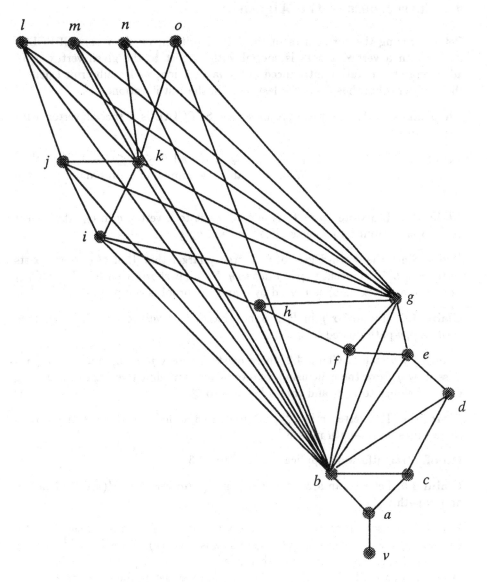

Fig. 1. *An asteroidal triple-free graph G*

364

4 Correctness of the Algorithm

Before proving the correctness of the DP algorithm, we show that SPECIAL does return a vertex w that is special with respect to the given vertex v. In addition to the notation introduced in the last section, we let subscript t denote the last iteration; thus L_t^* is the last layer in the last iteration.

Theorem 4.1. The vertex w returned by SPECIAL is a special vertex with respect to v.

Proof. Since $\mid P_{i+1} \cup Q_{i+1} \mid < \mid P_i \cup Q_i \mid$ for all $0 \le i \le t-1$, it is clear that SPECIAL terminates. We now establish a number of claims about paths in $H(v,C)$.

Claim 4.2. If a vertex p in P_i is non-adjacent to a vertex q in Q_i, then there exists a path from p to a vertex in L_i^0 missed by q.

Proof. Since the down-degree of p is strictly larger than that of q, there exists vertex r in L_i^{*-1} adjacent to p but not to q. Now any shortest path in $P_{i-1} \cup Q_{i-1}$ from r to a vertex in L_i^0 is missed by q and the proof is complete. □

Claim 4.3. If a vertex p in P_i is non-adjacent to a vertex q in Q_i, then there exists a p,v-path missed by q.

Proof. By virtue of Claim 4.2, there exists a vertex p' in L_i^0 and a p,p'-path missed by q. Now the conclusion follows by an easy inductive argument, noting that p' belongs to P_{i-1} and that q belongs to Q_{i-1}. □

Claim 4.4. If a vertex r in $L_{i-1}^* \setminus L_i^*$ is non-adjacent to a vertex s in L_i^*, then there exists an r,v-path missed by s.

Proof. Straightforward application of Claim 4.3. □

Claim 4.5. Let r be an arbitrary vertex in L_i^*. No vertex in $H(v,C) \setminus L_i^*$ misses an r,v-path.

Proof. Suppose that there exists a vertex s in $H(v,C) \setminus L_i^*$ missing such a path. Clearly s does not belong to $N(v)$, and so s is in $N'(v)$. If s is in L_i^{*-1} then by Claim 4.4, there exists an s,v-path missed by r. Such a path also exists for s anywhere else in $C \setminus (L_i^* \cup L_i^{*-1})$. Thus, we have an asteroidal triple on $\{r,s,v\}$. □

We now return to the proof of Theorem 4.1. We note that SPECIAL returns a vertex in one of the following two situations:

Case 1. $P_t \ne \emptyset$ (thus $\mid Q_t \mid = 1$)
Let $Q_t = \{w\}$. Suppose there is a w,v-path missed by a vertex r. By Claim 4.5, r belongs to P_t, but now Claim 4.3 shows that $\{r,v,w\}$ is an asteroidal triple.

Case 2. $P_t = \emptyset$

Note that this may happen either because all vertices in L_t^* have the same down-degree or because BFS* did not visit all the vertices in $G[P_{t-1} \cup Q_{t-1}]$.

Subcase 2.1. $L_t^* = Q_t$

We claim that every vertex w in Q_t is special with respect to v. Suppose not, and let some vertex r miss a w, v-path π. By Claim 4.5, r belongs to Q_t. Let w' be the last vertex on π that belongs to Q_t. The next vertex on π, $\tilde{w}$ belongs to L_k^{*-1} for some $k \leq t$. But both r and w' are in Q_k and thus have the same down-degree into L_k^{*-1}. Since r and $\tilde{w}$ are not adjacent, there exists vertex $\tilde{r}$ in L_k^{*-1} adjacent to r and not adjacent to w'. Now by Claim 4.4, there exists an $\tilde{r}, v$-path missed by $\tilde{w}$. Thus, $\{r, v, w'\}$ is an asteroidal triple, a contradiction.

Subcase 2.2. BFS* did not visit all vertices in $G[P_{t-1} \cup Q_{t-1}]$. Again, we claim that every vertex w in Q_t is special with respect to v. Assume to the contrary and let some vertex r miss a w, v-path π. By Claim 4.5, r does not belong to $H(v, C) \backslash L_{t-1}^*$. Furthermore, r does not belong to P_{t-1} nor may it be any vertex in L_{t-1}^* visited by BFS* starting with P_{t-1} since we may find an r, v-path missed by w. (This path would go directly, inside $L_{t-1}^* \backslash Q_t$, to a vertex in P_{t-1} and then follow a P_{t-1} to v path guaranteed by Claim 4.3.) Now, following a similar argument as in Subcase 2.1, we let w' be the last vertex on π that is in Q_t. The next vertex on π, $\tilde{w}$ belongs to L_k^{*-1} for some $k < t$. Again, both r and w' are in Q_k and the argument follows as in the previous subcase. □

We are now in a position to prove the correctness of the DP algorithm.

Theorem 4.6. The pair of vertices returned by the DP algorithm is a dominating pair in a connected AT-free graph G.

Proof. Clearly, this is true if (x, x) is returned in Step 1. We now examine the pair returned in Step 7 of the algorithm. Again, we proceed with some claims.

Claim 4.7. Let C be a component of $N'(x)$. If C is weak, then it contains a weak special vertex. Furthermore, the special vertex returned by SPECIAL is weak.

Proof. Let Y, W and S denote the set of special, weak and strong vertices in C respectively. If the first statement is false, then $Y \subseteq S$. Select a vertex w^* in W such that $D(w^*, x) \subset D(t, x)$ for no vertex t in W. If w^* does not belong to Y, then we find a vertex u in C that misses some w^*, x-path. By Proposition 2.1, $D(w^*, x) \subset D(u, x)$ thereby forcing u to belong to S. But now, we have a contradiction; u is strong, yet it misses some w^*, x-path. The fact that SPECIAL returns a weak special vertex in C follows from Theorem 4.1 and the fact that all vertices of maximum down-degree are initially placed in P and thus are eliminated from consideration as the vertex returned by SPECIAL. □

Claim 4.8. Let C be the component chosen in Step 3 and let B be any other component. Now $B \subset X$ unless both B and C are strong and $S_B = S_C$.

Proof. By the choice of C, every other component B of $N'(x)$ either has $S_B \setminus S_C \neq \emptyset$ or else $S_B = S_C$. In the former case, $B \subset X$. In the latter case, if C is strong and $S_B = S_C$, then by choice of C, B is also strong. If C is weak, then by Claim 4.7, y, the vertex returned in Step 4, is weak and thus there exists a vertex y' in $S_C \cap N'(y)$ non-adjacent to y. Since y' belongs to S_B, B has a vertex adjacent to y' and thus $B \subset X$. □

We now finish the proof of Theorem 4.6 by showing that (y, z), the pair returned in Step 7, is a dominating pair of G. Suppose not, and let π be a y, z-path missed by some vertex w. By Theorem 4.1, w does not belong to $H(y, X)$. Thus, w either belongs to $C \setminus X$ or to some component B of $N'(x)$ where, by Claim 4.8, $S_B = S_C$ and both B and C are strong. In this case, since S_C is a cutset separating z and y, all z, y-paths must pass through S_C and thus dominate all vertices in B.

Therefore, w belongs to $C \setminus X$. Let z' be the last vertex of π in S_C and let π' be the subpath of π from z' to y. Clearly, w must miss π' and thus must also miss the x, y-path consisting of π' augmented with the edge xz', contradicting the fact that y is a special vertex with respect to x in $H(x, C)$. □

5 Complexity Considerations

We now sketch the proof of the claim that the DP algorithm may be implemented to run in linear time. With the exception of the two calls to SPECIAL, it is clear that the other steps may be implemented in linear time by using Depth First Search and standard techniques.

To show that SPECIAL can also have a linear time implementation, we show that every edge of G will be "processed" a constant number of times. By keeping appropriate counters, the last layer of the BFS layering of a connected graph can be recognized without examining the edges inside the last layer. The calculation of the down-degrees can be "charged" to the edges between the last two layers. For each call to BFS* from SPECIAL, the set P consists of vertices on the previous last layer; thus each vertex belongs to at most one P set. Finally, we note that when we are using BFS* to layer L_k^* we must remove all edges from vertices in L_k^* to previous layers. This can be accomplished through standard linking techniques. To summarize our findings we state the following result.

Theorem 5.1. Given an AT-free graph G with n vertices and m edges as input, the DP algorithm produces a dominating pair in G in $O(n + m)$ time. □

6 Concluding Remarks

The class of asteroidal triple-free graphs (AT-free graphs) is a natural generalization of a number of classes of graphs including interval graphs, permutation graphs, trapezoid graphs, and cocomparability graphs. Recently the authors have argued [9] that the property of being asteroidal triple-free is responsible for the various linearity properties featured by all these classes of graphs.

An interesting result in [9] asserts that every connected AT-free graph contains a dominating path, that is, a path with the property that every vertex outside the path is adjacent to some vertex on the path. More recently, the authors have shown [10] that a dominating path in a connected AT-free graph can be computed in linear time.

Yet another interesting concept put forth in [9] is the notion of a *dominating pair*. Specifically, a pair (x, y) of vertices of a connected AT-free graph is a dominating pair if every x, y-path is dominating. In [9] it has been shown that every connected AT-free graph contains a dominating pair. Recently, Balakrishnan *et al.* [3] have exhibited a straightforward algorithm that finds all dominating pairs in an arbitrary n-vertex graph in $O(n^3)$ time. In particular, their algorithm can be used to find a dominating pair in a connected n-vertex AT-free graph in $O(n^3)$ time. Unfortunately, for large values of n this is prohibitively expensive. Second, their algorithm does not exploit the structure of AT-free graphs.

The main contribution of this paper is to show that the task of computing a dominating pair in an AT-free graph with n vertices and m edges can be computed in $O(n + m)$ time. An important side effect of our algorithm is to reveal intriguing structural properties of AT-free graphs. It is to be expected that these new insights will lead to efficient algorithms for a number of other computational problems for this class of graphs.

As a first step in this direction, the authors have recently developed another linear time algorithm [12], based on Lexicographic Breadth First Search (LBFS) to find a dominating pair in a connected AT-free graph. The LBFS algorithm is slightly simpler than the present algorithm but does not reveal the structural properties of AT-free graphs presented in Section 4. In [12] it is also shown that the LBFS algorithm can be extended to compute, in linear time, *all* the dominating pairs in a connected AT-free graph of diameter at least three.

There are a number of problems that we cannot solve efficiently. Perhaps the most natural of them is the task of recognizing AT-free graphs. It is not hard to devise a recognition algorithm that, with a graph with n vertices as input, decides whether the graph is AT-free in $O(n^3)$ time – such an algorithm proceeds, essentially, by brute-force. Is it the case that the algorithm in this paper can be modified to yield an efficient recognition algorithm?

Acknowledgements

D. G. Corneil and L. Stewart wish to thank the Natural Sciences and Engineering Research Council of Canada for financial assistance. S. Olariu was supported, in part, by the National Science Foundation under grant CCR-9407180.

References

1. A. V. Aho, J. E. Hopcroft and J. D. Ullman, *Data Structures and Algorithms*, Addison-Wesley, Reading, Massachusetts, 1983.
2. K. A. Baker, P. C. Fishburn and F. S. Roberts, Partial orders of dimension two, *Networks*, 2, (1971), 11–28.
3. H. Balakrishnan, A. Rajaraman and C. Pandu Rangan, Connected domination and Steiner set on asteroidal triple-free graphs, *Proc. Workshop on Algorithms and Data Structures, WADS'93*, Montreal, Canada, August 1993, LNCS, Vol. 709, F. Dehne, J.-R. Sack, N. Santoro, S. Whitesides (Eds.), Springer-Verlag, Heidelberg, Berlin, 1993, 131–141.
4. J. A. Bondy and U. S. R. Murty, *Graph Theory with Applications*, North-Holland, Amsterdam, 1976.
5. K. S. Booth and G. S. Lueker, Testing for the consecutive ones property, interval graphs and graph planarity using PQ-tree algorithms. *Journal of Comput. Syst. Sci.*, 13 (1976), 335–379.
6. K. S. Booth and G. S. Lueker, A linear time algorithm for deciding interval graph isomorphism, *Journal of the ACM*, 26 (1979), 183–195.
7. F. Cheah, A recognition algorithm for II-graphs, Doctoral thesis, Department of Computer Science, University of Toronto, (available as TR 246/90), 1990.
8. D.G. Corneil and P.A. Kamula Extensions of permutation and interval graphs, *Proceedings 18th Southeastern Conference on Combinatorics, Graph Theory and Computing* (1987), 267–276.
9. D.G. Corneil, S. Olariu and L. Stewart, Asteroidal triple-free graphs, *Proc. 19th International Workshop on Graph Theoretic Concepts in Computer Science, WG'93*, Utrecht, The Netherlands, June 1993, LNCS, Vol. 790, J. van Leeuwen (Ed.), Springer-Verlag, Berlin, 1994, 211–224.
10. D.G. Corneil, S. Olariu and L. Stewart, A linear time algorithm to compute a dominating path in an AT-free graph, *Information Processing Letters*, to appear.
11. D.G. Corneil, S. Olariu and L. Stewart, Asteroidal triple-free graphs, Technical Report TR-94-31, Department of Computer Science, Old Dominion University, November, 1994.
12. D.G. Corneil, S. Olariu and L. Stewart, Linear time algorithms for dominating pairs in asteroidal triple-free graphs, submitted for publication, (available as TR 294/95, Department of Computer Science, University of Toronto), extended abstract to appear in Proceedings of ICALP Conference, July 1995.
13. I. Dagan, M.C. Golumbic and R.Y. Pinter, Trapezoid graphs and their coloring, *Discrete Applied Mathematics* 21 (1988), 35–46.
14. S. Even, A. Pnueli and A. Lempel, Permutation graphs and transitive graphs, *Journal of the ACM* 19 (1972), 400–410.
15. M.C. Golumbic. *Algorithmic Graph Theory and Perfect Graphs*. Academic Press, New York, 1980.
16. M.C. Golumbic, C.L. Monma and W.T. Trotter Jr., Tolerance graphs, *Discrete Applied Mathematics* 9 (1984), 157–170.
17. D. Kratsch and L. Stewart, Domination on cocomparability graphs, *SIAM Journal on Discrete Mathematics*, 6 (1993) 400–417.
18. C.G. Lekkerkerker and J.C. Boland, Representation of a finite graph by a set of intervals on the real line, *Fundamenta Mathematicae* 51 (1962), 45-64.

A Linear Algorithm for the Maximal Planar Subgraph Problem *

HRISTO N. DJIDJEV

Department of Computer Science, Rice University
Houston, TX 77251, USA, email: hristo@cs.rice.edu

Abstract. We construct an optimal linear algorithm for the maximal planar subgraph problem: given a graph G, find a planar subgraph G' of G such that adding to G' any edge of G not present in G' leads to a non-planar graph. Our solution is based on a dynamic graph search procedure and a fast data structure for on-line planarity testing of triconnected graphs. Our algorithm can be transformed into a new optimal planarity testing algorithm.

1 Introduction

A graph is *planar* if it can be drawn in the plane so that no two edges intersect except at a common endpoint. Testing an n-vertex m-edge graph for planarity takes $O(n + m)$ time [11, 1].

If the graph is not planar, then often a problem arises of how to find a planar subgraph that is as close to the given graph, as possible. A problem of this type is called a *graph planarization problem*. For any n vertex graph G of genus g there exists a vertex set of size $O(\sqrt{ng})$ whose removal leads to a planar graph [5]. However, the linear implementation of the algorithm that finds such planarizing set requires a genus-g embedding of G as input; the best algorithm that finds such embedding [6] is polynomial in n, but doubly exponential in g. The problem of finding the smallest number of edges whose removal leaves a planar graph is known to be NP-complete [9].

Since finding a maximum planar subgraph is very hard, many researchers have investigated the problem of constructing, for a given n-vertex m-edge graph G, a planar subgraph G' of G such that adding to G' any edge of $E(G) - E(G')$ results in a non-planar graph. G' is called a *maximal planar subgraph* of G. This problem has been intensively investigated in relation to its applications to circuit layout. Recently, Cai, Han, and Tarjan [2] developed an $O(m \log n)$ algorithm for the maximal planar subgraph problem based on the Hopcroft-Tarjan planarity testing algorithm. Their result improved (if $m = o(n^2/\log n)$) the best previous $O(n^2)$ algorithm from [13] (based on the PQ-tree technique [1]). An algorithm with the same complexity bound of $O(m \log n)$ can also be derived from the incremental planarity testing algorithm of Di Battista and Tamassia [3]. Using

---

* This work is partially supported by National Scientific Foundation grant CCR-9409191.

an approach similar to [3], Westbrook [16] described an algorithm that works in $O(n \log n + m\alpha(m, n))$ worst-case time plus an additional $O(n)$ expected time. La Poutré [14] recently gave an incremental planarity testing algorithm that takes $O(\alpha(m, n))$ amortized time per operation, which can be transformed into an $O(n + m\alpha(m, n))$ time algorithm for the maximal planar subgraph problem.

In this paper we describe the first linear $O(n + m)$ time algorithm for the maximal planar subgraph problem. Our algorithm uses a tree-represented decomposition of a biconnected graph into triconnected components, a common feature of the incremental planarity testing algorithms [3, 4, 16, 14]. We use a variation of the decomposition tree of Di Battista and Tamassia, however any of the alternative representations could be used instead. Our algorithm has the following structure: (i) it initially constructs a depth-first spanning tree of G (we can assume that w.l.o.g. that G is connected) and uses it as an initial approximation of the maximal planar subgraph; (ii) it adds the edges one by one, making an on-line choice of the next edge to be added so that the testing time be appropriately small.

Our algorithm for the maximal planar subgraph problem can be transformed into a linear algorithm for planarity testing based on an approach entirely different from the existing ones. The previous algorithms of Hopcroft and Tarjan [11] and Booth and Lueker [1] (and their modifications) are based on the Jordan Curve Theorem which states that any closed curve in the plane divides it into exactly two connected regions. In contrast, our algorithm is based on the uniqueness of the planar embedding of any triconnected planar graph.

This paper is organized as follows. In Section 2 we describe a dynamic data structure that maintains a decomposition of a connected graph into biconnected and triconnected components. In Section 3 we develop an algorithm for on-line planarity testing in triconnected graphs in a constant amortized time which we use as a subroutine in the main algorithm. In Section 4 we give the overall structure of the algorithm as well as more details about individual data structures and update operations.

2 Preliminaries

In this section we give some basic definitions related to graph connectivity and graph orientation and describe briefly the data structure for maintaining the biconnected and triconnected components of a graph developed by Di Battista and Tamassia [3, 4].

A graph G is *connected*, if any two vertices of G are connected by a path. The maximal connected subgraphs of G are the *connected components* of G. A vertex v is a *cutvertex* if the removal of v increases the number of components. G is *biconnected*, if G is connected and G has no cutvertices. The maximal biconnected subgraphs of G are called *bicomponents*. A pair v, w of vertices of G is a *separation pair*, if the deletion of v and w disconnects G. G is *triconnected*, if G has no cutvertex and no separation pair. A triconnected planar graph has an unique planar embedding. The *triconnected components (or tricomponents)* of a graph are produced by a recursive procedure that finds a separation pair and divides G into two subgraphs. For the precise definition and a linear time algorithm see [10].

An *st-graph* is a directed acyclic graph with exactly one source and exactly one sink. Any biconnected graph can be converted into an *st*-graph using the linear time *st*-numbering algorithm of [7]. A *planar st-graph* is an *st*-graph that is embedded in the plane such that the source and the sink belong to the external face of the embedding.

Let G be an *st*-graph. A *split pair* $\{a, b\}$ of G is either a separation pair or a pair of adjacent vertices of G. A *split component* of a split pair $\{a, b\}$ is either an edge (a, b), or a maximal subgraph G' of G that is an *st*-graph with a source a and a sink b such that $\{a, b\}$ is not a split pair of G'. If there is no other split pair $\{a', b'\}$ such that $\{a, b\}$ is contained in a split component of $\{a', b'\}$, then $\{a, b\}$ is a *maximal split pair*.

2.1 Decompositions of biconnected graphs

First we consider the case where G is a biconnected graph. Let n be the number of vertices and m be the number of edges of G.

We recall the definition of SPQR trees from [3]. An *SPQR* tree for G is a recursively defined tree T closely related to the decomposition of G into tricomponents. T has four types of nodes S, P, Q, and R and there is an *st*-graph, $skeleton(\mu)$, associated with each node μ of T. The skeletons of the internal nodes of T are in one-to-one correspondence with the tricomponents of G and hence their number is $O(m)$. The endpoints of each edge e in the skeleton of the root of T correspond to a maximal split pair of G and e represents the set of split components of that split pair (see Figure 1). For the formal definitions see [3].

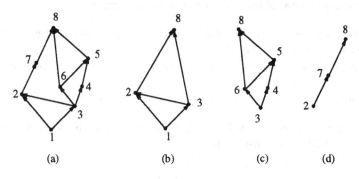

Fig. 1.

(a) A planar *st*-graph with source 1 and sink 8.

(b) The skeleton of the root μ of the SPQR tree for G (an R node).

(c) The split component corresponding to edge (3,8) of the skeleton of μ.

(d) The split component corresponding to edge (2,8) of the skeleton of μ.

A property of the SPQR trees that is relevant to planarity testing is that the skeleton of any internal node μ of a SPQR tree has either a unique planar embedding (if μ is an R node), or *any* two edges can be placed on the same face (if μ is a P or S node.) Our next goal is to show how to reduce a planarity testing in a graph to planarity testing in skeletons of nodes of its SPQR tree.

Planarity testing using SPQR trees

An *allocation node* of a vertex v of G is a node μ such that $skeleton(\mu)$ contains v. A *proper allocation node* of v, denoted by $proper(v)$, is the least common ancestor of all allocation nodes of v.

For any pair of vertices v_1 and v_2 we will define *projections* $pr(v_1)$ and $pr(v_2)$, any of which can be a vertex or an edge of the skeleton of an appropriate node μ of the SPQR tree. The relevant property of the projections of v_1 and v_2 is that $pr(v_1)$ and $pr(v_2)$ will belong to the same face of the skeleton of μ if and only if v_1 and v_2 belong to the same face of G.

Let v_1 and v_2 be two vertices of G and $proper(v_1)$ and $proper(v_2)$ be the proper allocation nodes of v_1 and v_2. Assume that $proper(v_1)$ and $proper(v_2)$ belong to a single tree path to the root of the SPQR tree. (In our algorithm described in Section 4.1 below this will always be the case.) Assume w.l.o.g. that $proper(v_1)$ is an ancestor of $proper(v_2)$. Define $\mu = \mu(v_1, v_2)$ as the nearest ancestor of $proper(v_2)$ whose skeleton contains v_1. Call a *dividing path* $p(v_1, v_2)$ the tree path in T between μ and $proper(v_2)$. For $i = 1$ and $i = 2$, if $skeleton(\mu)$ contains v_i, then define $pr(v_i) = v_i$, otherwise define $pr(v_i)$ to be the edge in $skeleton(\mu)$ corresponding to the subgraph containing v_i.

We define a *peripheral* vertex (resp. edge) of a planar graph to be a vertex (resp. edge) that appears on the external face of some planar embedding of the graph. A *peripheral node* is a node μ which is represented by a peripheral edge in the skeleton of its parent node.

The following lemma relates incremental planarity testing in an arbitrary graph to incremental planarity testing in its tricomponents.

Lemma 1. *[3] There exists a planar embedding of G such that v_1 and v_2 belong to the same face if and only if*

(i) $pr(v_1)$ and $pr(v_2)$ are on the same face of some planar embedding of $skeleton(\mu(v_1, v_2))$, and

(ii) all the nodes of the dividing path $p(v_1, v_2)$ are peripheral.

In the next sections we will describe data structures for answering queries of types (i) and (ii) in a constant time.

2.2 Decompositions of connected graphs

In order to handle connected graphs that are not necessarily biconnected we define the BC trees introduced in [4] which are extensions of the SPQR trees. To construct a BC tree of a connected graph G first find all bicomponents of G. Then construct a tree that contains a node of type B for any bicomponent b

and a node of type C for any cutvertex c of G. Associate with each B node b an SPQR tree representing b. Connect a C node c and a B node b iff c belongs to b. Finally root the tree at an arbitrary B node. Call the nodes of B *level-1* nodes and the nodes of the SPQR trees *level-2* nodes.

Suppose that an edge (v_1, v_2) has to be added to G. If v_1 and v_2 belong to the same bicomponent b of G then the BC tree of G is not changed after the insertion. In this case we use the SPQR tree associated with b and Lemma 1 to determine if (v_1, v_2) can be added while preserving the planarity and do the insertion by modifying the SPQR tree for b. Now assume that v_1 and v_2 belong to different bicomponents $b(v_1)$ and $b(v_2)$. Let $p = \{b_1 = b(v_1), c_1, b_2, c_2, \cdots, c_k, b_{k+1} = b(v_2)\}$ be the unique tree path between $b(v_1)$ and $b(v_2)$. If one of b_1 and b_{k+1} is an ancestor to the other and the edge (c_{i-1}, c_i) can be added to b_i while preserving planarity then we call b_i a *peripheral* level-1 node (with respect to path p.) We have the following lemma [4].

Lemma 2. *There exists a planar embedding of G such that v_1 and v_2 belong to the same face if and only if all edges $(v_1, c_1), (c_1, c_2), \ldots, (c_k, v_2)$ can be added to G while preserving planarity.*

For edges (v_1, c_1) and (c_k, v_2) we do planarity testing using the corresponding SPQR trees and for edges $(c_1, c_2), \ldots, (c_{k-1}, c_k)$ we use dynamically maintained maximal paths of edges (c_i, c_{i+1}) whose addition preserves planarity. We will give more details in Section 4.

In order to use the above data structure for the maximal planar subgraph problem we need also algorithms for efficiently updating the data structure after any insertion of an edge. Before discussing the update operations we will describe the data structures for planarity testing in 3-connected graphs and give an outline of the whole algorithm.

3 The triconnected case

We will give here an $O(n)$ solution to the following problem.

Problem 1 Let G be a planar triconnected n-vertex graph and E' be a set of edges between vertices of G. Find a maximal set $E'' \subset E'$ such that $G + E''$ is still planar.

We will use the solution of Problem 1, with some little modifications, to the problem of finding a maximal planar subgraph of a general graph.

Our solution is based on the fact that triconnected planar graphs have a unique planar embedding. Thus an edge (v, w) can be added to a triconnected embedded planar graph so that planarity is preserved, iff v and w belong to the same face of the embedding. To solve Problem 1 we need a fast procedure that tests if any pair of vertices belong to the same face. The next lemma concerns testing in a static graph.

Lemma 3. *For any triconnected planar n-vertex graph G there exists a data structure for G that can be constructed in $O(n)$ time, uses $O(n)$ space, and that provides answers in $O(1)$ time to the following two types of queries:*

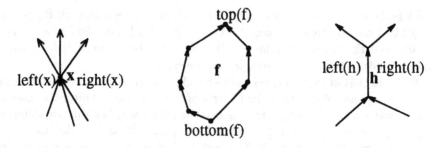

Fig. 2. Illustration to the definition of *left*, *right*, *top*, and *bottom* for vertices and *left* and *right* for edges.

(a) *If v and w are vertices of G and v has degree $O(1)$, check if v and w belong to the same face of G.*

(b) *If v is a vertex and e is an edge of G, check if v and e belong to the same face of G.*

Queries of type (b) will be used in the algorithms described in Section 4.

Proof: We use the data structure from [3]. Convert G into a planar st-graph. For any vertex x, the incoming edges in x appear consecutively around x and the edges outgoing from x also appear consecutively around x. Thus there is a single face, denoted by $left(x)$, that separates incoming and outgoing edges in a clockwise direction and there is a single face, $right(x)$, that separates incoming and outgoing edges in a counterclockwise direction (Figure 2). Furthermore, the vertices from the boundary of each face f form two directed paths. The common start vertex of these paths will be denoted by $bottom(f)$ and the common end-vertex will be denoted by $top(f)$. Furthermore, if h is an edge of G, we denote by $right(h)$ the face whose clockwise boundary contains h and by $left(h)$ the other face containing h. The values of $left$, $right$, $bottom$, and top are easily computed in linear time and space.

Consider now a query of type (a). Since the degree of v is $O(1)$, we can answer the query in a constant time by checking if, for any $f_v \in \{left(v), right(v)\}$ and any $f_w \in \{left(w), right(w)\}$, any of the following cases applies:

(i) $f_v = f_w$;

(ii) $top(f_v) = w$ or $bottom(f_v) = w$;

(iii) $top(f_w) = v$ or $bottom(f_w) = v$;

(iv) $\{v, w\} = \{top(f), bottom(f)\}$ for some face f incident to v.

Similarly, for queries of type (b), the problem is reduced to checking if the following condition is satisfied:

(v) for some f in $\{left(e), right(e)\}$ f belongs to $\{left(v), right(v)\}$, or $top(f) = v$, or $bottom(f) = v$. □

Note that the only condition that we would not be able to check in constant time if there have been no restrictions on the degree of v is condition (iv) of the proof of Lemma 3. Our next goal is to show that for solving Problem 1 an edge $(v, w) \in E'$ can always be chosen so that the number of faces f incident to either

v or w that are "relevant" in certain context to the planarity testing is $O(1)$. The idea of our solution is related to the observation that any n-vertex planar graph G has no more than $3n - 3$ edges and thus there exists a vertex of G of degree less or equal to 6.

Define a graph G_{tb} with a set of vertices $V(G)$ and a set of edges all pairs $(top(f), bottom(f))$ where f is a face of G. Note that G_{tb} is a planar graph (since any edge of G_{tb} can be drawn inside a distinct face of G) and its edges correspond to all pairs of vertices that satisfy condition (iv) above. We define a graph G'_{tb} to be the subgraph of G_{tb} induced by the set of vertices incident to at least one edge of E'. From the definition of G'_{tb} the next lemma follows.

Lemma 4. *For any edge $(v, w) \in E'$ vertices v and w belong to the same face f of G iff some of the conditions (i)–(iii) above is satisfied or (v, w) is in G'_{tb}. Furthermore, G'_{tb} always contains a vertex of degree $O(1)$.*

In our algorithm for solving Problem 1 described below we iteratively choose a new edge e of E' using information about the degrees of G'_{tb}. We add e to G if the planarity of the embedding is preserved and update G'_{tb}. The following procedure specifies the details.

Algorithm *Triconnected*

{Finds a maximal planar subgraph of $G + E'$ if G is triconnected}

1. Construct the data structures of Lemma 3.
2. Construct graphs G_{tb} and G'_{tb}.
3. For each vertex v of G construct the linked list of the edges of E' incident to v by a lexicographical sort. For each vertex v of G maintain the values $degree_1(v)$ of the number of edges from E' incident to v and $degree_2(v)$ of the degree of v in G'_{tb}. Also maintain a list $SmallDeg$ of all vertices whose degree in G'_{tb} is less or equal to 6.
4. Repeat until $E' = \emptyset$.
   4.1. Pick any vertex x in $SmallDeg$ and choose any edge $(x, y) \in E'$.
   4.2. If some of the conditions of Lemma 3 is satisfied for $x = v$ and $y = w$ then add (x, y) to G and update variables $left, right, top, bottom$, and the graph G'_{tb}.
   4.3. Remove (x, y) from E' and update G'_{tb} and variables $degree_1, degree_2$ and $SmallDeg$.

By the above analysis it is clear that if $E' \neq \emptyset$ then $SmallDeg \neq \emptyset$ and the conditions (i), (ii), (iii) of the proof of Lemma 3 can be checked in $O(1)$ time in Step 4.2. Furthermore, the initial construction of the data structures in Steps 1 and 2 requires in $O(n)$ time. Updating any of the data structures except $left$ and $right$ for vertices takes clearly $O(1)$ time. Updating $left$ and $right$ relations for vertices is more complex, because inserting a new edge in G splits a face f of G into two faces f_1 and f_2 which may require a potentially large number of vertices to change their $left$ or $right$ pointer from f to f_1 or f_2. We solve this problem by using the microset technique of Gabow and Tarjan [8]. Our structure is a modification of the split-find-insert data structure of Imai and Asano [12] maintaining a partition of a sorted sequence of integers under a sequence of split, find, and insert operations. We will give the details in the full version of the paper.

We summarize the results of this section in the following theorem.

Theorem 5. *Let G be a planar triconnected n-vertex graph and E' be a set of m edges between vertices of G. A maximal set $E'' \subset E'$ such that $G + E''$ is planar can be constructed in $O(n + m)$ time.*

4 Finding a maximal planar subgraph of an arbitrary graph

4.1 Outline of the algorithm

Our algorithm uses the decomposition tree described in the previous section to represent the tricomponents of the current planar subgraph. Recall that we can assume w.l.o.g. that the input graph is connected, because otherwise we can apply the same algorithm to each connected component. For maintaining the embeddings of skeletons and answering queries at each node of a SPQR tree we use a procedure similar to Algorithm *Triconnected*. At each iteration the algorithm chooses a new edge and checks if it is possible to add it to the subgraph so that planarity is preserved. The efficiency of our algorithm essentially depends on the order in which the edges are tested for insertion in the subgraph. Another feature of the algorithm is that it maintains a dynamic set *Upaths* of paths called *update paths* which will be our "working" paths, i.e. all essential information will be located on these paths and all updates will be done on these paths.

Algorithm *Maxplanar*
(Outline)

Input: A connected n-vertex m-edge graph G.
Output: A maximal planar subgraph G' of G.

1. Construct a depth-first spanning tree T of G. Associate a BC tree B with T whose root is the root of T. Let $E' = E(G) - E(T)$, $E^* = E(T)$, where E' denotes the set of edges of G not examined yet and E^* denotes the set of edges of the current approximation of the maximal planar subgraph.
2. Initialize for the skeleton of each level-2 node of B the data structures for on-line planarity testing from Steps 1, 2, and 3 of Algorithm *Triconnected*.
3. Use a variation of a postorder search to visit the nodes of B. Denote the current level-1 node by λ^* and the current level-2 node by μ^*.
   {**Comment:** The postorder will guarantee that any level-2 node that either is a descendant of μ^* or belongs to a level-1 node which is a proper descendant of λ^* is marked. (A level-2 node μ will be marked if no vertex of $skeleton(\mu)$ is incident to any edge from E'.)}

3.1. Update $Upaths$ and the associated data structures if a new node has been examined in the previous step (details to be given below.)

3.2. Pick any vertex x of the skeleton of μ^* belonging to the $SmallDeg$ list of μ^*.

3.3. Pick an edge $(x,y) \in E'$ and update $E' := E' - \{(x,y)\}$. If no vertex remains in $skeleton(\mu^*)$ that is incident to an edge of E' then mark μ^*. Let $\nu^* = proper(y)$. Check if (x,y) can be added to E^* by considering the following cases.

3.3.1. If $\nu^* = \mu^*$ then test whether y belongs to any of the faces incident to x by checking if the conditions of Lemma 4 for $x = v$ and $y = w$ are satisfied. If the answer is "yes", then add (x,y) to E^* and update the data structures associated with μ^*.

3.3.2. If ν^* is a proper ancestor of μ^* then let edge d be the projection $pr(x)$ of x on the skeleton of $\mu(x,y)$. (Recall that $\mu(x,y)$ was defined in Section 2 as a node on the tree path between μ^* and ν^*.) By Lemma 1, we have to check if y and d belong to the same face of $\mu(x,y)$ and if all nodes on the dividing path $p(x,y)$ are peripheral. If Condition (v) of the proof of Lemma 3 is satisfied for $v = y$ and $e = d$, then y and d belong to the same face of the skeleton of $\mu(x,y)$. Using $Upaths$ we decide whether all nodes on $p(x,y)$ are peripheral. If both queries give positive answers, then we add (x,y) to E^* and update the data structures as described in the next section.

3.3.3. If ν^* belongs to a level-1 node κ^* that is a proper ancestor of λ^* then, by Lemma 2, we perform on κ^* and λ^* two test operations of the type described in Step 3.3.2 and check if all other level-1 nodes on the tree path π^* between κ^* and λ^* are peripheral (using precomputed information stored with $Upaths$.) If all answers are positive we add (x,y) to E^* and merge into the SPQR tree of κ^* the other level-1 nodes of π^*.

Next we give more details about the implementation of some of the steps. The search of B in Step 3 is essentially a postorder search applied at two levels: first with respect to level-1 nodes and then, when the level-1 node is chosen, with respect to the level-2 nodes in its SPQR tree. Another feature is that the search is applied on-line to dynamic trees. Thus, if in Steps 3.3.2 or 3.3.3 a path of two or more level-1 or level-2 nodes has been shrunk, then the resulting node, μ, might have unmarked children (which must be visited before continuing with μ,) even if μ^* may have had no marked children before the shrinking.

In the next subsection we describe the data structures associated with $Upaths$ that will allow us to determine in constant time if a path of nodes contains only peripheral nodes. We will also show that it is possible to do updates on B and on the planar st-graphs associated with its nodes after shrinking of paths of level-1 and level-2 nodes in $O(n)$ total time.

4.2 Updating the data structures

Our update algorithms are simpler and more efficient than the algorithms of [3, 16, 14] because of our use of $Upaths$.

The update paths

$Upaths$ is a set of paths called *update paths* that includes the current path π of level-1 nodes of B from λ^* to the root of the tree and a path of level-2 nodes in the SPQR tree of each node in π. Let $\pi = \{b_1, c_1, b_2, c_2, \cdots, c_{k-1}, b_k\}$ where the path in node $b_1 = \lambda^*$ is called the *top update path* and b_k is the root of B. For λ^*, the corresponding path of level-2 nodes is from μ^* to the root of the SPQR tree of λ^*. The update path in b_i, for $2 \leq i \leq k$, is the path from the allocation node of c_{i-1} to the root of the SPQR tree for b_i. At any iteration we will use only π and the top update path. The other paths in $Upaths$ will be needed when we backtrack to an ancestor node during the postorder search. We prove the following important property of $Upaths$.

Lemma 6. *Let x be a vertex in μ^* and $(x, y) \in E'$ be the edge chosen in Step 3.3 of Algorithm* Maxplanar. *Then the proper allocation node proper(y) of y belongs to the update path of λ^* or to the SPQR tree of a node in π different from λ^*.*

The update paths change during the computation when a new node of B is visited and when a subpath of B is contracted. This requires that some information associated with $Upaths$ be dynamically updated, as described below.

Update algorithms

We need to dynamically maintain the following types of information:

(a) The proper allocation nodes of the vertices of G;

(b) For any level-1 or level-2 node μ, the nearest ancestor of μ that is not peripheral;

(c) A planar embedding of a triconnected planar st-graph G' (a skeleton of a level-2 R node ν) with respect to the structures described in Section 3 subject to the operation replacement of an edge of G' with a planar st-graph (the skeleton of a child of ν.)

Information about the proper allocation nodes of vertices of G is needed in Step 3.3 of Algorithm *Maxplanar*. We store for each vertex v of G a pointer to the representative of v in the skeleton of $proper(v)$. Furthermore, we dynamically maintain for each level-2 node μ belonging to a path of $Upaths$ a set of the vertices x of G such that $proper(x) = \mu$. This can be done by using the split-find-insert data structure described in the previous section. Hence one can find the proper allocation node μ of any vertex of G in $O(1)$ amortized time, provided that μ belongs to a path of $Upaths$. By the description of Algorithm *Maxplanar* and Lemma 6, the proper allocation nodes of the vertices x and y examined in Step 3.3 will always belong to a path of $Upaths$.

In order to maintain information about the nearest non-peripheral ancestor of any level-2 node of a path in $Upaths$, we define an array *nearest*. Whenever a new level-2 node μ is examined, we add μ to the top update path and we check if μ is peripheral. Depending on the value of *nearest* for the parent of μ (if μ is not the root of B,) the value of $nearest(\mu)$ is determined. Note that when a subpath of level-2 nodes is contracted, that subpath is always located at the end of the top update path. Thus at most one value of *nearest* needs to be updated which takes $O(1)$ time. The information about the nearest non-peripheral ancestors of level-1 nodes is maintained in a similar way.

Merging the skeleton of a level-2 node μ of B with the skeleton of its parent $parent(\mu)$ requires a replacement of an edge e of a planar st-graph G_e (the skeleton of $parent(\mu)$) with another st-graph (the skeleton of μ.) Consider the case where both μ and $parent(\mu)$ are R nodes (the most interesting case) and e is an internal edge. The faces of the resulting planar st-graph are all internal faces of the skeleton of $parent(\mu)$ and all faces of the skeleton of μ except the two faces, say f_1 and f_2, incident to e. In each of f_1 and f_2 we replace e by a path of vertices using the insert operation of the split-find-insert data structure described in the previous section. This might take time proportional to the sum of the lengths of the two paths. However, for the whole execution of the algorithm, the time needed for insertions of this kind will be $O(n)$, since no edge of p_1 or p_2 can be inserted again.

If e is on the periphery of G_e then the above argument for bounding the number of edges that need to be inserted does not apply because same edges may need to be re-inserted more than once. To handle this case we modify our data structure for maintaining the planar embeddings of the skeletons of level-2 nodes by defining an array *external* such that $external(v) = 1$ if v is on an external face of the skeleton of its allocation node and $external(v) = 0$, otherwise. The *left* and *right* values for vertices on the external faces of the skeletons will not be supported. Vertices v_1 and v_2 belong to the same external face iff $external(v_1) = external(v_2) = 1$ and v_1 and v_2 have the same allocation node. Maintaining *external* will take linear time since any vertex can change its *external* value no more than once.

We can summarize our main result as follows.

Theorem 7. *Given any n-vertex m-edge graph G, a maximal planar subgraph of G can be found in $O(n + m)$ time.*

We can also adapt our technique to find a maximal *outerplanar* subgraph of an n-vertex graph. We know of no previous algorithm for solving this problem. We create an additional vertex z and join z to all vertices of G. Then we find a maximal planar subgraph of the resulting graph by a similar procedure as Algorithm *Maxplanar*, however the initial tree constructed in Step 1 is the star graph with root z This guarantees that the maximal planar graph constructed by the modified algorithm will contain all additional edges. Removing at the end z and all incident edges clearly will result in a maximal outerplanar graph. We need to show that the time complexity of this algorithm is $O(n)$, since our initial subgraph was not a depth-first tree and the analysis of the original Algorithm *Maxplanar* (Lemma 6) can be no longer applied. In this case, however, we do not need the update paths since each level-1 or level-2 node can have only one ancestor and the conditions of Lemmas 1 and 2 can be directly checked. Thus we have the following theorem.

Theorem 8. *Given any n-vertex m-edge graph G, a maximal outerplanar subgraph of G can be found in $O(n + m)$ time.*

References

1. K. Booth, G. Lueker, *Testing for the consecutive ones property, interval graphs, and graph planarity using PQ-tree algorithm*, J. Comp. Syst. Sci. 13, 1976, pp. 335-379.
2. J. Cai, X. Han, and R.E. Tarjan, An O(m log n)-time algorithm for the maximal planar subgraph, *SIAM Journal on Computing*, 22 (1993), 1142-1162, .
3. G. Di Battista, R. Tamassia, Incremental planarity testing, *Proc. IEEE Symp. on Found. of Comp. Sci.*, (1989), 436-441.
4. G. Di Battista, R. Tamassia, On-line graph algorithms with SPQR trees, *Proc. Intern. Colloquium on Automata, Languages and Programming* (1990), 598-611.
5. H. N. Djidjev, On some properties of nonplanar graphs, *Compt. rend. Acad. bulg. Sci.*, vol. 37 (1984), 9, 1183-1185.
6. H.N. Djidjev, J. Reif, An efficient algorithm for the genus problem with explicit construction of forbidden subgraphs, *Proc. Annual ACM Symposium on Theory of Computing* (1991), pp.337-347.
7. S. Even and R.E. Tarjan, Computing an *st*-numbering, Theoretical Computer Science 2 (1976), 339-344.
8. H. Gabow and R.E. Tarjan, A linear-time algorithm for a special case of disjoint set union, *J. Compu. Syst. Sci.*, 30 (1985), 209-220.
9. M.R. Garey and D.S. Johnson, *Algorithms and Intractability: A Guide to the Theory of NP Completeness.* San Francisko, Freeman, 1979.
10. J. Hopcroft and R.E. Tarjan, *Dividing a graph into triconnected components*, SIAM J. Comput. 2, 1973, pp. 135-158.
11. J. Hopcroft and R.E. Tarjan, *Efficient planarity testing*, J.ACM, 21:4, 1974, pp. 549-568.
12. H. Imai and T. Asano, Dynamic orthogonal segment intersection search, in *Journal of Algorithms* 8, 1987, pp. 1-18.
13. R. Jayakumar, K. Thulasiraman, and M.N.S. Swamy, $O(n^2)$ algorithms for graph planarization, *IEEE Trans. on Comp.-Aided Design* 8 (1989), 257-267.
14. J.A. La Poutré, Alpha-algorithms for incremental planarity testing, *Proc. of the Ann. ACM Symp. on Theory of Comput.*, 1994, 706-715.
15. R.E. Tarjan, Efficiency of a good but not linear set union algorithm, *J. ACM*, 22 (1975), 215-225.
16. J. Westbrook, Fast incremental planarity testing, *Proc. Int. Col. on Automata, Languages, and Programming*, 1992, 342-353.

Topology B-Trees and Their Applications

Paul Callahan* Michael T. Goodrich** Kumar Ramaiyer***

Dept. of Computer Science, The Johns Hopkins Univ., Baltimore, MD 21218, USA

Abstract. The well-known B-tree data structure provides a mechanism for dynamically maintaining balanced binary trees in external memory. We present an external-memory dynamic data structure for maintaining arbitrary binary trees. Our data structure, which we call the *topology B-tree*, is an external-memory analogue to the internal-memory topology tree data structure of Frederickson. It allows for dynamic expression evaluation and updates as well as various tree searching and evaluation queries. We show how to apply this data structure to a number of external-memory dynamic problems, including approximate nearest-neighbor searching and closest-pair maintenance.

1 Introduction

The B-tree [8, 12, 14, 15] data structure is a very efficient and powerful way for maintaining balanced binary trees in external memory [1, 11, 13, 18, 19, 21, 22, 2]. Indeed, in his well-known survey paper [8], Comer calls B-trees "ubiquitous," for they are found in a host of different applications. Nevertheless, there are many applications that operate on unbalanced binary trees.

In this paper we describe a data structure, which we call the *topology B-tree*, for maintaining unbalanced binary trees in external memory. We allow for dynamic expression updates [7] and we consider a number of tree-search queries on arbitrary binary trees, which in turn can be used to solve a number of dynamic external-memory problems, including approximate nearest-neighbor searching and closest-pair maintenance. The topology B-tree is an external memory analogue to the *topology tree* data structure of Frederickson [10], which is an elegant internal-memory method for maintaining unbalanced binary trees.

Before we describe our results, let us review the model for external memory [1, 11, 13, 18, 19, 21, 22] that we will be assuming throughout this paper.

1.1 The External-Memory Model

We assume that the external-memory device (e.g., a disk) is structured so that seek time is much larger than the time needed to transfer a single record; hence,

* This research supported by the NSF under Grant CCR-9107293.
** This research supported by the NSF under Grants CCR-9300079, IRI-9116843 and CCR-9300079.
*** This research supported by the NSF under Grants CCR-9300079, IRI-9116843 and CCR-9300079.

to compensate for this time difference data is transferred between internal and external memory in *blocks* of records. We let B denote the number of records that can be transferred in a single external-memory input or output (i/o), and our measure of efficiency will be in terms of the total number of i/o's needed for a particular computation. Indeed, the model does not at all consider the number of internal computations performed by the CPU (provided this is kept within reason). This is motivated by the large difference in speed between modern CPU and disk technologies, for most computations on modern CPU's are measured in nanoseconds whereas most access times for modern disk drives are measured in milliseconds. As Comer[1] puts it, this is analogous to the difference in speed in sharpening a pencil by using a sharpener on one's desk or by taking an airplane to the other side of the world and using a sharpener on someone else's desk.

In addition to the parameter B, measuring block size, we also use M to denote the number of records that can fit in internal memory, and we use N to denote the total number of records i.e., input size. For the problems we consider, we make the reasonable assumptions that $M < N$, and $1 \leq B \leq M/2$.

1.2 Our Results

As mentioned above, in this paper we give an external-memory analogue to the topology tree data structure, which we call the topology B-tree. We show how use this data structure to dynamically maintain arbitrary binary trees, subject to the operations insertion and deletion of nodes, a generalized deepest-intersection search, and evaluation of arithmetic expressions, which we implement using $O(\log_B N)$ block i/o's. In addition, we show that each of the operations on dynamic expression trees require $\bar{O}(\log_B N)$ block i/o's[2]. Finally, using these primitives, we design optimal external-memory methods for dynamically solving the following geometric problems:

- Approximate nearest neighbor [3, 4]: given a set S of points in $\mathbb{R}^d$, for fixed d, a query point p, a metric L_t, and a parameter ϵ, find a point q in S that is within distance at most $(1 + \epsilon)$ times the distance of the actual nearest neighbor of p in S under L_t metric. We support this query under the operations of insertion and deletion of points in S.
- Closest pair [6, 5]: given a set S of points in $\mathbb{R}^d$, for fixed d, find a pair of points in S which are the closest among all pairs of points in S under the Euclidean distance metric. We support this operation under insertion and deletion of points from S.

Our query algorithms all use an optimal $O(\log_B N)$ external-memory i/o's.

2 The Topology Tree Data Structure

Before we describe our data structure in detail, however, let us first review the structure of the topology tree [10], and discuss how to implement insertion and

---

[1] Personal communication.

[2] We use the notation $\bar{O}(.)$ to describe amortized complexity.

deletion of nodes, a generalized deepest-intersection search, and the evaluation of arithmetic expressions.

Given any rooted tree $T = (V, E)$, the topology tree $\mathcal{T}$ is a balanced tree constructed on top of the nodes of T by repeated clustering. The topology tree $\mathcal{T}$ has multiple levels, and at each level there is a tree structure defined on the nodes at that level. Moreover, the nodes at any level define a partition of V. The rules for clustering the nodes are simple, and they enforce certain constraints on the resulting structure, which makes the topology tree balanced. The leaves of the topology tree $\mathcal{T}$ are the nodes V of tree T, and are at level 0. We refer to the tree $T_0 = T$ as the *base* tree of the topology tree. These nodes of T_0 are clustered to form bigger nodes, and result in a new tree structure T_1. The nodes of T_1 are the nodes at level 1 of the topology tree, and from each node v of T_1 there are edges (in $\mathcal{T}$) to the leaves of the topology tree which were combined to form v. Now clustering is done on nodes of T_1 to obtain the nodes for level 2 of the topology tree, and so on. We refer to the tree T_i as the *level i tree*, for its nodes are all at level i in the topology tree $\mathcal{T}$ (numbering up from the leaves). Eventually the clustering results in a single node which forms the root of the topology tree. The clustering is done according to the following simple rules:

1. Each cluster of degree 3 is of cardinality 1.
2. Each cluster of degree less than 3 is of cardinality at most 2.
3. No two adjacent clusters can be combined and still satisfy the above.

The first two rules guide the clustering operation, and the last one specifies the maximality property of clustering at each level. Based upon these clustering rules, it is fairly straightforward to show that the number of levels in a topology tree is $O(\log N)$, where N is the number of nodes in the base tree T. Frederickson [9] proves the following (stronger) lemma which relates the number of clusters at one level with the previous level:

Lemma 1. *[9] For any level $l > 0$ in a topology tree, the number of clusters at level l is at most $5/6$ of the number of clusters at level $l - 1$.*

2.1 Implementation of Primitives on Topology Tree

In this section, we discuss how to implement the dynamic operations on the topology tree. Our methods are very similar to those of Frederickson [10], but simpler, since we consider here only a subset of the operations he considers.

We consider the following operations on an arbitrary rooted binary tree T:

insert(T, v, w, pos): Insert the node v in the tree T as the *pos (left or right)* child of node w.

delete(T, v): Delete node v from the tree T.

swap(T, T_v, w): Given a tree T_v rooted at node v, replace the subtree rooted at w in T with T_v.

2.2 Augmenting the Tree for Generalized Searching

We augment the topology tree to perform a generalized searching computation and evaluate arithmetic expressions, under the dynamic operations outlined above. Additional operations we implement are as follows:

intersect(T, x, v): Suppose each node w of the tree T stores an $O(1)$-sized description of a set Q_w, such that the set stored at a node w always contains the sets stored at its children. This operation tests if an object x intersects a set Q_v for a given node v in T.

deepest-intersect(T, x): Suppose again that each node w of the tree T stores an $O(1)$-sized description of a set Q_w, such that the set stored at a node w always contains the sets stored at its children. This operation identifies each node v in the tree T in which x intersects Q_v, but x does not intersect the set associated with any of v's children (or v is a leaf).

eval-expression(T, v): Suppose the leaves of the tree T store values from a semiring $(S, +, *, 0, 1)$, and the internal nodes store the operations $+$ or $*$. This operation evaluates the arithmetic expression represented by the subtree T_v rooted at v in T.

Our implementation of the insert, delete, and swap operations is similar to Frederickson [10]. We implement these operations using constant number of *reclustering* operations i.e., removal of clusters along a root-to-leaf path in $\mathcal{T}$, and performing the clustering again. The complexity of reclustering operation is $O(\log N)$ as shown in the following lemma:

Lemma 2. *The reclustering operation along a path in a topology tree $\mathcal{T}$ uses a total of $O(\log N)$ pointers from $\mathcal{T}$ and from all the level trees. Moreover at each level, the number of pointers modified in the level tree is constant (at most 2).*

Hence the maintenance of the topology tree after any of the dynamic operations takes $O(\log N)$ time. We also show in the full version how the additional operations can be implemented on a topology tree in $O(\log N)$ time ($O(k*\log N)$ for deepest-intersect queries, where k is the size of the output).

3 B-Lists

In this section, we divert our attention and consider a method that is probably part of the folklore in external-memory algorithms, but which is applicable in the construction of our final data structure.

Suppose we are given a doubly-linked list of N weighted nodes, and a parameter B, where each node u in the list is of weight $w_u \leq B$. Let $W = \sum_{i=1}^{N} w_i$. The problem is to appropriately group the nodes in the list into *blocks* so that the weight of each resulting block is less than or equal B, and the total number of blocks is $O(W/B)$. Also, we require that the structure supports the operations of insertion and deletion of nodes in the list.

We solve this problem by simply grouping contiguous nodes into blocks, and maintain the following *weight invariant*: the sum of the weights of any two adjacent blocks is at least B, and the weight of each block is less than or equal to B. We refer to the resulting structure as a *B-list*.

We can easily show that insertion and deletion operations on B-lists manipulates only $O(1)$ blocks. Also, it is easy to show that the operations of weight updates of nodes can also be done similarly by changing only $O(1)$ blocks.

4 Hierarchical B-lists

In this section, we show how to build a structure using the B-list structures, which we call the *hierarchical B-list*. This structure is motivated by the skip list structure of Pugh [20].

The hierarchical B-list consists of a hierarchy of B-lists in which only the blocks of adjacent B-lists are connected. We assign a level to each B-list, and the level numbers increase from bottom to the top of the hierarchy. The pointers are directed, and we refer to them as *down* or *up* pointers based on the direction. We require the blocks in the underlying B-lists satisfy the following connectivity constraint: each block has at most B *down* pointers, and has at most constant number of *up* pointers (if present). We define the hierarchical B-lists to be *governed* if all the inter-level pointers are *down* pointers, and *ungoverned* otherwise.

The blocking on the individual B-lists are done independently as discussed in the previous section. When we split (merge) blocks the pointers get added (removed) to (from) the blocks in the next B-list which may require further splitting (merging). We can do update operations on hierarchical B-lists as in *hysterical B-trees* [15]. We give the details in full version.

In ungoverned hierarchical B-lists, during splitting and merging we may need to perform $O(B)$ pointer changes, since we need to add new *up* pointers to parent blocks. But using a result of hysterical B-trees [15], we can prove that the number of pointer changes during a split or merge is $\bar{O}(1)$.

We now consider hierarchical B-lists consisting of $O(\log_B N)$ B-lists, which we can easily show as requiring a storage of $O(N/B)$ i/o blocks. We can also show the following lemma for update operations on ungoverned hierarchical B-lists.

Lemma 3. *We can perform the operations of search and updates on a ungoverned hierarchical B-list requiring a storage of $O(N/B)$ i/o blocks, using $\bar{O}(\log_B N)$ i/o's.*

For governed hierarchical B-lists, however, we can show the following:

Lemma 4. *We can perform the operations of top-down search and updates on a governed hierarchical B-list requiring a storage of $O(N/B)$ i/o blocks, by performing only $O(\log_B N)$ i/o's.*

5 The Topology B-Tree

In this section we give details of the construction of our external-memory data structure, the *topology B-tree*, and we also discuss some of its properties.

Given a topology tree $\mathcal{T}$, we group the clusters of $\mathcal{T}$ to form a tree of bigger nodes, which we call *super clusters*. This process increases the degree of each node in the resulting tree. We prove bounds on the degree, the size of the new clusters, number of nodes, and the depth of the resulting tree. We also show how to implement dynamic operations on this topology tree of super clusters. We refer to this method of grouping of clusters into super clusters as *stratification*, and we call the resulting tree the *stratified topology tree*.

The lemma 1 shows that the number of clusters in a topology tree decreases in a geometric progression as we move from leaves to the root. This provides us a method for stratification, which we now discuss in detail. We split the levels of a topology tree into groups of contiguous $\log_2 B$ levels. We refer to each level of $\mathcal{T}$ that is a multiple of $\log_2 B$ as a *super level*. We refer to the contiguous group of $\log_2 B$ levels between two super levels, say i and $i+1$, in $\mathcal{T}$ as a *layer* i of $\mathcal{T}$. From every node u in each super level, we construct a super cluster by including all the descendants of u in $\mathcal{T}$ up to but not including the nodes of the next super level. We refer to the resulting tree of layers of super clusters as the *stratified topology tree*. To obtain our final structure, we construct a B-list on the super clusters in each layer of stratified $\mathcal{T}$ (ordered left to right), and then build a hierarchical B-lists structure over the B-lists constructed on all the layers of $\mathcal{T}$. We call the resultant structure the *topology B-tree*.

Now consider a block b at level i in the hierarchical B-lists. The block b contains one or more super clusters from layer i of $\mathcal{T}$. But the total number of nodes of $\mathcal{T}$ in b from these super clusters is at most B. These nodes have descendants which belong to at most B blocks at level $(i-1)$ of the hierarchical B-lists. We make the *down* pointers for the block b point to these blocks in the B-list at level $i-1$. Similarly we make the *up* pointers for a block point to the blocks containing the ancestor super clusters (if the application needs ungoverned hierarchical B-lists). We can easily bound the number of up pointers required for each block by at most 2.

We now prove some properties of the topology B-tree:

Lemma 5. *In a topology B-tree $\mathcal{T}'$ corresponding to a topology tree $\mathcal{T}$ of N nodes,*

1. *the number of blocks in $\mathcal{T}'$ is $O(N/B)$,*
2. *the depth of $\mathcal{T}'$ is $O(\log_B N)$, and*
3. *each super cluster belongs to exactly one block.*

Proof: These follow directly from the above discussions. ∎

We begin our discussion of the implementation of our dynamic operations by first proving an important bound on the number of blocks that may be modified in a reclustering operation performed on a topology B-tree due to an insertion or deletion of a node in T. When we access a block, we have information about adjacencies in the topology tree as well as information from all the level tree nodes in that blocks. When we perform the changes required for reclustering within a block, we use the level tree edges which point to other blocks. This operation could potentially access a large number of blocks. But, as we show in the following lemma, the number of blocks that may be accessed during the reclustering operation is not too large.

Lemma 6. *The total number of blocks accessed during a reclustering operation on a topology B-tree is $O(\log_B N)$.*

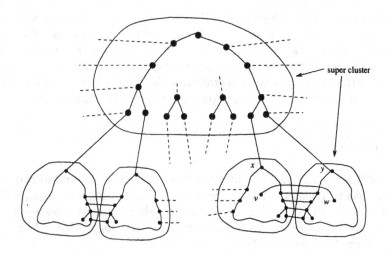

Fig. 1. The Structure of a Topology B-Tree (blocking not shown).

Proof: The structure of a topology B-tree $\mathcal{T}'$ is shown in Figure 1. Consider a super cluster x at layer l in the corresponding stratified topology tree $\mathcal{T}$. It contains part of $\mathcal{T}$, and also information about the level tree nodes contained in it. There are some level tree edges going out from x to other super clusters (see Figure 1). Consider a node v at level i within x. Suppose v has a edge e going to the node w in the super cluster y. There are two cases:

Case 1: The parent of node v at level $i+1$ is v itself in $\mathcal{T}$. In this case, the node v is not part of the clustering at level i. So, the level tree edge is inherited by the parent nodes of v and u, and hence by the corresponding super clusters.

Case 2: The parent of node v at level $i + 1$ is some other node, say u in $\mathcal{T}$. In this case, either the nodes v and w become part of the same super cluster or we fall back to Case 1.

Hence the total number of super clusters accessed during a reclustering operation is proportional to the number of layers or the depth of stratified topology tree $\mathcal{T}$, which is $O(\log_B N)$. Since each super cluster belongs to exactly one block in $\mathcal{T}'$ (see lemma 5), the number of blocks accessed during a reclustering operation on a topology B-tree is also $O(\log_B N)$. ■

Using the above lemmas we can show the following:

Theorem 7. *The dynamic operations insert, delete, and swap on the topology B-tree use $O(\log_B N)$ i/o's. The intersect operation at any node in the base tree uses $O(\log_B N)$ i/o's, and the deepest-intersect query uses $O(k * \log_B N)$ i/o's, where k is the number of nodes identified by the search. The arithmetic expression evaluation, and the maintenance of the dynamic expression tree uses $\bar{O}(\log_B N)$ i/o's.*

Proof: The claim follows from the lemmas 3, 4, 5, and 6, and from the discussions above. The topology tree built on an expression tree does not support search operation for a leaf node, and hence it requires ungoverned hierarchical B-lists for reclustering operation. As a result, we get amortized complexity as shown in lemma 3. However, for implementing other operations we assume the underlying tree supports search operation for locating a leaf. Once the search is done, we can use the path information obtained during reclustering. ■

6 Applications

In this section we consider two fundamental problems in computational geometry, and discuss dynamic solutions for those problems using our topology B-tree. Both the applications involve tree structure which supports top-down search from the root to locate any leaf. Hence, we use a topology B-tree which is built using governed hierarchical B-lists.

6.1 Dynamic Approximate Nearest Neighbor

The problem we consider here is as follows: Given a set S of points in d dimensions (d is a constant), a query point p, a metric L_t, and a parameter ϵ, find a point $q \in S$ such that $\frac{dist(p,q)}{dist(p,p^*)} \leq 1 + \epsilon$, where $dist(.,.)$ represents the distance between two points in L_t metric, and p^* is the actual nearest neighbor of p in S. Our goal is to come up with a data structure to answer this *approximate nearest neighbor* query, and to maintain the data structure under the operations of insertion and deletion of points in S.

Arya and Mount [3] first presented a (static) linear-space data structure for the approximate nearest neighbor problem that answered queries in $O(\log^3 N)$ time, which was later improved by Arya et al. [4] to $O(\log N)$ time and also made dynamic. All the previous work on this problem is for the internal memory model.

We give a brief outline of their method here. The set of points in S in d dimensions is partitioned into boxes of "good" aspect ratio. The partitioning is done by repeatedly splitting boxes of points into two boxes using hyperplanes parallel to one of the d dimensions. The boxes are arranged in a binary tree with leaves representing the boxes containing some constant number of points, and the internal nodes containing boxes which are the union of the boxes contained in the children[3]. The tree of boxes can have linear depth in the worst case. But a topology tree is constructed on top of it to obtain a balanced structure.

The algorithm of Arya et. al. [4] can be characterized as a method that performs constant number of point location queries on the topology tree constructed, maintaining the closest point found so far. This observation helps us to "externalize" the algorithm. We represent the tree of boxes obtained by partitioning the point space using a topology tree whose nodes are augmented with sets of constant size. The tree of boxes supports searching for a leaf node, and hence we use a topology B-tree built using governed hierarchical B-lists.

Using topology B-tree, we can compute the approximate nearest neighbor for a query point using $O(\log_B N)$ i/o's. We can also update the data structure using $O(\log_B N)$ i/o's, during the operations of insertion and deletion of points. We give the details in the full version.

6.2 Dynamic Closest Pair

Recently, Bespamyatnikh [5] has developed an algorithm to maintain the closest pair of points in a point set S in optimal worst case $O(\log N)$ time for insertions and deletions. The space requirement is linear in N. We adapt his algorithm to the present framework in order to externalize it, using the same box decomposition used in the preceding section for computing approximate nearest neighbor queries.

Callahan and Kosaraju [6] have shown how to maintain such a box decomposition of S under point insertions and deletions using only algebraic operations. In the present framework, this box decomposition corresponds to the tree T_0 in which each node v is labeled by a rectangle $R(v)$. The adapted algorithm can be modified to require $O(\log_B N)$ i/o's in the external-memory model.

Bespamyatnikh maintains a linear-size subset E of the set of distinct pairs of S such that E is guaranteed to contain the closest pair. As in the $O(\log^2 N)$ algorithm of [6], which solves a more general class of dynamic problems, these pairs are then maintained on a heap, resulting in the maintenance of the closest pair. The set E must satisfy certain invariants, which we now recast in the terminology of Callahan and Kosaraju [6].

Let $l_{\max}(R)$ denote the longest dimension of some rectangle R, let $p(v)$ denote the parent of v in T_0 (where the point a is used interchangeably with the leaf representing it), and let $d_{\min}$ and $d_{\max}$ denote, respectively the minimum and maximum distances between two point sets. We also introduce constant parameters α and β that must be adjusted to reconcile the new definitions with those of Bespamyatnikh.

First, we define a *rejected pair* to be an ordered pair (a, b) of points from S such that there exists v in the box decomposition T_0 satisfying the following:

---

[3] There are other types of nodes also, representing *doughnut cells*, but we omit the details here.

1. $a \notin R(v)$,
2. $l_{\max}(R(v)) \leq \alpha l_{\max}(R(p(a)))$,
3. $d_{\min}(R(p(a)), R(p(v))) \leq \beta l_{\max}(R(p(v)))$, and
4. $d_{\max}(a, R(v)) < d(a, b)$.

Then we maintain the invariant that for all $a, b \in S$, $\{a, b\} \in E$ unless (a, b) or (b, a) is a rejected pair. For sufficiently small α and β, the conditions for rejection are stronger than those of Bespamyatnikh, and will therefore suffice to prove correctness.

Second, we define E_p to be the set of all those pairs in E that contain the point p, and let N_d denote some d-dependent constant. We maintain the additional invariant that for all $p \in S$, $|E_p| \leq N_d$. Note that this gives us a linear bound on $|E|$. This requirement is justified by a theorem of Bespamyatnikh deriving a constant N_d such that for any p such that $|E_p| > N_d$, there is some $\{p, q\}$ in $|E_p|$ such that either (p, q) or (q, p) is a rejected pair.

There are two kinds of searches we must perform in order to maintain the set E. First, for any point p, we must be able to retrieve a set E_p containing at most N_d points. This is necessary for restricting the size of these sets under updates when we add new pairs to E. Second, we must be able to retrieve a set $A(v)$ for any v that contains all $p \in S$ such that there exists a (p, q) that is a rejected pair by virtue of the rectangle $R(v)$. This is necessary for determining when new pairs must be added to E to account for the deletion of some point. Bespamyatnikh has shown that the size of $A(v)$ is constant. Intuitively, this follows from conditions 2 and 3, which allow us to apply a packing argument. See [5] for a proof that these two operations are sufficient.

The above searches can be reduced to an invocation of an approximate nearest neighbor search of the preceding section and a search defined in [6] in which we construct a δ-*rendering* of a given d-cube C, denoted $\rho_\delta(C)$. Intuitively, $\rho_\delta(C)$ is an approximate covering of the points in C using a constant number of rectangles from T_0. More formally, $\rho_\delta(C)$ is a set containing all tree nodes w such that $l_{\max}(R(w)) \leq \delta l(C) < l_{\max}(R(p(w)))$, and $R(w)$ intersects C. It is straightforward to show by a packing argument that the size of a δ-rendering is $O(1)$ (with constants dependent on δ and d).

We can implement the construction of a δ-rendering as a search on the topology tree that is much like point location, but in which we may need to descend into both children of a cluster, resulting in a search subtree of the topology tree rather than a single path. The objects for such a "truncated" deepest-intersect query now correspond to rectangle intersection rather than point inclusion. Details of this search will be given in the final version. Because the number of leaves in such a search will be bounded by the size of the δ-rendering, the total number of i/o's will remain bounded by the depth of the search tree, and will therefore have complexity $O(\log_B N)$ in the external memory model.

Computing E_p: Given a point p, we compute E_p as follows. First, we find the approximate nearest neighbor of p using the algorithm of the preceding section. Let r denote the distance to this neighbor. Clearly r is at least the distance to the actual nearest neighbor. Moreover, it can be greater by a factor of at most $(1 + \epsilon)$. The value of ϵ used is not critical, though it may be chosen to optimize efficiency.

We now let C be the cube centered at p with sides of length $2r$, and compute $\rho_\delta(C)$ for δ sufficiently small that the diameter of each $R(w)$ is bounded above by $r(1 + \epsilon)^{-1}$. We let E_p consist of all those points q such that $w \in \rho_\delta(C)$ and $S \cap R(w) = \{q\}$. That is, we rule out any points contained in boxes in which there is more than one point. Note that for any $q \in S \cap R(w)$ such that $w \in \rho_\delta(C)$ and $|S \cap R(w)| > 1$, one can construct a v (a descendant of w) such that (q, p) is a rejected pair. Hence, we may maintain the first invariant while rejecting such q. It is even easier to verify that we may reject all points not covered by boxes in $\rho_\delta(C)$. We derive the constant N_d by bounding $|\rho_\delta(C)|$ in terms of d and δ.

Computing $A(v)$: For this computation, we recall conditions 2 and 3, and consider the set of all $a \in A(v)$. One can easily verify from condition 3 that $R(p(a))$ must intersect a cube C of length $(2\beta + 1)l_{\max}(R(p(v)))$ on a side. For sufficiently small δ, it suffices to consider those a such that there exists $w \in \rho_\delta(C)$ with $S \cap R(w) = \{a\}$. Once again, we may rule out any w such that $R(w)$ contains multiple points. In this case, the reason is that $R(p(a))$ would then violate condition 2.

Recall that the number of i/o's needed to perform an approximate nearest neighbor query and to construct $\rho_\delta(C)$ is $O(\log_B N)$. It follows that the above operations can be performed in $O(\log_B N)$ i/o's. We use standard B-trees to implement heap maintenance in the same i/o complexity. Combining this with the result of [5], we obtain an algorithm for closest-pair maintenance using $O(\log_B N)$ i/o's.

7 Conclusions

We give an efficient method for maintaining arbitrary rooted binary trees in external memory in a dynamic fashion. We show how to perform the dynamic expression tree updates and how these can be applied to solve some interesting dynamic computational geometry problems in external memory. We believe there are other applications, as well, such as approximate range searching [17].

Acknowledgements

We would like to thank David Mount for several helpful discussions concerning the topics of this paper.

References

1. A. Aggarwal and J. S. Vitter. The input/output complexity of sorting and related problems. *Communications of the ACM*, 31(9):1116–1127, 1988.
2. Lars Arge. The buffer tree: A new technique for optimal i/o algorithms. In *Proc. on Fourth Workshop on Algorithms and Data Structures*, 1995.
3. S. Arya and D. M. Mount. Approximate nearest neighbor queries in fixed dimensions. In *Proc. 4th ACM-SIAM Sympos. Discrete Algorithms*, pages 271–280, 1993.

4. S. Arya, D. M. Mount, N. S. Netanyahu, R. Silverman, and A. Wu. An optimal algorithm for approximate nearest neighbor searching. In *Proc. 5th ACM-SIAM Sympos. Discrete Algorithms*, pages 573–582, 1994.

5. Sergei N. Bespamyatnikh. An optimal algorithm for closest pair maintenance. In *Proceedings 11th Annual Symposium on Computational Geometry*, 1995.

6. P. B. Callahan and S. R. Kosaraju. Algorithms for dynamic closest pair and *n*-body potential fields. In *Proc. 6th ACM-SIAM Symp. on Discrete Algorithms*, pages 263–272, 1995.

7. R. F. Cohen and R. Tamassia. Dynamic expression trees and their applications. In *Proc. 2nd ACM-SIAM Sympos. Discrete Algorithms*, pages 52–61, 1991.

8. D. Comer. The ubiquitous B-tree. *ACM Comput. Surv.*, 11:121–137, 1979.

9. G. N. Frederickson. Ambivalent data structures for dynamic 2-edge connectivity and *k*-smallest spanning trees. In *Proc. 32nd Annu. IEEE Sympos. Found. Comput. Sci.*, pages 632–641, 1991.

10. G. N. Frederickson. A data structure for dynamically maintaining rooted trees. In *Proc. 4th ACM-SIAM Symp. on Discrete Algorithms (SODA)*, pages 175–184, 1993.

11. Michael T. Goodrich, Jyh-Jong Tsay, Darren E. Vengroff, and Jeffrey Scott Vitter. External-memory computational geometry. In *Proc. 34th Annu. IEEE Sympos. Found. Comput. Sci. (FOCS 93)*, pages 714–723, 1993.

12. O. Gunther and H.-J. Schek. Advances in spatial databases. In *Proc. 2nd Symposium, SSD '91*, volume 525 of *Lecture Notes in Computer Science*. Springer-Verlag, 1991.

13. P. C. Kanellakis, S. Ramaswamy, D. E. Vengroff, and J. S. Vitter. Indexing for data models with constraints and classes. In *Proc. 12th ACM SIGACT-SIGMOD-SIGART Conf. Princ. Database Sys.*, pages 233–243, 1993.

14. Robert Laurini and Derek Thompson. *Fundamentals of Spatial Information Systems*. A.P.I.C. Series. Academic Press, 1992.

15. D. Maier and S. C. Salveter. Hysterical B-trees. *Information Processing Letters*, 12(4):199–202, 1981.

16. J. Matoušek. Reporting points in halfspaces. *Comput. Geom. Theory Appl.*, 2(3):169–186, 1992.

17. D. Mount and S. Arya. Approximate range searching. In *Proc. 11th ACM Symp. on Computational Geometry*, 1995.

18. M. H. Nodine, M. T. Goodrich, and J. S. Vitter. Blocking for external graph searching. In *Proceedings of the 12th Annual ACM Symposium on Principles of Database Systems (PODS '93)*, pages 222–232, 1993.

19. M. H. Overmars, M. H. M. Smid, M. T. de Berg, and M. J. van Kreveld. Maintaining range trees in secondary memory, part I: partitions. *Acta Inform.*, 27:423–452, 1990.

20. W. Pugh. Skip lists: A probabilistic alternative to balanced trees. *Communications of the ACM*, 33(6):668–676, 1990.

21. M. H. M. Smid and M. H. Overmars. Maintaining range trees in secondary memory, part II: lower bounds. *Acta Inform.*, 27:453–480, 1990.

22. J. S. Vitter. Efficient memory access in large-scale computation. In *1991 Symposium on Theoretical Aspects of Computer Science (STACS)*, *Lecture Notes in Computer Science,*, Hamburg, 1991. Springer-Verlag.

In-Place Calculation of Minimum-Redundancy Codes

Alistair Moffat[1]   Jyrki Katajainen[2]

[1] Department of Computer Science, The University of Melbourne,
Parkville 3052, Australia
alistair@cs.mu.oz.au
[2] Department of Computer Science, University of Copenhagen,
Universitetsparken 1, DK-2100 Copenhagen East, Denmark
jyrki@diku.dk

Abstract. The *optimal prefix-free code problem* is to determine, for a given array $p = [p_i \mid i \in \{1 \ldots n\}]$ of n weights, an integer array $l = [l_i \mid i \in \{1 \ldots n\}]$ of n codeword lengths such that $\sum_{i=1}^{n} 2^{-l_i} \leq 1$ and $\sum_{i=1}^{n} p_i l_i$ is minimized. Huffman's famous greedy algorithm solves this problem in $O(n \log n)$ time, if p is unsorted; and can be implemented to execute in $O(n)$ time, if the input array p is sorted. Here we consider the space requirements of the greedy method. We show that if p is sorted then it is possible to calculate the array l in-place, with l_i overwriting p_i, in $O(n)$ time and using $O(1)$ additional space. The new implementation leads directly to an $O(n \log n)$-time and $n + O(1)$ words of extra space implementation for the case when p is not sorted. The proposed method is simple to implement and executes quickly.

Keywords. Prefix-free code, Huffman code, in-place algorithm, data compression.

1 Introduction

The algorithm introduced by Huffman [4, 7] for devising minimum-redundancy prefix-free codes is well known and continues to enjoy widespread use in data compression programs. Huffman's method is also a good illustration of the greedy paradigm of algorithm design and, at the implementation level, provides a useful motivation for the priority queue abstract data type. For these reasons Huffman's algorithm enjoys a prominence enjoyed by only a relatively small number of fundamental methods.

In this paper we examine the space-efficiency of this greedy algorithm for constructing optimal prefix-free codes. Textbooks describing the technique often provide pseudo-code rather than a complete implementation and draw figures showing forests of binary trees. These descriptions create the impression that the implementation of the greedy algorithm should be pointer-based and reliant upon a linear amount of auxiliary memory for node addresses and for internal tree nodes. This is, as we shall show, an erroneous impression. We describe an implementation of the greedy algorithm that, in addition to an input array storing the weights of the symbols to be coded, requires just $O(1)$ words of extra space if the input array is sorted and $n + O(1)$ words of extra space if the input array is not sorted, where n is the number of symbols for which the code is to be constructed. As for pointer-based implementations, the algorithms require $O(n)$ time for sorted input, and $O(n \log n)$ time for unsorted input. Moreover, implementation of the algorithms is straightforward, and they are suitable for practical use.

The main motivation for this study is our algorithmic curiosity. The best previous implementation of the greedy method for optimal prefix-free coding requires $n + O(1)$ words of extra memory and $O(n \log n)$ time for unsorted input arrays [10], so it was natural to ask whether these bounds could be improved if the input array is sorted. In particular, we were interested to know whether an in-place calculation was possible, since, for practical computation on large alphabets, the space constant is of overriding concern. For example, a typical textbook implementation of the greedy method requires around 20 megabytes of memory to calculate a code for a collection of one million symbols, whereas our implementation requires just 4 megabytes (one million rather than five million 4-byte words). Furthermore, recent research papers report (see, for example, [2]) that in-place algorithms can be faster in practice than their space-inefficient counterparts when run on a modern computer system with a hierarchical memory. Speed is one of the important characteristics of our implementation, too. We have calculated an optimal code for a set of over one million symbols in just a few seconds of CPU time.

2 Prefix Codes

Suppose that in some token stream there are n distinct symbols and that the ith least frequent symbol appears p_i times. That is, we suppose that $p = [p_i \mid i \in \{1 \ldots n\}]$ is a non-decreasing array of n positive integer *weights*, $p_1 \leq p_2 \leq p_3 \cdots \leq p_n$. A *code* is an array $l = [l_i \mid i \in \{1 \ldots n\}]$ of n integers, where the presumption is that the ith symbol is to be represented by an l_i-bit long binary *codeword* over the alphabet $\{0, 1\}$. A *prefix-free code* is a code for which $\sum_{i=1}^{n} 2^{-l_i} \leq 1$. For example, assigning $l_i = \lceil \log_2 n \rceil$ is a prefix-free code, since $n \cdot 2^{-\lceil \log_2 n \rceil} \leq 1$. Given a prefix-free code l, it is straightforward to determine a set of n codewords, one per distinct symbol, with the property that the codeword for symbol i is l_i bits long, and such that no codeword in the set is a proper prefix of any other.

An *optimal prefix-free code* is a set of codeword lengths l_i such that not only is $\sum_{i=1}^{n} 2^{-l_i} \leq 1$ satisfied, but also such that $B = \sum_{i=1}^{n} l_i p_i$ is minimized over all prefix-free codes. Quantity B is the number of output bits used by the code to represent the token stream in question; a code is optimal if there is no other code that results in an output representation requiring fewer than B bits. For any given array p there can be more than one optimal code; for the assignment $p = [1, 1, 2, 2]$ both $l = [2, 2, 2, 2]$ and $l = [3, 3, 1, 2]$ (and one other) result in compressed representations that require $B = 12$ bits. Note, however, that there is always at least one code for which $l_1 \geq l_2 \geq l_3 \cdots \geq l_n$, and it is such a code that we shall seek to calculate. Huffman's greedy algorithm [4] generates optimal prefix-free codes, and is sketched in Section 3; an alternative paradigm by which this problem may be solved has been articulated recently by Larmore and Przytycka [5].

Once an optimal prefix-free code has been determined and a set of codewords is known they can be used to generate an efficient representation of the token stream. If the original representation was not as economical then compression will result. However, we do not concern ourselves with the steps that actually assign final codewords or use them, and will regard our task as being over when, for each symbol, a codeword length is assigned. One method for assigning codewords that leads to fast decoding is summarized in Witten, Moffat, and Bell [10] (see also [3]). The decoder is also space-efficient—for the case of sorted symbol weights and ordinal symbol identifiers in $\{1 \ldots n\}$ the decoder requires just $O(\max_{i=1}^{n} l_i)$ words of memory.

We also need some terminology for describing regular binary trees: a *node s* is a *tree*, and if t_1 and t_2 are two trees then $t = s(t_1, t_2)$ is a tree, with node s as its *root*. If $t = s(t_1, t_2)$ and nodes s_1 and s_2 are the roots of trees t_1 and t_2 respectively, then s is the *parent* of nodes s_1 and s_2 in tree t. Similarly, nodes s_1 and s_2 are the *children* of node s. If node s is a singleton and has no children, then it is a *leaf* node of the tree, otherwise it is an *internal* node. The *depth* of any node is one greater than the depth of its parent; the depth of a root is zero. A *forest* is a set of trees.

The model of computation we assume is a unit-cost random access machine, in which values as large as U can be stored in a single word, where $U = \sum_{i=1}^{n} p_i$ is the sum of the input weights. That is, we suppose that addition and comparison operations on integer values in the range $1 \ldots U$ require $O(1)$ time each. At various stages of the algorithm we will store in these memory words partial sums of the input weights (integers in the range $1 \ldots U$), array indices (integers in the range $1 \ldots n$), and codeword lengths (integers in the range $1 \ldots n - 1$).

In all of the algorithms that follow we will assume at no cost the n words of storage for the input array p; this is the description of the problem and is "free" in the same way that in-place sorting algorithms such as Heapsort regard the input list as being "free". We also suppose that the algorithm may be destructive—that p_i can be overwritten by l_i and that the output array replaces the input array. What we seek to limit is the extra space required. As will be demonstrated in Section 4, $O(1)$ words of memory are sufficient to solve the optimal prefix-code problem as we have stated it here.

3 The Greedy Algorithm

Huffman's greedy algorithm [4] is widely known and descriptions appear in a wide range of algorithms textbooks (see, for example, [9]). In this greedy method a forest of trees is manipulated. At each step of the algorithm the two least weight trees are selected and melded, this continuing until a single tree remains. For the purposes of ordering the sequence of operations, the *weight* of a tree is the sum of the weights of symbols associated with the leaves of that tree, with ties broken arbitrarily. Initially each symbol is installed in a singleton tree, so at the commencement of the algorithm the forest contains n trees.

By the end of the melding process there is one tree remaining. This tree contains as subtrees all of the other trees constructed during the course of the algorithm; and the weight of the final tree is the sum of the set of initial weights, $\sum_{i=1}^{n} p_i$. The structure of the final tree defines an optimal code—symbol i of weight p_i should be allocated a codeword of l_i bits, where l_i is the depth in the tree of the leaf corresponding to the singleton tree p_i. To allow depths to be calculated, the structure of meldings during the melding loop is noted using *parent* pointers. A second loop then traces, for each symbol, the sequence of parent pointers through to the root of the final tree. The depth is the required codelength l_i.

A straightforward implementation of the greedy algorithm uses approximately $5n$ words—two words at each leaf node to store the initial weight and the parent pointer; $2n - 2$ words to store the weight and parent of the $n - 1$ internal nodes of the final tree; and n words for a heap of at most n items so that the priority queue operations can be performed efficiently. These operations require $O(\log n)$ time each, so $O(n \log n)$ time is sufficient for the main loop, since each iteration of the melding loop involves a constant number of priority queue operations. This is how the algorithm is described in most textbooks.

One small problem is that, as described, the second phase takes $O(\sum_{i=1}^{n} l_i)$ time, which might be as large as $\Theta(n^2)$ and could dominate the time required by the first phase. The solution to this problem is to label internal nodes with their depth the first time they are traversed, thereby short-circuiting subsequent traversals through that node. Since there are exactly $2n - 2$ edges and each edge is traversed once only, this variant of path-compression reduces the time for the depth-calculation phase to $O(n)$. This modification does not change the space complexity of the algorithm, as the weight fields can be used to record depth at both leaf and internal nodes.

Van Leeuwen [6] was apparently the first to note that if the input array p is in sorted order then the running time can be improved to $O(n)$. The reduction is achieved by keeping the leaf nodes distinct from the internal nodes formed during the melding, and maintaining two separate priority queues. The queue implementation can then be a linked list, since the sequence of internal nodes is formed in sorted order, and the input list is already in sorted order. At each melding stage the two items with the smallest weights are within the first two of the unprocessed section of the input list and the first two of the list of internal nodes, so all of the priority queue operations can be effected in $O(1)$ time. Implementation of this idea requires $4n$ words of memory—$2n$ to store the weights and parent pointers of the leaves and $2n - 2$ to store the weights and parent pointers of the internal nodes.

4 In-Place Implementation

Let us now focus on the implementation of van Leeuwen's $O(n)$ variant of the greedy algorithm. During the melding phase, two lists are manipulated—a sorted list of leaves that have not yet been processed and a sorted list of internal nodes. The first observation we make about this operation is that the weight of any node need be maintained only until that node is processed. At any given stage of the melding process there are thus at most n weights to be recorded; and by the end of this phase there is just one extant weight.

The second key observation is that it is not necessary to maintain parent pointers in both of these lists. If the depth of each internal node of the tree is known then the depth of each leaf can be inferred, since the codeword lengths can be assumed to be non-increasing. For example, a tree with internal node depths of $[3, 3, 2, 1, 0]$ must have leaves at depths $[4, 4, 4, 4, 2, 1]$. Furthermore, at the start of the melding phase there are no parent pointers in either list; and at the end there are $n - 2$ in the list of internal nodes, but none in the list of leaves. The combined total of weights (required for nodes yet to be processed) and parent pointers (required for internal nodes already processed) can never exceed n, so the parent pointers and weights can co-exist in the same array. If r indicates the next tree node to be processed, s indicates the next leaf node to be processed (singleton tree), and t indicates the next vacant position to be used for a tree node, then the array can be partitioned and processed as shown in the following diagram:

1		r		t	s		n
indices of parents of internal nodes		weights of non-singleton trees, non-decreasing			weights of singleton trees, non-decreasing		

Figure 1 describes this process in more detail. Initially $A[i]$ is assumed to store p_i, but the values are modified in-place as the procedure executes. At the completion of the loop, word $A[n]$ is unused, word $A[n - 1]$ stores the weight of

---

1. Set $s \leftarrow 1$ and $r \leftarrow 1$.
2. For $t \leftarrow 1$ to $n - 1$ do
   (a) If $(s > n)$ or $(r < t$ and $A[r] < A[s])$ then
       /* Select an internal tree node */
       Set $A[t] \leftarrow A[r]$, $A[r] \leftarrow t$, and $r \leftarrow r + 1$
   else
       /* Select a singleton leaf node */
       Set $A[t] \leftarrow A[s]$ and $s \leftarrow s + 1$.
   (b) Repeat Step 2a, but adding to $A[t]$ rather than assigning.

Fig. 1. In-place processing, phase one

the code tree, and words $A[1 \ldots n - 2]$ store parent pointers. Care must be taken that nodes and leaves are only examined if they logically exist, so the test at Step 2a includes a validity guard. Note that both "and" and "or" are assumed to be evaluated conditionally. Note also the strict inequality in the last clause of the test at Step 2a. If ties are broken in favour of leaf nodes then the resulting code has the smallest possible value of $l_1 = \max_{i=1}^{n} l_i$ amongst all minimum redundancy codes [6].

Figure 2a shows an example array of $n = 6$ weights prior to the execution of the procedure of Figure 1. Figure 2b indicates the state of processing at the commencement of Step 2a when $t = 4$ and $A[3]$ has just been computed, at which time $s = 5$ indicating that $A[5]$ is the next leaf to be processed, and $r = 3$, marking $A[3]$ as the next tree node to be considered. The two sets of double lines in Figure 2b indicate the three active zones in the array. Finally, Figure 2c shows the contents of the array at the completion of this first phase.

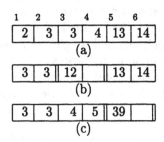

Fig. 2. Example of phase one on input array $[2, 3, 3, 4, 13, 14]$

In the second phase of the algorithm the array A must be converted into a array of codelengths. This process is described in Figure 3, and requires two further scans of the array A. In the first scan A is converted to an array of depths of internal nodes—Step 2 in Figure 3. The important observation here is that all of the array indices—that is, parent pointers—stored in $A[1 \ldots n - 2]$ point to the right, so that $A[i] > i$. Hence, if $A[n - 1]$ is assigned tree depth of 0, then a leftward scan in the array setting each depth to be one more than the depth of the parent node correctly converts parent pointers to node depths. By the completion of Step 2, $A[1 \ldots n - 1]$ is a list of depths of the internal nodes of the tree. The arrangement in array A during Step 2 in Figure 3 is:

1		t		$n-1$	n
indices of parents of internal nodes		depths of internal nodes			

Continuing the previous example, Figure 4a shows the result of applying this step to the array shown in Figure 2c.

1. Set $A[n-1] \leftarrow 0$.
2. For $t \leftarrow n-2$ downto 1 do
    Set $A[t] \leftarrow A[A[t]] + 1$.
3. Set $a \leftarrow 1$, $u \leftarrow 0$, $d \leftarrow 0$, $t \leftarrow n-1$, and $x \leftarrow n$.
4. While $a > 0$ do
    (a) While $t \geq 1$ and $A[t] = d$ do
        Set $u \leftarrow u + 1$ and $t \leftarrow t - 1$.
    (b) While $a > u$ do
        Set $A[x] \leftarrow d$, $x \leftarrow x - 1$, and $a \leftarrow a - 1$.
    (c) Set $a \leftarrow 2u$, $d \leftarrow d + 1$, and $u \leftarrow 0$.

Fig. 3. In-place processing, phase two

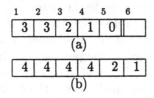

Fig. 4. Example of phase two on input array $[2, 3, 3, 4, 13, 14]$

Finally, the $n - 1$ internal node depths must be converted to n leaf node depths. This is accomplished by a further right-to-left scan using pointers t, which consumes internal nodes, and x, which indicates the index at which the next external node depth should be stored. The arrangement during this phase (Step 4 of Figure 3) is:

1		t	x		n
depths of internal nodes			codelengths (depths of leaves)		

The procedure used assumes that the internal node depths in $A[1 \ldots n - 1]$ form a non-increasing sequence. That this must be so is demonstrated by the following argument. To disambiguate the two different values stored in array A, let $parent[i]$ denote the value of $A[i]$ prior to Step 2 of Figure 3 and let $depth[i]$ denote the value stored in $A[i]$ after the execution of Step 2. Suppose, in contradiction of the claim that the $depth$ values are non-increasing, that $depth[i] < depth[j]$ for some $1 \leq i < j \leq n - 1$. Further, assume that j is the maximum value for which a corresponding i can be found. Note that neither i nor j can be the root: j cannot, since $depth[j] > depth[i] \geq 0$; and i cannot, since $i < n - 1$ and the root is, by definition, in $A[n - 1]$.

Consider the two values $i' = parent[i]$ and $j' = parent[j]$. If $i' = j'$ then $depth[i]$ and $depth[j]$ must be the same, since both are calculated as $depth[i'] + 1 = depth[j'] + 1$. Hence, $i' \neq j'$. Moreover, the strict first-in first-out nature of the queue in which internal nodes are stored means that when $i < j$ we have $parent[i] \leq parent[j]$. But, if $parent[i] \neq parent[j]$, then $i' < j'$. Moreover, $depth[i'] = depth[i] - 1$ and $depth[j'] = depth[j] - 1$, by the definition of $depth$ used during the calculation at Step 2. But this contradicts the assumption that j was the maximal value for which an i could found, $i < j$ and $depth[i] > depth[j]$, since we have just demonstrated that $i' < j'$ and $depth[i'] > depth[j']$. Thus, no such i and j could have existed in the first instance and the claim is correct—the list of internal node depths is non-increasing.

To perform the conversion from internal node depths to leaf node depths, the number u of internal nodes used at each depth d is counted and subtracted from the total number of nodes (including leaves) available (variable a) at that depth of the tree at Step 4a. Any nodes that were available for use at this level but not encountered as internal nodes must be leaf nodes and can be assigned; this is done at Step 4b. Depth d is then incremented and the next level of the tree is processed. The number of available nodes at any given depth is twice the number of internal nodes used at the previous depth; and initially there is one node of depth zero available. Figure 4b shows the state of the example array at the completion of Step 4. This final array is the desired set of codelengths.

To guarantee that Step 4 of Figure 3 is correct, we must be sure that $t < x$ at all times, as otherwise one or more unprocessed values might get overwritten. We show this by demonstrating that at the commencement of each loop iteration at Step 4 we have, as an invariant, that $t = x - a - u$. When $t = n - 1$, x, a, and u have the values n, 1, and 0 respectively and so the claim is true the first time Step 4 is executed. Consider now the effect of Step 4a. Each iteration of the inner loop increases u by one and decreases t by one, maintaining the invariant.

When t either reaches zero or a value at which $A[t] \neq d$ then x is decreased by $a - u$ during the course of the second inner loop at Step 4b, following which Step 4c sets a to twice the value of u and u to zero. If a prime indicates the value of a variable after this sequence of operations, then we have $t' = t$, $x' = x - a + u$, $u' = 0$, and $a' = 2u$. Hence, $t' = x' - a' - u'$ is true if $t = x - a + u - 2 \cdot u - 0$ holds. But the latter expression is true by assumption, so the claim of invariance is correct. Moreover, the variable u is non-negative throughout; and a is positive because of the guard at Step 4. Hence, $t < x$ holds until the loop terminates and the sequence of operations carried out by Step 4 is safe.

5 Other Considerations

An actual implementation of the complete algorithm differs only slightly from the pseudo-code shown in Figures 1 and 3 and is remarkably compact. For example, a test implementation in the language C is about 50 lines of code. Three straightforward scans over the input array are required, one in ascending order and two descending, meaning that locality of reference is high. The result is extremely fast execution. For example, codelengths for an array of 1,073,971 word frequencies (accumulated by processing three gigabytes of English text, see [10] for a description of this document collection) are calculated in just 1.4 seconds of CPU time on a Sun SparcStation 10/402.

If the input array is not sorted, we introduce an n-element auxiliary array B, initialized so that $B[i] = i$. We next sort A, taking care that $B[i]$ continues to record the location in A of weight p_i. The in-place Huffman algorithm is then executed on array A, and finally the required codelengths are determined by setting $l_i = B[A[i]]$. In this case the running time is dominated by the cost of sorting, and $O(n \log n)$ time is required; the space cost is $n + O(1)$ words of auxiliary storage provided an in-place sorting algorithm such as Heapsort is used, or $n + O(\log n)$ words if a stack-bounded Quicksort (which is usually faster) is used.

If an explicit sort must be performed, sorting is the dominant step. For the same list of 1,073,971 word frequencies it takes around 3.2 seconds for the Bentley-McIlroy Quicksort [1] to sort an array of "frequency, index" pairs, so overall code construction time is 4.6 seconds.[1] By way of comparison, the heap-based construction method described in [10] (which assumes the input is not sorted) requires 23.2 seconds to generate the same codelengths. The difference between the two alternatives—heap-based calculation, and Quicksort then in-place code calculation—is accounted for by the locality of reference exhibited by both Quicksort and the algorithm presented in this paper, and because the Bentley-McIlroy Quicksort exploits duplicate values in the input list, of which, for this data, there are many. Even so, for random integer keys without duplications Quicksort requires just 8.0 seconds to order 1,000,000 two-word records. We thus conclude that the new algorithm is the most effective way to calculate optimal prefix-codes, irrespective of whether or not the data is sorted.

Also worth noting is that although we have assumed throughout that an instance of the optimal prefix-code problem is specified by an n-array of symbol weights, other methods for describing problem instances are possible and lead to different time and space requirements. One alternative input formulation suitable for situations in which there many symbols sharing the same weight is a list of pairs $[(p_i, q_i) \mid i \in \{1 \dots r\}]$, where weight p_i has repetition factor q_i, there are r distinct symbol weights, and there are $n = \sum_{i=1}^{r} q_i$ symbols in total. If a similar list of "codelength, repetition count" pairs is the desired output, an optimal prefix-free code can be constructed in $O(r \log(n/r))$ time and space [8], which is $o(n)$ when r is $o(n)$.

It is also interesting to examine the memory requirements of the actual encoding and decoding processes. If we assume—as we have—that tokens are integers in the range $1 \dots n$ in increasing weight order, then both encoding and decoding can be carried out using two arrays each of l_1 words, where l_1 is the length of a longest codeword. These arrays are the only space requirement—in particular,

---

[1] Note, however, that the Bentley-McIlroy Quicksort is not stack-bounded, and in the worst case might require $O(n)$ words of auxiliary memory. Slightly increased times result if a stack-bounded variant is used.

there is no need to maintain an n-element array of codewords—and so if l_1 is $o(n)$ then the total encoding and decoding space requirement is sublinear. Witten, Moffat, and Bell [10] (see also Hirschberg and Lelewer [3]) describe a mechanism to achieve this. The time required by each encoding or decoding step is linear in the number of output bits, so the total time is $O(\sum_{i=1}^{n} p_i l_i)$. Additional memory is, of course, also required in both encoder and decoder if ordinal symbol numbers in increasing weight order must be mapped from or to actual compression tokens such as characters or words that are not naturally in weight order. The amount of memory required for this mapping and for storage of source tokens depends upon the compression model being used.

Acknowledgements

We gratefully acknowledge the assistance of Andrew Turpin. We also thank one of the referees, who provided incisive comments that improved our presentation. This work was supported by the Australian Research Council.

References

1. J.L. Bentley and M.D. McIlroy. Engineering a sorting function. *Software—Practice and Experience* **23** (1993) 1249–1265.
2. S. Carlsson, J. Katajainen, and J. Teuhola. In-place linear probing sort. Submitted. Preliminary version appeared in *Proceedings of the 9th Symposium on Theoretical Aspects of Computer Science*, Lecture Notes in Computer Science **577**, Springer-Verlag, Berlin/Heidelberg, Germany (1992) 581–587.
3. D. Hirschberg and D. Lelewer. Efficient decoding of prefix codes. *Communications of the ACM* **33** (1990) 449–459.
4. D.A. Huffman. A method for the construction of minimum-redundancy codes. *Proceedings of the Inst. Radio Engineers* **40** (1952) 1098–1101.
5. L.L. Larmore and T.M. Przytycka. Constructing Huffman trees in parallel. *SIAM Journal on Computing*. To appear.
6. J. van Leeuwen. On the construction of Huffman trees. In *Proceedings of the 3rd International Colloquium on Automata, Languages and Programming*, Edinburgh University Press, Edinburgh, Scotland (1976) 382–410.
7. D.A. Lelewer and D.S. Hirschberg. Data compression. *Computing Surveys* **19** (1987) 261–296.
8. A. Moffat, A. Turpin, and J. Katajainen. Space-efficient construction of optimal prefix codes. *Proceedings of the 5th IEEE Data Compression Conference*, IEEE Computer Society Press, Los Alamitos, California (1995) 192–201.
9. R. Sedgewick. *Algorithms in C*. 2nd Edition, Addison-Wesley, Reading, Massachusetts (1990).
10. I.H. Witten, A. Moffat, and T.C. Bell. *Managing Gigabytes: Compressing and Indexing Documents and Images*. Van Nostrand Reinhold, New York, New York (1994).

Regular-Factors In The Complements Of Partial k-Trees *

Damon Kaller, Arvind Gupta and Tom Shermer

School of Computing Science
Simon Fraser University
Burnaby, B.C., Canada, V5A 1S6
{kaller, arvind, shermer}@cs.sfu.ca

Abstract. We consider the problem of recognizing graphs containing an f-factor (for any constant f) over the class of partial k-tree complements. We also consider a variation of this problem that only recognizes graphs containing a *connected* f-factor: this variation generalizes the Hamiltonian circuit problem. We show that these problems have $O(n)$ algorithms for partial k-tree complements (on n vertices); we assume that the $\Theta(n^2)$ edges of such a graph are specified by representing the $O(n)$ edges of its complement. As a preliminary result of independent interest, we demonstrate a logical language in which, if a graph property can be expressed over the class of partial k-tree complements, then those graphs that satisfy the property can be recognized in $O(n)$ time.

1 Introduction

The f-factor problem (for fixed f) is to determine whether it is possible to delete a subset of the edges in a graph, so that exactly f edges remain incident to each vertex. The 1-factor problem is simply a reformulation of the *perfect matching* problem. A solution of the 2-factor problem is a cover of the vertices with disjoint cycles; if it is required that the 2-factor be connected, a solution is a *Hamiltonian circuit*. These problems find applications widely in scheduling theory, and in the design of networks.

f-Factors were first studied by Petersen [Pet91] in 1891. Tutte [Tut52] considered a more general problem, for which f is a (not necessarily constant) function associating a nonnegative integer with each vertex. For the general problem, Tutte's *f-Factor Theorem* elegantly characterizes all graphs that contain an f-factor. Such graphs can be recognized in polynomial time, by reducing the problem to recognizing graphs that contain a perfect matching (*i.e.* 1-factor); the details of the reduction can be found in [Bol78]. In the remainder of this paper, we are only concerned with f-factors for a fixed constant f.

It is much more difficult to recognize graphs with *connected* f-factors. For $f = 1$ the problem is trivial, but for $f \geq 2$ the problem is NP-complete. The

---

* Research supported by the Natural Sciences and Engineering Research Council of Canada.

Hamiltonian circuit (*i.e.* connected 2-factor) problem is one of the classic NP-complete problems [GJ79], and it is easily reducible to the connected f-factor problem for any $f \geq 3$. There are classes of graphs for which all members are known to contain Hamiltonian circuits: for example, Dirac [Dir52] showed that every graph with minimum degree $\frac{n}{2}$ contains a Hamiltonian circuit (where n is the number of vertices of the graph). Remarkably, it remains NP-complete to determine whether a graph with minimum degree δ_n has a Hamiltonian circuit, for any $\delta_n < \frac{n}{2}$ [DHK93].

Like many other graph problems, the f-factor problems can be phrased in terms of finding a subgraph of a graph given as the problem instance.

Definition 1. A *subgraph property* Π is a set of pairs (G, S), where G is a graph and S is a subgraph of G. If $(G, S) \in \Pi$, then S is called a *solution* of Π on the graph G. We denote the set of solutions of Π on G by $\Pi(G) = \{S | (G, S) \in \Pi\}$.

The decision problem corresponding to a subgraph property Π can be expressed as the question: Is $\Pi(G)$ nonempty for a given graph G? Over a large class of subgraph problems (many of which are NP-complete in general) this question can be decided in $O(n)$ time over the class of partial k-trees: these are graphs that can be decomposed to resemble a tree [RS86]. Finding such a *tree decomposition* is an important first step of many $O(n)$ algorithms for subgraph decision problems. Recently Bodlaender [Bod93] showed that this first step can be performed in $O(n)$ time. The algorithms then perform dynamic programming on the tree decomposition. This dynamic programming step can be modeled as a *tree automaton* [GS84] executing the tree decomposition in much the same way as a string is executed by a conventional finite-state automaton. It is known that this type of $O(n)$ algorithm exists for any subgraph property whose solutions exhibit some sort of regularity [BLW87] or locality [MP87] in their structure. It is also known that such an algorithm exists for those properties that can be encoded in one of several variations of the *monadic second-order logic* [ALS91, BPT92, Cou90]. Courcelle has shown that encodability of a property in the *counting* monadic second-order logic (CMS) is necessary and sufficient for such an algorithm to exist for partial 1-trees [Cou90] and partial 2-trees [Cou91]. It remains an open problem to find a complete characterization of these properties over partial k-trees.

Recently, Kaller *et al.* [KGS95] raised the following question: If a graph property can be encoded in CMS over the class of partial k-trees, then can its *complement property* also be encoded in CMS over that class of graphs? Equivalently, this question can be phrased in terms of determining which properties can be decided by tree automata over the class of partial k-tree complements. In this paper, we identify a subset of the CMS language, the *complement CMS* (CCMS), in which if a graph property can be encoded over the class of partial k-tree complements, then it can be decided by a tree automaton in $O(n)$ time over that class of graphs. Some problems (such as clique and independent set) can be easily encoded in CCMS over the class of all graphs. For other problems, however, it appears necessary to exploit the structure of the graph in order to obtain an encoding: for example, partition into constant-sized cliques [KGS95], as well as the

the f-factor problems (studied in this paper), have different CCMS encodings (dependent on the value of k) for each class of partial k-tree complements.

The rest of this paper is organized as follows: In Section 2 we review partial k-trees and CMS logic. In Section 3 we introduce the CCMS logic. In Section 4 we derive a CCMS formula to encode the property that the complement G of a partial k-tree contains a (not necessarily connected) f-factor. In Section 5 we derive a CCMS encoding of the property that G contains a Hamiltonian circuit. In Section 6 we show that CCMS can encode the property that G contains a connected f-factor, for constant $f \geq 3$.

2 Preliminaries

The graphs in this paper are finite, simple and undirected. If G is a graph, then $V(G)$ denotes its vertex set, $E(G)$ denotes its edge set, and $\overline{G}$ denotes its complement graph. For $u, v \in V(G)$, we write $u \sim_G v$ to indicate that u and v are adjacent, and $\delta_G(v)$ to denote the degree of v; when the underlying graph is clear from the context, we may drop the subscripts and simply write $u \sim v$ or $\delta(v)$. The expression $G' \sqsubseteq G$ is used to indicate that G' is a subgraph of G.

A *factor* of G is a subgraph of G that has vertex set $V(G)$. An *f-regular* graph is one in which every vertex has degree f, and an *f-factor* of G is a factor of G that is f-regular. A *bridge* of G is any edge whose removal increases the number of maximal connected components in G.

2.1 Partial k-Trees ($\mathcal{P}k\mathcal{T}$) and Their Complements ($\mathcal{C}\mathcal{P}k\mathcal{T}$)

A *k-tree* is either the clique on k vertices, or a graph that can be obtained (recursively) from a k-tree G by adding a new vertex v and edges between v and k distinct vertices that induce a clique in G. A *partial k-tree* is a subgraph of a k-tree. We denote the class of partial k-trees by $\mathcal{P}k\mathcal{T}$, and their complements by $\mathcal{C}\mathcal{P}k\mathcal{T}$. For example, $\mathcal{P}0\mathcal{T}$ is the class of edge-free graphs and $\mathcal{P}1\mathcal{T}$ is the class of forests. Series-parallel graphs and outerplanar graphs are subclasses of $\mathcal{P}2\mathcal{T}$.

The following proposition can be found in [KGS95].

Proposition 2. *For each graph G in $\mathcal{C}\mathcal{P}k\mathcal{T}$, there exists a partition $\mathcal{C}(G) = \{C_1, C_2, \ldots C_{k+1}\}$ of its vertex set, for which each C_i induces a clique in G and (more generally) for which the union of any $\ell + 1$ of these vertex sets induces the complement of a partial ℓ-tree. We will refer to such a partition $\mathcal{C}(G)$ as a standard partition of $V(G)$.*

Corollary 3. *Suppose C and C' are cliques in a standard partition of the vertex set of $G \in \mathcal{C}\mathcal{P}k\mathcal{T}$. If v_1, v_2 are distinct vertices of C, and v'_1, v'_2 are distinct vertices of C', then there is an edge $\{v_i, v'_j\} \in E(G)$, for some $1 \leq i, j \leq 2$.*

Proof. Let H be the subgraph of G induced by $C \cup C'$. By Proposition 2, H is the complement of a partial 1-tree: that is $\overline{H}$ is a partial 1-tree (or forest). Suppose none of the edges $\{v_i, v'_j\}$ ($1 \leq i, j \leq 2$) exist in G; then the forest $\overline{H}$ contains all 4 of those edges—which is a cycle. □

2.2   Counting Monadic Second-Order (CMS) Logic

A graph $G = (V, E)$ can be viewed as a logical structure over a universe consisting of a set V of vertices and a set E of edges. G is described by the predicate $Edge(e, v)$, which holds whenever $v \in V$ is incident with $e \in E$. The CMS logic [Cou90] is a predicate calculus which can express properties of such structures. This logic contains individual variables, used to represent vertices or edges; and set variables, used to represent sets of vertices or edges. Expressions describing graph properties can be built in CMS by using the variables, the $Edge$ predicate, the equality ($=$) and membership ($\in$) symbols, existential ($\exists$) and universal ($\forall$) quantifiers, and the logical connectives: $\wedge$ ("and"), $\vee$ ("or"), $\neg$ ("not"), $\Rightarrow$ ("implies") and $\Leftrightarrow$ ("if and only if"). In addition, CMS expressions may contain predicates of the form $\mathbf{card}_{\ell,t}(S)$, for constants $\ell < t \in \mathsf{N}$: this evaluates to true whenever the set S has cardinality ℓ (mod t). Many graph properties can be expressed in a very natural way using this formalism. In this paper, we will give only high-level descriptions of logical statements that can be easily encoded in CMS; we refer to [ALS91, BPT92, Cou90] for a discussion of this.

Given a graph G and a CMS formula Φ, we write $G \models \Phi$ to indicate that Φ is true for G. A graph property Π (see Definition 1) is said to be a *CMS property* over a class $\mathcal{K}$ of graphs whenever there exists a CMS formula Φ such that for each G in $\mathcal{K}$: $G \models \Phi$ iff $\Pi(G) \neq \emptyset$. Such a formula Φ is called an *encoding* of Π. The existence of a CMS encoding is sufficient to obtain a linear-time algorithm, over the class of partial k-trees [Cou90]; moreover, such an algorithm can be generated automatically from an encoding.

3   Complement Problems and Complement-CMS

We are interested in using tree automata to obtain $O(n)$ algorithms for decision problems on $\mathcal{CP}k\mathcal{T}$ graphs (with n vertices). We will use Courcelle's result [Cou90] to automatically obtain such an algorithm over $\mathcal{CP}k\mathcal{T}$ from a logical encoding of the problem. In fact, we will actually be solving a problem on $\mathcal{P}k\mathcal{T}$ — called the *complement property*.

Definition 4. Suppose Π is a graph property. The complement-property of Π (denoted $\overline{\Pi}$) consists of those pairs $(\overline{G}, S)$ for which $(G, S) \in \Pi$.

This definition allows us to use $\Pi(G)$ and $\overline{\Pi}(\overline{G})$ interchangeably. The following theorem gives a sufficient condition for a property to be linear-time decidable by a tree automaton over $\mathcal{CP}k\mathcal{T}$.

Definition 5. The *complement-CMS* (CCMS) language for graphs is identical to the CMS language except that

- CCMS does not allow variables to represent edges or sets of edges, and
- CCMS allows the adjacency symbol ($\sim$) to be used in subexpressions of the form $u \sim v$: this indicates that vertices u and v are adjacent.

Theorem 6. *Suppose Π is a graph property. If there exists a CCMS formula that encodes Π over the class $\mathcal{CP}k\mathcal{T}$, then there is an $O(n)$ decision algorithm for Π over $\mathcal{CP}k\mathcal{T}$.*

Proof. Let Φ' be the formula obtained from the CCMS formula Φ by replacing each occurrence of "$(u \sim v)$" with "$\neg(u \sim v)$". It is clear that $G \models \Phi$ iff $\overline{G} \models \Phi'$. Hence, for a graph G in $\mathcal{CP}k\mathcal{T}$: $\Pi(G) \neq \emptyset$ iff $G \models \Phi$ iff $\overline{G} \models \Phi'$.

The adjacency statement $u \sim v$ can be treated as a CMS macro:

$$u \sim v \equiv \neg(u = v) \wedge (\exists e)(Edge(e, u) \wedge Edge(e, v)) \tag{1}$$

Hence Φ' is a CMS formula and, by Courcelle's result [Cou90], there is a tree automaton to decide whether $\overline{G} \models \Phi'$ for $\overline{G} \in \mathcal{P}k\mathcal{T}$. By equivalence, this tree automaton decides Π on G. We need only assume that G is specified by representing the $O(n)$ edges of $\overline{G}$, rather that explicitly representing the $\Theta(n^2)$ edges of G. □

4 f-Factors

In this section, we derive a CCMS formula to encode the property that a graph of $\mathcal{CP}k\mathcal{T}$ contains an f-factor (for any fixed f); it then follows from Theorem 6 that this property can be decided in $O(n)$ time for any $\mathcal{CP}k\mathcal{T}$ graph on n vertices. CCMS does not allow us to explicitly represent all edges of an f-factor. However, we will show that an arbitrary f-factor can be transformed, by a series of *edge flips*, into a standardized f-factor in which most of the edges are contained within the cliques of a standard partition (see Proposition 2): these edges need not be explicitly enumerated by a CCMS formula since their existence is guaranteed whenever such a clique is big enough and certain parity conditions are satisfied.

Throughout this section, we let G be a given graph of $\mathcal{CP}k\mathcal{T}$, and let $\mathcal{C}(G)$ be a standard partition of its vertex set—this partition is not uniquely determined, but we shall use $\mathcal{C}(G)$ to refer to a fixed (arbitrarily-chosen) representative. The $k + 1$ cliques of $\mathcal{C}(G)$ are independent sets in the partial k-tree $\overline{G}$: as such, we refer to each of these sets as a *color class*.

Definition 7. An edge of G is called *monochromatic* if its endpoints are in the same color class of $\mathcal{C}(G)$; otherwise it is called *dichromatic*.

Definition 8. Two dichromatic edges are *parallel*, in a subgraph $H \sqsubseteq G$, if

- they pass between two fixed (and distinct) color classes
- all four of the endpoints are distinct
- there are no monochromatic edges induced in H by the four endpoints

A set of dichromatic edges is called parallel if its members are pairwise parallel.

Figure 1 illustrates dichromatic parallel edges e_1 and e_2 in a subgraph $H \sqsubseteq G$. Throughout this paper, solid lines are used in figures to represent edges and dashed lines are used to indicate that two vertices are not adjacent.

We easily obtain the following proposition.

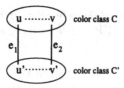

Fig. 1. Parallel edges

Proposition 9. *Suppose F is an f-factor of G, containing two parallel dichromatic edges e_1 and e_2. The graph obtained by the following sequence of operations is an f-factor of G.*

1. *add, to F, the two monochromatic edges between the endpoints of e_1 and e_2.*
2. *delete, from the resulting graph, the edges e_1 and e_2*

We will refer to this sequence of operations as a parallel flip *of e_1 and e_2.*

We wish to transform an arbitrary f-factor of G into an f-factor for which the number of dichromatic edges is bounded by a constant: to do this, we use Lemma 10 to identify $p = 2$ parallel dichromatic edges which can be flipped. Lemma 10 gives a more general result (allowing us to identify any constant number p of parallel edges) which will be useful in Section 6.

Lemma 10. *Let f, p be positive integers, and suppose F is an f-factor of G. If F has at least $2pf^2$ dichromatic edges between two fixed color classes, then p of these edges are pairwise parallel.*

Proof. The lemma is trivially true when $p = 1$. We inductively assume it is true for some p, and suppose there are $2(p + 1)f^2$ dichromatic edges between color classes C and C'. Let e be one of the these edges; now another edge e' ($e' \neq e$) can fail to be parallel to e only if both e' and e share an endpoint, or if they have adjacent like-colored endpoints. Since every vertex has degree f, there can be at most $2(f - 1)^2$ such edges. Therefore, there are at least $2(p + 1)f^2 - 2(f - 1)^2 - 1 > 2pf^2$ edges (excluding e) between C and C' that are parallel to e. Among these edges (inductively) there exist p pairwise parallel edges. $\qquad\square$

Lemma 11. *For fixed $f \in \mathbb{N}$, there exists a constant f' (depending only on f and k) such that: If G contains an f-factor then G contains an f-factor with fewer than f' dichromatic edges.*

Proof. Suppose there are $4f^2$ (or more) dichromatic edges between two fixed color classes; by Lemma 10, two of these edges are parallel. By Proposition 9, we can flip parallel edges until fewer than $4f^2$ dichromatic edges remain between any pair of color classes. Since there are $\binom{k+1}{2}$ distinct pairs of color classes, the resulting f-factor has fewer than $4f^2 \binom{k+1}{2}$ dichromatic edges. $\qquad\square$

We have now established that an f-factor with a bounded number of dichromatic edges necessarily exists if any f-factor exists in a graph of $\mathcal{CP}k\mathcal{T}$. In order to prove the sufficiency of representing only the dichromatic edges (and possibly also a constant number of monochromatic edges) we will need the following lemma—which is a consequence of Tutte's f-Factor Theorem [Tut52]. We give here a constructive proof, which will be helpful in Section 6.

Lemma 12. *Suppose H is a factor of G containing only a constant number of edges, and let f bound the maximum vertex-degree of H. There exists a constant f'' (depending only on f) such that if $C \in \mathcal{C}(G)$ is a color class with f'' (or more) vertices, and*

$$\sum_{v \in C}(f - \delta_H(v)) \quad \text{is even} \tag{2}$$

then it is possible to add monochromatic edges to H so that every vertex of C has degree f.

Proof. Suppose C is a color class that satisfies the parity condition (2). Since C induces a clique in G, we are free to choose any pair of vertices in C as the endpoints of a monochromatic edge in a factor. The following procedure adds monochromatic edges iteratively until all vertices are incident with f vertices. Provided C is large enough, the procedure is correct—this will be shown afterwards. A vertex will be called *light* as long as its degree is less than f.

1 If two light vertices are nonadjacent, then add an edge between them.
2 If there is only one light vertex $v \in C$, then select a monochromatic edge between two non-light vertices $u, u' \in C$, such that $u \not\sim v$ and $u' \not\sim v$. Now, delete the edge $\{u, u'\}$ from H, and add two new edges $\{v, u\}$ and $\{v, u'\}$.
3 Otherwise, there are two adjacent light vertices $v, v' \in C$. Select a monochromatic edge between two non-light vertices $u, u' \in C$, such that $u \not\sim v$ and $u' \not\sim v'$. Now, delete the edge $\{u, u'\}$ from H, and add two new edges $\{u, v\}$ and $\{u', v'\}$.

It is easy to verify that no vertex is made to exceed degree f, and the number edges in the factor is incremented at each step. We will now show that, in step **2**, there exists an edge $\{u, u'\}$, as specified. A similar argument guarantees the existence of the edge needed in step **3**.

In step **2**, the parity constraint (2) ensures that v (the only light vertex) has degree at most $f - 2$. Let $X \subseteq C - \{v\}$ be the set of those (non-light) vertices that are not adjacent to v. There are only a constant number of edges between X and $C - X$ (because $C - X$ contains at most $f - 1$ vertices) and, by assumption, there are only a constant number of dichromatic edges incident to vertices of $X \subset C$. Therefore, we need only choose the constant f'' large enough so that whenever $|C| \geq f''$, an edge of the factor was added, in a previous iteration of the procedure, between two vertices $u, u' \in X$. □

In Figure 2, we present a CCMS formula to encode the property that a graph $G \in \mathcal{CP}k\mathcal{T}$ contains an f-factor. Lemma 11 allows us to assume, without loss of

$$\exists\, C_j \subseteq V(G) \qquad\qquad 1 \le j \le k+1$$
$$\exists\, v_i, v_i' \in V(G) \qquad\qquad 1 \le i \le f_k$$
$$\exists\, E_j^1, E_j^2, \ldots, E_j^f \subseteq V(G)\; 1 \le j \le k+1$$

1. $\{C_1, C_2, \ldots, C_{k+1}\}$ is a partition of $V(G)$ into cliques
2. $v_i \sim v_i'$ (for $1 \le i \le f_k$)
3. if $|C_j| < f''$ (for $1 \le j \le k+1$) then
   (a) $\forall x \in C_j$: x is used exactly f times as an explicitly enumerated endpoint v_i, v_i'
4. otherwise (if $|C_j| \ge f''$)
   (a) $\forall x \in C_j$: x is used at most f times as an explicitly enumerated endpoint v_i, v_i'
   (b) $E_j^1, E_j^2, \ldots E_j^f \subseteq C_j$ and each $x \in C_j$ appears in exactly one of these sets for each appearance of x as an explicitly enumerated endpoint
   (c) $f|C| - |E_j^1| - |E_j^2| - \ldots - |E_j^f|$ is even

Fig. 2. CCMS formulation for f-factor in the complement G of a partial k-tree (constants f_k and f'' are dependent only on f and k)

generality, that there are only a constant number of dichromatic edges in this f-factor. We explicitly enumerate the endpoints v_i, v_i' of all dichromatic edges, and all monochromatic edges that are in "small" color classes (*i.e.* those whose size is bounded by the constant f'' of Lemma 12); we have used f_k to denote a constant bounding the number of these explicitly enumerated edges.

The sets $E_j^1, E_j^2, \ldots, E_j^f$ are used to count the number of explicitly enumerated edges that are incident to each vertex of C_j. For each "large" color class C_j, the modulo-counting feature of CMS can be used (item (4c) of Figure 2) to enforce the parity condition (2). Lemma 12 then assures the existence of a set of monochromatic edges within C_j to complete the f-factor.

Using Theorem 6, we can now conclude

Theorem 13. *There is an $O(n)$ algorithm to decide whether a graph of $CPkT$ contains an f-factor.*

5 Hamiltonian Circuits

In this section, we derive a CCMS formula encoding the property that a graph of $CPkT$ contains a connected 2-factor—also known as a *Hamiltonian circuit*. This provides an $O(n)$ algorithm for the Hamiltonian circuit problem over the class $CPkT$. As in Section 4, we let G denote a given graph of $CPkT$, and fix $C(G)$ as some standard partition of its vertex set. We will show that it is possible to flip pairs of parallel edges in any Hamiltonian circuit $H \sqsubseteq G$ in such a way that H does not become disconnected.

Definition 14. Suppose $H \sqsubseteq G$ contains two parallel edges e_1, e_2 between color classes $C, C' \in C(G)$. We say that e_1 and e_2 have an *N-configuration* in H, if H contains a path between the C-colored endpoint of one and the C'-colored endpoint of the other, such that this path passes through neither e_1 nor e_2.

For example, the edges e_1 and e_2 of Figure 1 would have an N-configuration if, after deleting e_1 and e_2 from the graph, u and v' (or u' and v) were in the same connected component.

Lemma 15. *If a Hamiltonian circuit of G has three dichromatic edges between two fixed color classes, then some pair of them can be flipped to give a (still connected) Hamiltonian circuit.*

Proof. It is readily verified that, if three dichromatic edges pass between two fixed color classes, then two of those edges have an N-configuration. Furthermore, a 2-factor cannot become disconnected as a result of making a parallel flip of edges in an N-configuration. □

Since there are only $\binom{k+1}{2}$ different pairs of color classes, we obtain

Lemma 16. *If G contains a Hamiltonian circuit, then G contains a Hamiltonian circuit with at most $2\binom{k+1}{2}$ dichromatic edges.*

Theorem 17. *There exists a CCMS formula encoding the Hamiltonian circuit problem over the class $\mathcal{CP}kT$.*

Proof. A CCMS formula can state that, for some $\ell \leq 6\binom{k+1}{2}$, there exist nonempty vertex subsets $X_1, X_2, \ldots X_\ell$ for which

(C1) the X_i partition the vertices of G, and
(C2) $X_i \cup X_{i+1}$ $(1 \leq i \leq \ell - 1)$ and $X_1 \cup X_\ell$ each induce a clique in G

When these conditions are satisfied, a Hamiltonian circuit of G can be constructed by first visiting all of the vertices of X_1 (in any order), then all of the vertices of X_2, and so on.

Conversely, suppose H is a Hamiltonian circuit of G. Lemma 16 allows us to assume, without loss of generality, that H has no more than $2\binom{k+1}{2}$ dichromatic edges. Let the circular sequence of vertices in H be $[v_1, v_2, \ldots v_n]$. These vertices can be packed into $\ell \leq 6\binom{k+1}{2}$ nonempty vertex sets $X_1, X_2, \ldots, X_\ell$ to satisfy conditions **C1** and **C2**. We treat $[X_1, X_2, \ldots, X_\ell]$ as a circular sequence, and pack every pair of consecutive vertices v_i, v_{i+1} either into the same set or into consecutive sets, such that each dichromatic edge has both endpoints in singleton sets. Since the union of any two consecutive sets is either a monochromatic set or a dichromatic edge, it follows that each such union is a clique, as required. □

6 Connected f-Factors

We now generalize the result of the previous section, to show that a CCMS formula can encode the property that a graph of $\mathcal{CP}kT$ contains a connected f-factor (for any fixed $f \geq 3$). By a series of edge flips, we show that there is a connected f-factor iff there is one in which the number of dichromatic edges is bounded by a constant. Again, we let G be a graph of $\mathcal{CP}kT$, and fix $\mathcal{C}(G)$ as some standard partition of its vertex set.

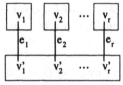

Fig. 3. Connected f-factor without N-configuration (Rectangles represent connected components resulting from removal of bridges $e_1, e_2, \ldots e_r$)

Definition 18. Suppose F is an f-factor of G. An edge in $E(G) - E(F)$ is said to be a *nonedge* of F. An *alternating circuit* (AC) of F is an even-length cycle of G that is composed by alternating edges of F with nonedges of F.

In order to transform the f-factor, we will repeatedly find an AC and *flip* its edges and nonedges. An AC of a connected f-factor will be called *useful*, if this flip operation results in a connected f-factor with fewer dichromatic edges. In Section 5 we saw an example of a useful AC consisting of two parallel edges in an N-configuration. In this section we also need other types of useful AC's.

Lemma 19. *Suppose F is a connected f-factor of G. If F contains a set of $\max\{4, \lceil \frac{k+1}{f-1} \rceil\}$ or more parallel edges between two fixed color classes of $\mathcal{C}(G)$, then there exists a useful AC in F.*

Proof. Suppose there are $r \geq \max\{4, \lceil \frac{k+1}{f-1} \rceil\}$ parallel edges between color classes C and C'. Let these edges be denoted $e_1, e_2, \ldots, e_r$, such that e_i has endpoints $v_i \in C$ and $v_i' \in C'$. If any two of these edges have an N-configuration, then their four endpoints give a useful AC.

Otherwise, it follows that each of the r edges is a bridge in F; furthermore, removing these r bridges from F would give a subgraph consisting of $r+1$ connected components (represented by rectangles in Figure 3) with either all of the C-colored endpoints, or all of the C'-colored endpoints, in the same component. Without loss of generality, we assume that the C'-colored endpoints $v_1', v_2', \ldots, v_r'$ are in the same component.

For $1 \leq i \leq r$, choose $T_i \sqsubseteq F$ as a maximal tree for which $v_i \in V(T_i)$, all vertices of T_i have color C, and T_i is a vertex-induced subgraph of F. We say that a vertex x is a *neighbor* of T_i, if x is not in T_i but there is an edge of F between x and some vertex of T_i. Clearly, each tree has at least $f-1$ neighbors, and no vertex is a neighbor of more than one tree. Therefore, there are at least $\lceil \frac{k+1}{f-1} \rceil (f-1) \geq k+1$ neighbors in total. We consider two cases:

Case 1. Some vertex v_0 of color C is a neighbor of one of the trees, say tree T_1. Let $v \in V(T_1)$ be a vertex adjacent to v_0. This is illustrated in Figure 4, where the connection labeled "*" indicates that there is a path in T_1, from v_1 to v, of length 0 or more (possibly $v = v_1$). Since T_1 is a maximal induced tree of color C, there must be a second vertex of T_1 that is adjacent to v_0. Hence, there is a path in T_1, from v_1 to v_0, of length 1 or more (this is indicated in Figure 4 by a connection labeled "+"). Therefore, the vertices $v_0, v, v_3, v_3', v_2', v_2$ induce a useful AC—the edges of which are labeled with triangles in Figure 4.

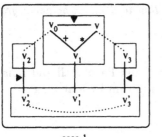 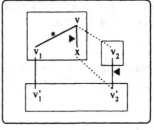

case 1   case 2

Fig. 4. Useful alternating circuits ("$*$" = 0 or more edges; "$+$" = 1 or more edges)

Case 2. None of the $k+1$ (or more) neighbors are of color C. By the pigeonhole principle, two of these neighbors x, y have the same color. Since there are at least 4 trees T_i, we can assume, without loss of generality, that x and y are neighbors of trees other than T_2 and T_3. By Corollary 3, there exists an edge of G between x (or y) and v_2' (or v_3'); without loss of generality assume this edge is $\{x, v_2'\}$ and that x is a neighbor of T_1. The vertices x, v, v_2, v_2' induce a useful AC (see Figure 4).   □

Combining Lemma 10 with Lemma 19, we see that whenever there are enough dichromatic edges in a connected f-factor, there exists a useful AC whose edges can be flipped to reduce the number of dichromatic edges:

Lemma 20. *For fixed $f \in \mathbb{N}$, there exists a constant f' such that: If G contains a connected f-factor then G contains a connected f-factor that has fewer than f' dichromatic edges.*

We encode the connected f-factor problem by augmenting the formulation in Figure 2 with an additional statement to express connectedness. The proof of correctness is very similar to the proof of Theorem 13. Connectedness can be enforced by a CCMS statement saying $\forall u, v \in V(G)$: "there is a path between u and v". A path can be represented by explicitly enumerating the sequence of vertices $[x_1, x_2, \ldots, x_\ell]$ where $u = x_1$, $v = x_\ell$ and (for $1 \leq i \leq \ell - 1$) either

- x_i and x_{i+1} are endpoints of an explicitly enumerated edge, or
- x_i and x_{i+1} belong to the same "large" color class, and neither is incident with f of the explicitly enumerated edges

In the latter case, we appeal to Lemma 12 to ensure that the represented f-factor ($f \geq 3$) has a monochromatic path connecting x_i and x_{i+1}. (The case of $f = 2$ has already been covered in Section 5.) Observe that connectedness is always preserved by the procedure given (in the proof of Lemma 12) to add monochromatic edges between those vertices of "large" color classes that are incident with fewer than f dichromatic edges. We just need to start with a connected graph among those vertices—which is easy to do when the color class is large enough and $f \geq 3$.

Using Theorem 6, we can now conclude

Theorem 21. *There is an $O(n)$ algorithm to decide whether a graph of $CP kT$ contains a connected f-factor.*

Acknowledgement. The authors wish to thank Pavol Hell and Luis Goddyn for pointers on solving the general f-factor problem by matching.

References

[ALS91] S. Arnborg, J. Lagergren, and D. Seese. Easy problems for tree decomposable graphs. *J. Algorithms*, 12:308–340, 1991.

[BLW87] M.W. Bern, E.L. Lawler, and A.L. Wong. Linear-time computation of optimal subgraphs of decomposable graphs. *J. Algorithms*, 8:216–235, 1987.

[Bod93] H.L. Bodlaender. A linear time algorithm for finding tree-decompositions of small treewidth. In *Proc. 25th STOC*, pages 226–234, 1993.

[Bol78] B. Bollobás. *Extremal Graph Theory*. Academic Press, London, 1978.

[BPT92] R.B. Borie, R.G. Parker, and C.A. Tovey. Automatic generation of linear-time algorithms from predicate calculus descriptions of problems on recursively constructed graph families. *Algorithmica*, 7:555–581, 1992.

[Cou90] B. Courcelle. The monadic second-order logic of graphs. I. Recognizable sets of finite graphs. *Information and Computation*, 85:12–75, 1990.

[Cou91] B. Courcelle. The monadic second-order logic of graphs. V. On closing the gap between definability and recognizability. *Theoret. Comput. Sci.*, 80:153–202, 1991.

[DHK93] E. Dahlhaus, P. Hajnal, and M. Karpinski. On the parallel complexity of Hamiltonian cycle and matching problem on dense graphs. *J. Algorithms*, 15:367–384, 1993.

[Dir52] G.A. Dirac. Some theorems on abstract graphs. *Proc. London Math. Soc. (Ser. 3)*, 2:69–81, 1952.

[GJ79] M.R. Garey and D.S. Johnson. *Computers and Intractability: A Guide to the Theory of NP-Completeness*. W.H. Freeman and Company, New York, 1979.

[GS84] F. Gécseg and M. Steinby. *Tree Automata*. Akadémiai Kiadó, Budapest, 1984.

[KGS95] D. Kaller, A. Gupta, and T. Shermer. The χ_t-coloring problem. In *Proc. 12th STACS*, pages 409–420, 1995.

[MP87] S. Mahajan and J.G. Peters. Algorithms for regular properties in recursive graphs. In *Proc. 25th Ann. Allerton Conf. Communication, Control, Comput.*, pages 14–23, 1987.

[Pet91] J. Petersen. Die Theorie der regularen Graphen. *Acta Math.*, 15:193–220, 1891.

[RS86] N. Robertson and P.D. Seymour. Graph minors. II. Algorithmic aspects of tree-width. *J. Algorithms*, 7:309–322, 1986.

[Tut52] W.T. Tutte. The factors of graphs. *Can. J. Math.*, 4:314–328, 1952.

Obstructions to Within a Few Vertices or Edges of Acyclic

Kevin Cattell[1]   Michael J. Dinneen[1,2]   Michael R. Fellows[1]

[1] Department of Computer Science, University of Victoria,
P.O. Box 3055, Victoria, B.C. Canada V8W 3P6
[2] Computer Research and Applications, Los Alamos National Laboratory,
M.S. B265, Los Alamos, New Mexico 87545 U.S.A.

Abstract. Finite obstruction sets for lower ideals in the minor order are guaranteed to exist by the Graph Minor Theorem. It has been known for several years that, in principle, obstruction sets can be mechanically computed for most natural lower ideals. In this paper, we describe a general-purpose method for finding obstructions by using a bounded treewidth (or pathwidth) search. We illustrate this approach by characterizing certain families of cycle-cover graphs based on the two well-known problems: k-FEEDBACK VERTEX SET and k-FEEDBACK EDGE SET. Our search is based on a number of algorithmic strategies by which large constants can be mitigated, including a randomized strategy for obtaining proofs of minimality.

1 Introduction

One of the most famous results in graph theory is the characterization of planar graphs due to Kuratowski: a graph is planar if and only if it does not contain either of $K_{3,3}$ or K_5 as a minor. The *obstruction set* for planarity thus consists of these two graphs.

The deep results of Robertson and Seymour [8] on the well-quasi-ordering of graphs under the minor (and other) orders, have consequence of establishing non-constructively that many natural graph properties have "Kuratowski-type" characterizations, that is, they can be characterized by finite obstruction sets in an appropriate partial order. Finite forbidden substructure characterizations of graph properties have been an important part of research in graph theory since the beginning, and there are many theorems of this kind.

We describe in this paper a theory of obstruction set computation, which we believe has the potential to automate much of the theorem-proving for this kind of mathematics. This approach has successfully been used to find the obstructions for the graph families k-VERTEX COVER, $k = 1, \ldots, 5$ (see [1]). The pinnacle of this effort would be a computation of the obstruction set for embedding of graphs on the torus.

The underlying theory for our obstruction set computations was first proved in [3], using the Graph Minor Theorem (GMT) to prove termination of the finite-state search procedure. The results in [6] can be used to prove termination without the GMT. The application of these results for the computation of any particular obstruction set requires additional problem-specific results. These results are nontrivial, but seem to be generally available (in one form or another) for virtually every natural lower ideal. Thus, this is (in principle) one route for establishing constructive versions of virtually all of the known complexity applications of the Robertson-Seymour results.

One of the curiosities of forbidden substructure theorems is the tendency of the number of obstructions for natural parameterized families of lower ideals to grow explosively as a function of the parameter k. For example, the number of minor-order obstructions for k-PATHWIDTH is 2 for $k = 1$, 110 for $k = 2$, and provably more than 60 million for $k = 3$ [5]. We favor the following as a working hypothesis: Natural forbidden substructure theorems of feasible size are feasibly computable.

The remaining sections of this paper are organized as follows. First, we formally define minor-order obstructions and the cycle-cover graph families that we characterize. Next, we present a family-independent method for finding obstruction sets. In the last two sections we present family-specific results along with obstruction sets for k-FEEDBACK VERTEX SET and k-FEEDBACK EDGE SET.

2 Preliminaries

Let $\leq_m$ be the *minor order* on graphs, that is, for two graphs G and H, $H \leq_m G$ if and only if a graph isomorphic to H can be obtained from G by a sequence of operations chosen from: (1) taking a subgraph, and (2) contracting an edge. A family of graphs $\mathcal{F}$ is a *lower ideal* with respect to $\leq_m$ if for all graphs G and H, the conditions (1) $H \leq_m G$ and (2) $G \in \mathcal{F}$ imply $H \in \mathcal{F}$. The *obstruction set* $\mathcal{O}_{\mathcal{F}}$ for $\mathcal{F}$ with respect to $\leq_m$ is the set of minimal elements of the complement of $\mathcal{F}$. This characterizes $\mathcal{F}$ in the sense that $G \in \mathcal{F}$ if and only if it is not the case that for some $H \in \mathcal{O}_{\mathcal{F}}$, $H \leq_m G$. The GMT states that $\leq_m$ is a well-partial order and hence $\mathcal{O}_{\mathcal{F}}$ is finite for all minor-order lower ideals $\mathcal{F}$.

The characterization of graph families based on the following two well-known problems (see [4]) is the focus of this paper.

Problem 1 FEEDBACK VERTEX SET (FVS)
Input: Graph $G = (V, E)$ and a positive integer $k \leq |V|$.
Question: Is there a subset $V' \subseteq V$ with $|V'| \leq k$ such that V' contains at least one vertex from every cycle in G?

A set V' in the above problem is called a *feedback vertex set* (witness set) for the graph G. The family of graphs that have a feedback vertex set of size at most k will be denoted by k-FVS. It is easy to verify that for each fixed k the set of graphs in k-FVS is a minor-order lower ideal. For a given graph G, let $FVS(G)$ denote the least k such that G has a feedback vertex set of cardinality k.

Problem 2 FEEDBACK EDGE SET (FES)
Input: Graph $G = (V, E)$ and a positive integer $k \leq |E|$.
Question: Is there a subset $E' \subseteq E$ with $|E'| \leq k$ such that $G \setminus E'$ is acyclic?

Since the this problem closely resembles the classic FEEDBACK VERTEX SET problem, this is called the FEEDBACK EDGE SET problem. The edge set E' is a *feedback edge set*. For a given graph G, let $FES(G)$ denote the least k such that G has a feedback edge set of cardinality k, and k-FES $= \{G \mid FES(G) \leq k\}$.

We conclude this section by formally defining the concept of graphs of bounded (combinatorial) width.

Definition 3 *A* tree decomposition *of a graph $G = (V, E)$ is a tree T together with a collection of subsets T_x of V indexed by the vertices x of T that satisfies:*
1. For every edge (u, v) of G there is some x such that $u \in T_x$ and $v \in T_x$.

2. *If y is a vertex on the unique path in T from x to z then $T_x \cap T_z \subseteq T_y$.*
The width *of a tree decomposition is the maximum over the vertices x of the tree T of the decomposition of $|T_x| - 1$. A graph G has* treewidth *at most k if there is a tree decomposition of G of width at most k.* Path decompositions *and* pathwidth *are defined by restricting the tree T to be simply a path.*

3 How To Find Obstructions Efficiently

We search for obstructions within the set of graphs of *bounded pathwidth* (and adaptable to *bounded treewidth*). We now describe an algebraic representation for these bounded-width graphs.

Definition 4 *A t-boundaried graph $G = (V, E, \partial, f)$ is an ordinary graph $G = (V, E)$ together with (1) a distinguished subset of the vertex set $\partial \subseteq V$ of cardinality t, the* boundary *of G, and (2) a bijection $f : \partial \to \{1, 2, \ldots, t\}$.*

The graphs of pathwidth at most t are generated exactly by strings of (unary) operators from the following *operator set* $\Sigma_t = V_t \cup E_t$:

$$V_t = \{⓪, \ldots ⓣ\} \quad \text{and} \quad E_t = \{\boxed{i\ j} : 0 \le i < j \le t\}.$$

To generate the graphs of treewidth at most t, an additional (binary) operator $\oplus$, called *circle plus*, is added to Σ_t. The semantics of these operators on $(t+1)$-boundaried graphs G and H are as follows:

$G ⓘ$ Add an isolated vertex to the graph G, and label it as the new boundary vertex i.

$G \boxed{i\ j}$ Add an edge between boundary vertices i and j of G (ignore if operation causes a multi-edge).

$G \oplus H$ Take the disjoint union of G and H except that equal-labeled boundary vertices of G and H are identified.

A graph described by a string (tree, if $\oplus$ is used) of these operators is called a *t-parse*, and has an implicit labeled boundary ∂ of $t + 1$ vertices. Throughout this paper, we refer to a t-parse and the graph it represents interchangeably. By convention, a t-parse always begins with the string $[⓪,①, \ldots ⓣ]$ which represents the edgeless graph of order $t + 1$.

For ease of discussion throughout the remaining part of this paper, we limit ourselves to bounded pathwidth in the obstruction set search theory and only point out places where any difficulty may occur with a bounded treewidth search.

Example 5 *A 2-parse and the graph it represents (the shaded vertices denote the final boundary).*

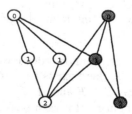

$[⓪,①,②, \boxed{0\ 1}, \boxed{1\ 2}, ①, \boxed{0\ 1}, \boxed{1\ 2}, ①, \boxed{0\ 1}, \boxed{1\ 2}, ⓪, \boxed{0\ 1}, \boxed{0\ 2}, ②, \boxed{0\ 2}, \boxed{1\ 2}]$

Definition 6 *Let* $G = (g_1, g_2, \ldots, g_n)$ *be a t-parse and* $Z = (z_1, z_2, \ldots, z_m)$ *be any sequence of operators over* Σ_t. *The* concatenation *(·) of* G *and* Z *is defined as*

$$G \cdot Z = (g_1, g_2, \ldots, g_n, z_1, z_2, \ldots, z_m).$$

The t-parse $G \cdot Z$ *is called an* extended t-parse, *and* $Z \in \Sigma_t^*$ *is called an* extension. *(For the treewidth case,* G *and* Z *are viewed as two connected subtree factors of a parse tree* $G \cdot Z$ *instead of two parts of a sequence of operators.)*

The following sequence of definitions and results forms our theoretical basis for computing minor-order obstruction sets.

Definition 7 *Let* G *be a t-parse. A t-parse* H *is a* ∂-minor *of* G, *denoted* $H \leq_{\partial m} G$, *if* H *is a combinatorial minor of* G *such that no boundary vertices of* G *are deleted by the minor operations, and the boundary vertices of* H *are the same as the boundary vertices of* G.

Definition 8 *Let* G *be a t-parse.* H *is a* one-step ∂-minor *of* G *if* H *is obtained from* G *by a single minor operation (one isolated vertex deletion, one edge deletion, or one edge contraction).*

Both k-PATHWIDTH, the family of graphs of pathwidth at most k, and k-TREEWIDTH are lower-ideals in the minor order so a ∂-minor H of a t-parse G can be represented as a t-parse. Our minor-order algorithms actually operate on the t-parses directly, bypassing any unnecessary conversion to and from the standard graph representations.

Definition 9 *Let* $\mathcal{F}$ *be a fixed graph family and let* G *and* H *be t-parses. We say* G *and* H *are* $\mathcal{F}$-congruent *(written* $G \sim_{\mathcal{F}} H$*) if for all extensions* $Z \in \Sigma_t^*$,

$$G \cdot Z \in \mathcal{F} \iff H \cdot Z \in \mathcal{F}.$$

If G *is not congruent to* H, *denoted by* $G \not\sim_{\mathcal{F}} H$, *then we say* G *is* distinguished *from* H *(by* Z*), and* Z *is a* distinguisher *for* G *and* H. *Otherwise,* G *and* H agree *on* Z.

Definition 10 *A set* $T \subseteq \Sigma_t^*$ *is a* testset *if* $G \not\sim_{\mathcal{F}} H$ *implies there exists* $Z \in T$ *that distinguishes* G *and* H.

In the more familiar and general setting of t-boundaried graphs (using an analogue of the Myhill-Nerode Theorem [3]), a test set T may be considered to be a subset of t-boundaried graphs where concatenation (·) is replaced solely by circle plus $\oplus$. As we will see later, a testset is only useful for finding obstruction sets if it has finite cardinality.

Definition 11 *A t-parse* G *is* nonminimal *if* G *has a* ∂-minor H *such that* $G \sim_{\mathcal{F}} H$. *Otherwise, we say* G *is* minimal. *A t-parse* G *is a* ∂-obstruction *if* G *is minimal and* $G \notin \mathcal{F}$.

In general, if a family $\mathcal{F}$ is a minor-order lower ideal and G is $\mathcal{F}$-minimal, then for each ∂-minor H of G, there exists an extension Z such that

$$G \cdot Z \notin \mathcal{F} \text{ and } H \cdot Z \in \mathcal{F}.$$

That is, there exists a distinguisher for each possible minor H of G.

The obstruction set $\mathcal{O}_{\mathcal{F}}$ for a family $\mathcal{F}$ is obtainable from the boundary obstruction set $\mathcal{O}_{\mathcal{F}}^{\partial}$ (set of ∂-obstructions) by contracting (possibly zero) edges on the boundaries of $\mathcal{O}_{\mathcal{F}}^{\partial}$, whenever the search space of width $\partial - 1$ is large enough. In our search for $\mathcal{O}_{\mathcal{F}}^{\partial}$, we must prove that each t-parse generated is minimal or nonminimal. The following two results drastically reduce the computation time required to determine these proofs.

Lemma 12 *A t-parse G is minimal if and only if G is distinguished from each one-step ∂-minor of G. Or equivalently, G is nonminimal if and only if G is $\mathcal{F}$-congruent to a one-step ∂-minor.*

Proof. We proof the second statement. Let G be nonminimal and suppose there exists two minors K and H of G such that $K \leq_{\partial m} H$ and $K \sim_{\mathcal{F}} G$. It is sufficient to show $H \sim_{\mathcal{F}} G$.

For all extensions $Z \in \Sigma_t^*$, if $G \cdot Z \in \mathcal{F}$ then $H \cdot Z \in \mathcal{F}$ since $H \cdot Z \leq_{\partial m} G \cdot Z$ and $\mathcal{F}$ is a ∂-minor lower ideal. Now let Z be any extension such that $G \cdot Z \notin \mathcal{F}$. Since $K \sim_{\mathcal{F}} G$, we have $K \cdot Z \notin \mathcal{F}$. And since $K \cdot Z \leq_{\partial m} H \cdot Z$, we also have $H \cdot Z \notin \mathcal{F}$. Therefore, G is $\mathcal{F}$-congruent to H. □

Lemma 13 (Prefix Lemma) *If $G_n = [g_1, g_2, \ldots, g_n]$ is a minimal t-parse then any prefix t-parse G_m, $m < n$, is also minimal.*

Proof. Assume G_n is nonminimal. It suffices to show that any extension of G_n is nonminimal. Without loss of generality, let H be a one-step ∂-minor of G_n such that for all $Z \in \Sigma_t^*$,

$$G_n \cdot Z \in \mathcal{F} \iff H \cdot Z \in \mathcal{F}.$$

Let $g_{n+1} \in \Sigma_t$ and $G_{n+1} = G_n \cdot g_{n+1}$. Now $H' = H \cdot g_{n+1}$ is a one-step ∂-minor of G_{n+1} such that for all $Z \in \Sigma_t^*$,

$$G_{n+1} \cdot Z = G_n \cdot (g_{n+1} \cdot Z) \in \mathcal{F} \iff H' = H \cdot (g_{n+1} \cdot Z) \in \mathcal{F}.$$

Thus, any extension of G_n is nonminimal. □

The above two lemmata also hold when the circle plus operator $\oplus$ is included in Σ_t. For illustration consider the Prefix Lemma: If G is a nonminimal t-parse with a $\mathcal{F}$-congruent minor G', and Z is any t-parse, then $(G \oplus Z)'$ is a $\mathcal{F}$-congruent minor of a nonminimal $G \oplus Z$, where we use the prime symbol to denote the corresponding minor operation done to the G part of $G \oplus Z$. (The awkward notation is needed since $G' \oplus Z$ may equal $G \oplus Z$ when common boundary edges exist in both G and Z.)

The Prefix Lemma implies that every minimal t-parse is obtainable by extending some minimal t-parse, providing a finite tree structure for the search space. In other words, the search tree may be pruned whenever a nonminimal t-parse is found. Since most $(t + 1)$-boundaried graphs have many t-parse representations, we can further reduce the size of the search tree by enforcing a canonical structure on the t-parses considered. To do this we have to ensure that every prefix of every canonic ∂-obstruction (a minimal leaf of the search tree) is also canonic.

We currently use the four techniques given in Figure 1 to prove that a t-parse in the search tree is minimal or nonminimal. They are listed in the order that they are attempted; if one succeeds, the remainder do not need to be performed. The first three of these may not succeed, though the fourth method always will. However, if we are fortunate to have a *minimal* finite-state congruence in step 2 of Figure 1 (i.e., not a refinement of the minimum automaton for $\sim_{\mathcal{F}}$) then we can stop at that step since distinct final states imply the existence of an extension to distinguish the two states (and their t-parse representatives) of the automaton. An example of such an finite-state algorithm was used in our k-VERTEX COVER characterizations [1].

1. *Direct nonminimal test.* These are easily observable properties of t-parses that imply t-parses nonminimal. For any k-FVS family, the existence of a degree one vertex is an example of such a property.
2. *Finite-state congruence algorithm.* Such an algorithm is a refinement of the minimal finite-state (linear/tree) automaton for $\sim_{\mathcal{F}}$. This means that if a t-parse G and a one-step ∂-minor G' of G have the same final state, then $G \sim_{\mathcal{F}} G'$, and G is nonminimal. If G and G' have distinct final states, no conclusion can be reached.
3. *Random minor-distinguisher search.* The proof that a t-parse G is minimal can consist of a distinguisher for each one-step ∂-minor G' of G. Such distinguishers can often be easily obtained by randomly generating a sequence of operators Z such that $G \cdot Z \notin F$, and then checking if $G' \cdot Z \in F$.
4. *Full test set proof.* We use a complete test set (see Definition 10) to determine if a t-parse G is distinguished from each of its one-step ∂-minors. A t-parse G is nonminimal if and only if it has a one-step ∂-minor G' such that G and G' agree on every test.

Fig. 1. Determining if a t-parse is minimal or nonminimal.

4 The FVS Obstruction Set Computation

In this section we focus on the problem-specific details for finding the k-FVS obstructions sets (i.e., steps 2 and 4 of Figure 1). First we describe a FVS finite-state congruence on graphs of bounded pathwidth/treewidth in t-parse form. Next we show how to produce complete testsets for the graph families k-FVS, $k \geq 0$, with respect to any boundary size t.

4.1 A FVS congruence

For a fixed t, let the current set of boundary vertices of a t-parse G_n be denoted by ∂. Our goal is to set up a dynamic-programming congruence/automaton where the state of the t-parse prefix G_{m+1}, $m < n$, can be computed in constant time (function of t) from the state of the prefix G_m. For any subset S of ∂, we define $F_m(S)$ to be the least k such that there is a FVS V of G_m with $V \cap \partial = S$ and $|V| = k$, and ∞ if no such k exists.

For any witness set V of G_m consisting of $F_m(S)$ vertices, there is an associated *witness forest* consisting of the trees that contain at least one boundary vertex in $G_m - V$. A witness forest tells us how tight the boundary vertices are held together. Some of these forests are more concise than others for representing how vertex deletions can break up the boundary.

For two witness forests A and B, with respect to $F_m(S)$, we say $A \leq_w B$ if the following two conditions hold:

1. For any two boundary vertices i and j, i and j are connected in A if and only if i and j are connected in B.
2. If for any t-parse extension Z where there exists some non-boundary vertex b of B such that $(B - b) \cdot Z$ is acyclic then there exists a non-boundary vertex a of A such that $(A - a) \cdot Z$ is acyclic.

Also two witness forests A and B are equivalent if $A \leq_w B$ and $B \leq_w A$. A witness forest in reduced form (minimal number of vertices) is called a *park*.

Lemma 14 *There are at most $3t - 3$ vertices in any park for boundary size t.*

Corollary 15 *The total number of parks with boundary size t is bounded above by $(t + 1)^{t-1} \cdot 2 \cdot (2t - 1)^{2t-3}$.*

The results of the previous lemma and its corollary may be strengthened. However, these bounds are sufficient for our purposes – to show that there is a manageable (constant) number of parks (i.e., these witness sets can be used as a finite-state congruence). For each subset S of the set of boundary vertices, we keep track of the parks with leaves and branches over $\partial \setminus S$ in the set $P_m(S)$.

In the same fashion that we converted our vertex cover algorithm in [1] to a finite-state congruence for a fixed upper-bound k, we can use the above sets, $F_m(S)$ and $P_m(S)$ for all $S \in 2^\partial$, to construct a finite-state congruence for k-FVS. This is accomplished by restricting the values of $F_m(S)$ to be in $\{0, 1, \ldots, k, k+1\}$ and setting any $P_m(S) = \emptyset$ for which $F_m(S) = k + 1$; we are only interested in knowing whether or not there exists a feedback vertex set of size at most k. (The value of $k + 1$ acts as ∞.) Two t-parses G_m and $G'_{m'}$ are congruent, $G_m \sim G'_{m'}$, if $F_m(S) = F'_{m'}(S)$ and $P_m(S) = P'_{m'}(S)$ for all $S \in 2^\partial$.

Notice that the k-FVS congruence $\sim$ is only a refinement of the $\mathcal{F}$-congruence $\sim_{\mathcal{F}}$ since $G \sim H$ implies that $G \sim_{\mathcal{F}} H$ but $G \not\sim H$ does not imply that $G \not\sim_{\mathcal{F}} H$. Thus, we will need to use a complete testset for k-FVS to prove t-parses nonminimal.

4.2 A complete FVS testset

Surprisingly, a finite test set for the FVS $\mathcal{F}$-congruence is easy to produce. The individual tests closely resemble the parks described above. The testset that we use consists of forests augmented with isolated triangles (and/or triangles solely attached to a single boundary vertex). Our k-FVS testset T_t^k consists of all t-boundaried graphs that have the following properties:

- Each graph is a member of k-FVS.
- Each graph is a forest with zero or more isolated triangles, K_3.
- Every tree component has at least two boundary vertices.
- Every isolated triangle has at most one boundary vertex.
- Every degree one vertex is a boundary vertex.
- Every non-boundary degree two vertex is adjacent to boundary vertices.

The above restrictions on members of T_t^k gives us an upper bound on the number of vertices, $|V| \leq 2t + 3(k - 1)$. Hence, T_t^k is a finite testset. Since this testset is based solely on t-boundaried graphs, it is useful for both pathwidth and treewidth searches for k-FVS.

Theorem 16 *The set of t-boundaried graphs T_t^k is a complete testset for the family k-FVS.*

Proof. Assume G and H are two t-boundaried graphs that are not $\mathcal{F}$-congruent for k-FVS. Without loss of generality, let Z be any t-boundaried graph that distinguishes G and H with $G \oplus Z \in \mathcal{F}$ and $H \oplus Z \notin \mathcal{F}$. We show how to build a t-boundaried graph $T \in T_t^k$ from Z that also distinguishes G and H. Let W be a set of k witness vertices such that $(G \oplus Z) \setminus W$ is acyclic. From W, let $W_G = W \cap G$, $W_\partial = W \cap \partial$ and $W_Z = W \cap Z$. Take T' to be $Z \setminus W$ plus $|W_Z|$ isolated triangles, plus $|W_\partial|$ triangles with each containing a single boundary vertex from W_∂. If T' contains any component $C \not\cong K_3$ without boundary vertices, replace it with $FVS(C)$ isolated triangles. Clearly, $G \oplus T' \in k$-FVS since W_G plus one vertex from each of the non-boundary isolated triangles of T' is a witness set of k vertices. If $H \oplus T' \in k$-FVS then this contradicts the fact that $H \oplus Z \notin k$-FVS with W_Z and W_∂ and the interior witness vertices of H (with respect to $H \oplus T'$). Finally, we construct a distinguisher $T \in T_t^k$ by minimizing T' to satisfy the 6 properties listed above. (Note that the extension T is created by not eliminating any cycles in the extension T'.) $\square$

For the graph family 1-FVS on boundary size 4, the above testset consists of only 546 tests. However, for 2-FVS on boundary size 5, the above testset contains a whopping set of 14686 tests. As can be seen by the increase in the number of tests, a more compact FVS testset would be needed (if possible) before we attempt to work with boundary sizes larger than 5. The large number of tests (especially T_5^2) for FVS indicates why using the testset step to prove t-parses minimal or nonminimal is the most CPU-intensive part of our obstruction set search (and is why it is attempted last in Figure 1).

4.3 The k-FVS obstructions

We now discuss the results of our search for the 1-FVS and 2-FVS obstructions. First, we need some type of lemma that bounds the search space. The following well-known treewidth bound can be found in [7] along with other introductory information concerning the minor order and obstruction sets.

Lemma 17 *A graph in k-FVS has treewidth at most $k + 1$.*

Corollary 18 *An obstruction for k-FVS has treewidth at most $k + 2$.*

Proof. Let v be any vertex of an obstruction G. Since $G' = G \setminus v \in k$-FVS has a tree decomposition T of width at most $k + 1$, adding the vertex v to each vertex of T yields a tree decomposition of width at most $k + 2$ for G. $\square$

We now consider when the pathwidth of a k-FVS obstruction G can be larger than the treewidth bound of $k + 2$. If we attempt to build a path decomposition like the tree decompositions in the proof of Lemma 4.3, we see that for the forest G' resulting by deleting an arbitrary vertex v and k witness vertices from G has to have pathwidth at least 2. From [2] we know that the forest will contain a subdivided $K_{1,3}$ for this to happen. So, such an obstruction must have at least $1 + k + 7$ vertices. And for pathwidth 3, the forest has to contain one of the tree obstructions of order 22, and hence G has to have at least $1 + k + 22$ vertices for pathwidth to be more than the treewidth plus one.

Lemma 19 *If O is an obstruction to 2-FVS and has pathwidth greater than 4, then O either has at least 24 vertices or is also an obstruction to k-PATHWIDTH, for some $k \geq 4$.*

Proof. Without loss of generality, assume that the pathwidth of O is 5 and is not a pathwidth obstruction. There must then exist a minor G of O with the same pathwidth as O. Since O is a 2-FVS obstruction, the minor G must have a feedback vertex set V of cardinality 2. If the forest $G' = G \setminus V$ has pathwidth 2 or less, we can build a path decomposition of G of width 4 by adding the two vertices of V to the sets of a path-decomposition of G' of width 2. So that leaves us with the case that G' must contain a tree of pathwidth at least 3. Such a tree must have at least 22 vertices so G must have at least 24 vertices. Since O has the same pathwidth as G, the obstruction O must also have 24 vertices. □

Any connected obstruction to 2-FVS can not contain 3 disjoint cycles, or any degree one vertices, or any consecutive degree two vertices, so having 24 or more vertices seems unreasonable. Observe that the graph K_5 is an obstruction to both 2-FVS and 3-PATHWIDTH (not 4!), and that most of the k-PATHWIDTH obstructions have degree one vertices (and other nonminimal FVS properties), so it is unlikely that the second case of the lemma is possible. Unfortunately at this time, we have not proven the impossibility of either of these two cases. We hope, with regards to 2-FVS, that we can find a definitive proof, and avoid a treewidth 4 search.

Besides the single obstruction K_3 for the trivial family 0-FVS, the connected obstructions for 1-FVS and the connected obstructions for 2-FVS (pathwidth ≤ 4) are shown in Figures 3 and 5. In our figures we have presented only the connected obstructions since any disconnected obstruction O of k-FVS is a union of graphs from $\bigcup_{i=0}^{k-1} \mathcal{O}(i\text{-FVS})$ such that $\text{FVS}(O) = k + 1$.

Example 20 *Since K_3 is an obstruction for 0-FVS, and K_4 is an obstruction for 1-FVS, the graph $K_3 \cup K_4$ is an obstruction for 2-FVS.*

Some patterns become apparent in these two sets of obstructions such as the following easily-proven observation.

Observation 21 *For the family k-FVS, the complete graph K_{k+3}, the augmented complete graph $A(K_{k+2})$ which has vertices $\{1, 2, \ldots, k+2\} \cup \{v_{i,j} \mid 1 \leq i < j \leq k+2\}$ and edges $\{(i,j) \mid 1 \leq i < j \leq k+2\} \cup \{(i, v_{i,j}) \text{ and } (v_{i,j}, j) \mid 1 \leq i < j \leq k+2\}$, and the augmented cycle $A(C_{2k+1})$ are obstructions.*

5 The FES Obstruction Set Computation

We now focus on the problem-specific details for finding the k-FES obstruction sets (i.e. steps 1 and 4 of Figure 1). We first describe a simple graph-theoretical characterization for the graphs that are within a few edges of acyclic. This trivial result also shows that Problem 2 has a linear-time recognition algorithm.

Theorem 22 *A graph $G = (V, E)$ with c components has $FES(G) = k$ if and only if $|E| = |V| - c + k$.*

Proof. For $k = 0$ the result follows from the standard result for characterizing forests. If $FES(G) = k$ then deleting the k witness edges produces an acyclic graph and thus $|E| = |V| - c + k$. Now consider a graph G with $|V| - c + k$ edges for some $k > 0$. Since G has more edges than a forest can have, there exists an edge e on a cycle. Let $G' = (V, E \setminus \{e\})$. By induction $FES(G') = k - 1$. Adding the edge e to a witness edge set E' for G' shows that $FES(G) = k$. □

Unlike k-FVS, it is not obvious that the k-FES graph family is a minor-order lower ideal. However, with the above theorem one can easily prove this.

Corollary 23 *For each $k \geq 0$, the family of graphs k-FES is a lower ideal in the minor order.*

Proof. We show that the three basic minor operations will not increase the number of edges required to remove all cycles of a graph. An isolated vertex deletion removes both a vertex and a component at the same time, so k is preserved in the formula $|E| = |V| - c + k$. For an edge deletion the number of components can increase by at most one, so with $|E|$ decreasing by one, the value of k does not increase. For an edge contraction, the number of vertices decreases by one, the number of edges decrease by at least one, and the number of components stays the same, so k does not increase. □

5.1 A direct nonminimal FES test and a complete FES testset

Corollary 23 allows us to characterize each k-FES family in terms of obstruction sets which we abstractly characterize below. The next theorem gives us a precise means of testing for nonminimal t-parses (see step 1 of Figure 1).

Theorem 24 *A connected graph $G = (V, E)$ is an obstruction for k-FES if and only if $FES(G) = k + 1$ and every edge contraction of G removes at least two edges (i.e., the open neighborhoods of adjacent vertices overlap).*

Proof. This follows from the fact that an edge contraction that does not remove at least two edges is the only basic minor operation that does not decrease the number of edges required to kill all cycles for a connected graph. □

Somewhat surprisingly, an usable testset for FES has already been presented in Theorem 16 of Section 4.2. These FVS tests can also be used here.

Lemma 25 *The testset T_t^k for the family k-FVS is also a testset for k-FES.*

It is interesting to notice that, in addition to the out-of-family tests, the isolated triangles in the tests for k-FES can be restricted to have no boundary vertices. Thus, the number of graphs in a testset for k-FES can be substantially smaller than our k-FVS testset.

5.2 The k-FES obstructions

Since the family k-FES $\subseteq k$-FVS we know that the maximum treewidth of any obstruction for k-FES is at most $k + 2$. Thus, the same arguments given in Section 4.3 regarding pathwidth apply to k-FES as well.

For the family 0-FES, it is trivial to show that K_3 is the only obstructions. The connected obstructions for the graph families 1-FES through 3-FES are shown in Figures 2, 4 and 6. There are well over 100 connected obstructions for the 4-FES family. Any disconnected obstruction for k-FES is easily determined by combining connected obstructions from j-FES, $j < k$, since $FES(G_1) + FES(G_2) = FES(G_1 \cup G_2)$.

An open problem is to determine a constructive method for finding the obstructions for k-FES directly from the j-FES, $j < k$. Some easily-observed partial results are given next.

Observation 26 *If a connected graph G is an obstruction for k-FES then the following are all connected obstructions for $(k+1)$-FES.*

1. G with an added subdivided edge attached to an edge of G.
2. G with an attached K_3 on one of the vertices of G.
3. G with an added edge (u, v) when there exists a path of length at least two between u and v in $G \setminus E$ for each feedback edge set E of $k + 1$ vertices.

It is easy to see that if an obstruction has a vertex of degree two then it is predictable by observations (1–2). The first 2-FES obstruction in Figure 4 (wheel W_3) and the second 3-FES obstruction in Figure 6 (W_4) are two examples of graphs where observation (3) predicts the graph. Those 4-FES and 5-FES obstructions (pathwidth bound of 4) without degree two vertices and cut-vertices are shown in Figures 7 and 8. Note that the third 4-FES obstruction in Figure 7 is not predicatable from the 3-FES obstructions by using any of the above observations since deleting any edge from this graph leaves a contractable edge that does not remove any cycles (see Theorem 24).

References

1. K. Cattell and M. J. Dinneen. A characterization of graphs with vertex cover up to five. *International Workshop on Orders, Algorithms, and Applications Proceedings (ORDAL '94)*, Springer-Verlag Lecture Notes in Computer Science, vol. 831, (1994), 86–99.
2. J. Ellis, I. H. Sudborough, and J. Turner. The vertex separation and and search number of a graph. *Information and Computation* 113 (1994), 50–79.
3. M. R. Fellows and M. A. Langston. An analogue of the Myhill-Nerode theorem and its use in computing finite-basis characterizations. *Proc. Symposium on the Foundations of Computer Science* (FOCS), IEEE Press (1989), 520–525.
4. M. R. Garey and D. S. Johnson. *Computers and Intractability: A Guide to the Theory of NP-Completeness.* W. H. Freeman and Company, 1979.
5. N. G. Kinnersley and M. A. Langston. Obstruction set isolation for the Gate Matrix Layout problem. Technical Report TR-91-5, Dept. of Computer Science, University of Kansas, January 1991, to appear *Annals of Discrete Math.*
6. J. Lagergren and S. Arnborg. Finding minimal forbidden minors using a finite congruence. *Proc. 18th International Colloquium on Automata, Languages and Programming* (ICALP), Springer-Verlag, Lecture Notes in Computer Science vol. 510 (1991), 533–543.
7. J. van Leeuwen, *Handbook of Theoretical Computer Science*, Volume A: Algorithms and Complexity, MIT Press, 1990.
8. N. Robertson and P. D. Seymour. Graph minors XVI: Wagner's conjecture. to appear.

Fig.2: Connected obstructions for
1-FEEDBACK EDGE SET

Fig.3: Connected obstructions for
1-FEEDBACK VERTEX SET

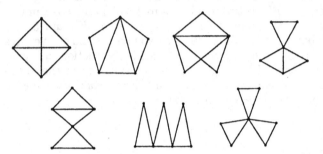

Fig.4: Connected obstructions for 2-FEEDBACK EDGE SET

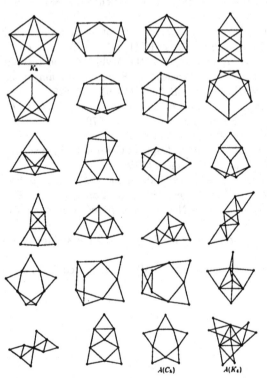

Fig.5: Connected obstructions for 2-FEEDBACK VERTEX SET, pathwidth ≤ 4

427

Fig.6: Connected obstructions for 3-FEEDBACK EDGE SET

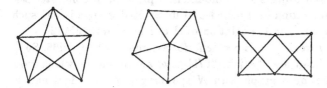

Fig.7: Biconnected 4-FES obstructions without degree 2 vertices

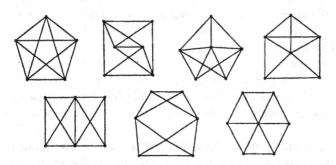

Fig.8: Biconnected 5-FES obstructions without degree 2 vertices, pathwidth ≤ 4

Faster Enumeration of All Spanning Trees of a Directed Graph

Ramesh Hariharan[1] and Sanjiv Kapoor[2] and Vijay Kumar[3]

[1] Max-Planck Institut für Informatik, Saarbrücken, Germany
[2] Indian Institute of Technology, New Delhi, India
[3] Northwestern University, Evanston, Illinois

Abstract. We present an algorithm for enumerating all spanning trees of a directed graph with V vertices, E edges and N spanning trees. The algorithm takes $O(\log V)$ time per spanning tree; more precisely, it runs in $O(N \log V + V^2 \alpha(V, V) + VE)$ time [4]. It first outputs a single spanning tree and then a list of edge swaps; each spanning tree can be generated from the first spanning tree by applying a prefix of this sequence of edge swaps. The total output size is $O(N)$ as against the $O(NV)$ size of all spanning trees put together. The previous best known algorithm for this problem [KR91] took $O(NV + V^3)$ time, even for generating the edge swap sequence.

1 Introduction

Enumerating combinatorial objects is a fundamental problem in computer science. Spanning tree enumeration in directed and undirected graphs is one such classical problem, which arises in the solution of electrical networks[M72].

There was much early work on this problem, for example, [Ch70, Mi65, S68]. For undirected graphs, Read and Tarjan[RT75] gave an algorithm which runs in $O(NE + V + E)$ time, on a graph with N spanning trees, E edges and V vertices. Gabow and Myers [GM78] refined this approach to obtain an algorithm which runs in $O(NV + V + E)$ time. This algorithm is optimal if all spanning trees have to be explicitly output. On the other hand, if only a computation tree which describes relative changes between spanning trees is desired, then the above algorithm is no longer optimal because the output has just $O(N)$ size. The algorithm of Gabow and Myers takes $O(V)$ time per spanning tree even to generate just the computation tree. Note that if desired, all spanning trees can be explicitly enumerated in $O(NV)$ time using the above computation tree. Kapoor and Ramesh [KR91, KR95] gave an algorithm to generate the computation tree of relative changes between spanning trees in $O(N + V + E)$ time, which is optimal.

The case of directed graphs seems to be harder. Shinoda[S68] gave an algorithm which could take exponential time per spanning tree in the worst case. Gabow and Myers [GM78] gave an algorithm which runs in $O(NE + V + E)$

---

[4] α is the Inverse Ackermann function.

time. Kapoor and Ramesh [KR91] gave an algorithm to generate the computation tree of relative changes between spanning trees in $O(NV + V^3)$ time. The question that then remained open was whether this computation tree could be generated in $o(V)$ time per spanning tree.

In this paper, we answer the above question in the affirmative by showing that the above computation tree can be generated using just $O(\log V)$ time per spanning tree. More precisely, we give a $O(N \log V + V^2 \alpha(V, V) + V E)$ algorithm for generating the computation tree. It is interesting to note that but for one component in the algorithm, the rest of the algorithm runs in just $O(\alpha(V, V))$ time per spanning tree. The "slow" component, which involves maintaining edges in a certain order, takes $O(\log V)$ time per spanning tree. We believe that this order can be maintained more efficiently but have not been able to give an algorithm to do so. An interesting side-effect of our algorithm is a procedure which, given vertex v of the graph, determines which edges occur in none of the spanning trees rooted at v in $O(V \alpha(V, V) + E)$ time.

We outline the techniques used in this paper in the rest of this section.

The algorithm of [KR91, KR95] introduced the *edge exchange* technique for enumerating spanning trees. First, consider undirected graphs. A spanning tree B can be obtained from another spanning tree A by adding an edge $f \notin A$ (called a *non-tree edge*) and removing an edge $e \in A$ (called a *tree-edge*) which is in the fundamental cycle of f with respect to A. This step is called an edge exchange. The algorithm of [KR91] starts with some spanning tree of the graph and obtains all other spanning trees by sequences of edge exchanges; duplications are avoided by an inclusion-exclusion scheme. Clearly, one needs to keep track of the fundamental cycles of the non-tree edges at each step in order to perform edge exchanges. The crux of the algorithm lies in maintaining these cycles efficiently.

Now consider directed graphs and the problem of enumerating all spanning trees rooted at some vertex v of the graph (repeating this process for all v gives all spanning trees). Here a spanning tree is defined to be a subgraph in which there is exactly one path from v to every other vertex.

The algorithm in [KR91] and the one in this paper follow the paradigm described above for undirected graphs. However, the notion of edge exchange is slightly different for directed graphs. Consider one spanning tree A rooted at some vertex v and let f be a non-tree edge, i.e., $f \notin A$. Recall that f is either a *back edge*, *cross edge*, or a *forward edge*. It is easy to observe that if f is a back edge then it cannot be exchanged with any of the edges A to get another spanning tree rooted at v; f is therefore *useless* for the purpose of generating another spanning tree. On the other hand, if f is a forward or a cross edge then it can be exchanged with exactly one edge in A to get a new spanning tree B rooted at v; this edge is the unique edge e in A with the same destination vertex as f. A complication is that after f is exchanged with e to get A, some edges not in A which were back edges with respect to A could now become forward or cross with respect to B and vice versa. The main challenge then is to maintain the set of forward and cross edges under edge exchange operations and to avoid processing back edges repeatedly, since they are useless for our purpose. The following main techniques are used to accomplish this.

As in [KR95], we order the exchanges in a *depth first* manner so that an exchange only converts back edges to forward and cross but not vice versa. There are two main issues now:

1. How to determine those edges which are converted from back to forward and cross by an exchange.

2. How to account for the time taken in processing back edges which are never converted to forward or cross and thus are useless.

In contrast to [KR91], we follow a *lazy* strategy for the first issue. We do not determine whether a given edge is converted from back to forward/cross as a result of an exchange when the exchange is made; instead. we postpone this computation to a later juncture. We then show that it suffices to answer *least common ancestor* (*lca* for short) queries efficiently in dynamic setting (as edge exchanges are performed) to perform this computation. Two tools are used to accomplish this. We organize the vertices into disjoint sets and use the *Union-Find* algorithm [TR75] to maintain these sets. Then we use one of the *lca* query algorithms [HT84, SV88] to answer lca queries. These algorithms preprocess a tree in linear time and then answer lca queries in constant time per query. However, we need them to work in the dynamic setting. We organize the computation so that:

(1) When the lca of vertices a, b is required, it suffices to compute the lcas of the sets (each set is named by a vertex) containing a and b, respectively.

(2) Lcas of sets are "static", so the initial lca preprocessing holds for them.

For the second issue, i.e., how to account for the time taken in processing back edges which are never converted to forward or cross, we give a non-trivial amortization argument. First, we order the exchanges such that useless edges are not processed too often. Second, we show that every time a useless edge is repeatedly processed, the work done can be charged to some spanning tree generated previously. We remark that ordering the exchanges as above is the only step in the algorithm which takes $O(\log V)$ time per spanning tree and that faster schemes for this step cannot be ruled out.

Section 2 gives some necessary definitions, section 3 gives an outline of the algorithm, section 4 describes the details of the scheme.

2 Definitions

An *exchange* for a spanning tree T of G rooted at v is a pair of edges (e, f) ,where $e \in T$, $f \in E - T$ and $T - \{e\} \cup \{f\}$ is a spanning tree rooted at v.

An edge not in a spanning tree T is a *back edge* relative to T if its destination is an ancestor of its source in T, a *forward edge* if its destination is a descendant of its source in T, and a *cross edge* otherwise. Forward and cross edges are collectively referred to as *non-back* edges.

The *least common ancestor (lca)* of two vertices in a tree is the last common vertex on the paths from the root to the two vertices. A vertex in a tree is considered to be an *ancestor* but not a *proper ancestor* of itself.

Destination(f) and *source(f)* refer to the destination and source vertices of edge f in G, respectively.

The *left subtree* of a vertex in a binary tree is the subtree rooted at the left child of that vertex. The *right subtree* is defined analogously.

3 Algorithm Outline

In this section, we present an outline of the algorithm. As in [KR91], the algorithm starts off with a directed spanning tree, T, rooted at particular vertex, v. All other spanning trees rooted at v are generated from T by exchanging non-tree edges with edges in T. All possible directed spanning trees may be generated by starting with directed spanning trees at each of the vertices. However note that the exchanges in the directed case are more specific.

Property 1: Every non-back, non-tree edge, f, relative to a spanning tree T, may replace exactly one tree edge, e, in T, namely the edge having the same destination, to result in a new spanning tree rooted at the same vertex as T.

Property 2: A back edge can not be exchanged for any edge in T to get a new spanning tree.

Let $CD(\mathrm{G}, v)$ be the computation tree which generates all spanning trees of the directed graph G with root v. At every node a of $CD(G, v)$, there is a spanning tree SD_a rooted at v. Node a has two children $b1$ and $b2$. SD_{b1} is obtained from SD_a by exchanging f with e, where f is a non-tree non-back edge and e is the unique tree edge with the same destination as f. SD_{b2} is the same as SD_a. The significance of $b2$ is that the subtree rooted at $b1$ will not include f in any spanning tree. This is captured by maintaining two sets, IN and OUT, with every node in the computation tree. IN_a is the set of all edges which must be present in the spanning trees that correspond to nodes in the subtree rooted at the node a and OUT_a represents edges which are precluded from these spanning trees. The IN and OUT sets at children $b1$ and $b2$ are obtained from the parent node a as follows:

$$IN_{b1} = IN_a \cup \{f\}$$
$$OUT_{b1} = OUT_a \cup \{e\} \cup$$
$$\qquad \{\text{all edges in } E \text{ incident upon } destination(e)\} - \{f\}$$
$$IN_{b2} = IN_a$$
$$OUT_{b2} = OUT_a \cup \{f\}$$

The IN and OUT sets for the root node are empty.

Lemma 1. $CD(G, v)$ *has at its nodes all directed spanning trees of G rooted at vertex v.*

The algorithm for constructing the computation tree follows a recursive strategy. At the root we start with some spanning tree. In general at each node, a, we have a spanning tree. A non-back edge, f, is chosen to construct a new spanning tree by the exchange (e, f) where e is the corresponding exchange edge given by property 1. The same procedure is repeated at the children $b1$ and $b2$ of the node a in the computation tree as described above. Note that to construct the entire sub-computation tree rooted at each node a, one needs to find the set of non-back, non-tree edges since every such edge leads to an exchange resulting in a new spanning tree. An exchange results in changing this set since some back edges may be converted to non-back or vice-versa. However we show that if we use a depth-first tree as the starting spanning tree at the root node and order non-back edges by the postorder number of their destination vertices in the spanning tree then no non-back edges are converted to back-edges. This simplifies the changes that need to be determined. We use this strategy in our algorithm in the next section.

Definition. Consider a node x in $CD(G, r)$ and an edge $e \in E - OUT_x - SD_x$. e is said to be *useful at x* if $e \in SD_{x'}$ for some node x' in the subtree of $CD(G, r)$ rooted at x, and to be *useless at x'* otherwise. Clearly, if $e \in E - OUT_x$ is useless at x then e must be a back edge at each of the nodes x' in the subtree rooted at x.

We define the *initial postorder number* of a vertex to be its rank in the list obtained by a postorder traversal of the DFS tree of G rooted at r.

4 Algorithm Description.

This section describes in detail an algorithm for generating all spanning trees of G rooted at a particular vertex r. For convenience, we assume that N is the number of spanning trees of G rooted at r and not the overall number of spanning trees.

The algorithm begins with a DFS tree T of G (rooted at r) at the root of the computation tree $CD(G, r)$. At any node x of $CD(G, r)$, there may be a number of edges in $E - IN_x - OUT_x$ which are non-back with respect to SD_x; each of these edges can serve as an exchange edge to give a new spanning tree. We consider these edges for exchange in increasing postorder number (with respect to SD_x) of their destination vertices; in addition, edges with the same destination are considered in increasing postorder number (with respect to SD_x) of the *lca* of their endpoints in T. With the above ordering, which we shall refer to as *exchange ordering* or *e-ordering*, Claim 1 holds.

Claim 1. *When edge f is used as the exchange edge to give a child z of x, then every other edge which is useful at x and is non-back with respect to SD_x will also be non-back with respect to SD_z.*

Thus no non-back edges are converted to back edges on an exchange. Some back edges may however be converted to non-back; these are governed by the following property.

Property 3: Let spanning tree T' be obtained from spanning tree T by applying the exchange (e, f). If g is a non-tree edge which is back with respect to T and non-back with respect to T', then $source(g)$ lies in the subtree of T rooted at $destination(f)$, and $destination(g)$ is a vertex which is a proper ancestor of $destination(f)$ and a proper descendant of $lca(source(f), destination(f))$ in T.

Next, note that when the exchange edge f is removed to generate the computation subtree rooted at the right child z of x, some edges in $E - IN_x - OUT_x$ which are back with respect to SD_x and useful at x will become useless at z. These edges must be identified and removed. Otherwise they might be repeatedly processed in the various subtrees of the computation subtree rooted at z which is expensive as these edges do not contribute to any spanning tree in this computation subtree. The processing of exchange edges in the previously specified order ensures the following property which facilitates this computation to be done easily.

Claim 2. *If a back edge with respect to SD_x is useful at the right child of x in $CD(G, r)$ then it is also useful at the left child of x.*

The three main issues in the algorithm now are:

(1). How to maintain the exchange edges so that the exchanges are performed in the above specified e-order.
(2). How to determine which back edges are converted to non-back on an exchange.
(3). How to determine which edges become useless when the exchange edge is removed.

For (2) and (3), we use a *lazy* scheme. In this scheme, an edge which is converted from back to non-back on an exchange is not detected at the time when the exchange is made; rather, it is determined to be non-back at a later instant when it itself is examined as a potential candidate for an exchange. The same is true for edges which become useless when an exchange edge is removed; these edges are determined to be useless when they themselves are examined as potential candidates for an exchange. More precisely, the lazy scheme is implemented as follows. We need to mention the following data structures before describing the lazy scheme.

Data Structures. The algorithm maintains a list X at each node x of $CD(G, r)$. At the root of $CD(G, r)$, X will contain those vertices upon which at least one edge that is useful at the root is incident. Further, X is organized in increasing initial postorder number. X will be updated in a manner to be described as the computation tree is generated; however, the vertices in X will always maintain their initial relative order. The algorithm also maintains two lists, $B[v]$ and $NB[v]$, for each vertex v in X. At the root of $CD(G, r)$, $NB[v]$ contains all edges in G which are non-back with respect to the spanning tree at the root and $B[v]$ contains all edges which are back edges with respect to this spanning tree and which are useful at the root. These sets will also be updated in a manner to be described as the computation tree is generated. The edges in $NB[v]$ will always be maintained in e-order. The following claim helps in this process. In particular, it ensures that the e-ordering for edges which are non-back edges with respect to the spanning tree at the root of $CD(G,r)$ is preserved as such as the computation proceeds.

Claim 3. *Consider the vertices in X at node x of $CD(G,r)$. The postorder ordering of these vertices with respect to SD_x is the same as their initial postorder ordering.*

Note that insertion and deletion of a particular vertex from X or a particular edge from NB or B takes constant time.

The Lazy Scheme. The lazy scheme is as follows. At each node x of $CD(G,r)$, the first vertex v in X is picked. The list $B[v]$ is examined. Recall that all edges in this list are back edges with respect to the spanning tree at the root of $CD(G,r)$. However, some of them might have been converted to non-back edges due to exchanges made along the path from the root to x. Those edges in $B[v]$ which are converted to non-back are identified, ordered in e-order and inserted into $NB[v]$ in a way which preserves the e-ordering of $NB[v]$; all this is done by procedures to be described. The remaining edges in $B[v]$ are discarded; clearly, these are useless at x. Then the first edge f in $NB[v]$ is picked as the exchange edge at x. f is exchanged with the unique edge in SD_x with the same destination as x to generate the spanning tree at the left son of x. As a result of this exchange, some edges g might have been converted from back to non-back. These edges will not be determined at the moment; they will determined only further down the computation tree at some node x' when the vertex *destination*(g) is encountered in X as X is processed at x'. The computation subtree rooted at the left son of X is generated recursively. Subsequently, edge f is removed from $NB[v]$ and the computation subtree rooted at the right son of x is generated recursively.

In the above algorithm, all the changes we make to the data structures B, NB, X at some node x of $CD(G,r)$ are saved on a stack; these changes are undone when we backtrack up from x.

Useless Edges are Detected Repeatedly. The algorithm, as described above, turns out to be expensive due to the following reason. Consider a node x in $CD(G,r)$ and let y be its right child. Let f be the exchange edge at x and suppose some back edge g with respect to SD_x is useful at x but not at both the children of x. By Claim 2, g is useful at the left child of x but useless at y. Then the exchange made at x converts g to non-back while none of the exchanges made at nodes in the subtree rooted at y convert g to non-back. So g becomes useless when edge f is removed to generate the computation subtree rooted at y. Since we are detecting useless edges lazily and also restoring all changes made to the data structures B and NB at any particular node while backtracking up from that node, g could possibly be detected as useless repeatedly in the subtrees rooted at the left children of each of the nodes on the rightmost path beginning at y. Since useless edges do not contribute to new spanning trees, the cost involved in this repeated detection cannot be accounted for. We use the following scheme to solve this problem.

We maintain a list called $ul(x)$ (short for *useless-list*) at each node x of the computation tree. Whenever an edge g is detected to be useless at some node w, it is added to $ul(w')$, where w' is the furthest (to w) ancestor of w such that all nodes on the path from w' to w (w' excluding) are left children of their respective parents. w' is called the *wake-up* node for w or $wake - up(w)$. We then mark g. This mark will be undone only just before the computation subtree rooted at the right child of w' is generated recursively. This mark has the effect that if g is again detected to be useless at some other node in the subtree rooted at the left child of w' then the above action is not taken. After the computation tree at the left child of x has been generated completely, the list $ul(x)$ is processed. For every edge $g \in ul(x)$, g is removed from $B[destination(g)]$ and g is unmarked. In addition, if there are no remaining edges in $NB[destination(g)]$ or in $B[destination(g)]$ then $destination(g)$ is removed from X. Subsequently, the subtree rooted at the right child of x is recursively generated following which all the above changes to B, NB and X are restored before backtracking up from x.

To illustrate why the above scheme is helpful, consider nodes x, y, g as in the paragraph preceding the previous one. Let z be the left child of y. When g is determined to be useless for the first time in the computation subtree rooted at z, it is added to $ul(y)$ and marked. Note that it may be detected as useless at various nodes in the subtree rooted at y; however, since it is marked the first time this event occurs, it is added to $ul(y)$ only once. After the computation subtree rooted at z has been generated, $ul(y)$ is processed and g is unmarked and removed from $B[destination(g)]$. As a result, g will not be encountered at all in the subtree rooted at the right child of y, which as it turns out, makes the algorithm efficient. However, note that g might still be detected as useless repeatedly in the subtree rooted at z; we will give a charging scheme later which will account for this repeated processing.

Detecting New Non-Back and Useless Edges. Consider node x of the computation tree and let v be a vertex in X processed at x. We show how to determine whether a given edge g in $B[v]$ is a non-back edge with respect to SD_x or an useless edge at x. Note that it suffices to be able to answer *lca* queries for SD_x in constant time. If x is the root of $CD(G, r)$ then this is done by simply preprocessing SD_x for *lca* queries using [HT84, SV88] in $O(V)$ time; subsequently *lca* queries for SD_x can be answered in constant time. Let dfs-lca(a, b) denote the constant time procedure which computes the *lca* of vertices a, b in the DFS tree at the root of $CD(G, r)$. To answer *lca* queries for spanning trees at the remaining nodes of $CD(G, r)$, the vertices in G are organized into disjoint sets. Each set carries the name of one of its vertices. These sets will be organized so that a crucial property which will be described in Claim 4 is satisfied. Thus each query takes only $\alpha(V, V)$ amortized time.

Claim 4. *Let v be a vertex in X at node x in $CD(G, r)$. Consider an edge $g = (u, v)$ in $B[v]$ at node x. If vertex u belongs to a set with name w at node x then g is back with respect to SD_x if and only if the dfs-lca$(w, v) = v$.*

E-Ordering Edges to be Transferred from $B[v]$ to $NB[v]$. This is the weak link in the algorithm. We use the following simple scheme which incurs a $O(\log V)$ overhead for each spanning tree generated. Note that the *lca*'s (with respect to SD_x) of the endpoints of the edges in $B[v]$ which are to be transferred to $NB[v]$ would have been computed above. From Claim 3, it follows that the postorder ordering of these *lca* nodes with respect to SD_x is the same as the initial postorder ordering. Then to e-order the relevant edges in $B[v]$, it suffices to sort them by the initial postorder number of these *lca* nodes.

Algorithm Details. The algorithm has two parts: a preprocessing part and the main procedure which generates the computation subtree rooted at any given node of the computation tree. We describe each in detail. We start with the preprocessing.

The Preprocessing Step. This step determines the spanning tree at the root of $CD(G, r)$ and sets up the required data structures. The procedure *Remove-useless-edges* removes all edges which do not occur in any spanning tree of G rooted at r and is skipped in this abstract. It takes $O(V\alpha(v, v) + E)$ time. We assume a procedure Union(u, v) which unions the sets with names u and v, the resulting set carrying the name of the vertex which has the *higher* initial postorder number.

$T \leftarrow$ DFS tree of G rooted at vertex r;
Preprocess T for *lca* queries.
Remove-useless-edges;
Compute NB and B with respect to T;
Create a set for each vertex;
For each vertex v
    If $NB[v] = B[v] = \Phi$, Union(find(u),find(v)), u is the parent of v;
$X \leftarrow$ A list of vertices v such that not both $NB[v]$ and $B[v]$ are empty
    Organized by increasing initial postorder number;

Algorithm 1: Preprocessing Algorithm.

The Main Step. The main procedure to generate the computation subtree rooted at some node x of $CD(G, r)$ is described in Algorithm 2. We assume that the path in $CD(G, r)$ from the root to x is available along with a pointer to $wake - up(x)$; clearly, this information is easy to maintain. We also skip the details of actually outputting the sequence of changes between spanning trees; again, this is easy to do. In Algorithm 2, let y be the left son of x and z be the right son of x.

This completes the algorithm description.

Repeat
  Remove the first vertex v from X;
  For each edge $g \in B[v]$ {*Detect useless edges*}
    If dfs-lca(find($source(g)$), v) = v
      {*i.e., g is back w.r.t SD_x and so useless at x*}
      If g is unmarked, add g to $ul(wake-up(x))$ and mark g;
      Remove g from $B[v]$;
  Sort remaining edges in $B[v]$ by e-order, remove them from $B[v]$ and merge .
    into $NB[v]$;
  If $NB[v]$ is empty then Union(v, w), w parent of v in T and in SD_x;
Until $NB[v]$ is not empty;
Pick the first edge f in $NB[v]$;
$SD_y = SD_x - \{e\} \cup \{f\}$, where e is the unique exchange edge for f;
Union($source(f), destination(f)$);
Recursively generate the computation subtree rooted at y;
Undo the effect of the above Union;
For each edge $g \in ul(x)$ {*Let u denote $destination(g)$*}
  Remove g from $B[u]$ and unmark g;
  If both $NB[u]$ and $B[u]$ are empty
    Remove u from X;
    Union(u, w), w the parent of u in T and SD_x;
Remove f from $NB[v]$;
If $NB[v]$ is not empty, restore v to X,
  else Union(v, w), w the parent of v in T and SD_x;
Recursively generate the computation subtree rooted at z;
Restore NB, B, X and the sets to their state at the beginning of this
  procedure;

Algorithm 2: Generating the Computation Subtree rooted at x.

4.1 Complexity

Consider the procedure for generating the computation subtree rooted at some node x of $CD(G, r)$. We account for the work done in this procedure (minus the recursive calls) next. We will assume each set operation takes $O(\alpha(V, V))$ time.

Work done in the Repeat Loop. Note that for each vertex v in X processed here, either $B[v]$ or $NB[v]$ is non-empty. The edges processed here can be divided into two groups, the first which are determined as useless and removed from B and the second which are determined as being useful and transferred to NB. If the above loop terminates at vertex v in X, all the edges in the latter group are moved to $NB[v]$. All edges in the first group incur $O(\alpha(V, V))$ cost per edge while edges in the second group incur $(\alpha(V, V) + \log V)$ cost per edge. Notice that each edge in the second group leads to a new spanning tree at the left child of one of the nodes along the rightmost path starting at x through an exchange;

the work done in processing it is then charged to that spanning tree. It is easily seen that each spanning tree gets charged at most $(\alpha(V, V) + \log V)$ in this way. It remains to account for edges in the first group.

Let g be an edge in the first group. Let y be the nearest ancestor of x such that g is useful at y. We claim that either x must be in the subtree rooted at z, the left child of the right child y' of y, or $x = y'$. To see this, note that by Claim 2, x must be in the subtree rooted at y'. Suppose $x \neq y'$ and x is not in the subtree rooted at the z'. Then g will be detected to be useless along the leftmost path from y', inserted into $ul(y')$ and subsequently, before the subtree rooted at the right child of y' is generated, g would have been removed from B. Thus g could not have been encountered at x, a contradiction. So either $x = y'$ or x is in the subtree rooted at z. Further, if the exchange edges at y' and y have the same destination vertex v then $x \neq y'$ as all edges in $B[v]$ would have been processed and removed at y itself.

We will define a one-to-one function $f(a, b)$, where a is an edge detected as useless at node b, $b = y'$ or b in the subtree rooted at z; the value of this function will be a spanning tree which is at the node in the subtree rooted at the left child y'' of y such that a is the exchange edge at y. Then the work done in processing g at x will be charged to the spanning tree at $f(g, x)$. Further, we will show that g is non-back with respect to $SD_{y''}$, where y'' is the left child of y. So g cannot be detected as useless anywhere in the subtree rooted at y''. From the above, it is clear that each spanning tree gets charged at most $(\alpha(V, V) + \log V)$ in this way.

The Function $f(g, x)$. Let $f_1, \ldots, f_k$ be the exchange edges on the path from y' to x inclusive. Let f be the exchange edge at y and f' the exchange edge at y' (note that $f' = f_1$). If the destination vertices of f, f' are the same then we define $f(g, x)$ be the spanning tree obtained from SD_y by the sequence of exchanges obtained by exchange edges $f, f_2, f_3, \ldots, f_k, g$. If the destination vertices of f, f' are different then we define $f(g, x)$ be the spanning tree obtained from SD_y by the sequence of exchanges obtained by exchange edges $f, f_1, f_2, f_3, \ldots, f_k, g$. Function $f()$ as defined above is clearly one-to-one. We show that the function is well-defined below.

Lemma 2. g is a non-back edge with respect to $SD_{y''}$.

Lemma 3. Suppose f, f' have the same destination. If edge q is non-back with respect to SD_z then it is also non-back with respect to $SD_{y''}$.

Lemma 4. Suppose f, f' have the same destination. Then each edge in the sequence $f, f_2, f_3, \ldots, f_k, g$ is a non-back edge with respect to the spanning tree obtained by exchanging all previous edges in sequence into SD_y.

Lemma 5. Suppose f, f' have different destinations. Then each edge in the sequence $f, f_1, f_2, f_3, \ldots, f_k, g$ is a non-back edge with respect to the spanning tree obtained by exchanging all previous edges in sequence into SD_y.

Work done in the other steps. All other steps, except for processing the list $ul(x)$ and restoring changes to NB, B, X and the sets, clearly take amortized $O(\alpha(V, V))$ time. The work done in processing $ul(x)$ is just $O(\alpha(V, V))$ per edge g in $ul(x)$. This can be accounted for exactly as we accounted for detecting g to be useless above.

Theorem 6. *The total work done by the algorithm to generate all spanning trees rooted at r is $O(N(\alpha(V, V) + \log V) + V\alpha(V, V) + E)$. The overall algorithm takes $O(N \log V + V^2\alpha(V, V) + VE)$ time and $O(V + E)$ space.*

5 Concluding Remarks

The existence of an $O(N)$ algorithm remains open. Whether the e-order defined above can be maintained more efficiently is another interesting question; this would of course improve the entire algorithm as the rest of the algorithm takes just $O(\alpha(V, V))$ time per tree.

References

[Ch70] S. M. Chase, Analysis for algorithms for finding all spanning trees of a graph, RC3190, IBM T.J. Watson Research Center, Yorktown Heights, NY, Dec. 1970.

[Ga77] H. N. Gabow, Two algorithms for generating weighted spanning trees in order, SIAM J. Comput., vol. 6, pp. 139-150, Mar 77.

[GM78] H. N. Gabow and E. W. Myers, Finding all spanning trees of directed and undirected graphs, SIAM J. Comput., vol. 7, no. 3, Aug 78.

[HT84] D. Harel, R. Tarjan. Fast algorithms for finding nearest common ancestors. SIAM J. Comput., 13, 1984, 338–355.

[KR91] S. Kapoor, H. Ramesh. Algorithms for generating all spanning trees of undirected, directed and weighted graphs, Workshop on Algorithms and Data Structures, LCNS 519, Ottawa, 1991.

[KR95] S. Kapoor, H. Ramesh. Algorithms for generating all spanning trees of undirected and weighted graphs, To appear in SIAM J. Comput., 1995.

[M72] W. Mayeda. Graph Theory, John Wiley, NY 1972, 252–264.

[Mi65] G.J. Minty, A simple algorithm for listing all trees of a graph, IEEE Trans. Circuit Theory, vol. CT-12, pp. 120, 1965.

[TR75] R. E. Tarjan, On the efficiency of a good but not linear set merging algorithm, J. of ACM, 22, 2, April 75.

[RT75] R. E. Tarjan, R. C. Read, Bounds on backtrack algorithms for listing cycles, paths and spanning trees, Networks, 5, 1975, pp. 237-252.

[SV88] B. Schieber, U. Vishkin. On finding lowest common ancestors: simplification and parallelization. SIAM J. Comput., 17, 1988, 1253–1262.

[S68] S. Shinoda. Finding all possible directed trees of a directed graph, *Electron Communication*, Japan, 51-A, 1968, 45–47.

A Simpler Minimum Spanning Tree Verification Algorithm

Valerie King

Department of Computer Science, University of Victoria
Victoria, BC, CANADA V8W 3P6

Abstract. The problem considered here is that of determining whether a given spanning tree is a minimal spanning tree. In 1984, Komlós presented an algorithm which required only a linear number of comparisons, but nonlinear overhead to determine which comparisons to make. We simplify his algorithm and give a linear time procedure for its implementation in the unit cost RAM model. The procedure uses table lookup of a few simple functions, which we precompute in time linear in the size of the tree.

1 Introduction

The problem of determining whether a given spanning tree in a graph is a minimal spanning tree has been studied by Tarjan[T] (1979), Komlós[Ko] (1984), and most recently by Dixon, Rauch, and Tarjan [DRT] (1992). Tarjan's 1979 algorithm uses path compression and gives an almost linear running time. Komlós's algorithm was the first to use a linear number of comparisons, but no linear time method of deciding which comparisions to make has been known. Indeed, a linear implementation of this algorithm was not thought possible, see [Ko] and [DRT]. The only known linear time algorithm for this problem, [DRT], combines the techniques of both [T1] and [Ko], using the Komlós algorithm to process small subproblems via preprocessing and table-lookup.

These verification methods and the method presented here use the fact that a spanning tree is a minimum spanning tree iff the weight of each non-tree edge $\{u, v\}$ is at least the weight of the heaviest edge in the path in the tree between u and v. These methods find the heaviest edge in each such path for each non-tree edge $\{u, v\}$ in the graph, and then compare the weight of $\{u, v\}$ to it.

The "tree path" problem of finding the heaviest edges in the paths between specified pairs of nodes ("query paths") arises in the recent randomized minimum spanning tree algorithms of Karger [Ka] and of Klein and Tarjan [KT]. The latter is the first algorithm to compute the minimum spanning tree in linear expected time, where the only operations allowed on edge weights are binary comparisions. The solution to the tree path problem is the most complicated part of these randomized algorithms, which are otherwise fairly simple.

The Komlós's algorithm is simplified by use of the following observation: If T is a spanning tree, then there is a simple $O(n)$ algorithm to construct a full branching tree B with no more than $2n$ edges and the following property:

Let $T(x, y)$ denote the set of edges in the path in T from node x to node y, and let $B(x, y)$ denotes the set of edges in the path in B from leaf x to leaf y.

The weight of the heaviest edge in $T(x, y)$ is the weight of the heaviest edge in $B(x, y)$.

Therefore it suffices to use the version of the Komlós algorithm for full branching trees only which is much simpler than his algorithm for general trees.

The second part of this paper is to show that this portion of Komlós's algorithm has a linear time implementation using table lookup of a few simple functions. These tables can be constructed in time linear in the size of the tree. As in the DRT algorithm, the model of computation is a unit cost RAM with word size $\Theta(\log n)$. The only operations used on edge weights are binary comparisons.

In contrast, the DRT algorithm separates the tree into a large subtree and many "microtrees" of size $O(\lg \lg n)$. Path compression is used on the large subtree. The comparison decision tree needed to implement Komlós's strategy for each possible configuration of microtree and possible set of query paths in the microtree is precomputed and stored in a table. Each microtree, together with its query paths in the input spanning tree, is encoded and then the table is used to look up the appropriate comparisons to make.

In the next section, the construction of B is described, and the property of B is proved. In section 3, we restate Komlós's algorithm for determining the maximum weighted edge in each of m paths of a full branching tree and describe its implementation.

2 Boruvka tree property

Let T be a spanning tree with n nodes. The tree B is the tree of the components that are formed when the Boruvka algorithm for finding a minimum spanning tree is applied to T.

The Boruvka algorithm, as applied to a tree $T = (V, E)$ is as follows (See [T2]): Initially there are n blue trees consisting of the nodes of V and no edges.

Repeat until there is one blue tree, i.e., T: For each blue tree, select a minimum weight edge incident to it. Color all selected edges blue.

Each repetition of these instructions will be referred to as a phase. We construct the tree B with nodeset W and edgeset F, by adding nodes and edges to B after each phase of the algorithm, so that there is a 1-1 correspondence between the nodes of B and the blue trees created during all the phases of the algorithm.

For each node $v \in V$ of T, we create a leaf $f(v)$ of B. Let A be the set of blue trees which are joined into one blue tree t in a phase i. Then we add a new node $f(t)$ to W and add to F $\{\{f(a), f(t)\}|$for all $a \in A\}$. Each edge $\{f(a), f(t)\}$ is labeled with the weight of the edge selected by a in phase i.

Note that B is a full branching tree, i.e., it is rooted and all leaves are on the same level and each internal node has at least two children.

Since T is a tree, B can be constructed in $O(n)$ time. This may be seen as follows: The cost of executing each phase is proportional to the number of uncolored edges in the tree during that phase. The number of uncolored edges is one less than the number of blue trees, since T is a tree. Finally, the number of blue trees drops by a factor of at least two after each phase.

For any tree T, let $T(x, y)$ denote the set of edges in the path in T from node x to node y.

We prove the following theorem:

Theorem 1. *Let T be any spanning tree and let B be the tree constructed as described above. For any pair of nodes x and y in T, the weight of the heaviest edge in $T(x, y)$ equals the weight of the heaviest edge in $B(f(x), f(y))$.*

Proof. We denote the weight of an edge e by $w(e)$. First we show that for every edge $e \in B(f(x), f(y))$, there is an edge $e' \in T(x, y)$ such that $w(e') \geq w(e)$.

Let $e = \{a, b\}$ and let a be the endpoint of e which is farther from the root. Then $a = f^{-1}(t)$ for some blue tree t which contains either x or y, but not both, and $w(e)$ is the weight of the edge selected by t.

Let e' be the edge in $T(x, y)$ with exactly one endpoint in t. Since t had the option of selecting e', $w(e') \geq w(e)$, which concludes the first part of the proof.

It remains to show the following:

Claim 1.1 *Let e be the a heaviest edge in $T(x, y)$. Then there is an edge of the same weight in $B(f(x), f(y))$.*

We assume for simplicity that there is a unique heaviest edge. The proof can easily be extended to the general case.

If e is selected by a blue tree which contains x or y then an edge in $B(f(x), f(y))$ is labeled with $w(e)$. Assume on the contrary that e is selected by a blue tree which does not contain x or y. This blue tree contained one endpoint of e and thus one intermediate node on the path from x to y. Therefore it is incident to at least two edges on the path. Then e is the heavier of the two, and is not selected, giving a contradiction.

3 Komlós's algorithm for a full branching tree

For a full branching tree of weighted edges with n nodes, and m query paths between pairs of leaves, Komlós has shown a simple algorithm to compute the heaviest edge on the path between each pair with $O(n \log(\frac{m+n}{n}))$ comparisons. He breaks up each path into two half-paths extending from the leaf up to the lowest common ancestor of the pair and finds the heaviest edge in each half-path, as follows:

Let $A(v)$ be the set of the paths which contain v restricted to the interval $[root, v]$.

Starting with the root, descend level by level and as each node v encountered, the heaviest edge in each path in the set $A(v)$ is determined, as follows.

Let p be the parent of v. Assume we know the heaviest edge in each path in the set $A(p)$. Note that the ordering of the weights of these heaviest edges can be determined by the length of their respective paths, since for any two paths s and t in $A(p)$, path s includes path t or vice versa. Let $A(v|p)$ be the set of the restrictions of each of the paths in $A(v)$ to the interval $[p, root]$. Since $A(v|p) \in A(p)$, the ordering of the weights of the heaviest edges in $A(v|p)$ is known. To determine the heaviest edge in each path in $A(v)$, we need only to compare $w(\{v,p\})$ to each of these weights. This can be done by using binary search. Komlos shows that $\sum_{v \in T} \lg |A(v)| = O(n \log(\frac{m+n}{n}))$ which gives the upper bound on the number of comparisons needed to find the heaviest edge in each half-path. Then the heaviest edge in each query path is determined with one additional comparison per path.

4 Implementation of Komlós's algorithm

The implementation of Komlós's algorithm requires the use of a few simple functions on words of size $O(\log n)$, such as a shift by a specified number of bits, the bit-wise OR of two words, $\lfloor \log n \rfloor$, the multiplication of two words and a few more functions which are less conventional and will be described below. All these functions can be precomputed in $O(n)$ time and stored in a table where they can be accessed in unit time. First, we present a description of the data structures we use, followed by a high level description of the algorithm, and then its implementation details.

4.1 Data Structures

We take the *wordsize* $= \lceil \lg n \rceil$ bits.

Node labels and edge tags: Following a modification of the scheme of Schieber and Vishkin [SV], we label the nodes with a $\lceil \lg n \rceil$ bit label and the edges with an $O(\log \log n)$ bit tag so that:

Label Property: Given the tag of any edge e and the label of any node on the path from e to any leaf, e can be located in constant time.

The labels are constructed as follows: Label the leaves 0, 1, 2,..., as encountered in a depthfirst traversal of the tree. Label each internal node by the label of the leaf in its subtree which has the longest all 0's suffix.

For each edge e, let v be its endpoint which is farther from the root and let $distance(v)$ be v's distance from the root and $i(v)$ be the index of the rightmost 1 in v's label. Then the *tag* of e is a string of $t = O(\lg \lg n)$ bits given by $< distance(v), i(v) >$.

We sketch the argument (see [SV]) that the Label Property holds: It is not hard to see that the label of an ancestor of a node w is given by a prefix of the label w possibly followed by a 1 and then all 0's. Also, nodes with the same label are connected by a path up the tree. Hence the label of w and the position of the rightmost 1 in an ancestor's label determine the ancestor's label, while its distance from the root uniquely determines the ancestor's identity, among those nodes with the same label. Once the lower endpoint v of an edge e is found, then e is the unique edge from v to its parent.

LCA: For each node v, $LCA(v)$ is a vector of length $\lceil lgn \rceil$ whose i^{th} bit of $LCA(v) = 1$ iff there is a path in $A(v)$ whose endpoint is at distance i from the root. That is, there is a query path with exactly one endpoint contained in the subtree rooted at v, such that the lowest common ancestor of its two endpoints is at distance i from the root. LCA is stored in a single word.

$BigLists$ and $smallLists$: For any node v, the ith longest path in $A(v)$ will be denoted by $A_i(v)$. The weight of an edge e is denoted $w(e)$. Recall that the set of paths in $A(v)$ restricted to $[a, root]$ is denoted $A(v|a)$. Call $A(v)$ big if $|A(v)| > (\lg n - 1)/t$; otherwise $A(v)$ is small.

For each node v such that $A(v)$ is big, we keep an ordered list whose i^{th} element is the tag of the heaviest edge in $A_i(v)$, for $i = 1, ..., |A(v)|$. This list is a referred to as $bigList(v)$. We may similarly define $bigList(v|a)$ for the set of paths $A(v|a)$. $BigList(v)$ is stored in up to $\lceil t|A(v)|/(\lg n - 1) \rceil = O(\log\log n)$ words, each containing up to $(\lg n - 1)/t$ tags.

For each v such that $A(v)$ is small, let a be the nearest big ancestor of v. For each such v, we keep an ordered list, $smallList(v)$, whose i^{th} element is either the tag of the heaviest edge e in $A_i(v)$, or if e is in the interval $[a, root]$, then the j such that $A_i(v|a) = A_j(a)$. That is, j is a pointer to the entry of $bigList(a)$ which contains the tag for e. $SmallList$ is stored in a single word.

4.2 The algorithm

The goal is to generate $biglist(v)$ or $smallList(v)$ in time proportional to $\log|A(v)|$, so that time spent implementing Komlos's algorithm at each node does not exceed the worst case number of comparisons needed at each node. We show that if $A(v)$ is big then the implementation time is $O(\log\log n)$, and if $|A(v)|$ is small, it is $O(1)$.

Initially, $A(root) = \emptyset$. We proceed down the tree, from the parent p to each of the children v. Depending on the $|A(v)|$, we generate either $bigList(v|p)$ or $smallList(v)$. We then compare $w(\{v, p\})$ to the weights of these edges, by performing binary search on the list, and insert the tag of $\{v, p\}$ in the appropriate places to form $bigList(v)$ or $smallList(v)$. We continue until the leaves are reached.

Let v be any node, p is its parent, and a its nearest big ancestor. To compute $A(v|p)$:

There are two cases if $A(v)$ is small:

- If $A(p)$ are small, we create $smallList(v|p)$ from $smallList(p)$ in $O(1)$ time.
- If $A(p)$ is big, we create $smallList(v|p)$ from $LCA(v)$ and $LCA(p)$ in $O(1)$ time.

If $A(v)$ is big:

- If v has a big ancestor, we create $bigList(v|a)$ from $bigList(a)$, $LCA(v)$, and $LCA(a)$ in $O(\lg \lg n)$ time.
  - If $p \neq a$ is small, we also create $bigList(v|p)$ from $bigList(v|a)$ and $smallList(p)$ in time $O(\lg \lg n)$.
- If v does not have a big ancestor, then $bigList(v|p) \leftarrow smallList(p)$

To insert a tag in its appropriate places in the list:

- Let $e = \{v, p\}$, and let i be rank of $w(e)$ as compared to the heaviest edges of $A(v|p)$. Then we insert the tag for e in positions i through $|A(v)|$, into our list data structure for v, in time $O(1)$, if $A(v)$ is small, or $O(\log \log n)$ if $A(v)$ is big.

4.3 Implementation details

The computation of the LCA's is straightforward. First, we compute all lowest common ancestors for each pair of endpoints of the m query paths using an algorithm that runs in time $O(n + m)$, see [SV] or [T2]. We form the vector $LCA(l)$ for each leaf l using this information, and then form the vector $LCA(v)$ for a node at distance i from the root by ORing together the LCA's of its children and setting the jth bits to 0 for all $j \geq i$.

To implement the remaining operations, we will need to preprocess a few functions so that we may do table look-up of these functions. We define a a $subword$ to be t bits and $h = \lfloor(\lg n - 1)/t\rfloor$. Each input and each output described below are stored in single words. The symbol $\cdot$ will denote "concatenated with".

$select_r$ takes as input $I \cdot J$, where I and J are two strings r bits. It outputs a list of bits of J which have been "selected" by I, i.e., let $< k_1, k_2, ... >$ be the ordered list of indices of those bits of I whose value is 1. Then the list is $< j_{k_1}, j_{k_2}, ... >$ where j_{k_i} is the value of the k_i^{th} bit of J.

$selectS_r$ takes as input $I \cdot J$, where I is a string of no more than r bits, no more than h of which are 1, and J is a list of h subwords. It outputs a list of the subwords of J which have been "selected" by I, i.e., let $< k_1, k_2, ... >$ be the ordered list of indices of those bits of I whose value is 1. Then the list is $< j_{k_1}, j_{k_2}, ... >$ where j_{k_i} is the k_i^{th} subword of J.

$weight_r$ takes as input a string of length r and outputs the number of bits set to 1.

$index_r$ takes a r bit vector with no more than h 1's and outputs a list of subwords containing the indices of the 1's in the vector.

$subword1$ is a constant such that for $i = 1, ..., h$, the $(i * t)^{th}$ bit is 1 and the remaining bits are 0. (I.e,. each subword is set to 1).

For each of these functions, it is not hard to see that the preprocessing takes $O(n)$ time, when the size of the input is no greater than $\lg n + c$ for c a constant. One can build a table for all inputs of length r by first building a table for inputs of size $r/2$, looking up the result for the two halves and in constant time, putting the results together to form the entry.

For example, for $index_r$, if a table is built for $index_{r/2}$, then one can easily construct the table for input strings of size r, in a constant number of operations per entry, as follows: Let I be the first half of the input and J be its second half. Add $weight_{r/2}(I)$ to each subword of $index_{r/2}(J)$ by adding $weight_{r/2}(I) * subword1$. to it. Let L be the string formed. Then concatenate the first $weight_{r/2}(I)$ subwords of $index(r/2)I$ with the first $weight_{r/2}(J)$ subwords of L.

Recall that the wordsize is $w = \lceil \lg n \rceil$. We cannot afford to build a table for $select_w$ and $selectS_w$ which takes inputs of $2w$ bits. But, as explained above, we can compute these functions as needed in constant time using table lookups of those functions on input size $w/2$ as described above.

We can now perform the operations needed for the data structures. (We omit the subscripts of the functions below, since they can be easily inferred from the size of their inputs.)

- Determine $|A(v)|$: $|A(v)| = weight(LCA(v))$.
- Create $smallList(v|p)$ from $smallList(p)$:
  $L \leftarrow select((LCA(p), LCA(v)))$;
  $smallList(v|p) \leftarrow selectS(L, smallList(p))$.
- Create $smallList(v|p)$ from $LCA(v)$ and $LCA(p)$
  $smallList(v|p) \leftarrow index(select(LCA(p), LCA(v)))$
- Insert tag k into positions i to j of $smallList(v|p)$ to form $smallList(v)$:
  Concatenate the first $i - 1$ subwords of $smallList(v|p)$ with the i through j subwords of $k * subword1$.
- Create $bigList(v|a)$ from $bigList(a)$, $LCA(v)$, and $LCA(a)$:
  Let $L = select(LCA(a), LCA(v))$;
  Partition L into strings L_i of h bits, and store each L_i in a word.
  Let $b_i(a)$ represent the ith word of $bigList(a)$;
  For each string L_i, do $selectS(L_i, b_i(a))$;
  Concatenate the outputs to form $bigList(v|a)$.
- Create $bigList(v|p)$ from $bigList(v|a)$ and $smallList(p)$ where p is the parent of v and $p \neq a$:
  Let f be the first subword of $bigList(p)$ which contains a tag, rather than a pointer.
  Replace all subwords in positions f or higher with $smallList(p)$.
  (Note that $A(v|p) = A(p)$ since this case only arises when $|A(v)| > |A(p)|$, so $smallList(v|p) = smallList(p)$.)
- Insert level k into the appropriate positions of $bigList(v|p)$ to form $bigList(v)$:
  Similar to item (2) above but must be done for each word in the list.

4.4 Analysis

When $|A(v)|$ is small, the cost of the overhead for performing the insertions by binary search is a constant. When $|A(v)| > wordsize/t = \Omega(\log n / \log\log n)$, the cost of the overhead is $O(\lg \lg n)$. Hence the implementation cost is $O(\lg(|A(v)|))$, which is proportional to the number of comparisons needed by the Komlós algorithm to find the heaviest edges in $2m$ half-paths of the tree in the worst case. Summed over all nodes, this comes to $O(n \log(\frac{m+n}{n}))$ as Komlós has shown.

The only additional costs are in forming the $LCA's$ which take $O(m+n)$ and in processing the tables which takes $O(n)$, and comparing the heaviest edges in each half-path, which takes $O(m)$.

Finally, to complete the minimum spanning tree verification algorithm, one compares the weight of each nontree edge to the weight of the heaviest tree edge in the tree path connecting its endpoints. for an additional $O(m)$ cost.

5   Conclusion and Open Problems

We have reduced Komlós's algorithm to the simpler case of the full branching tree. And, we have devised a novel data structure which gives the first algorithm with linear time overhead for its implementation.

It is still an open question as to whether one can find a linear time algorithm for a pointer machine. Such a result would imply a linear time algorithm for a pointer machine which can compute the lowest common ancestor. None is known for that problem which seems easier.

Given a static tree, the [SV] lowest common ancestor algorithm can process on-line query paths in constant time for each. An open problem is to solve the tree path problem in constant time per query path, where the query paths are given on-line.

The functions we use are in some sense natural. It is possible that they may be useful for implementing other algorithms which are not known to have linear implementations or whose implementations involve more specialized table lookup functions, as the DRT implementation did. (See [DRT] for references to some of these algorithms.)

Finally, any other applications of Theorem 1 would be of interest.

References

1. B. Dixon, M. Rauch, R. Tarjan, Verification and sensitivity analysis of minimum spanning trees in linear time, *SIAM Journal of Computing*, vol.21. Nov. 6, pp.1184-1192, (Dec. 1992).
2. D.Harel and R.E. Tarjan. Fast Algorithms for finding nearest common ancestors, *SIAM J. Computing*, vol. 13 (1984),pp.338-355.
3. D. Karger. Global min-cuts in RNC and other ramifications of a simple mincut algorithm," *Proc. 4th Annual ACM-SIAM Symposium on Discrete Algorithms*, 1993, pp.21-30.
4. P. Klein and R. Tarjan. A randomized linear-time algorithm for finding minimum spanning trees, *Twenty-Sixth Annual ACM Symposium on Theory of Computing*, (1994), pp. 9-15.
5. J. Komlós, Linear verification for spanning trees, *Combinatorica*, 5 (1985),pp.57-65.(Also in FOCS 1984.)

6. B. Schieber and U.Vishkin, On finding lowest common ancestors: simplification and parallelization, *SIAM J. Comput. 17* (1988), pp. 11253-1262.

7. R. Tarjan. Applications of path compressions on balanced trees, *J.Assoc. Comput. Mach. 26*(1979), pp.690-715.

8. R. Tarjan. *Data Structures and Network Algorithms*, CBMS-NSF Regional Conference Series in Applied Math. vol. 44, SIAM (1983).

On Approximation Properties of the Independent Set Problem for Degree 3 Graphs

Piotr Berman[1]* and Toshihiro Fujito[2]**

[1] Dept. of Computer Science and Engineering, The Pennsylvania State University,
University Park, PA 16802 USA
berman@cse.psu.edu
[2] Dept. of Electrical Engineering, Hiroshima University,
1-4-1 Kagamiyama, Higashi-Hiroshima 739 JAPAN
fujito@huis.hiroshima-u.ac.jp

Abstract. The main problem we consider in this paper is the Independent Set problem for bounded degree graphs. It is shown that the problem remains *MAX SNP*–complete when the maximum degree is bounded by 3. Some related problems are also shown to be *MAX SNP*–complete at the lowest possible degree bounds. Next we study better poly–time approximation of the problem for degree 3 graphs, and improve the previously best ratio, $\frac{5}{4}$, to arbitrarily close to $\frac{6}{5}$. This result also provides improved poly–time approximation ratios, $\frac{B+3}{5} + \epsilon$, for odd degree B.

1 Introduction

The area of efficient approximation algorithms for *NP*–hard optimization problems has recently seen dramatic progress with a sequence of breakthrough achievements. Even when restricted only to the area of constant bound approximation the following remarkable results have been obtained in the last few years. The subclass of *NP* optimization problems, called *MAX SNP*, consisting solely of constant ratio approximable problems was introduced and shown to have many natural complete problems by Papadimitriou and Yannakakis [14]. It turns out that actually all the *NP* optimization problems approximable within some constant factors belong to *MAX SNP* (via approximation preserving reduction) [11]. In 1992 the notion of *MAX SNP*–hardness became to bear much more significance when Arora et al. established that there do not exist polynomial time approximation schemes (PTAS) for *MAX SNP*–hard optimization problems unless $P = NP$ [1]. It has thus become possible to classify *qualitatively* many of *NP*–hard optimization problems according to their approximation properties, and as the area becomes more mature the research focus has to be shifted also to more *quantitative* classification of approximability.

The main problem we treat in this paper is a well–studied one: *bounded degree Independent Set problem* (called MAX IS-*B* when the maximum vertex degree

---

* This work was partially supported by NSF Grant CCR-9114545
** Part of this work was done while the author was at Dept. of CSE, Penn State.

of input graphs is bounded by B). This is one of the original and prototypical *MAX SNP*-complete problems [14], and its approximation ratio has been greatly improved over the years by a number of new techniques and analysis. The first nontrivial performance ratio B appeared implicitly in the Lovász's algorithmic proof [12] of Brooks' coloring theorem [5]. Hochbaum [9] developed a heuristic with a ratio $\frac{B}{2}$ using this coloring technique coupled with a method of Nemhauser and Trotter [13]. Halldórsson and Radhakrishnan [7] recently showed that the greedy heuristic actually delivers a better ratio, $\frac{B+2}{3}$. Very recently a progress in getting even better bounds became swift, probably in the wake of emergence of non–approximability results. Berman and Fürer [4] discovered new heuristics whose performance ratios are arbitrarily close to $\frac{B+3}{5}$ for even B and $\frac{B+3.25}{5}$ for odd B. Soon afterwards, Halldórsson and Radhakrishnan [8] obtained asymptotically better ratios, $\frac{B}{6} + o(1)$ and $O(\frac{B}{\log\log B})$.

In this paper we pay a special attention to MAX IS-3. MAX IS-B is NP-complete even when instance graphs are restricted to be cubic and planar [6]. It is also known that MAX IS (unbounded degree) admits a PTAS when graphs are planar [2]. In section 2 we will show, however, that MAX IS-3 is *MAX SNP*-complete. As by-products a few other problems (such as MAX 3–SET PACKING-2 and MAX TRIANGLE PACKING-4) are shown to remain *MAX SNP*-complete at the lowest possible degree bounds.

Next we study better approximation of MAX IS-3 in sections 3 through 5. The previously best ratio was $\frac{5}{4}$, and we improve it to arbitrarily close to $\frac{6}{5}$. Currently the best performance guarantee for MAX IS-B is given by Berman–Fürer's algorithm for B up to at least 613 [8]. The new ratio for MAX IS-3 provides further improvements on their ratios for odd B, matching their performance guarantee formula for even B. It should be also noted that with a method of Nemhauser–Trotter this result gives approximation of the Minimum Vertex Cover problem for graphs of degree B within a factor $2 - \frac{5}{B+3} + \epsilon$, which is an improvement over the previous best for small B.

2 *MAX SNP*-Completeness with the Lowest Degree Bounds

Many of *MAX SNP*-complete problems (especially graph problems) involve some parameters in their definitions, and even if they don't we may introduce such parameters to consider some restricted versions of original problems. It would be then important and interesting to know the exact boundaries of *MAX SNP*-completeness of those problems in terms of their parameters. Maximum Independent Set problem is known to remain *NP*-complete even when input graphs are restricted to be cubic and planar. However, for planar graphs (of unbounded degree) MAX IS admits a PTAS [2]. On the other hand we will show that it becomes *MAX SNP*-complete as soon as degree 3 nodes are allowed.

MAX 3SAT-B is a restriction of **MAX 3SAT** s.t. in any instance the number of occurrences of any variable is bounded by B. We reduce MAX 3SAT-B to MAX IS-3 using the "ring of trees" construction of Kann [10].

Theorem 1. *MAX IS-3 is MAX SNP-complete.*

Proof(Sketch). Suppose a variable u occurs d times in a given 3SAT–B instance. Let K be a large enough power of two (it suffices to take $K = 2^{\lfloor \log_2(\frac{3}{2}B+1) \rfloor}$). Prepare K identical cycles of length $2d$ (called "rings") and sequentially index the nodes in each cycle from 1 to $2d$. Also prepare $2d$ complete binary trees with K leaves each. Join these rings and trees by overlapping, in the identical fashion, leaves of each tree with nodes of the same index from each ring. Label the roots of these trees as u_i and $\bar{u}_i, i = 1, \cdots, d$, alternatively in the order of their indices. Construct a "ring of trees" this way for every variable.

Each clause c will be represented by a clique of size $|c|$. Suppose the ith occurrence of a variable u is in a clause c. Connect $\bar{u}_i$ or u_i, depending on whether u appeaars in positive or not, to the corresponding node in c-clique. This way clause cliques and rings of trees are connected together. Note that every node has its degree bounded by 3.

Let A be a (disjoint) union of rings of trees corresponding to all variables. An independent set is said to be *consistent* if it includes all u_i's and none of $\bar{u}_i$'s, or vice versa, for every variable u. For a MAX IS–3 instance thus constructed it can be shown that 1) An independent set maximum in A is cosistent, and 2) An independent set maximum in A is larger than an independent set not maximum in A. We deduce that an optimal solution for MAX IS–3 consists of a maximum independent set in A plus a collection of nodes, one each from a clique corresponding to a satisfied clause in an optimal solution for MAX 3SAT–B. It follows that an optimal value is scaled up only by some constant factor because the size of A can be bounded by K and $\sum d \leq 3 \cdot$ (number of clauses) and at least half of clauses can be always satisfied.

Secondly, from any MAX IS–3 solution we can find a consistent solution of no smaller size, and hence, a solution for MAX 3SAT–B. The value of a solution thus obtained is no further away from the optimum than the original one. $\square$

There are some other *MAX SNP*–complete problems whose structures are closely related to MAX IS–3 and MAX IS–B. Consider for instance the following problems:

MAX 3–DIMENSIONAL MATCHING–B Given three sets W, X, Y and a set $M \subseteq W \times X \times Y$ s.t. the number of occurrences of any element of $W, X,$ or Y in M is bounded by B, find the largest matching, i.e., a subset $M' \subseteq M$ s.t. no two elements of M' agree in any coordinate.

MAX 3–SET PACKING–B Given a collection C of subsets of a set S where every $c \in C$ contains at most three elements and every element $s \in S$ is contained in at most B of the subsets in C, find a largest collection of mutually disjoint sets in C.

MAX TRIANGLE PACKING–B Given a graph of maximum vertex degree bounded by B find a largest collection of mutually (vertex) disjoint 3–cliques.

Using *MAX SNP*-completeness of 3–DIMENSIONAL MATCHING–3 Kann showed that MAX IS–5, MAX 3–SET PACKING–3 and MAX TRIANGLE

PACKING–6 are *MAX SNP*–complete as well [10]. Reducing MAX IS–3 to these problems instead, we can improve the degree bounds in these problems to the best possible ones:

Corollary 2. *MAX 3-SET PACKING-2 and MAX TRIANGLE PACKING-4 are MAX SNP-complete.*

3 Better Approximation of MAX IS–3

The rest of the paper is devoted to proving the next theorem:

Theorem 3. *MAX IS-3 can be approximated within a factor $\frac{6}{5} + \epsilon$ in time $O(n^{2+\frac{1}{\epsilon}})$.*

Our algorithm, which is the subject of section 4, extends the idea of Berman and Fürer's heuristic given in [4]. However, to improve the existing approximation ratio we apply some general reductions, old and new, and construct solutions with care. Consequently much more careful and involved analysis is called for, and it will be given in section 5.

When combined with our algorithm for MAX IS–3, Berman–Fürer's algorithm for MAX IS–B does better for every odd B, giving the same performance guarantee formula as the one for even B. Therefore,

Corollary 4. *MAX IS-B can be approximated in poly-time within a factor arbitrarily close to $\frac{B+3}{5}$ for all $B \geq 2$.*

Definitions and Notation. For a graph $G = (V, E)$ and a node set $U \subseteq V$, $G(U)$ denotes a subgraph of G induced by U. The *neighborhood set* of U, denoted $N(U)$, is the set of nodes adjacent to U. The degree of a node $v \in V$ is $d(v) = |N(v)|$. A neighborhood set and degree can be given conditional to an arbitrary node set (instead of V). $N_W(U)$ denotes $N(U) \cap W$, and $d_W(v)$ is $|N_W(v)|$. An acronym *MIS* will be used for a maximum independent set. The *independence number* of a graph G is the cardinality of a MIS in G, and denoted $\alpha(G)$.

Our local search technique is based on augmentation of an independent set U by a node set I called an *improvement*. I is an improvement for U if $G(I)$ is connected and the symmetric difference $U \oplus I$ is a larger independent set. An *s-improvement* is the one that adds s and removes $s - 1$ from U, and a solution is *s-optimal* if it has no s-improvement.

4 Approximation Algorithm

We adopt two main ingredients of Berman–Fürer's algorithm for MAX IS–B: The first method is to find and apply every s-improvement to a current solution A, where $s = O(k \log n)$ for $|V| = n$ (Note: because the size of improvements is $O(\log n)$ the algorithm runs in polynomial time, as one can show that the number of "candidates" for s-improvements of any $U \subseteq V$ is smaller than $n3^s$). The second method is to find a MIS in $V \setminus A$, that is larger than A (Note: after failing with the first method, $G(V \setminus A)$ is a degree 2 graph). The resulting solution thus satisfies the two properties: (1) A is s-optimal, and (2) $\alpha(G(V \setminus A)) \leq |A|$.

The properties (1) and (2) assure that $(\frac{5}{4} + \frac{1}{k})|A| \geq \alpha(G)$; moreover, this inequality is tight. To improve the performance, we will assure that the output satisfies several additional properties that will enable us to prove a stronger inequality. Our algorithm (see Figure 1) has the following new features;

1. We add the first **Repeat**-loop as the preprocessing. As a result, we reduce the problem, without loss of approximation quality, to the case where
   (a) all nodes have degree 2 or 3, and nodes of degree 2 form an independent set (Branchy reduction).
   (b) $\alpha(G) \leq \frac{1}{2}|V|$ (Nemhauser-Trotter reduction).
   (c) for every node subset $U \subseteq V$ of size at most k, U is *not* a MIS in $G(U \cup N(U))$ (Small Commitment reduction).
2. Initial solutions are constructed in a special manner. First, all of the degree 2 nodes are collected in set A_1 (after Branchy reduction, A_1 is independent), and then, an independent set A_2 is found, recursively, from $G(V \setminus (A \cup N(A)))$. The union $A_1 \cup A_2$ is used as an initial solution.
   This feature allows us to analyze the performance of the algorithm only for the case when at most $\frac{4}{5}$ of degree 2 nodes belong to some MIS of G.
3. Before starting the local improvement procedure (in the second **Repeat**-loop), a current solution is replaced by an independent set A of no smaller size s.t. $G(V \setminus A)$ is acyclic.

Branchy Reduction. A graph G is called *branchy* if every node has degree 2 or more, and no two degree 2 nodes are adjacent (the notion of branchy graphs and reduction was used before in the context of weighted feedback vertex set problem, see [3]). The branchy reduction of an instance graph G for MAX IS is described as follows:

1. While there is a node of degree 0 or 1, remove it (along with its neighbor, if any) from G and store in set S.
2. While there is a path (v_1, v_2, v_3, v_4) where both v_2 and v_3 have degree 2, remove v_2 and v_3 from G, insert edge $\{v_1, v_4\}$ and store the path in set P.

The next lemma states that branchy reduction is indeed a lossless reduction.

Lemma 5. *Let $G' = (V', E')$ be a branchy reduction of $G = (V, E)$, and let S and P be the sets formed in that reduction. Then,*

1. *For any independent set A' for G', an independent set A for G can be constructed in linear time s.t. $|A| = |A'| + |S| + |P|$.*
2. *There is an optimal independent set A for G s.t. $A \cap V'$ is an independent set for G' with $|A| - |S| - |P|$ elements.*

```
Input: A degree 3 graph G = (V, E).
Output: An approximation of a maximum independent set.

   Repeat
        oldsize ← |V|
        Do Branchy reduction
        Do Nemhauser–Trotter reduction
        Do Small Commitment reduction
   until |V| = oldsize /* until no more reduction is applicable */
   A₁ ← {v ∈ V|d(v) = 2}
   A₂ ← a recursively computed independent set in G(V \ (A₁ ∪ N(A₁)))
   A ← A₁ ∪ A₂
   Repeat
        oldsize ← |A|
        Do Acyclic Complement procedure
        Do all possible improvements of size 3k log n to A
        Find an optimal solution A₃ in G(V \ A)
        If A₃ larger than A then A ← A₃
   until |A| = oldsize
```

Fig. 1. A $\frac{6}{5}$-Approximation Algorithm for MAX IS-3

Nemhauser–Trotter reduction. Nemhauser and Trotter [13] studied the solution to linear program relaxation of MAX IS problem, and showed that any graph $G(V)$ can be reduced to $G(V')$, without loss of approximation quality, s.t. $\alpha(G(V')) \leq \frac{1}{2}|V'|$.

Small Commitment reduction. This reduction repetitively looks for the following kind of situation: for some $A \subseteq V, |A| \leq k$, and A is a MIS for $G(A \cup N(A))$. If found we proceed exactly like in Nemhauser–Trotter reduction.

Acyclic Complement procedure. Given an independent set I in a connected degree 3 graph $G = (V, E)$, which is not K_4, this procedure finds an independent set I' in polynomial time s.t. 1) $|I'| \geq |I|$ and 2) $G(V \setminus I')$ is acyclic (details omitted in this short version).

5 Algorithm Analysis and Approximation Ratio

5.1 Node Type Classification and Normalization

To analyze the structural properties of approximate solutions produced by our algorithm, it will be convenient to compare the relative sizes of node subsets defined by a solution and one fixed optimal solution. Given a graph $G = (V, E)$, which is obtained from an input graph by preprocessing, V is partitioned into four sets $A, B, C,$ and D, with the following interpretations:

- $A \cup C$ is an independent set constructed by our algorithm (A for "approximate" solution).
- $B \cup C$ is a maximum independent set (B for "best" solution and C for "common" portion).
- D is $V \setminus (A \cup B \cup C)$, i.e., the set of remaining nodes.

Assuming that an approximate solution, $A \cup C$, is 1–optimal, the following observations are easy to verify;

1. an A–node cannot be adjacent to $A \cup C$ and must be adjacent to B.
2. a B–node cannot be adjacent to $B \cup C$ and must be adjacent to A.
3. a C–node must be nonadjacent to $A \cup B \cup C$.
4. a D–node must be adjacent to both $A \cup C$ and $B \cup C$.

Based on the partition of V thus defined, every node in D will be further classified according to its "connectivity pattern"; if a node is of degree 3 (2) and its three neighbors belong to node sets $X, Y,$ and Z (X and Y), respectively, we say the node has a type $[XYZ]$ ($[XY]$).

The use of preprocessing and the acyclic complement procedures as described in section 4 is to "normalize" an input graph and the final solution:

Lemma 6. *The node sets $A, B, C,$ and D satisfy the following properties:*

Norm 1. *C is maximal (given our solution, we consider a MIS with a maximum overlap).*
Norm 2. *$B \cup D$, the complement of a solution $A \cup C$, contains no cycles.*
Norm 3. *Degree 2 nodes form an independent set in graph G.*
Norm 4. *Every node in A has at least 2 neighbors in B.*
Norm 5. *There is no node of type $[AB]$.*

Now because of **Norm 5** each node in D is classified into one of the following types:

degree 2. $[AC][BC][CC][CD]$
degree 3. $[AAB]\ [AAC]\ [ABB]\ [ABC]\ [ABD]\ [ACC]\ [ACD]\ [BBC]\ [BCC]$
$[BCD]\ [CCC]\ [CCD]\ [CDD]$

5.2 Approximation Ratio of $\frac{6}{5}$

Denote the cardinalities of the sets, $A, B, C,$ and D by respective lower case letters, and set $i = b - a$. Also denote the number of degree 2 nodes in a set X by x_2. The number of D–nodes of type $[XYZ]$ ($[XY]$) is denoted $[xyz]$ ($[xy]$).

The (in)equalities given in Figure 2 will be proven in the subsections below. Assume for now that all these (in)equalities hold. Summing them up with the respective multiplicative factors of $\frac{7}{13}, \frac{6}{13}, \frac{12}{13}, 1, \frac{3}{13}, \frac{4}{13}, -\frac{3}{13},$ and $\frac{16}{13}$, yields the inequality

$$\frac{k+1}{k}(a+c) \geq 5\frac{1}{13}i + \frac{1}{13}(a_2 + c_2 + 27[aab] + 6[abb] + 10[abd] + 33[aac] + 6[acc]$$
$$+ 10[acd] + 13[cdd] + 6[bbc] + 20[ac] + [bc] + 14[cd])$$

Ineq 1. $\frac{k+1}{k}c \geq 3[bc] + 2[bbc] + [bcd] + [cdd] + [cd] + [bcc] + [cc] - (2[acc] + [aac] + [abc] + [acd] + [ac])$

Ineq 2. $\frac{k+1}{k}c \geq [bbc] + [bc] + [bcc] + [cc] + \frac{1}{2}([bcd] + [cdd] + [cd] + [ccd])$

Ineq 3. $c \geq i + [ccc] + [acc] + [aac] + [ac] + [cc] + \frac{1}{2}([cdd] + [ccd] + [acd] + [cd])$

Ineq 4. $\frac{k+1}{k}a \geq 3i + a_2 + 2[aab] + 2[aac] + [abb] + [abd] + [acc] + [acd] + [abc] + [ac]$

Ineq 5. $d \geq c + i$

Ineq 6. $b_2 = 3i + a_2 + ([aab] + 2[aac] + [acc] + [acd] + [ac]) - ([abb] + 2[bbc] + [bcc] + [bcd] + [bc])$

Ineq 7. $3c - c_2 = 3[ccc] + 2([acc] + [bcc] + [ccd] + [cc]) + [aac] + [abc] + [bbc] + [acd] + [bcd] + [cdd] + [ac] + [bc] + [cd]$

Ineq 8. $a_2 + [bc] + [cc] \geq \frac{1}{4}(b_2 + c_2 + [ac] + [cd])$

Fig. 2. List of inequalities relating node set sizes

Since all the variables are nonnegative, it follows that

$$\frac{k+1}{k}(a + c) \geq 5\frac{1}{13}i.$$

Therefore,

$$\frac{|B \cup C|}{|A \cup C|} = \frac{b+c}{a+c} = \frac{a+c+i}{a+c} \leq 1 + \frac{1}{\frac{k}{k+1}5\frac{1}{13}} < \frac{6}{5} + \frac{1}{5k}$$

and the desired ratio is obtained.

Proof of Ineq 1. The method of "local accounting" used here is also applied to proving **Ineq 2** and **4**. In a nutshell, we assign potential to every node in $C \cup D$ so that the inequality in question states that the total potential of $C \cup D$ cannot be positive. We will partition $C \cup D$ into "connected components" to study each of them one at a time. A component with positive potential will either contain an s–improvement, or a k–commitment, or we will be able to "factor it out" and reduce the problem to a smaller one.

There are 14 different D-node types that are adjacent to C; for the sake of the proof we name them as follows:

- *enforcers*
  - *solitaires:* $[BC], [BBC]$
  - *half-solitaires:* $[BCD], [CDD], [CD]$
  - *pairs:* $[BCC], [CC]$
- *absorbers:* $[ACC], [AAC], [ABC], [ACD], [AC]$
- *others:* $[CCC], [CCD]$

We will view pairs as "edges" connecting their neighbors in C; in this manner we divide C into connected components. Each enforcer will have a weight, which is initially 1; larger weights result from reductions that "factor out" a connected components. The potential is assigned to nodes of $C \cup D$ as follows:

- enforcer of type $[\alpha]$: $c_\alpha - \frac{w-1}{k}$ where c_α is the coefficient of $[\alpha]$ in **Ineq 1** and w is the weight.
- absorber of type $[\alpha]$: c_α (note that it is negative)
- C-node: $-\frac{k+1}{k}$
- other nodes: 0

Now **Ineq 1** is equivalent to $p(C \cup D) \le 0$.

Definition 7.

1. For a node set Y, $p(Y)$ denotes the sum of potentials of nodes in Y.
2. If $U \subseteq D$ then $I_U = U \cup N_C(U)$; if set U is independent, I_U is the improvement candidate defined by U.
3. If $U \subseteq D$ then $w(U)$ is the maximum weight of an independent subsest of U that consists of enforces only; given $X \subseteq C$, such a subset would provide "the best candidate" to define an improvement containing X.
4. For a subset X of C define $N_e(X)$ to be the set of enforcers adjacent to X and $ab(X)$ to be the number of edges that join X with absorbers.

We decompose $p(C \cup D)$ into a sum of expressions that refer to some connected fragments of $C \cup D$. Let X be a connected component of C defined by pairs. Let $N_e(X)$ be the set of enforcers adjacent to X and $ab(X)$ be the number of edges from X to adjacent absorbers. It is easy to see that $p(C \cup D)$ is the sum, over the components X of C, of

$$p_X = p(X \cup N_e(X)) - ab(X).$$

If no p_X is positive we are done. Otherwise, we apply a case analysis to positive p_X's; to classify the cases, we define $w_X = w(N_e(X))$.

· First we consider the cases when $w_X \le k$. Let $x = |X|$. Obviously, $N_e(X)$ contains at least $x - 1$ pairs. If $N_e(X)$ contains $x + 1$ (or more) pairs, these pairs, together with X, form a k–improvement, a contradiction. We get a similar contradiction if $N_e(X)$ contains x pairs and a (half-)solitaire, or $x - 1$ pairs and either of: 3 half-solitaires, one solitaire and one half-solitaire, two solitaires, or two nonadjacent half-solitaires. If $N_e(X)$ consists of pairs only, and $|N_e(X)| \le x$ then $p_X < 0$. As a conclusion we consider only the cases when $N_e(X)$ consists of $x - 1$ pairs and either one of: a solitaire, or two half-solitaires adjacent to each other.

Consider first the case when $N_e(X)$ consists of $x - 1$ pairs and a solitaire of type $[BC]$ (i.e., with coefficient $2 - (w - 1)/k$). We will remove X, $N_e(X)$ and the adjacent edges from consideration and assign the potential p_X (if positive) to nodes of type $[CCC]$ or $[CCD]$ that are adjacent to X. Below we analyze why it works.

As a technical preliminary, observe that at least two edges go from X to non-enforcers: if $X = \{u\}$ for some u, then u has three neighbors as a neighbor of a degree 2 node (**Norm 3**), hence two non-enforcer neighbors; otherwise (X,pairs) is a tree with at least two leaves and each leaf has a non-enforcer neighbor, in particular, a leaf adjacent to $[BC]$ has three neighbors—one pair, one $[BC]$ and one non–enforcer.

Next, one can easily compute that $p_X = 2 - w_X/k - ab(X)$. Thus if $ab(X) = 2$, $p_X < 0$ and we are satisfied. If $ab(X) = 1$, then an edge goes from X to a $[CCC]$ or $[CCD]$ node, say u. If u is of type $[CCC]$, then after removing $X \cup N_e(X)$ from considration u appears to be $[CC]$, a pair. As we observed above, pairs and other enforcers lead to small improvements if adjacent to the same component of C in excessive numbers. Assume that after removing $X \cup N_e(X)$, a set $I \subset C \cup N_e(C) \cup \{u\}$ becomes an improvement. If $u \notin I$, then I was an improvement even before the removal, otherwise $I \cup X \cup N_e(X)$ is an improvement. Thus an s-improvement containing u after the removal translates into $(s + w_X)$-improvement that is "genuine".

Therefore, after the removal we will measure the improvement size correctly if we give u the weight of $1 + w_X$. We also redefine $p(u)$ from 0 to $1 - w_X/k$. This way the total potential is preserved, and the potential of u agrees with the formula for pairs.

Observe that we can handle identically the case when u is of type $[CCD]$; now u appears to be a half-solitaire after the removal, and the potential of the half-solitaires has the same formula. In such cases we will say that u is *promoted* (from "other" to a pair or a half-solitaire).

Finally, when $ab(X) = 0$, X is adjacent to two "other" nodes and they both can be promoted. In the short version of this paper we skip the technicalities involved in the assignment of potential and weight in this case.

The case when $N_e(X)$ consists of $x - 1$ pairs and a solitaire of type $[BBC]$ is similar, only simpler. Now, $p_X = 1 - w_X/k - ab(X)$ and at least one edge goes from X to non-enforcers. If $ab(X) > 0$, then $p_X < 0$, otherwise the edge mentioned above goes to an "other" node and we can perform a promotion.

The case when $N_e(X)$ consists of $x - 1$ pairs and two half-solitaires adjacent to each other is very similar to the latter, but for one additional subcase—when no edge joins X with non-enforcers, i.e., when $N_e(X) = N(X)$. Let S be a maximum independent set in $X \cup N(X)$. If $|S| > x$, then $S \oplus X$ is a k-improvement—and a contradiction. If $|S| = x$, then X is a MIS for $X \cup N(X)$. Since $|X| = x \le k$, such situation would be eliminated by the Small Commitment reduction, so again, a contradiction. Observe that it is not possible that this situation occurred only after we performed some removals—removing a component does not change the set of neighbors of another (only the classification of the neighbors may change).

Now to prove **Ineq 1** it remains to handle the case when a component X has weight $w_X \ge k$ and positive potential p_X. It is easy to see that in this case $X \cup N_e(X)$ contains an improvement. Using a similar reasoning to that of Berman and Fürer [4] we can show that $X \cup N_e(X)$ contains a $(4k \log n)$-improvement. In a nutshell, we very easily find such improvements if even $1/(k \log n)$ proportion of $N_e(X)$ consists of (half-)solitaires: such an improvement is a path in $X \cup N_e(X)$ that joins two solitaires via C-nodes and pairs. In the remaining case $N_e(X)$ contains roughly $(1 + 1/k)x$ pairs and we can use Lemma 3.1 of [4]. [The detailed reasoning will be in the full version which contains an accounting necessitated by our "weight" system.]

Proof of Ineq 2. The proof of **Ineq 2** is quite similar to that of **Ineq 1**, but simpler, as we do not use the promotions. It is omitted in this short version.

Proof of Ineq 4. This inequality is proven in two stages. First, nodes in B with only one neighbor in A are called *solitaires* and those with exactly two neighbors are called *pairs*. Let $b_{(1)}$ and $b_{(2)}$ be their respective numbers. First we prove

Lemma 8. *If there is no improvement of size* $\max\{3k\log n, 4k + 2k\log n\}$,

$$2b_{(1)} + b_{(2)} \leq \frac{k+1}{k}a$$

The proof is similar to that of **Ineq 1**, but simpler because we do not have half-solitaires, solitaires with potential 3 and absorbers, and we have only one type of "other" node: $[AAA]$. The mechanism of promotions works as before, with one exception. Given a component X of A defined by pairs that is adjacent to $x - 1$ pairs and one solitaire ($x = |X|$), we must argue that this component is adjacent to at least one "other" node. When we dealt with components of C, this followed from the fact that the algorithm uses Small Commitment reduction, but now this argument is not applicable as X can have neighbors in D, and these cannot be promoted.

Nevertheless, we still can obtain a contradiction. Assuming that X is not adjacent to any "other" node, we have $|N_B(X)| = x$, consequently, $C \cup X \cup B \setminus N(X)$ is an independent set of the same size as $C \cup B$, but with a larger overlap with "our" independent set $C \cup A$, and that contradicts the way we have chosen $C \cup B$ among maximum independent sets of G (**Norm 1**).

Given Lemma 8, it suffices to show that

$$2b_{(1)} + b_{(2)} = 3i + a_2 + 2[aab] + 2[aac] + [abb] + [abd] + [acc] + [acd] + [abc] + [ac].$$

This fact follows simply by expanding the equality $\sum_{u \in A} d_B(u) = \sum_{u \in B} d_A(u)$.

Proofs of the remaining inequalities. **Ineq 3** follows from the fact that our solution, $A \cup C$, is at least as large as the largest independent set in $B \cup D$. Because $B \cup D$ contains no cycles the latter can be estimated as B, plus all the nodes in D without neighbors in $B \cup D$ (types $[CCC], [ACC], [AAC], [AC]$ and $[CC]$) plus half of the nodes in D without neighbors in B but with some in D (types $[CCD], [CDD], [ACD]$ and $[CD]$). Note that D contains no odd–length cycles because of **Norm 2**.

Ineq 5 follows from the fact that we use Nemhauser–Trotter reduction, consequently, the size of a MIS, $a + i + c$, does not exceed one half of the total number of nodes, i.e., $2a + i + c + d$.

Ineq 6 is an equality obtained from $\sum_{u \in A} d_B(u) = \sum_{u \in B} d_A(u)$ and $b = a + i$.

Similarly, Ineq 7 is an equality obtained from $\sum_{u \in C} d(u) = \sum_{u \in C} d_D(u) = \sum_{u \in D} d_C(u)$.

Lastly, Ineq 8 uses the fact that we reduced the problem to the case when no MIS contains more than 4/5 of degree 2 nodes (and Norm 5).

References

1. S. Arora, C. Lund, R. Motwani, M. Sudan and M. Szegedy. Proof verification and intractability of approximation problems. In *33rd IEEE Symp. on Foundations of Computer Science*, 1992.
2. B.S. Baker. Approximation algorithms for NP–complete problems on planar graphs. *Journal of the Association for Computing Machinery*, 41:153–180, 1994.
3. R. Bar-Yehuda, D. Geiger, J. Naor and R. M. Roth. Approximation algorithms for the vertex feedback set problem with applications to constraint satisfaction and bayesian inference. In *Proc. of the 5th Annual ACM-SIAM Symp. on Discrete Algorithms*, pages 344–354, 1994.
4. P. Berman and M. Fürer. Approximating maximum independent set in bounded degree graphs. In *Proc. of the 5th Annual ACM-SIAM Symp. on Discrete Algorithms*, 1994.
5. R.L. Brooks. On coloring the nodes of a network. In *Proc. Cambridge Philos. Soc.*, volume 37, pages 194–197, 1941.
6. M.R. Garey, D.S. Johnson and L. Stockmeyer. Some simplified NP–complete graph problems. *Theoretical Computer Science*, 1:237–267, 1976.
7. M.M. Halldórsson and J. Radhakrishnan. Greed is good: Approximating independent sets in sparse and bounded-degree graphs. In *Proc. of the 26th Annual ACM Symp. on Theory of Computing*, 1994.
8. M.M. Halldórsson and J. Radhakrishnan. Improved approximations of independent sets in bounded–degree graphs. In *SWAT 94, 6th Scandinavian Workshop on Algorithm Theory*, 1994.
9. D.S. Hochbaum. Efficient bounds for the stable set, vertex cover and set packing problems. *Discrete Applied Mathematics*, 6:243–254, 1983.
10. V. Kann. Maximum bounded 3–dimensional matching is MAX SNP–complete. *Information Processing Letters*, 37:27–35, 1991.
11. S. Khanna, R. Motwani, M. Sudan and U. Vazirani. On syntactic versus computation views of approximability. In *35th IEEE Symp. on Foundations of Computer Science*, pages 819–830, 1994.
12. L. Lovász. Three short proofs in graph theory. *Journal of Combinatorial Theory (B)*, 19:269–271, 1975.
13. G.L. Nemhauser and L.E. Trotter Jr. Vertex packings: structural properties and algorithms. *Mathematical Programming*, 8:232–248, 1975.
14. C. Papadimitriou and M. Yannakakis. Optimization, approximation and complexity classes. *Journal of Computer and System Sciences*, 43:425–440, 1991.

Approximation of Constraint Satisfaction via Local Search

(Extended Abstract)

Hoong Chuin LAU*

Dept. of Computer Science, Tokyo Institute of Technology
2-12-1 Ookayama, Meguro-ku, Tokyo 152, Japan

1 Introduction

The Constraint Satisfaction Problem (CSP) is defined by a set of variables, their domains and binary constraints governing assignment of values to variables. The output is an assignment which maximizes some linear function of the satisfied constraints. Many problems in Artificial Intelligence and Operations Research may be represented by instances of CSP, such as problems in machine vision, temporal reasoning, scheduling and timetabling.

We consider two problems in CSP, namely, the Maximum CSP (MAX-CSP) which seeks to maximize the total number of satisfied constraints, and the Weighted CSP (W-CSP) which seeks to maximize the sum of weights of satisfied constraints. Clearly, W-CSP is a generalization of the Maximum Cut problem and other related problems. While the Maximum Cut problem is well-studied in approximation [6, 14], surprisingly little work has been done to approximate the CSP. Recent related works are given as follows. Amaldi and Kann [1] considered the approximation of of finding maximum feasible subsystems of linear systems. Their problem may be seen as MAX-CSP with real number domains. They showed that even if the domains are 2-valued (i.e. {-1,+1}), and the constraints are binary and restricted to arithmetic inequalities of certain forms, the problem remains MAX SNP-hard. This means that there exists a constant $c \geq 0$ such that the problem cannot be approximated in polynomial time with ratio c unless P=NP. Khanna et al. [9] considered the approximation of W-CSP with 2-valued domains but the constraints are t-ary constraints (i.e. they connect t or less variables) for some fixed t. They showed that, for any fixed t, their problem is approximable within a factor of $1/2^t$ by local search with a fairly complicated objective function. Earlier, Berman and Schnitger [2], while studying the Maximum Independent Set problem, had obtained the same bound for a weaker version of Khanna et al.'s problem.

---

* email: hclau@cs.titech.ac.jp

In this paper, we will investigate the approximability of MAX-CSP and W-CSP by a simple local search strategy. The paper proceeds as follows. We show that MAX-CSP is MAX SNP-hard even in a restricted case. We prove tight approximation bounds for MAX-CSP and extend the analysis to handle W-CSP. Using the local optimal solutions of MAX-CSP, we devise an efficient partitioning strategy for approximating the bounded-degree the Maximum Cut and Graph Coloring problems. Finally, we give non-approximability results which show that our analysis is tight.

2 Preliminaries

We introduce terms and notations which will be used.

The *domain* of a variable i is the set of assignable values for i. An *assignment* σ is a mapping of variables to values in their respective domains. For technical simplicity, we assume that all domains have a fixed size k and are equal to the set $K = \{1, 2, \ldots, k\}$. All our results will still hold for varying-sized domains as long as the size of the largest domain does not exceed k. A *constraint* between two variables i_1 and i_2, denoted $R(i_1, i_2)$, is a binary relation on $K \times K$ which defines the *consistent* value pairs, i.e. the pairs of values that can be assigned to i_1 and i_2 simultaneously. Let σ_i denote the value assigned to the variable i. Given an assignment σ, a constraint $R(i_1, i_2)$ is said to be *satisfied* by σ if $(\sigma_{i_1}, \sigma_{i_2})$ is in $R(i_1, i_2)$.

Definition 1. The Maximum Constraint Satisfaction Problem (MAX-CSP) is defined as follows:

> **INSTANCE**: Variables $V = \{1, 2, ..., n\}$, integer k, and a set of constraints between variables in V.
> **SOLUTION**: An assignment such that the number of satisfied constraints is maximized.

Definition 2. The Weighted Maximum Constraint Satisfaction Problem (W-CSP) is the weighted version of MAX-CSP defined as follows:

> **INSTANCE**: Variables $V = \{1, 2, ..., n\}$, integer k, and a set of constraints R between variables in V, and a weight function $w : R \longrightarrow \mathbb{N}$.
> **SOLUTION**: An assignment such that the weighted sum of satisfied constraints is maximized.

Instances of CSP can be represented graphically. Precisely, the nodes and edges of a constraint graph represent the variables and constraints respectively.

Let m be the number of edges of the graph. Let m_i be the degree of i, i.e. the number of edges incident to variable i.

Definition 3. A constraint $R(i_1, i_2)$ is said to be *arc(r)-consistent* $(1 \le r \le k)$ iff, for all values $j_1 \in K$, there exists at least r values $j_2 \in K$ such that (j_1, j_2) is in $R(i_1, i_2)$. A constraint is *arc-consistent* iff it is arc(1)-consistent. A MAX-CSP instance is arc(r)-consistent iff all its constraints are arc(r)-consistent.

The notion of *arc-consistency* is well-studied and it is known that if a CSP instance x is *satisfiable* (i.e. all its constraints can be simultaneously satisfied), then we can construct an arc-consistent CSP instance x' such that:

1. all variables in x are in x';
2. each variable in x has a domain of size at most k;
3. x' contains a subset of the constraints in x; and
4. for any assignment σ valid for x' on x, a constraint in x' satisfied by σ is also satisfied in x, and all constraints not in x' are satisfied by σ.

Such transformation can be done in $O(nk^2)$ time [5].

Definition 4. The *Maximum k-Cut problem* (MAX k-CUT) is defined as follows:

> **INSTANCE**: Graph $G = (V, E)$, a weight function $w : E \longrightarrow \mathbb{N}$, and
> $k \in \{2, \ldots, |V|\}$.
> **SOLUTION**: A partition of V into k disjoint sets $V_1, V_2, \ldots, V_k$ such that the sum of weights of edges between the disjoint sets (*cut-edges*) is maximized.

The unweighted MAX k-CUT is MAX k-CUT with all weights equal 1.

The NOT-EQUAL constraint is a type of constraint such that the values of each pair must not be equal to each other. For example, for $k = 3$, the NOT-EQUAL constraint would be $\{(1,2), (1,3), (2,1), (2,3), (3,1), (3,2)\}$. Clearly, MAX k-CUT is equivalent to W-CSP with all NOT-EQUAL constraints. Let MAX-CSP(k, r) (resp. W-CSP(k, r)) denote MAX-CSP (resp. W-CSP) with domain size k and arc(r)-consistency.

Theorem 5. *MAX-CSP(k, r) is MAX SNP-hard, even for $k \ge 2$ and $r = k - 1$.*

Proof. This can be shown by a simple L-reduction from the unweighted MAX 2-CUT, which is known to be MAX SNP-complete [11]. Let graph G be an arbitrary instance x of unweighted MAX 2-CUT. Construct an instance y of MAX-CSP(2,1) with the same constraint graph G, domain size $k = 2$ and all constraints to be NOT-EQUAL constraints. Clearly, y represents x exactly and costs are preserved. □

Definition 6. Let A be an algorithm which computes a feasible solution $A(x)$ for any input x of a maximization problem X. We say that A *approximates* X *within* ϵ ($0 < \epsilon \leq 1$) iff for all inputs x, A computes a solution whose value is at least ϵ times the value of the optimal solution in polynomial time with respect to the size of x. That is, the performance ratio,

$$\phi_A = \min_x \frac{c_A(x)}{OPT(x)} \geq \epsilon$$

where $c_A(x)$ and $OPT(x)$ denote the value of the solution computed by A and optimal value for input x respectively. On the contrary, we say that A *cannot approxmiate* X *within* ϵ iff there exists an input x such that the above inequality does not hold.

3 Local Search Algorithm

In this section, we present a simple local search algorithm LS for solving MAX-CSP.

Let x be an instance of MAX-CSP with n variables m constraints and domain size k. Let Σ be the set containing all possible n-tuple assignments. Let σ and σ' be two arbitrary assignments in Σ. Let $f : \Sigma \longrightarrow \mathbb{N}$ be the objective function where $f(\sigma)$ counts the number of constraints which are satisfied by σ. The Hamming distance between σ and σ' is the number of variables whose assigned values are different. We say that σ and σ' are neighbors to each other iff their Hamming distance is exactly 1. We say that σ is a *local optimum* of x iff for all neighors σ' of σ, $f(\sigma') \leq f(\sigma)$.

Let Algorithm LS be the local hill-climbing procedure with objective function f. Thus, the worst-case time complexity of LS is $O(mt)$, where t is the time needed to find a better neighbor. By naive implementation $t = O(nk)$, and thus LS takes at most $O(mnk)$ time. Very often, if the problem is restricted, then by careful implementation, we can reduce the complexity of t. For instance, if the maximum degree of the constraint graph is Δ, then using lookup tables, t can be reduced to $O(\Delta k)$.

4 Approximation Results

In this section, we analyse the performance guarantee of MAX-CSP by counting the absolute number of constraints which can be satisfied by a locally optimal solution. By solving instances of MAX-CSP, we derive improved results for bounded-degree MAX k-CUT and graph coloring. Finally, we extend our result to approximate W-CSP in polynomial time.

4.1 MAX-CSP

The following is the key lemma to our analysis:

Lemma 7. *(Local Lemma). Let x be an instance of MAX-CSP(k, r) and σ be any local optimal solution computed by LS. Then, for all variables i, the number of constraints adjacent to i satisfied by σ is at least $\lceil \frac{rm_i}{k} \rceil$.*

Proof. Consider any variable i. Let $z_1, z_2, \ldots, z_{m_i}$ be the adjacent variables of i. By arc(r)-consistency, for each $1 \le t \le m_i$, the current assigned value of z_t must be consistent with at least r distinct values $j_t^1, j_t^2, \ldots, j_t^r$ assignable to i. Let J be the $r \times m_i$ matrix $[j_t^l]$, for all $1 \le l \le r$ and $1 \le t \le m_i$, i.e.,

$$
J = \begin{bmatrix}
j_1^1 & j_2^1 & \cdots & j_{m_i}^1 \\
j_1^2 & j_2^2 & \cdots & j_{m_i}^2 \\
\vdots & \vdots & \ddots & \vdots \\
j_1^r & j_2^r & \cdots & j_{m_i}^r
\end{bmatrix}
$$

By the pigeon-hole principle, there must exist a value $1 \le j' \le k$ which occurs at least $\lceil \frac{rm_i}{k} \rceil$ times in different columns of J. In other words, given any assignment to the adjacent variables, we can always find a value j' for i such that at least $\lceil \frac{rm_i}{k} \rceil$ constraints incident to it are satisfied. Since σ is locally optimal, i must be assigned to one such j'. □

Theorem 8. *LS approximates MAX-CSP(k, r) within $\frac{r}{k}$.*

Proof. This can be proved by contradiction. Given an instance and a locally optimal solution σ, suppose σ satisfies less than $\lceil \frac{rm}{k} \rceil$ constraints. Then, there must exist a variable i with degree m_i such that less than $\lceil \frac{rm_i}{k} \rceil$ constraints incident to it are satisfied. This cannot hold by the Local Lemma. □

Note that our bound of r/k is an absolute bound and thus the performance ratio is possibly higher in some cases. Note also that the approximation ratio holds even for MAX-CSP instances of varying domain sizes, as long as the largest domain size is k. This theorem leads to two corollaries. First, for constraint graphs which are regular, the approximation bound can be slightly improved:

For satisfiable instances of MAX-CSP, the following holds:

Corollary 9. *Satisfiable MAX-CSP can be approximated within $\frac{1}{k}$.*

Proof. Let x be a given instance of satisfiable MAX-CSP of m constraints. Let x' be the corresponding arc-consistent instance and let $m'(\leq m)$ be the number of constraints in x'. Suppose σ is the local optimum of x'. Then, σ satisfies at least $\lceil \frac{m'}{k} \rceil$ constraints in x' and the same σ satisfies at least $\lceil \frac{m'}{k} \rceil + (m - m')$ constraints in x. Therefore, the performance ratio is,

$$\frac{\lceil \frac{m'}{k} \rceil + (m - m')}{m} \geq \frac{\lceil \frac{m'}{k} \rceil + (m - m')}{m' + (m - m')} \geq \frac{1}{k}.$$

□

4.2 Bounded-Degree Maximum Cut and Graph Coloring

By Theorem 8, we can conclude the following for unweighted MAX k-CUT:

Corollary 10. *Given a graph of m edges and maximum degree Δ, $O(m\Delta)$ time suffices to construct a k-partition such that the number of cut-edges is at least $(m - \frac{1}{2} \sum_{i=1}^{n} \lfloor \frac{m_i}{k} \rfloor)$.*

Proof. Using LS, solve an instance of MAX-CSP$(k, k-1)$ with underlying graph G with all constraints being NOT-EQUAL constraints. Partition G into subgraphs $G_1, \ldots, G_k$ where each subgraph contains nodes assigned with the same values. Let the *indegree* of a node refer to the number of nodes adjacent to it within its subgraph. By the Local Lemma, every vertex has an indegree of at most $\lfloor \frac{m_i}{k} \rfloor$. Hence, the total number of edges within all subgraphs is at most $\frac{1}{2} \sum_{i=1}^{n} \lfloor \frac{m_i}{k} \rfloor)$ and the corollary follows. □

Setting $k = 2$, we can construct a 2-partition which contains at least $\frac{m}{2} + \frac{n}{4}$ edges for odd-degree graphs (i.e. all vertices have odd degrees). This is the best possible ratio because there exists an odd-degree graph, namely, a clique of even number of vertices, whose maximum cut is exactly $\frac{m}{2} + \frac{n}{4}$ edges. Our ratio for unweighted MAX 2-CUT on odd-degree graphs is hence $\frac{1}{2} + \frac{n}{4m}$ and is absolute. This improves the ratio of Poljak and Turzík [12] by a marginal additive factor of $\frac{1}{4m}$. Poljak and Turzík's algorithm runs in $O(n^3)$ time, while our algorithm requires $O(m\Delta)$ time. Unfortunately however, if we relax the odd-degree restriction, we can do no better than a ratio of $\frac{1}{2}$ using local search, as the next section on non-approximability (Theorem 16) would show.

Next, we consider bounded-degree graph coloring. The following result is due to Brooks [3]:

Proposition 11. *Let G be a graph with maximum degree $\Delta \geq 3$. If G does not contain a complete subgraph on $\Delta + 1$ nodes, then G can be colored with at most Δ colors in polynomial time.*

By Theorem 8, Brooks' result can be generalized as follows:

Corollary 12. *Let G be a graph with maximum degree $\Delta \geq 3$. If G does not contain a complete subgraph on r ($4 \leq r \leq \Delta + 1$) nodes, then G can be colored with at most $(\Delta + 1) - \lfloor \frac{\Delta + 1}{r} \rfloor$ colors in polynomial time.*

The proof is essentially the same as that for MAX k-CUT, namely, partition G into $k = \lceil \frac{\Delta + 1}{r} \rceil$ subgraphs so that every subgraph has a maximum indegree of at most $r - 1$. Hence, $r - 1$ colors are sufficient to color each subgraph by Brooks' Theorem. Clearly we need at most $k(r - 1) = (r - 1)\lceil \frac{\Delta + 1}{r} \rceil$ colors. By swapping nodes between subgraphs carefully using a slightly modified objective function, we can achieve a precise bound of $(\Delta + 1) - \lfloor \frac{\Delta + 1}{r} \rfloor$ [7].

This result has been independently discovered by Catlin [4] which employed a more elaborate local search technique originally due to Lovász [10]. By careful implementation, the worst-case time complexity of our local search is $O(m\Delta)$. On the other hand, Catlin's local search is $O(m\Delta^2)$ and each computation involves multiplications because the objective function is a sum of products.

4.3 W-CSP

Finally we extend our analysis to the weighted case W-CSP. By extending the proof given for MAX-CSP, one can show that, for W-CSP(k, r), LS always returns a solution whose value is at least $\frac{r}{k}$ of the optimal. Unfortunately, W-CSP belongs a class of PLS-hard problem, since it has been shown by Schaffer and Yannakakis [13] that MAX 2-CUT is PLS-hard. This means that if the edge weights are exponential in the input size n, then even finding a locally optimal solution is NP-hard. Thus, there is no guarantee in this case that LS would terminate in time polynomial in n. In fact, in the worst case, LS may take time which depends on the sum of edge weights.

How well can we do in polynomial time independent of the edge weights? For this purpose, we shall employ the technique of approximation with non-locally-optimal solution, proposed by Halldórsson [8]. We show that, using polynomial number of iterations, we can obtain a solution with *almost* the same quality as guaranteed by a local optimal.

We use the following notations. W denotes the sum of all edge weights. W_i denotes the sum of weights of edges incident to varaible i. For any assignment σ, W_i^σ denotes the sum of weights of edges incident to variable i that are satisfied by σ; and $W_{i,j}^\sigma$ denotes the sum of weights of satisfied edges incident to i when the current value of i is replaced by the value j. Let $\overline{w} = W/m$ denote the average edge weight.

To simplify discussion, we will prove a restricted version of the main theorem first, and then relax the restriction later. More precisely, we first consider instances in which the weight on each edge is at least some factor θ ($0 \le \theta \le 1$) of the average edge weight. Let the collection of such instances be denoted W-CSP(k, r, θ).

Consider a local search algorithm WLS with the following modifications from LS. Let $f : \Sigma \longrightarrow \mathbb{N}$ now be the objective function where $f(\sigma)$ gives the sum of weights of edges satisfied by σ. In order to ensure polynomial-time performance, each local improvement we now make must be a factor of W. Precisely, we seek a neighbor which improves the current assignment by at least $\mu = \epsilon\theta\overline{w}$ units.

Lemma 13. *(Weighted Local Lemma). Let x be an instance of W-CSP(k, r, θ) and σ be any local optimum computed by WLS described above. Then, for all variables i, the total weight of constraints adjacent to i satisfied by σ is at least $\lceil (\frac{r}{k} - \epsilon) W_i \rceil$.*

Proof. Consider any variable i in x and suppose the lemma does not hold. Then,

$$W_i^\sigma < \lceil \left(\frac{r}{k} - \epsilon\right) W_i \rceil.$$

Furthermore, since σ is locally optimal, reassigning i to any other value $j \neq \sigma_i$ will not increase the objective function by more than the amount μ. Thus, for all $j \neq \sigma_i$, ($1 \le j \le k$):

$$W_{i,j}^\sigma < \lceil \left(\frac{r}{k} - \epsilon\right) W_i \rceil + \mu.$$

Summing up the above k inequalities, we have,

$$\sum_{j=1}^{k} W_{i,j}^\sigma < rW_i - k\epsilon W_i + (k-1)\mu \le rW_i,$$

since $W_i \ge \theta\overline{w}$. On the other hand, we know,

$$\sum_{j=1}^{k} W_{i,j}^\sigma \ge rW_i$$

since each constraint must be satisfied at least r times with k different values assigned to i, by arc(r)-consistency. We thus arrive at a contradiction. $\square$

Theorem 14. *For any $0 < \epsilon \leq \frac{r}{k}$ and $0 \leq \theta \leq 1$, W-CSP(k, r, θ) can be approximated within $\left(\frac{r}{k} - \epsilon\right)$ in $\frac{m}{\epsilon\theta}$ local search iterations.*

Proof. Let x be an instance of W-CSP(k, r, θ). Consider the maximum number of iterations before WLS halts. Since $OPT(x) \leq W = \frac{\mu}{\epsilon\theta}m$, by the fact that each iteration increases the objective function by at least μ units, the total number of iterations cannot exceed $\frac{m}{\epsilon\theta}$. By the Weighted Local Lemma, when WLS halts, the total weight of satisfied constraints is at least $\lceil\left(\frac{r}{k} - \epsilon\right)W\rceil$. □

Now, we remove the restriction on weight distribution and prove our main theorem.

Theorem 15. *For any $0 < \epsilon \leq \frac{r}{k}$ W-CSP(k, r) can be approximated within $\left(\frac{r}{k} - \epsilon\right)$ in $O(m/\epsilon^2)$ local search iterations.*

Proof. Given ϵ, let $\hat{\epsilon} = \frac{1}{2}\epsilon$. Delete from the graph instance all edges whose weights are less than $\hat{\epsilon}\overline{w}$. In the resulting graph, all edges have weights at least $\hat{\epsilon}\overline{w}$, and the total edge weight is at least $(1 - \hat{\epsilon})W$. By Theorem 14, a solution with objective value at least $\left(\frac{r}{k} - \hat{\epsilon}\right)(1 - \hat{\epsilon})W \geq \left(\frac{r}{k} - 2\hat{\epsilon}\right)W$ can be obtained after $m/\hat{\epsilon}^2$ or $4m/\epsilon^2$ local search iterations. □

5 Non-Approximability

In this section, we show that our performance ratio is almost best possible in the sense that, any local search algorithm based on 1-neighborhood cannot guarantee a better performance ratio if it starts with bad initial solutions.

Theorem 16. *For $k \equiv 0 \pmod{r}$, MAX-CSP(k, r) cannot be approximated withi a factor more than $\frac{r}{k}$ by any local search algorithm using 1-neighborhood, even if the constraint graph is bipartite.*

Proof. Given k and r, we construct the following constraint graph G. G is a complete bipartite graph consisting of G_1 and G_2 having k and k/r nodes respectively. Constraints connecting G_1 nodes to G_2 nodes are identical and can be any exact arc(r)-consistent relation (i.e. all values in one domain are consistent with exactly r values in the other domain). Without loss of generality, let this relation be,

$$R = \{ (j_1, j_2) \in K \times K \mid j_2 - j_1 \equiv t \pmod{r}, \ 1 \leq t \leq r\}.$$

In words, R defines the relation where a value is consistent with the r values which are larger than itself cyclically.

Clearly, by assigning nodes in G_1 and G_2 to the values 1 and 2 respectively, we can obtain a solution which satisfies all edges in G. Now, a locally optimal solution is obtained as follows. Assign the k/r nodes in G_2 to the values $1, 1 + r, \ldots, 1 + (k-1)r$. Notice that since these values are distance at least r apart, for each node i in G_1, at most one edge incident to i can be satisfied, *independent of i's assigned value*. Now assign the k nodes in G_1 to $1, \ldots, k$ respectively. By this assignment, each node in G_1 has exactly one satisfied incident edge and each node in G_2 has exactly r satisfied incident edge. Hence, the assignment is locally optimal. The ratio of satisfied constraints is exactly $\frac{r}{k}$. □

Theorem 17. *MAX-CSP(k, r) cannot be approximated within more than $\left(\frac{r}{k} + \frac{k-r}{k^2} \right)$ by any local search algorithm using 1-neighborhood, even if the constraint graph is a tree.*

Proof. Given k and r, we construct the following constraint graph G (see Fig. 1(a)). G is a rooted tree T plus some sink nodes. The root of T has k children, which are respective roots of k complete subtrees of branch factor $(k-1)$ and height h, for some significantly large constant $h > 1$. All constraints are identical and defined by any exact arc(r)-consistent relation. Without loss of generality, let this relation be R as defined in Theorem 16.

Clearly, by assigning all nodes on alternate levels of G to the values 1 and 2, we can obtain a solution which satisfies all edges in G. Now, a locally optimal solution is obtained as follows. The root is assigned 1, and its k children are assigned $1, \ldots, k$ respectively. Each remaining node in T except the leaf nodes is assigned such that exactly r satisfied constraints are incident to it. This can be done by assigning values in a breadth-first manner such that for each node, all its neighboring values (including its parent) are distinct. For each leaf node, if the parent link is NOT satisfied, we connect it to a distinct sink node and assign any value to that sink node as long as the constraint between them is satisfied. We refer to the edges between the leaves and the sink nodes as *sink edges*. Let this locally optimal assignment be denoted as σ.

We prove the theorem by counting. Let x be the number of edges in T, which is exactly $k \left[(k-1)^h - 1 \right]$. Let y be the number of sink edges. One can verify that y is at most $k(k-1)^{h-2}(k-r)$ (the number of nodes on the level above the leaves times $(k-r)$). When h is significantly large, we can upper-bound y asymptotically by $\frac{1}{k-1}x$. The total number of edges in G is $x + y$, while the number of edges satisfied by σ is $\frac{r}{k}x + y$. Hence, the performance ratio,

$$\phi_{LS} = \frac{\frac{r}{k}x + y}{x + y} \leq \frac{\frac{r}{k}x + \frac{1}{k-1}x}{x + \frac{1}{k-1}x} \leq \frac{r}{k} + \frac{k-r}{k^2}$$

when h is sufficiently large. □

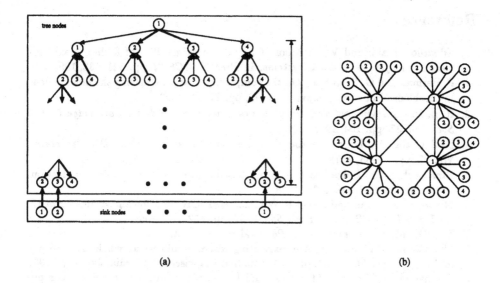

Fig. 1. (a) Constraint graph and a local optimal assignment, for the case of $k = 4$ and $r = 2$. Numbers in nodes represent the values assigned. Thickened arcs indicate satisfied constraints. (b) Constraint graph and a local optimal assignment, for the case of $k = 4$.

Corollary 18. *MAX k-CUT cannot be approximated within more than $\left(1 - \frac{1}{k} + \frac{1}{k^2}\right)$ by any local search algorithm using 1-neighborhood, even if the given graph is a tree.*

This is rather trivial if we let $k = 2$. For small values of k, we can establish a tighter non-approximation bound (albeit on general graphs):

Theorem 19. *MAX k-CUT cannot be approximated within more than $\left(1 - \frac{1}{2k-1}\right)$ by local search with 1-neighborhood.*

Proof. For this purpose, we construct the following constraint graph G (see Fig. 1(b)). Let all constraints be NOT-EQUAL constraints. G is composed of a k-clique plus k clusters. Each cluster consisting of $(k-1)^2$ nodes is connected to one clique node. Assign the values of clique nodes to be 1. Assign the nodes within a cluster to be $(k-1)$ number of 2's, $(k-1)$ number of 3's, ..., $(k-1)$ number of $(k-1)$'s. Surely, the assignment is locally optimal. Now total number of edges in G is $\binom{k}{2} + k(k-1)^2$ while the number of edges satisfied by σ is $k(k-1)^2$. Surely all edges are satisfied in the optimal solution. Thus, the performance ratio,

$$\phi_{LS} = \frac{k(k-1)^2}{\binom{k}{2} + k(k-1)^2} = 1 - \frac{1}{2k-1}$$

References

1. Edoardo Amaldi and Viggo Kann. On the approximability of finding maximum feasible subsystems of linear systems. In *Proc. STACS 94*, pp. 521–532, 1994.
2. P. Berman and G. Schnitger. On the complexity of approximating the independent set problem. *Infor. & Comput.*, Vol. 96, pp. 77–94, 1992.
3. R. L. Brooks. On colouring the nodes of a network. In *Proc. Cambridge Philos. Soc.*, Vol. 37, pp. 194–197, 1941.
4. Paul Catlin. A bound on the chromatic number of a graph. *Discrete Math.*, Vol. 22, pp. 81–83, 1978.
5. Rina Dechter and Judea Pearl. Network-based heuristics for constraint satisfaction. *Artif. Int.*, Vol. 34, pp. 1–38, 1988.
6. Michel X. Goemans and David P. Williamson. Approximation algorithms for MAX CUT and MAX 2SAT. In *Proc. STOC 94*, pp. 422–431, 1994.
7. Magnús M. Halldórsson. 1994. Personal communication.
8. Magnús M. Halldórsson. Approximating discrete collections via local improvements. In *Proc. SODA 95*, pp. 601–610, San Francisco, California, January 1995.
9. S. Khanna, R. Motwani, M. Sudan, and U. Vazirani. On syntactic versus computational views of approximability. In *Proc. FOCS 94*, 1994.
10. L. Lovász. On decomposition of graphs. *Studia Sci. Math. Hungar.*, Vol. 1, pp. 237–238, 1966.
11. Christos H. Papadimitriou and Mihalis Yannakakis. Optimization, approximation, and complexity classes. *J. Comput. Sys. Sci.*, Vol. 43, pp. 425–440, 1991.
12. Svatopluk Poljak and Daniel Turzik. A polynomial time algorithm for constructing a large bipartite subgraph, with an application to a satisfiability problem. *Can. J. Math*, Vol. 34, No. 3, pp. 519–524, 1982.
13. Alejandro A. Schaffer and Mihalis Yannakakis. Simple local search problems that are hard to solve. *SIAM J. Comput.*, Vol. 20, No. 1, pp. 56–87, 1991.
14. Paul Vitanyi. How well can a graph be n-colored? *Discrete Math.*, Vol. 34, pp. 69–80, 1981.

Acknowledgements

I would like to thank Osamu Watanabe for his advice and for verifying the proofs. Much appreciation to Magnús Halldórsson for constructive discussions, especially giving ideas on how to approximate the weighted CSP and references to results in bounded-degree graph coloring. Thanks also to the referees for comments and additional references.

On the Difficulty of Range Searching

Arne Andersson[*]   Kurt Swanson[*]

Dept. of Computer Science, Lund University,
Box 118, S-221 00 LUND, Sweden

Abstract. The problem of range searching is fundamental and well studied, and a large number of solutions have been suggested in the literature. The only existing non-trivial lower bound that closely matches known upper bounds with respect to time/space tradeoff is given for the pointer machine model. However, the pointer machine prohibits a number of possible and natural operations, such as the use of arrays and bit manipulation. In particular, such operations have proven useful in some special cases such as one-dimensional and rectilinear queries.

In this article, we consider the general problem of (2-dimensional) range reporting allowing arbitrarily convex queries. We show that using a traditional approach, even when incorporating techniques like those used in fusion trees, a (poly-) logarithmic query time can not be achieved unless more than linear space is used. Our arguments are based on a new non-trivial lower bound in a model of computation which, in contrast to the pointer machine model, allows for the use of arrays and bit manipulation. The crucial property of our model, *Layered Partitions*, is that it can be used to describe all known algorithms for processing range queries, as well as many other data structures used to represent multi-dimensional data.

We show that $\Omega\left(\frac{\log n}{\log T(n)}\right)$ partitions must be used to allow queries in $O(T(n) + k)$ time, where k is the number of reported elements, for any growing function $T(n)$. In some special cases, as for rectilinear queries, these partitions may be stored in compressed form, which has been exploited by the M-structure of Chazelle. However, so far there has been no indication that such compression would be feasible in the general case, in which case any algorithm based on our model, and supporting range searching in $O(\log^c n + k)$ time requires $\Omega\left(\frac{n \log n}{\log \log n}\right)$ space. (Note that it may be possible to obtain a better upper bound with an algorithm not adhering to the model of layered partitions.) Hence, we show that removing the restrictions of the pointer machine model does not help in obtaining a significantly improved time/space tradeoff — any solution based on traditional representations of point sets cannot combine linear space and polylogarithmic time.

1 Introduction

1.1 Discrepancy between upper and lower bound

The complexity of range searching has been a long standing open question. The problem is fundamental and easy to formulate: given a set of points in a multidimensional space, create a data structure that facilitates reporting of all points inside a given query region. This formulation is frequently called range reporting. Although many attempts have been made, the time-space tradeoff for this problem is still unclear.

---

[*] email: {arne, kurt}@dna.lth.se

Taking a general approach, we note the following trivial lower bounds: Let $F(n)$ be the time required to find *one* point in the query region—or to discover that the region is empty—in a set of n points. Then, an immediate lower bound on time complexity is $\Omega(F(n) + k)$, where k is the number of points to be reported. The same lower bound applies when $F(n)$ is the cost of counting the number of points in the region or computing the weighted sum of a set of weighted points. As an example, by a modification of the proof by Miltersen [13], a lower bound of $F(n) = \Omega(\log^{1/3 - o(1)} n)$ can be obtained [12]. (The original bound given in that article is expressed in terms of the size of the universe. This is also the case for similar lower bounds on *existential range searching*, which reports whether or not a given region is empty, given by Miltersen et al [14].) In the same way, the arithmetic lower bound by Chazelle [7] for the problem of *dominance searching* (where the sum of weights of all points dominated by a given point is computed), applies to our problem. However, these bounds are far from tight with respect to the time/space complexity of range reporting.

The only existing non-trivial lower bound that closely matches known upper bounds with respect to time/space tradeoff is given for the *pointer machine* model, where $F(n) = \Omega(\log n)$ even in the one-dimensional case. In this model, it has been shown [6] that $\Theta(n \log n / \log \log n)$ space is necessary and sufficient in order to achieve optimal query time complexity. In fact, not even polylogarithmic time can be achieved with less space.

However, the restrictions of the pointer machine model are not realistic. This weakness is particularly evident for range reporting since it has been explicitly demonstrated that the use of arrays and bit manipulation can help. In such a more general, and more realistic, model we can expect faster searching than $\Omega(\log n)$ [9]. As another possible improvement, we may reduce space requirements by packing information about more than one point into one machine word. This option of storing point sets in compressed form has been utilized by Chazelle [5] in the special case of *rectilinear* range queries; a query cost of $O(\log^4 n + k)$ can be achieved using only $O(n)$ space, and a query cost of $O(\log n + k)$ can be achieved using $O(n \log^\epsilon n)$ space on the RAM model. But what about the general problem?

1.2 A lower bound in a relevant model

We concentrate on two dimensional range reporting with convex query regions. It should be noted that our lower bound only holds for a (relevant) class of algorithms to solve range searching, and not the problem itself.

In examining the large set of known data structures, one finds that they all have one property in common: they may all be viewed as representing one or more partitions of the plane, where each partition divides the plane into $\Theta(n)$ convex areas. When a query is made, the answer is given by intersecting the query region with a selected subset of these partitions.

Based on this observation, we define the model of *Layered Partitions*, which can be used to emulate all known solutions to the range searching problem, as well as many other data structures used in computational geometry. Our lower bound on the time-space tradeoff is given in terms of the number of partitions needed in order to achieve a certain query cost. We show that, in order to support queries in time $O(T(n) + k)$, $\Omega(\log n / \log T(n))$ partitions must be represented. Hence, if each partition does require $\Theta(n)$ space (and there is no evidence pointing to the contrary for the general case of convex query regions), then any algorithm based on layered partitions, which supports range reporting in $O(\log^c n + k)$, $c = O(1)$, time requires $\Omega\left(\frac{n \log n}{\log \log n}\right)$ space.

Our model of computation is general in the sense that it allows all kinds of bit-manipulation techniques, such as fusion trees [9], to be used in order to speed up queries, thus avoiding inherent weaknesses in the pointer machine model.

2 Computational model

Our computational model is based on a data structure paradigm which can be used to describe all data structures for the range reporting problem found in the literature, as well as many other data structures used to represent multi-dimensional data.

A central part of our model is the *partition*. Given a set of points in the plane, we define the "universe" as the smallest enclosing rectangle containing all points in the set. A partition divides the universe in $\Theta(n)$ convex regions, each region contains at most one point.

A data structure in the model represents a set of partitions $P_1, P_2, \ldots$ in the plane. Range queries are processed in the following way:

1. Split the query region into m subregions $R_1, \ldots, R_m$.
2. Associate each R_i with a partition $P(R_i)$.
3. Examine all regions in $P(R_i)$ that intersect R_i and report which points are contained in R_i.

The cost of processing the query is defined as:

$$\sum_{i=1}^{m} \text{number of regions in } P(R_i) \text{ that intersect } R_i$$

Note that we only consider the time required to access information in partitions, and not the time needed to determine how to divide the query region into subregions, nor the time to determine which partitions to use, nor time spent searching in any ancillary data. Thus differences between the RAM and decision tree models are negated.

We claim that this model covers the classical data structures used to solve this, and similar, problems. Among others, the following data structures can be described as layered partitions: k-d-Tree [15], Multistage direct access (multilevel k-ranges) [2], Filtering search [3], Range Trees [1] (see also [16] and [10]), Quad trees [8], Priority search trees [11], Voronoi diagrams, and M-structures [5] (see also [4]).

As an example, we indicate how to describe, in terms of layered partitions, priority search trees as well as the data structure used in filtering search. In Figure 1, we illustrate how to view a priority search tree as a layered partition (a single layer). In a priority search tree, the point with highest y-coordinate is stored in the root. The rest of the points are divided between the two subtrees according to a *split value* which is also stored in the root. All points whose x-coordinate is less than the split value are stored in the left subtree, the other points are stored in the right subtree. A priority search tree supports range queries where the query region is a rectangle for which the topmost edge in the rectangle is located above all stored points.

In the figure, the universe covers $([0; 20], [0; 10])$ and the query region (shaded) is $([8; 18], [6; 10])$. In each tree node, the upper values are split values (not needed for the leaves) and the lower values are point coordinates. The partition created by the tree is illustrated below the tree; each node corresponds to one region. Vertical segments

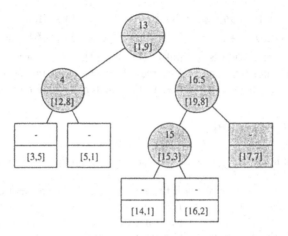

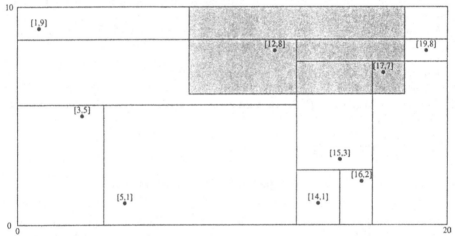

Fig. 1. Searching in a priority search tree

represent split values, and horizontal segments separate each node's point from those of its subtree. The horizontal segments are somewhat arbitrarily drawn, but conform to the nature of priority search trees as well as layered partitions. This particular query rectangle contains five regions, the corresponding nodes are shaded.

In filtering search, the data structure is organized in $\Theta(\log n/\log\log n)$ layers, each layer may be described as consisting of three partitions. At the ith layer, we have the following three partitions:

- The first partition divides the universe into $\Theta(\log^i n)$ vertical segments, each segment containing $\Theta(n/\log^i n)$ points. Each segment is in turn divided into horizontal segments, each segment containing one point.
- The second partition divides the universe into the same $\Theta(\log^i n)$ vertical segments. This time, however, each segment is represented as a priority search tree, based on the left edge of the segment. A priority search tree may in turn be described as a partition as previously shown.
- The third partition is similar to the second one, with the difference that the priority search trees are based on the right edge of their segments.

3 Lower bound

Our lower bound is based upon a specific example. We describe a simple layout pattern for points in the plane, and prove that, according to the above described model of computation, any algorithm that solves range searching in $O(T(n) + k)$ time, must represent $\Omega\left(\frac{\log n}{\log T(n)}\right)$ partitions.

For the sake of simplicity, we shall describe this layout in terms of rectangular queries. However, our lower bound construction can easily be extended to a set of convex non-rectangular queries. We indicate how to perform this extension below.

We arrange the point set to create classes of empty rectangles $R_1, R_2, R_3, \ldots$ We denote the entire set of rectangles as $R = R_1 \cup R_2 \cup R_3 \cup \ldots$ The class R_i is constructed recursively in the following way (see Figure 2):

1. Initially $i = 1$ and $R = R_1$ which contains one rectangle.
2. Set $i = i + 1$.
3. Make $T^3(n)$ copies of the entire set of rectangles R and place them on a horizontal line. This implies that the number of rectangles of class R_j, $(\forall j \mid 1 \le j < i)$ increase by a factor of $T^3(n)$.

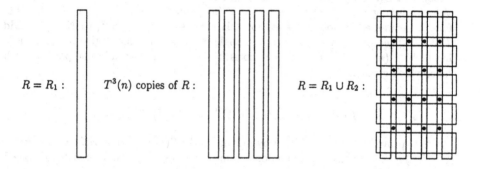

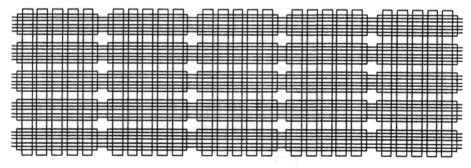

Fig. 2. The growth of R, for $T^3(n) = 5$, yielding 16 holes for $R = R_1 \cup R_2$, and 176 total holes for $R = R_1 \cup R_2 \cup R_3$. (The 25 rectangles in R_3 are shown as lines. Only points in R_2 are drawn.)

4. Add a class of rectangles R_i as $T^{3(i-1)}(n)$ long rectangles, evenly spaced over the universe from top to bottom, each one intersecting all copies made in the previous step (as shown in Figure 2).
5. Make the holes (rectangular regions between intersecting rectangles) small enough so that their total area is negligible. One point is placed in each hole.
6. If there are points left, go to 2.

We assume, without loss of generality, that the number of points, n, exactly fills the last class, without any remaining points. (We note that this provides for an infinite number of constructions).

We now indicate how this construction can be rephrased for a set of convex and non-rectangular queries. To do this, we observe that we have left small gaps between all rectangles. Hence, instead of placing our points on strict lines, we may arrange them in a slightly more irregular pattern, creating convex, but not necessarily rectangular, empty query regions.

Lemma 1. *The number of classes of rectangles that can be created by the above described process is* $\Omega\left(\frac{\log n}{\log T(n)}\right)$, *given n points.*

Proof. Let $S(i)$ equal the number of points required to create i classes of rectangles. When creating the ith class, we create $T^3(n)$ copies of everything that we had before, the number of points needed for this purpose is $S(i-1)T^3(n)$. Next, we add $T^{3(i-1)}(n)$ rectangles. Each of these rectangles crosses $T^3(n)$ rectangles in R_{i-1}, creating $(T^{3(i-1)}(n)-1)(T^3(n)-1)$ new holes for level R_i, and we add one point in each hole, which gives us:

$$S(i) = S(i-1)T^3(n) + (T^{3(i-1)}(n)-1)(T^3(n)-1) \tag{1}$$

We first prove that $S(i) < T^{4i}(n)$ by induction. As $S(1) = 0$, then $S(2) = (T^{3 \cdot 1}(n) - 1)(T^3(n)-1) < T^{4 \cdot 2}(n)$. By induction assume $S(i-1) < T^{4(i-1)}(n)$, then, for $T(n) > 1$ and $i > 2$:

$$S(i) < T^{4(i-1)}(n)T^3(n) + (T^{3(i-1)}(n)-1)(T^3(n)-1) \tag{2}$$
$$< T^{4i-1}(n) + T^{3i}(n) - T^{3(i-1)}(n) - T^3(n) + 1 < T^{4i}(n) \tag{3}$$

We now set $n = S(i)$ and solve for i:

$$n = S(i) < T^{4i}(n) \tag{4}$$
$$\log n < 4i \log T(n) \tag{5}$$
$$\frac{\log n}{\log T(n)} < 4i \tag{6}$$
$$i = \Omega\left(\frac{\log n}{\log T(n)}\right) \tag{7}$$

Next, we study how many partitions must be maintained in order to perform range queries efficiently. Intuitively, our goal is to show that there must be at least as many partitions as there are classes of empty rectangles.

We say that a rectangle used in a layered partition is *q-sized* if both its height and width is at least $1/T(n)$ times the height and width of a rectangle in R_q.

Lemma 2. *A q-sized rectangle used in a layered partition data structure is not s-sized if $q \neq s$.*

Proof. The proof follows from the way our R_q's are constructed and the fact that no rectangle used in a partition may contain more than one point.

Without loss of generality, assume $q < s$. The height of a q-sized rectangle is greater than $1/T(n)$ times the height of a rectangle in R_q, by definition. The height of a q-sized rectangle is greater than $T^2(n)$ times the height of a rectangle in R_s due to the recursive construction of R_q and R_s.

Assume a q-sized rectangle used in a layered partition is at least $1/T(n)$ times the width of a rectangle in R_s. Then the q-sized rectangle must cross over at least $T^2(n)$ rectangles in R_{s-1}. By construction, there are $\Omega(T^3(n))$ points between two rectangles in R_q. Therefore, due to its height, the q-sized rectangle must enclose at least $T^2(n)$ points in between each pair of rectangles it crosses in R_{s-1}. Thus the q-sized rectangle contains at least $T^2(n)(T^2(n) - 1) = T^4(n) - T^2(n)$ points. It can thereby not be used in a layered partition. This contradicts the assumption on its width, and thus, by definition, it cannot be s-sized.

Lemma 3. *For any solution to the range query problem, the following must hold: for each q, all but at most $1/T(n)$-th of the universe must be covered by q-sized rectangles represented by the solution.*

Proof. Assume that we chose to use an arbitrary rectangle in R_q as a query region. Then, in order to perform our query in time $T(n)$ our data structure must contain rectangles such that any rectangle in R_q can be covered by at most $T(n)$ rectangles.

By the construction of the example, all but a negligible part of the universe is covered by each set R_q. It thus suffices to show that for each rectangle in R_q, only $1/T(n)$-th of the rectangle may not be covered by q-sized rectangles in the solution. From Lemma 2 and the definition of q-sized, it follows that any s-sized rectangle, $(s \neq q)$, covers less than $\frac{1}{T^3(n)}$ of the rectangle. Thus, $\Theta(T(n))$ non-q-sized rectangles cover $O(\frac{1}{T^2(n)})$ of the rectangle. Therefore, the remainder of the rectangle must be covered by q-sized rectangles. If not, the cost of a query would exceed $O(T(n))$.

Theorem 4. *In order to search in $O(T(n)+k)$ time, where k is the number of elements in the query region, $\Omega\left(\frac{\log n}{\log T(n)}\right)$ partitions are required.*

Proof. It follows from lemma 3 that we need to store at least one partition for each separate class of rectangles in the construction, yielding $\Omega\left(\frac{\log n}{\log T(n)}\right)$ partitions.

The theorem yields the following corollary.

Corollary 5. *If each partition requires $\Theta(n)$ space, any algorithm based on layered partitions and supporting range reporting in $O(\log^c n + k)$, $c = O(1)$, time requires $\Omega\left(\frac{n \log n}{\log \log n}\right)$ space.*

4 Conclusion

We feel that our new lower bound provides new insight on the difficulty of range searching. Our model of computation, layered partitions, captures the inherent properties of a large class of data structures. In this model, we have shown that it is not possible to perform range queries in $O(\log^c n + k)$ time and linear space, unless partitions can be stored in compressed form. However, it seems infeasible to be able to apply the bit-encoding technique of M-structures [5] to other than orthogonal rectilinear queries, since the compression heavily exploits the fact that the queries are rectangular. When compression is not feasible, any algorithm based on layered partitions and supporting range reporting in $O(\log^c n + k)$, $c = O(1)$, time requires $\Omega\left(\frac{n \log n}{\log \log n}\right)$ space. Thus we show that no superior upper bound can be achieved using traditional methods and data structures for range searching in the general case.

One might also imagine that a possible way to achieve a better tradeoff between space and time would be to combine some classical data structure, such as range trees, with some sophisticated search method, such as the one used in fusion trees [9]. The number of possibilities seems to be very large and we believe that many researchers have tried methods like this. In this article, we have shown that such an approach would not be fruitful.

Acknowledgments

We would like to thank the referees and Dr. Ola Petersson for many insightful comments.

References

1. J. L. Bentley. Decomposable searching problems. *Inform. Process. Lett.*, 8:244–251, 1979.
2. J. L. Bentley and H. A. Maurer. Efficient worst-case data structures for range searching. *Acta Inform.*, 13:155–168, 1980.
3. B. Chazelle. Filtering search: a new approach to query-answering. In *Proc. 24th Annu. IEEE Sympos. Found. Comput. Sci.*, pages 122–132, 1983.
4. B. Chazelle. Slimming down search structures: A functional approach to algorithm design. In *Proc. 26th Annu. IEEE Sympos. Found. Comput. Sci.*, pages 165–174, 1985.
5. B. Chazelle. A functional approach to data structures and its use in multidimensional searching. *SIAM J. Comput.*, 17:427–462, 1988.
6. B. Chazelle. Lower bounds for orthogonal range searching, I: the reporting case. *J. ACM*, 37:200–212, 1990.
7. B. Chazelle. Lower bounds for orthogonal range searching: II. the arithmetic model. *Journal of the ACM*, 37(3):439–463, July 1990.
8. R. A. Finkel and J. L. Bentley. Quad trees: a data structure for retrieval on composite keys. *Acta Inform.*, 4:1–9, 1974.

9. M. L. Fredman and D. E. Willard. Blasting through the information theoretic barrier with fusion trees. In *Proc. 22nd Annu. ACM Sympos. Theory Comput.*, pages 1–7, 1990.

10. G. S. Lueker. A data structure for orthogonal range queries. In *Proc. 19th Annu. IEEE Sympos. Found. Comput. Sci.*, pages 28–34, 1978.

11. E. M. McCreight. Priority search trees. *SIAM J. Comput.*, 14:257–276, 1985.

12. P. B. Miltersen. Personal communication.

13. P. B. Miltersen. Lower bounds for union-split-find related problems on random access machines. In *Proc. 26th Ann. ACM STOC*, pages 625–634, 1994.

14. P. B. Miltersen, N. Nisan, S. Safra, and A. Wigderson. On data structures and asymmetric communication complexity. In *Proc. 27th Annu. ACM Sympos. Theory Comput.*, 1995. To appear.

15. J. B. Saxe and J. L. Bentley. Transforming static data structures to dynamic structures. In *Proc. 20th Annu. IEEE Sympos. Found. Comput. Sci.*, pages 148–168, 1979.

16. D. E. Willard. A new time complexity for orthogonal range queries. In *Proc. 20th Allerton Conf. Commun. Control Comput.*, pages 462–471, 1982.

Tables Should Be Sorted
(On Random Access Machines)

Faith Fich and Peter Bro Miltersen

Department of Computer Science,
University of Toronto.

Abstract. We consider the problem of storing an n element subset S of
a universe of size m, so that membership queries (is $x \in S$?) can be answered efficiently. The model of computation is a random access machine
with the standard instruction set (direct and indirect adressing, conditional branching, addition, subtraction, and multiplication). We show
that if s memory registers are used to store S, where $n \leq s \leq m/n^\epsilon$,
then query time $\Omega(\log n)$ is necessary in the worst case. That is, under
these conditions, the solution consisting of storing S as a sorted table
and doing binary search is optimal. The condition $s \leq m/n^\epsilon$ is essentially
optimal; we show that if $n + m/n^{o(1)}$ registers may be used, query time
$o(\log n)$ is possible.

1 Introduction

In Yao's influential paper "Should tables be sorted?" [Yao81], the following basic
data structure problem was considered: Given a subset S of size n of the universe
$U = \{0, \ldots, m-1\}$, store it as a data structure $\phi(S)$ in the memory of a unit cost
random access machine, using few memory registers, each containing an element
of U, so that membership queries "Is $x \in S$?" can be answered efficiently for
any value of x. The set S can be stored as a sorted table using n memory
registers. Then queries can be answered using binary search in $O(\log n)$ time.
Yao considered the possibility of improving this solution.

One of Yao's results was that, if for each S, $\phi(S)$ is a table of size n containing
the elements of S in some order (i.e. the data structure is *implicit*) and m is
sufficiently large compared to n, then query time $\Omega(\log n)$ is necessary and the
sorted table is optimal. The proof is an elegant Ramsey theoretic argument. The
lower bound holds in the *cell probe* model, i.e. only the number of memory cells
accessed is considered.

However, Yao also observed that by allowing one extra element of U to be
stored (which is interpreted as the name of a hash function), the lower bound can
be beaten and constant query time is possible, if m is sufficiently large compared
to n. This result was improved by Tarjan and Yao [TY79] and Fredman, Komlòs
and Szemerédi [FKS84]. The latter paper shows that, for *all* values of m and n,
there is a storage scheme using $n + o(n)$ memory cells, so that queries can be
answered in constant time.

For most practical purposes, this answers the question of whether tables
should be sorted: they should not. However, there are still some questions that

remain unanswered. One concerns the exact amount of extra memory needed to get constant query time. The upper bound in [FKS84] has been improved by [FNSS92] and [BM94]. It is still an open problem when exactly n memory cells are sufficient. In particular, Yao's lower bound does not apply if the implicitness restriction on ϕ is removed. Fiat, Naor, Schmidt, and Siegel [FNSS92], [FN93] consider bounds on the size of the universe m as a function of n for which there is an implicit data structure with constant query time. However, there is still a wide gap between their upper and lower bounds.

Instead of putting a restriction on the data structure, we can put a restriction on the query algorithm. The technique of [FKS84] is based on the family of hash functions $h_k(x) = (kx \bmod p) \bmod s$, i.e. integer division is used. However, the only arithmetic operations usually included in the instruction set of random access machines are addition, subtraction and multiplication. What can be done if only the standard instruction set is available? In this paper, we address this question, showing that on a unit cost random access machine with the standard instruction set, tables *should* be sorted. More precisely, we show:

- Let $U = \{0, \ldots, m-1\}$ and let $n \le s \le m/n^\epsilon$ for some constant $\epsilon > 0$. There is an n-element subset S of U, so that for any representation $\phi_S \in \mathbf{Z}^s$ of S as a sequence of s integers, the following is true. Consider any RAM program that, on inputs x and ϕ_S, accepts if $x \in S$ and rejects if $x \notin S$. Then, for some $x \in U$, the program uses $\Omega(\log n)$ steps on inputs x and ϕ_S.

We first prove that, for any suggested representation scheme, some set is hard (i.e. query time is $\Omega(\log n)$ in the worst case). Then, using the universality of the RAM model, we show that some specific set is hard no matter what representation is used.

Note that we do not restrict the contents of the registers in the data structure to be elements from the universe U, as in the cell probe model. These values can be arbitrary integers, as is customary in the random access machine model. Furthermore, we do not require any bound on the complexity of constructing ϕ_S from S. Finally, the space bound s only refers to the data structure itself. We do not need to limit the number of registers used by the query algorithm.

In Section 3, we show that there is a data structure for the membership problem using space $O(\max(n, m/2^t))$ and with query time $O(t)$. Thus, the space upper bound $s \in m/n^{\Omega(1)}$ in our theorem is essentially optimal.

Our proof technique has a strong communication complexity flavor and can, in fact, be viewed as a modification of the *richness* technique used for showing lower bounds on the communication complexity of membership in [MNSW95]. Communication complexity has previously been used for showing lower bounds for data structure problems in the cell probe model [MNSW95]. Our proof is the first application of this kind of technique taking advantage of a restricted instruction set, while allowing memory registers to contain arbitrary integers. Another lower bound proof technique has previously been transferred from the cell probe model to the random access machine model: Ben-Amram and Galil [BG91] modified Fredman and Saks' *time stamp* technique for the cell probe model [FS89] to obtain the same lower bounds for the random access machine model, with registers that can contain arbitrarily large integers. An interesting feature of our technique is that we can get larger lower bounds in the random access machine model than in the cell probe model (where the complexity of membership is constant).

2 The Random Access Machine Model

The random access machine (RAM) is an important and well studied model of sequential computation, first formalized by Cook and Reckow [CR73]. It has an infinite sequence of registers, indexed by the integers. Each register can contain an arbitrarily large integer. For ease of presentation, we include in our version of the RAM model two additional registers, the *accumulator* and the *pointer*. The accumulator is where arithmetic operations are performed. The pointer is used for indirect addressing.

The instruction set is described in Table 1. Here, as in [PS82, BG91, Maa88], we assume that addition, subtraction, and multiplication can be performed. In other papers, the RAM instruction set does not include multiplication [CR73] or restricts multiplication to reasonably small operands [AHU74].

Instruction	Semantics
load k	The accumulator is assigned the integer constant k.
direct read k	The accumulator is assigned the value in register k.
indirect read	The accumulator is assigned the value in the register whose index is the value in the pointer.
direct write k	Register k is assigned the value in the accumulator.
indirect write	The register whose index is the value in the pointer is assigned the value in the accumulator.
swap	The accumulator and the pointer exchange values.
add k	The value in register k is added to the accumulator.
subtract k	The value in register k is subtracted from the accumulator.
multiply k	The accumulator is multiplied by the value in register k.
conditional jump j	If the value in the accumulator is positive, then the program counter is assigned the value j.
accept	The program halts in the accept state.
reject	The program halts in the reject state.

Table 1. RAM Instruction Set

A RAM *program* is a finite sequence of instructions. The *program counter* indicates which instruction to execute. In most cases, the program counter is incremented at the completion of each instruction. However, if the instruction conditional jump j is performed and the value in the accumulator is positive, the program counter is assigned the value j. The program counter is not updated when the instruction accept or reject is performed. We say that a computation *accepts* if the program counter eventually points to an **accept** instruction and that the computation *rejects* if the program counter eventually points to a **reject** instruction. The running time of a computation is the number of instructions executed until the program counter points to an **accept** or **reject** instruction. Thus **accept** and **reject** are free and all other instructions have unit cost.

3 Upper bounds

In this section, we present data structures for representing a set S and algorithms that query these data structures to determine if a given element x is in S. Initially, register 0 contains the input x and registers $1, \ldots, s$ contain the cells of the data structure $\phi(S)$. All other registers have initial value 0. A correct algorithm must accept inputs x and $\phi(S)$ if $x \in S$ and must reject them if $x \notin S$.

Although binary search normally involves division by 2, it can be implemented on a RAM. The idea is to precompute the first $\lfloor \log_2 n \rfloor$ powers of 2. The initial comparison is performed at location $2^{\lfloor \log_2 n \rfloor}$ and the locations of subsequent comparisons are obtained by either adding or subtracting successively smaller powers of 2. (See [Knu73, vol. 3 pages 413-414].) Alternatively, the full binary search tree containing the values in S can be represented implicitly with the left and right children of the node in location l at locations $2l$ and $2l + 1$, respectively (as in a heap). (See [Ben86, pages 136,183–184] and [Knu73, vol. 1 page 401, vol. 3 pages 422,670].) Then the equivalent of binary search can be carried out using no extra registers.

Constant query time is possible with a bit vector representation, using m registers. By packing many bits together in one word, it is possible to use less space at the expense of more time. To do this, it is helpful to implement some functions which are not part of the standard RAM instruction set. We use the notation $[a..b]$ to denote the set of integers between a and b, inclusive.

Proposition 1. *A RAM can compute the quotient and remainder of x divided by y in time $O(\log(x/y))$.*

Proof. By repeated doubling, we construct an array containing the values y, $2y$, $4y$, $\ldots$, $2^{t-1}y$, where t is the smallest value such that $2^t y > x$. Note that $t \in O(\log(x/y))$. The quotient q of x divided by y is the largest integer such that $q \cdot y \leq x$. Using the array and a variant of binary search, q as well as qy can be computed in $O(t)$ steps. Then we can compute the remainder by subtracting qy from x.

A RAM can shift a number left k bit positions by multiplying the number by 2^k. This takes constant time, if the number 2^k is available. Shifting right is harder, but it can be done in constant time in restricted situations.

Proposition 2. *With tables of size 2^{2^t} and 2^{t-1}, a RAM can shift a $(2^t - k)$-bit number right k bit positions in constant time, for any $k \in [1..2^{t-1}]$.*

Proof. Use a table containing the first 2^{t-1} powers of 2 and a lookup table of size 2^{2^t} whose l'th entry is the left half (i.e. the 2^{t-1} most significant bits) of l, when viewed as a 2^t-bit number. Then a 2^t-bit number can be shifted right by 2^{t-1} positions using one **indirect read** operation.

A $(2^t - k)$-bit number can be shifted right by k positions by first multiplying the number by $2^{2^{t-1}-k}$ (to shift it left $2^{t-1} - k$ positions) and then shifting the result right 2^{t-1} positions using the lookup table, as above.

Proposition 3. *There is a data structure for storing subsets of $[0..m-1]$ using $m/2^t + 2^{2^t} + 2^{t-1} + O(1)$ registers and $O(t)$ query time on a RAM.*

Proof. The main part of the data structure $\phi(S)$ is an array of $\lceil m/2^t \rceil$ cells, each containing a 2^t-bit non-negative integer. Together, the bits of these integers form a bit vector representation of S, as follows: Let q and r denote the quotient and remainder when x is divided by $\lceil m/2^t \rceil$. Then $x \in S$ if and only if the $(q+1)$'st least significant bit in cell $r + 1$ of the array is 1. For example, if $m = 20$ and $t = 2$, the set $S = \{0, 1, 2, 3, 4, 5, 9, 11, 14, 19\}$ is represented by the following array.

$$\boxed{0011 \mid 0101 \mid 0001 \mid 0001 \mid 1111}$$

Given x, Proposition 1 can be used to compute r and q in time $O(t)$. Then the $(q+1)$'st least significant bit is extracted from the 2^t-bit integer in cell $r + 1$, as follows: Using Proposition 2, first shift the integer right $q + 1$ positions, then shift it left $q+1$ positions, and subtract the result from the integer. The resulting value is shifted right q positions to get the desired bit.

Division can be combined with binary search to obtain the following data structure. It improves the solution in Proposition 3 for most natural choices of the parameters.

Proposition 4. *There is a data structure for storing n-element subsets of $[0..m-1]$ using $m/2^t + n + O(1)$ registers and $O(t)$ query time on a RAM.*

Proof. The data structure $\phi(S)$ representing S consists of three arrays. One array contains the elements of S, arranged so that all elements that are equivalent modulo $\lceil m/2^{t+1} \rceil$ are grouped together and, within each group, the elements are in sorted order. The second array consists of $\lceil m/2^{t+1} \rceil$ pointers to the beginning of the regions of the first array that contain elements equivalent to r modulo $\lceil m/2^{t+1} \rceil$ for $r \in [0..\lceil m/2^{t+1} \rceil - 1]$. The third array contains the number of elements in S equivalent to r modulo $\lceil m/2^{t+1} \rceil$ for $r \in [0..\lceil m/2^{t+1} \rceil - 1]$. In this representation, with $m = 20$, $t = 1$, and $S = \{0, 1, 2, 3, 4, 5, 9, 11, 14, 19\}$, this is what $\phi(S)$ looks like.

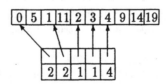

To determine whether x is in S, the remainder r of x divided by $\lceil m/2^{t+1} \rceil$ is computed in time $O(t)$ using Proposition 1. A pointer to the beginning of the relevant region of the first array and the size of this region are obtained from the second and third arrays. Binary search is then performed within this region. Since there are at most 2^{t+1} elements of S in the region, the search takes $O(t)$ time.

4 Lower Bounds

Throughout this section, we use the notation $U^{(n)}$ to denote the set of n-element subsets of U. We begin with two simple lemmas about low-degree polynomials.

Lemma 5. *Let $D, R \subseteq \mathbf{R}$ and let $p(x) \in \mathbf{R}[x]$ be a polynomial of degree at most d. If there are more than $d \cdot \#R$ elements of D that are mapped to R by the polynomial p, then p is a constant polynomial.*

Proof. Let $D' = \{x \in D \mid p(x) \in R\}$ and suppose $\#D' > d \cdot \#R$. Then there are at least $d + 1$ elements in D' that are mapped to the same element of R by p. Since p has degree at most d, it follows that p is constant.

Lemma 6. *Let $Z \subseteq \mathbf{Z}$ be a set of integers at least distance g apart from one another (i.e. if $x, y \in Z$ are distinct integers, then $|x - y| \geq g$). Let $p(x) \in \mathbf{Z}[x]$ be a nonconstant polynomial of degree at most d. If $d \cdot s \leq g$, then at most d elements of Z are mapped to $[1..s]$ by p.*

Proof. Suppose, to the contrary, that $d \cdot s \leq g$, but there exist $d + 1$ integers $x_0 < x_1 < \cdots < x_d \in Z$ that are all mapped to $[1..s]$ by p.

Let $i \in [1..d]$. Since p is nonconstant, it follows from Lemma 5 (with $D = [x_{i-1}..x_i]$ and $R = [0..s-1]$) that there is an integer $x \in [x_{i-1}..x_i]$ such that $p(x) \notin [1..s]$. If $p(x) \leq 0$, then there are two real numbers z_{2i-1} and z_{2i} such that $x_{i-1} < z_{2i-1} < x < z_{2i} < x_i$ and $p(z_{2i-1}) = p(z_{2i}) = \frac{1}{2}$. Otherwise $p(x) \geq s + 1$, since p has integer coefficients. In this case, there are two real numbers z_{2i-1} and z_{2i} such that $x_{i-1} < z_{2i-1} < x < z_{2i} < x_i$ and $p(z_{2i-1}) = p(z_{2i}) = s + \frac{1}{2}$.

Furthermore, since p is a nonconstant polynomial,

$$\lim_{x \to \infty} p(x), \ \lim_{x \to -\infty} p(x) \in \{-\infty, \infty\}.$$

Hence, there exist real numbers $z_0 < x_0$ and $z_{2d+1} > x_d$ such that $p(z_0), p(z_{2d+1}) \in \{\frac{1}{2}, s + \frac{1}{2}\}$. It follows from Lemma 5 (with $D = \{z_0, z_1, \ldots, z_{2d+1}\}$ and $R = \{\frac{1}{2}, s + \frac{1}{2}\}$) that p is constant, which is a contradiction.

We are now ready to present our main lemma, which is the same as our main theorem, except that the order of two quantifiers is switched; it states that in any representation, some set is hard.

Lemma 7. *Let $\phi : U^{(n)} \to \mathbf{Z}^s$ be a map that defines a representation of any n-element subset of $U = [0..m-1]$ as a sequence of s integers. Consider any correct RAM program for querying this data structure. For any $\epsilon > 0$, if $n \leq s \leq m/n^\epsilon$, there is a constant $\delta > 0$, an element $x \in U$, and a set $S \in U^{(n)}$ so that the program uses more than $\delta \log n$ steps on inputs x and $\phi(S)$.*

Proof. Let $l = \lfloor n^{\epsilon/4} \rfloor$. We assume, without loss of generality, that $\epsilon < 1/10$ and $l \geq 10$.

An essential part of our proof technique is to consider a subdomain of U where the elements are spaced widely apart. Then Lemma 6 can be applied to show that indirect reads to locations that are non-constant functions of x can essentially be ignored. This is because the range $[1..s]$, where the data structure is stored, is accessed for relatively few values of x. To achieve the optimal space bound $s \leq m/n^\epsilon$, we need wider spacing than can be achieved in a set of size n. Therefore, we restrict our attention to sets of size l. Since $\log l \in \Omega(\log n)$, the lower bound is not affected by more than a constant factor.

The data structure defined by ϕ can also be used for l-element sets from the universe $[0..m - (n - l) - 1]$. The representation $\phi'(S)$ of such a set S is simply $\phi(S \cup [m - (n - l)..m - 1])$. The original program is correct on all inputs x and $\phi'(S)$, where $x \in [0..m - (n - l) - 1]$ and $S \in [0..m - (n - l) - 1]^{(l)}$.

Let $g = l \cdot s$ and $U' = \{0, g, 2g, \ldots, (l^2 - 1)g\}$. Note that $(l^2 - 1)g \leq l^3 s \leq n^{3/4\epsilon}s \leq m/n^{\epsilon/4} \leq m/l \leq m - n$, so $U' \subseteq [0..m - (n - l) - 1]$.

Let $T = \lfloor \frac{\log l}{10} \rfloor$. To achieve a contradiction, suppose that on all inputs x and $\phi'(S)$, where S is an l-element subset of U', the RAM program reaches an **accept** or **reject** instruction within T steps.

At each step t, we choose a subdomain $U_t \subseteq U'$, a collection V_t of l-element subsets of U', and, for each $S \in V_t$, a small set of bad elements $B_{S,t} \subseteq U_t$ with the following property. For all $S \in V_t$ and all $x \in U_t - B_{S,t}$, the same sequence of instructions are performed and the outcomes of all tests are the same during the first t steps of the computation on inputs x and $\phi'(S)$. For each set $S \in V_t$, it is convenient to represent the values of the accumulator and the pointer at the end of step t by low degree polynomials, $a_{S,t}$ and $p_{S,t}$. The other registers to which values have been written are represented by a small set $Q_{S,t}$ of low degree integer polynomials. Specifically, for each element $x \in U_t - B_{S,t}$, $\{q(x) \mid q \in Q_{S,t}\}$ is the set of registers to which the algorithm writes during the first t steps on inputs x and $\phi'(S)$. In addition, for each polynomial $q \in Q_{S,t}$, the value of these cells is described by a low degree integer polynomial $v_{S,q,t}$ (i.e. $v_{S,q,t}(x)$ is the value in cell $q(x)$ after step t is performed on inputs x and $\phi'(S)$). The above discussion is formalized in the following claim.

Claim For each integer $t \in [0..T]$, there exist

- a subdomain $U_t \subseteq U'$,
- a collection V_t of l-element subsets of U',
- a set of bad elements $B_{S,t} \subseteq U_t$ for each $S \in V_t$
- two polynomials $a_{S,t}$ and $p_{S,t}$ for each set $S \in V_t$.

- a set of polynomials in $Q_{S,t} \subseteq \mathbf{Z}[x]$ for each set $S \in V_t$,
- a polynomial $v_{S,q,t}(x) \in \mathbf{Z}[x]$ for each set $S \in V_t$ and each polynomial $q \in Q_{S,t}$, and
- an integer c_t,

such that, for each set $S \in V_t$,

- $\#(U_t \cap S) \geq l/2^t$,
- $\#V_t \geq \binom{l^2}{l} 2^{-2t} (l^2)^{1-2^t}$,
- $\#B_{S,t} < 2^{2t}$,
- $\operatorname{degree}(a_{S,t}), \operatorname{degree}(p_{S,t}) \leq 2^t$.
- $\#Q_{S,t} \leq t+1$,
- $\operatorname{degree}(q), \operatorname{degree}(v_{S,q,t}) \leq 2^t$ for every polynomial $q \in Q_{S,t}$, and
- $q(x) \neq q'(x)$ for all $x \in U_t - B_{S,t}$ and all distinct polynomials $q, q' \in Q_{S,t}$,

and, for each set $S \in V_t$ and each element $x \in U_t - B_{S,t}$, after t steps on inputs x and $\phi'(S)$,

- the program counter has value c_t,
- the accumulator has value $a_{S,t}(x)$ and the pointer has value $p_{S,t}(x)$.
- register $q(x)$ has value $v_{S,q,t}(x)$ for each polynomial $q \in Q_{S,t}$,
- each register $r \in [1..s] - \{q(x) \mid q \in Q_{S,t}\}$ has value $\phi'(S)_r$, and
- each register $r \notin [1..s] \cup \{q(x) \mid q \in Q_{S,t}\}$ has value 0.

Proof of claim. By induction on t.

When $t = 0$, $U_0 = U'$, V_0 is the collection of all l-element subsets of U', $B_{S,0} = \emptyset$ for all $S \in V_0$, and c_0 is the initial value of the program counter, which is the same for all inputs. For each $S \in V_0$, let $a_{S,t} = p_{S,t} = 0$, $Q_{S,t} = \{0\}$, and $v_{S,0,0} = x$. Here 0 denotes the constant polynomial with value 0. In general, we will use k to denote the polynomial with constant value k. Then, $\#V_0 = \binom{\#U'}{l} = \binom{l^2}{l} = \binom{l^2}{l} 2^{-2 \cdot 0} (l^2)^{1-2^0}$ and for each set $S \in V_0$ we have $\#(U_0 \cap S) = \#S = l = l/2^0$, $\#B_{S,t} = 0 < 2^{2 \cdot 0}$, and $\#Q_{S,t} = 1$.

Now let $t < T$ and assume the claim is true for t. Since the program counter has the same value c_t for all $S \in V_t$ and $x \in U_t - B_{S,t}$, the same instruction is performed at step $t + 1$ on all these inputs. We consider a number of different cases, depending on this instruction. To avoid tedious repetition, we will only mention explicitly those things which change. For example, if $V_{t+1} = V_t$, we will not mention this. Also, unless we state otherwise, $c_{t+1} = c_t + 1$.

The accept and reject instructions do not change the value of the program counter or the contents of any register. Thus everything can remain unchanged.

When the load k instruction is performed, the accumulator is assigned the constant value k. We let $a_{S,t+1} = k$.

The swap instruction swaps the values of the accumulator and pointer. Thus $p_{S,t+1} = a_{S,t}$ and $a_{S,t+1} = p_{S,t}$.

When direct write k is performed, the value $a_{S,t}(x)$ in the accumulator is written to register k. If $Q_{S,t}$ contains the constant polynomial k, then no new polynomial is added to this set, but $v_{S,k,t+1} = a_{S,t}$.

Otherwise, $Q_{S,t+1} = Q_{S,t} \cup \{k\}$, $v_{S,k,t+1} = a_{S,t}$, and $B_{S,t+1} = B_{S,t} \cup \{x \in U_t | \, q(x) = k$ for some $q \in Q_{S,t}\}$. Since there are at most $t+1$ polynomials in $Q_{S,t}$, each having degree at most 2^t, it follows that $\#B_{S,t+1} \leq \#B_{S,t} + (t+1)2^t \leq 2^{2(t+1)}$.

When **direct read** k is performed, the value in register k is written to the accumulator. We will deal with each $S \in V_{t+1} = V_t$ one at a time. There are three cases: If $k \in Q_{S,t}$, then $a_{S,t+1} = v_{S,k,t}$. If $k \in [1..s] - Q_{S,t}$, let $a_{S,t+1}$ be the constant polynomial with value $\phi'(S)_k$. If $k \notin Q_{S,t} \cup [1..s]$, then let $a_{S,t+1} = 0$. In the last two cases, $B_{S,t+1} = B_{S,t} \cup \{x \in U_t | \, q(x) = k$ for some $q \in Q_{S,t}\}$ and, as above, $\#B_{S,t+1} \leq 2^{2(t+1)}$.

The **add** k, **subtract** k, and **multiply** k instructions are handled similarly to **direct read** k, except that the polynomial assigned to $a_{S,t+1}$ is first added to, subtracted from, or multiplied by the polynomial $a_{S,t}$. For example, for the case of **add** k, if $k \in Q_{S,t}$, let $a_{S,t+1}$ be the polynomial $v_{S,k,t} + a_{S,t}$. The degree can increase only when **multiply** is performed. In this case, since the multiplicands each have degree at most 2^t, the product has degree at most 2^{t+1}.

When **indirect write** is performed, the value in the accumulator is written to the register specified by the contents of the pointer. When $p_{S,t}(x)$ is a constant polynomial with value k, the operation is equivalent to **direct write** k and is handled in the same way. If $p_{S,t} \in Q_{S,t}$, the polynomial $v_{S,q,t+1}$ describing the contents of the cells $\{q(x) \mid x \in U_t - B_{S,t}\}$ is set equal to the polynomial $a_{S,t}$. Otherwise, let $Q_{S,t+1} = Q_{S,t} \cup \{p_{S,t}\}$ (so $\#Q_{S,t+1} \leq t+2$), $v_{S,p_{S,t},t+1} = a_{S,t}$, and

$$B_{S,t+1} = B_{S,t} \cup \{x \in U_t | \, p_{S,t}(x) = q(x) \text{ for some } q \in Q_{S,t}\}.$$

By construction, $p_{S,t}(x) \neq q(x)$ for each $q \in Q_{S,t}$ and $x \in U_{t+1} - B_{S,t+1}$. Each polynomial $q \in Q_{S,t}$ has degree at most 2^t, so $p_{S,t}$ and q intersect in at most 2^t places. Since $\#Q_{S,t} \leq t+1$, it follows that $\#\{x \in U_t | \, p_{S,t}(x) = q(x) \text{ for some } q \in Q_{S,t}\} \leq (t+1)2^t$. Thus $\#B_{S,t+1} < 2^{2t} + (t+1)2^t < 2^{2(t+1)}$.

When **indirect read** k is performed, the value in the register specified by the contents of the pointer is written to the accumulator. If $p_{S,t}(x)$ is a constant polynomial with value k, the operation is equivalent to **direct read** k and is handled in the same way. If $p_{S,t} \in Q_{S,t}$, the polynomial $a_{S,t+1}$ is set equal to the polynomial $v_{S,p_{S,t},t}$. Otherwise,

$$B_{S,t+1} = B_{S,t} \cup \{x \in U_t | \, p_{S,t}(x) \in [1..s]\}$$
$$\cup \{x \in U_t | \, p_{S,t}(x) = q(x) \text{ for some } q \in Q_{S,t}\}.$$

In this case, the value of the **indirect read** is 0 for all $x \in U_t - B_{S,t+1}$, so the polynomial $a_{S,t+1}$ is the constant 0 polynomial. Since $p_{S,t}$ has degree at most $2^t \leq g/s$, it follows from Lemma 6 that $\#\{x \in U_t | \, p_{S,t}(x) \in [1..s]\} \leq 2^t$. So we have $\#B_{S,t+1} < 2^{2t} + 2^t + (t+1)2^t < 2^{2(t+1)}$.

Finally, suppose the instruction executed is **conditional jump** j. For each $S \in V_t$, consider the sequence of test outcomes (either $a_{S,t}(x) > 0$ or $a_{S,t}(x) \leq 0$), for $x \in U_t$ taken in increasing order. Since a polynomial of degree at most 2^t

has at most 2^t roots and, hence, can change sign at most 2^t times along any increasing sequence of domain points, there are

$$2\sum_{i=0}^{2^t}\binom{\#U_t}{i} < 2\cdot(\#U_t)^{2^t} \le 2(l^2)^{2^t}$$

different sequences of test outcomes that can occur. Let V' be the largest subcollection of V_t such that all sets $S \in V'$ produce the same sequence of test outcomes. Then $\#V' \ge \#V_t/2(l^2)^{2^t}$.

Let $Y = \{x \in U_t \mid a_{S,t}(x) > 0 \text{ for all } S \in V'\}$ and $N = \{x \in U_t \mid a_{S,t}(x) \le 0 \text{ for all } S \in V'\}$. Then $Y \cup N = U_t$. For each $S \in V'$, the induction hypothesis says that $\#(U_t \cap S) \ge l/2^t$; so either $\#(Y \cap S) \ge l/2^{t+1}$ or $\#(N \cap S) \ge l/2^{t+1}$. If $\#(Y \cap S) \ge l/2^{t+1}$ for at least half the sets $S \in V'$, then $U_{t+1} = Y$, $V_{t+1} = \{S \in V' \mid \#(Y \cap S) \ge l/2^{t+1}\}$, $\#V_{t+1} \ge \#V'/2$, and $\#(U_{t+1} \cap S) \ge l/2^{t+1}$ for all sets $S \in V_{t+1}$. Also, for each element $x \in U_{t+1} - B_{S,t} \subseteq Y$ and each set $S \in V_{t+1}$, the test succeeds (i.e. $a_{S,t}(x) > 0$), so the jump is performed and the program counter is assigned the value j (i.e. $c_{t+1} = j$). Otherwise, $\#(N \cap S) \ge l/2^{t+1}$ for at least half the sets $S \in V'$. Then $U_{t+1} = N$, $V_{t+1} = \{S \in V' \mid \#(N \cap S) \ge l/2^{t+1}\}$, $\#V_{t+1} \ge \#V'/2$, and $\#(U_{t+1} \cap S) \ge l/2^{t+1}$ for all sets $S \in V_{t+1}$. For each element $x \in U_{t+1}$ and each set $S \in V_{t+1}$, the test fails (i.e. $a_{S,t}(x) \le 0$), so the jump is not performed and the program counter is incremented (i.e. $c_{t+1} = c_t + 1$). In both cases, $B_{S,t+1} = B_{S,t} \cap U_{t+1}$ (so $\#B_{S,t+1} \le 2^{2t}$) and

$$\#V_{t+1} \ge \#V'/2 \ge \#V_t/4(l^2)^{2^t} \ge \binom{l^2}{l}2^{-2(t+1)}(l^2)^{1-2^{t+1}}.$$

Since all the desired conditions are true no matter which instruction is performed at step $t+1$, the claim is true for $t+1$ and, by induction, for all integers $t \in [0..T]$.

To end the proof, we consider the meaning of the claim for $t = T$. We have a subdomain $U_T \subseteq U'$, a collection V_T of l-element subsets of U', and, for each $S \in V_T$, a set of bad points $B_{S,T} \subseteq U_T$ satisfying the following properties: For each set $S \in V_T$ and each element $x \in U_T - B_{S,T}$, $\#(U_T \cap S) \ge l/2^T$, $\#V_T \ge \binom{l^2}{l}2^{-2T}(l^2)^{1-2^T}$, $\#B_{S,T} < 2^{2T}$, and, after T steps on inputs x and $\phi'(S)$, the program counter has value c_T.

By assumption, c_T is either an **accept** or **reject** instruction. For any $S \in V_T$,

$$\#((U_T - B_{S,T}) \cap S) = \#((U_T \cap S) - B_{S,T}) \ge l/2^T - 2^{2T} > 0,$$

so there is some $x \in U_T - B_{S,T}$, such that $x \in S$. Thus c_T is an **accept** instruction.

In other words, the program accepts inputs x and $\phi'(S)$ for all $S \in V_T$ and $x \in U_T - B_{S,T}$. Since the program is correct, we must have $x \in S$ for all $S \in V_T$ and $x \in U_T - B_{S,T}$. Thus $U_T - B_{S,T} \subseteq S \subseteq U'$ for all $S \in V_T$. Furthermore, $\#U_T \ge l/2^T$ and $|U'| = l^2$. It follows that

$$\#V_T \le \sum_{i=0}^{2^{2T}}\binom{l/2^T}{i}\binom{l^2-l/2^T}{l-l/2^T+i} \le 2\binom{l/2^T}{2^{2T}}\binom{l^2-l/2^T}{l-l/2^T+2^{2T}}.$$

Combined with the lower bound $\#V_T \geq \binom{l^2}{l} 2^{-2^T} (l^2)^{1-2^T}$, this yields

$$\binom{l^2}{l} 2^{-2^T} (l^2)^{1-2^T} \leq 2\binom{l/2^T}{2^{2T}}\binom{l^2-l/2^T}{l-l/2^T+2^{2T}}.$$

By elementary estimates of binomial coefficients, this inequality can be shown to be false for $T = \lfloor \frac{\log l}{10} \rfloor$. Therefore, our assumption that the program always accepts or rejects within T steps must be false. This concludes the proof of Lemma 7.

Our main theorem follows easily from Lemma 7.

Theorem 8. *Let $n \leq s \leq m/n^\epsilon$ for some constant $\epsilon > 0$. There is a set $S \in U^{(n)}$, so that for any representation $\phi_S \in \mathbf{Z}^s$ the following is true. Consider any RAM program that, on inputs x and ϕ_S, accepts if $x \in S$ and rejects if $x \notin S$. Then, for some $x \in U$, the program uses $\Omega(\log n)$ steps on inputs x and ϕ_S.*

Proof. Given a program A with p instructions, we can encode A as a string of $2p$ integers, representing each instruction by an integer in $[1..12]$ that specifies the instruction type (i.e. 1 for load, 2 for direct read, etc.) and its argument, if any. Denote this encoding by $\tau(A)$. Cook and Rechow [CR73] show that there exists a universal RAM interpreter with the property that if the interpreter is executed with inputs $\mathbf{z} \in \mathbf{Z}^*$ and $\tau(A)$ (stored in an interleaved fashion), the result is the same as if A was executed on input $\mathbf{z}$. Furthermore, if A uses times T, then the interpreter uses time $O(T)$.

Given any positive constant $\epsilon \leq \frac{1}{2}$, let $\epsilon' = \epsilon/2$. Let n, m, and s be given and assume, without loss of generality, that $n^{\epsilon'} \geq 3$. Suppose that, for all $S \subseteq U$, there exists a representation ϕ_S and a program A_S that runs in time $T < \frac{\log n}{2}$ and accepts inputs x and ϕ_S if and only if $x \in S$. We can assume, without loss of generality, that A_S contains at most $2^T < n^{1/2}$ instructions. For any S, define $\phi(S)$ to consist of $\tau(A_S)$ and ϕ_S interleaved. The size of this data structure is at most $s' = 2\max(2n^{1/2}, s) < m/n^{\epsilon'}$. When the interpreter is run on inputs $x \in U$ and $\phi(S)$, it accepts if and only if $x \in S$. Furthermore, it accepts or rejects within $O(T)$ steps. From Lemma 7, it follows that $T \in \Omega(\log n)$.

Acknowledgments

We are indebted to Dany Breslauer for suggesting how to remove the restriction on the number of registers used by the query algorithm that appeared in a previous version of our theorem.

The first author was supported in part by Natural Science and Engineering Research Council of Canada grant A-9176 and the Information Technology Research Centre of Ontario. The second author was supported by a postdoctoral fellowship from the Danish Natural Science Research Council through BRICS, University of Aarhus.

References

[AHU74]   A. Aho, J. Hopcroft, and J. Ullman, *The Design and Analysis of Computer Algorithms*, Addison-Wesley, Reading, MA, 1974.

[BG91]   A.M. Ben-Amram and Z. Galil, Lower bounds for data structure problems on RAMs. In *Proc. 32th IEEE Symposium on Foundations of Computer Science*, 1991, pages 622–631.

[Ben86]   J.L. Bentley, *Programming Pearls*. Addison-Wesley, Reading, MA, 1986.

[BM94]   A. Brodnik and J. Ian Munro, Membership in constant time and minimum space. In *Proc. 2nd European Symposium on Algorithms* 1994, pages 72–81.

[CR73]   S.A. Cook and R.A. Reckhow, Time bounded random access machines. *JCSS*, vol. 7, 1973, pages 354–375.

[FN93]   A. Fiat and M. Naor, Implicit $O(1)$ probe search. *SIAM J. Computing* vol. 22, 1993, pages 1–10.

[FNSS92] A. Fiat, M. Naor, J.P. Schmidt, and A. Seigel, Nonoblivious hashing. *J. ACM* vol. 39, 1992, pages 764–782.

[FKS84]   M.L. Fredman, J. Komlòs, and E. Szemerédi, Storing a sparse table with $O(1)$ worst case access time. *J. ACM*, vol. 31, 1984, pages 538–544.

[FS89]   M.L. Fredman and M.E. Saks, The cell probe complexity of dynamic data structures. In *Proc. 21st Ann. ACM Symp. on Theory of Computing*, 1989, pages 345–354.

[Knu73]   D.E. Knuth, *The Art of Computer Programming*. Addison-Wesley, Reading, MA, 1973.

[Maa88]   W. Maass, On the use of inaccessible numbers and order indiscernibles in lower bound arguments for random access machines. *J. Symbolic Logic*, vol. 53, 1988, pages 1098–1109.

[MNSW95] P.B. Miltersen, N. Nisan, S. Safra, and A. Wigderson, On data structures and asymmetric communication complexity. In *Proc. 27th ACM Symposium on Theory of Computing*, 1995, to appear.

[PS82]   W. Paul and J. Simon, Decision trees and random access machines. In *Logic and Algorithmic*, monograph no. 30 de l'enseignement mathématique, Univeristé de Genève, 1982.

[ST85]   D.D. Sleator and R.E. Tarjan, Self-Adjusting Binary Search Trees. *J. ACM*, vol. 32, 1985, pages 652-686.

[TY79]   R.E. Tarjan and A.C. Yao, Storing a sparse table. *C. ACM*, vol. 22, 1979, pages 606–611.

[Yao81]   A.C. Yao, Should tables be sorted? *J. ACM*, vol. 28, 1981, pages 615–628.

Improved Length Bounds for the Shortest Superstring Problem

(extended abstract)

Chris Armen[1][*] and Clifford Stein[2][**]

[1] University of Hartford, W. Hartford, CT 06117-1599, USA
[2] Dartmouth College, Hanover, NH 03755-3510, USA

Abstract. Given a collection of strings $S = \{s_1, \ldots, s_n\}$ over an alphabet Σ, a *superstring* α of S is a string containing each s_i as a substring; that is, for each i, $1 \leq i \leq n$, α contains a block of $|s_i|$ consecutive characters that match s_i exactly. The *shortest superstring problem* is the problem of finding a superstring α of minimum length. This problem is NP-hard [6] and has applications in computational biology and data compression. The first $O(1)$-approximation algorithms were given in [2]. We describe our $2\frac{3}{4}$-approximation algorithm, which is the best known. While our algorithm is not complex, our analysis requires some novel machinery to describe overlapping periodic strings. We then show how to combine our result with that of [11] to obtain a ratio of $2\frac{50}{69} \approx 2.725$. We describe an implementation of our algorithm which runs in $O(|S| + n^3)$ time; this matches the running time of previous $O(1)$-approximations.

1 Introduction

Given a set of strings $S = \{s_1, \ldots, s_n\}$ over an alphabet Σ, a *superstring* α of S is a string containing each s_i as a substring, that is, for $1 \leq i \leq n$, α contains $|s_i|$ consecutive characters that match each s_i exactly. The *shortest superstring problem* is the problem of finding a superstring α of minimum length.

The shortest superstring problem has applications in both computational biology [4, 12, 15] and data compression [6, 17]. DNA sequencing is the task of determining the sequence of nucleotides in a section of DNA. These nucleotides are typically represented by the alphabet $\{a, c, g, t\}$. The sequence of DNA to be determined may be up to 50,000 nucleotides long [9], but current laboratory procedures can directly determine the nucleotides of a fragment up to only about 600 nucleotides long. In *shotgun sequencing*, several copies of a DNA molecule are fragmented using various restriction enzymes, each of which breaks a copy of the DNA molecule in different places.

---

[*] Email: armen@hartford.edu. This work was done while the author was at Dartmouth College.

[**] Email: cliff@cs.dartmouth.edu. Research partly supported by NSF Award CCR-9308701, a Walter Burke Research Initiation Award and a Dartmouth College Research Initiation Award.

Once the nucleotides of all of the fragments have been determined, the *sequence assembly problem* is the computational task of reconstructing the original molecule from the overlapping fragments. The shortest superstring problem is an abstraction of this problem, in which the shortest reconstruction is assumed to be the most likely on the grounds that it is the most parsimonious.

The shortest superstring problem is MAX SNP-hard [2]; several heuristics and approximation algorithms have been proposed. One often used algorithm is a greedy algorithm that repeatedly merges a pair of strings with the maximum amount of overlap. Turner [20] and Tarhio and Ukkonnen [18] independently proved that the greedy algorithm finds a superstring that has at least half as much overlap as an optimal superstring. This does not, however, guarantee a constant approximation with respect to the length of the resulting superstring.

The first bound on the length approximation of the greedy algorithm was provided by Blum et al.[2], who showed that the greedy algorithm returns a string whose length is no more than four times the length of an optimal superstring; they also gave a modified greedy algorithm that achieves a 3-approximation. Teng and Yao [19] gave a nongreedy $2\frac{8}{9}$-approximation algorithm; independently of our work, Czumaj et al.[3] refined this algorithm to achieve a $2\frac{5}{6}$-approximation. Recently a result by Kosaraju et al. for the maximum traveling salesman problem has been used to improve the algorithm of [2] to obtain an approximation slightly better than 2.8 [11].

In this paper, we study the structure of periodic strings with large amounts of overlap. These have been studied in other contexts, e.g. [13, 16]; here we prove several new structural properties of such strings. We use these properties to guide an algorithm that finds a superstring whose length is no more than $2\frac{3}{4}$ times the optimal superstring. We also show that this result can be combined with that of [11] to achieve a bound of $2\frac{50}{69} \approx 2.725$. We believe that these properties of overlapping strings are important beyond the particular improved bound that we obtain, and feel that this structure will ultimately lead to even better algorithms. The implementation of our algorithm provides an illustration of this structure; we show how our algorithm can be implemented to run in $O(|S| + n^3)$ time, which equals the time required by the other $O(1)$-approximation algorithms.

2 Preliminaries

For consistency, we use some notation and definitions from [2] and [19]. We can assume that the set S of strings is *substring free* [18, 20]; i.e. no s_j is a substring of s_i, $i \neq j$. We use $|s_i|$ to denote the length of string s_i, $|S|$ to denote the sum of the lengths of all the strings, and opt(S) to denote the length of the shortest superstring of S.

Given two strings s and t, we define ov(s, t), the *overlap* between s and t, to be the length of the longest string x, such that there exist non-empty u and v with $s = ux$ and $t = xv$. We call u the *prefix* of s with respect to t, pref(s, t), and refer to $|u|$ as the distance from s to t, d(s, t). Observe that for any s and t,

$\mathrm{ov}(s,t) + \mathrm{d}(s,t) = |s|$. String uxv, the shortest superstring of s and t in which s appears before t is denoted by $\langle s,t \rangle$, and $|\langle s,t \rangle| = |s| + |t| - \mathrm{ov}(s,t)$.

We can map the superstring problem to a graph problem by defining the *distance graph*. We create a graph $G = (V,E)$ with a vertex $v_i \in V$ for each string $s_i \in S$. For every ordered pair of vertices v_i, v_j, we place a directed edge of length $\mathrm{d}(s_i, s_j)$ and label the edge with $\mathrm{pref}(s_i, s_j)$. We can now observe that a minimum length Hamiltonian cycle (traveling salesman tour) $v_{\pi_1}, \ldots, v_{\pi_n}, v_{\pi_1}$, in G, with edge i,j labeled by $\mathrm{pref}(s_{\pi_i}, s_{\pi_j})$, almost corresponds to a superstring in S, the only difference being that we must replace $\mathrm{pref}(s_{\pi_n}, s_{\pi_1})$ with s_{π_n}. Since $\mathrm{pref}(s_i, s_j) \leq |s|$, we can conclude that $\mathrm{opt}(TSP) \leq \mathrm{opt}(S)$, where $\mathrm{opt}(TSP)$ is the optimal solution to TSP defined above. This TSP is directed (sometimes called *asymmetric*); thus the best known approximation [5] is only within a factor of $O(\log n)$. Therefore, we must exploit more of the structure of the problem in order to achieve better bounds.

Given a directed graph G, with weights on the edges, a *cycle cover* C is a set of cycles such that each vertex is in exactly one cycle. A minimum-cost cycle cover is a cycle cover such that the sum of the weights of the edges in all the cycles is minimized. A minimum-cost cycle cover $\mathrm{opt}(C)$ can be computed in $O(n^3)$ time by a well-known reduction to the assignment problem [14]. Since a tour is a cycle cover, $\mathrm{opt}(C) \leq \mathrm{opt}(TSP)$. When we say that a string s_i is in a cycle c of cycle cover C, we mean that the vertex v_i with which s_i is associated is in cycle c. When we refer to a cycle, we will be referring to a cycle that is in a minimum-cost cycle cover in the distance graph.

Following is a generic algorithm used, in some form, in [2],[19] and [3]. We state the algorithm and summarize its analysis in a way which anticipates our improvements.

GENERIC SUPERSTRING ALGORITHM
1) Find a minimum cost cycle cover C in the distance graph.
2) For each cycle $c \in C$, choose one string to be a representative r_c.
   Let G' be the subgraph induced by the representative set R.
3) Compute a cycle cover CC on G'.
4) In each cycle $\gamma \in CC$, delete one edge to form a string u_γ.
5) Concatenate the strings u_γ for all $\gamma \in CC$ to form $\bar{\alpha}$.
6) Extend each representative r_c by the concatenation of the prefixes around c;
   Return the resulting string α.

The first cycle cover identifies sets of strings that have large amounts of overlap. Breaking each cycle γ in Step (4) is like making a Hamiltonian path from a Hamiltonian cycle as discussed above; if we number the vertices of γ as $r_1, r_2, \ldots, r_m$, we must replace $\mathrm{pref}(r_{m-1}, r_m)$ with r_m. Let R_γ be the strings in cycle γ; each string u_γ in Step (4) is a superstring of the strings in R_γ; therefore $\bar{\alpha}$ in Step (5) is a superstring of R. Step (6) extends $\bar{\alpha}$ into a superstring for S [19].

For a cycle γ, let ov_γ^n denote the overlap in the edge deleted in Step (4), let ov_γ be the total overlap in cycle γ, and let $\mathrm{Ext}(\gamma)$ be the cost of extending all cycles $c \in C$ s.t. $r_c \in \gamma$. Note that $\mathrm{opt}(CC) \leq \mathrm{opt}(R)$ by the same analysis as above with the first cycle cover C and the original set S. The length of $\bar{\alpha}$ in Step

(5) will be as short as opt(CC) except for the overlap which is lost by discarding an edge in Step (4). Then we can bound the length of the solution α by

$$|\alpha| \leq \text{opt}(R) + \sum_{\gamma \in CC} \left(\text{ov}_\gamma^n + \text{Ext}(\gamma) \right) \tag{1}$$

Let $d(c)$ be the sum of the weights of the edges of a cycle $c \in C$ and let $d(C) = \sum_{c \in C} d(c)$. To obtain a 3-approximation, it can be shown that $\sum_{\gamma \in CC} \text{Ext}(\gamma) = d(C) \leq \text{opt}(S)$. At worst, Step 4 eliminates half of the overlap in a cycle in CC (in the case of a 2-cycle); the following key lemma from [2] allows us to conclude that $\sum_{\gamma \in CC} \text{ov}_\gamma^n \leq \frac{1}{2} \sum_{\gamma \in CC} \text{ov}_\gamma \leq d(C) \leq \text{opt}(S)$.

Lemma 1 [2]. *Let c, c' be cycles in a minimum cycle cover C with strings $s \in c$ and $s' \in c'$. Then the overlap between s, s' is less than $d(c) + d(c')$.*

From (1) we see that the cycle cover CC actually partitions the cycles in the cycle cover C, and hence each cycle in CC can be analyzed separately. As was observed by [19] in their $2\frac{8}{9}$ algorithm, if γ has three or more vertices, then $\text{ov}_\gamma^n \leq \frac{2}{3} \sum_{c \in \gamma} d(c)$. We obtain a $2\frac{3}{4}$ bound by proving structural properties of 2-cycles and analyzing each 2-cycle separately. Given a representative $v = r_c$ for some cycle c, we use c_v to denote the cycle c of which v is a representative. We summarize this discussion with the following lemma:

Lemma 2. *An algorithm following the framework of the generic algorithm above, that, for each 2-cycle γ in CC consisting of vertices v and t, attains a bound of $\text{ov}_\gamma^n + \text{Ext}(\gamma) \leq \beta(d(c_v) + d(c_t))$, for some $\beta \geq \frac{5}{3}$, is a $(1 + \beta)$-approximation algorithm for the shortest superstring problem.*

We define a few terms describing the structure of cycles. (See [2] for a more complete discussion.) We call a string s *irreducible* if all cyclic shifts of s yield unique strings, and *reducible* otherwise. Let $\text{gen}(\varsigma)$ be the string formed by an infinite repetition of a string ς. Let $\text{per}(c)$ be the string formed by concatenating all the labels of the edges on a cycle c, then for each string $s \in c$, s is a substring of $\text{gen}(\text{per}(c))$. We define $\overset{\infty}{\text{per}}(c)$ to be $\text{gen}(\text{per}(c))$. Note that $\text{per}(c)$ must be irreducible; otherwise a cycle with less total distance could generate the same strings, contradicting the minimality of the cycle cover.

3   The Structure of High-Overlap 2-Cycles

In the previous section we saw that in order to obtain a better length approximation it is sufficient to consider 2-cycles in the second cycle cover of the generic superstring algorithm. In this section we present new structural lemmas concerning 2-cycles.

Suppose we choose v and t as representatives of two cycles of the first cycle cover C, and they form a 2-cycle in CC in which one of $\text{ov}(v, t)$ or $\text{ov}(t, v)$ is large but the other is small. In Step 4 we will break the 2-cycle to form a string, and since we are trying to maximize overlap, the obvious choice is to keep the

$z =$ abab<u>abrst</u>ababab $z =$ <u>ababadababadab</u>ababadababadabab

) (( )   ( )   (

$y = y_\ell =$ ababab $y = y_\ell =$ ababadababadababa

$y_r =$ ababab $y_r =$ ababadababadabab

$\sigma =$ ab $\sigma =$ ababad

              (a)   (b)

Fig. 1. Positive and Negative Characteristics. Per(c) is underlined. (a) shows a negative characteristic. (b) shows a positive characteristic. y and σ are also shown.

high-overlap edge and discard the other. But if both edges have high overlap, we must discard one of them. In a 2-cycle this will cost us up to half of the overlap, which is the "worst case" of the generic algorithm.

Our strategy is to anticipate, when we choose representatives, the potential of each string to participate in a high-overlap 2-cycle. In particular we evaluate the potential of each string to play the role of the larger-period string in the 2-cycle. Such a string must have both a significant prefix and suffix with some smaller period, which corresponds to the period of another cycle in the cover and hence some other representative. We require some notation for this potential.

Definition 3. Let z be a string in cycle c and let σ be an irreducible string with $|\sigma| < \mathrm{d}(c)$. Then σ is a (g, h)-*repeater of* z if there exist witnesses y_ℓ and y_r, such that

1. y_ℓ is a prefix of z and y_r is a suffix of z.
2. y_ℓ and y_r are substrings of gen(σ).
3. $|y_\ell|, |y_r| > g\mathrm{d}(c) + h|\sigma|$.

Consider the string z in Fig. 1b and let $g = h = \frac{3}{4}$. As pictured, $|y_\ell|, |y_r| > \frac{3}{4}\mathrm{d}(c) + \frac{3}{4}|\sigma|$, and we say that σ is a $(\frac{3}{4}, \frac{3}{4})$-repeater of z. Note that in our example y_ℓ and y_r are almost the same; all the repeaters we consider in this paper will have $g \geq \frac{1}{2}$ and hence y_ℓ and y_r *must* overlap, often significantly (as in this example). For convenience we will define one witness y_σ which contains both y_ℓ and y_r; that is we define y_σ to be the maximum-length substring of gen(σ) that is also a substring of $\overset{\infty}{\mathrm{per}}(c)$. In other words, if you took σ and tried to repeat it as many times as possible, in both directions, while being consistent with c, you get y_σ. In the example above $y = y_\ell$. When the context is clear, we will drop the σ and just refer to witness y. Henceforth when discussing and proving properties of cycles, we will refer to the maximal witness y_σ rather than to the underlying pair of witnesses y_ℓ and y_r. This simplification is conservative.

The idea behind (g, h)-repeaters is to identify periodic substrings of the period of a cycle in C. We will also be interested in identifying that portion of a cycle that is *not* consistent with some (g, h)-repeater σ. Note that a copy of y_σ begins every $\mathrm{d}(c)$ in $\overset{\infty}{\mathrm{per}}(c)$, and that $|y| < 2\mathrm{d}(c)$.

Definition 4. Let c be a cycle with (g,h)-repeater σ and maximal witness y. Fix a copy of y in $\overset{\infty}{\text{per}}(c)$. The point just to the left of the first character of y is the *leftish of y*. Index this point as 0 and continue the indices between each character leftward and rightward to cover the interval $[-d(c)..d(c)]$. Now mark the point $|y| - d(c)$ and call it the *rightish of σ*. The *characteristic of σ*, X_σ, is the interval from the leftish to the rightish. If $|y| - d(c) > 0$ we call $[0..|y| - d(c)]$ a *positive characteristic X_σ*. If $|y| - d(c) \le 0$ we call $[|y| - d(c)..0]$ a *negative characteristic X_σ*.

We can picture the characteristics of the repeaters of a cycle c in terms of parentheses. Fig. 1b illustrates this idea for positive characteristics. The left and right ends of y_σ are marked with left and right parentheses; these correspond to the leftish and rightish of adjacent copies of X_σ.

A negative characteristic appears in Fig. 1a and can be pictured as the gap (perhaps of size 0) between copies of y. In this example rst is the negative characteristic. Each characteristic appears once every $d(c)$. Recall that we defined (g,h)-repeaters (Def. 3) in terms of some string z in a cycle c which contained witnesses y_ℓ and y_r as a prefix and suffix. In general there might be several such strings in c which could satisfy the definition. We say that σ is *active* in each of these strings. We say that two characteristics X_{σ_i}, X_{σ_j} are *properly nested* if X_{σ_i} is a positive characteristic and X_{σ_j} falls strictly within X_{σ_i}. We say that two characteristics X_{σ_i}, X_{σ_j} are *disjoint* if their intervals are disjoint.

We will be particularly interested in $(\frac{3}{4},\frac{3}{4})$-repeaters. We show that any two positive characteristics of $(\frac{3}{4},\frac{3}{4})$-repeaters are either nested or disjoint. This implies that any set of positive characteristics is well-parenthesized. We call X_σ a *major characteristic* if it is not nested within any other characteristic. A *minor characteristic* X_σ is one which is nested within some positive characteristic. We will say that σ is a *major (minor) repeater* if X_σ is a major (minor) characteristic.

This parenthesis structure naturally gives rise to a forest representation of the nesting of minor characteristics within major ones. We can view each major characteristic as the root of a parse tree, and each minor characteristic as another node in the tree according to its nested position, in the usual manner.

For any string in any cycle c, we can prove properties about the structure and size of possible (g,h)-repeaters and their characteristics. The following four lemmas provide this characterization, which shows that there can be only a small number of small repeaters and that all $(\frac{3}{4},\frac{3}{4})$-repeaters are nicely parenthesized.

Lemma 5. *Let c be an irreducible cycle. Then there is at most one σ such that σ is a $(\frac{1}{2},2)$-repeater of c.*

Lemma 6. *Let c be an irreducible cycle. Then there are at most two $(\frac{3}{4},\frac{3}{4})$-repeaters of c, σ_1 and σ_2, such that $|\sigma_i| \le \frac{1}{3}d(c), i \in \{1,2\}$.*

Lemma 7. *Let σ,σ' be $(\frac{3}{4},\frac{3}{4})$-repeaters in cycle c, $|\sigma| > |\sigma'|$, with witnesses y, y'. If both $y, y' \le d(c)$, then X_σ and $X_{\sigma'}$ are disjoint.*

Lemma 8. *Let σ,σ' be $(\frac{3}{4},\frac{3}{4})$-repeaters in cycle c, $|\sigma| > |\sigma'|$, with witnesses y, y'. If both $y, y' > d(c)$, then X_σ and $X_{\sigma'}$ are disjoint or properly nested.*

4 The Algorithm

4.1 Algorithm SHORTSTRING

Our algorithm, like the generic one described in Sect. 2, begins by forming a cycle cover on the distance graph, choosing a set of representatives, and then forming a second cycle cover on the representatives. We choose representatives by identifying $(\frac{3}{4}, \frac{3}{4})$-repeaters and their corresponding characteristics.

Let v and w be the representatives of two cycles in a distance graph and β the string formed by merging v and w to form $\langle v, w \rangle$ and extending it to the left to include each string in v's cycle and to the right to include each string in w's cycle. Then the extension cost $\mathrm{Ext}(v, w) = |\beta| - |\langle v, w \rangle|$. If γ is the two-cycle containing v and w, we will sometimes also write also write $\mathrm{Ext}(\gamma)$, meaning $\min(\mathrm{Ext}(v, w), \mathrm{Ext}(w, v))$. By the discussion in Sect. 2 we know that $\mathrm{Ext}(v, w) \leq \mathrm{d}(v) + \mathrm{d}(w)$. For cycles of size 3 and larger that is sufficient to achieve our bound. For 2-cycles we will be able to bound $\mathrm{Ext}(\gamma)$ more tightly, by taking advantage of the freedom to extend at either end.

Our algorithm, SHORTSTRING appears below. At a high level it resembles the generic algorithm, but in Step (2) we are more careful about choosing representatives and in Step (4), we are more careful about how we extend.

Algorithm SHORTSTRING
(1) Form a minimum cycle cover C on the distance graph.
(2) Call FINDREPS(c) on each cycle $c \in C$ to choose representatives R.
(3) Form minimum cycle cover CC on the graph induced by R.
(4) Break each cycle γ in CC:
        if γ is a 2-cycle (v, t) such that $\min(\mathrm{ov}(v, t), \mathrm{ov}(t, v)) > \frac{3}{4}(\mathrm{d}(c_v) + \mathrm{d}(c_t))$
    (a)   then if $\mathrm{Ext}(v, t) \leq \mathrm{Ext}(t, v)$
            then Discard edge (t, v) ; Extend $\langle v, t \rangle$ by $\mathrm{Ext}(v, t)$
            else Discard edge (v, t); Extend $\langle t, v \rangle$ by $\mathrm{Ext}(t, v)$
    (b) else discard the edge of cycle γ with least overlap;
        Extend each vertex $w \in \gamma$ by $\mathrm{d}(c_w)$.
(5) Concatenate strings from (4) to form superstring α.

Our procedure FINDREPS(c) is the key to our improved approximation bound. We begin by identifying all of the $(\frac{3}{4}, \frac{3}{4})$-repeaters of the cycle, and the corresponding major and minor characteristics. In order to do this, we need to more precisely relate a string to the characteristics in its cycle.

Definition 9. Suppose a cycle c contains a characteristic X_σ and consider a string z in c. Then $t_z(\sigma)$ is the number of times z *touches* σ where $t_z(\sigma)$ is computed as follows:

1. Each copy of X_σ which is strictly contained in z contributes 1 to $t_z(\sigma)$.
2. If X_σ is negative, then each end of z which begins within X_σ contributes 1 to $t_z(\sigma)$.

For each major anomaly X_{σ_i}, let $t^*(\sigma_i) = \max\{t_z(\sigma_i) : z \text{ is a string in } c\}$, that is, the maximum number of times any string touches σ_i. If a string z touches each characteristic σ_i exactly $t^*(\sigma_i)$ times, then z is called a *consensus candidate*.

FIND REPS(c) chooses one of the following, in order of preference:

1. A string without a $(\frac{3}{4}, \frac{3}{4})$-repeater.
2. A consensus candidate.
3. A string with the longest active $(\frac{3}{4}, \frac{3}{4})$-repeater.

Any string which satisfies (1) is sufficient. If more than one string satisfies (2) or (3), we consider a set Φ of candidate strings. In order to choose among the strings in Φ we examine the minor characteristics, using the parse tree representation of their nesting described in Sect. 3. The set of $(\frac{3}{4}, \frac{3}{4})$-repeaters for which a string is active must all be nested within each other. Thus a string defines a path in the tree. Such a path is unique because positive characteristics are disjoint by Lemma 8. We associate a string with the lowest node on this path. It is then fairly simple to choose one of the strings in Φ; for details see [1].

4.2 The Approximation Ratio

We sketch the analysis of the algorithm. Recall from Sect. 2 that given a 2-cycle γ in CC, ov_γ^n denotes the overlap of the discarded edge. Recall also from Lemma 2 that in order to improve the approximation bound from 3 down to $1 + \beta$ for $\beta \geq \frac{5}{3}$, we need only to show that for all 2-cycles γ composed of vertices v and t, $ov_\gamma^n + Ext(\gamma) \leq \beta(d(c_v) + d(c_t))$. If $\min(ov(v,t), ov(t,v)) \leq \frac{3}{4}(d(c_v) + d(c_t))$ then $ov_\gamma^n \leq \frac{3}{4}(d(c_v) + d(c_t))$ and we can achieve the bound of $\frac{7}{4}(d(c_v) + d(c_t))$ with an extension cost of $d(c_v) + d(c_t)$. Either our algorithm succeeded in finding a representative with no $(\frac{3}{4}, \frac{3}{4})$-repeaters, or there was not an r_v available such that $per(v) = \sigma$ for any $(\frac{3}{4}, \frac{3}{4})$-repeater in t. Thus we have

Lemma 10. *Let γ be a 2-cycle in CC with v the representative of cycle c_v and t the representative of c_t, and let $\min(ov(v,t), ov(t,v)) < \frac{3}{4}(d(c_v) + d(c_t))$. Then $ov_\gamma^n + Ext(\gamma) \leq \frac{7}{4}(d(c_v) + d(c_t))$.*

When there is high overlap on both edges of a 2-cycle, we can do even better due to our choice of representative. The proof of one case of the following lemma is included below; the remaining cases are omitted for brevity.

Lemma 11. *Let γ be a 2-cycle in CC with v the representative of cycle c_v and t the representative of c_t, and let $\min(ov(v,t), ov(t,v)) \geq \frac{3}{4}(d(c_v) + d(c_t))$. Then $ov_\gamma^n + Ext(\gamma) \leq \frac{5}{3}(d(c_v) + d(c_t))$.*

Proof. Assume without loss of generality $d(c_t) \geq d(c_v)$. Since v achieves high overlap at both ends of t, there must be at least one $(\frac{3}{4}, \frac{3}{4})$-repeater σ' in c_t, and in fact $\sigma' = per(v)$. Furthermore, we observe that all strings in c_t must have at least one $(\frac{3}{4}, \frac{3}{4})$-repeater; if some string t' did not, we would have chosen it as the representative of c_t and this high-overlap two-cycle could not have occurred.

We consider three cases which depend on the number and size of repeaters found in FIND REPS(c_t):

1. One repeater.
2. Two repeaters $|\sigma'| < |\sigma| < \frac{1}{2}\mathrm{d}(c_t)$.
3. At least two repeaters, with larger repeater $|\sigma| > \frac{1}{2}\mathrm{d}(c_t)$.

Case 1. Since we only found one repeater σ in $\mathrm{FIND\,REPS}(c_t)$, and t then appeared in a high-overlap two-cycle with a vertex v, then it must be the case that $\mathrm{per}(v) = \sigma$. Furthermore, since there was only one repeater t must have been chosen as a consensus candidate.

To extend t to include another string t' in c_t, we align the copies of X_σ in t' with those in t. Figures 2a and 2b illustrate this situation when σ has, respectively, a negative and positive characteristic. The figures also suggest the tradeoff at work in the analysis; recall that ov_γ^n is the edge of the 2-cycle in the second cycle cover CC which is not used in forming our superstring. As the figures suggest, as ov_γ^n increases, the remaining portion of the cycle to be covered by extension decreases. We bound the overlap and extension costs first for the case of a negative and then for a positive characteristic.

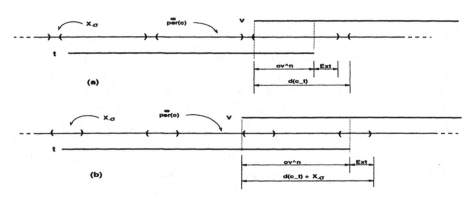

Fig. 2. Cases 1a and 1b from Proof of Lemma 11

Case 1a. Since t was a consensus candidate, no string t' can touch X_σ more times than t. Our extension cost therefore cannot exceed $\mathrm{d}(c_t) - \mathrm{ov}_\gamma^n$ as dimensioned in the figure. Allowing as well for extending v to cover the remaining strings in c_v at the cost of $\mathrm{d}(c_v) = |\sigma|$ we have:

$$\mathrm{ov}_\gamma^n + \mathrm{Ext}(\gamma) \leq \mathrm{ov}_\gamma^n + \mathrm{d}(c_t) - \mathrm{ov}_\gamma^n + \mathrm{d}(c_v) = \mathrm{d}(c_t) + \mathrm{d}(c_v) \ . \qquad (2)$$

Case 1b. Now X_σ is a positive characteristic. However, since t was chosen as a consensus candidate no string t' can extend beyond X_σ. This amount of extension, as dimensioned in Fig. 2b, is $\mathrm{d}(c_t) + |X_\sigma| - \mathrm{ov}_\gamma^n$. Again we allow for extending by $\mathrm{d}(c_v) = |\sigma|$, giving us:

$$\mathrm{ov}_\gamma^n + \mathrm{Ext}(\gamma) \leq \mathrm{ov}_\gamma^n + \mathrm{d}(c_t) + |X_\sigma| - \mathrm{ov}_\gamma^n + \mathrm{d}(c_v) \leq \mathrm{d}(c_t) + 2\mathrm{d}(c_v) \leq \frac{3}{2}(\mathrm{d}(c_t) + \mathrm{d}(c_v))$$
$$(3)$$

The remaining cases are similar in spirit to Case 1 but require additional technical lemmas. $\square$

We now combine Lemmas 2, 10, and 11 with the results of Sect. 3 to obtain:

Theorem 12. *Algorithm ShortString is a $2\frac{3}{4}$-approximation for the shortest superstring problem.*

4.3 Improving the Approximation Ratio

By combining algorithm SHORTSTRING with the max-TSP algorithm due to Kosaraju et al.[11], we can achieve a better bound because the two algorithms have complementary worst cases. We have shown (Lemma 11) that when 2-cycle γ has very high overlap we achieve the bound of $\mathrm{ov}_\gamma^n + \mathrm{Ext}(\gamma) \leq \frac{5}{3}(\mathrm{d}(c_v)+\mathrm{d}(c_t))$. Our worst case occurs when $\min(\mathrm{ov}(v,t), \mathrm{ov}(t,v)) \leq \frac{3}{4}(\mathrm{d}(c_v)+\mathrm{d}(c_t))$. In this case we can obtain a better ratio by running the max-TSP algorithm on the set R of representatives. Balancing the two algorithms gives us:

Theorem 13. *Algorithm SHORTSTRING augmented by the max-TSP algorithm of KPS as a subroutine achieves an approximation ratio of $2\frac{50}{69} \approx 2.725$ for the shortest superstring problem.*

4.4 Analysis of Running Time

The running time of our algorithm is dominated by three tasks: distance graph construction, the computation of the two cycle covers, and choosing representatives. Gusfield et al.[8] have given a nice solution to the first problem which runs in time $\Theta(|S|+n^2)$. As noted above, a cycle cover can be computed in $O(n^3)$ [14]. The essential step in choosing representatives is to identify the $(\frac{3}{4}, \frac{3}{4})$-repeaters in a cycle. We show in this section that they can be found in $O(|S|)$ time.

A repeater by definition must be active in at least one string, so it suffices to look for $(\frac{3}{4}, \frac{3}{4})$-repeaters which are witnessed by a prefix and suffix y_ℓ and y_r of some string rather than arbitrary points in per(c). We note that the characteristics of all repeaters active for a given string must be nested. For each string z, we will first examine it for large repeaters $(|\sigma| > \frac{1}{3}\mathrm{d}(c))$ and then for small ones. We describe our method for finding large repeaters, followed by a remark on the slight alteration required for small repeaters.

We outline our method for finding large repeaters as follows:

1. Find a set L of candidate pairs $(\sigma_i, y_\ell(\sigma_i))$.
2. Find a set R of candidate pairs $(\sigma_i, y_r(\sigma_i))$.
3. Remove from L and R candidate pairs which do not satisfy the $(\frac{3}{4}, \frac{3}{4})$-repeater bound.
4. $L \cap R$ is the set of $(\frac{3}{4}, \frac{3}{4})$-repeaters.

Step 3 requires testing each candidate pair for whether it meets the repeater bound. Each test takes time $O(1)$, and there are $O(|s|)$ of them. Step 4, computing the intersection of L and R, is also straightforward. It can easily be shown that $|\sigma_i|$ uniquely determines σ_i, and all of the σ_i are ordered, so computing the intersection is a simple $O(\mathrm{d}(c))$ operation. Steps 1 and 2 are symmetric; without loss of generality we describe Step 1. We will examine a series of candidates for y_ℓ. This series will be chosen in such a way that it will be sufficient to determine the smallest period of each candidate. That is, given a candidate witness y_ℓ, we wish to determine the smallest σ_i such that $y_\ell = (\sigma_i)^{x_i}$ for some $x_i \in \mathbb{R}^+$.

We will use the pre-processing step of the string-matching algorithm due to Knuth, Morris and Pratt [10] and will refer to it as KMP-P. In what follows, let $s[1..j]$ denote the prefix of length j of some string s. The subroutine KMP-P accepts as input a string z of length k. It computes for each position i in z a value $\pi[i] = \text{ov}(z[1..i], z)$; that is, the length of the longest suffix of $z[1..i]$ which is also a prefix of z. Note that $\pi[k] = \text{ov}(z, z)$. As noted by Gusfield in [7], this self-overlap implies that z has period $|\sigma_1| = k - \pi[k]$; since $\pi[k]$ is the largest self-overlap, σ_1 is the smallest period of z. This subroutine runs in time $O(|z|)$.

The range of π can be partitioned into subranges; each subrange consists of a sequence which increases by exactly 1. Each of these subranges corresponds to a single alignment of z with itself. We augment KMP-P to compute these subranges. In particular for any index i we wish to know the end of the subrange containing i; that is, let $\psi[i]$ be the smallest index $j > i$ such that $\pi[j] \geq \pi[j+1]$. We can compute ψ with an additional pass over π.

Let the *modulus* of string s be given by $m_s = |s| \% d(c)$. If z has at least one large $(\frac{3}{4}, \frac{3}{4})$-repeater, let σ_1 be the smallest such $(\frac{3}{4}, \frac{3}{4})$-repeater. We observe that $z[1..m_z + d(c)]$ must be a substring of $y_\ell(\sigma_1)$; that is, it must be periodic in σ_1.

In order to find set L we first run KMP-P on z, computing π and ψ. Now let $h_0 = m_z + d(c)$. Then $|\sigma_1| = h_0 - \pi[h_0]$, with σ_1 itself given by the first $|\sigma_1|$ characters of z. Now we find the rightish of $y_\ell(\sigma_1)$ by finding the next place where the sequence of π values is broken, that is $\psi(h_0)$. Any choice of h_0 up to and including $\psi(h_0)$ would have given us the same σ_1, and any $h_0 > \psi(h_0)$ would have given us some $|\sigma'| > |\sigma_1|$. We have now found the first candidate pair $(\sigma_1, y_\ell(\sigma_1))$.

We observed above that the characteristics of all $(\frac{3}{4}, \frac{3}{4})$-repeaters which are active in z must be nested. We can also show that if z has two $(\frac{3}{4}, \frac{3}{4})$-repeaters with X_{σ_1} nested within X_{σ_2}, then $|\sigma_2| > |\sigma_1|$. Therefore the rightish at the end of $y_\ell(\sigma_2)$ will be strictly to the right of that of $y_\ell(\sigma_1)$. To find σ_2, let $h_1 = \psi(h_0) + 1$. We get $|\sigma_2| = h_1 - \pi[h_1]$, and the rightish of $y_\ell(\sigma_2)$ is at $\psi(h_1)$.

In general, $|\sigma_{i+1}| = h_i - \pi[h_i]$, $|y_\ell(\sigma_i)| = \psi(h_i)$, and $h_{i+1} = \psi[h_i]$. We terminate when $|\sigma_{i+1}| \geq d(c)$. To find small repeaters, we repeat the procedure outlined above with $h_0 = m_z$ and terminating when $|\sigma_{i+1}| \geq \frac{1}{3}d(c)$.

Since we can find all of the $(\frac{3}{4}, \frac{3}{4})$-repeaters in any string s in $O(|s|)$, we can find all of the $(\frac{3}{4}, \frac{3}{4})$-repeaters in all of the strings in $O(|S|)$ time. Thus we can choose representatives in $O(|S|)$ time.

Acknowledgements

We thank Rao Kosaraju for pointing out a flaw in an earlier proof of this result, Shanghua Teng for helpful discussions and for sharing his unpublished work on superstrings, Bill Smyth for helpful discussions, and James Park and Perry Fizzano for many helpful discussions and reading drafts of this paper,

References

1. C. Armen and C. Stein. Short supertrings and the structure of overlapping strings. To appear in J. of Computational Biology, 1995.
2. A. Blum, T. Jiang, M. Li, J. Tromp, and M. Yannakakis. Linear approximation of shortest superstrings. *Journal of the ACM*, 41(4):630–647, July 1994.
3. A. Czumaj, L. Gasieniec, M. Piotrow, and W. Rytter. Parallel and sequential approxmations of shortest superstrings. In *Proceedings of Fourth Scandinavian Workshop on Algorithm Theory*, pages 95–106, 1994.
4. A. Lesk (edited). *Computational Molecular Biology, Sources and Methods for Sequence Analysis*. Oxford University Press, 1988.
5. A.M. Frieze, G. Galbiati, and F. Maffoli. On the worst case performance of some algorithms for the asymmetric travelling salesman problem. *Networks*, 12:23–39, 1982.
6. J. Gallant, D. Maier, and J. Storer. On finding minimal length superstrings. *Journal of Computer and System Sciences*, 20:50–58, 1980.
7. D. Gusfield. Faster implementation of a shortest superstring approximation. *Information Processing Letters*, (51):271–274, 1994.
8. D. Gusfield, G. Landau, and B. Schieber. An efficient algorithm for the all pairs suffix-prefix problem. *Information Processing Letters*, (41):181–185, March 1992.
9. John D. Kececioglu. *Exact and approximation algorithms for DNA sequence reconstruction*. PhD thesis, University of Arizona, 1991.
10. D.E. Knuth, J.H.Morris, and V.B. Pratt. Fast pattern matching in strings. *SIAM Journal on Computing*, 6:189–195, 1977.
11. R. Kosaraju, J. Park, and C. Stein. Long tours and short superstrings. In *FOCS*, November 1994.
12. M. Li. Towards a DNA sequencing theory (learning a string). In *FOCS*, pages 125–134, 1990.
13. L.J.Cummings. Strongly qth power-free strings. *Annals of Discrete Mathematics*, 17:247–252, 1983.
14. Christos H. Papadimitriou and Kenneth Steiglitz. *Combinatorial Optimization, Algorithms and Complexity*. Prentice-Hall, Englewood Cliffs, NJ, 1982.
15. H. Peltola, H. Soderlund, J. Tarjio, and E. Ukkonen. Algorithms for some string matching problems arising in molecular genetics. In *Proceedings of the IFIP Congress*, pages 53–64, 1983.
16. Graham A. Stephen. *String searching algorithms*. World Scientific, 1994.
17. J. Storer. *Data compression: methods and theory*. Computer Science Press, 1988.
18. J. Tarhio and E. Ukkonen. A greedy approximation algorithm for constructing shortest common superstrings. *Theoretical Computer Science*, 57:131–145, 1988.
19. Shang-Hua Teng and Frances Yao. Approximating shortest superstrings. In *Proceedings of the 34th Annual Symposium on Foundations of Computer Science*, pages 158–165, November 1993.
20. J. Turner. Approximation algorithms for the shortest common superstring problem. *Information and Computation*, 83:1–20, 1989.

Nonoverlapping Local Alignments (Weighted Independent Sets of Axis Parallel Rectangles) *

Vineet Bafna[1] and Babu Narayanan[2], and R. Ravi[3]

[1] DIMACS, P.O. Box 1179, Piscataway, NJ 08855-1179.
email:bafna@dimacs.rutgers.edu
[2] DIMACS, P.O. Box 1179, Piscataway, NJ 08855-1179.
email: bon@dimacs.rutgers.edu
[3] DIMACS, Department of Computer Science, Princeton University, NJ 08544.
email: ravi@cs.princeton.edu

Abstract. We consider the following problem motivated by an application in computational molecular biology. We are given a set of weighted axis-parallel rectangles such that for any pair of rectangles and either axis, the projection of one rectangle does not enclose that of the other. Define a pair to be independent if their projections in both axes are disjoint. The problem is to find a maximum-weight independent subset of rectangles.
We show that the problem is NP-hard even in the uniform case when all the weights are the same. We analyze the performance of a natural local-improvement heuristic for the general problem and prove a performance ratio of 3.25. We extend the heuristic to the problem of finding a maximum-weight independent set in $(d+1)$-claw free graphs, and show a tight performance ratio of $d-1+\frac{1}{d}$. A performance ratio of $\frac{d}{2}$ was known for the heuristic when applied to the uniform case. Our contributions are proving the hardness of the problem and providing a tight analysis of the local-improvement algorithm for the general weighted case.

1 Introduction

Let S be a set of axis-parallel rectangles, such that for any pair $a, b \in S$ of rectangles, the interval defined by projecting a on an axis does not include the interval defined by projecting b on the same axis. If the two intervals intersect, then we say that a and b are *conflicting*. A set S of rectangles is *independent* if no pair of rectangles in S is conflicting.

Definition 1. Independent subset of rectangles (IR): Given a set S of axis-parallel rectangles and an integer k, does there exist a subset $S' \subseteq S$, such that S' is independent and $|S'| > k$.

---

* All the authors were supported by a DIMACS postdoctoral fellowship under grants STC-88-09648 and 91-19999.

The extension of the problem when the rectangles are weighted is immediate. This problem is motivated by an application in molecular biology in which rectangles correspond to regions of high local similarity, and the problem is to find a large number of such regions that are independent.

Theorem 2. *IR is NP-complete.*

We construct a *conflict graph* from the given set of rectangles. Each node in the graph corresponds to a rectangle in the set and every two conflicting rectangles have an edge between them in the conflict graph. The *IR* problem can be phrased as the maximum independent set problem for the conflict graph. While the maximum independent set problem in arbitrary graphs is well known to be notoriously hard to approximate [ALM+92], we use the structure of the graphs arising from our problem to provide good approximation algorithms. Define a d-claw as the graph $K_{1,d}$, i.e., a star with d leaves. A graph is d-clawfree if has no induced d-claw. A key property that we use in devising our approximation algorithms and analyzing them is that a conflict graph of non-overlapping axis-parallel rectangles is 5-clawfree. A simple consequence of 5-clawfree property of the conflict graph is that a greedy algorithm that picks a node of maximum weight to add to the solution and continues by deleting the picked node and its neighborhood has a performance ratio of 4.

We consider a simple local improvement heuristic, t-opt, for the problem parameterized by the size, t, of the improvement. We shall describe it informally here for the unweighted problem. Begin with an arbitrary maximal independent set I in the graph. If there is an improvement that involves swapping at most t nodes into I, then we perform such an improvement. In other words, if there is an independent set A of at most t nodes in $V - I$ whose neighborhood in I has size less than that of A, then this set may be added and its neighborhood deleted from I. This results in a net increase in the size of I. The local improvement algorithm performs such t-improvements as long as they are available. It is not hard to argue that this algorithm runs in polynomial time for any fixed t. Halldórsson [Hal95] has shown that the t-opt heuristic when applied to a $d+1$-clawfree graph achieves a performance ratio of $\frac{d}{2} + \epsilon$ for any fixed $\epsilon > 0$ and in fact ϵ decreases exponentially in t. In Section 4, we provide a simple construction that shows that the performance ratio of $\frac{d}{2}$ is the best possible for the heuristic.

The local improvement heuristic can be extended in a natural way to weighted graphs. An independent set A of size at most t provides a t-improvement if the total weight of its neighborhood in I is less than the weight of A. When all the weights are polynomially bounded, the local improvement algorithm runs in polynomial time. We prove the following theorem improving the trivial performance ratio of d for the local improvement heuristic.

Theorem 3. *Let I be a locally optimal independent set for d-opt, and I^* be the optimal independent set in a node-weighted $d + 1$-clawfree graph. Then $w(I^*) \leq (d - 1 + \frac{1}{d})w(I)$, where $w(S)$ denotes the sum of the weights of the nodes in S.*

Note that in the biological example that motivated this research, $d = 4$, and the above theorem shows a performance bound of 3.25 implying an 18% improvement in the worst-case quality of the output solution. Though the improvement is modest, we also demonstrate that the bound is almost best possible for the local improvement heuristic that we analyze.

Theorem 4. *For all positive integers d, t and for all $\epsilon > 0$, there exist node-weighted $d + 1$-claw free graphs with a maximum weight independent set I^*, an independent set I that is locally optimal with respect to t-opt but $w(I^*) \geq (d - 1 - \epsilon) \cdot w(I)$.*

The class of d-clawfree graphs includes two other important classes of graphs: graphs with degree at most d and unit disk graphs. The latter is the family of intersection graphs of unit disks in the plane and can be shown to be 6-clawfree by a simple geometric argument. Thus our results provide a tight analysis of the local heuristic for the weighted independent set problem in these classes of graphs. Note that there has also been work on obtaining better ratios for the unweighted independent set problem in bounded degree graphs [BF94].

In Section 2, we describe in more detail how the IR problem arises in the application to molecular biology. In Section 3, we present the NP-hardness proof of Theorem 2. In Section 4, we sketch the basic local improvement algorithm for the unweighted (uniform) case. We then extend the heuristic to the weighted case and present an analysis of the same. We generalize the analysis to arbitrary clawfree graphs and show its tightness. Finally, in Section 5, we conclude with open issues.

2 Motivation

A fundamental problem that arises in the analysis of genetic sequences is to assess the similarity between two such sequences. Traditional notions of similarity have suggested aligning the sequences to reflect globally [NW70] or locally [SW81] similar regions in the string. A global alignment arranges the two strings with spaces inserted within them, so that the characters are organized in columns and most columns contain identical or similar characters in both strings. Such alignments tend to reflect similar regions between the two strings that have remained conserved over the evolutionary process of point mutations that has led to the divergence between the two sequences.

Recent studies on genome rearrangements [BP93, BP95, HP95, KS93, KS94, KR95] have addressed the notion of distances between sequences under more large-scale mutational operations. An example is a "reversal" that works on a large contiguous block of a genomic sequence and reverses the order of certain "markers" in the fragment. Another macro-mutational operation is a transposition that transfers a block of sequence to another position. These rearrangements have been postulated and confirmed to occur in the evolutionary history between several existing species [HCKP94]. The body of work mentioned above addresses the computation of a minimal set of such rearrangement operations to transform an initial sequence A to a final sequence B. The input to such a procedure is a set of disjoint fragments that occur in both the strings, their relative order and orientation in the two strings. When these fragments code for some genetic information, they are termed *genes* and what is supplied in this case is the gene order and orientation in the two strings for a set of common genes. Thus what is required is a set of fragments which remain highly conserved in both strings (the orientation may be reversed in the two strings), such that the similarity between the two copies of a fragment is appreciable and a large number of such fragments are available for investigation of genome rearrangements. Moreover, no two fragments selected for comparison must overlap in either string, since rearrangements work on segments of the string and therefore cannot separate overlapping fragments.

The problem of selecting fragments of high local similarity between two strings can be tackled by applying one of several known methods for local alignment [SW81] in the literature. The output of such a method is a set of pairs of substrings from A and B that have high local similarity. However, the projection of these pairs in the two strings may not be disjoint as required. It is useful to picture these regions of local similarity as axis-parallel rectangles in the plane where the axes are the two strings A and B being compared. A pair of substrings of high local similarity identifies the rectangle formed by the intersection of the horizontal and vertical slabs corresponding to these substrings in A and B. The rectangle may be weighted with the strength of the local similarity. The resulting problem is to find a maximum-weight set of rectangles whose projections are disjoint in both the axes. This leads to the IR problem introduced earlier. The non-enclosing condition on the projections of the rectangles translates to disallowing similarity pairs in which a substring in one pair is completely contained in that of the other pair. This is a reasonable assumption for data from sequences because the input data can be pruned to eliminate similarities that disobey this requirement.

3 NP-completeness of IR: Proof of Theorem 2

IR is trivially in the class NP. We shall show NP-hardness by transforming from 3SAT.

Let U be an instance of $3SAT$ with m clauses $c_1, \ldots, c_m$ and n variables. For each variable x, define a *cycle gadget* as follows (see Fig. 1). The cycle gadget has exactly $2m$ rectangles arranged in a cycle so that only conflicting pairs are the ones that appear consecutively in the cycle. Label the rectangles in the cycle gadget for x as $x_j, \bar{x}_j$, for $1 \leq j \leq m$. The following lemma is immediate:

Proposition 5. *A cycle gadget with $2m$ rectangles has a maximum independent subset of size m. Further, there are only two such subsets of maximum size, either the set of all $x'_j s$ or the set of all $\bar{x}'_j s$.*

For each clause c_j, $1 \leq j \leq m$, we define a clause gadget as set of three rectangles (see Fig. 1), one for each literal in the clause, that are pairwise conflicting. If literal x appears in clause c_j, label the corresponding rectangle in the clause gadget as $c_{x,j}$. Finally, place all the rectangles on the plane as follows (see Fig. 1): A pair (a, b) of rectangles conflicts if and only if

- a, b belong to the same clause.
- a, b are adjacent rectangles in a cycle gadget, i.e. $a = x_j$ and $b = \bar{x}_j$ or $b = \bar{x}_{j-1}$.
- $a = c_{x,j}$ and $b = \bar{x}_j$.

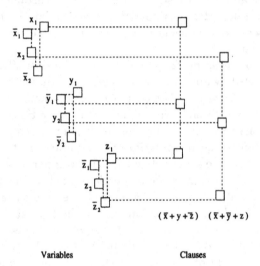

$$(\bar{x}+y+\bar{z}) \quad (\bar{x}+\bar{y}+z)$$

Variables   Clauses

Fig. 1. An instance of 3SAT with $n = 3, m = 2$ and $U = (\bar{x} + y + \bar{z})(\bar{x} + \bar{y} + z)$, transformed to an instance of IR

Figure 1 gives a layout for the case $n = 3, m = 2$ and $U = (\bar{x}+y+\bar{z})(\bar{x}+\bar{y}+z)$.

Therefore, we have transformed an instance U of $3SAT$ to an instance S of IR, such that $|S| = 2mn + 3m$.

Proposition 6. $U \in SAT$ if and only if there exists a independent subset $S' \subseteq S$ such that $|S'| \geq mn + m$.

Proof : Let $U \in 3SAT$ be satisfiable. For any variable x that is TRUE in a valid truth assignment, pick all the rectangles x_j for $1 \leq j \leq m$, otherwise pick $\bar{x}_j$ and for all $1 \leq j \leq m$. Clearly, m rectangles are picked from each of the n cycle gadgets, and they are independent. For each clause c_j, there is at least one literal $x \in c_j$ that is TRUE. By construction, rectangle $c_{x,j}$ only conflicts with other rectangles in the same clause gadget and with $\bar{x}_j$, none of which has been selected. Therefore, one rectangle from each of the clause gadgets can be picked for a total of $mn + m$ rectangles.

Correspondingly, let $S' \subset S$ be conflicting and $|S'| \geq mn + m$. Now, each cycle gadget can contribute at most m rectangles and each clause can contribute at most 1 rectangle to an independent set. Therefore, in order to get $mn + m$ rectangles each cycle gadget must supply m and each clause must supply 1 rectangle. We consider the following truth assignment. For each clause gadget, if the rectangle chosen is $c_{x,j}$, then set x to be TRUE. Clearly, each clause has at least one TRUE literal, and we only need to ensure that both x and $\bar{x}$ are not set to TRUE. Suppose that was the case, implying that for some $1 \leq j, j' \leq m$, $c_{x,j}$ and $c_{\bar{x},j'}$ were selected. Then, in the cycle gadget of x, neither $\bar{x}_j$ nor $x_{j'}$ can be selected. By proposition 5, this cycle gadget does not supply m independent rectangles.

Theorem 2 follows. □

4 Approximating independent sets in clawfree graphs

We begin with some formal definitions.

Definition 7.

1. Consider a set S of axis-parallel rectangles. Each rectangle may be identified by a pair of intervals (I_x, I_y) defining its projections on the two axes. Rectangle b *overlaps* rectangle a if one of its intervals contains an interval of a. S is *non-overlapping* if no rectangle overlaps another. Two rectangles b and a *conflict* if at least one of their intervals intersect.
2. Define the conflict graph $G_S(V, E)$ of a set S of axis-parallel rectangles as follows: each rectangle corresponds to a vertex $v \in V$, and $(v, w) \in E$ iff a and b are conflicting. In the following, we will drop the subscript S when the context is clear. For $X \subseteq V$, let $G(X)$ be the graph induced by the vertices in X.
3. Let $w : V \to \mathcal{R}^+$ be the weight function on rectangles. For $X \subseteq V$, $w(X) = \sum_{x \in X} w(x)$.
4. Define the neighborhood of a vertex $v \in V$ as $N(v) = \{x \in V | (v, x) \in E\}$. For $X \subseteq V$, $N(X) = \cup_{x \in X} N(x)$. Also, define $N^i(x) = N(N^{i-1}(x))$ for $i > 0$ and $N^0(x) = \{x\}$.

As we observed earlier, the problem of finding an independent set of rectangles is that of finding a maximum weighted independent set in the corresponding conflict graph. In order to provide good approximate solutions, we make the following observation.

Lemma 8. *A conflict graph of non-overlapping axis-parallel rectangles is 5-clawfree.*

Proof (by contradiction): Assume the statement is not true. There is an independent set of 5 rectangles, all conflicting with one rectangle s. Let s be defined by the interval pair $((x_1, x_2), (y_1, y_2))$. Each rectangle that conflicts with but is not overlapped by s must contain at least one of the 4 points x_1, x_2, y_1, y_2. Assuming 5 such rectangles, one of these points must be contained in two of these rectangles. These two rectangles conflict, a contradiction. □

Consider the problem of finding a maximum weight independent set in a $d + 1$-clawfree graph. One simple heuristic is the greedy one: Add a vertex of maximum weight to the current independent set I, discard all its neighbors and continue. This greedy heuristic performs quite well.

Lemma 9. *Let I^* be a maximum weighted independent set in a $d + 1$-clawfree graph G, and I be an independent set selected by the greedy heuristic. Then $w(I^*) \leq d \cdot w(I)$.*

Proof : The proof is straightforward and hence omitted. $\square$

In the following discussion, we shall attempt to find better algorithms for finding maximum weighted independent sets in $d + 1$ clawfree graphs. Even constant factor improvements are desirable, especially when d is small (Note that it is 4 in our application). Specifically, we will focus on a natural heuristic, which is based on iteratively improving the solution through some local changes. This heuristic for computing maximum weight independent sets in $d+1$-clawfree graphs is described in figure 3.

```
Procedure t-opt(I)
begin
    I ← maximal-independent-set (I)
    while ∃ independent set A ⊂ V − I, |A| ≤ t
        and w(A) > w(N(A) ∩ I)
            I ← I ⊕ A
    endwhile
    return I
end;
```

Fig. 2. A local improvement algorithm for node weighted graphs

Note that this algorithm runs in polynomial time if the weights are uniform or if they are polynomial functions of n.

Let us assume for the moment that all rectangles have the same weight. By Theorem 2, the problem remains NP-hard. Halldórsson [Hal95] has shown that t-opt, when applied to a $d + 1$-clawfree graph, achieves a performance ratio of $\frac{d}{2} + \epsilon$ for any fixed $\epsilon > 0$. It is interesting to note that his analysis uses only a restricted form of improvements that he calls t-ear-improvements. We present below a simple construction that shows that the performance ratio of $\frac{d}{2}$ is the best possible for the local improvement heuristic. To this end, we use the following result of Erdös and Sachs, which can be found in [Bol78].

Lemma 10. *Given positive integers d and g, for all n sufficiently large, there exist d-regular graphs on $2n$ vertices with girth at least g.*

Theorem 11. *For all positive integers d and t, there exist d+1-claw free graphs with an independent set I, where I is locally optimal with respect to t-opt but $|I^*| \geq \frac{d}{2}|I|$.*

Proof : By Lemma 10, we have a d-regular graph $G = (V, E)$ on n vertices with girth t (for all sufficiently large even n). Construct a new graph G' on vertex set $V \cup E$, and connect vertices x, y in G' if $x \in V$, $y \in E$ and y is incident on x in G. Intuitively, this corresponds to subdividing every edge in G by addition of a new vertex of degree 2. Clearly, G' is bipartite and $d + 1$-clawfree. Also, the girth of G' is at least $2t$. Let $I = V$ and $I^* = E$. Since the minimum degree of a vertex in G' is 2, the girth condition implies that every subset of E of size at most t has a neighborhood of size at least $t + 1$ in V. Hence, the independent set I is optimal with respect to t-opt. Noting that $|I^*| = |E| = \frac{d}{2}|V| = \frac{d}{2}|I|$ completes the proof. □

Weighted Independent Sets

We now turn to analyze the performance of t-opt for weighted $d + 1$-clawfree graphs and show that its performance is provably inferior to the performance for the unweighted case, even when the weights are a polynomial function of n. We also provide matching upper bounds. The following lemma provides a simple upper bound of d and motivates the detailed analysis that follows.

Lemma 12. *Let I be a locally optimal solution for 1-opt in a $d + 1$-clawfree graph. Then if I^* is the optimal solution,*

$$w(I^*) \leq d \cdot w(I)$$

Proof : Consider the bipartite graph $G(I \cup I^*)$. By local optimality, we know that for all $v \in V - I$ (in particular, for all $v \in I^*$), $w(v) \leq w(N(v))$, where $N(v)$ refers to the neighborhood of v in $G(I \cup I^*)$. Therefore,

$$w(I^*) = \sum_{v \in I^*} w(v) \qquad \leq \sum_{v \in I^*} \sum_{u \in N(v)} w(u)$$
$$= \sum_{u \in I} \sum_{v \in N(u)} w(u) \leq d \cdot w(I)$$

□

Next, we show that the performance of t-opt improves somewhat as we increase t. While the improvement is somewhat modest, it might still be useful for small values of d.

Let I be a locally optimal independent set for d-opt implying that for all $X \subseteq V - I$, $|X| \leq d$, $w(X) \leq w(N(X) \cap I)$. Let $d(v)$ be the degree of v in $G(I \cup I^*)$. Note that we can without loss of generality, assume that I and I^* are disjoint sets. Otherwise, we work with the graph $G((I \cup I^*) - J)$, where $J = I \cap I^*$. Define $I_i^* = \{v \in I^* | d(v) = i\}$. Clearly, I^* is partitioned into exactly d sets. For $v \in I$, let $d_i(v)$ be the degree of v in $G(I \cup I_i^*)$.

Lemma 13. *Let I be a locally optimal independent set for d-opt. For $1 \leq i \leq d$, let $f_i(u) = 1$ if $d_i(u) > 0$ and 0 otherwise. Then,*

1. $i \cdot w(I_i^*) \le \sum_{u \in I}[d_i(u) \cdot (i-1) + f_i(u)] \cdot w(u), \quad \text{for all } i \le d$
2. $\sum_{i=1}^{d} i \cdot w(I_i^*) \le \sum_{u \in I}[(\sum_{i=1}^{d} d_i(u) \cdot (i-1)) + 1] \cdot w(u)$

Proof : Observe that $G(I \cup I_i^*)$ has exactly $i|I_i^*|$ edges. Therefore,

$$i \cdot w(I_i^*) = \sum_{v \in I_i^*} \sum_{u \in N(v)} w(v) = \sum_{u \in I} w(N(u))$$

Further, any element $u \in I$ has at most d neighbors, therefore by local optimality for d-opt, $w(N(u)) \le w(N^2(u))$ for all $u \in I$. Using this and rearranging terms, we get

$$i \cdot w(I_i^*) \le \sum_{u \in I} w(N^2(u))$$

$$= \sum_{u \in I, d_i(u) > 0} (d_i(u)(i-1) + 1)w(u)$$

The last equality follows from the fact that for an $u \in I$ such that $d_i(u) > 0$, the number of times this u is counted in the sum is exactly $d_i(u)(i-1)+1$. This proves the first proposition. The second follows by a similar argument on the graph $G(I \cup I^*)$. $\square$

Next, we prove a technical lemma that we will use to bound the value of $w(I^*)$.

Lemma 14. *For arbitrary integer $d > 0$, consider the following integer program*

$$IP(d) = \max \sum_{i=1}^{d} \frac{(i-1) \cdot d \cdot d_i + (d-i) \cdot f_i}{i}$$
$$s.t.$$
$$\sum_{i=1}^{d} d_i \le d$$
$$\forall i, f_i \le d_i$$
$$\forall i, 0 \le f_i \le 1$$
$$\forall i, d_i \in \{0, 1, 2, \ldots, d\}$$

Then, $IP(d) = d(d-1)$.

Proof : We will prove that the integer program is maximized when $d_i = 1, f_i = 1$ for all i. Clearly, this solution is feasible. Also, observe that any optimal solution will have the property that $\sum_{i=1}^{d} d_i = d$ and $f_i = 1$ for all i such that $d_i > 0$. If this was not true, there would exist some d_i or f_i that could be incremented to increase the value of the objective function. Therefore, it is sufficient to prove that there exists an optimal solution in which $d_i \le 1$ for all i.

Consider an optimal solution in which this is not true, so that $d_i > 1$ for some i. Then, as $\sum_i d_i \le d$, there exists j such that $d_j = 0, f_j = 0$. Then, if we decrement d_i by 1, and set $d_j = 1, f_j = 1$, it is easy to see that the solution remains feasible.

Now, the objective function is the sum of d terms, where the contribution of the ith term is

$$\left(d - \frac{d}{i}\right) d_i + \left(\frac{d}{i} - 1\right) f_i$$

Furthermore, the new solution affects only the ith and j^{th} terms of this function. The net change is

$$-\left(d - \frac{d}{i}\right) + \left(d - \frac{d}{j}\right) + \left(\frac{d}{j} - 1\right) = \left(\frac{d}{i} - 1\right)$$

which is non-negative, so the new solution remains optimal. Continuing in this fashion, we eventually get an optimal solution in which all $d_i \leq 1$. $\square$

We now restate and prove Theorem 3.

Theorem 15. *Let I be a locally optimal independent set for d-opt, and I^* be the optimal independent set. Then $w(I^*) \leq (d - 1 + \frac{1}{d})w(I)$.*

Proof : As the sets I_i^* partition I^*, we have the identity

$$d \cdot w(I^*) = \sum_{i=1}^{d} i \cdot w(I_i^*) + \sum_{i=1}^{d-1}(d - i) \cdot w(I_i^*)$$

Applying the bounds obtained from lemma 13, we get

$$d \cdot w(I^*) \leq \sum_{u \in I} \left[\sum_{i=1}^{d} \left(d_i(u) \cdot (i - 1) + (d - i)\frac{d_i(u)(i - 1) + f_i(u)}{i} \right) + 1 \right] \cdot w(u)$$

$$= \sum_{u \in I} \left[\sum_{i=1}^{d} \left(\frac{(i - 1) \cdot d \cdot d_i(u) + (d - i) \cdot f_i(u)}{i} \right) + 1 \right] \cdot w(u)$$

$$\leq (IP(d) + 1) \cdot w(I)$$

where $IP(d)$ is the optimum value of the integer program described in lemma 14. Therefore, $w(I^*) \leq (d - 1 + \frac{1}{d})w(I)$. $\square$

Next, we show that our analysis is tight, by demonstrating the existence of claw-free graphs for which the heuristic cannot achieve a performance better than $d - 1$. First, we present a technical lemma describing the existence of bipartite graphs with an expansion property. Its proof is implicit in proofs for existence of expander graphs (see for example, Chung[Chu78]).

Lemma 16. *For all positive integers d, t, and for all $\epsilon > 0$ there exists an integer n, and bipartite graphs with bipartition (I, O) with the following properties.*

- $|I| = |O| = n$.
- *For all vertices $v \in I \cup O$, $deg(v) \leq d$.*
- *For all $X \subseteq O$, $|X| \leq t$, $|N(X)| \geq (d - 1 - \epsilon) \cdot |X|$.*

Note that these graphs are different from expander graphs in that the expansion is large (close to the maximum degree) but is required only for subsets of some constant size t. As a consequence of the existence of such graphs, we can derive Theorem 4. We restate and prove it below.

Theorem 17. *For all positive integers d, t and for all $\epsilon > 0$, there exist $d + 1$-claw free graphs with an independent set I, such that I is locally optimal with respect to t-opt but $w(I^*) \geq (d - 1 - \epsilon) \cdot w(I)$.*

Proof :

Let (I, O) be a bipartite graph with the expansion property described in lemma 16. Further, for all elements $v \in I$, let $w(v) = 1$, and for all elements $u \in O$, let $w(u) = d - 1 - \epsilon$. By the third condition in Lemma 16, in the graph (I, O), I is a locally optimal solution with respect to t-opt, and $w(O) = (d - 1 - \epsilon) \cdot w(I)$. □

5 Concluding Remarks

We conclude by describing many problems that arise naturally from this work. The problem we study is geometric, and we suspect that it might have applications to problems in computational geometry. However, the only related work that we found was a study of intersecting rectangles (for hidden surface removal) which corresponds to the case when *both* projections intersect. On the other side, can geometric techniques be applied to improve the quality of our solution?

Indeed, the only property we have exploited in finding approximate solutions is claw-freeness in the associated conflict graph. An interesting area of research is to investigate more properties of conflict graphs, and use these properties to find better algorithms or hardness of approximation results.

We have discussed the problem only in the context of pairwise alignments. It is often the case that $k > 2$ sequences are aligned, and biologists are interested in extracting meaningful blocks of locally aligned sequences, which correspond to hypercubes of dimension k. This natural extension to multiple alignment complicates the problem considerably, as the conflict graph of a set of k-dimensional cubes is only $2^k + 1$-clawfree. Different ideas are needed to provide meaningful approximations. It is also possible that general graphs are conflict graphs of some higher dimensional cubes, which might imply some hardness of approximation results for the problem.

Finally, local improvement algorithms have recently been studied extensively, and some interesting positive results have been obtained for related problems, such as independent sets and vertex covers in degree bounded graphs, 3-DM matching, k-set-packing etc. [BF94, Hal95]. Halldórsson [Hal95] shows reducibilities between these problems and uses these reductions to analyze local improvement heuristics for the unweighted case. We hope that the ideas in our analysis can be extended to analyzing heuristics for the weighted versions of these problems. This is particularly interesting for the case of independent sets in bounded degree graphs, where a slightly better local improvement can be applied to improve performance in the unweighted case [BF94], but nothing is known about the weighted version.

Acknowledgement

We would like to thank Dan Gusfield for explaining the biological motivation for the problem and Steve Skiena for useful discussions regarding the NP-completeness of the problem.

References

[ALM+92] S. Arora, C. Lund, R. Motwani, M. Sudan, and M. Szegedy. Proof verification and intractability of approximation problems. In *33rd IEEE Symp. on Foundations of Computer Science*, 1992.

[BF94] P. Berman and M. Fürer. Approximating maximum independent set in bounded degree graphs. In *Fifth ACM-SIAM Symp on Discrete Algorithms*, pages 365–371, 1994.

[Bol78] B. Bollobas. *Extremal Graph Theory*. Academic Press, 1978.

[BP93] V. Bafna and P. Pevzner. Genome rearrangements and sorting by reversals. In *34th IEEE Symp. on Foundations of Computer Science*, pages 148–157, 1993.

[BP95] V. Bafna and P. Pevzner. Sorting permutations by transpositions. In *The sixth annual ACM-SIAM symposium on discrete algorithms*, pages 614–623, 1995.

[Chu78] F. R. K. Chung. On Concentrators, Superconcentrators, Generalizers, and Nonblocking Networks. *The Bell Systems Technical Journal*, 58:1765–1777, 1978.

[Hal95] M. M. Halldórsson. Approximating discrete collections via local improvements. *The sixth annual ACM-SIAM symposium on discrete algorithms*, pages 160–169, 1995.

[HCKP94] S. Hannenhalli, C. Chappey, E. Koonin, and P. Pevzner. Scenarios for genome rearrangements: Herpesvirus evolution as a test case. In *Proc. of 3rd Intl. Conference on Bioinformatics and Complex Genome Analysis*, 1994.

[HP95] S. Hannenhalli and P. Pevzner. Transforming cabbage into turnip. In *27th Annual ACM Symposium on Theory of Computing*, 1995.

[KR95] J. D. Kececioglu and R. Ravi. Of mice and men: Evolutionary distances between genomes under translocations. *The sixth annual ACM-SIAM symposium on discrete algorithms*, pages 604–613, 1995.

[KS93] J. Kececioglu and D. Sankoff. Exact and approximation algorithms for the inversion distance between two permutations. In *Proc. of 4th Ann. Symp. on Combinatorial Pattern Matching*, Lecture Notes in Computer Science 684, pages 87–105. Springer Verlag, 1993.

[KS94] J. Kececioglu and D. Sankoff. Efficient bounds for oriented chromosome inversion distance. In *Lecture notes in computer science*, volume 807, pages 307–325, 1994.

[NW70] S. B. Needleman and C. D. Wunsch. A general method applicable to the search for similarities in the amino acid sequence of two proteins. *Journal of Molecular Biology*, 48:443–453, 1970.

[SW81] T. F. Smith and M. S. Waterman. The identification of common molecular sequences. *Journal of Molecular Biology*, 147:195–197, 1981.

Experiences with the Implementation of Geometric Algorithms

Kurt Mehlhorn

We review some of the experiences made with the implementation of geometric algorithms in LEDA, in particular with the problems of degeneracy and precision, and report on the conclusions that we have drawn from these experiences.

- We handle degeneracies as first class citizens, i.e., before starting to implement an algorithm we redo the theory so as to include degenerate cases.

- We implement all basic primitives using exact arithmetic. To gain speed we use floating-point filters.

- We added several data types to LEDA to support the preceding item: bigints, rationals, bigfloats, reals (the rationals closed under square roots), points and hyperplanes with rational coordinates and coefficients, linear algebra over the integers. Some of these classes incorporate a floating point filter in a way transparent to the user.

- We implemented algorithms for line segment intersection, 2d and 3d convex hulls, 2d Voronoi diagrams of points, and convex hulls (in arbitrary dimension) using these primitives.

- We are working on a program for Voronoi diagrams of line segments. This involves exact computation with algebraic numbers (class real mentioned above).

References

1. Ch. Burnikel, J. Könemann, K. Mehlhorn, St. Näher, St. Schirra, and Ch. Uhrig. Exact geometric computation in LEDA. In *Proc. COMPGEO 95*. To appear.

2. Ch. Burnikel, K. Mehlhorn, and St. Schirra. On degeneracy in geometric computations. In *Proc. SODA 94*, pages 16–23, 1994.

3. Ch. Burnikel, K. Mehlhorn, and St. Schirra. How to compute the Voronoi diagram of line segments: Theoretical and experimental results. In *LNCS*, volume 855, pages 227–239. Springer-Verlag Berlin/New York, 1994. Proceedings of ESA'94.

4. K. Mehlhorn and St. Näher. Implementation of a sweep line algorithm for the straight line segment intersection problem. Technical Report MPI-I-94-160, Max-Planck-Institut für Informatik, Saarbrücken, 1994.

5. K. Mehlhorn and St. Näher. The implementation of geometric algorithms. In *13th World Computer Congress IFIP94*, volume 1, pages 223–231. Elsevier Science B.V. North-Holland, Amsterdam, 1994.

6. K. Mehlhorn and St. Näher. LEDA: A library of efficient data types and algorithms. *CACM*, 38(1):96–102, 1995.

7. St. Näher. LEDA Manual Version 3.1. Technical Report MPI-I-95-1-002, Max-Planck-Institut für Informatik, 1995.

Author Index

Lecture Notes in Computer Science

For information about Vols. 1–890

please contact your bookseller or Springer-Verlag